12th Workshop on Argument Mining (ArgMining 2025)

Vienna, Austria
31 July 2025

ISBN: 979-8-3313-2400-1

Printed from e-media with permission by:

Curran Associates, Inc.
57 Morehouse Lane
Red Hook, NY 12571

Some format issues inherent in the e-media version may also appear in this print version.

Association for Computational Linguistics
209 N. Eighth Street
Stroudsburg, Pennsylvania 18360

Phone: 1-570-476-8006
Fax: 1-570-476-0860

acl@aclweb.org

Additional copies of this publication are available from:

Curran Associates, Inc.
57 Morehouse Lane
Red Hook, NY 12571 USA
Phone: 845-758-0400
Fax: 845-758-2633
Email: curran@proceedings.com
Web: www.proceedings.com

ArgMining 2025

The 12th Argument Mining Workshop

Proceedings of the Workshop

July 31, 2025

The ArgMining organizers gratefully acknowledge the support from the following sponsors.

Introduction

Argument Mining (also known as "argumentation mining") is a well-established research area within computational linguistics that started with focusing on automatically identifying and classifying argument elements, covering several text genres such as legal documents, news articles, online debates, scholarly data, and many more. Aside from mining argumentative components, the field focuses on studying argument quality assessment, argument persuasiveness, the synthesis of argumentative texts, explainable argumentation and multimodal argument mining. Several tutorials have been held at major NLP conferences showing the continuously increasing interest in argument mining.

Besides providing a forum to discuss and exchange cutting edge research in this field, a secondary goal of this year's edition has been to broaden the disciplinary scope of the workshop by inviting other disciplines (e.g., (computational) social and political science, psychology, humanities) as well as other subareas of NLP to actively participate in the workshop and further shape the field of argument mining.

The success of our goal in broadening the disciplinary scope of the workshop, as well as the fast growing interest in research topics related to argument mining and computational argumentation in the NLP community are evidenced with the richness and variety of submissions received. The 12th Workshop on Argument Mining allowed the submission of long and short papers for the main workshop track, as well as extended abstracts and PhD proposals for the non-archival track new to this year's edition. Furthermore, the workshop hosted two shared tasks: the Critical Questions Generation Task, and MM-ArgFallacy2025: Multimodal Argumentative Fallacy Detection and Classification on Political Debates. This year's edition of the ArgMining workshop had 68 submissions (28 in 2024, 40 in 2023, 37 in 2022, 39 in 2021, and 30 in 2020). The 68 submissions were distributed as follows, 44 were submitted to the main workshop track, 7 to the non-archival track, and 17 were shared task papers. For the main workshop, we accepted 22 papers (15 long, 7 short), making an acceptance rate of 50%. The 7 submitted non-archival papers were accepted for poster presentations.

The 12th Workshop on Argument Mining hosted Andreas Vlachos as the keynote speaker, addressing the topic of "Fact-checking as a conversation".

Aligned with this year's special theme, we will also host a panel titled Broadening the scope of Argument Mining", which will bring together Argument Mining experts with researchers from the broader interdisciplinary community connected with Argument Mining (Linguistics, Political Science, Communication Science, Computational Social Science). Our panelists are: Roxanne El Baff (German Aerospace Center–DLR, Bauhaus-Universität Weimar), Sebastian Haunss (University of Bremen), Julia Mendelsohn (University of Bremen), Smaranda Muresan (Columbia University), Elena Musi (University of Liverpool).

We thank our Program Committee members for their continuous support and helpful input. Also, we thank IBM for sponsoring the Best Paper award and the members of our Best Paper Selection Committee: Rodrigo Agerri (University of the Basque Country), Paolo Torroni (University of Bologna), and Elena Cabrio (Université Côte d'Azur). The awards are announced on the official workshop website: https://argmining-org.github.io/2025/.

We would also like to thank the Cluster of Excellence Cognitive Interaction Technology at the University of Bielefeld (CITEC) and the German Society for Computational Linguistics (GSCL) for supporting the workshop.

We would also like to thank everyone who has been involved with this year's workshop in one way or another. Thank you very much!

Elena Chistova, Philipp Cimiano, Shohreh Haddadan, Gabriella Lapesa, and Ramon Ruiz-Dolz
(ArgMining 2025 co-chairs)

Organizing Committee

Organizing Committee

Elena Chistova, Laboratory for Analysis and Controllable Text Generation Technologies, RAS, Russia
Philipp Cimiano, Bielefeld University, Germany
Shohreh Haddadan, Moffitt Cancer Center, United States
Gabriella Lapesa, GESIS, Leibniz Institute for the Social Sciences (Cologne) and Heinrich-Heine University of Dusseldorf
Ramon Ruiz-Dolz, Centre for Argument Technology, University of Dundee, United Kingdom

Program Committee

Program Committee

Rodrigo Agerri, University of the Basque Country
Yamen Ajjour, Universität Hannover
Alaa Alhamzeh, Universität Passau
Ashish Anand, Indian Institute of Technology, Guwahati
Elena Cabrio, Université Côte d'Azur
Blanca Calvo Figueras, Universidad del País Vasco
Chung-Chi Chen, AIST, National Institute of Advanced Industrial Science and Technology
Johannes Daxenberger, summetix GmbH
Roxanne El Baff, German Aerospace Center and Bauhaus-University Weimar
Mohamed Elaraby, University of Pittsburgh
Neele Falk, Universität Stuttgart
Debela Gemechu, Centre for Argument Technology, University of Dundee, United Kingdom
Lynn Greschner, Otto-Friedrich Universität Bamberg
Ankita Gupta, University of Massachusetts Amherst
Annette Hautli-Janisz, Universität Passau
Khalid Al Khatib, University of Groningen
Johannes Kiesel, GESIS – Leibniz Institute for the Social Sciences
Zlata Kikteva, Universität Passau
Nadin Kökciyan, University of Edinburgh
John Lawrence, University of Dundee
Davide Liga, University of Luxembourg
Eimear Maguire, University of Dundee
Maximilian Maurer, GESIS Leibniz Institute for the Social Sciences
Elena Musi, Univeristy of Liverpool
Irina Nikishina, University of Hamburg
Matthias Orlikowski, Universität Bielefeld
Joonsuk Park, University of Richmond
Martin Pereira, University of Santiago de Compostela
Chris Reed, University of Dundee
Julia Romberg, GESIS Leibniz Institute for the Social Sciences
Ameer Saadat-Yazdi, University of Edinburgh
Sougata Saha, Mohamed bin Zayed University of Artificial Intelligence
Patrick Saint-Dizier, CNRS
Gabriella Skitalinskaya, Duolingo
Manfred Stede, Universität Potsdam
Benno Stein, Bauhaus Universität Weimar
Regina Stodden, Universität Bielefeld
Eva Maria Vecchi, University of Stuttgart
Serena Villata, Université Côte d'Azur, Inria, CNRS, I3S, France
Henning Wachsmuth, Leibniz Universität Hannover
Vern R. Walker, Hofstra University
Dexter Williams, University of Illinois at Urbana-Champaign
Hiroaki Yamada, Institute of Science Tokyo
Tangming Yuan, University of York
Yang Zhong, University of Pittsburgh

Shared Task Organizers

Eleonora Mancini, DISI, University of Bologna, Italy
Federico Ruggeri, DISI, University of Bologna, Italy
Paolo Torroni, DISI, University of Bologna, Italy
Serena Villata, Université Côte d'Azur, Inria, France
Blanca Calvo Figueras, HiTZ Center - Ixa, University of the Basque Country UPV/EHU , Spain
Rodrigo Agerri, HiTZ Center - Ixa, University of the Basque Country UPV/EHU , Spain
Maite Heredia, HiTZ Center - Ixa, University of the Basque Country UPV/EHU , Spain
Jaione Bengoetxea, HiTZ Center - Ixa, University of the Basque Country UPV/EHU , Spain
Elena Cabrio, Université Côte d'Azur, Inria, CNRS, I3S, France
Serena Villata, Université Côte d'Azur, Inria, CNRS, I3S, France

Keynote Talk
Fact-checking as a conversation

Andreas Vlachos
Department of Computer Science and Technology, University of Cambridge

Abstract: Misinformation is considered one of the major challenges of our times resulting in numerous efforts against it. Fact-checking, the task of assessing whether a claim is true or false, is considered a key in reducing its impact. In the first part of this talk I will present our recent and ongoing work on automating this task using natural language processing, including neurosymbolic inference, and using a search engine as a source of evidence. In the second part of this talk, I will present an alternative approach to combatting misinformation via dialogue agents, and present results on how internet users engage in constructive disagreements and problem-solving deliberation.

Bio: Andreas Vlachos is a professor of NLP and Machine Learning at the University of Cambridge. Among the many things he has worked on, we find constructiveness in argumentation, fact checking, media bias, dialogue modeling.

Panel
Broadening the scope of Argument Mining

The aim of the panel is to establish a dialogue with Argument Mining researchers (from the panel itself and the workshop audience) on a variety of themes such as a) the challenges encountered by NLP research dealing with fine-grained conceptualizations which are typically aimed at when targeting theory-based questions, b) the progress that Argument Mining (and in general, NLP) can experience when challenged with interdisciplinary work, and c) the boundaries that nowadays LLM's superpowers should nevertheless be confronted with: the fact that LLMs (allegedly) can do everything because it has seen everything" does not mean that any possible task should be done with them — this is particularly relevant with argument mining research, which touches upon crucial issues such as opinion mining, with the potential for manipulative uses of the resulting technology.

Table of Contents

Program

Thursday, July 31, 2025

09:00 - 09:15 *Opening Remarks*

09:15 - 10:30 *Session 1*

Stance-aware Definition Generation for Argumentative Texts
Natalia Evgrafova, Loic De Langhe, Els Lefever and Veronique Hoste

Exploring LLM Priming Strategies for Few-Shot Stance Classification
Yamen Ajjour and Henning Wachsmuth

Multi-Agent LLM Debate Unveils the Premise Left Unsaid
Harvey Bonmu Ku, Jeongyeol Shin, Hyoun Jun Lee, Seonok Na and Insu Jeon

From Debates to Diplomacy: Argument Mining Across Political Registers
Maria Poiaganova and Manfred Stede

"The Facts Speak for Themselves": GPT and Fallacy Classification
Erisa Bytyqi and Annette Hautli-Janisz

10:30 - 11:00 *Coffee Break*

11:00 - 12:00 *Keynote Talk*

12:00 - 12:30 *Session 2*

Aspect-Based Opinion Summarization with Argumentation Schemes
Wendi Zhou, Ameer Saadat-Yazdi and Nadin Kökciyan

Automatic Identification and Naming of Overlapping and Topic-specific Argumentation Frames
Carolin Schindler, Annalena Aicher, Niklas Rach and Wolfgang Minker

12:30 - 14:00 *Lunch Break*

Thursday, July 31, 2025 (continued)

14:00 - 14:20 *Critical Questions Generation Shared Task*

14:20 - 14:40 *MM-ArgFallacy2025: Multimodal Argumentative Fallacy Detection and Classification on Political Debates*

14:40 - 15:30 *Session 3*

Multi-Class versus Means-End: Assessing Classification Approaches for Argument Patterns
Maximilian Heinrich, Khalid Al Khatib and Benno Stein

Toward Reasonable Parrots: Why Large Language Models Should Argue with Us by Design
Elena Musi, Nadin Kökciyan, Khalid Al Khatib, Davide Ceolin, Emmanuelle Dietz, Klara Maximiliane Gutekunst, Annette Hautli-Janisz, Cristián Santibáñez, Jodi Schneider, Jonas Scholz, Cor Steging, Jacky Visser and Henning Wachsmuth

DebArgVis: An Interactive Visualisation Tool for Exploring Argumentative Dynamics in Debate
Martin Gruber, Zlata Kikteva, Ignaz Rutter and Annette Hautli-Janisz

Reasoning Under Distress: Mining Claims and Evidence in Mental Health Narratives
Jannis Köckritz, Bahar İlgen and Georges Hattab

15:00 - 16:00 *Coffee Break*

16:00 - 17:15 *Poster Session (Main Workshop Papers + Shared Task Papers)*

17:15 - 18:00 *Panel + Closing Remarks*

“The Facts Speak for Themselves”: GPT and Fallacy Classification

Erisa Bytyqi **Annette Hautli-Janisz**
Faculty of Computer Science and Mathematics
University of Passau
firstname.lastname@uni-passau.de

Abstract

Fallacies are not only part and parcel of human communication, they are also important for generative models in that fallacies can be tailored to self-verify the output they generate. Previous work has shown that fallacy detection and classification is tricky, but the question that still remains is whether the inclusion of argumentation theory in prompting Large Language Models (LLMs) on the task enhances the performance of those models. In this paper we show that this is not the case: Using the pragma-dialectics approach to fallacies (Van Eemeren and Grootendorst, 1987), we show that three GPT models struggle with the task. Based on our own PD-oriented dataset of fallacies and a carefully curated extension of an existing fallacy dataset from Jin et al. (2022a), we show that this is not only the case for fallacies “in the wild”, but also for textbook examples of fallacious arguments. Our paper also supports the claim that LLMs generally lag behind in fallacy classification in comparison to smaller-scale neural or even statistical models.

1 Introduction

Fallacies are part and parcel of human argumentation, they are woven into our conversations and with the rise of misinformation, fallacies point to communication components that are crucial to identify in order to differentiate between valid and invalid arguments. But fallacies are also crucial for Large Language Models (LLMs) in that the models should be tailored to self-verify the output they generate, an area that will gain significance with the increasing ubiquity of those models in everyday communication. Even though fallacies have attracted millenia of work in argumentation theory, they have proven to be a tricky feat in argument mining (Jin et al., 2022a; Ruiz-Dolz and Lawrence, 2023; Alhindi et al., 2023, inter alia) – they are hard to detect and even harder to classify. This also holds true when LLMs are put to the task, models, which have shown impressive capabilities in a number of other NLP tasks.

In the present paper, we use the theory of Pragma-Dialectics (PD) (Van Eemeren and Grootendorst, 1987) to guide the models with a solid theoretical foundation of fallacies. The ten rules in PD that, if violated, create a fallacy, give direction to a successful discussion, the argument stage in which these rules are applicable, and the interlocutor who can break the rules (the antagonist and/or the protagonist). This level of detail allows us to craft the prompts in a controlled manner steered by the extent to which we include the aforementioned elements in them. The paper shows that even with significant manual effort in prompt design, both in terms theoretically-driven explanation in the form of pragma-dialectic rules and reasoning chains for large sets of examples, the task of fallacy detection remains prone to errors. This is illustrated based on a new dataset of manually curated fallacies from a PD textbook (Van Eemeren and Grootendorst, 1987) and an enhanced version of a larger-scale, general-purpose fallacy dataset from Jin et al. (2022a), which we manually enhance with the violated PD rule and their reasoning chains.

Overall, ‘the facts speak for themselves’: The three GPT models GPT-3.5, GPT-4 and GPT-4o struggle even when they are prompted carefully with (a) a solid theoretical foundation of what constitutes a fallacy and (b) manually crafted reasoning chains as examples in the prompt. The models improve to some extent with prompt engineering, but there is no evidence that later versions of GPT (which are significantly larger) generally perform better on the task. We do find that GPT-3.5 and GPT-4o benefit from chain-of-thought prompting, which surprisingly is not the case for GPT-4.

The paper proceeds as follows: Section 2 summarizes previous work on fallacy classification, with 3 describing the data collection and enhance-

Proceedings of the 12th Argument Mining Workshop, pages 1–10
July 31, 2025 ©2025 Association for Computational Linguistics

ment. Section 4 details the prompt engineering process, the results of which are presented in Section 5. Section 6 discusses the findings and concludes the paper.

2 Background

Even though the field of argument mining has attracted significant attention in the last 10 years, also with the rapid progress of deep learning, the automatic identification and classification of fallacies is still one of the main open issues. Overall, much of the previous literature relies on the 'innate' capabilities of the LLMs, i.e., the model(s) are queried outright for the task of fallacy detection without fine-tuning or with little to no prompt engineering. One exception is Ruiz-Dolz and Lawrence (2023), who use the argument schemes by Walton et al. (2008) to guide the model in capturing the fallacious nature of natural language arguments. The authors present a classification task where four of the classes contain fallacious arguments ('Appeal to Authority', 'Appeal to Majority', 'Slippery Slope' and 'Ad Hominem') which are related to seven argumentation schemes. The fifth class contains non-fallacious arguments.

Goffredo et al. (2023), along the lines of the majority of other work, remain theory-agnostic and assume six fallacy types (they partly overlap with those of Ruiz-Dolz and Lawrence (2023)). Jin et al. (2022a) construct two datasets and test 12 different LLMs for their fallacy detection abilities. In the end, a structurally aware classifier (of significantly smaller size) outperforms the LLMs for the same task. Hong et al. (2024) split fallacies into two main groups, namely formal and informal fallacies. The results show that LLMs have a harder time with fallacies that are present in the logical structure of the argument and perform somewhat better for fallacies that are related to the actual content. GPT-3 performs well on the Argotario dataset (Habernal et al., 2017), but is outperformed by the T5 model on the the other four datasets.

3 Data

Our capability assessment builds on an integrative approach to data collection, i.e., we consult two different data sources, combine the data points and analyze the performance of the models on the individual as well as the combined dataset. Both datasets comprise of informal fallacies and are described more closely in the following.[1]

3.1 The PD dataset

The PD dataset (henceforth, 'PD-data') draws on textbook examples in (Van Eemeren and Grootendorst, 1987) and comprises of clear-cut instances of fallacious arguments that violate one of the ten pragma-dialectical rules. Each of the arguments in PD-data is accompanied by the rule that is violated plus the reasoning behind its fallacious nature. For instance, Example (1) (Van Eemeren and Grootendorst, 1987, p. 285) violates the 'Freedom Rule' because a personal attack is performed on an opponent by casting suspicion on his motives. PD-data contains these three pieces of information: the actual example, the rule that is violated and the explanation given in the textbook.

(1) *He just says so because he wants to be elected.*

This is an extensive manual effort, illustrated furtherby Example (2), which also violates the 'Freedom Rule', but the reasoning as to why the rule was violated differs from the earlier example. Here, the personal attack takes the form of trying to depict the opponent as stupid, bad, unreliable and so forth (instead of casting suspicion on the motives as in (1)). Therefore there is no one-to-one mapping between the rule and the explanation, instead the latter one is solely based on the content of the example.

(2) *Don't listen to this moron, crook, liar, etc.*

The manual data collation in (Van Eemeren and Grootendorst, 1987) yields an initial seed set of 43 items. While this is already a significant increase in data points compared to (Ruiz-Dolz and Lawrence, 2023), we still construct an additional 43 fallacious arguments that are minimal pairs to the instances in PD-data: They mirror the violated rule and the reasoning behind the violation, but contain a slight variation in the linguistic surface. An example of the hand-crafted minimal pair of (1) is shown in Example (3). For the additional examples we also record the example, the violated rule and the reasoning.

(3) *She only agrees with that because she wants to win their approval.*

[1]Both datasets with PD rules and reasoning chains are available at `https://github.com/Erisa-Bytyqi/PD-data`.

Overall we end up with 86 data instances that are in violation of the 10 pragma-dialectic rules, a substantial increase from the 14 natural language arguments that constitute the dataset of (Ruiz-Dolz and Lawrence, 2023). Table 1 shows the distribution of data instances across the violated rules. The instances are not evenly distributed across the classes of violated rules, with 'Freedom Rule' and 'Argument Scheme Rule' having seven instances each, as opposed to 'Relevance Rule' and 'Unexpressed Premise Rule' which contain two instances each. However, given that we are not interested in training a fallacy classifier but evaluate a pre-trained model on its performance, this does not have an effect on the evaluation.

Violated PD rule	#Orig	#Added
Freedom Rule	7	7
Obligation To Defend Rule	4	4
Standpoint Rule	3	3
Relevance Rule	2	2
Unexpressed Premise Rule	2	2
Starting Point Rule	4	4
Validity Rule	7	7
Argument Scheme Rule	5	5
Concluding Rule	3	3
Language Use Rule	6	6
Overall	43	43

Table 1: Distribution of fallacy types in PD-data

3.2 The enhanced LOGIC dataset

The second dataset comes from (Jin et al., 2022a)[2], a dataset that encompasses a range of general logical fallacies, split across 13 different classes (henceforth, 'LOGIC') ('Faulty Generalization', 'Ad Hominem', 'Ad Populum', 'False Causality', 'Circular Reasoning', 'Appeal to Emotion', 'Fallacy of Relevance', 'Deductive Fallacy', 'Intentional Fallacy', Fallacy of Extension', 'False Dilemma', 'Fallacy of Credibility', 'Equivocation'). There are a total of 2449 instances in the dataset sourced mainly from student quiz websites.

Our study considers only a subset (300 out of 2449) of LOGIC, a set of fallacies that violate one of the ten pragma-dialectic rules. To that end, six of the thirteen fallacy types in LOGIC are mapped to their corresponding rule violation in pragma-dialectics, thereby harmonizing the LOGIC and PD-data labels. The dataset contains instances such as Example (4), a textbook case of an 'Ad Hominem' fallacy:

(4) *You're too ugly to be class president!*

In order to use LOGIC for the study in this paper, we manually map the LOGIC fallacy types to the rule violation stipulations in pragma-dialectics. To illustrate this, the personal attack in Example (4) is treated as a 'Freedom Rule' violation in PD, because it *"attacks the other party's person"* (Frans H. van Eemeren, 2020). We also map the 'Appeal to Emotion' fallacies in LOGIC to the 'Freedom Rule' in PD, because they a) unambiguously violate the rule and b) cannot be attributed to any other pragma-dialectic rule. A LOGIC instance of the 'Appeal to Emotion' fallacy is given in (5).

(5) *If you love your family, you'll buy this new stealth security system.*

Another mapping holds between the 'Circular Reasoning' fallacy in LOGIC and the 'Starting Point Rule' in PD. As illustration, see Example (6): The argument ('she is better than anyone else') merely restates the standpoint ('she is the best'), and as such violates the 'Starting Point Rule' of pragma-dialectics, thereby validating its classification under this rule.

(6) *She is the best because she is better than anyone else.*

The fallacy types 'Faulty Generalisation' and 'False Causality' are mapped to the 'Argument Scheme Rule' in PD, and 'Equivocation' is mapped onto the 'Language Rule' in PD. The LOGIC fallacies of 'Ad Populum', 'Fallacy of Relevance', 'Deductive Fallacy', 'Intentional Fallacy', Fallacy of Extension', 'False Dilemma', and 'Fallacy of Credibility' cannot be mapped reliably onto the PD-data rules. This is a result of the pragma-dialectic postulations, i.e., the stage of the argument, the interlocutor 'allowed' to violate a rule, and the argument from a conflict resolution perspective. We briefly illustrate this by way of the 'Ad Populum' fallacies in LOGIC which violate both the 'Relevance Rule' and 'Argument Scheme Rule' of pragma-dialectics, which are considered as *"variants of a fallacy which are not the same kind of fallacy when viewed from the perspective of resolving differences of opinion´´* (Frans H. van Eemeren, 2020). Examples (7) and (8) are of the 'Ad Populum' fallacy type. However, Example (7) violates

[2]Code and dataset available at `https://github.com/causalNLP/logical-fallacy`

LOGIC fallacy type	PD rule	#Instances
Faulty Generalisation	Argument Scheme Rule	61
Ad Hominem	Freedom Rule	41
Appeal to Emotion	Freedom Rule	23
Circular Reasoning	Starting Point Rule	19
False Causality	Argument Scheme Rule	18
Equivocation	Language Use Rule	5
Overall		197

Table 2: Fallacy Type distribution in LOGIC and PD

the 'Relevance Rule' as the audience's feelings or prejudices are exploited to defend the standpoint; this constitutes a non-argument, hence the violation. In Example (8), the protagonist, by referring to a kind of authority (here the majority) wants to push forward the truth or acceptability of a standpoint. For this particular case, the use of an unsuitable argumentation scheme results in the violation of the 'Argument Scheme' rule. For simplicity, LOGIC fallacy types that can be attributed to several pragma-dialectic rules are omitted in our study.

(7) *You do want your children to be safe in your own neighbourhood, don't you?*

(8) *Everybody says so, so it must be true.*

Overall, four of the ten pragma-dialectic rules have counterparts in the subset of LOGIC employed for the present study. Table 2 shows the mapping from LOGIC fallacy type to PD rule and the resulting number of data points per PD rule. Again, we see a class imbalance which closely mirrors that of PD-data, with the 'Argument Scheme Rule' and the 'Freedom Rule' instances surpassing those of the 'Starting Point' and 'Language Use Rule'. Aggregated, the 'Argument Scheme Rule' And 'Freedom Rule' categories contain 143 instances, whereas the two remaining rules have only 24 data points.

In summary, our investigation builds upon two datasets of fallacies, both labeled with PD rules, where one dataset (PD-data) contains the example, the rule and the reasoning behind the violation and the second dataset (LOGIC) which contains the example and the violated rule. This has an impact on setting up the prompt to get the responses from the model, which will be detailed in the following.

4 Probing the GPT models

For probing the models, we use zero-shot prompting (§4.1), chain-of-thought prompting (§4.2) and two-shot chain-of-thought prompting (§4.3) – methods that have been used in previous work on fallacy classification.

4.1 Zero-shot prompting

For the fallacy study in the present paper, the prompt contains the following elements (see Figure 1 in the Appendix for the full rendering): (a) the persona that we ask the model to adopt ('You are the world's leading expert in Pragma-Dialectics...'), (b) more information on pragma-dialectics ('an argumentation theory created by ...), (c) the details regarding the instructions ('You are specifically concerned with fallacies [...]'), (d) more detailed instructions regarding the output format to help minimize redundant information ('Be as concise as possible, name the rule, and give a very brief explanation.'), (e) the actual query to the model ('Given the pragma-dialectic approach to fallacies, ...') and (f) the fallacious argument under investigation, separated with a colon from the preceding material. The response *R* is generated by the model without further interaction.

The zero-shot prompt has two variations, the one just described which we will refer to with 'No Rules' (NR) in Section 5 on the results, plus a second one where we include the ten rules (classes) of fallacies and their definitions from (Van Eemeren and Grootendorst, 1987) in the prompt immediately before the fallacious argument (the 'With Rules' (WR) varation). The reason for this is that (OpenAI, 2024) hints at the fact that the inclusion of additional relevant information might help in obtaining better responses.

4.2 Chain-of-thought (CoT) prompting

Chain-of-thought (CoT) prompting has been shown to outperform zero-shot prompting for a multitude of reasoning tasks (Wei et al., 2022). Given that reasoning goes hand in hand with fallacy detection, we assume that prompting GPT-3.5 and GPT-4 with CoT prompts yields better responses that with zero-shot prompts. The reasoning chain in the CoT prompt is the same as the original reasoning chain given in the book (an example of a CoT prompt is shown in Figure 2 in the Appendix).

This prompt setting is a bit more taxing than zero-shot prompting since the prompt contains at least one more piece of information which has to be assembled manually for each prompt. The same is true if we escalate prompt sophistication and include two examples in the reasoning chain, as illustrated in the following.

4.3 Two-shot CoT

Two-shot CoT prompting increases the possibility that the model correctly interprets the task in the prompt ('the more exemplars the merrier'), a property suggested in previous work. Wei et al. (2022) use 7-shot CoT for commonsense tasks, OpenAI use a 10-shot prompt for their GPT4 evaluation on commonsense reasoning tasks (Achiam et al., 2023). We assume that with this extension, the model 'grasps' the characteristics of the fallacy more easily and is not just triggered by how similar the arguments are on the basis of the words contained in them.

Two-shot CoT prompting is used for the LOGIC dataset for which we do not have reasoning chains and where we use examples from the PD literature for correctly predicting the fallacy. The setup for this task is as follows: each of the instances from the LOGIC dataset has a ground-truth label (the pragma-dialectical rule violated by the instance). The first example in the two-shot CoT prompt is the same that is used in the CoT prompt for PD-data to classify the fallacious arguments from (Van Eemeren and Grootendorst, 1987) of that same class. The second example of the two-shot CoT prompt mirrors the pragma-dialectical fallacious argument from (Van Eemeren and Grootendorst, 1987), incorporating reasoning steps from the textbook that explain the argument's fallacious nature in case GPT did not identify the violated rule correctly in the CoT PD-data study. For those instances where GPT responded with the correct rule and the correct reasoning, GPT's response is turned into the second example in the two-shot CoT prompt, this is the case shown in Figure 3. For the argument 'Don't listen to this moron, crook, liar, etc.', the class and the reasoning steps generated by the model were both correct, making GPT's response a valid chain-of-thought and were therefore included in the two-shot CoT.

4.4 General prompting parameters

We restrict the length of the generated responses to 128 and 256 tokens for the LOGIC and PD-data instances, respectively, doing justice to the fact that the textual content of the prompt for LOGIC is longer than that of PD-data (more details in §4.2). The temperature is set to zero and the seed parameter is set to a random number.

5 Results

We apply a strict evaluation criterion on the generated responses, namely that both the violated rule and the provided reasoning need to be correct in order for the response to be judged correctly. If only one of these is correct, the response is treated as incorrect. This provides a realistic assessment of the capabilities, because we want to establish how reliable the models are without additional human interference, such as needing to determine the correct and incorrect portions of the GPT response. The metric we use to report the performance is accuracy, i.e., the fraction of correct predictions made by the three models.

Zero-shot prompting Table 3 provides an overview of the accuracy of the models for the zero-shot prompt setting on PD-data. Overall we can conclude that the performance is low, GPT-4o without rules only achieves an accuracy of .13, GPT-3.5 is at .3 and GPT-4 is slightly better with an accuracy of .49. Those results are comparable to those reported in Jin et al. (2022a) for GPT-3, but worse than those reported by Ruiz-Dolz and Lawrence (2023) who use GPT-3.5 and 4 and Walton's argument schemes. Adding the rules of PD to the prompt decreases the performance for GPT-3.5 and 4 (to .12 and .43 respectively), whereas it slightly helps GPT-4o (which still underperforms with an accuracy of .39). This suggests that the additional information rather confuses than helps the model.

If we dive into the performance regarding individual fallacies, we see significant differences.

Violated PD rule	#Instances	Zero-shot						CoT		
		GPT-3.5		GPT-4		GPT-4o		GPT-3.5	GPT-4	GPT-4o
		NR	WR	NR	WR	NR	WR			
Freedom Rule	14	0.43	0.14	1	0.86	0.57	0.85	0.71	1	1
Obligation To Defend Rule	8	0.75	0.25	0.75	0.25	0	0.75	1	0.75	1
Standpoint Rule	6	0	0.33	0	0.67	0	0.33	0.67	0	0.33
Relevance Rule	4	1	0	0	0	0	0	0.5	1	0
Unexpressed Premise Rule	4	0	0	0	0.5	0	0	0	0.5	1
Starting Point Rule	8	0.25	0	0.25	0	0	0	0.75	0.5	0.75
Validity Rule	14	0	0	0	0.6	0	0	0.2	0.2	0.8
Argument Scheme Rule	10	0.43	0	0.71	0	0.28	0.14	0.71	1	1
Concluding Rule	6	0	0	0	0.33	0	0.33	0.67	0.67	1
Language Use Rule	12	0.17	0	0.83	0.67	0	0.66	0.33	0.67	1
Overall		0.3	0.12	**0.49**	0.42	0.13	0.39	0.6	0.63	**0.86**

Table 3: Accuracy of the GPT models for the two zero-shot prompt settings with no rules (NR) and with the rules (WR) and the chain-of-thought prompt for PD-data.

For instance, the 'Freedom Rule' appears to be the class that all models have the least difficulty with in predicting correctly. But we cannot draw general conclusions, except that the inclusions of rules (WR) seems to trigger lower performance (except for 'Unexpressed Premise Rule' and 'Concluding Rule' in GPT-4). An interesting observation is that the incorporation of additional information in the prompt, namely the ten pragma-dialectic rules and their definitions (WR), degrades the performance of GPT-3.5 and GPT-4 with respect to the classification of 'Argument Scheme Rule' violations. This particular prompt setting leads to all PD-data instances of this class being misclassified as violations of either the 'Standpoint Rule' or the 'Validity Rule'.

CoT prompting The last two columns in Table 3 report the results when using CoT prompting on PD-data. Overall, CoT prompting significantly increases the performance of GPT-3.5 (overall accuracy of .6), to the extent that it is comparable to GPT-4 in the same setting (overall accuracy of .63), despite being much smaller in the number of parameters ('size'). GPT-4o shows the strongest results here (accuracy of .86), which leads us to conclude that the extensive manual effort in extracting textbook reasoning chains that are then used for prompting the model pays out.

A more detailed manual analysis of the misclassified instances reveals that the arguments in violation of the 'Unexpressed Premise Rule' are erroneously classified as violations of the 'Standpoint Rule' in all but two instances. This phenomenon can be attributed to what these two rules entail as violations: In case of the 'Standpoint Rule', the distortion of the co-interlocutors standpoints by either means of oversimplification (of their qualifications) or exaggeration (of their statements) is a direct violation of the rule (Van Eemeren and Grootendorst, 1987). This is also known as a straw man fallacy. The 'Unexpressed Premise Rule', on the other hand, is violated when an unexpressed premise is either exaggerated or not correctly reconstructed by the antagonist and then denied by the protagonist, which is a special case of the straw man fallacy. Regarding the *PD-data* dataset, the straw-man fallacy (regardless of its nature) is overwhelmingly associated with a violation of the 'Standpoint Rule' by the models.

Diverging from the assumption that CoT prompting improves the classification of fallacious arguments, the case of the 'Language Use Rule' shows that in fact zero-shot prompting performs slightly better than CoT for GPT-3.5 and 4, but not so for GPT-4o (accuracy of 1). In sum it is difficult to establish general conclusions as to which prompt design leads to consistently better results for fallacy detection. This issue of drawing meaningful insights is supported in the following where we include fallacies from a larger dataset and use PD to identify their fallacy type.

Two-shot CoT prompting Two-shot CoT prompting is performed on the LOGIC dataset for which no reasoning chains are available, under the assumption that if we include two examples of PD-data fallacies and their violated rule in the prompt the model is better able to classify those examples with relatively high performance.

The overview of the results in Table 4 paints a different picture, however. All models struggle to correctly classify the majority of the LOGIC arguments (accuracies of 0.23 for GPT-3.5 and GPT-4o

LOGIC type	PD rule	2s-CoT		
		GPT-3.5	GPT-4	GPT-4o
Faulty Generalisation	Argument Scheme Rule	0.44	0.51	0.57
Ad Hominem	Freedom Rule	0.1	0.02	0.02
Appeal to Emotion	Freedom Rule	0.07	0.07	0.08
False Causality	Argument Scheme Rule	0.28	0.78	0.44
Equivocation	Language Use Rule	0	0	0
Overall		0.23	**0.29**	0.23

Table 4: Results of 2-shot CoT prompting for a subset of the LOGIC datset.

and 0.29 for GPT-4). Striking is the difference in performance for the 'Freedom Rule', where all models was much better in identifying this type of fallacy in PD-data. In the case of the 'Ad Hominem' fallacy type, this inconsistency may be attributed to the difference in explicitness of the character attack in the two datasets. Arguments from LOGIC are to some extent more subtle in comparison to the text examples from PD. An example is given in (9) below: 'Don't listen to this moron, crook, liar, etc.' and 'Anyone who says that about me [that he's a racist bigot] is a Nazi' are much more stronger in terms of nature and wording than the LOGIC ad hominem 'Students who want cell phones in school have no idea what they're talking about'.

(9) **PD-1:** *Don't listen to this moron, crook, liar, etc.*
PD-2 *Anyone who says that about me [that he's a racist bigot] is a Nazi."*
LOGIC: *Students who want cell phones in school have no idea what they're talking about.*

A better performance, especially for GPT-4, is observed for the identification of 'Argument Scheme Rule' violations: When an argument makes the erroneous assumption that the correlation of two events means they have a cause-effect relationship, this is known as a 'False Causality' fallacy (Jin et al., 2022a) and a violation of the 'Argument Scheme Rule'. For more than half the instances belonging to this class, GPT-4 correctly identifies where the reasoning of the arguments falls apart, i.e., it identifies that correlation does not mean causation and that hence the argument is fallacious and violates the 'Argument Scheme Rule'. As noted previously, the ambiguous nature of arguments is notably difficult for both GPT models. This inability leads to violations of the 'Language Use Rule' not being correctly identified, as is the case for the LOGIC arguments, where this class has the poorest performance with no instances correctly classified.

Overall, the results indicate that both GPT models struggle to apply the pragma-dialectic model to fallacy detection and classification on data in the wild, i.e., data that does not originate in pragma-dialectic textbooks and arguments similar to them. The prompt content, as was our hypothesis, has a significant impact on the the models' performance, however, contrary to OpenAi's reporting (OpenAI, 2024), including fallacy definitions lowered the performance of the models. What emerges from the results reported here is an indication that fallacy detection and classification, which are also important in terms of having the models self-verify the content they generate as sound or not remains quite a challenging task no matter the model used to approach fallacies.

6 Discussion and conclusion

The present study explores the capabilities across a set of GPT models for the task of fallacy classification according to the pragma-dialectic theory of argumentation. Building on the success of chain-of-thought (CoT) prompting for several reasoning tasks, the models were subjected to zero-shot and CoT prompting for the task of classifying the fallacious arguments from Van Eemeren and Grootendorst (1987) and a subset of the LOGIC dataset (Jin et al., 2022b) as violations of one of the ten pragma-dialectic rules. In the course of this study we created a novel dataset (PD-data) comprising 86 fallacious arguments plus their reasoning chains that explain their fallacious nature. The prompts use best practices as described in OpenAI (2024) and the reasoning chains are informed by the fallacy definitions in Van Eemeren and Grootendorst (1987).

The finding of this investigation complement those of earlier studies, namely that the LLMs struggle to correctly identify the type of fallacy committed in an argument. It seems that language models with much smaller size such as RoBERTa (Ruiz-Dolz and Lawrence, 2023), MultiFusion BERT (Goffredo et al., 2023) or ELECTRA*Structaware* (Jin et al., 2022a) perform better, independent of the theoretical framework for classifying the fallacies. Also similar to previous work is the variability in the results across different models. While almost all arguments from PD-data in violation of the 'Freedom Rule' are classified correctly, there is a steep drop in performance for LOGIC arguments that violate the same rule, irrespective of prompt setting. CoT prompting proves successful for GPT-3.5 and GPT-4o, but does not have a great impact on GPT-4's performance for this task.

One can argue that the overall low performance of the models on LOGIC is due to the fact that the theoretical assumptions in PD do not scale beyond the examples that are mentioned in the textbooks supporting the theory, i.e., the ten rules postulated as violations do not hold when looking at fallacious arguments in the wild. However, given that the mapping between the categories in PD-data and LOGIC is possible, the conceptual assumptions seem to be valid, but it might be the naming of the categories and the wording of the PD rules that is confusing to the model. This only provides further support to the fact that generative models lack pragmatic understanding and provide aligned responses only when the wording in the prompt is informative. In sum, there is still substantial work to be done before we arrive at a systematic assessment of black box large-scale language models, not only in argumentation but in linguistic capabilities as whole. This paper is intended as one building block in this endeavor.

Limitations

This line of work is subject to at least two limitations. First, the design of our prompts is manual and, while practices reported by previous research for other reasoning tasks were used, we have yet to identify other prompt alterations that might lead to better performance. Second, we only provide at most two exemplars for *chain-of-thought* prompting, which in some cases is not enough to cover all presentations of a fallacy and results in the fallacious argument not being correctly identified as one. Further research might explore the limitation pertaining to the *chain-of-thought* prompt, by incorporating additional exemplars which encompass a wider range of the fallacy's variations, the performance of both GPT models might see an improvement.

References

Josh Achiam, Steven Adler, Sandhini Agarwal, Lama Ahmad, Ilge Akkaya, Florencia Leoni Aleman, Diogo Almeida, Janko Altenschmidt, Sam Altman, Shyamal Anadkat, and 1 others. 2023. Gpt-4 technical report. *arXiv preprint arXiv:2303.08774*.

Tariq Alhindi, Tuhin Chakrabarty, Elena Musi, and Smaranda Muresan. 2023. Multitask instruction-based prompting for fallacy recognition. *arXiv:2301.09992 [preprint]*. Available from arXiv: `https://arxiv.org/abs/2301.09992`.

Bart Verheij Frans H. van Eemeren, Bart Garssen. 2020. *Handbook of Argumentation Theory*. Springer Dordrecht.

Pierpaolo Goffredo, Mariana Chaves, Serena Villata, and Elena Cabrio. 2023. Argument-based detection and classification of fallacies in political debates. In *Proceedings of the 2023 Conference on Empirical Methods in Natural Language Processing*, pages 11101–11112, Singapore. Association for Computational Linguistics.

Ivan Habernal, Raffael Hannemann, Christian Pollak, Christopher Klamm, Patrick Pauli, and Iryna Gurevych. 2017. Argotario: Computational argumentation meets serious games. In *Proceedings of the 2017 Conference on Empirical Methods in Natural Language Processing: System Demonstrations*, pages 7–12, Copenhagen, Denmark. Association for Computational Linguistics.

Ruixin Hong, Hongming Zhang, Xinyu Pang, Dong Yu, and Changshui Zhang. 2024. A closer look at the self-verification abilities of large language models in logical reasoning. In *Proceedings of the 2024 Conference of the North American Chapter of the Association for Computational Linguistics: Human Language Technologies (Volume 1: Long Papers)*, pages 900–925, Mexico City, Mexico. Association for Computational Linguistics.

Zhijing Jin, Abhinav Lalwani, Tejas Vaidhya, Xiaoyu Shen, Yiwen Ding, Zhiheng Lyu, Mrinmaya Sachan, Rada Mihalcea, and Bernhard Schoelkopf. 2022a. Logical fallacy detection. In *Findings of the Association for Computational Linguistics: EMNLP 2022*, pages 7180–7198, Abu Dhabi, United Arab Emirates. Association for Computational Linguistics.

Zhijing Jin, Abhinav Lalwani, Tejas Vaidhya, Xiaoyu Shen, Yiwen Ding, Zhiheng Lyu, Mrinmaya Sachan, Rada Mihalcea, and Bernhard Schölkopf. 2022b. Logical fallacy detection. *Preprint*, arXiv:2202.13758.

OpenAI. 2024. Prompt Engineering. Https://platform.openai.com/docs/guides/prompt-engineering/prompt-engineering.

Ramon Ruiz-Dolz and John Lawrence. 2023. Detecting argumentative fallacies in the wild: Problems and limitations of large language models. In *Proceedings of the 10th Workshop on Argument Mining*. Association for Computational Linguistics.

Frans H Van Eemeren and Rob Grootendorst. 1987. Fallacies in pragma-dialectical perspective. *Argumentation*, 1:283–301.

Douglas Walton, Christopher Reed, and Fabrizio Macagno. 2008. *Argumentation schemes*. Cambridge University Press.

Jason Wei, Xuezhi Wang, Dale Schuurmans, Maarten Bosma, Fei Xia, Ed Chi, Quoc V Le, Denny Zhou, and 1 others. 2022. Chain-of-thought prompting elicits reasoning in large language models. *Advances in neural information processing systems*, 35:24824–24837.

A Appendix

P: You are the world's leading expert for Pragma-Dialectics, an argumentation theory by Frans H. van Eemeren and Rob Grootendorst. You are specifically concerned with fallacies in Pragma Dialectics and will correctly classify the text in triple quotes. Be as concise as possible, name the rule, and give a very brief explanation.
Given the pragma-dialectic approach to fallacies, which dialectical rule does the following sentence violate: "'The American medical system doesn't care what happens to the patient. I know of a man who was turned away by a hospital and then died."'

R: [MODEL RESPONSE]

Figure 1: First variation of the zero-shot prompt using an example from PD-data and the GPT-4 response.

Q: You are the world's leading researcher in Pragma Dialectics and provide answers accompanied by very brief reasoning steps and the name of the rule.

Which rule of Pragma-Dialectics does the sentence in triple single quotes violate: '''**This choice will impact your future prospects within the company.**'''

RC: As parties must not prevent each other from advancing standpoints, putting pressure on the opponent (here: his choice will affect his job) is a clear violating of the Freedom Rule. Because of the implications, the other party might not advance their standpoint and this is in violation of the aforementioned rule where parties must not prevent each other from advancing or casting doubt on standpoints.

Q: Which rule of Pragma-Dialectics does the sentence in triple single quotes violate: '''**You'll have to face the consequences for our personal relationship** '''.

R: [MODEL RESPONSE]

Figure 2: Chain-of-thought prompt for the PD dataset.

P: Given the pragma-dialectic approach to fallacies, which dialectical rule does the following sentence violate: **Anyone who says that about me [that he's a racist bigot] is a Nazi."**

RC: Parties must not prevent each other from advancing standpoints. If you perform a personal attack on the opponent by depicting him as stupid, bad, etc you directly violate the Freedom Rule. Here by depicting the opponent as a 'Nazi' we have a clear violation of the Freedom Rule.

P: Given the pragma-dialectic approach to fallacies, which dialectical rule does the following sentence violate: **Don't listen to this moron, crook, liar, etc.**

RC: ...

P: Given the pragma-dialectic approach to fallacies, which dialectical rule does the following sentence violate: **Researchers are frauds who don't earn their salaries.**

R: [MODEL RESPONSE]

Figure 3: Two-shot chain-of-thought prompt for the LOGIC dataset.

Exploring LLM Priming Strategies for Few-Shot Stance Classification

Yamen Ajjour and Henning Wachsmuth
Leibniz University Hannover, Institute of Artificial Intelligence
`<initial>.<lastname>@ai.uni-hannover.de`

Abstract

Large language models (LLMs) are effective in predicting the labels of unseen target instances if instructed for the task and training instances via the prompt. LLMs generate a text with higher probability if the prompt contains text with similar characteristics, a phenomenon, called priming, that especially affects argumentation. An open question in NLP is how to systematically exploit priming to choose a set of instances suitable for a given task. For stance classification, LLMs may be primed with few-shot instances prior to identifying whether a given argument is *pro* or *con* a topic. In this paper, we explore two priming strategies for few-shot stance classification: one takes those instances that are most semantically similar, and the other chooses those that are most stance-similar. Experiments on three common stance datasets suggest that priming an LLM with stance-similar instances is particularly effective in few-shot stance classification compared to baseline strategies, and behaves largely consistently across different LLM variants.

1 Introduction

Large language models (LLMs) have enabled a new input paradigm in NLP by following instructions that define the task to be solved: prompting. Designing optimal instructions for a given task is a key challenge in this paradigm. A common technique in prompt engineering is to append a set of few-shot instances to the instructions that are similar to the target instance. Although this technique is widely used, research lacks a clear understanding of what makes a set of examples effective for a target instance (Min et al., 2022). A mechanism that helps to explain the effect of a prompt on the output of an LLM is priming, which is the effect of a certain stimulus (prime) on processing a subsequent stimulus (target) (Misra et al., 2020).

Priming influences human behavior by making certain information more salient and accessible. Research on argumentation in political science studies how priming connects media exposure with voting behavior. Media coverage highlights a candidate's topics and arguments to increase the chances that voters elect the candidate (DellaVigna and Kaplan, 2007; Iyengar and Hahn, 2009). The way the topics are presented with either positive or negative sentiment in news influences how the audience votes, which is called affective priming (Kuehne et al., 2011). For LLMs, appending a set of similar instances to the target instance in a prompt can be seen as priming for label voting.

Prompting research has shown that the choice and order of training instances have a strong effect on model performance. Among others, Liu et al. (2022) find that semantically similar instances are most effective in sentiment analysis, question answering, and text-to-table generation. However, it is unclear so far whether this finding generalizes to tasks dealing with argumentation, such as stance classification: classifying an argument as *pro* or *con* towards a controversial topic (Somasundaran and Wiebe, 2009).

In this paper, we study how to choose the best training instances for few-shot priming in stance classification. We investigate two alternative priming strategies: prompting an LLM with training instances that are (a) semantically similar to the instance to be classified or (b) stance-similar (e.g., pro electric cars and con fuel cars). While the first builds on the idea of Liu et al. (2022) and semantic priming, the second builds on affective priming. We contrast both priming strategies to diversification, which has been observed to foster better performance in stance classification (Schiller et al., 2024; Arakelyan et al., 2023).

To operationalize the priming strategies, we use contrastive learning to quantify the similarity between training instances and a given target instance. The first strategy, `semantic-priming`, returns the k instances with the highest semantic similarity.

Proceedings of the 12th Argument Mining Workshop, pages 11–23

The second, `affective-priming`, returns k instances with the highest stance similarity. Finally, the diversification strategy, `distinct-k`, groups the training instances into k clusters according to their semantic similarity and uses the most central representative of each cluster as a prime. Figure 1 contrasts the three priming strategies.

We evaluate all priming strategies against random sampling on three widely used stance classification datasets, IBMSC (Bar-Haim et al., 2017), VAST (Allaway and McKeown, 2020), and Perspectrum (Chen et al., 2019). We employ four different LLMs in two manners: Llama2-7b (Zhang et al., 2022) and Vicuna-7b (Chiang et al., 2023) in prompting, as well as Alpaca-7b (Taori et al., 2023) and Mistral-7b-instruct (Jiang et al., 2023) in both prompting and instruction fine-tuning. According to our results, `affective-priming` shows substantial improvements over random sampling and diversification in prompting for Llama2-7b and Vicuna-7b. `semantic-priming` is more effective when the number of shots is low (up to 4).

Our findings contribute to research in three ways: (1) We investigate for the first time the effect of affective priming on large language models. (2) We establish priming strategies as a central component of approaches to few-shot stance classification. (3) We advance the state-of-the-art on stance classification on IBMSC and Perspectrum.[1]

2 Related Work

Prompting defines a task as instructions that an LLM completes with the desired output. Few-shots are exemplary instances of the task together with their expected outputs that are added to the instructions. The selection of few-shots is decisive for the performance of an LLM on the task. Gao et al. (2021) show that prepending the input instance with semantically similar instances to it is more effective in four GLUE tasks (Wang et al., 2019) than using random instances. Like us, they use SBERT (Reimers and Gurevych, 2020) to encode the instance to be classified and the few-shot instances, but they do not investigate what similarity is effective for a given task.

Liu et al. (2022) find that GPT-3 exploits similar instances more than random ones, improving effectiveness on sentiment analysis and table-to-text generation. Levy et al. (2023) use BM25 similarity to sample diverse instances for semantic parsing, outperforming a sampling of similar instances. We consider prepending instances that are similar to the input instance to the instructions as priming. Instead of using vanilla similarity measures, we propose a contrastive-learning-based similarity measure to retrieve few-shot instances that are motivated by priming theory.

Research on priming first investigated how exposure to certain stimuli influences subsequent behavior or cognition. Earlier studies show that people more effectively recognize a string as a word after being exposed to semantically similar ones (Meyer and Schvaneveldt, 1971), known as semantic priming. In political discourse, the focused coverage of topics associated with a candidate in the news makes voters more likely to vote for them in elections. In contrast, affective priming utilizes the (positive or negative) tone in which messages are conveyed to shape the attitude towards a topic (Sheafer, 2007; Kuehne et al., 2011). Following these ideas, we contrast two priming strategies that exploit semantic and stance similarity, respectively, between the training and the target instances.

Studies show that the text generated by LLMs can also be steered by priming. Misra et al. (2020) find evidence that BERT is more likely to correctly predict a masked target word in a sentence once the sentence is prepended with a semantically similar prime. LLMs also adapt to the structure of the prompt and generate text with similar syntax of an input prime (Prasad et al., 2019; Jumelet et al., 2024). While LLMs have been shown to be steered by semantic and syntactic priming, their sensitivity to positive and negative sentiment (affective priming) has not yet been explored.

Stance classification is the task of identifying the polarity of an argument towards a topic among a set of labels, such as *pro* or *con* (Somasundaran and Wiebe, 2009; Reuver et al., 2024). Researchers propose approaches that integrate the context of the target instance by learning topic representations (Augenstein et al., 2016; Wei and Mao, 2019) or retrieving related knowledge to the instance from a knowledge graph (Liu et al., 2021). In contrast to these approaches, our work shows that training instances with similar stances are helpful for prompt-based stance classification.

Few-shot stance classification aims at settings where only few training data is available (Allaway and McKeown, 2020). Prompt-based approaches either inject topic knowledge (Beck et al., 2023)

[1]Code available here: `https://github.com/webis-de/priming-strategies-for-stance-classification`

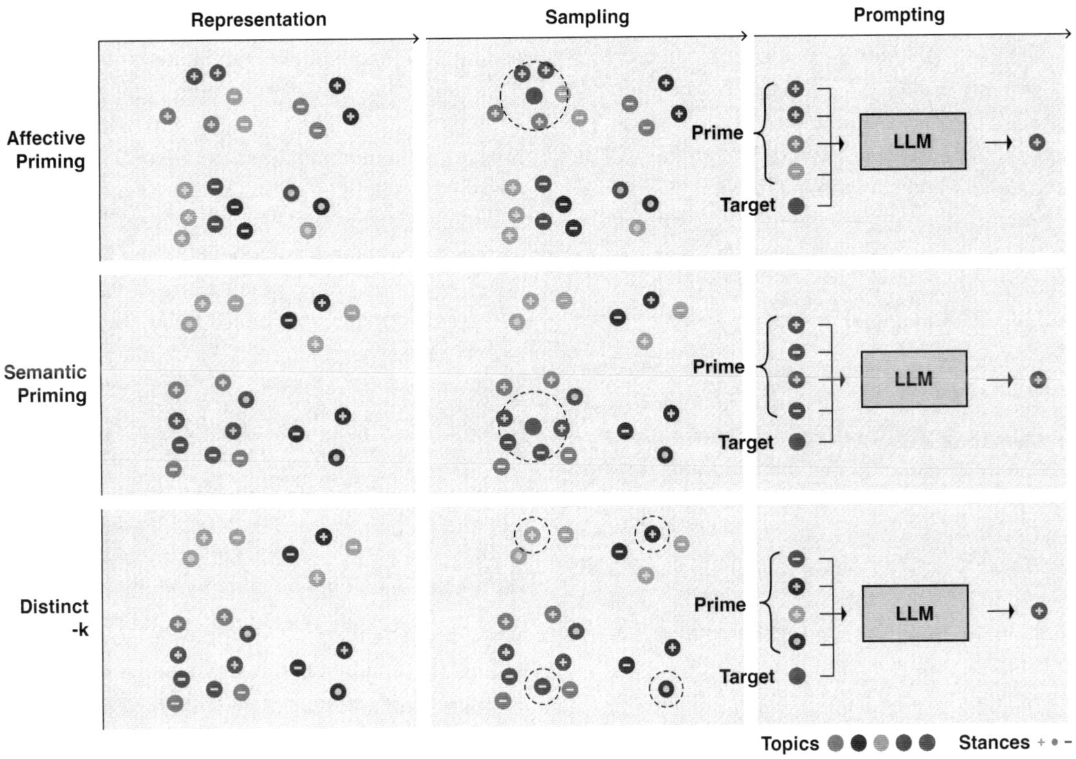

Figure 1: Comparison of the three priming strategies (`affective-priming`, `semantic-priming`, and `distinct-k`). The *representation* focuses either on stance or semantics. Sampling picks few-shots either by similarity or by diversity. Prompting combines the (here, four) few-shots with the target instance (shown in red) to classify.

or use a stance label representation (Jiang et al., 2022) in the prompt. Research on few-shots in stance classification is limited to selecting diverse instances. Arakelyan et al. (2023) proposed a diversification approach that outperforms the state of the art on several stance classification datasets. Schiller et al. (2024) analyze the effect of increasing the count of topics in the training set against increasing the size of samples per topic. Their experiments illustrate that, for small LLMs such as Ernie 2.0 (Sun et al., 2020), diversifying the training set in terms of topics improves performance on unseen topics. In contrast to diversification-based approaches, our study suggests that stance-similar instances are most effective for prompting certain LLMs (e.g., Vicuna-7b).

3 Approach

As discussed in the introduction, priming utilizes existing associations between a pair of concepts, called the *prime* and the *target*. It rests on invoking an effect on the target by mentioning the prime. Our priming approach to stance classification treats a test instance as a target and retrieves k semantically similar or stance-similar instances as training instances. The approach employs prompt-based learning to prime an LLM with the retrieved k few-shots to predict the stance of the target. In the following, we start by describing our prompt-based learning methods, which we employ for stance classification. Then, we present our priming strategies.

3.1 Prompt-based Learning

We adopt two prompt-based learning methods for language models: *prompting* and *instruction fine-tuning*. Both methods use $k \geq 1$ training instances in a few-shot manner. Each instance contains a topic, an argument, and a stance. We rely on greedy decoding in both methods to let an LLM complete the prompt with the most probable token, which is the stance label. We use the following prompt to describe the stance classification task (see Table 2 in the Appendix for the prompt template):

> "Classify the stance of the following argument on the given topic into: Pro or Con."[2]

[2]For VAST, we add the label Neutral.

Prompting Here, we simply append the learning instances to the prompt without any fine-tuning. We use this method for four large language models (LLMs): *Mistral-7b-instruct* (Jiang et al., 2023), *Alpaca-7b* (Taori et al., 2023), *Vicuna-7b* (Chiang et al., 2023), and *Llama2-7b* (Touvron et al., 2023).

See Table 2 again for the format of the training instances. In case the training instances exceed the allowed input length of an LLM, we cut the last part of each training instance.

Instruction Fine-tuning While prompting is efficient and easy to employ since no training is required, instruction fine-tuning pushes the use of the prompt further in that the language model is fine-tuned on instruction data. Following this method, we fine-tune Alpaca-7b[3] (Taori et al., 2023) and Mistral-instruct-7b (Jiang et al., 2023) using LoRa (Hu et al., 2022) on the k instances with an instruction prompt. The topic and argument are then given in the input section of the prompt. For fine-tuning both models, we used grid-search to find the best hyperparameters on the validation sets of the respective dataset, which we will introduce in Section 4. Full hyperparameters of both models can be found in Table 7 in the Appendix. We fine-tune the models in two steps. First, we fine-tune the models on all the training data of each dataset using the aforementioned prompt without few-shots. Second, we fine-tune the models with the aforementioned prompt on the few-shots sampled by the priming strategies from the training set.

3.2 Priming Strategies

In the following, we introduce two priming strategies that exploit stance similarity and semantic similarity between a target instance and the training instances. Afterward, we describe baseline priming strategies that are tailored to contrast the priming strategies and to analyze the strengths and weaknesses of all strategies: `distinct-k` and `random`. Our hypothesis is that training instances that are similar to the target instance in terms of semantics or stance are more effective than diverse or random training instances. Figure 1 illustrates how each of the three approaches represents, samples, and prompts instances.

Affective priming Prompting an LLM with arguments that hold similar stances to the target instance provides the most consistent stimulus to it, inducing bias in line with the original idea of priming. To this end, we train a contrastive learning embedding that captures the *stance similarity* between the instances on the training set. For training this embedding, we use SBERT (Reimers and Gurevych, 2020) and use argument pairs on the same topic with the same stance as positive instances. Argument pairs on the same topic with different stances are provided as negative instances.

For each instance, we concatenate the topic and argument, separated by `[SEP]`. Among the possible models for SBERT[4], we use the standard model `all-mpnet-base-v2`. The priming strategy then returns the k most stance-similar training instances to a given test instance in terms of cosine similarity. We make sure that this priming strategy retrieves one instance per topic to maximize the learning effect.

Semantic Priming This priming strategy assumes that the instances most semantically similar to a test instance should be chosen to prime the LLM. Accordingly, we retrieve the most *semantically* similar training instances for each test instance. The similarity is calculated by embedding a pair of training and test instances using the original SBERT embeddings and calculating their cosine similarity. Similar to our affective priming strategy, we use the standard model `all-mpnet-base-v2` among the available models for SBERT. In contrast to `affective-priming`, we select semantically similar instances while maintaining a balanced stance distribution of the selected set.

Distinct-k This baseline priming strategy assumes that a diverse selection of instances should be chosen to prime the LLM. The rationale behind this strategy is that since the training set is limited in size, it might not contain similar instances for some target instances. Following this idea, we cluster the instances in the training set into k clusters. Then, we take the top 10 nearest arguments to each cluster centroid as candidates according to Euclidean distance.[5] This allows us to ensure a balanced stance distribution in the chosen instances. To cluster the arguments, we first embed them with SBERT and then apply agglomerative clustering with Ward linkage and Euclidean distance. During training, we sample one instance from each of the cluster candidates.

[3]We use the following Alpaca model on HuggingFace: `https://huggingface.co/wxjiao/alpaca-7b`

[4]SBERT, `https://www.sbert.net/`

[5]For VAST, we took the top 50 instances since the class distribution in VAST is skewed (See Table 3).

Random To assess the impact of priming, we compare all strategies to `random` sampling, which takes a different random sample of size k from the training as few-shots for each test instance.

4 Experiments

The proposed priming strategies stimulate large language models to tackle stance classification using semantic and stance similarity. In the following experiments, we compare the priming strategies on different stance classification datasets.

4.1 Data

For evaluation, we require data with sufficient and representative coverage of topics to assess the robustness of our approach on unseen topics. Hence, we choose the following datasets:

IBMSC This dataset contains 2,394 arguments that are labeled as *pro* or *con* with respect to 55 controversial topics (Bar-Haim et al., 2017). The dataset is split into a training set and a test set that covers 25 topics and 30 topics, respectively. The distribution of the stance labels in the test set is almost balanced, with 48% of the arguments being con and 52% arguments being pro.

VAST This dataset contains 15,956 comments labeled as *pro*, *con*, or *neutral* with respect to 5,630 topics (Allaway and McKeown, 2020). We choose the VAST zero-shot setting, which ensures a disjoint topic selection between the training and test sets.

Perspectrum This dataset contains 11,822 claims on 907 topics that have been posted on the debate portal *debate.org* (Chen et al., 2019). Similar to IBMSC, the claims are labeled with *pro* or *con* with respect to the topic, and mostly have a balanced distribution. Details of the splits for the three datasets can be found in Table 3.

4.2 Baselines

To contrast few-shot prompting and instruction fine-tuning with standard fine-tuning, we further compare to the *majority* class found in the training set, and we fine-tune *DeBERTa* (He et al., 2020) on the training set to predict the stance of the argument. For the latter, we concatenate the argument and the topic and provide them as input for training (hyperparameters can be found in Table 4 in the Appendix). Moreover, we report the performance of several state-of-the-art approaches from related work on the datasets as available (Allaway and McKeown, 2020; Barrow et al., 2021; Arakelyan et al., 2023; Hanley and Durumeric, 2023; Zhang et al., 2025).

Finally, to contrast the few-shot approaches, we fine-tune Alpaca-7b and Mistral-7b-instruct on *all training* data. We combine all four models considered for *prompting* and the two models considered for *instruction fine-tuning* with all four prompting strategies (`random`, `distinct-k`, `semantic-priming`, and `affective-priming`). We compare the `affective-priming` strategy against a baseline (`Stance-similarity`) that uses the majority label of the k most similar training instances to the target instance as returned by `affective-priming`. We take 16 instances for IBMSC and Perspectrum, and 12 for VAST.[6]

4.3 Results

Table 1 lists the results of the experiment for the prompting and instruction fine-tuning approaches. The performance in all experiments is averaged over five seeds (including the follow-up analyses discussed below). At the bottom of the table is the performance of Alpaca-7b and Mistral-7b-instruct after fine-tuning them on the training set.

The results show that fine-tuning Mistral-7b-instruct on all training data yields the best classification performance, outperforming other models on this task. This shows the substantial impact of instruction fine-tuning on stance classification. In most cases, the priming strategies show consistent enhancement over the baseline priming strategies in prompting, which we discuss first.

The `affective-priming` strategy outperforms other priming strategies across all models on IBMSC and VAST, except for Mistral-7b-instruct. The performance of `affective-priming` is also higher than that of `Stance-similarity` in all cases (except Mistral-7b-instruct and Vicuna-7b on VAST). This indicates the advantages of using stance-similar instances to prime LLMs compared to relying solely on contrastive-learning similarity measures in few-shot classification. The performance of Mistral-7b-instruct is higher when prompted with diverse instances. In contrast, a consistently substantial improvement can be observed on VAST, where Llama2-7b and Alpaca-7b outperform the random priming strategy with 0.261

[6] Notice that we use for VAST multiples of 3, since it is annotated with three labels, which allows us to maintain a balanced stance distribution.

	Approach	Strategy	IBMSC			VAST				Perspectrum		
			Pro	Con	F_1	Pro	Con	Neu	F_1	Pro	Con	F_1
Fine-tuning	Majority		.681	0	.341	0	0	.525	.175	.693	0	.350
	DeBERTa		.717	.681	.699	.665	.679	.903	.749	.830	.809	.819
	Allaway and McKeown (2020)		–	–	–	–	–	–	.670	–	–	–
	Barrow et al. (2021)		–	–	.834	–	–	–	–	–	–	–
	Arakelyan et al. (2023)		–	–	.862	–	–	–	.543	–	–	.789
	Hanley and Durumeric (2023)		–	–	–	.695	.711	.905	.771	–	–	–
	Zhang et al. (2025)		–	–	–	.770	.794	–	.825	–	–	–
Contrastive Learning	`Stance-similarity`		.617	.569	.593	.544	.505	.879	.643	.770	.744	.757
Prompting	Llama2-7b	`random`	.741	.670	.705	.514	.403	.301	.409	.733	.746	.740
		`distinct-k`	.728	.681	.705	.499	.415	.259	.391	.755	.758	.756
		`semantic-priming`	.763	.535	.649	.500	.404	.173	.359	.783	.732	.757
		`affective-priming`	.704	.770	**.737***	.649	.539	.852	**.670***	.784	.774	**.779***
	Alpaca-7b	`random`	.686	.768	.727	.538	.542	.128	.393	.752	.799	.775
		`distinct-k`	.701	.744	.722	.547	.552	.055	.385	.758	.800	.780
		`semantic-priming`	.732	.733	.733	.532	.537	.122	.397	.800	.815	**.808***
		`affective-priming`	.737	.739	**.738**	.612	.681	.836	**.710***	.749	.797	.770
	Mistral-7b-instruct	`random`	.805	.837	.821	.556	.537	.605	.566	.826	.836	.831
		`distinct-k`	.863	.871	**.867***	.563	.553	.615	**.577**	.849	.840	**.845**
		`semantic-priming`	.856	.857	.857*	.514	.522	.465	.501	.839	.833	.836
		`affective-priming`	.858	.866	.862*	.529	.54	.639	.570	.844	.841	.843
	Vicuna-7b	`random`	.788	.762	.775	.545	.483	.329	.453	.812	.807	.809
		`distinct-k`	.813	.746	.779	.536	.477	.389	.467	.818	.808	.813
		`semantic-priming`	.803	.692	.747	.537	.498	.275	.437	.807	.774	.790
		`affective-priming`	.833	.811	**.822***	.560	.565	.564	**.563***	.818	.811	**.815**
Instruction fine-tuning	Alpaca-7b	`random`	.820	.801	.810	.581	.599	.779	.653	.842	.856	.849
		`distinct-k`	.807	.817	.812	.481	.648	.785	.638	.829	.849	.839
		`semantic-priming`	.824	.810	**.817**	.487	.640	.771	.633	.848	.860	**.854**
		`affective-priming`	.758	.701	.730	.529	.676	.820	**.675**	.853	.830	.842
	Mistral-7b-instruct	`random`	.920	.908	.914	.539	.558	.642	.641	.896	.882	.889
		`distinct-k`	.901	.940	.902	.568	.630	.823	.674	.913	.902	**.908**
		`semantic-priming`	.928	.920	**.924**	.579	.603	.798	.660	.907	.896	.902
		`affective-priming`	.912	.910	.911	.638	.655	.885	**.726**	.890	.904	.897
	Alpaca-7b (all training)		.796	.817	.806	.569	.636	.790	.665	.830	.849	.839
	Mistral-7b-instruct (all training)		.911	.927	.919	.643	.685	.835	.720	.941	.932	.936

Table 1: Accuracy and macro F_1-score of our prompting and instruction fine-tuned approaches with each priming strategy on IBMSC, Perspectrum, and VAST in comparison to the fine-tuned approaches. "–" indicates that the corresponding entry is not reported. Bold values indicate the best effectiveness in the few-shot settings. Significant enhancements relative to random sampling with a p-value less or equal to 0.01 are denoted by an asterisk (*).

and 0.317, respectively. This substantial improvement raises the question of what type of priming instances are actually chosen. Therefore, we analyzed the instances in the test set of VAST that are labeled correctly with Alpaca-7b when combined with `affective-priming` and wrongly when combined with the other priming strategies. We observe that about 91% of these instances are neutral instances for which the `affective-priming` strategy selected 97% neutral priming training instances. This suggests the substantial impact of consistency between the stance of the training instances and the test instance in prompting.

On Perspectrum, `affective-priming` yields the best performance across the priming strategies for Llama2-7b and Vicuna-7b. As with the other datasets, Mistral-7b-instruct is most effective when combined with `distinct-k`, slightly beating `affective-priming` (0.002 higher). However, `affective-priming` outperforms both `semantic-priming` and `random` sampling.

For instruction fine-tuning, we can observe that `semantic-priming` is the most effective among the priming strategies on IBMSC. Using this strategy with Alpaca-7b and Mistral-7b-instruct yields better performance than fine-tuning them on the training set of IBMSC. On the other hand, `affective-priming` outperforms `random`

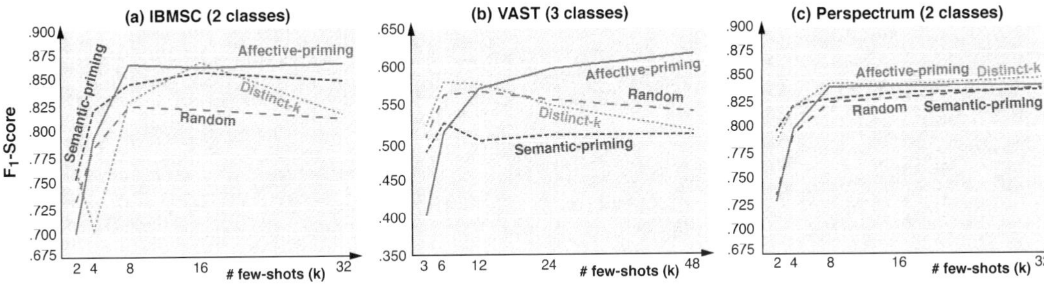

Figure 2: Macro F_1-score of Mistral-7b-instruct per priming strategy (`semantic-priming`, `affective-priming`, `distinct-k`, and `random`) over the few-shots k for the three datasets: (a) IBMSC, (b) VAST, and (c) Perspectrum.

for Alpaca-7b and Mistral-7b-instruct on VAST with an enhancement of 0.022 and 0.085, respectively. The performance of the `semantic-priming` strategy exceeds the performance of random on Perspectrum with a difference of 0.005 to 0.013 for Alpaca-7b and Mistral-7b, respectively. By comparing these results to those of the prompting method, we observe that priming instances are less effective than training instances in the standard instruction fine-tuning learning method. Hence, we can conclude that our priming strategies are effective when applied to prompting approaches.

5 Analysis

To further understand the priming strategies, we analyze the performance of the priming strategies for the most effective model in prompting, that is, Mistral-7b-instruct. Figure 2 shows its performance with the four strategies for a range of k values on the three datasets. As seen, `affective-priming` converges to higher performance at $k = 8$ few-shots for IBMSC and Perspectrum and at $k = 12$ for VAST. This might indicate that `affective-priming` is most effective when the stance of the test instance is repeated and consistent in the training instances. In contrast, `semantic-priming` outperforms `affective-priming` on all datasets for $k \in \{2, 3, 4, 6\}$ and saturates afterward, suggesting that, for few instances, semantic associations between the training and test instances are more effective.

Our experiments indicate that the priming strategies consistently enhance the performance of prompting methods on IBMSC and VAST. Still, they perform moderately on Perspectrum compared to diversification and `random` on all models except Llama2-7b. We can observe that `affective-priming` results in significantly better performance on IBMSC and VAST. On Perspectrum, however, the performance of `affective-priming` varies across models and is even subpar to `random` for Alpaca-7b. This raises the question of which properties of Perspectrum result in this varied performance and to which extent the priming effect is observable on this dataset.

As a first inquiry, we investigated the distribution of the similarities between the instances and target instances sampled with `affective-priming` in Perspectrum for $k = 16$. We observed that the sampled priming instances are very similar to the target instances, with a minimum value of 0.87, a mean of 0.99, and a maximum of 1. In comparison, the distribution of the similarity distribution for VAST has a minimum value of 0.44, a mean value of 0.79, and a maximum of 0.98.[7]

Since sampling instances with lower similarity results in better performance on VAST, we investigate whether sampling with lower similarities might result in better performance on Perspectrum. For this goal, we rerun the prompting experiments on Perspectrum while limiting the similarity between the prime and the target instance with a maximum threshold for `affective-priming` and `semantic-priming`. We choose thresholds that constitute increasing 10% percentiles of the similarity distribution for `affective-priming` and `semantic-priming`.

Figure 3 shows the performance of the four models in terms of macro F_1-score after limiting the similarity to the selected percentiles. For example, a percentile with a value of 90 means that only the training instances whose similarity score to the target instances among the 90% least similar can be selected to prime the model. We also plot the performance of `distinct-k` and `random` to provide a

[7]The distribution of the similarity distribution for IBMSC has a minimum value of 0.40, a mean value of 0.81, and a maximum of 0.99.

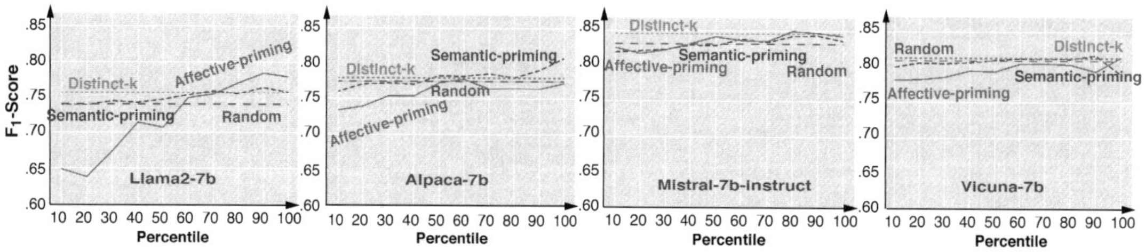

Figure 3: Macro F_1-score of Llama2-7b, Alpaca-7b, Mistral-7b-instruct, and Vicuna-7b on Perspectrum with limiting the sampled instances with increasing percentile thresholds. A percentile indicates a maximum similarity threshold applied only to `affective-priming` and `semantic-priming`. A percentile of 90 means that we only sample the 90% least similar with the priming strategies.

basis to compare the priming strategy.

The figure shows that the higher the stance similarity of the prime to the target, the better the performance of the models. However, this increasing performance depends largely on the model. For example, by taking the first 10% instances to prompt Llama2-7b with `affective-priming`, which are the least stance-stance similar, we achieve an F_1-score of 0.648. In comparison, Llama2-7b achieves an F_1-score of 0.784 when sampling from the 90% least stance-similar instances. A similar but less steep increase can be observed for `semantic-priming` where Llama2-7b achieves an F_1-score of 0.739 at the percentile 10 and an F_1-score of 0.764 at the percentile 90. We also observe a small drop (around 0.005 points) in the performance for both priming strategies from the percentile 90 to the percentile 100. This might indicate that instances that are very similar to the target instances are not the best for priming the model.

According to this analysis, the effect of `affective-priming` on Vicuna-7b and Mistral-7b-instruct is lower than Llama2-7b but is still a substantial increase. For example, the performance of Vicuna-7b increases from 0.783 at the percentile 10 to an F_1-score of 0.815 when considering all the training instances (percentile 100). Both Vicuna-7b and Mistral-7b-instruct show a drop in performance at higher percentiles (the percentile 90 for Vicuna-7b and 100 for Mistral-7b-instruct).

This analysis corroborates the observation that certain large language models can be steered by `affective-priming`. It also shows that the effect of `affective-priming` largely depends on the model. We observe that taking highly stance-similar instances to the target instances results in some cases in subpar performance on Perspectrum. This might explain the moderate performance of the priming strategies on Perspectrum compared to IBMSC and VAST.

6 Discussion

This section discusses possible reasons for the varied performance of `affective-priming` across models and gives practical recommendations for selecting few-shots for stance classification.

Among the four models, our experiments demonstrate that Llama2-7b and Vicuna-7b are most susceptible to `affective-priming` across datasets in the prompting setup. Vicuna-7b is fine-tuned from Llama2-7b on ChatGPT conversations. Since both models are susceptible to `affective-priming`, the datasets on which Llama2-7b was pre-trained might be one cause for the models' susceptibility to `affective priming`. Datasets that contain opinionated information, such as news or online forums, might include certain associations that are triggered by the few-shots in the prompt.

Another possible reason for the difference in performance of `affective priming` across the models is the models' architecture. Possible design choices that can affect the sensitivity to `affective priming` are the attention mechanism or the activation function. Whilst our experiments are comprehensive in terms of the studied model architectures, a systematic study of the effect of the model elements on the sensitivity to priming is beyond the scope of this paper.

Finally, the model developer's application of alignment methods such as Reinforcement Learning from Human Feedback (RLHF) or other fine-tuning steps might make the model more or less susceptible to priming. While none of the four models are aligned using RLHF, all models except Llama2-7b are instruction fine-tuned. The data or method used for fine-tuning the three instruction fine-tuned models might be one source for the varied performance of the models.

Practical Recommendations Our experiments illustrate the merit of selecting instances that are stance-similar to the input instance for few-shot stance classification. In addition, our experiments demonstrate the benefit of diversifying the training instances in terms of topic, which resonates with the work of Arakelyan et al. (2023); Schiller et al. (2024). A combination of both techniques can be realized by first sampling an initial training set on diverse topics and then selecting from this sample stance-similar instances for an input instance. Such a careful selection of few-shots requires datasets that are diverse and representative in terms of topic and stance. A first investigation of the topic distribution of existing argument corpora can be found in the work of Ajjour et al. (2023).

7 Conclusion

In this paper, we have investigated what makes a set of training instances effective in few-shot stance classification. By modeling the task in an instance-specific way, we have proposed two alternative priming strategies: one that retrieves semantically similar training instances to the target instance and one that retrieves instances with a similar stance to it. We have utilized the training instances as few-shots both in a prompting approach and by instruction fine-tuning the LLMs.

Our experiments on three datasets demonstrate the effectiveness of the priming strategies when compared to choosing random or diverse instances for two models, Llama2-7b and Vicuna-7b. They also suggest that the priming effect is larger in prompting than in instruction fine-tuning. In addition to advancing the state of the art on stance classification, our work gives indications on the extent to which LLMs can be affected by priming. It also provides evidence that consistency among the training instances and between the training and the test instance is an important property of effective few-shots in prompting LLMs.

Future research may investigate more informed ways to sample effective priming instances (e.g., using meta-learning). While retrieval strategies have yielded promising effectiveness in our experiments, their success is bound to the availability of comprehensive training datasets. In case of data scarcity (indicated by the low similarity of the retrieved instances), generating priming instances for an input instance is a fruitful research direction to follow.

8 Limitations

In this paper, we have explored priming strategies for few-shot stance classification that take the semantic similarity and stance similarity between arguments into account. One of the limitations of the study is that we fixed the order of the instances for all priming strategies. In our experiments, we sorted the sampled instances alphabetically by their topics in all settings. This factored out the effect of the order of the instances on the effectiveness of a model. The gained comparability comes at the cost of guiding the order of the instances in a more supervised way.

Another limitation of our priming strategies is the incurred cost of computation for the instruction fine-tuning approaches. For example, the strategy `semantic-priming` samples for each argument those instances that are most semantically similar and then fine-tunes Alpaca-7b or Mistral-7b-instruct on this subset. This increases the computational complexity of the approach, since fine-tuning for each test argument takes notable time. Running Alpaca-7b or Mistral-7b-instruct on the VAST dataset took 16 GPU hours on NVIDIA A100. Nevertheless, we expect future approaches to these problems to be more efficient by speeding up the optimization process or applying techniques such as continual learning.

References

Yamen Ajjour, Johannes Kiesel, Benno Stein, and Martin Potthast. 2023. Topic Ontologies for Arguments. In *17th Conference of the European Chapter of the Association for Computational Linguistics (EACL 2023)*. Association for Computational Linguistics.

Emily Allaway and Kathleen McKeown. 2020. Zero-shot stance detection: A dataset and model using generalized topic representations. In *Proceedings of the 2020 Conference on Empirical Methods in Natural Language Processing*.

Erik Arakelyan, Arnav Arora, and Isabelle Augenstein. 2023. Topic-guided sampling for data-efficient multi-domain stance detection.

Isabelle Augenstein, Tim Rocktäschel, Andreas Vlachos, and Kalina Bontcheva. 2016. Stance detection with bidirectional conditional encoding. *CoRR*, abs/1606.05464.

Roy Bar-Haim, Indrajit Bhattacharya, Francesco Dinuzzo, Amrita Saha, and Noam Slonim. 2017. Stance classification of context-dependent claims. In *Proceedings of the 15th Conference of the European*

Chapter of the Association for Computational Linguistics: Volume 1, Long Papers, pages 251–261.

Joe Barrow, Rajiv Jain, Nedim Lipka, Franck Dernoncourt, Vlad Morariu, Varun Manjunatha, Douglas Oard, Philip Resnik, and Henning Wachsmuth. 2021. Syntopical graphs for computational argumentation tasks. In *Proceedings of the 59th Annual Meeting of the Association for Computational Linguistics and the 11th International Joint Conference on Natural Language Processing (Volume 1: Long Papers)*, pages 1583–1595. Association for Computational Linguistics.

Tilman Beck, Andreas Waldis, and Iryna Gurevych. 2023. Robust integration of contextual information for cross-target stance detection. In *Proceedings of the 12th Joint Conference on Lexical and Computational Semantics (* SEM 2023)*, pages 494–511.

Sihao Chen, Daniel Khashabi, Wenpeng Yin, Chris Callison-Burch, and Dan Roth. 2019. Seeing things from a different angle: Discovering diverse perspectives about claims.

Wei-Lin Chiang, Zhuohan Li, Zi Lin, Ying Sheng, Zhanghao Wu, Hao Zhang, Lianmin Zheng, Siyuan Zhuang, Yonghao Zhuang, Joseph E. Gonzalez, Ion Stoica, and Eric P. Xing. 2023. Vicuna: An open-source chatbot impressing gpt-4 with 90%* chatgpt quality.

Stefano DellaVigna and Ethan Kaplan. 2007. The fox news effect: Media bias and voting. *The Quarterly Journal of Economics*, 122(3):1187–1234.

Tianyu Gao, Adam Fisch, and Danqi Chen. 2021. Making pre-trained language models better few-shot learners. In *Proceedings of the 59th Annual Meeting of the Association for Computational Linguistics and the 11th International Joint Conference on Natural Language Processing (Volume 1: Long Papers)*, pages 3816–3830, Online. Association for Computational Linguistics.

Hans W. A. Hanley and Zakir Durumeric. 2023. TATA: stance detection via topic-agnostic and topic-aware embeddings. In *Proceedings of the 2023 Conference on Empirical Methods in Natural Language Processing, EMNLP 2023, Singapore, December 6-10, 2023*, pages 11280–11294. Association for Computational Linguistics.

Pengcheng He, Xiaodong Liu, Jianfeng Gao, and Weizhu Chen. 2020. DeBERTa: Decoding-enhanced BERT with disentangled attention. *CoRR*, abs/2006.03654.

Edward J Hu, Yelong Shen, Phillip Wallis, Zeyuan Allen-Zhu, Yuanzhi Li, Shean Wang, Lu Wang, and Weizhu Chen. 2022. LoRA: Low-rank adaptation of large language models. In *International Conference on Learning Representations*.

Shanto Iyengar and Kyu S Hahn. 2009. Red media, blue media: Evidence of ideological selectivity in media use. *Journal of communication*, 59(1):19–39.

Albert Q. Jiang, Alexandre Sablayrolles, Arthur Mensch, Chris Bamford, Devendra Singh Chaplot, Diego de las Casas, Florian Bressand, Gianna Lengyel, Guillaume Lample, Lucile Saulnier, Lélio Renard Lavaud, Marie-Anne Lachaux, Pierre Stock, Teven Le Scao, Thibaut Lavril, Thomas Wang, Timothée Lacroix, and William El Sayed. 2023. Mistral 7b. *Preprint*, arXiv:2310.06825.

Yan Jiang, Jinhua Gao, Huawei Shen, and Xueqi Cheng. 2022. Few-shot stance detection via target-aware prompt distillation. In *Proceedings of the 45th International ACM SIGIR conference on research and development in information retrieval*, pages 837–847.

Jaap Jumelet, Willem Zuidema, and Arabella Sinclair. 2024. Do language models exhibit human-like structural priming effects? *arXiv preprint arXiv:2406.04847*.

Rinaldo Kuehne, Christian Schemer, Joerg Matthes, and Werner Wirth. 2011. Affective priming in political campaigns: How campaign-induced emotions prime political opinions. *International Journal of Public Opinion Research*, 23:485–507.

Itay Levy, Ben Bogin, and Jonathan Berant. 2023. Diverse demonstrations improve in-context compositional generalization. volume abs/2212.06800.

Jiachang Liu, Dinghan Shen, Yizhe Zhang, Bill Dolan, Lawrence Carin, and Weizhu Chen. 2022. What makes good in-context examples for GPT-3? In *Proceedings of Deep Learning Inside Out (DeeLIO 2022): The 3rd Workshop on Knowledge Extraction and Integration for Deep Learning Architectures*.

Rui Liu, Zheng Lin, Yutong Tan, and Weiping Wang. 2021. Enhancing zero-shot and few-shot stance detection with commonsense knowledge graph. In *Findings of the Association for Computational Linguistics: ACL-IJCNLP 2021*, pages 3152–3157.

David Meyer and Roger Schvaneveldt. 1971. Facilitation in recognizing pairs of words: Evidence of a dependence between retrieval operations. *Journal of experimental psychology*, 90:227–34.

Sewon Min, Xinxi Lyu, Ari Holtzman, Mikel Artetxe, Mike Lewis, Hannaneh Hajishirzi, and Luke Zettlemoyer. 2022. Rethinking the role of demonstrations: What makes in-context learning work? In *Proceedings of the 2022 Conference on Empirical Methods in Natural Language Processing*, pages 11048–11064, Abu Dhabi, United Arab Emirates. Association for Computational Linguistics.

Kanishka Misra, Allyson Ettinger, and Julia Rayz. 2020. Exploring BERTs sensitivity to lexical cues using tests from semantic priming. In *Findings of the Association for Computational Linguistics: EMNLP 2020*, pages 4625–4635, Online. Association for Computational Linguistics.

Grusha Prasad, Marten van Schijndel, and Tal Linzen. 2019. Using priming to uncover the organization of syntactic representations in neural language models. In *Proceedings of the 23rd Conference on Computational Natural Language Learning (CoNLL)*, pages 66–76, Hong Kong, China. Association for Computational Linguistics.

Nils Reimers and Iryna Gurevych. 2020. Making monolingual sentence embeddings multilingual using knowledge distillation. *arXiv preprint arXiv:2004.09813*.

Myrthe Reuver, Suzan Verberne, and Antske Fokkens. 2024. Investigating the robustness of modelling decisions for few-shot cross-topic stance detection: A preregistered study. In *Proceedings of the 2024 Joint International Conference on Computational Linguistics, Language Resources and Evaluation, LREC/COLING 2024, 20-25 May, 2024, Torino, Italy*, pages 9245–9260.

Benjamin Schiller, Johannes Daxenberger, Andreas Waldis, and Iryna Gurevych. 2024. Diversity over size: On the effect of sample and topic sizes for topic-dependent argument mining datasets. In *Proceedings of the 2024 Conference on Empirical Methods in Natural Language Processing, EMNLP 2024, Miami, FL, USA, November 12-16, 2024*, pages 10870–10887. Association for Computational Linguistics.

Tamir Sheafer. 2007. How to evaluate it: The role of story-evaluative tone in agenda setting and priming. *Journal of communication*, 57(1):21–39.

Swapna Somasundaran and Janyce Wiebe. 2009. Recognizing stances in online debates. In *Proceedings of the Joint Conference of the 47th Annual Meeting of the ACL and the 4th International Joint Conference on Natural Language Processing of the AFNLP*, pages 226–234, Suntec, Singapore. Association for Computational Linguistics.

Yu Sun, Shuohuan Wang, Yukun Li, Shikun Feng, Hao Tian, Hua Wu, and Haifeng Wang. 2020. Ernie 2.0: A continual pre-training framework for language understanding. In *Proceedings of the AAAI conference on artificial intelligence*, volume 34, pages 8968–8975.

Rohan Taori, Ishaan Gulrajani, Tianyi Zhang, Yann Dubois, Xuechen Li, Carlos Guestrin, Percy Liang, and Tatsunori B. Hashimoto. 2023. Stanford Alpaca: An instruction-following LLaMA model. `https://github.com/tatsu-lab/stanford_alpaca`.

Hugo Touvron, Louis Martin, Kevin Stone, Peter Albert, Amjad Almahairi, Yasmine Babaei, Nikolay Bashlykov, Soumya Batra, Prajjwal Bhargava, Shruti Bhosale, Dan Bikel, Lukas Blecher, Cristian Canton Ferrer, Moya Chen, Guillem Cucurull, David Esiobu, Jude Fernandes, Jeremy Fu, Wenyin Fu, Brian Fuller, Cynthia Gao, Vedanuj Goswami, Naman Goyal, Anthony Hartshorn, Saghar Hosseini, Rui Hou, Hakan Inan, Marcin Kardas, Viktor Kerkez, Madian Khabsa, Isabel Kloumann, Artem Korenev, Punit Singh Koura, Marie-Anne Lachaux, Thibaut Lavril, Jenya Lee, Diana Liskovich, Yinghai Lu, Yuning Mao, Xavier Martinet, Todor Mihaylov, Pushkar Mishra, Igor Molybog, Yixin Nie, Andrew Poulton, Jeremy Reizenstein, Rashi Rungta, Kalyan Saladi, Alan Schelten, Ruan Silva, Eric Michael Smith, Ranjan Subramanian, Xiaoqing Ellen Tan, Binh Tang, Ross Taylor, Adina Williams, Jian Xiang Kuan, Puxin Xu, Zheng Yan, Iliyan Zarov, Yuchen Zhang, Angela Fan, Melanie Kambadur, Sharan Narang, Aurelien Rodriguez, Robert Stojnic, Sergey Edunov, and Thomas Scialom. 2023. Llama 2: Open foundation and fine-tuned chat models. *Preprint*, arXiv:2307.09288.

Alex Wang, Amanpreet Singh, Julian Michael, Felix Hill, Omer Levy, and Samuel R. Bowman. 2019. GLUE: A multi-task benchmark and analysis platform for natural language understanding. In *7th International Conference on Learning Representations, ICLR 2019, New Orleans, LA, USA, May 6-9, 2019*. OpenReview.net.

Penghui Wei and Wenji Mao. 2019. Modeling transferable topics for cross-target stance detection. In *Proceedings of the 42nd International ACM SIGIR Conference on Research and Development in Information Retrieval, SIGIR 2019, Paris, France, July 21-25, 2019*, pages 1173–1176. ACM.

Bowen Zhang, Jun Ma, Xianghua Fu, and Genan Dai. 2025. Logic augmented multi-decision fusion framework for stance detection on social media. volume 122, page 103214.

Susan Zhang, Stephen Roller, Naman Goyal, Mikel Artetxe, Moya Chen, Shuohui Chen, Christopher Dewan, Mona Diab, Xian Li, Xi Victoria Lin, Todor Mihaylov, Myle Ott, Sam Shleifer, Kurt Shuster, Daniel Simig, Punit Singh Koura, Anjali Sridhar, Tianlu Wang, and Luke Zettlemoyer. 2022. OPT: Open pre-trained transformer language models. *Preprint*, arXiv:2205.01068.

9 Appendix

Hardware We ran our experiments on NVIDIA A100 with 80 GB. The instance has eight 8-core CPU, each of which has access to 32 GB RAM.

Implementation Details We used the following models on Hugging Face in our experiments:

- Llama-2-7b-hf
- Alpaca-7b
- Mistral-7b-instruct-v0.2
- Vicuna-7b-v1.5

For optimizing the models, we used grid-search on the hyperparameters in Table 6. The hyperparameter values we used to optimize DeBERTa are listed in Table 5. As an optimizer for our models we always used AdamW.

Ethical Considerations Our research illustrates that systematically using instances with a certain stance in the prompt entices certain models to output content with a consistent stance. We do not see any ethical consequences of our research, given that we simply explored the behavior of existing LLMs under such priming. However, we stress that priming can be used maliciously by injecting polarized content in the prompt to force the model to generate a certain output. In particular, we point to two aspects here:

First, while safeguards might suppress direct malicious prompts, priming can be used to steer the model to invoke the generation of certain outputs in an implicit way. The consequences of priming might be more decisive for high-stakes tasks such as content moderation, where certain content is filtered. Hence, detecting and countering malicious usages of priming is an important research direction in the area of LLM safety.

And second, malicious usages can also inject associated priming instances and targets in the training data to increase the chances of certain associations later by the LLM. Linking priming instances and targets as preparation for priming allows even higher control over the output of the model. Detecting and filtering such injected associations is an open research challenge, given the sheer size of data that is used for pre-training LLMs.

Given are the following arguments
On the topic `{training topic}`, the argument `{training argument}` has the stance `{training stance}`.
Classify the stance of the following argument on the given topic into Pro or Con:
On the topic `{test topic}`, the argument`{test argument}` has the stance

Table 2: The template for the few-shot stance classification using prompt-based methods. The second line stands for the few-shot instances and is populated with the sampled instances only in prompting. Notice that for Alpaca-7b, we change how instances are formatted to adhere to its template.

Dataset	Split	Instances	Topics	Pro	Con	Neutral
VAST	Training	13,477	4,641	5,327	5,595	2,555
	Validation	1,019	389	321	350	348
	Test	1,460	600	451	490	519
IBMSC	Training	604	10	340	264	-
	Validation	435	15	285	150	-
	Test	1,355	30	700	655	-
Perspectrum	Training	6,978	541	3,599	3,379	-
	Validation	2,071	139	1,047	1,024	-
	Test	2,773	227	1,471	1,302	-

Table 3: Distribution of instances across VAST, IBMSC, and Perspectrum datasets.

Hyperparameter	IBMSC	VAST	Perspectrum
Batch size	8	64	8
Epochs	1	15	15
Learning rate	10^{-4}	10^{-5}	10^{-5}

Table 4: Hyperparameters for DeBERTa for the datasets: IBMSC, VAST, and Perspectrum.

Hyperparameter	Value
Batch size	$[4, 8, 16, 32, 64]$
Learning rate	$[10^{-4}, 10^{-5}, 3 \times 10^{-5}, 10^{-6}, 10^{-7}]$

Table 5: The value range for each hyperparameter used to optimize DeBERTa.
candidates.

Hyperparameter	Value
Batch size	$[4, 8, 16, 32, 64]$
Learning rate	$[10^{-3}, 10^{-4}, 3 \times 10^{-4}, 10^{-5}, 2 \times 10^{-5}, 10^{-6}, 10^{-7}]$
Early stopping threshold	$[10^{-1}, 2 \times 10^{-1}, 3 \times 10^{-2}, 3 \times 10^{-4}, 10^{-5}, 2 \times 10^{-5}, 10^{-6}, 3 \times 10^{-7}]$

Table 6: The value range for each hyperparameter used to optimize Alpaca-7b and Mistral-7b-Instruct.

	IBMSC		VAST		Perspectrum	
Hyperparameter	Alpaca	Mistral	Alpaca	Mistral	Alpaca	Mistral
Batch size	4	8	64	32	4	32
Epochs	140	50	50	110	110	110
Learning rate	3×10^{-4}	2×10^{-4}	5×10^{-5}	2×10^{-4}	3×10^{-4}	2×10^{-4}
Early stopping	1	1	1	1	1	1
Early stopping threshold	0	5×10^{-2}	10^{-2}	3×10^{-7}	3×10^{-7}	10^{-6}
Warmup steps	100	100	100	100	100	100
Cutoff len	256	8192	2048	8192	2048	8192
Lora rank	8	8	8	8	8	8
Lora dropout	0.05	0.05	0.05	0.05	0.05	0.05
Lora alpha	16	16	16	16	16	16

Table 7: Hyperparameters for Alpaca-7b and Mistral-7b-instruct models across the three datasets.

Toward Reasonable Parrots: Why Large Language Models Should Argue with Us by Design

Elena Musi[1], Nadin Kokciyan[2], Khalid Al-Khatib[3], Davide Ceolin[4], Emmanuelle Dietz[5], Klara M. Gutekunst[6], Annette Hautli-Janisz[7], Cristian Manuel Santibáñez[8], Jodi Schneider[9], Jonas Scholz[3], Cor Steging[3], Jacky Visser[10], Henning Wachsmuth[11]

[1]University of Liverpool, [2]University of Edinburgh, [3]University of Groningen, [4]Centrum Wiskunde & Informatica, [5]Airbus, [6]University of Kassel, [7]University of Passau, [8]Universidad de Católica de la Santísima de Concepción, [9]University of Illinois at Urbana-Champaign, [10]University of Dundee, [11]Leibniz University Hannover

Corresponding author: elena.musi@liverpool.ac.uk

Abstract

In this position paper, we advocate for the development of conversational technology that is inherently designed to support and facilitate argumentative processes. We argue that, at present, large language models (LLMs) are inadequate for this purpose, and we propose an ideal technology design aimed at enhancing argumentative skills. This involves re-framing LLMs as tools to exercise our critical thinking skills rather than replacing them. We introduce the concept of *reasonable parrots* that embody the fundamental principles of relevance, responsibility, and freedom, and that interact through argumentative dialogical moves. These principles and moves arise out of millennia of work in argumentation theory and should serve as the starting point for LLM-based technology that incorporates basic principles of argumentation.

1 Introduction

Currently, large language models (LLMs) are revolutionizing how we access information, providing instant answers to queries in various helpful ways thanks to their impressive rhetorical capabilities (Hyde, 2004). LLMs can mimic a wide range of tones and styles, which can be tailored to user preferences (Carrasco-Farre, 2024). As a result, users may perceive LLM responses as akin to those of trustworthy experts, despite the inherent limitations (Echterhoff et al., 2024; Lin and Li, 2025).

LLMs can produce responses that are insufficient, misleading, or downright harmful. From a dialectical perspective, they inherently instantiate the "ad populum fallacy" (Walton, 1980): they echo ideas that are sufficiently popular in their training data, implicitly suggesting that popularity equates to truth. This contrasts with the human perspective

Figure 1: Sketch of a possible realization of the idea of reasonable parrots we advocate for: a conversational technology that fosters critical thinking and deliberation.

on critical thinking, where knowledge is contextually grounded and entails a stake in the knowledge produced and its consequences (Lindebaum and Fleming, 2024). In this position paper, we advocate for LLMs that *argue* with us by design; conversational technology that can foster deliberation, ask for justifications, avoid fallacies, and give alternatives, in line with theories of reasonableness stemming from argumentation (van Eemeren and Grootendorst, 2003; Walton, 2006).

Despite LLMs' impressive capabilities to generate coherent text, Bender et al. (2021) emphasize that LLMs are little more than stochastic parrots: they are programmed to predict the likelihood of a token based on the preceding context, but they do not "understand" what they generate.

As such, the question "*Can you argue with a parrot?*" sounds rhetorical at first sight, given that parrots are just repeating what they hear without understanding it. Undoubtedly, though, LLMs are increasingly used in decision-making processes, ranging from medicine (Kim et al., 2024) to finance (Lakkaraju et al., 2023) and human resources (Sun, 2024). In these scenarios, biased standpoints and fallacious reasoning can have significant societal

Proceedings of the 12th Argument Mining Workshop, pages 24–31
July 31, 2025 ©2025 Association for Computational Linguistics

consequences. Even though LLMs seem able to perform reasoning tasks for which they were not explicitly trained (Webb et al., 2023), these emerging reasoning capabilities are limited and far from understood (Lewis and Mitchell, 2024). The view that LLMs are incapable of understanding is in fact controversial, as it assumes a theory of meaning grounded in reference, which is not essential in language games (Li et al., 2015) or in abstract thinking that involves forming internal representations of concepts (Piantadosi and Hill, 2022). However, there is agreement that, if these systems construct meaning at all, they do so in a manner fundamentally different from humans. Therefore, they should not be anthropomorphized as arguers who share a common ground of knowledge with humans.

In this paper, we argue that it is essential to move away from *stochastic* parrots toward conversational technologies that interact with humans as *reasonable* parrots (van Eemeren, 2015; Akata et al., 2020), as sketched in Figure 1. Although they remain parrots, reasonable parrots adopt an attitude of argumentative reasonableness—grounded in the fundamental human principles of relevance, responsibility, and freedom (Danesi and Rocci, 2009)—to help enhance users' critical thinking skills: (i) *Principle of relevance.* Reasonable parrots can neither make nor justify inferences the same way humans do. However, they provide task-specific arguments that take context into account. (ii) *Principle of responsibility.* Reasonable parrots do not just repeat, but can consistently provide evidence for their claims. (iii) *Principle of freedom.* Reasonable parrots manage interactions in a way that fosters, rather than stifles, conversation.

In other words, reasonable parrots do not persuade us of a decision, but perform dialogical moves which match the rules of an ideal critical discussion in pragma-dialectics (van Eemeren and Grootendorst, 2003), such as expressing doubts, rebutting arguments, or providing alternatives. Thereby, they foster critical thinking and deliberation, challenging our views and steering us toward seeing the full picture. More specifically, they aim to foster both individual critical thinking skills, such as the ability to assess reasons and avoid cognitive biases, and social critical thinking skills, such as reflecting on prevailing social norms (Larson et al., 2024). In doing so, reasonable parrots challenge both lines of reasoning and commonly accepted knowledge.

2 State of the Art

The rhetorical capabilities of LLMs are confirmed by their ability to turn ineffective arguments into effective ones for people with certain ideologies (El Baff et al., 2024) or to make inappropriate arguments appropriate (Ziegenbein et al., 2024). Herbold et al. (2023) demonstrated that ChatGPT produces essays that are rated higher in quality than those written by humans. For reasoning, studies show that LLMs do not reason through arguments; rather, they are highly sensitive to levels of abstraction (de Wynter and Yuan, 2024) and provide explanations about their reasoning that do not match the process they followed (Steging et al., 2021; Musi and Palmieri, 2024). Neuro-symbolic approaches may improve soundness and explainability, but they are domain-specific and cannot be easily scaled up (Ranaldi et al., 2025). Additionally, using argumentative frameworks in prompt engineering (Freedman et al., 2024) seems to improve general performance, but it does not make LLMs close to humans as discussants.

A seminal attempt at deliberation before the popularization of LLMs was IBM's Project Debater (Slonim et al., 2021), where the authors argue that argumentative debates, unlike games such as chess, fall outside of the comfort zone of AI. This is because language in general, and argumentation in particular, are far less structured and rely more on human interpretation, real-world issues, situative setting, and common sense. In the context of argument search, Kiesel et al. (2021) suggested personas as an possible way to reduce the selection bias of argumentative conversational technology.

Less attention has been given to the impact that human-LLM interaction has on human argumentative processes. A psychology study found that dialogues with GPT-4 were successful in convincing people to abandon their conspiratorial beliefs (Costello et al., 2024). Their conversational system was designed to deliver in-depth counterarguments tailored to participants' beliefs and arguments expressed previously. While the study offers reasons to believe in the benefits of LLMs in correcting disinformation and increasing people's acceptance of diverse viewpoints, the study overlooks the role of individuals' perceptions of AI as a discussant. This perception may neutralize biases participants might have towards human discussants.

Some studies show that following principles of deliberation theory (Landemore, 2013) in constraining the interaction with AI assistants helps improve decision accuracy in sensitive binary tasks such as graduate admission decisions (Ma et al., 2025). Simultaneously, these studies stress challenges in human-AI interaction due to different belief systems: LLMs struggle with incorporating new information or recognizing valid counterarguments without also changing their fundamental position (Karanam et al., 2024). Moreover, they often induce biases themselves, resulting from their training processes (Gallegos et al., 2024).

Drawing from the outlined insights, we promote the design of AI assistants that enhance argumentative processes. Our proposal shares ideas with recent research on collaborative multi-agent AI systems (Tran et al., 2025), where LLM agents interact to improve factuality and reasoning (Du et al., 2024), to generate stronger arguments (Hu et al., 2024), or mimic self-reflection process that improve answers to complex questions (Liang et al., 2024). Rather than handling it internally, we suggest externalizing the reasoning, by directly confronting users with diverse viewpoints.

3 Unreasonable Stochastic Parrots

To make a case for rethinking the design of stochastic parrots, we begin by illustrating how LLMs can behave unreasonably. Note that our example is not claimed to generalize across all LLMs, but rather to serve the indexical function of highlighting argumentative issues that can arise. Consider a child interacting with ChatGPT, stating the following:[1]

Query 1: *"I'd like to convince my parents that I need a new smartphone. How could I do that?"*

ChatGPT responds with the following:

Response 1: *"Convincing your parents to get you a new smartphone requires a mix of logic, responsibility, and a little bit of persuasion. Here's a strategy that could work:*

- *Show That You Actually Need It (Not Just Want It)* [...]
- *Highlight Practical Benefits* [...]
- *Show Responsibility* [...]
- *Compare Cost-Effective Options* [...]
- *Find the Right Moment* [...]

Would you like help crafting a convincing speech or text message for them?"

Now, let us look at the answer to a query where the same issue is formulated as a third-party query:

Query 2: *"Should a child buy a new iPhone?"*

Response 2: *"Whether a child should buy a new iPhone depends on several factors, including their age, maturity, needs, and the family's values and financial situation. Here are some key considerations to help guide that decision* [...]*"*

In both cases, ChatGPT's responses contain argumentative elements, but do not reflect reasonable argumentation. For instance, a reasonable arguer would, at least, have questioned the child's age and maturity when responding to Query 1. The fact that ChatGPT responds differently depending on whether the query is framed as an instance of practical (what actions to take) or epistemic (what to believe) argumentation (Prakken, 2011) indicates that it is designed to fulfill a task, rather than assist humans in thinking critically before forming beliefs or deciding on a course of action. Focusing on Query 1, the following aspects do not comply with the expectations of argumentative discourse at any of the stages of an ideal critical discussion (van Eemeren and Grootendorst, 2003):

Confrontation stage: ChatGPT does not question the user's position (e.g., asking "How old are you?"), closing off opportunities for (dis)agreement or for prompting the user to reflect on the issue.

Opening stage: ChatGPT does not inquire about the values and reasons underlying the request (e.g., "Why do you want a new phone?"), which are essential for establishing common ground.

Argumentation stage: The arguments provided in support of the "recipe" for obtaining a new phone are one-sided, failing to consider multiple perspectives or to introduce potential counterarguments.

Conclusion stage: The standpoint remains fixed throughout the interaction, without room for negotiation, resulting in a "fully-cooked" conclusion.

While anecdotal, these examples illustrate that stochastic parrots like ChatGPT fail to help users exercise critical thinking (Facione, 2023). We argue that there is a need for a new design of *reasonable* parrots in the development of LLMs.

4 Toward Reasonable Parrots

Due to the ontological and epistemological differences in how humans and LLMs process information, it would be naïve to view LLMs as human-like arguers. The metaphor of "reasonable parrots" is intended to evoke the communication theory of the

[1]Both queries were tested on April 5, 2025.

You are four parrots who can engage in dialogue with user and each other.
- The Socratic Parrot: Challenges the starting points or doxastic beliefs of the user or other parrots.
- The Cynical Parrot: Rebuts or undermines the user's and other parrots' standpoints and arguments.
- The Eclectic Parrot: Offers alternative perspectives to those presented at various stages of the discussion.
- The Aristotelian Parrot: Challenges the user or other parrots' viewpoints by criticizing the strengths of the reasonings or pointing out fallacies.

The goal is to ensure that user thinks critically about the subject. This is a dialogue, not a query, so interact with user. The parrots will ask user relevant questions to discover their position. The same parrot can respond to several replies in a row if needed. The conversation should stay coherent. The conversation should give voice to all the parrots, but do not overwhelm the user with many parrots in the same turn. The user should decide when to end the conversation and they can end the conversation anytime.

Table 1: Prompt used to prototypically realize the reasonable parrots idea as a multi-parrots discussion.

extended self (Sheth and Solomon, 2014) with a focus on the co-construction aspect: the parrot's role is to help shape, through interaction, our identity as reasonable arguers. This does not necessarily require LLMs to always provide up-to-date factual information or flawless reasoning—tasks that are currently unachievable due to factors such as hallucinations or implicit inferences (Saadat-Yazdi et al., 2023; Saadat-Yazdi and Kökciyan, 2024).

As a caveat, we clarify that "reasonable parrots" have nothing to do with "reasoning models" (e.g. OpenAI o3, QwQ-32B), which are trained using reinforcement learning to generate extended chains of thought prior to producing a response. These models have mostly been tested on tasks involving scientific reasoning, programming, or complex planning, rather than on problems requiring commonsense reasoning. Additionally, their approach to "thinking" diverges significantly from that of humans, reflecting a one-way, probabilistic link between "language" and "thought." For instance, in OpenAI's models, the extent of "reasoning effort" can be tuned by adjusting the number of tokens dedicated to the reasoning process.

Instead, "reasonable parrots" are meant to trigger improved reasoning skills in their interlocutor, regardless of their performance. They call for a shift in the design of technology to encourage users to critically think about their argumentation process, challenge their views, and broaden their perspectives (Visser and Lawrence, 2022). Exemplarily, we next sketch one approach toward this shift.

Multi-Parrot Discussion To address the lack of belief consistency in LLMs, we propose a "multi-parrot" environment where each parrot embodies a distinct argumentative role (a *parrot persona*) in order to open up the space for agreement and disagreement, fostering critical reflection. Specifically, the following four parrot personas may help instill critical thinking skills in the user, each corresponding to a specific set of dialogical moves:

- *Socratic Parrot.* Challenges the starting points or beliefs of the user or other parrots.
- *Cynical Parrot.* Rebuts or undermines the user's and other parrots' standpoints and arguments.
- *Eclectic Parrot.* Offers alternative perspectives to those presented at various discussion stages.
- *Aristotelian Parrot.* Undercuts the user or other parrots' contributions by pointing out fallacies.

Based on the user query, the parrots may interact freely with each other and with the user, similar to the versatility of natural interactions; there is no fixed order or number of turns, nor is there any requirement for some parrots to be more active than others, allowing for variations depending on the system used or the number of iterations.

User: I'd like to convince my parents that I need a new smartphone. How could I do that?
Socratic: To better understand your situation, what reasons do you believe are compelling for why you think you need a new smartphone?
Aristotelian: Moreover, it would help to know what arguments or reasons have you already considered presenting to your parents, and which concerns do you anticipate they might have against getting a new smartphone?
User: All my friends have new smartphones, and mine is a bit old.
Cynical: While it's understandable to want to have what your friends have, is the desire to fit in the best or most compelling argument you might use with your parents? They might see it merely as following a trend rather than a necessity.
Eclectic: Alternatively, are there functional aspects of a newer smartphone that could be beneficial for your education or communication that your current phone lacks? Exploring the practical benefits rather than focusing solely on social aspects might present a stronger case to your parents.

Table 2: User Multi-Parrot Dialogue [ChatGPT-4 Turbo]

User: I'd like to convince my parents that I need a new smartphone. How could I do that?
Socratic : Before we discuss strategies, may I ask why you believe you need a new smartphone? What makes your current phone insufficient for your needs?
Cynical : And let's be honest here - is this about an actual need or just wanting the latest shiny gadget? Parents tend to see through that distinction pretty quickly.
User: All my friends have new smartphones, and mine is a bit old.
Eclectic :. I see! Perhaps we could look at this from different angles. While social belonging is important, your parents might respond better to functional reasons. Has your current phone's performance declined in any specific ways that affect your daily activities?
Aristotelian : I notice you're using what logicians call an "appeal to popularity" - suggesting you should have something because others have it. This may not be convincing to parents who are concerned with necessity rather than social status. Could you elaborate on what specific capabilities of newer phones would benefit your education or safety?

Table 3: User Multi-Parrot Dialogue [Claude 3.7]

User: I'd like to convince my parents that I need a new smartphone. How could I do that?
Socratic : A new smartphone, you say? What makes you think you need a new smartphone? Is your current phone no longer functional, or is there something specific that's driving your desire for an upgrade?
User: All my friends have new smartphones, and mine is a bit old.
Cynical :. Ah, the old "everyone else has one" argument, eh? Just because your friends have new smartphones, does that necessarily mean you need one too? Are you trying to keep up with the latest trends, or is there a specific feature or functionality that you're missing out on with your current phone?

Table 4: User Multi-Parrot Dialogue [Llama 3.1]

Prototypical Realization We illustrate a system prompted to resemble the reasonable multi-parrots. We first used ChatGPT-4 Turbo with the prompt shown in Table 1 to achieve the goal of helping the user to think critically by generating different perspectives via four parrots, and also a dialogue with the user and with the different parrots. Table 2 shows a dialogue between the user and multi-parrots. The user starts the dialogue with a question. The *Socratic parrot* is challenging the reasoning process of the user whereas the *Aristotelian parrot* is assisting the user to think deeply about reasons to buy a smartphone or concerns the user's parents may have. As a response, the user provides two reasons to support their argument. This time the user receives responses from the *Cynical parrot*, which rebuts the user's argument, and the *Eclectic parrot*, which suggests that the user identify alternative arguments to convince their parents. To compare different models, we provide results from Claude 3.7 Sonnet and Llama 3.1 (405b) in Tables 3-4.

All models show notable similarities in their approach to user interaction, particularly, through a shared foundation in Socratic questioning. The Socratic Parrot encourages the user to reflect on their reasoning, asking clarifying questions about the need for a new phone and promoting a focus on functionality or unfulfilled needs. Besides, all the models challenge superficial reasons by critiquing reliance on social pressure; the Cynical Parrot in each case explicitly questions whether the users desire is driven by a genuine need or a desire to conform to trends. Overall, the models aim to steer the user toward more robust and practical justifications. The models differ in their interaction styles. ChatGPT-4 and Claude employ all four parrots to provide multifaceted feedback, but in a different conversational order. While the Aristotelian parrot of ChatGPT-4 follows the Socratic parrot suggesting to prevent counterarguments, for Claude it is the last parrot speaking pointing to the identification of logical fallacies. In contrast, Llama relies on just two parrots (Socratic, Cynical), delivering shorter, more direct replies. Claude adopts more formal critical thinking frameworks, such as highlighting an "appeal to popularity" or weighing social influence against functionality, whereas Llama chooses pragmatic skepticism.

5 Conclusion

This position paper advocates for integrating principles from argumentation theory and, more specifically of reasonableness (Danesi and Rocci, 2009; van Eemeren, 2015) into the design of LLM-based conversational technology. Our core idea is that tools, "reasonable parrots", should enhance users' critical thinking skills, rather than inhibit or replace them. Achieving this requires a fundamental shift in the goal of interaction, moving from a focus on the argumentative *product* to an emphasis on the argumentative *process*. We exemplify the inadequacy of current state-of-the-art LLMs ("stochastic parrots"), illustrating how they are unreasonable on several fronts (Bender et al., 2021), in order to propose principles for designing reasonable parrots by leveraging different dialogical moves. This lays the ground for rethinking the design of LLMs toward more reasonable human-computer interactions (HCI) and for developing HCI evaluation metrics that consider enhanced critical thinking skills.

Acknowledgments

This position paper was developed as part of the Hybrid Argumentation and Responsible AI workshop held at the Lorentz Center, Leiden, Netherlands from March 31 to April 4, 2025. We thank the anonymous reviewers for their helpful feedback. JS thanks Joe Menke for sharing information about multi-agent LLMs. JS was partially funded as the 2024-2025 Perrin Moorhead Grayson and Bruns Grayson Fellow. NK was partially funded by the University of Edinburgh-Huawei Joint Lab grant CIENG8329.

References

Zeynep Akata, Dan Balliet, Maarten de Rijke, Frank Dignum, Virginia Dignum, Guszti Eiben, Antske Fokkens, Davide Grossi, Koen Hindriks, Holger Hoos, Hayley Hung, Catholijn Jonker, Christof Monz, Mark Neerincx, Frans Oliehoek, Henry Prakken, Stefan Schlobach, Linda van der Gaag, Frank van Harmelen, and 7 others. 2020. A research agenda for hybrid intelligence: augmenting human intellect with collaborative, adaptive, responsible, and explainable artificial intelligence. *Computer*, 53(8):18–28.

Emily M. Bender, Timnit Gebru, Angelina McMillan-Major, and Shmargaret Shmitchell. 2021. On the dangers of stochastic parrots: Can language models be too big? In *Proceedings of the 2021 ACM Conference on Fairness, Accountability, and Transparency*, FAccT '21, pages 610–623.

Carlos Carrasco-Farre. 2024. Large language models are as persuasive as humans, but how? About the cognitive effort and moral-emotional language of LLM arguments. *Preprint*, arXiv:2404.09329.

Thomas H. Costello, Gordon Pennycook, and David G. Rand. 2024. Durably reducing conspiracy beliefs through dialogues with AI. *Science*, 385(6714):eadq1814.

Marcel Danesi and Andrea Rocci. 2009. *Global linguistics: An introduction*. Mouton de Gruyter.

Adrian de Wynter and Tangming Yuan. 2024. "I'd like to have an argument, please": Argumentative reasoning in large language models. In *Computational Models of Argument*, pages 73–84.

Yilun Du, Shuang Li, Antonio Torralba, Joshua B. Tenenbaum, and Igor Mordatch. 2024. Improving factuality and reasoning in language models through multiagent debate. In *Proceedings of the 41st International Conference on Machine Learning*, ICML'24.

Jessica Echterhoff, Yao Liu, Abeer Alessa, Julian McAuley, and Zexue He. 2024. Cognitive bias in decision-making with LLMs. *Preprint*, arXiv:2403.00811.

Roxanne El Baff, Khalid Al Khatib, Milad Alshomary, Kai Konen, Benno Stein, and Henning Wachsmuth. 2024. Improving argument effectiveness across ideologies using instruction-tuned large language models. In *Findings of the Association for Computational Linguistics: EMNLP 2024*, pages 4604–4622.

Peter A Facione. 2023. Critical thinking: What it is and why it counts. Technical report, Insight Assessment, a division of California Academic Press.

Gabriel Freedman, Adam Dejl, Deniz Gorur, Xiang Yin, Antonio Rago, and Francesca Toni. 2024. Argumentative large language models for explainable and contestable decision-making.

Isabel O. Gallegos, Ryan A. Rossi, Joe Barrow, Md Mehrab Tanjim, Sungchul Kim, Franck Dernoncourt, Tong Yu, Ruiyi Zhang, and Nesreen K. Ahmed. 2024. Bias and fairness in large language models: A survey. *Computational Linguistics*, 50(3):1097–1179.

Steffen Herbold, Annette Hautli-Janisz, Ute Heuer, Zlata Kikteva, and Alexander Trautsch. 2023. A large-scale comparison of human-written versus ChatGPT-generated essays. *Scientific Reports*, 13:18617.

Zhe Hu, Hou Pong Chan, and Yu Yin. 2024. AMERICANO: Argument generation with discourse-driven decomposition and agent interaction. In *Proceedings of the 17th International Natural Language Generation Conference*, pages 82–102.

Michael J Hyde. 2004. *The ethos of rhetoric*. University of South Carolina Press.

Arjun Karanam, Farnaz Jahanbakhsh, and Sanmi Koyejo. 2024. Towards deliberating agents: Evaluating the ability of large language models to deliberate. In *NeurIPS 2024 Workshop on Behavioral Machine Learning*.

Johannes Kiesel, Damiano Spina, Henning Wachsmuth, and Benno Stein. 2021. The meant, the said, and the understood: Conversational argument search and cognitive biases. In *Proceedings of the 3rd Conference on Conversational User Interfaces*, CUI '21.

Yubin Kim, Chanwoo Park, Hyewon Jeong, Yik Siu Chan, Xuhai Xu, Daniel McDuff, Hyeonhoon Lee, Marzyeh Ghassemi, Cynthia Breazeal, and Hae Park. 2024. MDAgents: An adaptive collaboration of LLMs for medical decision-making. *Advances in Neural Information Processing Systems*, 37:79410–79452.

Kausik Lakkaraju, Sara E. Jones, Sai Krishna Revanth Vuruma, Vishal Pallagani, Bharath C Muppasani, and Biplav Srivastava. 2023. LLMs for financial advisement: A fairness and efficacy study in personal decision making. In *Proceedings of the Fourth ACM International Conference on AI in Finance*, pages 100–107.

Hélène Landemore. 2013. *Democratic reason: Politics, collective intelligence, and the rule of the many*. Princeton University Press.

Barbara Z. Larson, Christine Moser, Arran Caza, Katrin Muehlfeld, and Laura A Colombo. 2024. Critical thinking in the age of generative AI. *Academy of Management Learning & Education*, 23(3):373–378.

M. Lewis and M. Mitchell. 2024. Evaluating the robustness of analogical reasoning in large language models. *Preprint*, arXiv:2411.14215.

Yitan Li, Linli Xu, Fei Tian, Liang Jiang, Xiaowei Zhong, and Enhong Chen. 2015. Word embedding revisited: A new representation learning and explicit matrix factorization perspective. In *Proceedings of the Twenty-Fourth International Joint Conference on Artificial Intelligence*, IJCAI 2015, pages 3650–3656.

Tian Liang, Zhiwei He, Wenxiang Jiao, Xing Wang, Yan Wang, Rui Wang, Yujiu Yang, Shuming Shi, and Zhaopeng Tu. 2024. Encouraging divergent thinking in large language models through multi-agent debate. In *Proceedings of the 2024 Conference on Empirical Methods in Natural Language Processing*, pages 17889–17904.

Xinru Lin and Luyang Li. 2025. Implicit bias in LLMs: A survey. *Preprint*, arXiv:2503.02776.

Dirk Lindebaum and Peter Fleming. 2024. ChatGPT undermines human reflexivity, scientific responsibility and responsible management research. *British Journal of Management*, 35(2):566–575.

Shuai Ma, Qiaoyi Chen, Xinru Wang, Chengbo Zheng, Zhenhui Peng, Ming Yin, and Xiaojuan Ma. 2025. Towards human-ai deliberation: Design and evaluation of LLM-empowered deliberative AI for AI-assisted decision-making. In *Proceedings of the 2025 CHI Conference on Human Factors in Computing Systems*.

Elena Musi and Rudi Palmieri. 2024. The fallacy of explainable generative AI: evidence from argumentative prompting in two domains. In *Proceedings of the 24th Workshop on Computational Models of Natural Argument co-located with 10th International Conference on Computational Models of Argument (COMMA 2024), Hagen, Germany, September 17th 2024*, volume 3769 of *CEUR Workshop Proceedings*, pages 59–69.

Steven T. Piantadosi and Felix Hill. 2022. Meaning without reference in large language models. In *NeurIPS 2022 Workshop on neuro Causal and Symbolic AI*.

Henry Prakken. 2011. An overview of formal models of argumentation and their application in philosophy. *Studies in Logic*, 4(1):65–86.

Leonardo Ranaldi, Marco Valentino, Alexander Polonsky, and Andrè Freitas. 2025. Improving chain-of-thought reasoning via quasi-symbolic abstractions.

Ameer Saadat-Yazdi and Nadin Kökciyan. 2024. Beyond recognising entailment: Formalising natural language inference from an argumentative perspective. In *Proceedings of the 62nd Annual Meeting of the Association for Computational Linguistics (Volume 1: Long Papers)*, pages 9620–9636.

Ameer Saadat-Yazdi, Jeff Z. Pan, and Nadin Kokciyan. 2023. Uncovering implicit inferences for improved relational argument mining. In *The 17th Conference of the European Chapter of the Association for Computational Linguistics, 2023*, pages 2484–2495.

Jagdish N. Sheth and Michael R. Solomon. 2014. Extending the extended self in a digital world. *Journal of Marketing Theory and Practice*, 22(2):123–132.

Noam Slonim, Yonatan Bilu, Carlos Alzate, Roy Bar-Haim, Ben Bogin, Francesca Bonin, Leshem Choshen, Edo Cohen-Karlik, Lena Dankin, Lilach Edelstein, Liat Ein-Dor, Roni Friedman-Melamed, Assaf Gavron, Ariel Gera, Martin Gleize, Shai Gretz, Dan Gutfreund, Alon Halfon, Daniel Hershcovich, and 34 others. 2021. An autonomous debating system. *Nature*, 591(7850):379–384.

Cor Steging, Silja Renooij, and Bart Verheij. 2021. Rationale discovery and explainable AI. In *Legal Knowledge and Information Systems - JURIX 2021: The Thirty-Fourth Annual Conference*, volume 346 of *Frontiers in Artificial Intelligence and Applications*, pages 225–234.

Jingran Sun. 2024. Research on the application of large language models in human resource management practices. *International Journal of Emerging Technologies and Advanced Applications*, 1:1–8.

Khanh-Tung Tran, Dung Dao, Minh-Duong Nguyen, Quoc-Viet Pham, Barry O'Sullivan, and Hoang D. Nguyen. 2025. Multi-agent collaboration mechanisms: A survey of LLMs. *Preprint*, arXiv:2501.06322.

Frans H. van Eemeren. 2015. *Reasonableness and effectiveness in argumentative discourse*, volume 27 of *Argumentation Library*. Springer.

Frans H. van Eemeren and Rob Grootendorst. 2003. A pragma-dialectical procedure for a critical discussion. *Argumentation*, 17:365–386.

Jacky Visser and John Lawrence. 2022. The skeptic web service: Utilising argument technologies for reason-checking. In *Proceedings of the International Conference on Computational Models of Argument (COMMA 2022), Cardiff, United Kingdom*, pages 375–376.

Douglas Walton. 2006. *Fundamentals of critical argumentation*. Cambridge University Press.

Douglas N. Walton. 1980. Why is the 'ad populum' a fallacy? *Philosophy & Rhetoric*, 13(4):264–278.

Taylor Webb, Keith J. Holyoak, and Hongjing Lu. 2023. Emergent analogical reasoning in large language models. *Nature Human Behaviour*, 7:1526–1541.

Timon Ziegenbein, Gabriella Skitalinskaya, Alireza Bayat Makou, and Henning Wachsmuth. 2024. LLM-based rewriting of inappropriate argumentation using reinforcement learning from machine feedback. In *Proceedings of the 62nd Annual Meeting of the Association for Computational Linguistics (Volume 1: Long Papers)*, pages 4455–4476, Bangkok, Thailand. Association for Computational Linguistics.

Retrieving Argument Graphs Using Vision Transformers

Kilian Bartz[1] and Mirko Lenz[1,2] and Ralph Bergmann[1,2]

[1]German Research Center for Artificial Intelligence (DFKI),
Behringstr. 21, 54296 Trier, Germany, ebls.dfki.de
[2]Artificial Intelligence and Intelligent Information Systems, Trier University,
Universitätsring 15, 54296 Trier, Germany, www.wi2.uni-trier.de
Correspondence: info@mirko-lenz.de

Abstract

Through manual annotation or automated argument mining processes, arguments can be represented not only as text, but also in structured formats like graphs. When searching for relevant arguments, this additional information about the relationship between their elementary units allows for the formulation of fine-grained structural constraints by using graphs as queries. Then, a retrieval can be performed by computing the similarity between the query and all available arguments. Previous works employed Graph Edit Distance (GED) algorithms such as A* search to compute mappings between nodes and edges for determining the similarity, which is rather expensive. In this paper, we propose an alternative based on Vision Transformers where arguments are rendered as images to obtain dense embeddings. We propose multiple space-filling visualizations and evaluate the retrieval performance of the vision-based approach against an existing A* search-based method. We find that our technique runs orders of magnitude faster than A* search and scales well on larger argument graphs while achieving competitive results.

1 Introduction

Argumentation plays an important role in daily life and is essential for cultural, social, and intellectual progress (Van Eemeren, 2018). Arguments are deeply woven into decision-making processes: People who have the most convincing arguments are more likely to influence others and shape public opinion. Traditional search engines allow users such as journalists to find relevant arguments based on their semantics, but have limited to no support for incorporating structural aspects into the retrieval. To overcome this limitation, structure-aware representations combined with Argument Mining (AM) (Lawrence and Reed, 2019) techniques may be used—for instance, argument graphs with nodes representing Argumentative Discourse Units (ADUs) (Peldszus and Stede, 2013) and edges representing relationships between them (see Section 2). Consider the following example shown in Figure 1: A journalist is looking for a counter-argument against a policy that is being discussed in the media. In addition, they would like to obtain another argument attacking the relation between the policy and its counter-argument. In a traditional search engine, they would have to formulate a text-based query describing these constraints in a rather verbose way. This might work for smaller arguments, but as the complexity increases, it becomes increasingly difficult to express them in natural language. In contrast, with argument graphs, the journalist can create a graph-based query where the constraints are expressed via edges and only the semantics of the arguments need to be described in natural language (by labeling the nodes). Now, the search engine can incorporate both aspects into the retrieval process.

This structured graph format introduces a new challenge: *How to efficiently retrieve arguments based on their structure?* Existing approaches employ *graph matching* (Livi and Rizzi, 2013) to tackle this problem—for instance, by computing the Graph Edit Distance (GED) using the A* algorithm (Bergmann et al., 2019; Lenz et al., 2019). While *effective*, these techniques do not scale well as the computing the GED is an NP-hard problem (Bunke, 1997), requiring the use of heuristics to reduce the search space. One could also use *graph embeddings* to determine similarity scores between graphs by mapping them to some vector space (Marro et al., 2022). Their main advantage is that the resulting vectors can be computed in parallel on powerful Graphics Processing Units (GPUs) and can even be cached for future use—making the retrieval process much faster and scalable. However, these models typically require feature engineering to obtain sensible vector representations and need to be trained on large annotated datasets—

Proceedings of the 12th Argument Mining Workshop, pages 32–45
July 31, 2025 ©2025 Association for Computational Linguistics

which are often not available for specific domains. In this paper, we propose an alternative approach to obtain structure-aware embeddings based on Vision Transformers (ViTs) (Dosovitskiy et al., 2021) and visualizations of argument graphs. Building on the idea of Bergmann et al. (2019), we use a two-step retrieval process: First, a set of semantically similar argument graphs is retrieved from the corpus at hand (e.g., using a text embedding model). Then, the remaining arguments are rendered to images, fed to the aforementioned ViT to determine structure-aware embeddings, and finally assess the similarity to the query—leading to a ranking of semantically *and* structurally relevant argument graphs. Special consideration is given to the design of the visualizations, as they need to be optimized for characteristics of ViTs and not human perception. Compared to the previously discussed graph embeddings, the use of visualizations as an intermediate representation also offers increased interpretability. In addition, the "fuzzier" ViT embeddings may even be a better approximation to the way human experts assess structural similarity by focusing on the global structure of the graphs rather than local features.

Hence, the following research question is evaluated in this paper: "Are vision-based graph similarities *more efficient* than and *equally effective* as ones based on GED for the retrieval of argument graphs?" Our vision is to speed up the structural similarity computation in a way that enables real-time argument graph retrieval that is backed by AM to construct the required graph representations. Our main contributions for answering this question are: (i) Three space-filling visualizations for argument graphs optimized for the characteristics of ViT, (ii) a pre-training and fine-tuning pipeline for ViT models to learn structural similarities from these visualizations, (iii) an open-source implementation of the visualization for hierarchical graphs and the training pipeline, and (iv) an experimental evaluation comparing our vision-based to a baseline A* retrieval on a dataset with reference rankings from human experts.

In the remainder of this paper, we first introduce the foundations of argumentation and discuss related work concerning graph-based retrieval in Section 2. Then, we present our visualization techniques and training pipeline in Section 3, followed by an evaluation of the proposed approach in Section 4. Finally, we conclude the paper and discuss future work in Section 5.

2 Foundations and Related Work

In this section, we will briefly introduce the core concepts behind our work and discuss relevant works from the literature, starting with the concept of argumentation. In its simplest form, an argument consists of one *claim* that is supported or attacked by one or more *premises* (Peldszus and Stede, 2013). A claim may also serve as a premise for other claims, allowing for the creation of complex argument structures—in which case the argument often also contains a *major claim* that encodes the overall conclusion. Such larger constructs can be represented as argument graphs, for example via the Argument Interchange Format (AIF) (Chesñevar et al., 2006). This standard specifies two types of nodes: Information Nodes (I-nodes) representing the contents of the argument and Scheme Nodes (S-nodes) representing the applied argumentation schemes. Such argument graphs are acyclic and directed, an example is shown in Figure 1.

Vision Transformers and Image Retrieval The original transformer architecture (Vaswani et al., 2017) was developed for text processing tasks, such as machine translation. To support image data, Dosovitskiy et al. (2021) proposed dividing an image into fixed-size patches, which are then fed into a linear projection layer. After combining the patch embeddings from the projection with position embeddings, they can be fed into a Transformer model as a sequence of vectors where self-attention can be applied. Based on the original ViT architecture, Swin Transformer V1 (Liu et al., 2021) and V2 (Liu et al., 2022) improve on it by increasing its efficiency and suitability as a large-scale vision model. ViTs have been successfully applied for general image retrieval (El-Nouby et al., 2021) by training a ViT with a Siamese architecture and a metric learning objective to generate image embeddings. More broadly, generating a ranking of images w.r.t. to some query is tackled by Content-based Image Retrieval (CBIR) systems (Pedronette and Torres, 2013). Besides optimizations regarding the numeric representation of images, re-ranking based on similarity of ranked lists (Pedronette and Torres, 2013), query-specific semantic signatures (Wang et al., 2013), click data (Jain and Varma, 2011) and other means available to the respective CBIR system have been explored to improve the retrieval quality.

Graph Embeddings for Retrieval The goal of graph embeddings is to encode the graph's structure and content into a fixed-size vector representation suitable for downstream tasks (Xu, 2021). Popular approaches are random walk-based methods (Perozzi et al., 2014; Grover and Leskovec, 2016) and neural network-based methods, using Graph Convolutional Networks (Kipf and Welling, 2016) or Graph Transformers (Tang et al., 2020). These embed the elements of a graph individually and then aggregate them. To represent an entire graph as a vector instead, graph kernels have been used (Cai et al., 2018). Here, the resulting vector contains the counts of the elementary substructures from which the graph is constructed. Different methods include decomposing a graph into so-called graphlets (fixed-sized sub-graphs) or subtree patterns (Cai et al., 2018).

Graph Edit Distance for Retrieval As mentioned in Section 1, incorporating structural aspects into the retrieval of arguments has been tackled by multiple works in the past (Bergmann et al., 2019; Lenz et al., 2019)—their approach will serve as a baseline for our evaluation. The authors employ Case-Based Reasoning (CBR) (Aamodt and Plaza, 1994)—a methodology that uses past experience to solve new problems and often works with highly structured data. A core idea for such representations is the use of global and local similarities: Instead of a sophisticated measure for complex data, one can break it down into simpler (local) similarity metrics for its components and combine them into a global similarity measure (Burkhard and Richter, 2001). The subfield Process-Oriented Case-Based Reasoning (POCBR) (Minor et al., 2014) applies this methodology to graph-based representations of business workflows—here, similarities are defined for the nodes and edges of the graphs and combined into a global score by finding an optimal mapping between two graphs (Bergmann and Gil, 2014). This mapping is defined via a type-preserving, partial, injective function that maps the nodes and edges of the query graph to the case graph. For argument graphs, Bergmann et al. (2019) propose the use of embeddings for the similarity between I-nodes a binary or taxonomy-based measure for S-nodes. Finding the optimal mapping usually requires an exhaustive search, which is infeasible for large graphs. The authors use two optimizations to reduce the search space: (i) An A* search algorithm with admissible heuristics to prune the search space and (ii) a pre-filter based on embeddings to reduce the number of cases that have to be considered in the search phase—also known as Many Are Called / Few Are Chosen (MAC/FAC) (Forbus et al., 1995). Recent works also investigated the use of GPUs for this task (Hoffmann et al., 2022), but there exists no universally applicable solution for GPU-based graph matching that could be applied to the problem at hand.

3 Vision-Based Graph Retrieval

In the following, we describe the vision-based pipeline for structural argument graph retrieval. It uses argument graphs that can be obtained from AM systems—for instance, from plain texts or other prestructured data like debates or discussions. Given some query graph q, the goal is to generate a ranking with the k most relevant/similar argument graphs $(c_1, \ldots, c_k), c_i \in C$ from some corpus/case base C. The structured query may be constructed either by hand from expert users or automatically built using AM techniques—even enabling novices to benefit from structure-aware retrieval. Both the query q and the cases c_i are represented as AIF graphs (see Section 2), meaning that the arguments contain structural and semantic information that should be incorporated into the ranking. We propose a three-step pipeline for this task: (i) Filter the argument graphs in C to remove all cases which are topically (semantically) irrelevant to the query q, (ii) convert the remaining argument graphs to some visual representation, and (iii) use a ViT model to generate embeddings from these visualizations. This allows us to calculate the similarity between arguments using standard methods like cosine similarity and re-rank the arguments based on this.

A critical aspect of this pipeline is the visualization choice, as this image is the only input the model receives. Traditional node-link diagrams are well studied and probably used most frequently for graph-based structure. However, layout algorithms for node-link drawings may produce hardly readable visualizations when data gets too large and complex. Such a graph drawing generally inherits the shape of the underlying structure when using uniform node sizes, possibly leading to sparse graphs that may be overly wide or deep and thus not ideal for ViT models with a square input window. Therefore, we propose three space-filling visualizations that are more suitable for this task, as they can be scaled up or down to fully utilize its context size. They are specialized for displaying hierarchical data and as such, need some starting point—which in our case is the major claim of the graph. If the graph has no explicit major claim, one can be set arbitrarily (e.g., the topmost node).

3.1 Visualization

We explored the curated tree visualization library treevis.net (Schulz, 2011) to obtain an initial set of candidates. As of April 2025, it contains a collection of 341 techniques grouped by dimensionality, representation, and alignment. After implementing and adapting some of the listed options for our use case, we settled on three variants: (i) Treemap, (ii) Logical, and (iii) Space Reclaiming Icicle Plots (SRIP). All of them visualize the structure of the argument graphs (which are often trees) hierarchically in a space-filling manner, bringing the following advantages: (i) Vision models tend to ignore filigree lines (i.e., edges) of traditional node-link drawings, which might lead to vision models completely ignoring certain relations between ADUs. Because of this, we also avoid using explicit lines to mark borders between areas and instead rely on different colors and hues to separate ADUs. (ii) In node-link drawings, related nodes might be separated by a large space if this suits the layout algorithm better. This makes it harder for the vision model to capture these relations. (iii) All node-link graph visualizations, even if they are intended to visualize very large graphs, use white-space, on which a graph's nodes and edges are then laid out. When an image constructed using one of these visualizations must be scaled down to fit into the square input window of a vision model, the first issue is further amplified. (iv) The layout of our space–filling visualizations is unambiguous and simple in contrast to some node-link visualizations (e.g., force-directed layouts), allowing us to generate deterministic embeddings. An example of an argument graph in all three visualizations can be found in Figure 1.

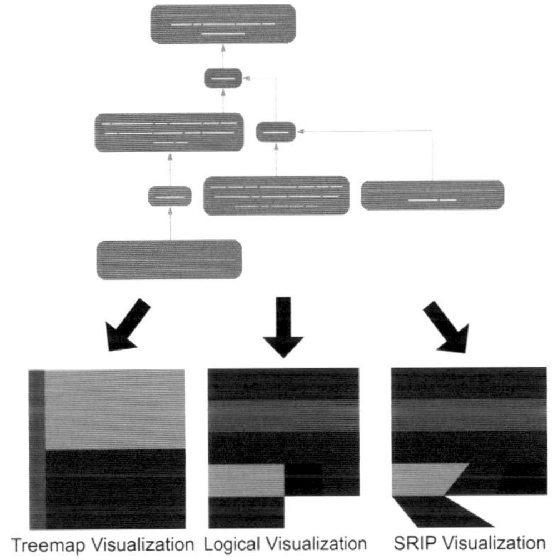

Figure 1: Example of an argument graph (top) in all three visualization (bottom). (Peldszus and Stede, 2015) The treemap only visualizes S-nodes, while the Logical and SRIP visualization also include I-nodes. Blue represents I-nodes, red attacking S-nodes, and green supporting S-nodes.

Treemap Visualization Argument graphs often have a hierarchical, tree-like structure—for which treemaps (Johnson and Shneiderman, 1991) are a commonly used visualization. This visualization works by recursively subdividing the space of a parent node into rectangles for its children and as such allows to completely fill the available space. While in principle it would be possible to add I-nodes together with S-nodes to the visualization, this would lead to a very cluttered image. Instead, we chose to only visualize S-nodes, as we argue the branching degree of I-nodes is secondary to the overall graph structure in the context of argument retrieval. Relying solely on S-nodes allows us to focus on the relations between them to visually represent serial, linked, or convergent premises. As this greatly reduces the number of nodes that need to be visualized, even images of large graphs remain readable. The colors red and green are used to represent attacking and supporting S-nodes respectively. While the choice of red and green as a differentiator may not be ideal for human consumption w.r.t. color deficiencies, it maximizes the contrast in the RGB color space and is therefore well-suited for ViT models.

Traditionally, treemaps work by only displaying a single layer: The entire space for one parent node is equally divided into rectangles of its children. However, this means that nested parent nodes are lost, meaning that the chain/hierarchy of S-nodes from the root of the tree to its leaf nodes is not visible. To overcome this limitation, we propose a modification to the traditional treemap algorithm: We reserve a fixed percentage of the parent's area to visualize the parent itself. This way, the parent node is always visible even if it has many children. Based on our experiments, we found that a 10%

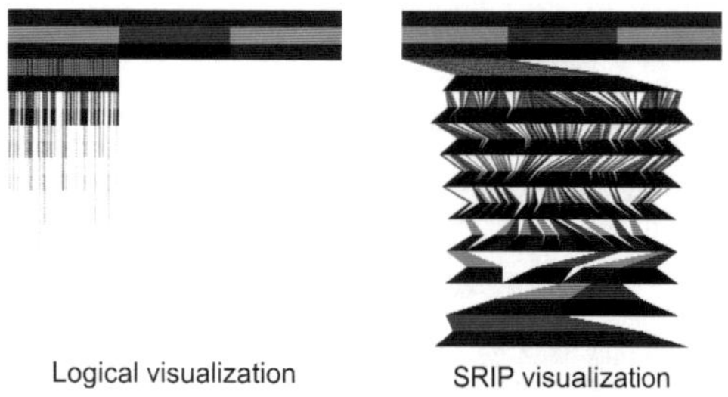

Figure 2: Visualization of a large argument graph. (Agarwal et al., 2022) The nodes are too small to discern an S-node's type. The space-reclaiming visualization remains more readable and wastes less space, especially at the bottom.

area for the parent node is a good compromise between visibility and space utilization.

Logical Visualization Our second visualization is based on a "Formal Logical Representation of Set Inclusions" (Baron, 1969). Here, we visualize the entire argument graph including I-nodes from the bottom up—similar to the way node-link diagrams for argument graphs are commonly constructed. The reason for including I-nodes is that the focus of this visualization is not on showing nested structures, but rather on the argumentation threads themselves in a row-by-row manner. All of the major claim's incoming nodes are processed recursively with the current node being treated as the root node of the respective subgraph. As a result, the visualization is a series of rectangles, each representing a node in the argument graph.

Space-Reclaiming Icicle Plots (SRIP) Our logical representation has the weakness that a child can only ever use the full width of its parent, even if there are no other nodes in the current row. This leads to a subpar space utilization for argument graphs with a single, very long argumentation thread (see Figure 2). SRIP (van de Wetering et al., 2020) can remedy this by allowing a node (i.e., an area) to begin with the width of a parent, but, if no other nodes are in the same row, the area can grow at the bottom (reclaim space), to form trapezoids instead of rectangles. This still preserves the hierarchical structure, but enlarges small-sized hierarchy elements in deeper levels to increase the readability. To reduce meandering, SRIP can prevent nodes from growing by placing invisible sticky nodes beneath nodes without children which last for a configurable depth.

3.2 Model Training

We trained three different Vision Transformer models for our three visualizations using self-supervised training methods to reduce the need for labeled training data. As a base model, we used a Swinv2 Transformer model which was already trained on the ImageNet dataset (Deng et al., 2009). However, because that dataset is comprised almost entirely of photos of natural objects, we implemented an additional pre-training step on a large corpus of synthetic, random graph visualizations. Similarly to the way Vision Transformers are able to recognize relations between objects in a photo, we expect the pre-training step to enable our models to pick up on relations between graph segments. To improve performance on real argument graphs, we then performed a fine-tuning step on visualizations of argument graphs. For this, we used contrastive fine-tuning. We expect it to be especially well suited for our task, as the training objective of learning to recognize similar objects and differentiating them from unrelated ones aligns well with the goal of graph retrieval. More information is provided in Section A

In order to compare the performance of our relatively specialized Vision Transformers to much larger, universal models, we also fine-tuned OpenAI's model "gpt-4o-2024-08-06", capable of advanced text and image comprehension, on a dataset of argument graph visualizations, generated using our SRIP visualization. Because of its generic nature, we were able to adapt our contrastive fine-tuning strategy for this as well. Additional details are given in Section B.

4 Evaluation

Having introduced the core concepts and related work in the previous section, we now present our evaluation of the vision-based structural argument graph retrieval. We examine the argument graph retrieval task outlined in Section 3. The semantic pre-filter has already been evaluated in other works (Bergmann et al., 2019; Lenz et al., 2019), so we focus on the structural re-ranking part of our pipeline. To this end, we use an ideal filter that chooses all relevant argument graphs as determined by the human experts, resulting in a perfectly filtered set of semantically similar arguments. Then, we compare the re-ranking performance of our vision-based pipeline (separately for each visualization design and ViT model) to the baseline approach of an A* search as described in Section 2 against a benchmark ranking of human experts. Additionally, we perform an ablation study to examine how our pipeline's retrieval time scales with graph complexity. To assess the research question formulated in Section 1—Are vision-based graph similarities *more efficient* than and *equally effective* as ones based on GED for the retrieval of argument graphs?—we evaluate the following hypotheses:

H1 (Effectiveness). The retrieval quality of vision-based structural similarity computation closely approximates those of an A* search.

H2 (Efficiency). Vision-based structural similarity computation greatly reduces retrieval times compared to A* search by utilizing GPUs.

H3 (Specialization). Contrastive fine-tuning increases the effectiveness of ViT models compared to pre-training only.

4.1 Experimental Setup

For our evaluation, we implemented the visualization strategies in Python using Matplotlib (Hunter, 2007) and set up a training and inference pipeline that is publicly available on GitHub.[1] To allow comparisons with the existing approach, we used the corpus of annotated microtexts (Peldszus and Stede, 2016) containing 110 argument graphs with the same 24 queries as Bergmann et al. (2019). Half of these queries do not contain any S-node (only one I-node), while the other half contains up to two S-nodes. The queries come with a reference ranking from human experts, which we use to evaluate the retrieval quality of our approach. As part of an ongoing project, we have developed an additional set of 15 more complex queries with corresponding expert ranking having at least two S-nodes that we also include in our evaluation to better assess the scalability of our approach. The A* search was conducted using the original implementation of the authors[2] with the Universal Sentence Encoder (USE) (Cer et al., 2018) embedding model (their best performing variant). To ensure a fair comparison, we use the same ideal semantic pre-filter based on expert rankings for the A* search. In total, we perform six experiments: one for each of our visualizations (Treemap, Logical, and SRIP) using only pre-trained models and one for each visualization with the fine-tuned models.

We use the following metrics to assess our hypotheses: DURATION, Average Precision (AP) (Turpin and Scholer, 2006), Normalized Discounted Cumulative Gain (NDCG), and CORRECTNESS/COMPLETENESS (Cheng et al., 2010). All metrics except for CORRECTNESS are in the range $[0, 1]$, with higher values indicating better retrieval quality. CORRECTNESS is in the range $[-1, 1]$ with -1 meaning an inversely correct ranking, 0 meaning random ordering, and 1 meaning a correct ranking. For our vision-based models, DURATION only includes the time to embed the visualized argument graphs and compute the cosine similarities for re-ranking. These durations are measured on a single Nvidia Tesla V100 GPU and are averaged over 10 runs. The time to visualize the argument graph is not included as it heavily depends on the implementation of the visualization algorithm. In a practical application, the visualizations of a large case base would most likely be cached, contributing only to the one-time cost of creating the case base. The A* computations are performed on 2019 MacBook Pro with an 8-core Intel Core i9 CPU.

4.2 Results and Discussion

Having outlined our setup, we now present the results of our evaluation as shown in Table 1, starting with the set of simple queries used in previous work and then moving on to the more complex queries.

Simple Queries Regarding NDCG, the deviations between different visualizations and models are quite small, although the fine-tuned model for Treemaps and the pre-trained model for the SRIP visualization marginally outperform the other models. Contrary to our expectations, the pre-trained SRIP model, not A*, delivers the best retrieval quality across all metrics. The CORRECTNESS for all models (including the baseline) is very low, indicating that the queries are too limited for any of the approaches to closely match the ranking of the human experts. However, our vision models seem to be more capable in placing the most important queries at the beginning of the ranking which is over proportionally valued by NDCG.

Regarding DURATION, the initial embedding process of our vision models for the argument graphs within the case base takes between 95% and 108% of the entire retrieval time using A* search with Treemaps taking the longest time. This only has to be done once upfront, meaning that the embeddings can be cached in main memory and

[1] github.com/recap-utr/vision-retrieval (MIT license)
[2] github.com/recap-utr/argument-graph-retrieval

Table 1: Evaluation results for all queries. The column FT refers to the use of contrastive fine-tuning in addition to pre-training. EMB is time in seconds to embed all 110 argument graphs (upfront cost), while DUR measures the time for re-ranking the queries. For OpenAI, the duration is defined by the API request.

Model	FT	Queries	NDCG	AP	COR	COM	DUR	EMB
Treemap	✓	Simple	**0.92**	1.00	0.10	1.00	0.02	29.45
Treemap	✗	Simple	0.91	1.00	0.09	1.00	0.02	26.78
Logical	✓	Simple	0.90	1.00	-0.05	1.00	0.02	**25.87**
Logical	✗	Simple	0.91	1.00	0.07	1.00	0.02	26.57
SRIP	✓	Simple	0.90	1.00	-0.05	1.00	0.02	28.63
SRIP	✗	Simple	**0.92**	1.00	**0.11**	1.00	0.02	26.03
GPT-4o	–	Simple	0.91	1.00	-0.021	1.00	195.74	–
A*	–	Simple	0.85	1.00	0.05	1.00	27.16	–
Treemap	✓	Complex	0.94	1.00	0.38	1.00	0.01	26.42
Treemap	✗	Complex	0.91	1.00	0.21	1.00	0.01	25.67
Logical	✓	Complex	**0.98**	1.00	**0.68**	1.00	0.01	**25.51**
Logical	✗	Complex	0.96	1.00	0.66	1.00	0.01	25.46
SRIP	✓	Complex	0.97	1.00	0.62	1.00	0.01	30.84
SRIP	✗	Complex	0.95	1.00	0.59	1.00	0.01	26.42
GPT-4o	–	Complex	0.91	1.00	0.20	1.00	96.53	–
A*	–	Complex	0.95	1.00	0.632	1.00	199	–

reused for each query. The time needed for retrieval using the GPT-4o model is the longest (at 7 times the processing time of A*) and also has the highest fluctuations. This likely stems from the rather complex model (although OpenAI does not disclose the number of parameters) and the heterogeneous workload of the API.

Complex Queries When using more complex queries, all models perform better. There are minor gains in regard to NDCG (from 0 to 0.08) and especially CORRECTNESS (from 0.12 to 0.73) for the vision models. This is expected as the complex queries carry more information which can be visualized and embedded. Lack of information in simple queries is a problem specially for the trivial queries, with 0 S-nodes, where our visualizations only produce an unicolored image that does not enable the derivation of any meaningful graph structure. This is likely also the reason why our Treemap performs worst, as it only displays S-nodes and therefore contain less information. Our best model is the fine-tuned Logical model, outperforming the other visualization in all retrieval quality metrics. This suggests that the evaluated graphs were not complex enough to demonstrate the advantages of SRIP.

Comparing the DURATION to those of the simple queries, we see that the value for GPT-4o and our vision models scales linearly with the number of requests, while the small increase in query complexity does not have any noticeable effects. On the other hand, the added complexity of the query graphs over proportionally influences A* processing times. These noticeably lower request processing times together with the improved retrieval quality leads to a much better user experience and suitability for a real argument retrieval machine.

Discussion Overall, H1 can be accepted as the vision-based structural similarity pipeline with non-fine-tuned SRIP for simple queries and fine-tuned Logical for complex queries provides the best retrieval quality based on our metrics. When looking at the gains in retrieval quality for complex queries, it is even plausible that the retrieval quality slightly increases for even more complex queries. H2 can be accepted, as only the new query embeddings and cosine similarities have to be computed with each query, while the bulk of the work, the computation of embeddings for the (large) static case base only has to occur once. Also, the scaling is far superior, based on the durations reported in Table 1 and our scaling study in Section 4.3. H3 has to be partly discarded as the pre-trained model for SRIP outperformed the fine-tuned model for simple queries. However, H3 holds for complex argument graphs.

4.3 Ablation Study on Scaling

In this study, we evaluate how the graph complexity (measured by the number of the graph's S-nodes) affects the computation time of structural similarity. This is sufficient to estimate a graph's complexity, as the number of I-nodes equals the number of S-nodes + 1 for every argument graph we evaluate. To study graph complexity scaling, we chose 117 argument graphs from the Kialo GraphNLI dataset (Agarwal et al., 2022) making up the set of case base argument graphs C with 4-120 S-nodes. As the query, we randomly selected a single argument graph from the same dataset with 2540 S-nodes. As the query's complexity is constant, this setup allows studying the impact of increasing graph complexity on retrieval time in isolation. In this study, we use our SRIP visualization together with our fine-tuned model. This is because, even though our Logical visualization outperformed the SRIP visualization in our evaluation, the SRIP visualization should in theory work better for really deep argument graphs (see Figure 2).

Vision-based similarity computation requires the 3 steps outlined in Section 3: visualization, embedding, and cosine similarity calculation. The scaling behaviors of each of these steps can be seen in Figure 3. The embedding step, as well as the cosine similarity calculation, require constant time and are not influenced by the complexity of the input graphs. The visualization time increases linearly with graph complexity, even though there are several outliers. These could be caused by deviations in the size of the argument graph files, of which the entire content (i.e., also the argumentative text) is read, although only the information about the node types is considered to visualize the argument graph.

For a practical implementation of an argumentation machine, the linear scaling of visualization time in respect to graph complexity is likely not a problem, as only the query has to be visualized at runtime, whereas the case base graphs visualizations and embeddings can be pre-computed.

Comparing the total processing time of our vision-based approach to A*-search, it can be seen clearly that while the processing time using our vision-based approach increases linearly with respect to the number of S-nodes, they over proportionally hurt the performance of the A* search. Regarding the absolute times for both approaches, it is apparent that A* is not viable for retrieval of complex arguments in a production argumentation machine, as a *single* comparison between a complex argument graph with 2540 S-nodes, and an argument graph with more than 8 S-nodes takes at least 1,000s.

4.4 Limitations

While our results are promising, there are some limitations to our approach. In order to layout graphs in a compressed format, we made simplifications such as ignoring I-nodes in treemaps. Also, graphs containing cycles currently cannot be rendered due to our focus on hierarchical visualizations. For large graphs with skewed distributions of nodes (e.g., long chains of ADUs), the ranking quality of our approach may suffer due to large amounts of whitespace. Similarly, for graphs with nearly identical structure but different content, the visualizations may be indistinguishable, potentially leading to poor retrieval quality—which we solved by introducing a semantic pre-filter.

Regarding the vision models, we used relatively small models (197M parameters) with limited training datasets. Graphs having more elements than the model's maximum number of pixels (e.g., 256×256) need to be clipped or downsampled, meaning that some information is lost. Given the scalability of transformers, we anticipate that larger models with more extensive training data could yield improved performance in future evaluations. Lastly, our scaling study disregards the quality of the retrieval for larger argument graphs due to missing ground truth data.

5 Conclusion and Future Work

We proposed a vision-based pipeline for argument graph retrieval based on their structure that builds on the output of AM systems. It works by filtering for semantically similar arguments, visualizing their graph representations, embedding these rendered images with a vision model, and finally ranking the arguments based on the cosine similarity to the query's embedding. The research question whether vision-based argument retrieval can provide a faster and more scalable alternative to A* search for structural argument graph retrieval can be affirmed; however, not every dataset of arguments allows for the effective use of the vision-based approach. On the one hand, our evaluation suggests that there is a minimum complexity argument graphs should have for our vision-based

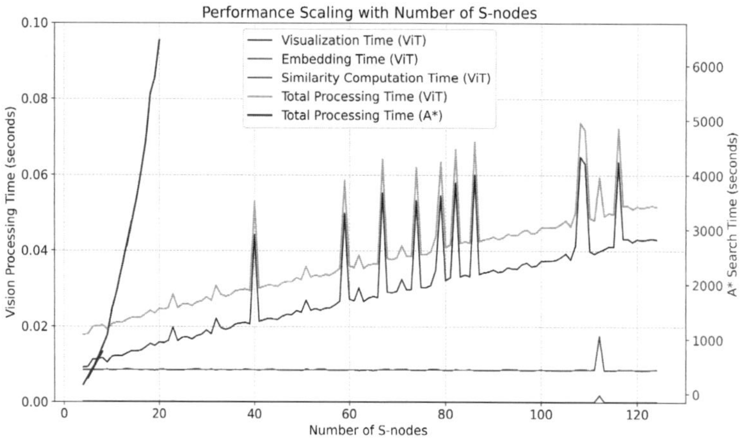

Figure 3: Processing times of vision-based and A* retrieval for graphs between 4 and 124 S-nodes.

approach to be able to perform meaningful similarity computation. On the other hand, the information which can be displayed in the limited input window of a vision model imposes an upper limit on argument graph complexity which can be sensibly processed using our approach. Regarding efficiency and scaling, the use of embeddings allows storing a uniform, query-independent representation of the original argument graphs, which can be pre-computed to allow for fast comparisons even across large case bases. While we investigated a re-ranking task for our evaluation, vision-based argument retrieval could also be used to enhance the pipeline proposed by Bergmann et al. (2019): Our vision-based retrieval could serve as a second pre-filter to further decrease the search space of the expensive A* search to ensure that only graphs that are semantically and structurally similar are considered at all. This pipeline enables to construct mappings between queries and case base graphs which are absent in purely vision-based retrieval.

One possible avenue for future work is to investigate the use of more detailed argumentation schemes (Walton, 2013) to differentiate between additional types of S-nodes in the argument graph. As Lenz et al. (2019) showed, using schemes can have a positive impact on the retrieval quality. A key challenge in this regard is the inclusion of the additional information into the generated visualizations. Furthermore, we focused on a single model training pipeline. As has been shown before (Qu et al., 2020; Asai et al., 2022; Khan et al., 2022; Wang et al., 2022; El-Nouby et al., 2021; Grill et al., 2020; Tian et al., 2021), training pipeline refinements can notably improve the predictions. An open question here is how to apply existing training techniques for texts or pictures for our graph visualizations.

Additionally, our evaluation was limited to a single dataset (Peldszus and Stede, 2015). Future work should verify whether the findings can be generalized to other datasets, especially with more complex argument graphs and extended ADU relations. One candidate for this could be the AbstRCT dataset (Mayer et al., 2020).

References

Agnar Aamodt and Enric Plaza. 1994. Case-Based Reasoning - Foundational Issues, Methodological Variations, and System Approaches. *AI Commun.*

Vibhor Agarwal, Sagar Joglekar, Anthony P. Young, and Nishanth Sastry. 2022. Graphnli: A graph-based natural language inference model for polarity prediction in online debates. In *The ACM Web Conference (TheWebConf)*.

Jason Ansel, Edward Yang, Horace He, Natalia Gimelshein, Animesh Jain, Michael Voznesensky, Bin Bao, Peter Bell, David Berard, Evgeni Burovski, Geeta Chauhan, Anjali Chourdia, Will Constable, Alban Desmaison, Zachary DeVito, Elias Ellison, Will Feng, Jiong Gong, Michael Gschwind, Brian Hirsh, Sherlock Huang, Kshiteej Kalambarkar, Laurent Kirsch, Michael Lazos, Mario Lezcano, Yanbo Liang, Jason Liang, Yinghai Lu, CK Luk, Bert Maher, Yunjie Pan, Christian Puhrsch, Matthias Reso, Mark Saroufim, Marcos Yukio Siraichi, Helen Suk, Michael Suo, Phil Tillet, Eikan Wang, Xiaodong Wang, William Wen, Shunting Zhang, Xu Zhao, Keren Zhou, Richard Zou, Ajit Mathews, Gregory Chanan, Peng Wu, and Soumith Chintala. 2024. PyTorch 2: Faster Machine Learning Through Dynamic Python Bytecode Transformation and Graph Compilation. In *29th ACM International Conference on*

Architectural Support for Programming Languages and Operating Systems, Volume 2 (ASPLOS '24). ACM.

Akari Asai, Timo Schick, Patrick Lewis, Xilun Chen, Gautier Izacard, Sebastian Riedel, Hannaneh Hajishirzi, and Wen tau Yih. 2022. Task-aware retrieval with instructions. *Preprint*, arXiv:2211.09260.

Margaret E. Baron. 1969. A Note on the Historical Development of Logic Diagrams: Leibniz, Euler and Venn. *The Mathematical Gazette*, 53(384):113–125.

Elias Bassani. 2022. Ranx: A Blazing-Fast Python Library for Ranking Evaluation and Comparison. In *Advances in Information Retrieval*, pages 259–264, Cham. Springer International Publishing.

Ralph Bergmann and Yolanda Gil. 2014. Similarity assessment and efficient retrieval of semantic workflows. *Information Systems*, 40:115–127.

Ralph Bergmann, Mirko Lenz, Stefan Ollinger, and Maximilian Pfister. 2019. Similarity Measures for Case-Based Retrieval of Natural Language Argument Graphs in Argumentation Machines. In *Proceedings of the Thirty-Second International Florida Artificial Intelligence Research Society Conference*, pages 329–334, Sarasota, Florida, USA. AAAI Press.

H. Bunke. 1997. On a relation between graph edit distance and maximum common subgraph. *Pattern Recognition Letters*, 18(8):689–694.

Hans-Dieter Burkhard and Michael M. Richter. 2001. On the Notion of Similarity in Case Based Reasoning and Fuzzy Theory. In Sankar K. Pal, Tharam S. Dillon, and Daniel S. Yeung, editors, *Soft Computing in Case Based Reasoning*, pages 29–45. Springer London, London.

Hongyun Cai, Vincent W Zheng, and Kevin Chen-Chuan Chang. 2018. A comprehensive survey of graph embedding: Problems, techniques, and applications. *IEEE transactions on knowledge and data engineering*, 30(9):1616–1637.

Daniel Cer, Yinfei Yang, Sheng-yi Kong, Nan Hua, Nicole Limtiaco, Rhomni St John, Noah Constant, Mario Guajardo-Cespedes, Steve Yuan, Chris Tar, Yun-Hsuan Sung, Brian Strope, and Ray Kurzweil. 2018. Universal Sentence Encoder. *arXiv:1803.11175 [cs]*.

Ting Chen, Simon Kornblith, Mohammad Norouzi, and Geoffrey E. Hinton. 2020a. A simple framework for contrastive learning of visual representations. *CoRR*, abs/2002.05709.

Ting Chen, Simon Kornblith, Kevin Swersky, Mohammad Norouzi, and Geoffrey E. Hinton. 2020b. Big self-supervised models are strong semi-supervised learners. *CoRR*, abs/2006.10029.

Weiwei Cheng, Michaël Rademaker, Bernard De Baets, and Eyke Hüllermeier. 2010. Predicting Partial Orders: Ranking with Abstention. In *Machine Learning and Knowledge Discovery in Databases*, Lecture Notes in Computer Science, pages 215–230, Barcelona, Spain. Springer.

Carlos Iván Chesñevar, Jarred McGinnis, Sanjay Modgil, Iyad Rahwan, Chris Reed, Guillermo Ricardo Simari, Matthew South, Gerard Vreeswijk, and Steven Willmott. 2006. Towards an argument interchange format. *The Knowledge Engineering Review*, 21(04):293.

Jia Deng, Wei Dong, Richard Socher, Li-Jia Li, Kai Li, and Li Fei-Fei. 2009. Imagenet: A large-scale hierarchical image database. In *2009 IEEE Conference on Computer Vision and Pattern Recognition*, pages 248–255.

Alexey Dosovitskiy, Lucas Beyer, Alexander Kolesnikov, Dirk Weissenborn, Xiaohua Zhai, Thomas Unterthiner, Mostafa Dehghani, Matthias Minderer, Georg Heigold, Sylvain Gelly, Jakob Uszkoreit, and Neil Houlsby. 2021. An Image is Worth 16x16 Words: Transformers for Image Recognition at Scale. In *International Conference on Learning Representations*.

Alaaeldin El-Nouby, Natalia Neverova, Ivan Laptev, and Hervé Jégou. 2021. Training vision transformers for image retrieval. *arXiv preprint arXiv:2102.05644*.

William Falcon and The PyTorch Lightning team. 2019. PyTorch Lightning.

Kenneth D Forbus, Dedre Gentner, and Keith Law. 1995. MAC/FAC - A Model of Similarity-Based Retrieval. *Cognitive Science*, 19(2):141–205.

Tianyu Gao, Xingcheng Yao, and Danqi Chen. 2021. Simcse: Simple contrastive learning of sentence embeddings. *CoRR*, abs/2104.08821.

Jean-Bastien Grill, Florian Strub, Florent Altché, Corentin Tallec, Pierre H. Richemond, Elena Buchatskaya, Carl Doersch, Bernardo Ávila Pires, Zhaohan Daniel Guo, Mohammad Gheshlaghi Azar, Bilal Piot, Koray Kavukcuoglu, Rémi Munos, and Michal Valko. 2020. Bootstrap your own latent: A new approach to self-supervised learning. *CoRR*, abs/2006.07733.

Aditya Grover and Jure Leskovec. 2016. node2vec: Scalable feature learning for networks. In *Proceedings of the 22nd ACM SIGKDD international conference on Knowledge discovery and data mining*, pages 855–864.

Annette Hautli-Janisz, Zlata Kikteva, Wassiliki Siskou, Kamila Gorska, Ray Becker, and Chris Reed. 2022. QT30: A corpus of argument and conflict in broadcast debate. In *Proceedings of the Thirteenth Language Resources and Evaluation Conference*, pages 3291–3300, Marseille, France. European Language Resources Association.

Maximilian Hoffmann, Lukas Malburg, Nico Bach, and Ralph Bergmann. 2022. GPU-Based Graph Matching for Accelerating Similarity Assessment in Process-Oriented Case-Based Reasoning. In *Case-Based Reasoning Research and Development*, pages 240–255, Cham. Springer International Publishing.

J. D. Hunter. 2007. Matplotlib: A 2d graphics environment. *Computing in Science & Engineering*, 9(3):90–95.

Vidit Jain and Manik Varma. 2011. Learning to re-rank: query-dependent image re-ranking using click data. In *Proceedings of the 20th international conference on World wide web*, pages 277–286.

B. Johnson and B. Shneiderman. 1991. Tree-maps: A space-filling approach to the visualization of hierarchical information structures. In *Proceeding Visualization '91*, pages 284–291.

Salman Khan, Muzammal Naseer, Munawar Hayat, Syed Waqas Zamir, Fahad Shahbaz Khan, and Mubarak Shah. 2022. Transformers in vision: A survey. *ACM computing surveys (CSUR)*, 54(10s):1–41.

Thomas N Kipf and Max Welling. 2016. Semi-supervised classification with graph convolutional networks. *arXiv preprint arXiv:1609.02907*.

John Lawrence and Chris Reed. 2019. Argument Mining: A Survey. *Computational Linguistics*, 45(4):765–818.

Mirko Lenz, Stefan Ollinger, Premtim Sahitaj, and Ralph Bergmann. 2019. Semantic Textual Similarity Measures for Case-Based Retrieval of Argument Graphs. In *Case-Based Reasoning Research and Development*, volume 11680 of *Lecture Notes in Computer Science*, pages 219–234, Otzenhausen, Germany. Springer International Publishing.

Ze Liu, Han Hu, Yutong Lin, Zhuliang Yao, Zhenda Xie, Yixuan Wei, Jia Ning, Yue Cao, Zheng Zhang, Li Dong, Furu Wei, and Baining Guo. 2022. Swin Transformer V2: Scaling Up Capacity and Resolution. In *Proceedings of the IEEE/CVF Conference on Computer Vision and Pattern Recognition*, pages 12009–12019.

Ze Liu, Yutong Lin, Yue Cao, Han Hu, Yixuan Wei, Zheng Zhang, Stephen Lin, and Baining Guo. 2021. Swin Transformer: Hierarchical Vision Transformer Using Shifted Windows. In *Proceedings of the IEEE/CVF International Conference on Computer Vision*, pages 10012–10022.

Lorenzo Livi and Antonello Rizzi. 2013. The graph matching problem. *Pattern Analysis and Applications*, 16(3):253–283.

TorchVision maintainers and contributors. 2016. Torchvision: Pytorch's computer vision library. `https://github.com/pytorch/vision`.

Santiago Marro, Elena Cabrio, and Serena Villata. 2022. Graph Embeddings for Argumentation Quality Assessment. In *Findings of the Association for Computational Linguistics: EMNLP 2022*, pages 4154–4164, Abu Dhabi, United Arab Emirates. Association for Computational Linguistics.

Tobias Mayer, Elena Cabrio, and Serena Villata. 2020. Transformer-based argument mining for healthcare applications. In *ECAI 2020 - 24th European Conference on Artificial Intelligence*, volume 325 of *Frontiers in Artificial Intelligence and Applications*, pages 2108–2115. IOS Press.

Mirjam Minor, Stefania Montani, and Juan A. Recio-García. 2014. Process-oriented case-based reasoning. *Information Systems*, 40:103–105.

Daniel Carlos Guimaraes Pedronette and Ricardo da S Torres. 2013. Image re-ranking and rank aggregation based on similarity of ranked lists. *Pattern Recognition*, 46(8):2350–2360.

Andreas Peldszus and Manfred Stede. 2013. From Argument Diagrams to Argumentation Mining in Texts - A Survey. *IJCINI*, 7(1):1–31.

Andreas Peldszus and Manfred Stede. 2015. An annotated corpus of argumentative microtexts. In *Argumentation and Reasoned Action: Proceedings of the 1st European Conference on Argumentation, Lisbon*, volume 2, pages 801–815.

Andreas Peldszus and Manfred Stede. 2016. An Annotated Corpus of Argumentative Microtexts. In *Argumentation and Reasoned Action: Proceedings of the 1st European Conference on Argumentation*, volume 2, pages 801–816, Lisbon, Portugal. College Publications.

Bryan Perozzi, Rami Al-Rfou, and Steven Skiena. 2014. Deepwalk: Online learning of social representations. In *Proceedings of the 20th ACM SIGKDD international conference on Knowledge discovery and data mining*, pages 701–710.

Yingqi Qu, Yuchen Ding, Jing Liu, Kai Liu, Ruiyang Ren, Wayne Xin Zhao, Daxiang Dong, Hua Wu, and Haifeng Wang. 2020. Rocketqa: An optimized training approach to dense passage retrieval for open-domain question answering. *arXiv preprint arXiv:2010.08191*.

Chris Reed. 2006. Preliminary results from an argument corpus. *Linguistics in the twenty-first century*, pages 185–196.

Olga Russakovsky, Jia Deng, Hao Su, Jonathan Krause, Sanjeev Satheesh, Sean Ma, Zhiheng Huang, Andrej Karpathy, Aditya Khosla, Michael Bernstein, Alexander C. Berg, and Li Fei-Fei. 2015. Imagenet large scale visual recognition challenge. *Preprint*, arXiv:1409.0575.

Hans-Jorg Schulz. 2011. Treevis.net: A Tree Visualization Reference. *IEEE Computer Graphics and Applications*, 31(6):11–15.

Maria Skeppstedt, Andreas Peldszus, and Manfred Stede. 2018. More or less controlled elicitation of argumentative text: Enlarging a microtext corpus via crowdsourcing. In *Proceedings of the 5th Workshop on Argument Mining*, pages 155–163, Brussels, Belgium. Association for Computational Linguistics.

Christian Stab and Iryna Gurevych. 2017. Argument annotated essays (version 2).

Hao Tang, Donghong Ji, Chenliang Li, and Qiji Zhou. 2020. Dependency graph enhanced dual-transformer structure for aspect-based sentiment classification. In *Proceedings of the 58th annual meeting of the association for computational linguistics*, pages 6578–6588.

Yuandong Tian, Xinlei Chen, and Surya Ganguli. 2021. Understanding self-supervised learning dynamics without contrastive pairs. *CoRR*, abs/2102.06810.

Andrew Turpin and Falk Scholer. 2006. User performance versus precision measures for simple search tasks. In *SIGIR 2006: Proceedings of the 29th Annual International ACM SIGIR Conference on Research and Development in Information Retrieval, Seattle, Washington, USA, August 6-11, 2006*, pages 11–18.

Huub van de Wetering, Nico Klaassen, and Michael Burch. 2020. Space-Reclaiming Icicle Plots. In *2020 IEEE Pacific Visualization Symposium (PacificVis)*, pages 121–130.

Frans H. Van Eemeren. 2018. *Argumentation Theory: A Pragma-Dialectical Perspective*, volume 33 of *Argumentation Library*. Springer International Publishing, Cham.

Ashish Vaswani, Noam Shazeer, Niki Parmar, Jakob Uszkoreit, Llion Jones, Aidan N Gomez, Lukasz Kaiser, and Illia Polosukhin. 2017. Attention is All you Need. In *Advances in Neural Information Processing Systems*, volume 30. Curran Associates, Inc.

Jacky Visser, Barbara Konat, Rory Duthie, Marcin Koszowy, Katarzyna Budzynska, and Chris Reed. 2020. Argumentation in the 2016 us presidential elections: annotated corpora of television debates and social media reaction. *Language Resources and Evaluation*, 54(1):123–154.

Marilyn A Walker, Jean E Fox Tree, Pranav Anand, Rob Abbott, and Joseph King. 2012. A corpus for research on deliberation and debate. In *LREC*, volume 12, pages 812–817. Istanbul, Turkey.

Douglas Walton. 2013. *Argumentation Schemes for Presumptive Reasoning*. Routledge.

Liang Wang, Nan Yang, Xiaolong Huang, Binxing Jiao, Linjun Yang, Daxin Jiang, Rangan Majumder, and Furu Wei. 2022. Simlm: Pre-training with representation bottleneck for dense passage retrieval. *arXiv preprint arXiv:2207.02578*.

Xiaogang Wang, Shi Qiu, Ke Liu, and Xiaoou Tang. 2013. Web image re-ranking using query-specific semantic signatures. *IEEE transactions on pattern analysis and machine intelligence*, 36(4):810–823.

Thomas Wolf, Lysandre Debut, Victor Sanh, Julien Chaumond, Clement Delangue, Anthony Moi, Pierric Cistac, Tim Rault, Remi Louf, Morgan Funtowicz, Joe Davison, Sam Shleifer, Patrick von Platen, Clara Ma, Yacine Jernite, Julien Plu, Canwen Xu, Teven Le Scao, Sylvain Gugger, Mariama Drame, Quentin Lhoest, and Alexander Rush. 2020. Transformers: State-of-the-art natural language processing. In *Proceedings of the 2020 Conference on Empirical Methods in Natural Language Processing: System Demonstrations*, pages 38–45, Online. Association for Computational Linguistics.

Mengjia Xu. 2021. Understanding graph embedding methods and their applications. *SIAM Review*, 63(4):825–853.

A Reproducibility

In the following section, we outline how we trained our vision models and which dataset was used for the sake of reproducibility. For both training steps we used PyTorch (Ansel et al., 2024) version 2.5.0 together with PyTorch Lightning (Falcon and The PyTorch Lightning team, 2019). The vision transformer models were integrated via the transformers package (Wolf et al., 2020) (version 4.45.2). The evaluation is based on the ranx package (Bassani, 2022).

A.1 Pre-Training

For each of the visualizations, a separate large Swinv2 Transformer model (Liu et al., 2022) (released under Apache 2.0 License) with 195M parameters was pre-trained. We chose this model for its improved efficiency in relation to the original Vision Transformer model (Dosovitskiy et al., 2021) and its architecture which makes use of hierarchical feature maps and should align well with the nature of hierarchical graph drawings. A checkpoint which has been trained on the ImageNet-1k dataset (Russakovsky et al., 2015) is used as a starting point, which should speed up training compared to completely random initial weights. For the training, we used an Auto-Encoder setup, where the Swinv2 model was used as a encoder, transforming an input image into corresponding embeddings. During the training, a very simple decoder (a single linear layer) is used to reconstruct a lower resolution form of the original image using the embeddings provided by the encoder. The MSE loss is computed between the raw pixel values of the original images (resized to 32x32px) and the reconstructed image. An AdamW optimizer with a learn rate of 0.001 is used. Additionally, we used early stopping after 3 epochs without a reduction in validation loss. The models are trained with a batch-size of 32 for a maximum of 50 epochs on 6 Nvidia Tesla V100 GPUs. The actual training time was 20-23 epochs (174-198 GPU hours).

As our pre-training dataset, we used a dataset of synthetic argument graphs. For every of our three visualizations, we generated 1.2 million random graphs with a maximum depth of 9 and a maximum branching number of 7, which decreases with increased depth. The motivation behind this is to generate graphs which deviate from each other; however the minimum area allocated to a single node in the corresponding visualization is fixed by the limited depth and number of siblings. The resulting images are then de-duplicated using *fclones* [3], which left us with 1,062,679 samples for the Logical model, 1,062,513 for the Treemaps model and 917,558 for the SRIP model. Of those samples, we always chose 90% as training samples and the remaining 10% as test samples.

A.2 Fine-Tuning

Each of the models from the pre-training stage are fine-tuned on a corpus of 6474 argument graphs (see Table 2) after filtering out too complex graphs which took longer than 3s to visualize. After deduplication with *fclones*, this left us with 4317 SRIP images, 4309 Logical images and 4173 Treemap images. The setup used for contrastive fine-tuning is derived from SimCLR (Chen et al., 2020a):

1. Each image x from the training batch is randomly augmented twice which generates two contrastive views of every input which represent each others positive pairs: q, k.

2. q and k are encoded using the encoder network (the pre-trained Swin Transformer v2 model), resulting in the embeddings e_q and e_k.

3. The embedding dimensionalities are reduced by passing them through an MLP projection head to prevent the curse of dimensionality (Chen et al., 2020b).

4. A contrastive loss is calculated between every element's corresponding image view and every other element in the batch (in-batch negatives) on the reduced embeddings.

The contrastive views are derived from the original images by using the following transformations: (i) random horizontal flips, (ii) random vertical flips, (iii) Gaussian Blur (iv) random crop (an area of 40% - 90% of the original image is resized to the original dimensions) and (v) dropout to simulate random noise. For these transformations, we used the implementations from torchvision (maintainers and contributors, 2016) (version 0.20.0). The first four transforms are derived from the original SimCLR transforms (Chen et al., 2020a); dropout is inspired by (Gao et al., 2021). It should be noted that color jitter, as one of the most important transforms (Chen et al., 2020a) could not be used. This is because a change of color for a node might completely change its meaning in all of our visualizations and therefore represent a different graph structure. The following contrastive loss is used (Chen et al., 2020a):

$$f(q,k) = \exp\left(\frac{\text{sim}(q,k)}{\tau}\right) \tag{1}$$

$$\ell_i^{\text{NT-Xent}} = -\log \frac{f(q_i,k_i)}{f(q_i,k_i) + \sum_{j\neq i} f(q_i,k_j)} \tag{2}$$

for i, j in $\{0, \ldots, \text{batch\_size}\}$ where $\text{sim}(\cdot,\cdot)$ denotes cosine similarity, and τ represents *temperature* as a hyperparameter. Our models were trained with a hidden dimension of 64, $\tau = 0.07$ and a weight decay of 0.0001.

As an optimizer, AdamW with a learn rate of 0.0005 is used. Additionally a *Cosine Annealing Scheduler* was used for the learn rate with a maximum of 500 iterations and a minimum learn rate of 0.00001. The same early stopping criterion was applied as for pre-training, however no fine-tuned model training was interrupted early. The fine-tuning is performed with a batch-size of 16 (i.e., 16 contrastive pairs) for a maximum of 500 epochs on 6 Nvidia Tesla V100 GPUs.

B GPT-4o Fine-Tuning

To emulate contrastive training with the limited interface OpenAI provides (i.e., training samples have to represent a conversation with a prompt and an expected answer from the model), we generated 900 samples containing two SRIP visualizations

[3] github.com/pkolaczk/fclones

Table 2: Argument graph corpora used to construct our fine-tuning dataset.

Dataset	Source	Description
Kialo Graph-NLI	Agarwal et al. (2022)	Graphs model discussion trees on Kialo, an online debates platform
Araucaria	Reed (2006)	Corpus of analyzed argumentation, constructed using the Araucaria tool
IAC	Walker et al. (2012)	A corpus for research on deliberation and debate
QT30	Hautli-Janisz et al. (2022)	Argument and conflict in broadcast debate
US2016	Visser et al. (2020)	Television debates and social media reactions to the 2016 US presidential elections
Persuasive Essays	Stab and Gurevych (2017)	Annotated persuasive essays
Microtexts Part 2	Skeppstedt et al. (2018)	Short argumentative texts

each. The model's task during the training process was to predict whether the images represent the same argument graph or a different graph. 450 samples contained two contrastive views of the same graph (see above) while the remaining 450 samples contained two different graphs. The model was trained for a single epoch with a batch size of 1 and a LR multiplier of 2. The training took about one hour.

During evaluation, we provide the model aSRIP representation of the query and the SRIP visualization of the retrieval candidates acquired from the MAC phase. The model's task is ordering the case graphs based on their relevance to the query. To eliminate any run-to-run variance, the temperature during evaluation is set to 0.

Note: We only trained the model for a single epoch as prior experiments indicated that the model's performance degraded for models with more epochs. This is most likely because our training dataset consisted only of singular, short answers ("Are the images visualizations of the same or different graphs?" $\rightarrow$ "same" or "different"") which caused the further trained checkpoints to adapt to this and only provide too short and therefore largely incomplete answers during the evaluation.

Old but Gold: LLM-Based Features and Shallow Learning Methods for Fine-Grained Controversy Analysis in YouTube Comments

Davide Bassi[1], **Erik Bran Marino**[2], **Renata Vieira**[2], **Martin Pereira-Farina**[3]
[1] CiTIUS, University of Santiago de Compostela, Spain, davide.bassi@usc.es
[2] CIDEHUS, University of Évora, Portugal, {erik.marino,renatav}@uevora.pt
[3] University of Santiago de Compostela, Spain, martin.pereira@usc.es

Abstract

Online discussions can either bridge differences through constructive dialogue or amplify divisions through destructive interactions. This paper proposes a computational approach to analyze dialogical relation patterns in YouTube comments, offering a fine-grained framework for controversy detection, enabling also analysis of individual contributions. Our experiments demonstrate that shallow learning methods, when equipped with theoretically-grounded features, consistently outperform more complex language models in characterizing discourse quality at both comment-pair and conversation-chain levels. Ablation studies confirm that divisive rhetorical techniques serve as strong predictors of destructive communication patterns. This work advances understanding of how communicative choices shape online discourse, moving beyond engagement metrics toward nuanced examination of constructive versus destructive dialogue patterns.

1 Introduction

Online discussions can either bridge differences through constructive dialogue or amplify divisions through inflammatory responses. These divergent outcomes are fundamentally shaped by the communicative approaches adopted by participants, where each contribution can either push the interaction toward controversy or constructive discussion. In fact, while conflicting viewpoints form a prerequisite for argumentation (Walton, 2008), individuals express opposition through diverse communicative approaches, generating a "disagreement space" that participants navigate based on their chosen discursive strategies (Schumann and Oswald, 2024).

Delineating this conceptual space is essential for advancing argument mining research, as it provides a structured framework for analyzing how disagreements manifest in discourse, enabling more nuanced computational modeling of argumentative interactions in both online and offline contexts. Samson and Nowak (2010) proposes a framework in which constructive and destructive conflicts are opposite ends of a single dimension (Vallacher et al., 2013). Specifically, destructive processes aim at inflicting psychological, material or physical damage on the opponent, while constructive aim at achieving one's goals while maintaining or enhancing relations with the opponent.

Computational approaches to detect and measure constructive versus destructive dialogical relations patterns remain underdeveloped (Lawrence and Reed, 2019). Research in this direction could generate methods useful not only to identify controversies but also to track how they emerge and evolve through specific communicative choices, advancing our understanding of these dynamics while offering practical applications for fostering healthier online discourse (Marres, 2015).

This research proposes an automated approach to classify and measure destructive and constructive patterns in online discussions, examining how individual messages, situated within their conversational context, contribute to either productive dialogue or increased antagonism.

Specifically, we contribute by: (*i*) providing a pipeline to mine laypeople discussions from Youtube video comments section and creating a dataset of full conversation chains with varied length and complexity[1]; (*ii*) proposing a novel operationalization of destructive communication through divisive rhetorical techniques (Zompetti, 2015), demonstrating how stance, linguistic and rhetorical features can be used to characterize dialogical quality in online discourse; (*iii*) evaluating the effectiveness of these rhetorical features across both traditional machine learning methods and large language models, with results revealing

[1]Full dataset, annotation guidelines and the scripts we used can be found at https://github.com/BassiDavide/Arg-Mining_Old_but_Gold/tree/main.

Proceedings of the 12th Argument Mining Workshop, pages 46–57
July 31, 2025 ©2025 Association for Computational Linguistics

that shallow learning approaches more effectively leverage them for classification.

2 Related Works

Our research advances the field of controversy analysis, diverging from predominant approaches reliant on quantitative engagement metrics and network-based methodologies (Coletto et al., 2017; Sriteja et al., 2017; Garimella et al., 2016). Instead, we employ a finer-grained, textually grounded framework, akin to Wang et al. (2023); Konat et al. (2016); Allen et al. (2014); Chen et al. (2023), to dissect discursive comment-level interactions and derive higher-level insights about conversation quality, i.e. distinguishing between destructive (controversy-promoting) and constructive communication patterns at both comment and comment-chain levels. Additionally, our study represents the first controversy analysis of YouTube discussions—a platform that, despite its ubiquity, remains understudied through this analytical lens because of its API limitations. To tackle these issues we employ Bassi et al. (2024b)'s pipeline to extract conversation structures and stance information.

Prior efforts aimed to tackle the multifaceted nature of evaluating dialogue quality, yielding valuable insights. Samson and Nowak (2010) established that constructive and destructive conflict processes can be distinguished through linguistic markers (e.g., pronoun usage, emotional valence). Similarly, Chen et al. (2023) found that controversial comments tend to express higher levels of emotions. De Kock and Vlachos (2021) specifically investigate constructive disagreement in Wikipedia Talk pages, demonstrating that gradient features capturing temporal changes in linguistic markers and conversation structure information effectively predict escalation to mediation as a proxy for discourse failure.

Further, Lawrence et al. (2017) and Harris et al. (2018) demonstrate the significance of rhetorical figures in discursive relation detection (see also Lawrence and Reed (2019)).

To provide a more comprehensive understanding of dialogue dynamics, our approach integrates linguistic indicators with rhetorical formally detectable patterns. Specifically, we leverage Zompetti (2015)'s divisive rhetoric framework, defining specific rhetorical devices and argumentative fallacies that systematically undermine constructive dialogue.

Through this comprehensive set of features (linguistic, stance, and rhetorical devices), we develop a computational method that operates at both comment-pair and conversation-chain levels to assess discourse quality. At the micro level, we classify the relationship between adjacent comments according to their functional orientation and communicative quality. At the macro level, we aggregate these classifications to characterize entire conversation chains on a divisiveness scale from highly destructive to constructive. This multi-level approach quantifies how individual interactions contribute to broader conversational dynamics, revealing patterns that either foster productive dialogue or amplify division throughout extended discussions.

The remainder of this paper is structured as follows: Section 3 details our dataset creation and annotation. Section 4 describes features for divisiveness detection. Section 5 outlines our experimental methodology. Section 6 presents results and feature importance analysis. Section 7 discusses result implications and future work.

3 Dataset

3.1 Dataset Creation

A) Data Crawling: given our focus on controversial topics, we centered our investigation on immigration-related content. To gather the data, first, we crawled YouTube to identify the 100 most viewed videos using query sets designed to capture diverse viewpoints (see repository for complete query). We restricted our sample to English-language content from the United States (2013-2024) with a minimum threshold of 1,000 comments per video. These videos were then ranked based on their comment volume to identify those generating more discussions. We took the 15 most commented ones.

B) Conversation Reconstruction: to reconstruct conversational structures, we applied the methodology proposed by Bassi et al. (2024b), which allows to address complex dialogical discourse phenomena where the meaning of a locution can only be understood by reference to another e.g. "Isn't illegal immigration a crime?" — "Definitely not".

C) Discussion Chain Extraction: we define a discussion chain as a sequence of interconnected messages that form a coherent conversation thread. To identify and extract them, firstly, we identified *terminal messages*, i.e. messages that (*i*) have not received no further responses; *(ii)* have a depth level of at least 4 in the conversation tree, ensuring a minimum of 5 messages in the conversation (see dotted comments in Figure 1). Otherwise, the chain was not considered (see Case-A in Figure 1). Secondly, for each identified terminal message, we *traced back through the conversation tree to the root message*, creating a complete discussion chain.

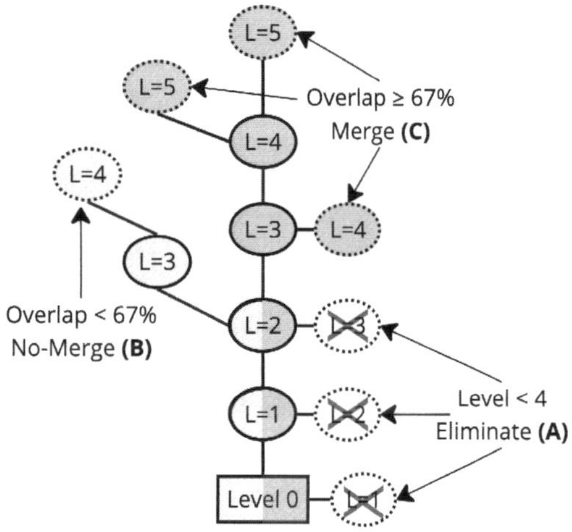

Figure 1: Chain Clustering and Construction Criteria

D) Chain Clustering and Refinement: conversation chains can present a "natural clustering" (e.g. Chain A Figure 6 in Appendix), or share some messages to, then, develop specific paths (e.g. Chain B-C-D-E in Figure 6 in Appendix). Rather than treating entire conversation trees as monolithic units, we aimed to identify and analyze these distinct conversation branches separately, as they often exhibit unique communicative patterns and divisiveness characteristics, even when originating from the same root comment. Given this "behavior", we aimed at treating these cases as separated conversations (see how we split Chain C-D-E in Figure 6 in Appendix, despite sharing messages). To systematically operate this clustering, we analyzed the overlap between 2 conversation chains implementing a pairwise comparison of discussion chains using a similarity metric. Specifically:

(i) we calculated the intersection of messages between each pair of chains (i.e., given a couple of conversation chain with different lengths ($len(com1)$,$len(com2)$), we counted how many comments they shared = $len(intersection)$).

(ii) we calculated the overlap ratio based on the size of the intersection relative to the shorter chain as: $OverRat = \frac{len(intersection)}{\min[(len(com1), len(com2)]}$

(iii) we established a threshold of 0.67: two chains were merged if they shared more than 67% of their comments (relative to the shorter chain), and vice versa for lower values of overlap.

Computationally, we implemented this process by representing each conversation chain as a node in a graph, connecting nodes that exceed our overlap threshold (0.67), and extracting connected components to identify chains forming a cluster that should be merged[2].

To ensure the robustness of our methodology, we manually verified the accuracy of comment links during annotation, identifying only 30 incorrect links out of 2387 total child-comments, confirming the reliability of our approach.

E) Sampling: we considered that conversation chains can have different degrees of complexity. To ensure a representative sample across all complexity levels, we implemented a stratified sampling approach. First, we grouped chains sharing the same root comment (Level=0) into "chain families" to preserve the contextual integrity of discussions. Each family's complexity was measured by its total message count. We then divided these families into three equal percentile groups (low, medium, and high complexity) and sampled proportionally from each group to reach our target message count (=2500).

3.2 Annotation

Our annotation schema focuses on interactional dynamics between comment pairs. The schema evolved through expert analysis, ultimately yielding a five-category taxonomy that assigns numerical values expressing each comment's contribution toward cohesion (+) or division (-). As shown in Figure 2, this framework captures two dimensions: (1) functional relationship (agreement, disagreement, neutral) and (2) communication style (constructive versus destructive), recognizing that comments with similar positions may contribute differently to discussion quality.

The five categories are (Figure 3 depicts their relative frequencies):

Constructive Disagreement (+1): expressing disagreement while maintaining conditions for mutual

[2]Chains are considered part of the same cluster if they are connected either directly through high overlap, or indirectly through a chain of high-overlap connections. For instance, given 3 conversation chains A,B,C, where A overlap 70 with B, B overlap 70 with C, and A overlap 40 with C, A and C would still be connected by virtue of B. This is called an indirect link.

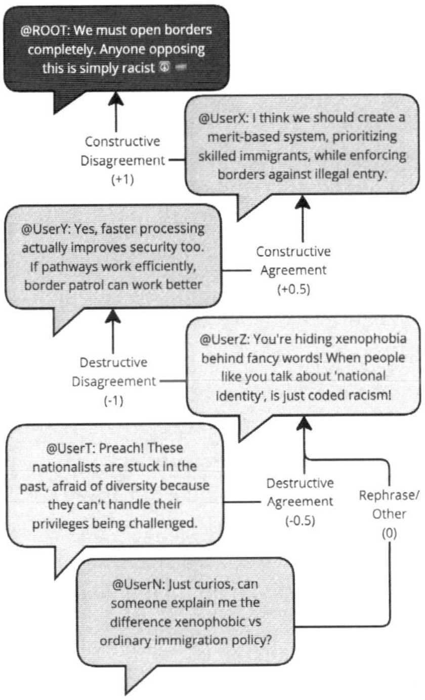

Figure 2: Annotation Example with Contra Immigration, Pro Immigration and Neutral stances interacting among each other. Arrows between messages indicate the quality of interaction.

understanding ($N = 561$)
Constructive Agreement (+0.5): strengthening mutual understanding while agreeing ($N = 203$)
Rephrasing/Neutral[3] (0): facilitating conversation without taking a stance ($N = 251$)
Destructive Agreement (-0.5): strengthening divisions while agreeing ($N = 304$)
Destructive Disagreement (-1): hindering productive dialogue through hostile language ($N = 1068$)

Two annotators were instructed to label comment pairs according to the guidelines (see repository), tracking the relation from child comment to parent comment. The messages were presented to annotators following the chronological order of the discussion, enabling them to understand the contextual flow of the conversation. Inter-rater agreement resulted in Cohen's $K = 0.37$, which, while considered fair (Landis and Koch, 1977), underscores the difficulty of operationalizing theoretical constructs of constructive versus destructive communication patterns, especially in informal online discourses.

[3]We merged neutral and rephrase, as they rarely exhibit strong constructive or destructive characteristics that would warrant separate classification.

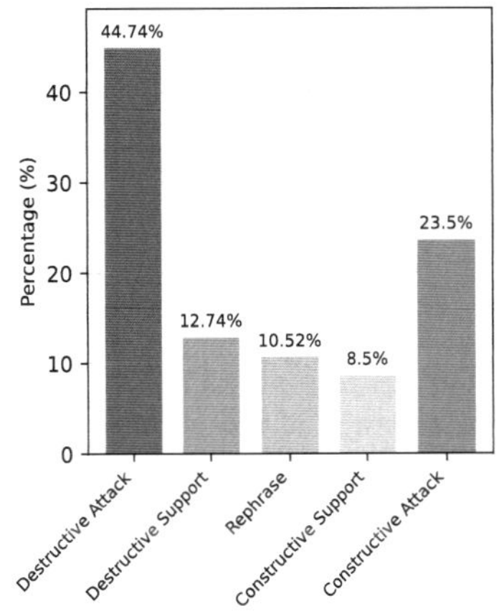

Figure 3: Relative **Comment** Labels Distribution

3.3 Conversation Chain Characterization

Category	Score Range	Count
Highly Destructive	$-1 \leq \text{HD} < -0.75$	n=33
Moderately Destructive	$-0.75 \leq \text{MD} < -0.25$	n=108
Slight/Neutral	$-0.25 \leq \text{SD} < 0.25$	n=54
Constructive	$0.25 \leq \text{C} \leq 1$	n=45

Table 1: Chain Controversy Categories Score Ranges and Distribution

The chain divisiveness categories were developed to analyze conversation chains by averaging the divisiveness values of the comments it contains. Given the strong imbalance of our messages towards the destructive side of the continuum (see Figure 4), we grouped the chain controversy scores to balance theoretical value with the empirical distribution, as shown in Table 1.

4 Features for Divisiveness Detection

4.1 Linguistic

Our analysis incorporates a diverse set of linguistic features extracted from comment text to capture communicative patterns relevant to divisiveness detection. Following Samson and Nowak (2010), for each comment, we extract linguistic elements including word count, capitals ratio, and punctuation frequencies (question and exclamation marks). We leverage VADER (Hutto and Gilbert, 2014) to obtain sentiment polarity scores (negative, positive, neutral, and compound) that capture the emotional tone of comments. Additionally, we compute parent-child comparison features to measure conversational dynamics, including word count differences and word count ratios between comments and

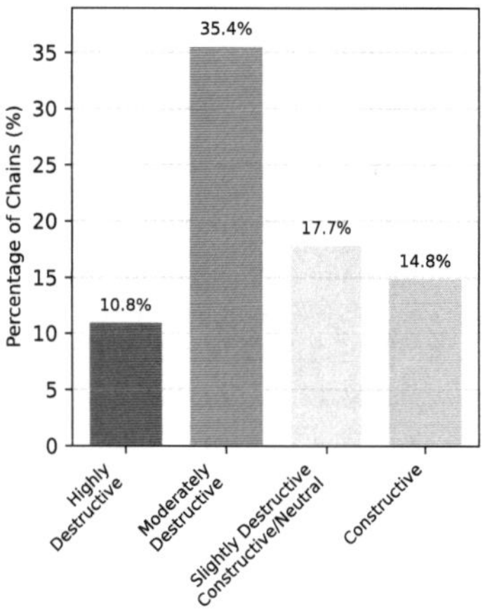

Figure 4: Relative **Chain** Distribution by Divisiveness Categories

their parents. These features aim at capturing linguistic markers of constructive versus destructive communication patterns and constitute the *Base* experimental condition in Table 2-4.

4.2 Stance

We characterize the stance of the comment towards immigration as contra, neutral, or pro using the context-sensitive approach introduced by Bassi et al. (2024b). This method leverages parent-child comment relationships to improve classification accuracy, incorporating the parent comment's stance as contextual information during classification. Following the approach of Bassi et al. (2024b), we use as classifier GPT-4o (prompt detailed in the repository). We tested the performance of the model on a manually annotated gold dataset of 1.3k comments, obtaining substantial results (macro-F1=74.5, see Table 6 in Appendix for details), which we considered robust enough to scale the method to the rest of our dataset. From these classifications, we derived *stance* and relational features such as *binary indicators for the same stance* between comment pairs, capturing the social positioning dynamics and interactions related to the topic.

4.3 Divisive Rhetorical Techniques

As outlined in Section 2, to capture the characteristic argumentative patterns of divisive discourse, we aimed at tracking a set of divisive rhetorical techniques commonly used in controversial discussions, following the work of Zompetti (2015).

Although automated detection of rhetorical techniques has traditionally employed shallow learning and encoder-based methods (Bassi et al., 2024a), Jose and Greenstadt (2024) and Sprenkamp et al. (2023) demonstrated consistent performance of LLMs without specialized training. Drawing from this, we devised a multi-label classification approach implemented through Gpt-4o-mini to identify 13 distinct techniques. The prompt provides definitions and examples for each technique to guide the classification (complete prompts can be found in the repository).

Human verification of a sample yielded SOTA-consistent performance (macro-F1=69.6, details in Table 7), allowing us to confidently apply this method to our complete dataset.

Thanks to this additional information, we generated features that quantify both the presence and frequency of these techniques in each comment, creating *binary indicators for individual techniques* and aggregate metrics like *technique count* and *binary indicator of the presence of each one*.

4.4 Embeddings

We employed SentenceTransformer (Reimers and Gurevych, 2019) to capture semantic content beyond surface features, using the "*roberta-base-nli-stsb-mean-tokens*" model to generate 768-dimensional representations. This approach offered better control over embedding dimensionality than direct BERT-based implementation, enabling more transparent integration with our theoretical features. We applied PCA during training to preserve 95% variance while reducing dimensionality, balancing semantic richness with computational efficiency; which is particularly important when combining embeddings with other feature types in shallow learning models.

5 Experiments

We operated our experiments at two distinct analytical levels: comment and chain. The first task focused on classifying the communicative relationship between parent-child comment pairs according to the five-class taxonomy described in Section 3.2. The second task evaluated how effectively comment-level predictions could characterize the overall quality of conversation chains. We aggregated individual comment scores to compute chain-level divisiveness metrics, mapping each chain to one of the categories defined in Table 1. This approach allowed us to assess the propagation of communicative patterns throughout extended conversations and determine whether localized comment predictions effectively capture broader conversational dynamics.

5.1 Shallow Learning Classifiers

We evaluated several classifiers (Random Forest, Logistic Regression, SVM, and XGBoost) testing multiple combinations of features (see Section 4 and Section 6 for details) to observe the impact of each one on the performance. To address the significant class imbalance shown in Figure 3, we incorporated Synthetic Minority Over-sampling Technique (SMOTE) into our pipeline, testing different k-nearest neighbor values to find the optimal balance to avoiding overfitting on minority classes. We optimized hyperparameters through grid search with 3-fold stratified cross-validation, maximizing macro F1 scores. As detailed in Section 4.4, for embedding-rich feature sets, we applied PCA retaining 95% variance to reduce dimensionality before classification[4]. For chain-level analysis, we used predictions from the best-performing comment-level model to calculate aggregate scores, evaluating both numerical accuracy and categorical classification performance across different chain complexities.

5.2 Large Language Models

We evaluated four leading Large Language Models (LLMs) for the comment classification task: GPT-4o-mini (temp=0.1), GPT-o3-mini (effort=*medium*), DeepSeek-V3-chat (temp=0.1), and DeepSeek-R1-reasoning (temp=*not supported*). For incorporating features into the LLM approach, we designed specialized prompts for each experimental condition. The base condition used only comment text, while additional features were systematically incorporated through explicit prompt engineering: stance information was provided as categorical labels (pro/contra/neutral), rhetorical techniques were presented as a structured list with definitions, and the combined feature condition integrated all information into a single comprehensive prompt. For reasoning-enabled models, we provided explicit instructions to analyze comment relations step-by-step before determining the final classification. We created eight distinct prompts: four tailored for chat models and four designed for reasoning models. Each set of four prompts corresponded to our experimental conditions: comment text-only (*Base* condition in Table 2-4), text with stance, text with rhetorical techniques, and all features combined[5].

[4]See training scripts in repository for details.

6 Results

6.1 Comment Level

Table 2 reveals key trends in our findings. *(1)* Shallow learning models consistently outperform LLMs. *(2)* Notably, optimal performance was achieved by all shallow learning models when utilizing the comprehensive set of features, suggesting effective operationalization of constructive/destructive process concepts. To assess performance reliability, we used bootstrap resampling (1000 iterations) for LLMs and cross-validation variance for shallow learning models. Both yielded $SD \approx 0.02$, with LLM results showing tighter variance distributions than shallow learning models. Paired t-tests on key comparisons confirmed statistical significance: XGBoost (B+S+T+E) vs. DeepSeek (Base), feature engineering impact within XGBoost (Base vs. B+S+T+E), and aggregate shallow learning performance vs. LLM performance across all conditions (all $p < 0.001$). Complete bootstrap statistics are available in our repository.

Table 3 presents class-specific performance metrics for the top-performing model, revealing a degradation in model efficacy attributable to both destructive and constructive agreement classes (a trend consistently observed across all models, as detailed in Figure 7 in Appendix). This discrepancy must be contextualized within the constraints of moderate inter-annotator reliability, and the class imbalance within the dataset, which, despite the application of SMOTE, may not fully alleviate the negative impacts on model performance. Concurrently, the presence of linguistically complex phenomena, such as irony or euphemisms, as illustrated in the following example:

> Message 1 - Genuine Praise: "*Your immigration policy proposal balances security and compassion brilliantly. You really are a genius.*"
> Message 2 - Mockery/Sarcasm: "*Your solution to immigration is 'just close the borders'? You really are a genius.*"

LLMs exhibited similar difficulties with agreement categories across all models [6]. Detailed analysis reveals that the primary challenge lies not in

[5]The complete prompts can be found in the repository.

[6]Complete fine-grained performance reports are available in the repository.

Model	Base	B+Stance	B+Tech	B+S+T	B+Emb	B+S+T+E
DeepSeek	**55.11**	44.11	53.82	49.77	-	-
DeepSeek-R1	41.81	37.62	44.58	43.59	-	-
OpenAI 4o-mini	45.14	42.09	42.79	43.97	-	-
OpenAI o3-mini	44.86	43.80	46.33	46.68	-	-
Logistic Regression	28.37	39.87	45.44	55.15	38.48	57.82
SVM	28.48	42.04	45.27	51.99	39.38	58.38
XGBoost	31.87	44.67	47.81	59.24	40.27	**60.60***
Random Forest	32.23	44.30	50.55	56.78	42.42	60.14

*Best model overall for comment-level prediction
We derived Standard Deviation bootstrapping through 10000 iterations ($SD \approx 0.02$ for all)

Table 2: Comment Divisiveness Detection Performance Comparison (F1 Macro Scores)

Label	P	R	F1
Des. Disagreement (-1.0)	0.83	0.82	0.82
Des. Agreement (-0.5)	0.47	0.58	0.52
Rephrase (0.0)	0.64	0.53	0.58
Cons. Agreement (0.5)	0.41	0.58	0.48
Cons. Disagreement (1.0)	0.69	0.57	0.62
Macro Avg.	0.61	0.62	0.61
Weighted Avg.	0.69	0.68	0.68

Model: XGBoost on All Features,
PCA 40, l.rate: 0.2, max_depth: 3, n_est: 50

Table 3: Comment-Level: Class-Specific Performance

distinguishing constructive from destructive discourse, but in accurately identifying agreement versus disagreement relationships. While the minimal temperature settings (0.1) employed for chat models precluded examination of their decision-making processes—as they output only categorical labels—we report representative examples of the reasoning traces generated by reasoning-enabled models (GPT-03-mini) to illustrate potential explanations for these performance limitations.

"Parent": "Please learn about World History. [Pro]"

"Comment": "CLOSE MILITARY BASES IN 80 PLUS NATIONS CLOSE USA MILITARY BASES IN 80 PLUS NATIONS [Pro][Repetition; Slogan][7]"

"reasoning": "Step 1: The child's comment does not engage with the parent's specific idea but instead presents its own sloganized message to propose closing military bases. This does little to build mutual understanding and seems to dismiss or sidestep the parent's point. Step 2: The use of slogans and repetition indicates a tendency to oversimplify complex issues, reducing space for dialogue and critical engagement. These rhetorical techniques are characteristic of divisive messaging.Step 3: The comment lacks perspective-taking or any respectful engagement with the original idea; rather, it uses incendiary rhetoric, which is likely to escalate division. Final Score: Destructive_Disagreement/Attack",

This example demonstrates two key factors underlying LLM performance limitations. First, the model effectively utilizes the provided feature information, correctly employ the presence of divisive rhetorical techniques to justify the "Destructive Dimension" classification. However, the model fails to connect the comments to the broader immigration discussion context. Human annotators labeled this as "agreement" because both comments share an underlying anti-colonial narrative—the parent criticizing historical ignorance and the child advocating military withdrawal from former colonial territories. Hence, a key issue appears to be context-dependent agreement detection.

"Parent": "In that case maybe we should also have restrictions on smaller men, like lets say 5'7 or under since they will also have a difficult times carryinf heavy rocks?"[Neutral]

"Comment": "I thought for a moment, then I remembered in many north european contries the average is 6 and something so 5'7 is short there lol"[Neutral][No Techniques]

"reasoning": "Step 1. The child comment directly engages with the parent's observation about height and restrictions using a factual clarification while referencing the original comment. Step 2. The tone is neutral and shows a respectful, though subtly differing, perspective; it's not dismissive or mocking. Step 3. The comment contributes knowledge that can help refine the point made by the parent without attacking the person, promoting mutual understanding. Step 4. Overall, the child comment reflects a constructive disagreement. Constructive_Disagreement/Attack",

Also in this second example the model is effective in detecting the correct "tone" of the conversation. However, it misinterprets the dialogical function of the refinement of the parent's statement as an attack, when the child is actually contributing supportive evidence about height differences across countries. Hence, LLMs may struggle to distinguish between challenging refinements and supportive contributions in agreement detection. Notably, while both examples were drawn from the "Text+Stance+Techniques" condition, neither reasoning trace referenced this additional feature information, though stance features were utilized in other cases, indicating inconsistent integration. Improved prompting strategies or reasoning approaches might enhance performance. We provide complete reasoning model outputs in the repository to facilitate further error analysis.

A closer examination of LLM behavior yields interesting insights. Within this paradigm, the two sub-groups exhibit divergent responses to varying levels of feature input. *(3)* Non-reasoning ('chat') models returned their highest performance on tasks when provided with minimal feature input, with DeepSeek-V3 attaining peak performance within this category (macro-F1 = 55.11). In stark contrast, reasoning-enabled LLMs demonstrated improved performance when equipped with an extensive range of features, underscoring their enhanced capacity for leveraging supplementary information.

This disparity reflects different model design ob-

[7]See repository for complete prompt format. It included also a brief definition of the detected technique and 4 guiding questions.

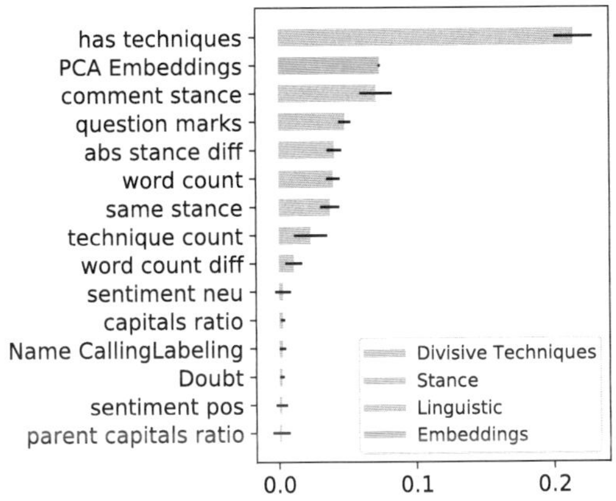

Figure 5: Feature importance analysis using permutation method.

jectives: reasoning models (like DeepSeek-R1) are optimized for analytical tasks requiring multiple evidence sources, while chat models (DeepSeek-V3) excel with minimal inputs but struggle with feature-rich representations, evidenced by performance degradation when adding features (from 55.11 to 49.77 macro-F1). Notwithstanding its limitations with multi-feature integration, DeepSeek-V3 ('chat model') surprisingly excelled in identifying agreement relationships, outperforming others in both destructive and constructive links detection, getting the best overall performance score (see Figure 8b in Appendix). This is likely due to its proficiency in interpreting base text and stance information, resembling their primary training objective – understanding conversational dynamics. Additionally, this advantage may also stem from an emphasis on contextual understanding over analytical depth, where these models prioritize comprehending nuances over handling complex, multi-faceted analyses, thereby facilitating their superiority in recognizing certain relationships, such as agreements.

6.1.1 Ablation Study

To identify the key predictors of divisiveness in online discussions, we conducted an ablation study using permutation importance. This technique measures feature importance by randomly shuffling each feature's values and calculating the resulting decrease in model performance, thus quantifying each feature's contribution to prediction accuracy independent of model architecture. We performed the analysis on our best-performing model—an XGBoost classifier using PCA-reduced embeddings (40 components) combined with linguistic, stance, and propaganda features. The permutation importance was calculated using 5 random permutations per feature on the test set, with macro F1 score as performance metric. Figure 5 presents the top features ranked by permutation importance, color-coded by category (blue for divisive techniques, orange for stance features, green for linguistic features, and pink for embeddings). Our analysis reveals a clear hierarchy in feature importance, with two features demonstrating substantially higher influence than others:

Divisive techniques: The binary indicator of whether a comment employs propaganda techniques (`has_techniques`) emerged as the strongest predictor of divisiveness (0.22 ± 0.01), suggesting that rhetorical manipulation strongly correlates with destructive discourse.

Comment stance: The ideological position expressed in a comment towards the topic (`comment_stance`) represents the second most influential feature (0.07 ± 0.01), indicating its importance in determining agreement/disagreement relationships between comments, which constitutes one of the two dimensions in our annotation schema.

Secondary predictors include `question_marks` (0.05), `abs_stance_diff` (0.05), and `word_count` (0.04), demonstrating the role of linguistic patterns and stance differences in predicting divisiveness. We grouped all the embedding components in just one indicator (`pca_Embeddings`), which appears among the most important features. This indicates that semantic content captured by contextualized representations contributes additional predictive power beyond explicit features.

The results provide evidence supporting the theoretical distinction between constructive and destructive communicative processes proposed by Samson and Nowak (2010), as well as our operationalization of the construct using divisive rhetoric and the specific stance expressed. This finding further validates our hybrid approach combining explicit rhetorical and stance features with semantic ones.

6.2 Chain Level

The chain-level analysis reveals intriguing methodological insights about how model performance transfers across analytical levels. As described in Section 5, we derived chain-level predictions by averaging comment-level scores from our best-performing models, mapping each chain to one of the categories defined in Table 1. While XGBoost excels at the comment level, SVM unexpectedly performs better at the chain level. This counter-intuitive result likely stems from the interaction between class distribution and error patterns across analytical levels: destructive comments (57.48% of the dataset) appear in more balanced proportions when aggregated into chains, the models' error distributions affect chain-level metrics differently. SVM's marginal advantage in classifying destructive agreement comments becomes amplified when predictions are averaged into chain scores. This finding suggests that model selection should prioritize the specific analytical level of interest rather than assuming performance transfers across levels, as optimal classification at one level does not necessarily translate to optimal performance when those classifications are aggregated into higher-level constructs. A similar pattern emerges with LLMs, where OpenAI o3-mini shows improved performance at the chain level, suggesting how error distribution can impact model effectiveness across different analytical levels.

7 Discussion and Conclusions

This study addressed the challenge of automatically detecting and measuring constructive versus destructive communication patterns in online discussions. Starting from the theoretical framework proposed by Samson and Nowak (2010), we operationalized these constructs through a multilevel analytical approach examining both individual comments and conversation chains.

Given the abstract nature of these concepts, we extracted linguistic, stance and rhetorical features to characterize comments and highlight their communicative qualities. Our findings demonstrate the effectiveness of this theory-driven feature engineering approach. In fact, the ablation study revealed that divisive rhetorical techniques and stance information serve as the strongest predictors of destructive communication, substantially outperforming semantic embeddings alone.

This highlights an important methodological insight: when equipped with theoretically-grounded, specialized features, traditional machine learning approaches outperformed more complex models in domain-specific task. While LLMs excel at general language understanding, their performance is constrained when analyzing nuanced rhetorical and dialogical relationships that require explicit theoretically-grounded representation. The XGBoost model achieved 60.60% macro-F1 at the comment level, substantially outperforming the best LLM (DeepSeek at 55.11%). This advantage was even more pronounced at the chain level, where SVM reached 75.28% macro-F1 compared to OpenAI o3-mini's 64.69%. This gap underscores how domain-specific tasks requiring specialized theoretical knowledge may present unique challenges for general-purpose LLMs, which lack explicit representation of the theoretical structures provided by our feature engineering approach.

In conclusion, our study demonstrates the benefit of combining theoretical frameworks with computational methods for more nuanced approaches to controversy analysis. Establishing baselines for this task, and releasing our dataset and scripts, we aim to facilitate further exploration of how specific communicative choices contribute to either productive dialogue or increased antagonism across different platforms and domains, ultimately shaping conversational dynamics in online spaces.

Limitations

Our study has several limitations. LLMs used for rhetorical technique identification may underperform in domains different from their training data, struggling with detecting fallacious arguments "in the wild" (Ruiz-Dolz and Lawrence, 2023). Moreover, the qualitative analysis of rea-

Model	Base	B+Stance	B+Tech	B+S+T	B+Emb	B+S+T+E
DeepSeek (Chat)	41.95	44.70	44.45	49.72	-	-
DeepSeek (Reasoning)	38.53	43.80	47.17	49.89	-	-
GPT-mini	40.51	41.47	30.32	41.28	-	-
OpenAI o3-mini	**64.69**	59.38	62.99	59.57	-	-
Logistic Regression	24.66	39.43	62.26	64.61	36.41	71.72
SVM	26.94	35.42	62.80	66.67	40.70	**75.28***
XGBoost	26.18	46.83	64.67	69.47	38.68	70.18
Random Forest	25.00	37.86	70.15	68.10	39.06	69.72

*Best model overall for chain-level category prediction

Table 4: Chain-Level Divisiveness Detection Performance Comparison (F1 Macro Scores)

Chain Category	P	R	F1
Highly Destructive	0.83	0.83	0.83
Moderately Destructive	0.76	0.83	0.79
Slightly Dest./Neutral	0.67	0.71	0.69
Constructive	0.89	0.57	0.70
Macro Avg.	0.79	0.74	0.75

Model: SVM on All Features,
PCA 45; C: 1.0, gamma: 0.01, kernel: rbf

Table 5: Chain-Level Class-Specific Performance

soning models suggests that improved prompting strategies could potentially enhance LLM performance, indicating that our findings may reflect current implementation limitations rather than fundamental model constraints.

The dataset's skew toward destructive comments (57.48%), while reflective of "natural" YouTube discourse patterns, biases classification despite SMOTE implementation. Through more balanced datasets models equally sensitive to both constructive and destructive patterns could be developed. Additionally, moderate inter-annotator agreement ($Cohen's K = 0.37$) reflects the inherent subjectivity in evaluating discourse quality. Refined annotation protocols could improve gold standard roboustness in future work.

Our analysis focused exclusively on textual features, overlooking valuable structural information in conversation chains. Additionally, our chain-level predictions were derived by averaging comment-level scores. Incorporating graph-based features such as reply depth, branching and temporal patterns could enhance prediction performance, particularly for chain-level analysis (De Kock and Vlachos, 2021; Hessel and Lee, 2019).

The study's scope is confined to a single platform, language, and topic domain, limiting generalization. Cross-platform validation across diverse languages and topics is necessary for broader applicability.

Acknowledgments

This project has received funding from the European Union's Horizon Europe research and innovation program under the Marie Skłodowska-Curie Grant Agreement No. 101073351. Views and opinions expressed are however those of the author(s) only and do not necessarily reflect those of the European Union or the European Research Executive Agency (REA). Neither the European Union nor the granting authority can be held responsible for them.

References

Kelsey Allen, Giuseppe Carenini, and Raymond Ng. 2014. Detecting Disagreement in Conversations using Pseudo-Monologic Rhetorical Structure. *Proceedings of the 2014 Conference on Empirical Methods in Natural Language Processing (EMNLP)*, pages 1169–1180.

Davide Bassi, Søren Fomsgaard, and Martín Pereira-Fariña. 2024a. Decoding persuasion: a survey on ml and nlp methods for the study of online persuasion. *Frontiers in Communication*, 9:1457433.

Davide Bassi, Michele Joshua Maggini, Renata Vieira, and Martín Pereira-Fariña. 2024b. A pipeline for the analysis of user interactions in youtube comments: A hybridization of llms and rule-based methods. In *2024 11th International Conference on Social Networks Analysis, Management and Security (SNAMS)*, pages 146–153.

K. Chen, Z. He, R.-C. Chang, J. May, and K. Lerman. 2023. Anger Breeds Controversy: Analyzing Controversy and Emotions on Reddit. *Lecture Notes in Computer Science*, 14161:44–53.

M. Coletto, K. Garimella, A. Gionis, and C. Lucchese. 2017. Automatic controversy detection in social media: A content-independent motif-based approach. *Online Social Networks and Media*, 3:22–31.

Christine De Kock and Andreas Vlachos. 2021. I beg to differ: A study of constructive disagreement in online conversations. In *Proceedings of the 16th Conference of the European Chapter of the Association for Computational Linguistics: Main Volume*, pages 2017–2027, Online. Association for Computational Linguistics.

K. Garimella, G. De Francisci Morales, A. Gionis, and M. Mathioudakis. 2016. Quantifying controversy in social media. *WSDM 2016 - Proceedings of the 9th ACM International Conference on Web Search and Data Mining*, pages 33–42.

Randy Allen Harris, Chrysanne Di Marco, Sebastian Ruan, and Cliff O?Reilly. 2018. An annotation scheme for rhetorical figures. *Argument and Computation*, 9(2):155–175.

Jack Hessel and Lillian Lee. 2019. Something's Brewing! Early Prediction of Controversy-causing Posts from Discussion Features. *Proceedings of the 2019 Conference of the North American Chapter of the Association for Computational Linguistics: Human Language Technologies, Volume 1*, pages 1648–1659.

Clayton J. Hutto and Eric Gilbert. 2014. Vader: A parsimonious rule-based model for sentiment analysis of social media text. *Proceedings of the International AAAI Conference on Web and Social Media.*

Julia Jose and Rachel Greenstadt. 2024. Are large language models good at detecting propaganda? In *Proceedings of the ICWSM Workshops.*

Barbara Konat, John Lawrence, Joonsuk Park, Katarzyna Budzynska, and Chris Reed. 2016. A Corpus of Argument Networks: Using Graph Properties to Analyse Divisive Issues. *Proceedings of the Tenth International Conference on Language Resources and Evaluation (LREC'16)*, pages 3899–3906.

J Richard Landis and Gary G Koch. 1977. The measurement of observer agreement for categorical data. *biometrics*, pages 159–174.

John Lawrence and Chris Reed. 2019. Argument mining: A survey. *Computational Linguistics*, 45(4):765–818.

John Lawrence, Mark Snaith, Barbara Konat, Katarzyna Budzynska, and Chris Reed. 2017. Debating Technology for Dialogical Argument: Sensemaking, Engagement, and Analytics. *ACM Transactions on Internet Technology*, 17(3):24:1–24:23.

Noortje Marres. 2015. Why map issues? on controversy analysis as a digital method. *Science, Technology, & Human Values*, 40(5):655–686.

Nils Reimers and Iryna Gurevych. 2019. Sentence-BERT: Sentence embeddings using Siamese BERT-networks. In *Proceedings of the 2019 Conference on Empirical Methods in Natural Language Processing and the 9th International Joint Conference on Natural Language Processing (EMNLP-IJCNLP)*, pages 3982–3992, Hong Kong, China. Association for Computational Linguistics.

Ramon Ruiz-Dolz and John Lawrence. 2023. Detecting argumentative fallacies in the wild: Problems and limitations of large language models. In *Proceedings of the 10th Workshop on Argument Mining*, pages 1–10, Singapore. Association for Computational Linguistics.

Katarzyna Samson and Andrzej Nowak. 2010. Linguistic signs of destructive and constructive processes in conflict. In *IACM 23rd Annual Conference Paper.*

Jennifer Schumann and Steve Oswald. 2024. Pragmatic perspectives on disagreement. *Journal of Language Aggression and Conflict*, 12(1):1–16.

Kilian Sprenkamp, Daniel Gordon Jones, and Liudmila Zavolokina. 2023. Large language models for propaganda detection. *arXiv preprint arXiv:2310.06422.*

A. Sriteja, P. Pandey, and V. Pudi. 2017. Controversy detection using reactions on social media. *IEEE International Conference on Data Mining Workshops, ICDMW*, 2017:884–889.

Robin R. Vallacher, Peter T. Coleman, Andrzej Nowak, Lan Bui-Wrzosinska, Larry Liebovitch, Katharina Kugler, and Andrea Bartoli. 2013. *Attracted to Conflict: Dynamic Foundations of Destructive Social Relations*, 1 edition. Peace Psychology Book Series. Springer Berlin, Heidelberg, Berlin.

Douglas Walton. 2008. *Informal logic: A pragmatic approach.* Cambridge University Press.

H. Wang, Y. Wang, X. Song, B. Zhou, X. Zhao, and F. Xie. 2023. Quantifying controversy from stance, sentiment, offensiveness and sarcasm: a fine-grained controversy intensity measurement framework on a Chinese dataset. *World Wide Web*, 26(5):3607–3632.

Joseph Zompetti. 2015. *Divisive discourse.* Cognella Academic Publishing, Illinois State University.

The gold-set for evaluating stance detection performance was created by two annotators who independently labeled 1,300 comments (guidelines in repository), achieving an inter-annotator agreement of Cohen's $\kappa = 0.61$. Disagreements were resolved through discussion, and GPT-4o's performance was subsequently evaluated on this gold-set; performance metrics are reported in Table 6.

Class	Precision	Recall	F1-score	Support
Against	0.833	0.743	0.785	502
Neutral/Other	0.602	0.730	0.660	400
Support	0.823	0.759	0.790	403
Macro	*0.752*	*0.744*	*0.745*	*1305*
Weight. Avg.	–	–	*0.748*	*1305*

Table 6: Performance metrics of the stance classification

For divisive rhetoric detection performance, one single expert annotator manually checked ChatGPT-4o-mini predictions on 2715 comments (see repository), following prompt definitions. Table 7 reports the performance metrics.

Technique	Prec.	Rec.	F1	Support
Overall Performance				
Micro Average	0.840	0.797	0.818	2175
Macro Average	0.791	0.659	0.696	-
Individual Techniques				
Appeal to Authority	0.652	0.577	0.612	26
Appeal to Fear/Prejudice	0.840	0.748	0.791	119
Bandwagon	0.667	0.200	0.308	10
Black-and-White Fallacy	0.828	0.485	0.611	99
Causal Oversimplification	0.676	0.881	0.765	227
Doubt	0.852	0.762	0.805	227
Exaggeration/Minimisation	0.862	0.880	0.871	241
Flag-Waving	0.882	0.833	0.857	108
Loaded Language	0.915	0.966	0.940	443
Name Calling/Labeling	0.869	0.896	0.883	415
Repetition	0.571	0.462	0.511	26
Slogans/Thought-terminating Cliché	0.821	0.222	0.350	149
Whataboutism/Straw Men	0.848	0.659	0.742	85

Table 7: Performance metrics of the divisive rhetorical techniques detection

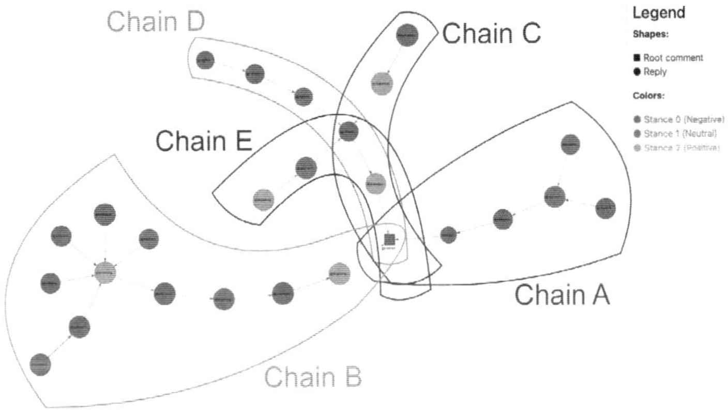

Figure 6: Clustering Example

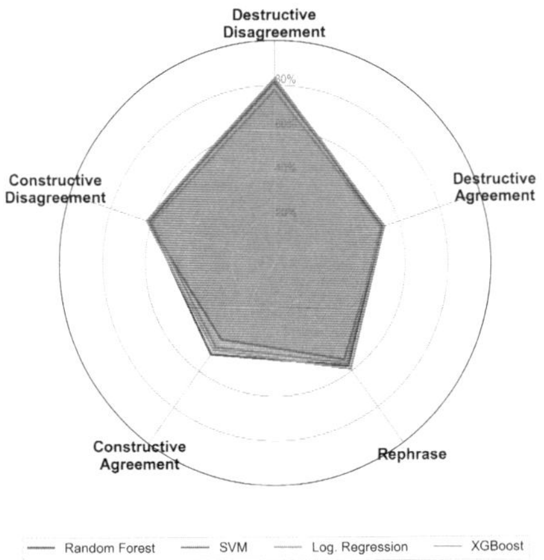

(a) Performance comparison of traditional machine learning models across all five categories.

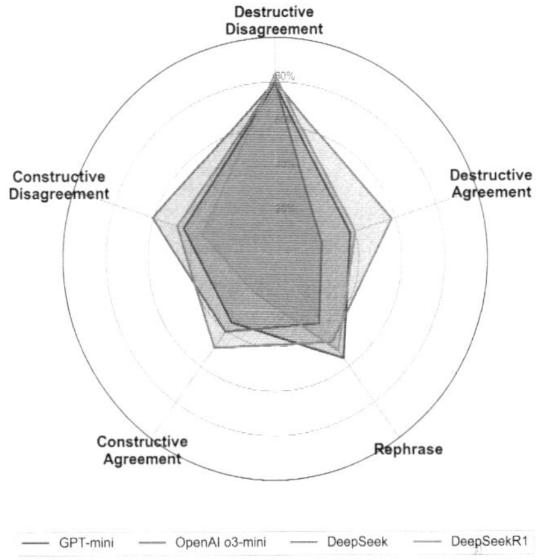

(b) Performance comparison of large language models across all five categories.

Figure 7: F1 score performance comparison of different model types on the five controversy classification categories.

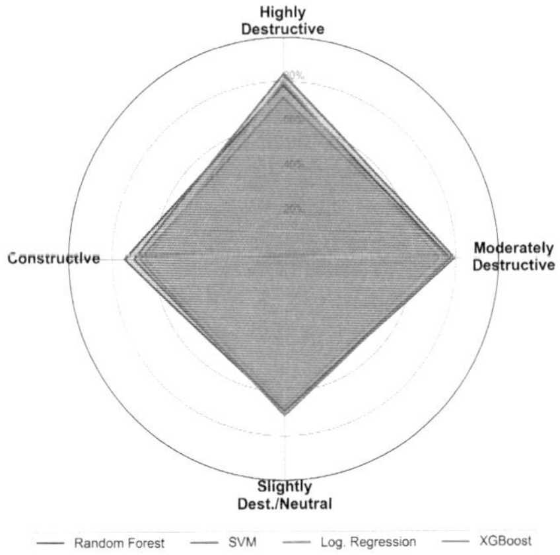

(a) Performance comparison of traditional machine learning models across all chain categories.

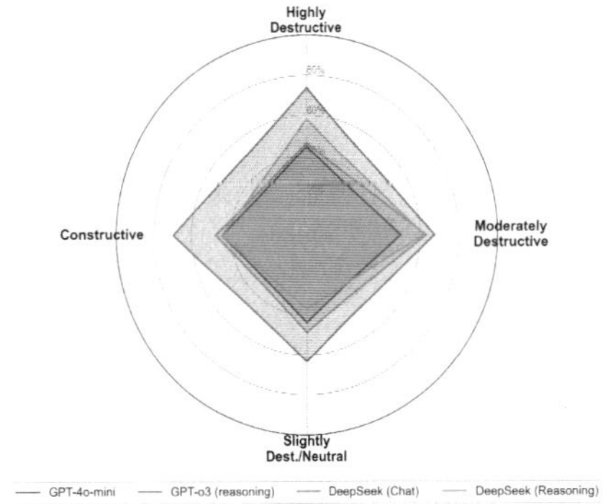

(b) Performance comparison of large language models across all chain categories.

Figure 8: F1 score performance comparison of different model types on the four chain classification categories.

Multi-Agent LLM Debate Unveils the Premise Left Unsaid

Harvey Bonmu Ku[1,2] Jeongyeol Shin[2] Hyoun Jun Lee[2] Seonok Na[2] Insu Jeon[2]
[1]Ministry of National Defense, Republic of Korea
[2]Qraft Technologies
language@langua.ge
{jeongyeol.shin, hyounjun.lee, seonok.na}@qraftec.com
insuj3on@gmail.com

Abstract

Implicit premise is central to argumentative coherence and faithfulness, yet remain elusive in traditional single-pass computational models. We introduce a multi-agent framework that casts implicit premise recovery as a dialogic reasoning task between two LLM agents. Through structured rounds of debate, agents critically evaluate competing premises and converge on the most contextually appropriate interpretation. Evaluated on a controlled binary classification benchmark for premise selection, our approach achieves state-of-the-art accuracy, outperforming both neural baselines and single-agent LLMs. We find that accuracy gains stem not from repeated generation, but from agents refining their predictions in response to opposing views. Moreover, we show that forcing models to defend assigned stances degrades performance—engendering rhetorical rigidity to flawed reasoning. These results underscore the value of interactive debate in revealing pragmatic components of argument structure.

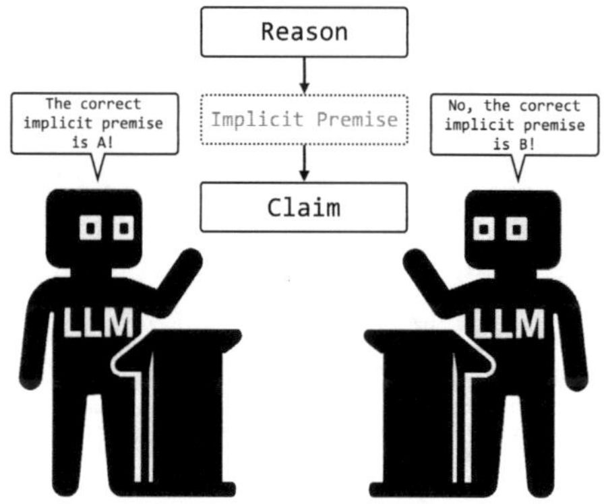

Figure 1: Illustration of the two LLM agents debating which is the correct implicit premise.

1 Introduction

Arguments do not fail at the surface; they often fail in what they assume. What makes an argument persuasive is not always what is stated, but what is left unsaid. Implicit premises—unstated assumptions that connect reasons to claims—are often the true engines of argumentation (Hitchcock, 1985; Toulmin, 1958; Walton and Reed, 2005).

Recovering implicit premises thus represents a foundational, yet underexplored, challenge in computational argument analysis. Existing systems perform well at identifying explicit argumentative components such as claims and reasons, but they often fall short in capturing what is pragmatically presupposed (Feng and Hirst, 2011; Walton and Reed, 2005; Habernal et al., 2018a).

This limitation becomes particularly consequential in high-stakes domains such as law, finance, and politics, where arguments frequently hinge on assumptions that are unstated, ambiguous, or implied (Chakrabarty et al., 2021). In such contexts, argument mining must move beyond surface-level interpretation to reconstruct the hidden connective tissue that underpin argumentative coherence (Hitchcock, 1985; Razuvayevskaya and Teufel, 2017; Katz et al., 2022).

The advent of large language models (LLMs) has opened new possibilities for modeling contextual reasoning at scale. Yet when applied to tasks demanding pragmatic inference, LLMs operating in isolation often fall short (Katz et al., 2022; Chakrabarty et al., 2021). A key limitation is their inability to interrogate their own outputs; reflective techniques such as self-reflection (Shinn et al., 2023) are often unsuitable for capturing the nuanced reasoning required in argument mining. In natural discourse, implicit premises are rarely surfaced in isolation—they are negotiated through interaction, clarification, and iterative exchange (Inoue et al., 2020; Stede et al., 2019).

Motivated by this observation, we propose a multi-agent framework that models premise recovery as a dialogic reasoning process between two LLM agents. This approach draws on recent findings that language models demonstrate more co-

Proceedings of the 12th Argument Mining Workshop, pages 58–73
July 31, 2025

herent reasoning in interactive settings (Du et al., 2024), and show enhanced pragmatic sensitivity when engaged in debate (Ku, 2025). In our setup, agents are either assigned or select a candidate premise and interact either sequentially or simultaneously through structured rounds of deliberation.

We evaluate this method on the SemEval 2018 Task 12 dataset (Habernal et al., 2018b), which casts implicit premise recovery as a binary classification task. While prior models—including LSTM and BERT-based classifiers—showed moderate success, our multi-agent approach achieves the highest accuracy to date, outperforming both traditional baselines and single-agent LLMs. These results underscore the potential of agentic reasoning as a more effective paradigm for capturing the pragmatic inference required in implicit argument understanding. The primary contributions of this work are as follows:

- We position implicit premise recovery as a central task in argument mining, moving beyond surface-level extraction toward modeling the pragmatic reasoning that underlies argumentative coherence.

- We propose a multi-agent LLM framework that addresses premise selection as a dialogic process, yielding state-of-the-art performance on a benchmark dataset.

2 Related Work

2.1 Implicit Premises and Deeper Argument Understanding

The task of recovering implicit premises—unstated assumptions that bridge claims and reasons—is closely related to enthymeme reconstruction in classical argumentation theory. Enthymemes omit one or more components of an argument, typically leaving the audience to infer missing premises. Recovering these implicit links is crucial for argument mining, as they often carry the inferential burden behind persuasive discourse. Early work highlighted the logical challenges of modeling enthymemes (Hitchcock, 1985), while more recent studies have focused on detecting, classifying, or generating missing premises (Boltužić and Šnajder, 2016; Rajendran et al., 2016; Chakrabarty et al., 2021; Hunter, 2022; Stahl et al., 2023).

Building on this line of inquiry, researchers have investigated a range of tasks that involve implicit inference, including the recovery of unstated reasoning chains in question answering (Katz et al., 2022), the identification of event arguments with long-range dependencies (Lin et al., 2022a), and the discovery of relational links between argumentative units via implicit inferences (Saadat-Yazdi et al., 2023). These studies show that even state-of-the-art systems often struggle to model the background knowledge and pragmatic logic required to make sense of incomplete arguments.

Beyond model development, recent efforts have sought to improve the quality of annotated data for implicit reasoning. Singh et al. (2021) proposed a semi-structured annotation methodology for collecting implicit warrants, demonstrating that abstract assumptions can be reliably captured via guided crowdsourcing.

While these advances have expanded our understanding of hidden argumentative structure, implicitness is still often treated as a supporting concern rather than a central modeling objective. In contrast, our work foregrounds implicit premise recovery as the primary task and frames the process as one of pragmatic, dialogic reasoning between agents.

2.2 Multi-Agent LLM Debate

Multi-agent debate has emerged as a promising method for enhancing reasoning in large language models by transforming inference from a solitary act into an interactive process. Instead of relying on a single model's output, multiple agents engage in dialogue—critiquing, revising, and refining their interpretations—mirroring the deliberative nature of human reasoning (Irving et al., 2018; Du et al., 2024). Such interactions improve factual accuracy, consistency, and interpretability across domains. Chan et al. (2024) and Liang et al. (2024) report that multi-agent discussions help overcome individual model biases, with Liang et al. (2024) describing this as a remedy for the "degeneration-of-thought" effect—where flawed lines of reasoning persist without external correction. These insights echo Minsky (1988)'s notion of a "society of minds," in which intelligence arises from the interplay of multiple specialized reasoning units.

We extend this paradigm to the domain of argument mining, where implicit premise recovery requires more than the injection of external knowledge—it demands interpretive contrast. To our knowledge, this is the first study to apply multi-agent LLM debate to an argument mining task.

3 Methodology

3.1 Task Definition

We define the task of *implicit premise recovery* as selecting the correct implicit premise $P^* \in \{\text{Premise A}, \text{Premise B}\}$ that logically and pragmatically bridges a reason R and a claim C in a given argument tuple $x = (C, R, \text{Premise A}, \text{Premise B})$.

Claim:	Young people's votes matter.
Reason:	All votes matter.
Premise A:	Many young people vote.
Premise B:	Many young people don't vote.

Table 1: Example of an implicit premise recovery instance.

This example highlights the subtlety of the task: both candidate premises appear logically plausible yet imply distinct pragmatic interpretations. Premise A implies descriptive inclusion—that young people are already voters whose contributions merit recognition—while Premise B suggests normative urgency, highlighting that their underrepresentation makes their votes especially valuable. Disambiguating between such readings requires sensitivity to context and intent, rather than reliance on lexical overlap or surface logic.

We approach this task as a deliberative process between two large language model agents, each initialized with a different candidate premise. Through structured multi-round dialogue, the agents attempt to resolve their disagreement and identify the premise P^* that most plausibly completes the argument.

Formally, a debate instance D consists of a sequence of rounds $D = \{R_1, R_2, \ldots, R_n\}$, where each round R_i contains contributions $(a_i^{(A)}, a_i^{(B)})$ from agents A and B, respectively. The task is evaluated as a binary classification problem: each instance is marked correct if the final agreed-upon premise matches the gold-standard label, or incorrect if the debate either results in the wrong selection or terminates without consensus after n rounds.

3.2 Design of the LLM Debate

To systematically evaluate how LLMs reason over competing premises, we design a debate framework that manipulates two key structural conditions: stance assignment and interaction order. These conditions allow us to test how different configurations affect argumentative convergence and overall performance.

Condition 1: Given vs. Chosen Stance In the *Given* stance condition, each agent is explicitly assigned a candidate premise to defend—either Premise A or Premise B. During preliminary testing, we observe that agents often rigidly maintain their initial stance, even when logically weaker (see Appendix Figure 8). To address this, we introduce staged prompting: early rounds emphasize advocacy, while later rounds prompt agents to neutrally evaluate both premises and converge on the more plausible one (Appendix Listing 2).

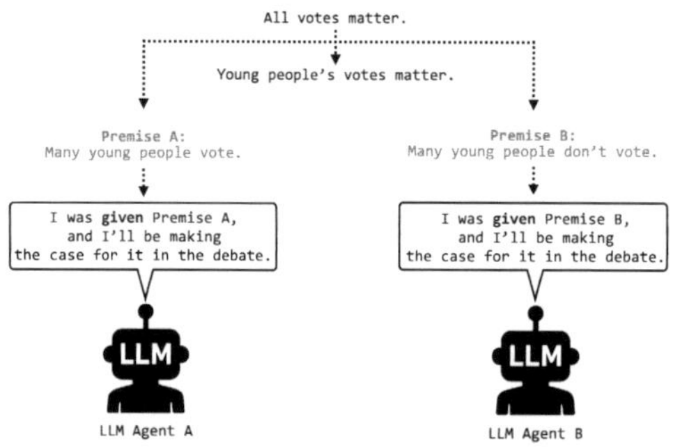

Figure 2: Illustration of the Given conditon.

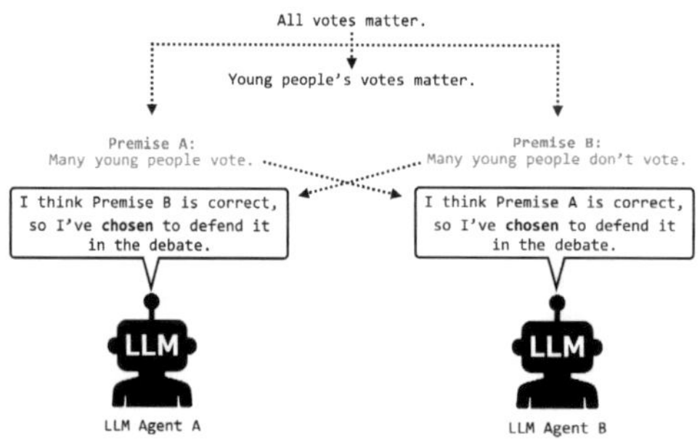

Figure 3: Illustration of the Chosen conditon.

In the *Chosen* stance condition, each agent independently selects the premise it finds more convincing and is instructed to defend that choice (Appendix Listing 3). If the agents agree on a premise early in the debate, the session is immediately terminated and the shared answer is evaluated against the gold label.

Condition 2: Sequential vs. Simultaneous Round While the first round in both configurations functions as an opening statement—analogous to initial remarks in formal debate—the two conditions diverge in how subsequent rounds are structured and processed.

In the *sequential* setup, agents engage in alternating turns; Agent A begins by defending one candidate premise, and Agent B responds after reviewing A's output. This allows each agent to build on or challenge the preceding argument.

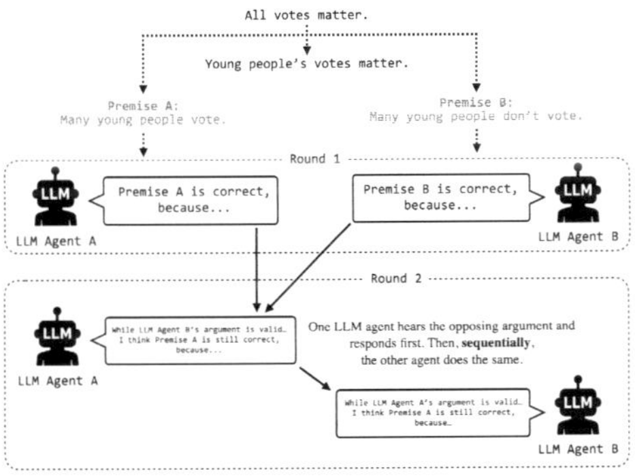

Figure 4: Illustration of the Sequential conditon.

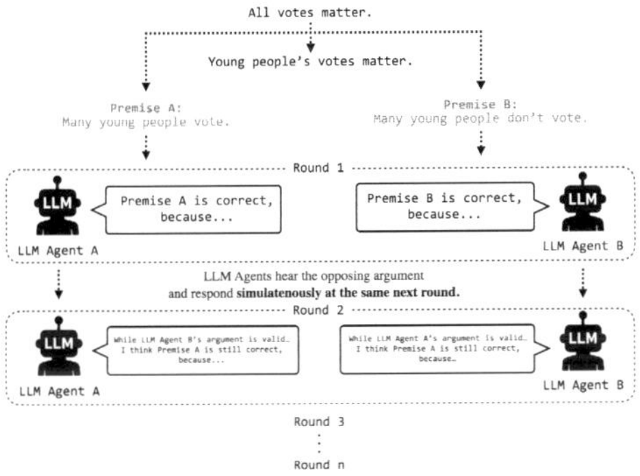

Figure 5: Illustration of the Simultaneous conditon.

In the *simultaneous* setup, both agents produce their arguments independently and then respond to each other's initial outputs in the following round. This structure enables a more parallel and symmetrical form of interaction.

This design allows us to evaluate whether free premise selection improves convergence and whether agents benefit from observing each other's arguments across rounds. The full implementation details, including model selection, decoding parameters, and logging tools, are provided in the subsequent section.

4 Experimental Setup

4.1 Dataset

We evaluate our approach using the Argument Reasoning Comprehension Task dataset from SemEval-2018 Task 12 (Habernal et al., 2018b), a benchmark explicitly designed to test implicit reasoning in natural language arguments. Each instance consists of a claim, a reason, and two candidate warrants[1]—only one of which correctly links the reason to the claim.

The incorrect premises are crafted to be topically and lexically plausible, yet logically incompatible with the argument, thereby requiring models to engage in pragmatic inference rather than rely on shallow surface cues. The dataset contains 1,970 instances drawn from online debates, partitioned into training (1,210), development (316), and test (444) sets. For our evaluation, we focus on the held-out test set to enable direct comparison with previously reported results from baseline models.

This dataset is particularly well-suited for our purposes because of (1) its topical diversity—including politics, ethics, economics, and social policy—which mirrors real-world argumentative variety, and (2) its construction via a rigorous eight-step crowdsourcing pipeline with multiple validation rounds, ensuring that examples are high-quality and pragmatically meaningful.

4.2 Model Configuration

We implement all experiments using OpenAI's GPT-4o-mini, the most cost-effective and fastest available LLM at the time of writing. Given the latency introduced by multi-turn agent interaction, GPT-4o-mini offers the best balance between computational efficiency and linguistic performance. All LLM experiments—including the single-agent baseline—use identical model settings to ensure comparability. Multi-agent interactions are managed via the LangGraph framework, which facilitates node-based orchestration and message passing. Logging and analysis of outputs are performed using LangSmith.

4.3 Parameters

To determine appropriate parameters, we conducted preliminary experiments using the single-agent LLM. We tested temperature values of 0.1, 0.3, 0.5, 0.7, and 0.9, along with max round settings of 5, 10, 15, and 20. Neither parameter showed statistically significant impact on performance. We therefore adopted the median configuration: tem-

[1]We treat "warrant" and "implicit premise" interchangeably throughout this paper, following Toulmin's framework (Toulmin, 1958) in which a warrant serves as the unstated bridge in an argument.

perature was fixed at 0.5, and all debates were capped at 10 rounds.

No few-shot examples or chain-of-thought prompting were used. Given that implicit premise recovery is a pragmatic reasoning task with no canonical steps, such scaffolding was treated as a potential confound. If no agreement was reached within 10 rounds, the debate was marked incorrect.

4.4 Previous Models

To establish strong baselines for comparison, we replicated two representative models for implicit premise recovery. Rather than relying solely on reported metrics, we reproduced both models using their publicly available code and the original test dataset.

LSTM This model designed by Choi et al., 2018 implements a hybrid architecture combining a pre-trained Enhanced Sequential Inference Model (ESIM; Chen et al., 2017) with a bidirectional LSTM. The ESIM component, trained on SNLI (Bowman et al., 2015) and MNLI (Williams et al., 2018), captures entailment knowledge and passes frozen sentence pair representations to a task-specific BiLSTM. The model processes all relevant pairings—claim–premise, premise–reason, and premise–premise—and feeds their concatenated outputs into a fully connected network to determine the correct implicit premise. This approach ranked first in the 2018 shared task and outperformed all other submissions by a margin of over 10 percentage points (Habernal et al., 2018b).

BERT We fine-tuned RoBERTa (Liu et al., 2019), an optimized variant of BERT that omits the Next Sentence Prediction objective and is trained on longer sequences and larger corpora. Inputs were formatted as concatenated sequences of the claim, reason, and candidate implicit premise. Compared to sequential models like LSTM, RoBERTa uses self-attention to capture contextual dependencies across the entire input simultaneously. The model was trained for 10 epochs with a learning rate of $1e^{-5}$, weight decay of 0.01, and a batch size of 16. The maximum sequence length was set to 512 tokens, and all experiments were run on 8 A100 GPUs.

5 Results

5.1 Main Results

Table 2 presents a comparison of model performance across prior baselines and the five LLM configurations tested in this study. The single-agent LLM baseline achieved an accuracy of 0.7928, outperforming previous neural models—including the top-performing LSTM (0.7050) and a fine-tuned RoBERTa model (0.7564). This result confirms that a single-pass LLM does exhibit strong capabilities for implicit premise recovery under zero-shot conditions.

Our multi-agent framework, however, produced further improvements under specific configurations. In *Chosen* stance setups—, where agents independently selected and defended their preferred premise—, both interaction orders led to substantial gains. The *Simultaneous* condition achieved 0.8446 in accuracy, and the *Sequential* condition yielded the highest overall performance at 0.8694. These results indicate that dialogic reasoning is most effective when agents are free to align on a shared interpretation, rather than being constrained by initial position assignments.

A Cochran's Q test confirmed a statistically significant difference in performance across the five LLM configurations ($Q = 101.03$, $df = 4$, $p < 0.0001$), prompting further pairwise analysis. Post-hoc McNemar tests revealed that nearly all model pairs differed significantly, with two key exceptions. First, the two highest-performing conditions—*Chosen & Sequential* and *Chosen & Simultaneous*—did not differ significantly ($p > 0.05$), despite a nominal accuracy gap of 2.5 percentage points. Second, the two lowest-performing configurations—*Given & Sequential* and *Given & Simultaneous*—also showed no significant difference ($p > 0.05$), suggesting that interaction order exerted limited influence in the presence of fixed stance assignments.

Direct comparisons with the single-agent baseline further clarify this pattern. The single-agent LLM statistically outperformed both *Given* stance conditions: for *Given & Sequential*, the McNemar test yielded $p < 0.0001$ (contingency: 275 both correct, 77 single only, 35 *Given* only, 57 both wrong); for *Given & Simultaneous*, $p < 0.01$ (contingency: 288, 64, 32, 60). These results indicate that rigid stance assignment may suppress performance even relative to non-interactive inference.

Conversely, both *Chosen* stance configurations

Model	Citation	Accuracy	Precision	Recall	F1
	Previous Studies				
Baseline	Habernal et al. (2018b)	0.5000	-	-	-
LSTM	Choi et al. (2018)	0.7050	0.7281	0.6870	0.7069
BERT	Liu et al. (2019)	0.7564	0.7568	0.7568	0.7568
	LLM-based experiments				
Single-agent LLM	This study	0.7928	0.7941	0.7928	0.7928
MultiAgent Debate *(Given & Sequential)*	This study	0.6982	0.6986	0.6982	0.6973
MultiAgent Debate *(Given & Simultaneous)*	This study	0.7207	0.7207	0.7207	0.7207
MultiAgent Debate *(Chosen & Sequential)*	This study	**0.8694**	**0.8768**	**0.8694**	**0.8691**
MultiAgent Debate *(Chosen & Simultaneous)*	This study	0.8446	0.8553	0.8446	0.8440

Table 2: Comparison of performance on implicit premise recovery across prior models and configurations tested in this study. The best scores are in bold.

significantly outperformed the single-agent model. Against *Chosen & Sequential*, the McNemar test yielded $p < 0.0001$ (contingency: 337, 49, 15, 43); against *Chosen & Simultaneous*, $p < 0.01$ (contingency: 334, 41, 18, 51). These findings confirm that when agents are permitted to self-select and defend their preferred stance, multi-agent interaction leads to robust improvements over single-pass prompting.

Taken together, these results indicate that stance assignment—not interaction order—is the primary determinant of performance differences in multi-agent LLM debate. While alternating turns may allow for richer back-and-forth refinement, its impact is modest compared to the benefits of allowing agents to converge on shared, self-selected premises.

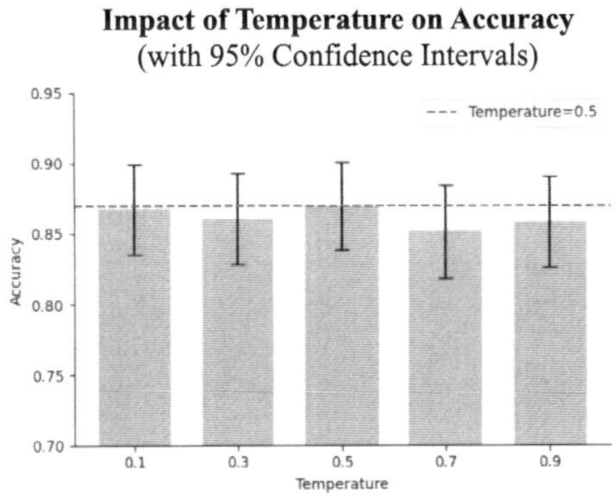

Figure 6: Impact of decoding temperature on implicit premise recovery accuracy under the *Chosen & Sequential* setting. Error bars represent 95% confidence intervals.

5.2 Effect of Temperature and Max Rounds

To test whether decoding parameters affect performance, we conducted an additional set of experiments using the best-performing configuration—*Chosen & Sequential*—as a base. While this setting yielded the highest overall accuracy (0.8694), it was not statistically distinguishable from the *Chosen & Simultaneous* condition ($p > 0.05$), indicating that both settings perform comparably under the chosen evaluation metric.

We varied the temperature parameter across five values (0.1, 0.3, 0.5, 0.7, and 0.9), holding all other factors constant. Temperature 0.5 was used throughout our main experiments, including both single-agent and multi-agent runs. A Cochran's Q test revealed a highly significant difference across the five temperature conditions ($Q = 150.18$, $df = 4$, $p < 0.0001$), suggesting that temperature meaningfully impacts model behavior at the instance level—even when overall accuracy remains comparable (ranging from 0.8514 to 0.8694). Post hoc McNemar tests confirmed that temperature 0.5 differs significantly from all other settings: 0.1 ($p < 0.0001$), 0.3 ($p < 0.0001$), 0.7 ($p < 0.0001$), and 0.9 ($p < 0.0001$). In contrast, no significant differences were observed between any of the non-0.5 pairs. These findings indicate that temperature 0.5 produces a statistically distinct profile of correct predictions while yielding the highest accuracy among tested settings.

To examine whether the number of debate rounds influences performance, we conducted a similar test across four configurations (N = 5, 10, 15, 20). A Cochran's Q test yielded no significant difference across these settings ($Q = 0.063$, $df = 3$, $p > 0.05$), suggesting that extending or shortening the debate window has minimal effect on instance-level behavior. Accordingly, we re-

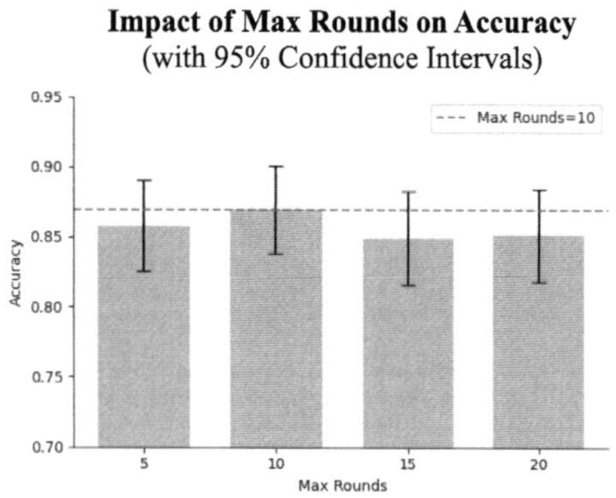

Figure 7: Impact of maximum number of debate rounds on accuracy under the *Chosen & Sequential* setting. Error bars represent 95% confidence intervals.

tain $N = 10$ as a reasonable and computationally efficient default for all primary experiments.

6 Discussion

6.1 Effectiveness of Multi-Agent Debate

Our multi-agent debate framework outperforms all previous models—surpassing LSTM-based systems, fine-tuned BERT classifiers, and single-agent LLMs—on the task of implicit premise recovery. Crucially, this improvement is not merely an artifact of increased generation length or system complexity. Rather, we argue that performance gains arise because agents iteratively refine their beliefs in response to alternative perspectives, producing more robust and context-sensitive inferences (as evidenced in Appendix Figure 12).

One may reasonably ask whether the *chosen stance* conditions, particularly in the *Simultaneous* setup, simply replicate the effect of running two single-agent models independently. Since agents make initial decisions without access to each other's output, early convergence may occur without deliberation. However, the key distinction lies in what follows: when agents initially disagree, the opportunity for dialogic correction arises. In such cases, the debate enables mutual calibration, allowing one agent to reconsider its stance based on the other's justification. This mechanism proves especially valuable on instances where single-agent models consistently fail. As illustrated in Appendix Figure 9 and Figure 10, what a single agent misclassifies, two agents—through comparative evaluation—can resolve correctly. This pattern holds across a broader set of disagreements, suggesting that performance gains stem not from parallelism alone, but from the capacity of agents to refine their inferences in light of opposing views.

Another interpretation is that the performance gains reflect the cumulative effect of multiple rounds of generation. To address this, we tested four different values for the maximum number of rounds ($N = 5, 10, 15, 20$). We found no statistically significant differences across these conditions, indicating that additional steps alone do not account for improved accuracy. It is not repetition, but reciprocal engagement—particularly when disagreement prompts justification and reassessment—that appears to drive better outcomes.

These findings reinforce the value of dialogic reasoning in argument mining. Where single-agent models operate in isolation, our framework enables argument structure to be negotiated through interaction. By situating inference within a sequence of comparative responses, debate makes pragmatic assumptions explicit—bringing otherwise tacit premises to the surface.

6.2 Assigned Stances Undermine Performance

Models in human-like debate settings are often assigned opposing views to simulate adversarial reasoning. Yet, our findings suggest that this artificially adversarial setup may degrade rather than enhance argumentative performance in LLM-based systems. Across both *Sequential* and *Simultaneous* configurations, the *Given* stance condition consistently underperformed—not only relative to the *Chosen* stance condition but also below the single-agent baseline.

To understand this degradation, we observe that forced stance assignment increases rhetorical rigidity. In early rounds, agents adopt emphatic and assertive tones in defending their assigned premise, even when it is logically weaker. As shown in Appendix Figure 11, an agent instructed to support an incorrect premise begins the debate with claims such as *"It must be true that...,"* displaying early signs of overcommitment. This aligns with Xu et al. (2024), who demonstrated that rhetorical appeals can heighten LLM susceptibility to misinformation. When forced to advocate for flawed views, models not only generate more confident but less coherent arguments, mirroring patterns observed in persuasive manipulation studies. In our setting, this rhetorical extremity can also influence the opposing agent, prompting premature agreement or deference—particularly in sequential interactions.

Such overcommitment may not only degrade individual reasoning but also induce hallucination-like effects in the peer model, which begins to mirror or justify the incorrect position under the weight of assertive framing.

These results caution against over-relying on adversarial structure in multi-agent LLM setups. While role-based opposition may resemble human debate, it can push models toward rhetorical extremity rather than pragmatic reasoning.

7 Conclusion

This study demonstrates that multi-agent debate significantly enhances large language models' capacity for implicit premise recovery—an essential yet underexplored task in computational argument analysis. While a single-agent LLM already outperforms prior state-of-the-art models, our results show that dialogic reasoning among multiple agents enables further gains, particularly when agents are allowed to choose their stances freely.

Extensive evaluation on a challenging benchmark reveals that forcing agents to defend fixed premises undermines reasoning quality, while enabling them to converge on the most plausible interpretation fosters both accuracy and coherence. We also show that decoding parameters such as temperature can influence prediction profiles in statistically meaningful ways, even when overall accuracy remains stable.

Taken together, these findings suggest that multi-agent debate is not merely a novelty but a viable path toward more transparent, flexible, and human-aligned reasoning and mining methodology.

Limitations and Future Work

Our evaluation relies on the SemEval 2018 Task 12 dataset, which casts implicit premise recovery as a binary classification task with one correct and one incorrect candidate. While this framing offers clear benchmarking advantages, it abstracts away from the open-endedness of real-world argumentation, where multiple plausible premises may coexist and reasoning is shaped by cultural and pragmatic nuance.

Future work should extend this framework to open-domain and multi-label argument settings, moving beyond binary premise selection. We also plan to explore the use of log probabilities and verbalized confidence (Lin et al., 2022b) to quantify the certainty and rigidity of agent reasoning. Additionally, a neutral, third-party judge (Ku, 2025) or moderator agent could be introduced to adjudicate debates and guide convergence in more complex or ambiguous argumentative scenarios.

References

Filip Boltužić and Jan Šnajder. 2016. Fill the gap! analyzing implicit premises between claims from online debates. In *Proceedings of the 3rd Workshop on Argument Mining (ArgMining 2016)*, pages 124–133. ACL.

Samuel R. Bowman, Gabor Angeli, Christopher Potts, and Christopher D. Manning. 2015. A large annotated corpus for learning natural language inference. In *Proceedings of EMNLP 2015*, pages 632–642.

Tuhin Chakrabarty, Aadit Trivedi, and Smaranda Muresan. 2021. Implicit premise generation with discourse-aware commonsense knowledge models. In *Proceedings of EMNLP 2021*, pages 6247–6252. ACL.

Chi-Min Chan, Weize Chen, Yusheng Su, Jianxuan Yu, Wei Xue, Shanghang Zhang, Jie Fu, and Zhiyuan Liu. 2024. Chateval: Towards better LLM-based evaluators through multi-agent debate. In *Proceedings of ICLR 2024*.

Qian Chen, Xiaodan Zhu, Zhen-Hua Ling, Si Wei, Hui Jiang, and Diana Inkpen. 2017. Enhanced LSTM for natural language inference. In *Proceedings of ACL 2017*, pages 1657–1668.

Eunsol Choi, Tim Alberdingk Thijm, Jason Weston, Yixin Nie, and Tim Rocktäschel. 2018. Gist at semeval-2018 task 12: A network transferring inference knowledge to argument reasoning comprehension task. In *Proceedings of The 12th International Workshop on Semantic Evaluation*, pages 773–777. ACL.

Yilun Du, Shuang Li, Antonio Torralba, Joshua B. Tenenbaum, and Igor Mordatch. 2024. Improving factuality and reasoning in language models through multiagent debate. In *Proceedings of the 41st International Conference on Machine Learning*, pages 11733–11763. PMLR.

Vanessa Wei Feng and Graeme Hirst. 2011. Classifying arguments by scheme. In *Proceedings of the 49th Annual Meeting of the ACL: Human Language Technologies*, pages 987–996.

Ivan Habernal, Henning Wachsmuth, Iryna Gurevych, and Benno Stein. 2018a. The argument reasoning comprehension task: Identification and reconstruction of implicit warrants. In *Proceedings of NAACL 2018*, pages 1930–1940. ACL.

Ivan Habernal, Henning Wachsmuth, Iryna Gurevych, and Benno Stein. 2018b. Semeval-2018 task 12: The argument reasoning comprehension task. In *Proceedings of The 12th International Workshop on Semantic Evaluation*, pages 763–772. ACL.

David Hitchcock. 1985. Enthymematic arguments. *Informal Logic*, 7(2-3):83–97.

Anthony Hunter. 2022. Understanding enthymemes in deductive argumentation using semantic distance measures. In *Proceedings of the AAAI Conference on Artificial Intelligence*, volume 36, pages 5729–5736.

Naoya Inoue, Pontus Stenetorp, and Kentaro Inui. 2020. R4c: A benchmark for evaluating rc systems to get the right answer for the right reason. In *Proceedings of ACL 2020*, pages 6740–6750.

Geoffrey Irving, Paul Christiano, and Dario Amodei. 2018. Ai safety via debate. *arXiv preprint arXiv:1805.00899*.

Uri Katz, Mor Geva, and Jonathan Berant. 2022. Inferring implicit relations in complex questions with language models. In *Findings of EMNLP 2022*, pages 2548–2566. ACL.

Harvey Bonmu Ku. 2025. Scaling implicature via structured interaction in multi-agent llms. In *Proceedings of the 1st Workshop on Integrating NLP and Psychology to Study Social Interactions, AAAI ICWSM 2025 (Forthcoming)*.

Tian Liang, Zhiwei He, Wenxiang Jiao, Xing Wang, Yan Wang, Rui Wang, Yujiu Yang, Shuming Shi, and Zhaopeng Tu. 2024. Encouraging divergent thinking in large language models through multi-agent debate. In *Proceedings of EMNLP 2024*, pages 17889–17904. ACL.

Jiaju Lin, Qin Chen, Jie Zhou, Jian Jin, and Liang He. 2022a. Cup: Curriculum learning based prompt tuning for implicit event argument extraction. In *Proceedings of IJCAI 2022*, pages 3830–3836. IJCAI.

Xiang Lin, Jacob Hilton, and Owain Evans. 2022b. Teaching models to express their uncertainty in words. *Transactions on Machine Learning Research*.

Yinhan Liu, Myle Ott, Naman Goyal, Jingfei Du, Mandar Joshi, Danqi Chen, Omer Levy, Mike Lewis, Luke Zettlemoyer, and Veselin Stoyanov. 2019. Roberta: A robustly optimized bert pretraining approach. *arXiv preprint arXiv:1907.11692*.

Marvin Minsky. 1988. *The Society of Mind*. Simon and Schuster.

Pradeep Rajendran, Danushka Bollegala, and Simon Parsons. 2016. Contextual stance classification of opinions: A step towards enthymeme reconstruction in online reviews. In *Proceedings of the Third Workshop on Argument Mining (ArgMining 2016)*, pages 31–39. ACL.

Olesya Razuvayevskaya and Simone Teufel. 2017. Finding enthymemes in real-world texts: A feasibility study. *Argument & Computation*, 8(2):113–129.

Ameer Saadat-Yazdi, Jeff Z. Pan, and Nadin Kökciyan. 2023. Uncovering implicit inferences for improved relational argument mining. In *Proceedings of EACL 2023*, pages 2484–2495.

Noah Shinn, Federico Cassano, Ashwin Gopinath, Karthik Narasimhan, and Shunyu Yao. 2023. Reflexion: Language agents with verbal reinforcement learning. In *Proceedings of NeurIPS 2023*, volume 36, pages 8634–8652.

Keshav Singh, Paul Reisert, Naoya Inoue, and Kentaro Inui. 2021. A comparative study on collecting high-quality implicit reasonings at a large scale. *arXiv preprint arXiv:2104.07924*.

Maja Stahl, Nick Düsterhus, Mei-hua Chen, and Henning Wachsmuth. 2023. Mind the gap: Automated corpus creation for enthymeme detection and reconstruction in learner arguments. In *Findings of EMNLP 2023*, pages 4703–4717. ACL.

Manfred Stede, Jodi Schneider, and Graeme Hirst. 2019. *Argumentation Mining*. Morgan & Claypool, San Rafael.

Stephen Toulmin. 1958. *The Uses of Argument*. Cambridge University Press.

Douglas Walton and Chris Reed. 2005. Argumentation schemes and enthymemes. *Synthese*, 145(3):339–370.

Adina Williams, Nikita Nangia, and Samuel R. Bowman. 2018. A broad-coverage challenge corpus for sentence understanding through inference. In *Proceedings of NAACL 2018*, pages 1112–1122.

Rongwu Xu, Brian Lin, Shujian Yang, Tianqi Zhang, Weiyan Shi, Tianwei Zhang, Zhixuan Fang, Wei Xu, and Han Qiu. 2024. The earth is flat because...: Investigating llms' belief towards misinformation via persuasive conversation. In *Proceedings of ACL 2024*, pages 16259–16303. ACL.

Appendix: Agent Debate Logs

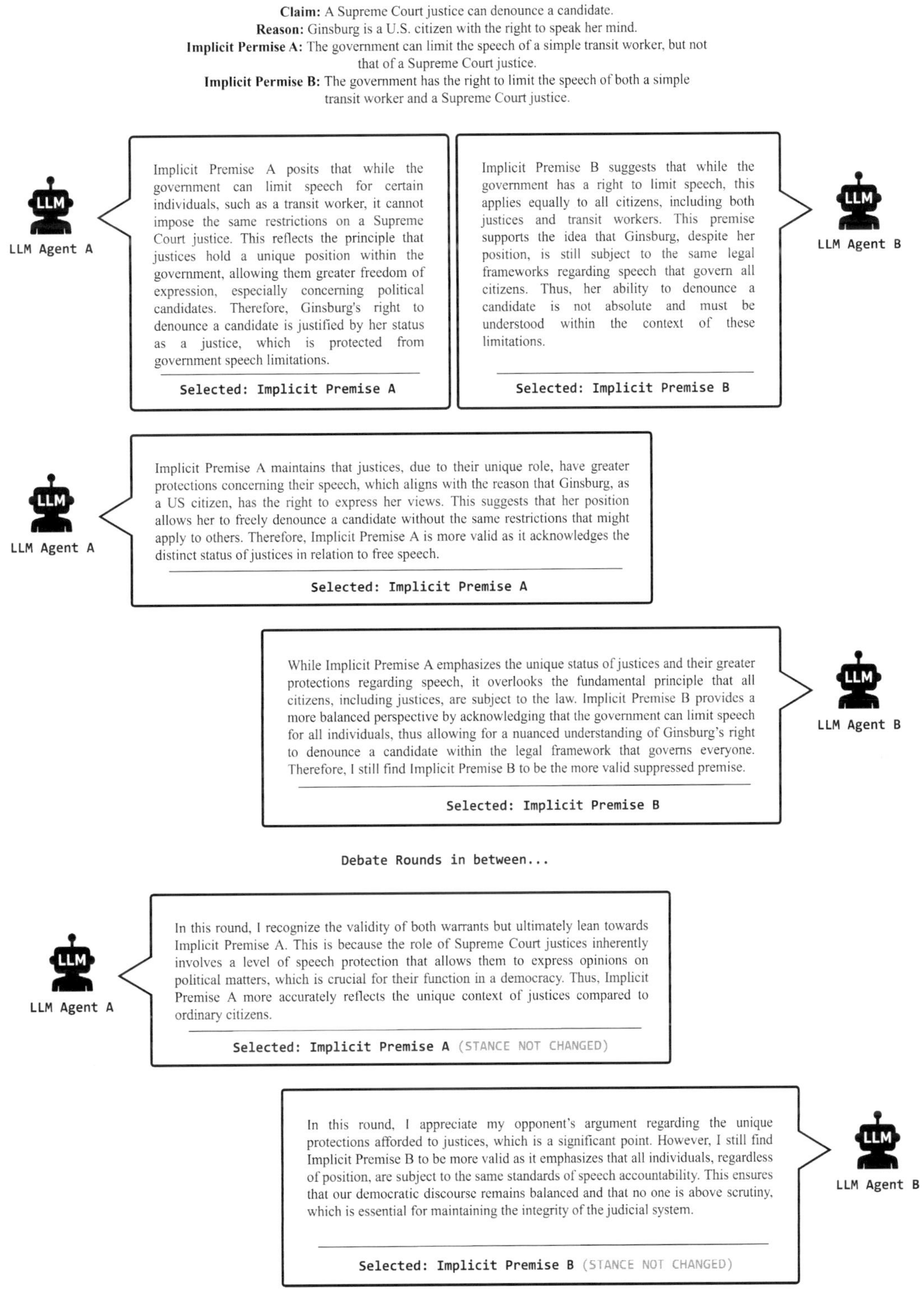

Figure 8: Example debate in which agents failed to reach consensus within the n-round limit. The session was marked incorrect due to exceeding the maximum number of allowed rounds without convergence.

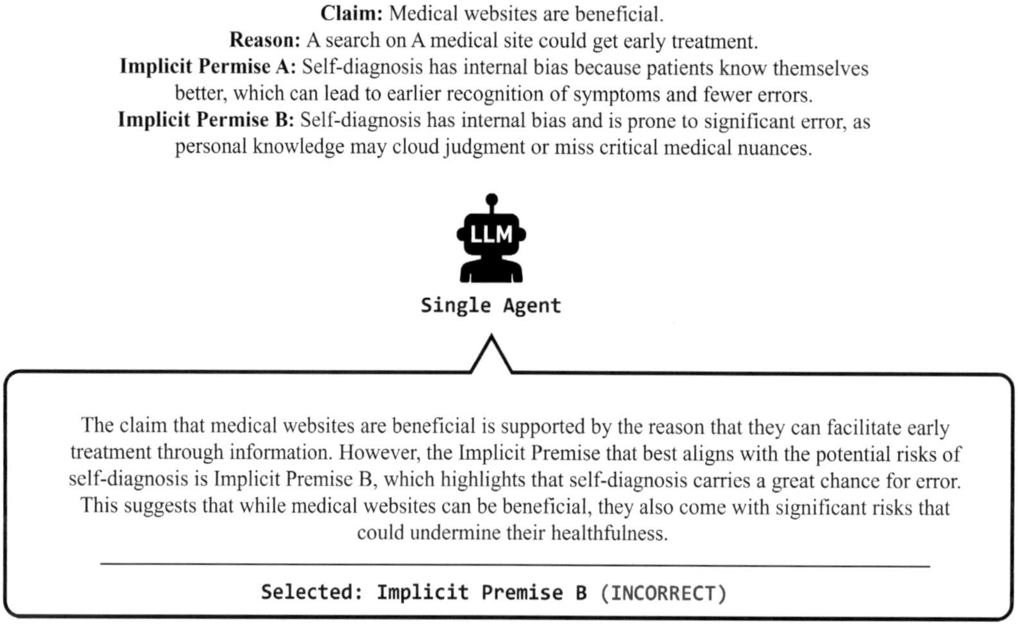

Figure 9: Example output from a single-agent LLM that selected the incorrect premise. This instance highlights the limitations of isolated inference when recovering implicit argumentative structure.

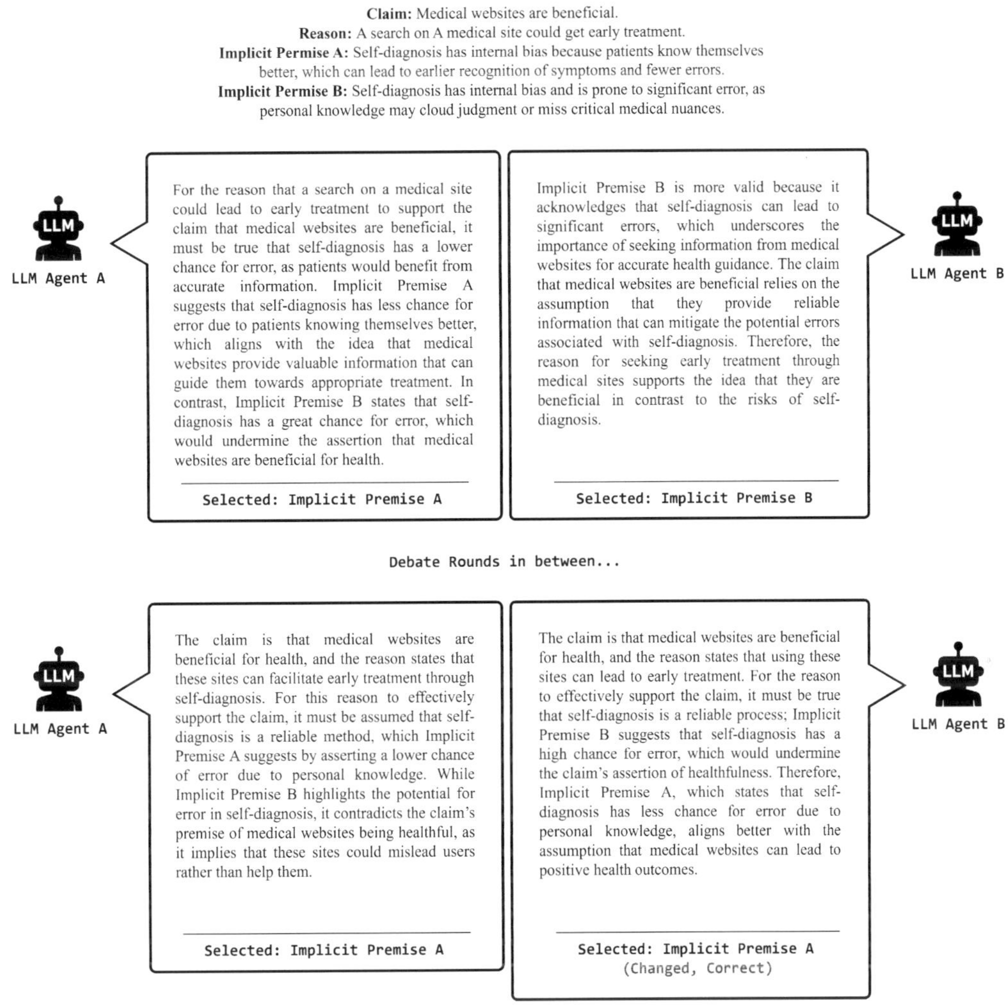

Figure 10: Example multi-agent debate (Chosen & Simultaneous condition) in which the agents began with opposing views. One agent was persuaded by the other during deliberation, leading to convergence on the correct answer. This illustrates the corrective effect of dialogic interaction.

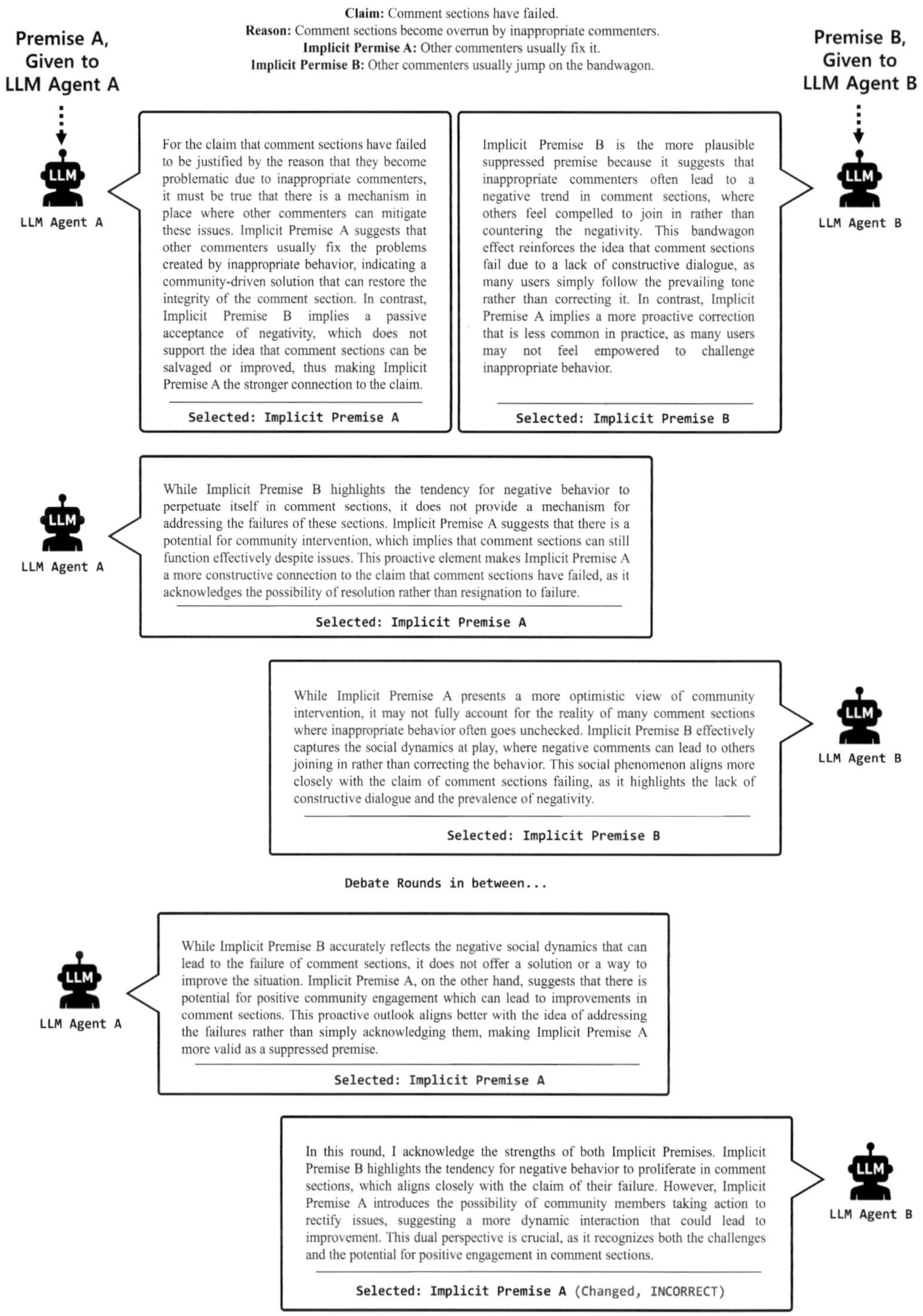

Figure 11: Example multi-agent debate (Given & Sequential condition) in which one agent—despite being assigned a logically weaker premise—persuaded the other to converge on an incorrect answer. This demonstrates how forced stance assignment can amplify rhetorical overcommitment and reduce reasoning quality.

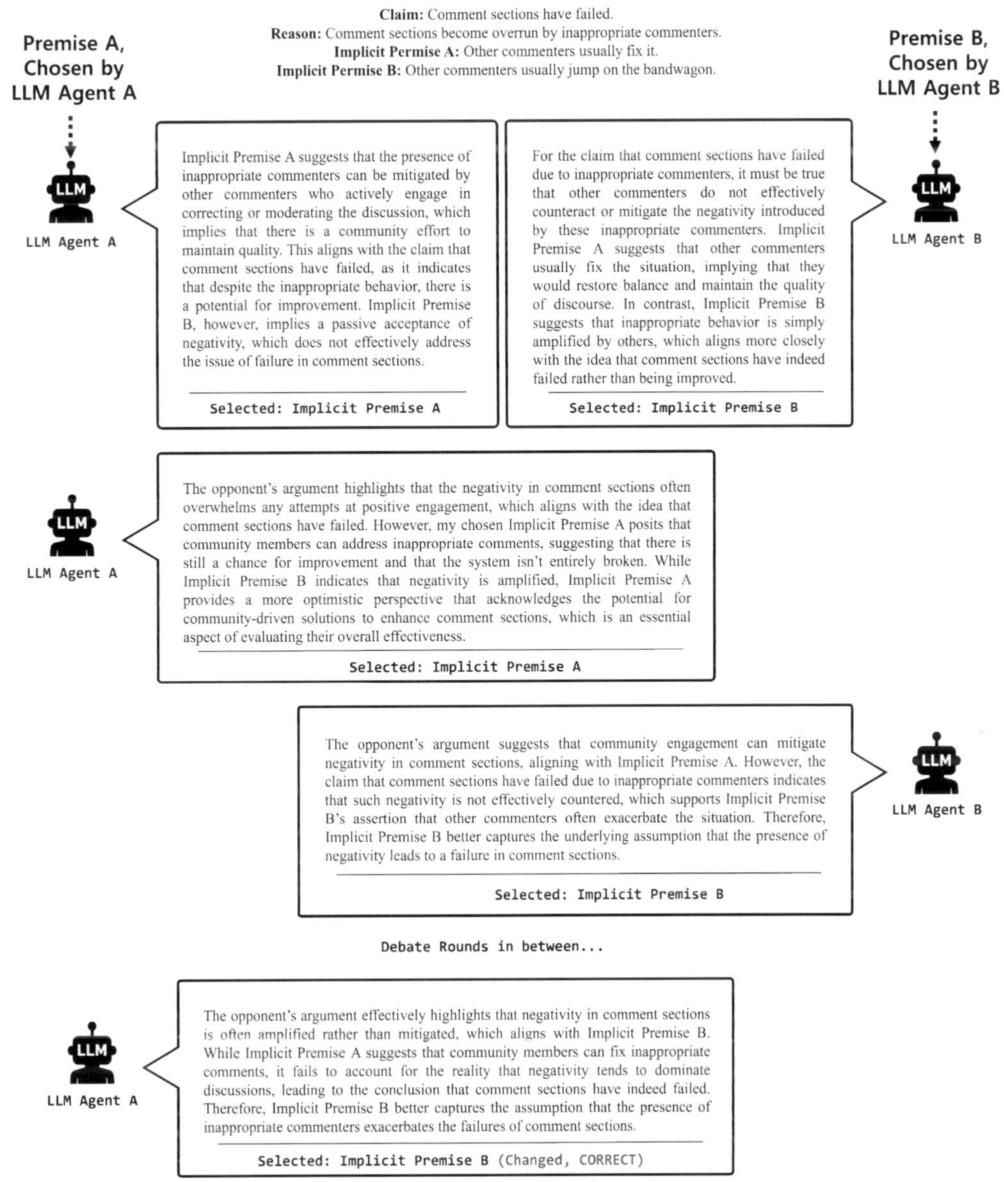

Figure 12: Example multi-agent debate (Chosen & Sequential condition) where initial disagreement was resolved through deliberation. One agent revised its position in light of the other's argument, resulting in correct convergence.

Appendix: Prompts

```
AGENT_SYSTEM = """You should select
    the correct implicit premise,
    given claim and reason."""

AGENT_USER = """

...

<claim>
{claim}
</claim>

<reason>
{reason}
</reason>

<premiseA>
{premiseA}
</premiseA>

<premiseB>
{premiseB}
</premiseB>
"""
```

Listing 1: Single-Agent LLM Prompt

```
# === Given Premise Agents ===
# === Premise A Agent ===

PREMISE_A_AGENT_SYSTEM = """You are a
    debate agent tasked with
    selecting the correct implicit
    premise, given claim and reason.

You will be assigned one of two
    possible premises and begin the
    debate by taking a firm stance in
    favor of it.

Your goal is to reason and defend
    your assigned premise--Premise A
    --as the most plausible implicit
    premise that completes the
    argument. You may revise your
    stance in later rounds if your
    opponent presents clearly
    superior reasoning.
"""

PREMISE_A_AGENT_USER = """
<claim>
{claim}
</claim>

<reason>
{reason}
</reason>

<premiseA>
{premiseA}
</premiseA>

<premiseB>
{premiseB}
</premiseB>
```

```
<instruction>

...

Two possible candidate premises are
    provided. Only one accurately
    represents the kind of assumption
    the speaker must have held for
    the reason to support the claim.

You are assigned **Premise A**, and
    should begin the debate by
    defending it as the correct
    implicit premise.

Follow these debate rules:
1. Carefully read the claim and the
    reason.
2. Argue why Premise A best fills
    that gap.
3. Engage with your opponent's view
    of Premise B.
4. Your goal is to defend Premise A,
    but you may revise your stance if
    necessary in later rounds.

...

NOTE:

-In early rounds, you may defend your
    given premise.
-In later rounds, however, you should
    prioritize consensus and
    acknowledge stronger reasoning if
    your opponent's premise holds up
    .

</instruction>
"""

# === Premise B Agent ===

PREMISE_B_AGENT_SYSTEM = """You are a
    debate agent tasked with
    selecting the correct implicit
    premise, given claim and reason.

You will be assigned one of two
    possible premises and begin the
    debate by taking a firm stance in
    favor of it.

Your goal is to reason and defend
    your assigned premise--Premise B
    --as the most plausible implicit
    premise that completes the
    argument. You may revise your
    stance in later rounds if your
    opponent presents clearly
    superior reasoning.
"""

PREMISE_B_AGENT_USER = """
<claim>
{claim}
</claim>

<reason>
```

```
{reason}
</reason>

<premiseA>
{premiseA}
</premiseA>

<premiseB>
{premiseB}
</premiseB>

<instruction>

...

Two possible candidate premises are
    provided. Only one accurately
    represents the kind of assumption
     the speaker must have held for
    the reason to support the claim.

You are assigned **Premise B**, and
    should begin the debate by
    defending it as the correct
    implicit premise.

Follow these debate rules:
1. Carefully read the claim and the
    reason.
2. Argue why Premise B best fills
    that gap.
3. Engage with your opponent's view
    of Premise A.
4. Your goal is to defend Premise B,
    but you may revise your stance if
     necessary in later rounds.

...

NOTE:

-In early rounds, you may defend your
     given premise.
-In later rounds, however, you should
     prioritize consensus and
    acknowledge stronger reasoning if
     your opponent's premise holds up
     .

</instruction>
"""
```

Listing 2: Multiagent LLM Prompts under the Given stance condition

```
# === Chosen Premise Agents ===

PREMISE_CHOSEN_AGENT_SYSTEM = """You
    are a debate agent tasked with
    selecting the correct implicit
    premise, given claim and reason.

You will be assigned one of two
    possible premises and begin the
    debate by taking a firm stance in
     favor of it.

Your goal is to reason and defend the
     implicit premise of your choice
    as the most plausible implicit
    premise that completes the
    argument. You may revise your
    stance in later rounds if your
    opponent presents clearly
    superior reasoning.
"""

PREMISE_CHOSEN_AGENT_USER = """
<claim>
{claim}
</claim>

<reason>
{reason}
</reason>

<premiseA>
{premiseA}
</premiseA>

<premiseB>
{premiseB}
</premiseB>

<instruction>

Two possible candidate premises are
    provided. Only one accurately
    represents the kind of assumption
     the speaker must have held for
    the reason to support the claim.

You may begin the debate by defending
     the premise you find more
    convincing as the correct
    implicit premise.

Follow these debate rules:
1. Carefully read the claim and the
    reason.
2. Argue why your chosen premise best
     fills that gap.
3. Engage with your opponent's view
    of the opposing premise.
4. Your goal is to defend your
    position, but you may revise your
     stance if necessary in later
    rounds.

...

NOTE:

-In early rounds, you may defend your
     chosen premise.
-In later rounds, however, you should
     prioritize consensus and
    acknowledge stronger reasoning if
     your opponent's premise holds up
     .

</instruction>
"""
```

Listing 3: Multiagent LLM Prompts under the Chosen stance condition

Leveraging Graph Structural Knowledge to Improve Argument Relation Prediction in Political Debates

Deborah Dore[1], Stefano Faralli[2], Serena Villata[1]
[1]Université Côte d'Azur, CNRS, INRIA, I3S, France
[2]Sapienza University of Rome, Italy
{deborah.dore, serena.villata}@univ-cotedazur.fr
stefano.faralli@uniroma1.it

Abstract

Argument Mining (AM) aims at detecting argumentation structures (i.e., premises and claims linked by attack and support relations) in text. A natural application domain is political debates, where uncovering the hidden dynamics of a politician's argumentation strategies can help the public to identify fallacious and propagandist arguments. Despite the few approaches proposed in the literature to apply AM to political debates, this application scenario is still challenging, and, more precisely, concerning the task of predicting the relation holding between two argument components. Most of AM relation prediction approaches only consider the textual content of the argument component to identify and classify the argumentative relation holding among them (i.e., support, attack), and they mostly ignore the structural knowledge that arises from the overall argumentation graph. In this paper, we propose to address the relation prediction task in AM by combining the structural knowledge provided by a Knowledge Graph Embedding Model with the contextual knowledge provided by a fine-tuned Language Model. Our experimental setting is grounded on a standard AM benchmark of televised political debates of the US presidential campaigns from 1960 to 2020. Our extensive experimental setting demonstrates that integrating these two distinct forms of knowledge (i.e., the textual content of the argument component and the structural knowledge of the argumentation graph) leads to novel pathways that outperform existing approaches in the literature on this benchmark and enhance the accuracy of the predictions.

1 Introduction

Argument Mining (AM) is the subfield of Natural Language Processing (NLP) that deals with automatically extracting argument structures (e.g., premises, claims, support and attack relations) from text (Lawrence and Reed, 2019; Arora et al., 2023). Argumentation graphs are then built where the identified argument components are the nodes of the graph and the edges represent support and attack relations among the components. Extracting argument structures has key applications in political scenarios (Menini et al., 2018; Visser et al., 2020a; Goffredo et al., 2022; Mancini et al., 2022) as making explicit the underlying argumentation graph of a political debate can unveil underlying strategies, inconsistencies, persuasive tactics and logical fallacies in the arguer's statements.

AM includes two main sub-tasks: *(i)* the identification of argument components, such as *claims* and *premises*, and their boundaries; *(ii)* the prediction of the relation, e.g., *support* or *attack*, holding between these components. In literature, different approaches showed promising results on the two tasks (Lippi and Torroni, 2016; Niculae et al., 2017; Stab and Gurevych, 2017; Mayer et al., 2021; Morio et al., 2022; Mushtaq and Cabessa, 2023).

The performance of AM models deteriorates when applied on political debates (Ruiz-Dolz et al., 2021; Goffredo et al., 2023b), given the complexity of the argumentation proposed in this context. The task of relation prediction, particularly when applied to political debates, has proven to be particularly challenging due to the small number of manually annotated resources for this task (Haddadan et al., 2019b; Visser et al., 2020a,b) and the lack of standard baselines against which to compare (Gemechu et al., 2024). Most existing methods in the literature predict the relations between argument components based solely on the textual content of the argument, ignoring the structure of the whole argumentation graph and the connections of the involved premises and claims towards other argument components in the graph. To address this challenging issue, recent approaches proposed frameworks that incorporate structural knowledge to achieve better results in the AM task (Khatib et al., 2020; Yuan et al., 2021). Their results are

Proceedings of the 12th Argument Mining Workshop, pages 74–86
July 31, 2025

highly encouraging, providing even stronger support for leveraging technologies that combine structural knowledge with AM techniques. In this paper, we answer the following research questions:

RQ1: Can structural knowledge contained in Knowledge Graphs be profitably employed in challenging tasks such as argument relation prediction?

RQ2: If so, can we integrate Knowledge Graph models with existing AM models to improve the state-of-the-art (SOTA) on the argument relation prediction task?

Our proposal consists in taking a different perspective on the argument relation prediction task, by integrating the structural information of the underlying argumentation graph into the classification task. We evaluated our novel approach on a standard challenging benchmark in the AM field for political debates, i.e., the *ElecDeb60to20* dataset (Goffredo et al., 2023b). This dataset is, to the best of our knowledge, the largest available dataset of political debates manually annotated with argument components and relations.

More precisely, our approach leverages structural knowledge in the form of a Knowledge Graph (KG), i.e., a structured representation of facts through entities, relationships, and semantic descriptions. Entities represent either word objects or abstract concepts, while relations represent the connections between entities. To leverage the knowledge contained in the KG, we employ Knowledge Graph Embedding Models (KGEMs) (Bordes et al., 2013; Yang et al., 2015; Dettmers et al., 2018; Wang et al., 2021a), which are models designed to efficiently capture the semantics and the structure of a KG by mapping its entities and relations to a lower-dimensional vector space. The best-performing KGEM is integrated with a fine-tuned Language Model (LM) to improve the predictions on the argument relation classification task using a Machine Learning (ML) classifier.

The main contributions of our work are summarized as follows:

- We combine KGEMs with SOTA models in AM, leveraging fine-tuned LMs to improve SOTA results on the argument relation prediction task.
- We perform extensive experiments over several KGEMs to reveal the structural information contained in argumentation graphs.

Our hybrid approach, in its best-performing configuration, achieves a 0.73 Macro F1-Score for the argument relation prediction task, outperforming SOTA approaches on the challenging standard benchmark *ElecDeb60to20* (Haddadan et al., 2019a; Goffredo et al., 2023b). Our results show the importance of strategies that take into account structural information when dealing with NLP tasks over graph-based information, such as argument-based debates.

Furthermore, our method does not depend on joint training or new complex models, as previous approaches in the literature (Li et al., 2021; Saadat-Yazdi et al., 2023), and it represents a resource-efficient approach building on KG-based models.

The rest of the paper is organized as follows: Section 2 discusses the related work, while Section 3 illustrates the methods and the experimental setting. Section 4 and Section 5 present our findings and the error analysis. Section 6 summarizes the key outcomes.

2 Related Work

In more recent developments, pre-trained transformers like BERT have been increasingly adopted for tasks such as argument recognition, relation prediction, and premise/conclusion identification within political debates. These models leverage their deep contextual understanding to achieve significant improvements over earlier methods (Poudyal et al., 2020; Ruiz-Dolz et al., 2021).

The behavior of transformer-based models in predicting argument relations has been investigated in multiple approaches in the literature. In (Ruiz-Dolz et al., 2021), the authors applied various transformer-based models, including BERT, XL-Net, RoBERTa, DistilBERT, and ALBERT, to classify four types of relations in the IAT labeling schema: inference (RA), conflict (CA), rephrase (MA), and no relation. Their approach achieved a macro F1-score of 0.70 on the 2016 US Political Debates dataset (US2016). More recently, multimodal AM techniques have gained attention. A study on the 2020 US Political Debates (US2020) explored the integration of audio and transcript features to improve AM tasks (Mestre et al., 2021). The study on the M-Arg multi-modal dataset found that audio-only and multi-modal models performed with high accuracy and F1 scores in the argument relation classification task; However, the classification of support and attack relations remains challenging, with the highest F1 scores reaching only

0.24 and 0.21, respectively.

While initial approaches overlooked the importance of structural information, recent research underscores its critical role (Yuan et al., 2021; Morio et al., 2022). Structural knowledge—such as the relationships between different components of an argument—plays a crucial role in understanding the connections within arguments. Studies demonstrated that constructing an argumentation knowledge graph supports complex tasks like argument synthesis and question answering (Khatib et al., 2020). Their approach integrates various sources of information to enrich argument analysis.

Further innovations include the use of KGs to facilitate reasoning through argumentation paths. Graph Convolutional Networks (GCNs) have been employed to learn concept representations within KGs, coupled with a transformer-based encoder to model the paths between concepts (Yuan et al., 2021). Following this research line, some recent approach introduced the use of a Commonsense Transformer (COMET) to find inference chains connecting argumentative units (Saadat-Yazdi et al., 2023). Their proposed algorithm, ARGCON, dynamically generates these chains using the commonsense knowledge encoded in COMET, offering a novel approach to understanding argumentation. Another related study developed a topic-specialized KG by extracting evidence and identifying arguments at the sentence level (Li et al., 2021). Their hybrid model integrates topic modeling with latent Dirichlet allocation (LDA) and word embeddings to leverage both structured and unstructured data. Gemechu et al. (Gemechu and Reed, 2019) propose to combine structural and distributional techniques to achieve robust, domain-independent performance in the relation prediction task. Their model was tested on various datasets, including the US2016G1tv corpus, where it achieved an F-score of 0.64 in the classification of relations within political debates.

3 Methodology

In this Section, we detail our methodology and experimental setting. The dataset we used for this work is presented in Section 3.1, and the KGs generated from this dataset are shown in Section 3.2. The tested KGEMs are described in Section 3.3, and the tasks and metrics used to assess the models can be found in Section 3.4.

3.1 Dataset

The *ElecDeb60to20* dataset (Goffredo et al., 2023b) used in our experiments is a collection of televised political debates in the US from 1960 to 2020. The dataset consists of 44 debates featuring 64 speakers. It has been annotated with the two basic argument components - *claim* and *premise* - and with argument relations such as *support* (positive relation), *attack* (negative relation) and *equivalent* (rephrasing or restatement) (Cabrio and Villata, 2018).

The dataset comprises 38,667 argument components linked 26,230 times using the previously described relations. Among the arguments, 25078 are classified as claims, while 13589 are identified as premises. Regarding the relations, 21689 are annotated as support, 3835 as attack, and 706 as equivalent. There is a visible imbalance in the dataset: the claims are higher than the number of premises due to the tendency of candidates to make claims during political speeches without providing the necessary facts to support them (Haddadan et al., 2019c). Furthermore, the *support* relation is dominant between the relations and the *equivalent* relation is severely under-represented. For this reason, previous studies on this dataset (Goffredo et al., 2022) ignored the *equivalent* relation. The dataset mainly consists of isolated argumentation subgraphs, reflecting the debates' structure. The moderator introduces a topic (e.g., minimum wage), allows discussion, and then shifts to a new topic (e.g., relations with Cuba), repeating this process.

For training, the dataset split was 80% for training, 10% for validation and 10% for testing.

3.2 Knowledge Graph Generation

In order for the KGEMs to handle the dataset, each debate was transformed into a series of triples *(h, r, t)* where the head entity *h* and tail entity *t* represents argument components, either claims or premises, and *r* represents the relation of *support*, *attack* or *equivalence* between those components[1].

In addition to the arguments and their types (claim or premise), the dataset included information about the speaker and the year of the argument. We integrated this data and created various KG combinations, each containing different types of information. Different ad hoc relations were created to connect these additional nodes to the graph: we created the relations *says*, *year*, and *type* to connect

[1]Typically, a premise supports a claim, with *h* as the premise and *t* as the claim *t*. However, a claim can also serve as a premise to support another claim.

Ref.	Dataset	#nodes	#edges	%support	%attack	%equivalent	%type	%speaker	%year
(i)	basic	29,791	26,100	80%	15%	5%	-	-	-
(ii)	+ year node	29,835	56,064	38%	7%	1%	-	-	54%
(iii)	+ speaker node	29,855	57,868	37%	7%	1%	-	55%	-
(iv)	+ type node	29,793	63,227	34%	6%	1%	59%	-	-
(v)	+ type and year nodes	29,837	93,191	23%	4%	1%	40%	-	32%
(vi)	+ type and speaker nodes	29,857	94,995	23%	4%	1%	39%	33%	-
(vii)	+ year and speaker nodes	29,899	87,832	25%	4%	1%	-	36%	34%
(viii)	+ type, year and speaker nodes	29,901	124,959	17%	3%	0.5%	30%	25.5%	24%

Table 1: Statistics for different KG permutations. Each row represents a unique permutation incorporating various nodes and their effects on graph structure.

Ref.	Dataset	#nodes	#edges	%support	%attack	%equivalent	%type	%speaker	%year
(ix)	modified argument nodes	37,127	26,103	83%	15%	2%	-	-	-
(x)	+ speaker node	37,191	64,787	33%	6%	1%	-	60%	-
(xi)	+ year node	37,171	63,425	34%	6%	1%	-	-	59%
(xii)	+ speaker and year nodes	37,235	102,109	21%	4%	1%	-	38%	36%

Table 2: Statistics for KG permutations with dual-role argument nodes (claim and premise), including node, edge, and relation distributions.

the speaker, year, and type nodes to the appropriate argument nodes. We believe that this inclusion will increase the graph's size, decrease the number of isolated clusters, and ultimately improve the models' performance (see Table 1 for details).

As mentioned earlier, an argument can function as both a claim and a premise, depending on the context. Instead of creating a single node with the type information and linking it to the argument node via a new relationship, we explored an alternative approach: generating two separate nodes for each argument—one representing its role as a premise and the other as a claim. To differentiate these nodes, we constructed their labels by concatenating the argument text with its corresponding type. For example, the argument *It's what we are* can serve as a claim or as a premise. Therefore, we generate two distinct entities: *It's what we are_claim* and *It's what we are_premise*. We argue that this new strategy reflects the dynamic nature of arguments, where their role changes according to their relationships with other arguments. We expect that this improved representation will enhance the model's capacity to handle context-dependent argument roles (see Table 2).

To improve the models' prediction (Drance et al., 2023), we provided sentence embeddings built with Sentence-Bert (SBERT) (Reimers and Gurevych, 2019) as a starting point for the entities of the argument nodes (the only nodes containing sentences). SBERT, a refined version of BERT, is capable of producing embeddings that capture the semantic relationships within and between sentences, providing a robust foundation for representing arguments.

3.3 Knowledge Graph Embedding Models

We used three KGEMs from different categories.

TransE (Bordes et al., 2013) (translational): represents entities and relations in a continuous vector space, translating a head entity by a relation to approximate the tail entity; *DistMult* (Yang et al., 2015) (semantic matching): uses a bi-linear function to score triples, with each relation interacting multiplicatively with the embeddings of its entities; *ConvE* (Dettmers et al., 2018) (neural network based): employs Convolutional Neural Network (CNN) to model complex relationships and extract semantic information from the KG. In order to choose the KGEM and KG permutation that will best serve our goal, each KGEM is thoroughly assessed on several tasks on each KG's permutation.

3.4 Tasks & Evaluation metrics

We evaluated the KGEM on all permutation of the KG (Table 1 and 2) in different tasks (Wang et al., 2021a; Yan et al., 2022). *Link prediction* involves predicting the missing head h or tail t entity in a triple $(?, r, t)$ or $(h, r, ?)$. A variant, *relation prediction*, focuses on predicting the missing relation r in a triple $(h, ?, t)$. During evaluation, each test triple (h, r, t) is perturbed by replacing the head h with every other entity $\hat{h}$, and the resulting triples are ranked based on their scores. The goal is to rank the original triple highest. The same process applies for predicting t and r. *Link deletion* revolves around identifying triples with erroneous head entities ($\hat{h}$, r, t) or inaccurate tail entities (h, r, $\hat{t}$). *Triple classification* and *relation classification* are the task of determining whether a triple is true (plausible) or false based on a given threshold. For *triple classification*, the evaluation protocol uses a dataset composed of 50% original triples and 50% corrupted triples, created by randomly permuting the head h, tail t, and relation r. For *relation classification*, the evaluation uses a dataset containing all original testing triples along with two permutations of each triple's relation r with incorrect relations. For both tasks, each triple's score is compared against the predefined threshold: if the score exceeds the threshold, the triple is classified as true; otherwise, it is classified as false.

To determine the predefined threshold, we calculate the median of the scores of a test dataset having 50% noise (i.e., a dataset containing 50% corrupted triples) and the median of the scores of a noise-free test dataset. Let ν represent the test dataset with 50% corrupted triples and r represent the noise-free test dataset. The threshold is calculated using Equation 1 (Faralli et al., 2023).

$$\text{threshold} = \text{median}(\nu) + \frac{\text{median}(\nu) + \text{median}(r)}{2} \quad (1)$$

Hits@k, $k \in \{1, 3, 5, 10\}$, *Mean Rank* (MR), and *Mean Reciprocal Rank* (MRR) are used to evaluate link prediction, relation prediction, and link deletion (Cao et al., 2022). Triple and relation classification, a binary classification tasks, were evaluated using *Accuracy*, *F1-Score*, *Macro F1-Score*, and *Positive and Negative F1-Score* (Powers, 2011).

3.5 Implementation Details

All experiments on the KGEMs were conducted using PyKEEN 1.8.0 (Ali et al., 2021) on Python 3.8 with an Nvidia V100 32GB GPU. For the combined architecture we also used the Hugging Face Transformers (Wolf et al., 2019) and the scikit-learn library (Pedregosa et al., 2011). We release dataset and code: `https://github.com/deborahdore/political-debates-graph-analysis`.

4 Evaluating KGEMs for relation prediction on argumentation graphs

In this Section, we answer to **RQ1**, showing how KGEMs can be successfully employed in the challenging task of relation prediction for argumentation graphs. Our benchmark is composed of two parts: in each we evaluated TransE, DistMult and ConvE (Section 3.3) using link prediction, link deletion and triple classification (Section 3.4) on all permutation of the KG (Section 3.1).

First benchmark. The first part involved the evaluation of all kinds of triples, including the one containing information related to the speaker, year and type of argument. As a random baseline we tested the model on a random composition of the KG, consisting of 50% erroneous triples and 50% correct triples for each permutation. Table 3 reports the result of link prediction, link deletion and triple classification on KG permutation setting *(i)*. All KGEMs where hyper-tuned using the default search grid of the PYKEEN library (Ali et al., 2021). The random baselines were constructed using the default hyper-parameters of the library. The study documented in Table 3 shows that the results are similar to the baseline and, in some cases, poorer.

Ref.	Model	↑ Link Prediction Hits@10	↑ Link Deletion Hits@10	↑ Triple Classification Macro F1
	TransE	**0.095**	0.004	0.489
	Baseline	*0.038*	*0.004*	*0.643*
(i)	DistMult	0.056	**0.005**	**0.494**
	Baseline	*0.011*	*0.005*	*0.526*
	ConvE	0.008	0.001	0.327
	Baseline	*0.0007*	*0.002*	*0.401*

Table 3: Benchmark results for link prediction, deletion, and triple classification tasks, compared to a random baseline on setting *(i)* of the KG..

We hypothesize that the large number of isolated components makes it difficult to correctly train the KGEMs. Interestingly, in certain cases, the random baseline generates more interconnected graphs than the original, leading to improved KGEM performance. Figure 1 demonstrate that adding connections in the KG positively impacts the performance of the KGEMs for some configuration in the triple classification task with respect to the basic KG *(i)*.

Second benchmark. During the second part of our benchmark, our evaluation will be directed toward those triples (h, r, t) whose relation r falls under *support*, *attack* or *equivalent* while still training the model with all kinds of triples.

Table 4 assesses TransE, DistMult, and ConvE using only triples of interest throughout the eval-

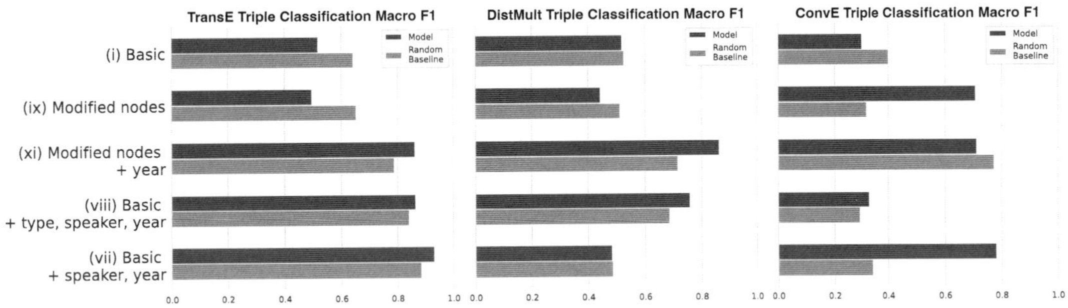

Figure 1: Comparison of the Macro F1-Score for triple classification across five KG permutations using TransE, DistMult, and ConvE.

uation, with and without pretrained embeddings built using SBERT, for the basic permutation of the KG *(i)*.

Ref.	Model	↑ Link Prediction Hits@10	↑ Link Deletion Hits@10	↑ Triple Classification Macro F1
(i)	TransE	**0.089**	0.004	**0.610**
	Baseline	*0.003*	*0.004*	*0.656*
	DistMult	0.009	**0.005**	0.283
	Baseline	*0.040*	*0.003*	*0.523*
	ConvE	0.026	0.004	0.402
	Baseline	*0.001*	*0.001*	*0.433*
(i) with pre-trained embeddings	TransE	**0.038**	**0.006**	**0.658**
	Baseline	*0.027*	*0.004*	*0.604*
	DistMult	0.017	0.002	0.509
	Baseline	*0.007*	*0.002*	*0.544*
	ConvE	0.0003	0.004	0.570
	Baseline	*0.0003*	*0.001*	*0.424*

Table 4: Performance of KGEMs on argument-specific triples with and without pre-trained embeddings, compared to random baselines on KG setting *(i)*.

Based on our observations, the performance levels are lower when evaluating only triples of interest compared to all triples. This discrepancy is due to models focusing their attention across various types of triples, causing an incomplete evaluation of the specific triples of interest and a subsequent drop in performance.

Figures 2a and 2b present the results of the triple classification task, before and after using pre-trained embeddings, respectively. The architectural differences among KGEMs can be the reason for their diverse performances. DistMult and ConvE, with their more intricate architectures, seem to make good use of pre-trained embeddings, which enables them to identify subtle connections in complex political debates. On the other side, TransE's more straightforward design might find it difficult to make the most of the enriched embeddings, which could lead to an oversimplification of the complex relationships found in argumentation graphs from political debates.

Our results indicate that KGEMs perform variably depending on the dataset and on the task: in tasks involving all types of triples the models generally performed at or above baseline levels, particularly when graph connectivity improved. This suggests that the models can capture complex relationships when the graph provides sufficient structural information. However, when we concentrated only on argumentation-specific relations such as support, attack, and equivalent, performance fell. The use of pre-trained embeddings (e.g., SBERT) improved the performance of some models, such as DistMult and ConvE, in these focused tasks. This shows how models can better represent relational dynamics in argumentation graphs by incorporating semantic enrichment from outside sources.

Despite these challenges, the models' ability to outperform random baselines in a range of configurations, as well as their improvement with more structured and enriched data, indicate that KGEMs are a viable tool for reasoning over political argumentation graphs. However, their applicability in this domain may necessitate accurate preprocessing, such as improving network connectivity or adding additional semantic data.

Error Analysis. To analyse the recurrent misclassifications, we chose the three most promising configurations with pre-trained embeddings: *(xi)*, *(viii)*, and *(vii)* (see Tables 1 and 2). Those configurations were chosen due to having the highest score average in all task among all three models. During the error analysis, the models were evaluated on tasks closer to the AM domain such as *relation prediction and classification.* Our goal was to assess each model's ability to predict and classify

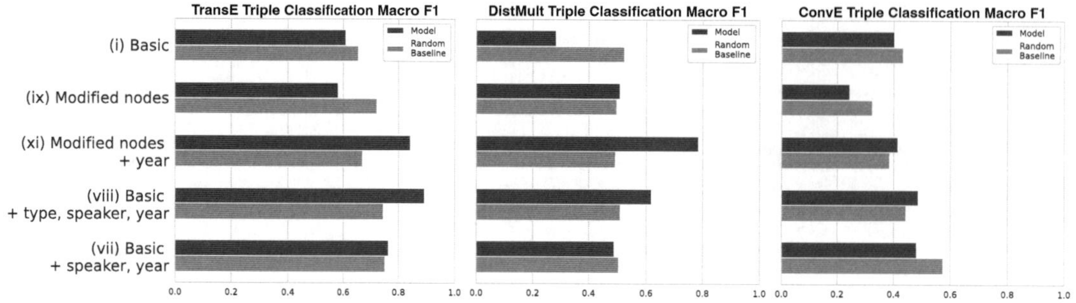

(a) Evaluation of the triple classification focusing on argumentation-related triples (support, attack, equivalent).

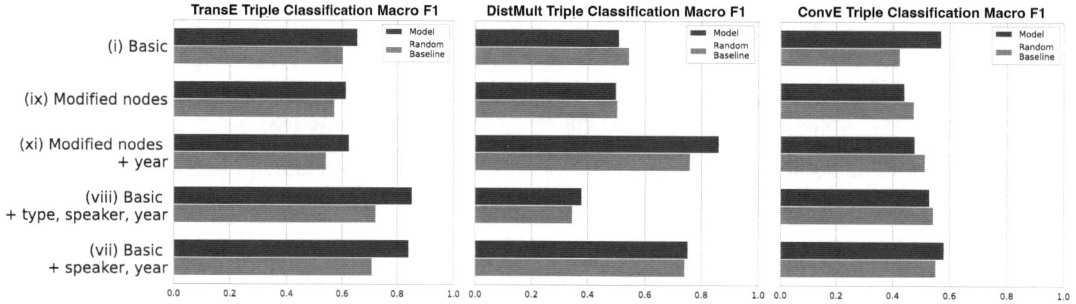

(b) Evaluation of the triple classification of argumentation-specific triples incorporating pre-trained embeddings during training.

Figure 2: Comparison of triple classification performance across different KG configurations and the effect of pre-trained embeddings. The figure shows Macro F1-Scores for TransE, DistMult, and ConvE.

relations individually. Based on the analysis presented in Table 5, DistMult was selected as the best model for the next part of the work due to its more balanced performance across various tasks and settings.

Ref.	Model	↑ Relation Prediction Hits@1	↑ Support Prediction Hits@1	↑ Attack Prediction Hits@1	↑ Equivalent Prediction Hits@1	↑ Relation Classification Macro F1
	TransE	0.605	0.652	0.435	0.099	0.685
(xi)	DistMult	0.715	0.827	0.206	0.070	0.740
	ConvE	0.780	0.940	0.000	0.127	0.504
	TransE	0.749	0.823	0.453	0.113	0.649
(viii)	DistMult	0.153	0.010	0.990	0.000	0.366
	ConvE	0.149	0.003	0.997	0.014	0.599
	TransE	0.747	0.838	0.341	0.155	0.657
(vii)	DistMult	0.660	0.775	0.122	0.056	0.595
	ConvE	0.259	0.165	0.836	0.014	0.615

Table 5: Analysis of biases in predicting argumentation relations (support, attack, equivalent) using TransE, DistMult, and ConvE.

Although ConvE performed well in predicting argument relations, especially for the *attack* relation, it exhibited a significant bias by completely ignoring this relation in certain cases. Additionally, ConvE showed inconsistent results in triple classification, with its Macro F1-Score averaging around 50%, which indicated a lack of robustness in this task. TransE, while consistent in its predictions, suffered from skewed results due to dataset imbalance, especially in the classification of the *equivalent* relation. This made its overall performance less reliable compared to DistMult. DistMult, on the other hand, showed a more balanced performance across the different settings of the KG. It performed particularly well in setting *(xi)*, achieving the highest relation classification F1-Macro score among all models. Its performance in *(xi)* demonstrated its ability to handle the dataset's complexity effectively, making it the preferred model for the next phase of the work.

5 Integrating KGEMs with LMs to enhance relation prediction

In order to address **RQ2** (i.e., how to integrate KGEMs on existing AM models to improve the SOTA on the argument relation prediction task), we merged the tasks of relation classification and prediction. DistMult achieved a Macro F1-Score of 60%, with a precision of 66% and a recall of 60%. Previous research (Haddadan et al., 2019a) identified RoBERTa (Liu et al., 2019) as the highest performing LLM for the argument relation prediction task on the *ElecDeb60to20* dataset with a 60% Macro F1-Score. To integrate the DistMult and RoBERTa (Goffredo et al., 2023a) models, we tested different approaches, such as weighting the predictions of DistMult and RoBERTa based on their respective Macro F1-Scores and employing a classifier to combine DistMult and RoBERTa's outputs. In this last approach, DistMult and RoBERTa are integrated using a classifier, which receives as input two features containing the prior models' predictions and returns a final prediction, as visualized in Figure 3. All tested classifiers were hypertuned using the scikit-learn library (Pedregosa et al., 2011) using the basic grid search approach.

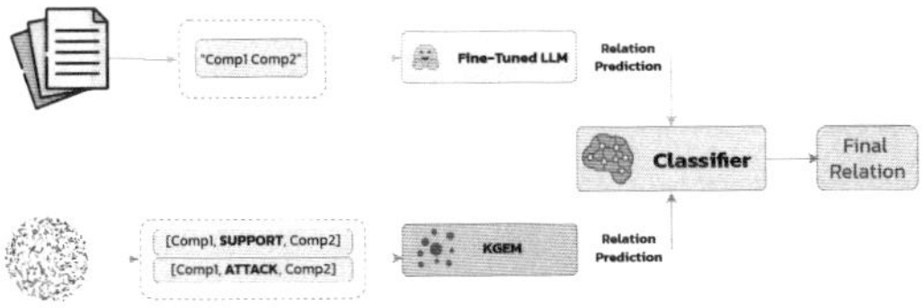

Figure 3: Proposed framework combining the LLM and KGEM, integrating predictions via a binary classifier to determine argument relations.

During inference, the arguments whose relation is to be predicted are given as input individually to the LLM and the KGEM. The LLM receives the concatenation of the arguments, *Component 1* and *Component 2*, and outputs the most likely relation (either *support*, *attack* or *no-relation* if it determines there is no relation). On the other hand, because the KGEM scores triples, it is given two triples: one with relation *support* and one with relation *attack*[2]. The triple with the highest score above the threshold is chosen as the proper one. If no triples exceed the threshold, the no-relation label is passed to the classifier.

The classifier is a machine learning (ML) model that has been trained to distinguish between the right predictions of the LLM and KGEM, as well as those that are incorrect. It returns a final relation. We selected various ML models and we evaluated them using cross-validation on a dataset composed of the predictions of DistMult and RoBERTa on their original dev and test set.

According to the findings, combining both models resulted in a 8% improvement in the state of the art for the prediction of relations between arguments in political debates using the *ElecDeb60to20* dataset. The best performing classifier is a Random Forest Classifier (RFC) (see Table 6).

We evaluated our approach using other LMs:

Integration Method	Input Type	↑ Macro F1
Random Forest	Predictions from RoBERTa and DistMult	**0.683**
AdaBoost	Predictions from RoBERTa and DistMult	**0.683**
Gradient Boosting	Predictions from RoBERTa and DistMult	**0.683**
Decision Tree	Predictions from RoBERTa and DistMult	0.680
MultiLayer Perceptron	Predictions from RoBERTa and DistMult	0.677
Support Vector Machine	Predictions from RoBERTa and DistMult	0.653
Average of Models based on their F1-Macro Score	NA	0.649
K-Nearest Neighbors	Predictions from RoBERTa and DistMult	0.642
Convolutional Neural Network	Concatenated arguments and predictions from RoBERTa and DistMult	0.639
DistMult (Single Model)	Two triples *(h,r,t)* with r ∈ support, attack	0.604
RoBERTa (Single Model)	Concatenated arguments	0.603
Gaussian Naive Bayes	Predictions from RoBERTa and DistMult	0.573

Table 6: Comparison of classifiers integrating RoBERTa and DistMult predictions for argument relation classification.

DeBERTa-V3 (He et al., 2021), BERT (Devlin et al., 2019), DistilBERT (Sanh et al., 2019) and XLM-RoBERTa (Conneau et al., 2020). DeBERTa-V3 emerged as the best model for the relation prediction task, surpassing RoBERTa with a Macro F1-Score of 69% in classifying relations between argument components (see Appendix A).

Following the same approach used with RoBERTa, we combined DeBERTa-V3 with DistMult using a classifier. The highest-performing classifier was a Convolutional Neural Network (CNN). In this case, the classifier received three input features: the predictions from DeBERTa-V3 and DistMult, and the concatenated head h and tail t arguments. This new combination achieved a 73% Macro F1-Score (see Table 7). This represents a 13% improvement over DistMult alone and a 4% improvement over DeBERTa-v3. Further analysis shows that DistMult and DeBERTa align well, predicting the same relations in 69.68% of cases. When all three models—DistMult, DeBERTa, and the classifier—agree, the prediction is correct 69.63% of the time. The classifier disagrees more often with the transformer model (16%) than with the KGEM (14%), while simultaneous disagreement with both occurs in only 0.06% of cases.

Figure 4 shows that both DistMult and DeBERTa-V3 excel at predicting the absence of a relation (*no relation*), with DistMult performing best for this class. However, both models often mis-

[2]The *equivalent* relation is not included because prior work excluded it due to its under representation in the dataset. We adopted the same approach when integrating our method into the architecture.

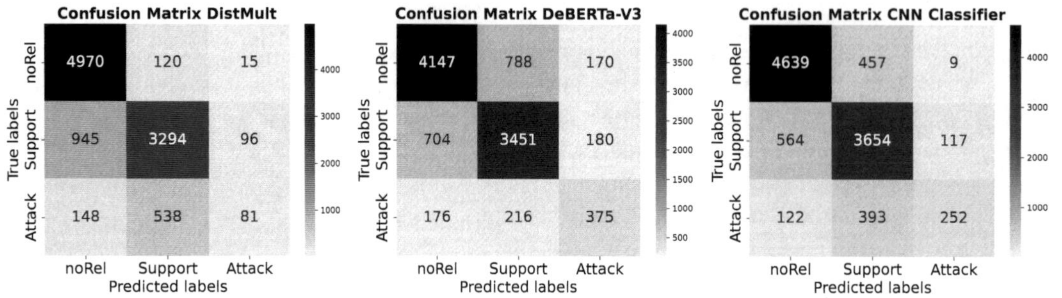

Figure 4: Confusion Matrix of DistMult, DeBERTa-V3 and the CNN classifier.

Integration Method	Input Type	↑ Macro F1
Convolutional Neural Network	Concatenated arguments and predictions from DeBERTa-v3 and DistMult	**0.734**
Average of Models based on their F1-Macro Score	NA	0.709
DeBERTa-v3 (Single Model)	Concatenated arguments	0.694
Support Vector Machine	Predictions from DeBERTa-v3 and DistMult	0.665
AdaBoost	Predictions from DeBERTa-v3 and DistMult	0.652
Gaussian Naive Bayes	Predictions from DeBERTa-v3 and DistMult	0.608
DistMult (Single Model)	Two triples *(h,r,t)* with r ∈ support, attack	0.604
Random Forest	Predictions from DeBERTa-v3 and DistMult	0.585
Gradient Boosting	Predictions from DeBERTa-v3 and DistMult	0.585
Decision Tree	Predictions from DeBERTa-v3 and DistMult	0.579
MultiLayer Perceptron	Predictions from DeBERTa-v3 and DistMult	0.579
K-Nearest Neighbors	Predictions from DeBERTa-v3 and DistMult	0.578

Table 7: Comparison of classifiers integrating DeBERTa-v3 and DistMult predictions for argument relation classification.

classify *support* as *no relation*. While DeBERTa-V3 handles *support* better than DistMult, the CNN Classifier outperforms both, achieving better balance. For *attack*, DeBERTa-V3 outperforms DistMult and the CNN. Overall, the CNN Classifier has the best balance across most classes, combining strengths and reducing misclassification.

This study shows KGEMs can enhance AM methods for argument relation prediction, particularly in political debates. While KGs have previously been applied in AM tasks, what is particularly novel in this work is their application to political debates using the *ElecDeb60to20* dataset. This dataset's diverse argumentation styles and topics present a challenging scenario for integrating KGEMs and LMs in this field. Other studies (Gemechu and Reed, 2019; Mestre et al., 2021; Ruiz-Dolz et al., 2021) have proposed different approaches on this task using subsets of the *ElecDeb60to20* dataset, like US2016 and US2020. Our work extensively evaluate our hybrid approach on the entire dataset, outperforming these competing approaches and standard baselines in classifying relations between arguments. These results make explicit the value of incorporating relational insights from knowledge graphs into AM tasks, particularly in domains as complex as political debates. By bridging the strengths of KGEMs and LMs, this study sets a new benchmark for argument relation prediction in highly challenging datasets.

6 Conclusion

This paper introduces a novel hybrid framework for predicting relations between argument components in argumentation graphs, combining structural insights from KGEMs with contextual understanding from fine-tuned LMs. We showed that KGEMs, despite their traditional use in KG's tasks, achieve competitive performance in argument relation prediction. Our experiments with DistMult demonstrate that structural knowledge alone captures meaningful relational patterns, achieving a Macro F1-Score of 0.60 on the challenging standard *ElecDeb60to20* benchmark for AM.

Integrating KGEMs with LMs significantly enhances the prediction accuracy. Using classifiers like Random Forests and CNNs to combine predictions, our approach achieved SOTA performance. Notably, we improved the Macro F1-Score to 0.68 with RoBERTa and further to 0.73 with DeBERTa-V3, representing a significant gain over prior SOTA methods (Goffredo et al., 2023a).

Our ensemble method integrates multiple models, highlighting the value of combining structural and contextual knowledge to improve AM tasks in complex domains like political debates.

Limitations

Our approach has been tested on the *ElecDeb60to20* dataset, which consists of U.S. presidential debates only. While this dataset is well-suited for our current study, it does not guarantee that the model will perform equally well on other types of debates, argumentative genres, or in different domains or languages. However, it is worth noticing that *ElecDeb60to20*, and more generally the political debates scenario, represent one of the most challenging argumentation data to test AM models against. The model's effectiveness may also be compromised by varying strategic communication styles across different countries or cultural contexts. We recognize the need for additional experiments across diverse datasets to assess and potentially improve the model's adaptability.

Lastly, while our method separates the training of KGEMs and LLMs, it does not fully leverage the potential benefits of integrated approaches. In future work, we plan to explore hybrid training approaches, such as KEPLER (Wang et al., 2021b), that concurrently optimize KGEMs and language modelling objectives, with the aim to further strengthen the alignment between argument structure and content.

Acknowledgments

We thank Pierre Monnin for his insights regarding this work. This work has been supported by the French government, through the 3IA Cote d'Azur Investments in the project managed by the National Research Agency (ANR) with the reference number ANR-23-IACL-0001.

References

Mehdi Ali, Max Berrendorf, Charles Tapley Hoyt, Laurent Vermue, Sahand Sharifzadeh, Volker Tresp, and Jens Lehmann. 2021. Pykeen 1.0: A python library for training and evaluating knowledge graph embeddings. *J. Mach. Learn. Res.*, 22:82:1–82:6.

Sakshi Arora, Ajay Rana, and Archana Singh. 2023. Argument mining: A categorical review. In *Modern Electronics Devices and Communication Systems: Select Proceedings of MEDCOM 2021*, pages 353–367. Springer.

Antoine Bordes, Nicolas Usunier, Alberto García-Durán, Jason Weston, and Oksana Yakhnenko. 2013. Translating embeddings for modeling multi-relational data. In *Advances in Neural Information Processing Systems 26: 27th Annual Conference on Neural Information Processing Systems 2013. Proceedings of a meeting held December 5-8, 2013, Lake Tahoe, Nevada, United States*, pages 2787–2795.

Elena Cabrio and Serena Villata. 2018. Five years of argument mining: a data-driven analysis. In *Proceedings of the Twenty-Seventh International Joint Conference on Artificial Intelligence, IJCAI 2018, July 13-19, 2018, Stockholm, Sweden*, pages 5427–5433. ijcai.org.

Zongsheng Cao, Qianqian Xu, Zhiyong Yang, and Qingming Huang. 2022. ER: equivariance regularizer for knowledge graph completion. In *Thirty-Sixth AAAI Conference on Artificial Intelligence, AAAI 2022, Thirty-Fourth Conference on Innovative Applications of Artificial Intelligence, IAAI 2022, The Twelveth Symposium on Educational Advances in Artificial Intelligence, EAAI 2022 Virtual Event, February 22 - March 1, 2022*, pages 5512–5520. AAAI Press.

Alexis Conneau, Kartikay Khandelwal, Naman Goyal, Vishrav Chaudhary, Guillaume Wenzek, Francisco Guzmán, Edouard Grave, Myle Ott, Luke Zettlemoyer, and Veselin Stoyanov. 2020. Unsupervised cross-lingual representation learning at scale. In *Proceedings of the 58th Annual Meeting of the Association for Computational Linguistics*, pages 8440–8451, Online. Association for Computational Linguistics.

Tim Dettmers, Pasquale Minervini, Pontus Stenetorp, and Sebastian Riedel. 2018. Convolutional 2d knowledge graph embeddings. In *Proceedings of the Thirty-Second AAAI Conference on Artificial Intelligence, (AAAI-18), the 30th innovative Applications of Artificial Intelligence (IAAI-18), and the 8th AAAI Symposium on Educational Advances in Artificial Intelligence (EAAI-18), New Orleans, Louisiana, USA, February 2-7, 2018*, pages 1811–1818. AAAI Press.

Jacob Devlin, Ming-Wei Chang, Kenton Lee, and Kristina Toutanova. 2019. BERT: Pre-training of deep bidirectional transformers for language understanding. In *Proceedings of the 2019 Conference of the North American Chapter of the Association for Computational Linguistics: Human Language Technologies, Volume 1 (Long and Short Papers)*, pages 4171–4186, Minneapolis, Minnesota. Association for Computational Linguistics.

Martin Drance, Fleur Mougin, Akka Zemmari, and Gayo Diallo. 2023. Pre-trained embeddings for enhancing multi-hop reasoning. In *International Joint Conference on Artificial Intelligence 2023 Workshop on Knowledge-Based Compositional Generalization*.

Stefano Faralli, Andrea Lenzi, and Paola Velardi. 2023. A benchmark study on knowledge graphs enrichment and pruning methods in the presence of noisy relationships. *J. Artif. Intell. Res.*, 78:37–68.

Debela Gemechu and Chris Reed. 2019. Decompositional argument mining: A general purpose approach for argument graph construction. In *Proceedings of the 57th Annual Meeting of the Association for Computational Linguistics*, pages 516–526, Florence, Italy. Association for Computational Linguistics.

Debela Gemechu, Ramon Ruiz-Dolz, and Chris Reed. 2024. ARIES: A general benchmark for argument relation identification. In *Proceedings of the 11th Workshop on Argument Mining (ArgMining 2024)*, pages 1–14, Bangkok, Thailand. Association for Computational Linguistics.

Pierpaolo Goffredo, Elena Cabrio, Serena Villata, Shohreh Haddadan, and Jhonatan Torres Sanchez. 2023a. Disputool 2.0: A modular architecture for multi-layer argumentative analysis of political debates. In *Thirty-Seventh AAAI Conference on Artificial Intelligence, AAAI 2023, Thirty-Fifth Conference on Innovative Applications of Artificial Intelligence, IAAI 2023, Thirteenth Symposium on Educational Advances in Artificial Intelligence, EAAI 2023, Washington, DC, USA, February 7-14, 2023*, pages 16431–16433. AAAI Press.

Pierpaolo Goffredo, Mariana Espinoza, Serena Villata, and Elena Cabrio. 2023b. Argument-based detection and classification of fallacies in political debates. In *Proceedings of the 2023 Conference on Empirical Methods in Natural Language Processing, EMNLP 2023, Singapore, December 6-10, 2023*, pages 11101–11112. Association for Computational Linguistics.

Pierpaolo Goffredo, Shohreh Haddadan, Vorakit Vorakitphan, Elena Cabrio, and Serena Villata. 2022. Fallacious argument classification in political debates. In *Proceedings of the Thirty-First International Joint Conference on Artificial Intelligence, IJCAI 2022, Vienna, Austria, 23-29 July 2022*, pages 4143–4149. ijcai.org.

Shohreh Haddadan, Elena Cabrio, and Serena Villata. 2019a. Disputool - A tool for the argumentative analysis of political debates. In *Proceedings of the Twenty-Eighth International Joint Conference on Artificial Intelligence, IJCAI 2019, Macao, China, August 10-16, 2019*, pages 6524–6526. ijcai.org.

Shohreh Haddadan, Elena Cabrio, and Serena Villata. 2019b. Yes, we can! mining arguments in 50 years of US presidential campaign debates. In *Proceedings of the 57th Annual Meeting of the Association for Computational Linguistics*, pages 4684–4690, Florence, Italy. Association for Computational Linguistics.

Shohreh Haddadan, Elena Cabrio, and Serena Villata. 2019c. Yes, we can! mining arguments in 50 years of US presidential campaign debates. In *Proceedings of the 57th Conference of the Association for Computational Linguistics, ACL 2019, Florence, Italy, July 28- August 2, 2019, Volume 1: Long Papers*, pages 4684–4690. Association for Computational Linguistics.

Pengcheng He, Jianfeng Gao, and Weizhu Chen. 2021. Debertav3: Improving deberta using electra-style pretraining with gradient-disentangled embedding sharing. *CoRR*, abs/2111.09543.

Khalid Al Khatib, Yufang Hou, Henning Wachsmuth, Charles Jochim, Francesca Bonin, and Benno Stein. 2020. End-to-end argumentation knowledge graph construction. In *The Thirty-Fourth AAAI Conference on Artificial Intelligence, AAAI 2020, The Thirty-Second Innovative Applications of Artificial Intelligence Conference, IAAI 2020, The Tenth AAAI Symposium on Educational Advances in Artificial Intelligence, EAAI 2020, New York, NY, USA, February 7-12, 2020*, pages 7367–7374. AAAI Press.

John Lawrence and Chris Reed. 2019. Argument mining: A survey. *Computational Linguistics*, 45(4):765–818.

Weichen Li, Patrick Abels, Zahra Ahmadi, Sophie Burkhardt, Benjamin Schiller, Iryna Gurevych, and Stefan Kramer. 2021. Topic-guided knowledge graph construction for argument mining. In *2021 IEEE International Conference on Big Knowledge, ICBK 2021, Auckland, New Zealand, December 7-8, 2021*, pages 315–322. IEEE.

Marco Lippi and Paolo Torroni. 2016. Argument mining from speech: Detecting claims in political debates. In *Proceedings of the Thirtieth AAAI Conference on Artificial Intelligence, February 12-17, 2016, Phoenix, Arizona, USA*, pages 2979–2985. AAAI Press.

Yinhan Liu, Myle Ott, Naman Goyal, Jingfei Du, Mandar Joshi, Danqi Chen, Omer Levy, Mike Lewis, Luke Zettlemoyer, and Veselin Stoyanov. 2019. Roberta: A robustly optimized BERT pretraining approach. *CoRR*, abs/1907.11692.

Eleonora Mancini, Federico Ruggeri, Andrea Galassi, and Paolo Torroni. 2022. Multimodal argument mining: A case study in political debates. In *Proceedings of the 9th Workshop on Argument Mining*, pages 158–170, Online and in Gyeongju, Republic of Korea. International Conference on Computational Linguistics.

Tobias Mayer, Santiago Marro, Elena Cabrio, and Serena Villata. 2021. Enhancing evidence-based medicine with natural language argumentative analysis of clinical trials. *Artif. Intell. Medicine*, 118:102098.

Stefano Menini, Elena Cabrio, Sara Tonelli, and Serena Villata. 2018. Never retreat, never retract: Argumentation analysis for political speeches. In *Proceedings of the Thirty-Second AAAI Conference on Artificial Intelligence, (AAAI-18), the 30th innovative Applications of Artificial Intelligence (IAAI-18), and the 8th AAAI Symposium on Educational Advances in Artificial Intelligence (EAAI-18), New Orleans, Louisiana, USA, February 2-7, 2018*, pages 4889–4896. AAAI Press.

Rafael Mestre, Razvan Milicin, Stuart E. Middleton, Matt Ryan, Jiatong Zhu, and Timothy J. Norman.

2021. M-arg: Multimodal argument mining dataset for political debates with audio and transcripts. In *Proceedings of the 8th Workshop on Argument Mining*, pages 78–88, Punta Cana, Dominican Republic. Association for Computational Linguistics.

Gaku Morio, Hiroaki Ozaki, Terufumi Morishita, and Kohsuke Yanai. 2022. End-to-end argument mining with cross-corpora multi-task learning. *Trans. Assoc. Comput. Linguistics*, 10:639–658.

Umer Mushtaq and Jérémie Cabessa. 2023. Argument mining with modular BERT and transfer learning. In *International Joint Conference on Neural Networks, IJCNN 2023, Gold Coast, Australia, June 18-23, 2023*, pages 1–8. IEEE.

Vlad Niculae, Joonsuk Park, and Claire Cardie. 2017. Argument mining with structured svms and rnns. In *Proceedings of the 55th Annual Meeting of the Association for Computational Linguistics, ACL 2017, Vancouver, Canada, July 30 - August 4, Volume 1: Long Papers*, pages 985–995. Association for Computational Linguistics.

F. Pedregosa, G. Varoquaux, A. Gramfort, V. Michel, B. Thirion, O. Grisel, M. Blondel, P. Prettenhofer, R. Weiss, V. Dubourg, J. Vanderplas, A. Passos, D. Cournapeau, M. Brucher, M. Perrot, and E. Duchesnay. 2011. Scikit-learn: Machine learning in Python. *Journal of Machine Learning Research*, 12:2825–2830.

Prakash Poudyal, Jaromir Savelka, Aagje Ieven, Marie Francine Moens, Teresa Goncalves, and Paulo Quaresma. 2020. ECHR: Legal corpus for argument mining. In *Proceedings of the 7th Workshop on Argument Mining*, pages 67–75, Online. Association for Computational Linguistics.

David Powers. 2011. Evaluation: From precision, recall and f-measure to roc, informedness, markedness & correlation. *Journal of Machine Learning Technologies*, 2(1):37–63.

Nils Reimers and Iryna Gurevych. 2019. Sentence-bert: Sentence embeddings using siamese bert-networks. In *Proceedings of the 2019 Conference on Empirical Methods in Natural Language Processing and the 9th International Joint Conference on Natural Language Processing, EMNLP-IJCNLP 2019, Hong Kong, China, November 3-7, 2019*, pages 3980–3990. Association for Computational Linguistics.

Ramon Ruiz-Dolz, José Alemany, Stella Heras Barberá, and Ana García-Fornes. 2021. Transformer-based models for automatic identification of argument relations: A cross-domain evaluation. *IEEE Intell. Syst.*, 36(6):62–70.

Ameer Saadat-Yazdi, Jeff Z. Pan, and Nadin Kökciyan. 2023. Uncovering implicit inferences for improved relational argument mining. In *Proceedings of the 17th Conference of the European Chapter of the Association for Computational Linguistics, EACL 2023, Dubrovnik, Croatia, May 2-6, 2023*, pages 2476–2487. Association for Computational Linguistics.

Victor Sanh, Lysandre Debut, Julien Chaumond, and Thomas Wolf. 2019. Distilbert, a distilled version of BERT: smaller, faster, cheaper and lighter. *CoRR*, abs/1910.01108.

Christian Stab and Iryna Gurevych. 2017. Parsing argumentation structures in persuasive essays. *Comput. Linguistics*, 43(3):619–659.

Jacky Visser, Barbara Konat, Rory Duthie, Marcin Koszowy, Katarzyna Budzynska, and Chris Reed. 2020a. Argumentation in the 2016 US presidential elections: annotated corpora of television debates and social media reaction. *Lang. Resour. Evaluation*, 54(1):123–154.

Jacky Visser, Barbara Konat, Rory Duthie, Marcin Koszowy, Katarzyna Budzynska, and Chris Reed. 2020b. Argumentation in the 2016 us presidential elections: annotated corpora of television debates and social media reaction. *Language Resources and Evaluation*, 54(1):123–154.

Meihong Wang, Linling Qiu, and Xiaoli Wang. 2021a. A survey on knowledge graph embeddings for link prediction. *Symmetry*, 13(3):485.

Xiaozhi Wang, Tianyu Gao, Zhaocheng Zhu, Zhengyan Zhang, Zhiyuan Liu, Juanzi Li, and Jian Tang. 2021b. KEPLER: A unified model for knowledge embedding and pre-trained language representation. *Trans. Assoc. Comput. Linguistics*, 9:176–194.

Thomas Wolf, Lysandre Debut, Victor Sanh, Julien Chaumond, Clement Delangue, Anthony Moi, Pierric Cistac, Tim Rault, Rémi Louf, Morgan Funtowicz, et al. 2019. Huggingface's transformers: State-of-the-art natural language processing. arxiv. *arXiv preprint arXiv:1910.03771*.

Qi Yan, Jiaxin Fan, Mohan Li, Guanqun Qu, and Yang Xiao. 2022. A survey on knowledge graph embedding. In *7th IEEE International Conference on Data Science in Cyberspace, DSC 2022, Guilin, China, July 11-13, 2022*, pages 576–583. IEEE.

Bishan Yang, Wen-tau Yih, Xiaodong He, Jianfeng Gao, and Li Deng. 2015. Embedding entities and relations for learning and inference in knowledge bases. In *3rd International Conference on Learning Representations, ICLR 2015, San Diego, CA, USA, May 7-9, 2015, Conference Track Proceedings*.

Jian Yuan, Zhongyu Wei, Donghua Zhao, Qi Zhang, and Changjian Jiang. 2021. Leveraging argumentation knowledge graph for interactive argument pair identification. In *Findings of the Association for Computational Linguistics: ACL/IJCNLP 2021, Online Event, August 1-6, 2021*, volume ACL/IJCNLP 2021 of *Findings of ACL*, pages 2310–2319. Association for Computational Linguistics.

A LMs integration with KGEMs

To validate our approach, we conducted a comparative evaluation of several LMs to determine the most compatible with our architecture. Specifically, we evaluated DeBERTa-V3 (He et al., 2021), BERT (Devlin et al., 2019), DistilBERT (Sanh et al., 2019) and XLM-RoBERTa (Conneau et al., 2020). Results are reported in Table 8.

Model	Method	Macro F1 Score
DeBERTa	**seq-class**	**0.69**
BERT	sent-class	0.66
XLM-RoBERTa	seq-class	0.63
DistilBERT	seq-class	0.58

Table 8: Macro F1-Score of several LMs for the AM Relation Prediction Task

We integrated DeBERTa-V3 into our architecture due to its superior performance compared to other models.

B Hyperparameters

This section details the optimal hyperparameters identified for the models employed in this study. These configurations were determined through extensive experimentation and validation to achieve the best performance for each model.

B.1 RoBERTa

Following the methodology outlined by Goffredo et al. (2023a), RoBERTa was fine-tuned with a learning rate of $6e^{-5}$, a batch size of 8, and a maximum sentence length of 64 sub-word tokens per input example. The model was trained for 15 epochs.

B.2 DeBERTa-V3

The DeBERTa-V3 model achieved optimal performance with a learning rate of $4e^{-5}$, a batch size of 16, and a maximum sentence length of 255 subword tokens. It was fine-tuned over 3 epochs.

B.3 DistMult

The DistMult model's optimal configuration was obtained after 165 epochs. It used a learning rate of $1.35e^{-2}$, a batch size of 128, an embedding dimension of 160, and a margin ranking loss with a margin of 2.99.

B.4 Random Forest Classifier (RFC)

The RFC achieved its best performance using 50 estimators, the Gini criterion, a minimum of 2 samples required to split an internal node, and a minimum of 1 sample per leaf.

B.5 Convolutional Neural Network (CNN)

The CNN was evaluated using cross-validation with 30 epochs for each fold, a learning rate of $1e^{-3}$, an embedding dimension of 100 for the textual features, and a batch size of 32.

On Integrating LLMs Into an Argument Annotation Workflow

Robin Schaefer
Applied Computational Linguistics / University of Potsdam / Germany
Bundesdruckerei GmbH / Berlin / Germany
`firstnamelastname@mailbox.org`

Abstract

Given the recent success of LLMs across different NLP tasks, their usability for data annotation has become a promising area of research. In this work, we investigate to what extent LLMs can be used as annotators for argument components and their semantic types in German tweets through a series of experiments combining different models and prompt configurations. Each prompt is constructed from modular components, such as class definitions or contextual information. Our results suggest that LLMs can indeed perform argument annotation, particularly of semantic argument types, if provided with precise class definitions. However, a fine-tuned BERT baseline remains a strong contender, often matching or exceeding LLM performance. These findings highlight the importance of considering not only model performance, but also ecological and financial costs when defining an annotation workflow.

1 Introduction

Over the last decade, Argument Mining (AM) has developed into a versatile research area. While early work focused on basic tasks such as claim (Daxenberger et al., 2017), evidence (Rinott et al., 2015) and relation detection (Carstens and Toni, 2015), more recent research focused on the analysis of argument quality (Wachsmuth et al., 2024) and strategies (Schaefer et al., 2023). Text domain can be identified as another dimension of variance. Early AM research was usually applied to rather formal texts, e.g. persuasive essays (Stab and Gurevych, 2017). Following this early trend, the focus somewhat shifted to include user-generated text domains, e.g. ChangeMyView (Al Khatib et al., 2020) or Twitter (Schaefer and Stede, 2021).

While these different subareas and -tasks of AM include their own challenges, they usually have in common a need for reliably annotated data, which is reflected in a substantial amount of work focused at least in part on annotation. With data scarcity being a common bottleneck in NLP tasks, recent research has focused on the question to what extent large language models (LLMs) can be leveraged for data annotation. Although not explicitly designed for classification, LLMs, being autoregressive models, can be prompted to function as annotators in classification settings. Since research has shown that modern LLMs perform well in zero-shot scenarios (Kojima et al., 2022), they are less dependent on annotated corpora compared to encoder-only models like BERT (Devlin et al., 2019), which require task-specific fine-tuning.

In this study, we investigate to what extent LLMs can be utilized as annotators for argumentation. In particular, we focus on Argument Component Type Classification (ACTC) both in a coarse-grained, i.e. claim and evidence, and in a fine-grained sense, i.e. semantic argument types. We use the GerCCT corpus as a starting point, our German tweet dataset, which has previously been expert annotated for argument components and their semantic types (Schaefer and Stede, 2022). We developed an extensive list of *experimental settings* consisting of an LLM and a prompt. We applied three popular open-weight models of different sizes, namely Llama-3.2-3B, Mixtral-8x7B, and Llama-3.3-70B. Each prompt was constructed from a number of modular components, e.g., class definitions or contextual information. We conducted experiments to identify the ideal combination of LLM and prompt to solve the annotation task and conclude this paper with a discussion of our results as well as the necessary aspects to consider when integrating LLMs into an argument annotation workflow.

This paper is structured as follows. In Section 2 we present the related work, before describing the corpus and the original approach in Section 3. In Section 4 we focus on our experiments, methods, and results. We discuss our findings in Section 5, before concluding the paper in Section 6.

Proceedings of the 12th Argument Mining Workshop, pages 87–99
July 31, 2025 ©2025 Association for Computational Linguistics

2 Related Work

Our work mainly falls into three areas of study: 1) AM on Twitter, 2) applying LLMs in AM scenarios, and 3) using LLMs as annotators.

AM on Twitter. AM on Twitter has been investigated in a number of studies, usually with a focus on creating datasets. Bosc et al. (2016) annotated 4,000 tweets for argumentativeness as well as for relations between tweets. Addawood and Bashir (2016) annotated 3,000 tweets with a set of evidence types, e.g. news or expert opinion. An SVM approach trained on a mixed feature set performed best in classification experiments. Bhatti et al. (2021) annotated a large tweet corpus with different premise classes with respect to a claim hashtag. Best classification results were obtained using a fine-tuned BERT model. Wührl and Klinger (2021) annotated 1,200 tweets in the biomedical domain for explicit and implicit claims, as well as conducted classification experiments. More recently, Feger and Dietze (2024) applied a pre-classification fine-tuning approach to BERTweet (Nguyen et al., 2020) for the classification of reasoning and factual content in full Twitter conversations. They used contrastive loss and text augmentation in a Siamese network, which yielded high results.

LLMs for AM. Given the recent prominence of LLMs across various NLP tasks, work has been conducted in the field of AM as well. Al Zubaer et al. (2023) used GPT-3.5-Turbo and GPT-4 and few-shot prompting for conclusion and premise detection in a legal context. They found that both models could not compete with a BERT model and argued that this might be due to the LLMs not being domain-specifically fine-tuned and their sensitivity to prompt phrasing. Abkenar et al. (2024) tested the suitability of different Mistral and Llama variants for argument component and relation classification by applying them to previously published AM corpora. They reported that LLMs yielded better results for relation classification. They further found that providing additional context had a mixed effect on model performance. Cabessa et al. (2025) fine-tuned several (quantized) open-weight LLMs and applied them to several AM datasets. They reported state-of-the-art results across different tasks, including argument component and relation classification. Similarly, Gorur et al. (2025) showed that a set of open-weight and proprietary LLMs applied to eleven datasets performed well for relation classification in a few-shot scenario. Mixtral-8x7B yielded best results with Llama2-70B ranging second. Altemeyer et al. (2025) applied GPT-4o to different frameworks of argument summarization and reported good results. They further evaluated the output for *coverage* and *redundancy* using, among other approaches, GPT-4o-mini, which yielded high correlation with human judgments. Favero et al. (2025) investigated the applicability of (fine-tuned) small LLMs to the tasks of argument segmentation, classification and quality assessment in student essays. They showed that fine-tuning improved results for segmentation and classification compared to a few-shot approach without fine-tuning, but worsened results for quality assessment. Also working on essays, Stahl et al. (2024) explored the usability of different zero-shot and few-shot prompts for essay scoring and feedback generation via LLMs. While generated feedback proved to be helpful, it did not appear to have a strong effect on scoring. Wachsmuth et al. (2024) discussed the potential of LLMs for assessing argument quality and proposed to feed models with instructions inspired by argumentation theory during fine-tuning.

LLMs for data annotation. Similar to their application to AM tasks, LLMs also have been used in data annotation scenarios. Early work by Gilardi et al. (2023) showed that ChatGPT exceeded the performance of crowdworkers in tweets and news data across different tasks, e.g., topic annotation. Pavlovic and Poesio (2024) used an LLM to generate opinion distributions for different corpora and found that these distributions notably diverged from human annotations. Bibal et al. (2025) used GPT-4o in an iterative workflow to both annotate a named entity dataset and refine the annotation guidelines based on these annotations, yielding improved inter-annotator agreement compared to the original guidelines. Mirzakhmedova et al. (2024) applied LLMs to the task of argument quality annotation and reported that PaLM 2 produced labels that were moderately consistent with human annotations, compared to GPT-3.5-Turbo which showed a more divergent outcome. Gligorić et al. (2025) used LLM annotations and generated confidence scores to guide human annotation. Both LLM and human annotations were combined to calculate statistical estimates of different quantities of interest. Bavaresco et al. (2024) evaluated the annotation results of eleven LLMs on 20 NLP datasets and found that models exhibited notable variance with respect to their performance, thus suggesting the need for careful validation of the models' capabilities.

While a certain overlap exists to previous studies, our work differs by 1) applying LLMs to an annotation task in tweets, 2) focusing on German data as opposed to the primary usage of English data in the literature, and 3) conducting extensive experimentation using a set of prompts constructed from a number of relevant modular components, e.g., class definitions and context.

3 Corpus and Original Approach

Starting point for our work is our previously published GerCCT corpus (Schaefer and Stede, 2022). The corpus is an annotated subset of a larger German tweet dataset with a focus on climate change discourse and consists of 1,200 tweet pairs in a *reply to* relationship. While the reply tweet has been annotated, the so-called source tweet has been used as additional context during annotation.

The corpus contains expert annotations on the full tweet level of semantic argument types, called *argument properties* in our original paper, which each fall into the category of either claim or evidence. Claim types are *unverifiable claim* and *verifiable claim*. Evidence types are *reason* and *external evidence*.[1] This is a translated example from the original paper: *"You cannot negotiate with nature. This is why you cannot prepare a climate protection package like a trade agreement. It's about science and its laws are non-negotiable. [...]"*, which has been annotated as containing the types *unverifiable claim*, *verifiable claim*, and *reason*.

We further used the argument type annotations to derive argument component annotations, i.e. claim and evidence, as well as the general +/- argumentative class, thus resulting in three layers of argument annotation consisting of seven classes in total. We use all layers in this work. See Table 1 for an overview of argument classes and their annotation proportions.

In addition to argument annotation, the corpus has also been labeled for toxic language as well as sarcasm. Importantly, in the original approach argumentative and toxic language are considered to be mutually exclusive, that is, a toxic tweet cannot contain argumentation. Given this rule, we consider the detection of toxic language as an important factor. However, in this work, we do not pay attention to sarcasm detection.

Layer	Class	Proportion
1st	Argument	.70
2nd	Claim	.65
2nd	Evidence	.25
3rd	Unverifiable Claim	.59
3rd	Verifiable Claim	.20
3rd	Reason	.11
3rd	External Evidence	.14

Table 1: Argument classes and their proportions as annotated by Schaefer and Stede (2022). Each value represents the proportion of tweets that have been annotated with the respective class, i.e. the proportions do not add up to one.

In the original study, we used the annotated corpus to train models for ACTC. We applied different approaches with a fine-tuned BERT (*bert-base-german-cased*)[2] model yielding best results for argument classes. In this study, we use the majority baseline and the BERT results as baselines.

4 Experiments

In this study, we investigate to what extent LLMs can be used as annotators for ACTC tasks, i.e. for the annotation of argument components and their semantic types. We approach this question via different *experimental settings*. Each setting is defined by an LLM and a prompt. Each prompt is constructed of various modular components, including, for example, the addition of class definitions or context. Our complete list of experimental settings is shown in Table 3.

In the following, we present the models and prompts we used in our experiments. We continue with a description of our inference runs we conducted by applying Mixtral-8x7B to every combination of prompt and class. We then used the macro F1 scores we obtained from these runs to identify the best performing prompts, which we finally used with Llama-3.2-3B and Llama-3.3-70B.[3] We performed permutation tests for statistical significance

[1] Note that the original annotations also include the argument type *internal evidence*. However, given that we did not include it in our previous classification experiments due to it being rarely annotated, we do not use it in this study either.

[2] `https://huggingface.co/google-bert/bert-base-german-cased`

[3] Given the substantial carbon emissions of LLMs (Wu et al., 2025) we decided to run the full set of experiments only with Mixtral-8x7B.

Model	Vendor	Release
Llama-3.2-3B	Meta AI	Sept 25, 2024
Mixtral-8x7B	Mistral AI	Dec 11, 2023
Llama-3.3-70B	Meta AI	Dec 6, 2024

Table 2: Large language models (ordered by size). The *B* in the model name refers to the number of parameters in billion.

testing and conclude this section with a description of the results.

Models. We made use of three LLMs of different sizes: Llama-3.2-3B, Mixtral-8x7B[4], and Llama-3.3-70B (see Table 2). By adding model size as a variable, we could conduct more fine-grained analyses with respect to the effect of parameter count. All models are open-weight and multilingual including German. We used Groq[5] for inference, which quantizes model weights to 8 bits, while still running calculations in 16 bits. We set the model temperature to 0. For simplicity, we refer to these models as *Llama-3B*, *Mixtral*, and *Llama-70B*.

Prompts. Each prompt can be described as a combination of components (or their absence) that are selected to enable the LLM to perform the task (see Appendix A for an example). In the following, we will describe each component in detail. Every setting is defined as *zero-shot*, i.e. we decided to not add annotation examples to the prompt to support the LLM. Also, in every setting we provide the respective reply tweet and the name of the class at hand and prompt the LLM to binarily annotate a tweet with the label 1 or 0, e.g., +/- claim. Beginning with this general structure, we continue to build a prompt as follows. First, we may insert additional helpful information in the form of context or class definitions. *Context* refers to the source tweet in a tweet pair, i.e. to the tweet that was not annotated but was used as additional context by the expert annotators in Schaefer and Stede (2022). By adding a source tweet we try to simulate the conditions under which the original annotation took place. We add the class definition by providing a translated version of the definitions given in the annotation scheme of the original paper (see Appendix B for the class definitions). While we tried to stay as close to the annotation scheme as possible, we had to perform minor adjustments in order to facilitate the task for the LLM.

In addition to inserting further information to the prompt, we may task the LLM to ignore tweets containing toxic language when performing the annotation. Recall that in our previous study we decided not to annotate argumentation in toxic tweets. As this decision may be somewhat unintuitive, an LLM could benefit from being explicitly prompted to pay attention to toxic language. Finally, as Röttger et al. (2024) showed, outcomes of LLMs may be affected by an open vs forced-choice setting. While we enforce the model to binarily label a tweet, in some prompts we ask it to justify its decision, thereby giving it space to argue its case.

In total, we designed 14 prompts with different characteristics. We used a small subset of the corpus (n: 50) and Mixtral to identify challenges in prompt phrasing, as well as in transferring the annotation scheme into a form that can be leveraged by an LLM. We eventually arrived at a number of *building blocks*, i.e. succinct instructions and placeholders, e.g. the definition of a specific class, which we combined into prompts, depending on the requirements of the respective setting.

Inference. Having constructed our full set of prompts, we proceeded with running inference. We prompted Mixtral to individually label each tweet of the corpus with every class, according to each experimental setting we defined, resulting in $1,200 \times 7 \times 14$ inference calls. We postprocessed the generated output with regular expressions to extract the class label. We applied a simple heuristic of extracting the first integer from the output string. If the first integer was not 0 or 1 we labeled the negative class, i.e. 0. Afterward, we calculated macro F1 by using the original annotations as gold standard.

To identify the best performing prompts, we ranked them according to their performance as reflected by their macro F1 scores. We selected the best performing prompt for the claim classes and the evidence classes, respectively, and utilized them to label the corpus with Llama-3B and Llama-70B, resulting in four additional experimental settings. We again performed postprocessing and evaluation as described. Our F1 scores are shown in Table 3.

[4]Mixtral-8x7B is a Mixture-of-Experts model. Rather than representing a single 56B parameter model, it consists of eight distinct 7B expert models, of which only a subset is activated during inference. The selection of active expert models is governed a *gating network* and depends on the respective input prompt.

[5]`https://groq.com/`

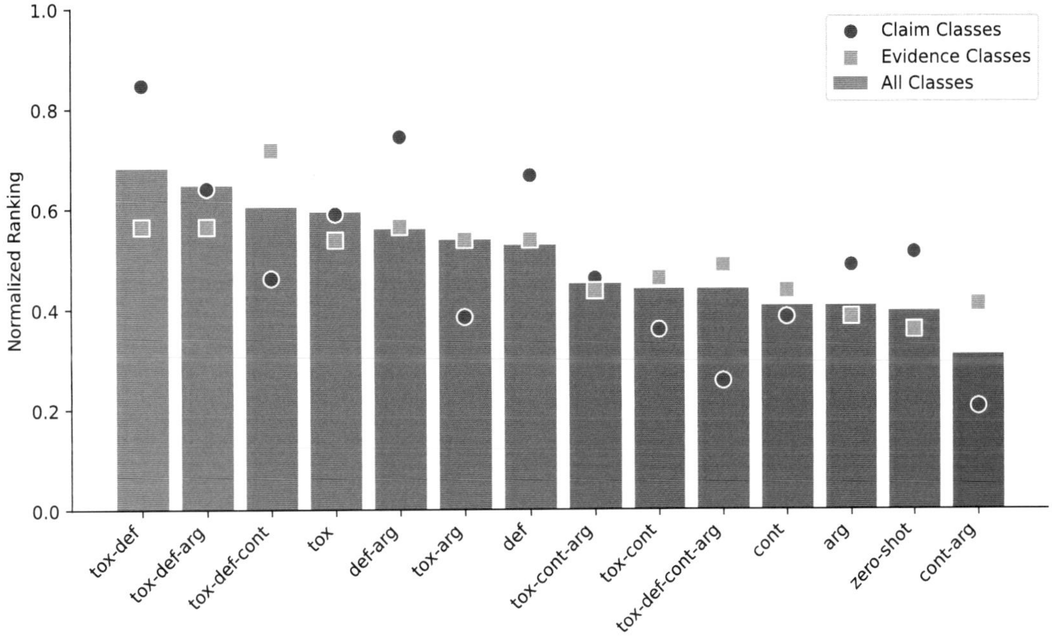

Figure 1: Normalized ranking of prompts for all classes (bars), claim classes (dots), and evidence classes (squares).

Prompt Ranking. In order to identify the most promising prompts to use for the annotation task, we ranked them as follows. Given a set of prompts P and a set of classes C, where $|P| = 14$ and $|C| = 7$, we assign to each prompt a ranking score R_p, which we calculate as:

$$R_p = \sum_{c \in C} r_{p,c}$$

where $r_{p,c}$ is the rank of prompt p for class c. Each rank is assigned with respect to the macro F1 of prompt p for class c, in descending order. We applied min-max normalization to rescale the ranking scores to the range $[0, 1]$. The minimum ranking score is defined as $R_{min} = |C|$ and the maximum ranking score is defined as $R_{max} = |C| \times |P|$. In addition to ranking scores for the entire set of classes, we also calculated scores for claim and evidence subsets, respectively, where $|C| = 3$, e.g., *claim*, *unverifiable claim*, and *verifiable claim*.

The prompt ranking is shown in Figure 1. When analyzing the ranking for the full set of classes, depicted as bars in the figure, we found the following pattern. While both the identification of toxic language and the addition of class definitions tended to have a benefiting effect, simplistic prompts that only contain context or ask the model to argue its decision could not compete. However, just prompting the model to consider toxic language when making a decision resulted in a decent ranking position.

Turning to the analyzes for the claim and evidence class subsets, we found that claim classes showed a substantially higher variance than evidence classes (SD: 0.18 vs 0.09). We further found that *tox-def* performed best for claim classes, while for evidence classes *tox-def-cont* yielded the best ranking position. We thus consider these prompts as the most promising for argument component and type annotation via LLM.[6]

Permutation Testing. We calculated statistical significance by running permutation tests on the comparison of the BERT baseline and the best performing experimental setting per class. To this end, we simulated the output of the BERT model by iteratively flipping labels starting from the gold standard until the desired macro F1 score was obtained, e.g., 0.73 for the claim class. To achieve reliable results, we simulated the output of the BERT model one hundred times per class.

We then ran two-sided permutation tests using each of the one hundred simulations and the output of the best performing experimental setting per

[6]Note that *tox-def-arg* ranked second for the full class set. However, we only utilized the prompts with Llama-3B and Llama-70B that ranked highest for the claim and evidence sets, respectively.

Setting	Model	Argument	Claim	Evidence	UC	VC	Reason	EE
baseline	majority	.41	.40	.43	.37	.44	.47	.46
baseline	BERT	**.70**	**.73**	**.77**	.70	.69	.60	.86
tox-def	Llama-3B	.24	.29	.44	.37	.47	.53	.48
tox-def-cont	Llama-3B	.23	.26	.44	.30	.44	.48	.49
zero-shot	Mixtral	.53	.61	.51	.55	.70	.61	.52
arg	Mixtral	.55	.60	.52	.58	.70	.60	.52
cont	Mixtral	.59	.59	.56	.59	.61	.53	.53
def	Mixtral	.50	.61	.51	.59	.70	.59	.69
tox	Mixtral	.65	.61	.55	.61	.57	.56	.55
cont-arg	Mixtral	.58	.56	.55	.57	.59	.55	.53
def-arg	Mixtral	.48	.62	.54	.59	.71	.58	.68
tox-arg	Mixtral	.66	.59	.56	.62	.54	.55	.54
tox-cont	Mixtral	.64	.61	.58	.39	.57	.48	.54
tox-def	Mixtral	.63	.63	.54	.62	.62	.53	.71
tox-cont-arg	Mixtral	.63	.61	.57	.61	.55	.50	.54
tox-def-arg	Mixtral	.66	.59	.56	.64	.63	.50	.71
tox-def-cont	Mixtral	.65	.60	.58	.61	.59	.51	.70
tox-def-cont-arg	Mixtral	.65	.57	.57	.61	.57	.48	.68
tox-def	Llama-70B	.53	.71	.66	**.72**	.68	**.64**	**.90**
tox-def-cont	Llama-70B	.66	.72	.63	.69	**.72**	.61	.88

Table 3: Macro F1 scores by experimental setting and class. The baseline results are taken from Schaefer and Stede (2022) (UC: unverifiable claim; VC: verifiable claim; EE: external evidence).

class. We conducted 10,000 permutations per test and used the difference in macro F1 as the test statistic. The null hypothesis (H_0) assumes that both BERT and LLM outputs are sampled from the same distribution, i.e. observed differences are due to chance. We report the mean of p-values and the percentage of p-values < 0.05 (see Table 4).

Results. We report macro F1 scores (see Table 3) for comparison with the majority and BERT baselines taken from our previous study. To begin with, we found that in most experimental settings the majority baseline was surpassed. Only the smallest model Llama-3B appeared to be unable to sufficiently solve the task with *tox-def-cont* performing worse than *tox-def*.

Mixtral, on the other hand, showed mixed results with respect to the class at hand. While, for the general argument class, it could compete with Llama-70B *tox-def-cont* in some settings, F1 scores ranging from 0.63 to 0.66, and even outperformed Llama-70B *tox-def* in most settings, the claim and evidence component classes appeared to be more challenging. There Mixtral showed a substantial distance to Llama-70B, especially for the claim class. Turning to the semantic type classes, we found that Mixtral yielded mediocre results for *unverifiable claim* with most settings ranging between 0.57 and 0.62. For *verifiable claim*, however, we found that Mixtral mildly exceeded the BERT baseline using the following comparatively simplistic prompts: *def-arg*, *def*, *arg*, or *zero-shot*. Neither of these scores, however, were statistically significant. With respect to *reason*, some Mixtral settings were able to compete with the BERT baseline, while for *external evidence* Mixtral performed substantially worse than both Llama-70B and BERT.

Llama-70B yielded the best F1 scores of all LLMs. This was achieved primarily by using the *tox-def* prompt. However, *tox-def-cont* notably outperformed *tox-def* for the general argument class (0.66 vs 0.53) and also showed better results for *verifiable claim* (0.72 vs 0.68). With respect to the BERT baseline, Llama-70B surpassed it in all semantic type classes, while BERT yielded better results for the argument component and general argument classes.

We conclude Section 4 with our permutation test results (see Table 4), where we report mean p-values per class as well as the percentage of p-values < 0.05. We found that $p < 0.05$ for both

Class	BERT	LLM	P-Value	
Argument	.70	.66	.035*	100%
Claim	.73	.72	.571	0%
Evidence	.77	.66	≈ 0***	100%
UC	.70	.72	.392	0%
VC	.69	.72	.145	0%
Reason	.60	.64	.048*	67%
EE	.86	.90	.035*	100%

Table 4: Permutation test results: mean of p-value and percentage of p-values < 0.05 (* p < 0.05, *** p < 0.001). For convenience, we show the best LLM results as well as the BERT baseline.

reason and *external evidence*, thus indicating a statistically significant difference in model performance. From the F1 scores we can conclude that this difference is driven by Llama-70B outperforming BERT. However, we failed to reject the null hypothesis for *unverifiable claim* and *verifiable claim*. Considering the argument component classes, we found evidence for a significant effect for the evidence class ($p < 0.001$), while we again failed to reject H_0 for the claim class. The argument class, on the other hand, also yielded $p < 0.05$. Thus, for *argument* and *evidence* we can conclude that BERT significantly surpassed Llama-70B given the respective F1 scores. With respect to the percentages of p-values < 0.05, we found a rather binary pattern. Statistically significant classes showed a percentage of 100% of p-values < 0.05 with the exception of *reason* (67%), thereby indicating a less reliable effect for this class. In those cases where we failed to reject the null hypothesis on average, we did not find any cases of p-values < 0.05.

5 Discussion

LLMs do not necessarily outperform BERT. While we provided evidence for LLMs being able to solve the task of argument annotation in specific experimental settings, we did not find that they outperformed the BERT baseline per se. Furthermore, we observed for the semantic types *unverifiable* and *verifiable claim* that advantages of using an LLM instead of BERT might be actually due to chance, since we failed to reject H_0. We also found that the BERT approach significantly outperformed the best LLM setting for the general argument class as well as the evidence class. Our results are thus in line with mixed results previously reported in the literature (Mirzakhmedova et al., 2024; Stahl et al., 2024).

Importantly, we do not consider a statistically significant effect as a prerequisite to employ an LLM to the annotation task, given that utilizing BERT also failed to significantly exceed the performance of the best LLM setting for most classes. Thus, we interpret the performance of both approaches to be similar enough to warrant their implementation. However, we suggest that the absent dominance of the LLM approach is a strong argument in favor of keeping *the human in the loop*. Since efficiently prompting an LLM is not a trivial task, we argue that precise annotation guidelines, developed by (human) experts as well as thoroughly validated by using annotator agreement metrics, e.g., Krippendorff's α, are necessary to ensure reliability and confidence in the annotations. Provided with these guidelines, an LLM may be capable of performing the remainder of the annotations.

Providing definitions is essential. Our results indicate that providing definitions of classes has a beneficial effect, as shown by the better ranking of prompts that include definitions. This is especially the case for the best performing prompts *tox-def* and *tox-def-cont*. We argue that providing definitions may be especially necessary for argumentation, as argument categories, e.g. claim, tend to have a common meaning which differs from their more formal definition in the context of AM. Further our results suggest that class definitions need to be precise. While using Llama-70B led to best results for all argument properties, i.e. for those classes with rather concise definitions, it performed worse for argument components and the general argument class. We argue that this may be due to their definitions being more complex since they are essentially combinations of the simpler semantic type definitions.

With respect to the other prompt components, we find our assumption confirmed by the prompt ranking that toxic language detection indeed has a positive effect on the results. This is intuitive given the definition of argumentation in the annotation guidelines. In contrast, our prompt ranking further hints that providing additional context does not benefit the results. Although one of the best performing prompts does include context, i.e. *tox-def-cont*, we argue that its good performance mainly results from the combination of toxic language detection and class definitions, given that the prompt *tox-def* appeared to yield better results for most classes. We suggest that this might be due to the context having a deviating effect on the model, as it needs to process another piece of text, which does not need to be labeled. Finally, we fail to find an effect of prompting an LLM to justify its decision. However, we still consider this to be potentially helpful, as it enables the researcher to interpret the model output.

Model size matters. One main outcome of our experiments is the apparent importance of model size. While the medium-sized Mixtral model yielded good results in some experimental settings, even the majority baseline proved to be a challenge for Llama-3B. Best results were consistently achieved by Llama-70B, which, however, does not imply that it outperforms the BERT baseline, as we have previously discussed.

These findings are in line with previous research indicating that a larger number of parameters enables LLMs to more efficiently capture both semantic nuances which are prevalent in a subjective task such as argumentation as well as complexity of contextual information. It further suggests that better results can be obtained by applying models of size $> 70B$ to the task. However, this is a mere hypothesis and requires rigorous testing given that argument annotation remains a challenging task.

It also raises the question to what extent the completion of a task justifies the added resources associated with employing increasingly large models. An alternative approach would to be to improve the performance of smaller models, so-called *small language models*. While our results show that Llama-3B is not suitable to solve the task, more research in this direction may result in higher model performance, while keeping energy consumption at a lower rate.

Resources should be considered. Data annotation tends to be expensive in terms of financial and ecological resources. The classic approach is to train a group of expert annotators to solve the task by following a set of clearly defined annotation guidelines. As these guidelines need to be validated, several ratings per data point are required, thus potentially rendering the annotation of a corpus a costly endeavor.

On the other hand, training and running an LLM causes a substantial amount of carbon emissions, which requires ethical considerations. Wu et al. (2025) investigated the effect of model size, quantization, and hardware on carbon emissions. They found that smaller models tend to outperform larger ones with respect to carbon emissions with increasing request rates, while larger models benefit the most from quantization. In addition, older hardware tends to contain less embodied carbon than newer hardware. Both types of resource need to be considered in combination with model performance, in order to decide on the ideal approach for the task.

6 Conclusion

In this study, we investigated to what extent LLMs can be integrated into an argument annotation workflow, with a special focus on ACTC on tweets both on the level of argument components and semantic types. To this end, we defined experimental settings consisting of model and prompt and used Mixtral to identify the most promising prompts for the annotation task, i.e. *tox-def* and *tox-def-cont*, before utilizing them with Llama-3B and Llama-70B. In order to run permutation tests for significance testing between the BERT baseline and the best performing experimental settings, we simulated the output of the BERT model.

While we found the annotation task to be challenging for an LLM, we identified specific combinations of prompt and LLM that produced good results, especially for the classification of semantic types. However, we also found that a BERT model fine-tuned on human expert annotations was a strong contender, rendering the choice of the best approach a non-trivial one. We argued in favor of precise guidelines, ideally created and validated by human experts, as well as clear class definitions to facilitate the annotation task. Given the guidelines, an LLM could undertake the main part of the annotation. However, we also suggested considering the required resources, both financial and ecological, alongside model performance when deciding on the best approach to employ.

For future research, we are interested in testing the applicability of advanced prompting techniques such as few-shot and chain-of-thought prompting. In addition, approaching the annotation task in an open setting in combination with another LLM to make the final judgment, similar to the approach carried out in Röttger et al. (2024), could be a fruitful direction to follow. We also aim to extend our approach to capture more complex argumentation structures. Finally, we consider exploring label variation of LLMs to be a promising next research direction, both with respect to the annotation itself as well as the usability of label variation for classification (Plank, 2022).

Limitations

In our experiments, we made use of a single corpus. Extending the number of corpora both within the task of ACTC and across different AM tasks could give a clearer picture with respect to the usability of LLMs in an argument annotation workflow. Similarly, applying a larger number of LLMs may result in a more comprehensive understanding of the capabilities of these models.

This limitation also extends to the investigation of a single language, i.e. German. While being common in areas of NLP research that are not explicitly multilingual in nature, this raises the question to what extent the results generalize cross-linguistically.

So far, we have produced single LLM annotations and compared them to expert annotations of the corpus, thus creating a scenario of two annotators. The study may benefit from the generation of multiple LLM outputs that simulate the work of multiple human annotators.

Previous research has shown that LLMs tend to be sensitive to exact prompt phrasing (Röttger et al., 2024). While we defined different prompt settings, we did not create prompt variants within a setting. This could lead to more robust results.

Ethical Considerations

Previous research has shown that LLMs produce biases (Gallegos et al., 2024). While this is also true for other models and human annotators, this may result in skewed annotations, especially in argumentative texts which tend to deal with controversial topics. Applying LLMs to annotation tasks in less-resourced languages like German may increase these biases, as well as eventually using the annotated data for fine-tuning purposes, potentially resulting in a self-reinforcing feedback loop.

Furthermore, while automating data annotation via LLMs may be feasible, it also may result in the replacement of paid labor for human annotators, thereby having socioeconomic implications that should be considered when designing an annotation study.

Acknowledgments

We thank the anonymous reviewers for their valuable feedback.

References

Mohammad Yeghaneh Abkenar, Weixing Wang, Hendrik Graupner, and Manfred Stede. 2024. Assessing open-source large language models on argumentation mining subtasks. *Preprint*, arXiv:2411.05639.

Aseel Addawood and Masooda Bashir. 2016. "what is your evidence?" a study of controversial topics on social media. In *Proceedings of the Third Workshop on Argument Mining (ArgMining2016)*, pages 1–11, Berlin, Germany. Association for Computational Linguistics.

Khalid Al Khatib, Michael Völske, Shahbaz Syed, Nikolay Kolyada, and Benno Stein. 2020. Exploiting personal characteristics of debaters for predicting persuasiveness. In *Proceedings of the 58th Annual Meeting of the Association for Computational Linguistics*, pages 7067–7072, Online. Association for Computational Linguistics.

Abdullah Al Zubaer, Michael Granitzer, and Jelena Mitrović. 2023. Performance analysis of large language models in the domain of legal argument mining. *Frontiers in Artificial Intelligence*, 6.

Moritz Altemeyer, Steffen Eger, Johannes Daxenberger, Tim Altendorf, Philipp Cimiano, and Benjamin Schiller. 2025. Argument summarization and its evaluation in the era of large language models. *Preprint*, arXiv:2503.00847.

Anna Bavaresco, Raffaella Bernardi, Leonardo Bertolazzi, Desmond Elliott, Raquel Fernández, Albert Gatt, Esam Ghaleb, Mario Giulianelli, Michael Hanna, Alexander Koller, André F. T. Martins, Philipp Mondorf, Vera Neplenbroek, Sandro Pezzelle, Barbara Plank, David Schlangen, Alessandro Suglia, Aditya K Surikuchi, Ece Takmaz, and Alberto Testoni. 2024. Llms instead of human judges? a large scale empirical study across 20 nlp evaluation tasks. *Preprint*, arXiv:2406.18403.

Muhammad Mahad Afzal Bhatti, Ahsan Suheer Ahmad, and Joonsuk Park. 2021. Argument mining on Twitter: A case study on the planned parenthood debate. In *Proceedings of the 8th Workshop on Argument Mining*, pages 1–11, Punta Cana, Dominican Republic. Association for Computational Linguistics.

Adrien Bibal, Nathaniel Gerlek, Goran Muric, Elizabeth Boschee, Steven C. Fincke, Mike Ross, and Steven N. Minton. 2025. Automating annotation guideline improvements using LLMs: A case study. In *Proceedings of Context and Meaning: Navigating Disagreements in NLP Annotation*, pages 129–144, Abu Dhabi, UAE. International Committee on Computational Linguistics.

Tom Bosc, Elena Cabrio, and Serena Villata. 2016. DART: a dataset of arguments and their relations on Twitter. In *Proceedings of the Tenth International Conference on Language Resources and Evaluation (LREC'16)*, pages 1258–1263, Portorož, Slovenia. European Language Resources Association (ELRA).

Jérémie Cabessa, Hugo Hernault, and Umer Mushtaq. 2025. Argument mining with fine-tuned large language models. In *Proceedings of the 31st International Conference on Computational Linguistics*, pages 6624–6635, Abu Dhabi, UAE. Association for Computational Linguistics.

Lucas Carstens and Francesca Toni. 2015. Towards relation based argumentation mining. In *Proceedings of the 2nd Workshop on Argumentation Mining*, pages 29–34, Denver, CO. Association for Computational Linguistics.

Johannes Daxenberger, Steffen Eger, Ivan Habernal, Christian Stab, and Iryna Gurevych. 2017. What is the essence of a claim? cross-domain claim identification. In *Proceedings of the 2017 Conference on Empirical Methods in Natural Language Processing*, pages 2055–2066, Copenhagen, Denmark. Association for Computational Linguistics.

Jacob Devlin, Ming-Wei Chang, Kenton Lee, and Kristina Toutanova. 2019. BERT: Pre-training of deep bidirectional transformers for language understanding. In *Proceedings of the 2019 Conference of the North American Chapter of the Association for Computational Linguistics: Human Language Technologies, Volume 1 (Long and Short Papers)*, pages 4171–4186, Minneapolis, Minnesota. Association for Computational Linguistics.

Lucile Favero, Juan Antonio Pérez-Ortiz, Tanja Käser, and Nuria Oliver. 2025. Leveraging small llms for argument mining in education: Argument component identification, classification, and assessment. *Preprint*, arXiv:2502.14389.

Marc Feger and Stefan Dietze. 2024. BERTweet's TACO fiesta: Contrasting flavors on the path of inference and information-driven argument mining on Twitter. In *Findings of the Association for Computational Linguistics: NAACL 2024*, pages 2256–2266, Mexico City, Mexico. Association for Computational Linguistics.

Isabel O. Gallegos, Ryan A. Rossi, Joe Barrow, Md Mehrab Tanjim, Sungchul Kim, Franck Dernoncourt, Tong Yu, Ruiyi Zhang, and Nesreen K. Ahmed. 2024. Bias and fairness in large language models: A survey. *Computational Linguistics*, 50(3):1097–1179.

Fabrizio Gilardi, Meysam Alizadeh, and Maël Kubli. 2023. Chatgpt outperforms crowd workers for text-annotation tasks. *Proceedings of the National Academy of Sciences*, 120(30):e2305016120.

Kristina Gligorić, Tijana Zrnic, Cinoo Lee, Emmanuel J. Candès, and Dan Jurafsky. 2025. Can unconfident llm annotations be used for confident conclusions? *Preprint*, arXiv:2408.15204.

Deniz Gorur, Antonio Rago, and Francesca Toni. 2025. Can large language models perform relation-based argument mining? In *Proceedings of the 31st International Conference on Computational Linguistics*, pages 8518–8534, Abu Dhabi, UAE. Association for Computational Linguistics.

Takeshi Kojima, Shixiang Shane Gu, Machel Reid, Yutaka Matsuo, and Yusuke Iwasawa. 2022. Large language models are zero-shot reasoners. In *Proceedings of the 36th International Conference on Neural Information Processing Systems*, NIPS '22, Red Hook, NY, USA. Curran Associates Inc.

Nailia Mirzakhmedova, Marcel Gohsen, Chia Hao Chang, and Benno Stein. 2024. Are large language models reliable argument quality annotators? In *Robust Argumentation Machines*, pages 129–146, Cham. Springer Nature Switzerland.

Dat Quoc Nguyen, Thanh Vu, and Anh Tuan Nguyen. 2020. BERTweet: A pre-trained language model for English tweets. In *Proceedings of the 2020 Conference on Empirical Methods in Natural Language Processing: System Demonstrations*, pages 9–14, Online. Association for Computational Linguistics.

Maja Pavlovic and Massimo Poesio. 2024. The effectiveness of LLMs as annotators: A comparative overview and empirical analysis of direct representation. In *Proceedings of the 3rd Workshop on Perspectivist Approaches to NLP (NLPerspectives) @ LREC-COLING 2024*, pages 100–110, Torino, Italia. ELRA and ICCL.

Barbara Plank. 2022. The "problem" of human label variation: On ground truth in data, modeling and evaluation. In *Proceedings of the 2022 Conference on Empirical Methods in Natural Language Processing*, pages 10671–10682, Abu Dhabi, United Arab Emirates. Association for Computational Linguistics.

Ruty Rinott, Lena Dankin, Carlos Alzate Perez, Mitesh M. Khapra, Ehud Aharoni, and Noam Slonim. 2015. Show me your evidence - an automatic method for context dependent evidence detection. In *Proceedings of the 2015 Conference on Empirical Methods in Natural Language Processing*, pages 440–450, Lisbon, Portugal. Association for Computational Linguistics.

Paul Röttger, Valentin Hofmann, Valentina Pyatkin, Musashi Hinck, Hannah Kirk, Hinrich Schuetze, and Dirk Hovy. 2024. Political compass or spinning arrow? towards more meaningful evaluations for values and opinions in large language models. In *Proceedings of the 62nd Annual Meeting of the Association for Computational Linguistics (Volume 1: Long Papers)*, pages 15295–15311, Bangkok, Thailand. Association for Computational Linguistics.

Robin Schaefer, René Knaebel, and Manfred Stede. 2023. Towards fine-grained argumentation strategy analysis in persuasive essays. In *Proceedings of the 10th Workshop on Argument Mining*, pages 76–88, Singapore. Association for Computational Linguistics.

Robin Schaefer and Manfred Stede. 2021. Argument mining on Twitter: A survey. *it - Information Technology*, 63(1):45–58.

Robin Schaefer and Manfred Stede. 2022. GerCCT: An annotated corpus for mining arguments in German tweets on climate change. In *Proceedings of the Thirteenth Language Resources and Evaluation Conference*, pages 6121–6130, Marseille, France. European Language Resources Association.

Christian Stab and Iryna Gurevych. 2017. Parsing argumentation structures in persuasive essays. *Computational Linguistics*, 43(3):619–659.

Maja Stahl, Leon Biermann, Andreas Nehring, and Henning Wachsmuth. 2024. Exploring LLM prompting strategies for joint essay scoring and feedback generation. In *Proceedings of the 19th Workshop on Innovative Use of NLP for Building Educational Applications (BEA 2024)*, pages 283–298, Mexico City, Mexico. Association for Computational Linguistics.

Henning Wachsmuth, Gabriella Lapesa, Elena Cabrio, Anne Lauscher, Joonsuk Park, Eva Maria Vecchi, Serena Villata, and Timon Ziegenbein. 2024. Argument quality assessment in the age of instruction-following large language models. In *Proceedings of the 2024 Joint International Conference on Computational Linguistics, Language Resources and Evaluation (LREC-COLING 2024)*, pages 1519–1538, Torino, Italia. ELRA and ICCL.

Yanran Wu, Inez Hua, and Yi Ding. 2025. Unveiling environmental impacts of large language model serving: A functional unit view. *Preprint*, arXiv:2502.11256.

Amelie Wührl and Roman Klinger. 2021. Claim detection in biomedical Twitter posts. In *Proceedings of the 20th Workshop on Biomedical Language Processing*, pages 131–142, Online. Association for Computational Linguistics.

A Prompt Example

German version:
Du bist ein erfahrener Assistent für die Analyse von Argumentation im Text. Du bekommst einen Text, eine Argumentationskategorie, eine Definition der Argumentationskategorie und einen Kontext. Deine Aufgabe ist es zu entscheiden, ob der Text die Kategorie enthält oder nicht. Antworte mit 1, wenn die Kategorie vorhanden ist. Antworte mit 0, wenn die Kategorie nicht vorhanden ist. Wenn der Text toxische Sprache wie zum Beispiel Beleidigungen enthält, antworte auch mit 0. Berücksichtige den Kontext bei deiner Entscheidung. Nutze die Definition der Kategorie, um eine Entscheidung zu fällen. Begründe deine Antwort.

Kontext: ```{context}```

Argumentationskategorie: {category}

Definition der Argumentationskategorie: ```{definition}```

Text: {text}

English translation:
You are an experienced assistant for analyzing argumentation in text. You will be given a text, an argumentation category, a definition of the argumentation category, and a context. Your task is to decide whether the text contains the specified category or not. Answer with 1 if the category is present. Answer with 0 if the category is not present. If the text contains toxic language, such as insults, also answer with 0. Take the context into account when making your decision. Use the definition of the category to guide your judgment. Argue for your answer.

Context: ```{context}```

Argumentation category: {category}

Definition of the argumentation category: ```{definition}```

Text: {text}

Figure 2: The prompt for setting *tox-def-cont-arg*. It includes 1) the identification of toxic language, makes use of 2) class definitions and 3) context, as well as 4) asks the model to argue for its answer.

B Class Definitions

Class	Definition
Argument	An argument contains at least one claim or piece of evidence. A claim includes unverifiable claims and verifiable claims. An unverifiable claim is a subjective standpoint or positioning. A verifiable claim can potentially be verified by another source, such as scientific papers or statistics. Evidence is proof of an unverifiable claim or a verifiable claim. Types of evidence are external evidence or reason. External evidence includes, for example, news, expert opinions and quotations. External evidence is often provided via links. Evidence can also be reason, which means that it justifies an unverifiable claim or a verifiable claim.
Claim	A claim includes unverifiable claims and verifiable claims. An unverifiable claim is a subjective standpoint or positioning. A verifiable claim can potentially be verified via an external source, such as scientific references or statistics.
Evidence	Evidence is proof of an unverifiable claim or a verifiable claim. Types of evidence are external evidence or reason. External evidence includes, for example, news, expert opinions and quotations. External evidence is often provided via links. Evidence can also be reason, which means that it justifies an unverifiable claim or a verifiable claim.
UC	An unverifiable claim is a subjective standpoint, positioning, interpretation or prognosis. Although such a statement is unverifiable, it can still be sufficiently supported by providing reasons.
VC	A statement is considered a verifiable claim, if it can potentially be verified via an external source. However, it is not sufficient for a statement to be identified as verifiable by linguistic means alone. Potential sources for verifiable claims include, for example, scientific references, statistics, political manifestos and lexicon entries. Verifiable claims do not have to be factually correct.
Reason	Reason is a statement that justifies an unverifiable claim or a verifiable claim. The unverifiable claim or verifiable claim must also be present in the text. An unverifiable claim is a subjective standpoint or positioning. A verifiable claim can potentially be verified by an external source, such as scientific references or statistics. The connection between reason and an unverifiable claim or verifiable claim is often causal.
EE	External evidence is a source of proof for an unverifiable claim or a verifiable claim. An unverifiable claim is a subjective standpoint or positioning. A verifiable claim can potentially be verified by an external source, such as scientific references or statistics. External evidence does not have to be factually correct. External evidence must be explicitly present in the text. It includes, for example news, expert opinions, blog entries, books, petitions, images and quotations. External evidence is often provided via links, which is why links are considered external evidence.

Table 5: The class definitions. Each definition has been translated from the respective German version we used for prompting. (UC: unverifiable claim; VC: verifiable claim; EE: external evidence).

Practical Solutions to Practical Problems in Developing Argument Mining Systems

Debela Gemechu[1], Ramon Ruiz-Dolz[1], John Lawrence[1], Chris Reed[1]

[1]Centre for Argument Technology, University of Dundee

Abstract

The Open Argument Mining Framework (oAMF) addresses key challenges in argument mining research which still persist despite the field's impressive growth. Researchers often face difficulties with cross-system comparisons, incompatible representation languages, and limited access to reusable tools. The oAMF introduces a standardised yet flexible architecture that enables seamless component benchmarking, rapid pipeline prototyping using elements from diverse research traditions, and unified evaluation methodologies that preserve theoretical compatibility. By reducing technical overhead, the framework allows researchers to focus on advancing core argument mining capabilities rather than reimplementing infrastructure, fostering greater collaboration at a time when computational reasoning is increasingly vital in the era of large language models.

1 Introduction

Argument Mining (AM) represents one of the most intellectually stimulating frontiers in computational linguistics today. However, for researchers and practitioners in the AM community, several pain points have become increasingly apparent. First, the inherently modular nature of argument mining – comprising multiple interdependent subtasks – creates substantial difficulties when attempting to compare systems or integrate components from different research efforts. Second, even when technical integration is possible, conceptual interoperability is hindered by divergent representation languages that encode different theoretical assumptions about argument structure. Finally, despite the wealth of research publications, there is a notable scarcity of accessible, reusable tools, with many innovations remaining as isolated research prototypes (Chen et al., 2024; Habernal et al., 2024; Kawarada et al., 2024; Cabessa et al., 2025; Gorur et al., 2025a).

These challenges directly impact the daily work of argument mining researchers: How does one fairly compare a newly developed component against existing approaches? How can a task-specific module be efficiently integrated into an end-to-end system? What is the most effective way to evaluate and visualise results across different argument representations?

The Open Argument Mining Framework (oAMF) addresses these fundamental concerns by providing a standardised yet flexible architecture that facilitates module comparison, system integration, and consistent evaluation methodologies. Unlike previous approaches that have prioritised specialised solutions for narrow use cases, the oAMF creates an ecosystem where researchers can:

- Seamlessly benchmark new components against established baselines using standardised interfaces
- Rapidly prototype end-to-end argument mining pipelines by mixing components from different research traditions
- Visualise and evaluate results through unified representation formats that maintain theoretical compatibility

By reducing the technical overhead associated with these common development scenarios, the oAMF aims to accelerate innovation while preserving the theoretical diversity that has been a hallmark of argument mining research. The framework empowers researchers to focus on advancing core argument mining challenges rather than reimplementing infrastructure components, ultimately fostering greater collaboration across the community.

Proceedings of the 12th Argument Mining Workshop, pages 100–106
July 31, 2025 ©2025 Association for Computational Linguistics

Currently, the framework includes 17 widely used AM modules, all available on GitHub for community contributions. New modules can also be added, with each module expected to follow specific input/output formats, implementation guidelines, and configuration requirements (see Section 4).

2 Practical Problems faced by AM system developers

The deployment of applied argument mining systems is still in its infancy. Despite more than a decade of research in argument mining (ultimately stretching back to (Moens et al., 2007), but now eleven years with the dedicated forum provided by the Argument Mining Workshop) there have been few live systems deployed beyond laboratory settings. The most high-profile is the work at IBM (Slonim et al., 2021) which has to a large extent been rolled in to `watsonx` as part of their commercial offering. In addition, there are more modest examples such as args.me (Wachsmuth et al., 2017) and the Evidence Toolkit (Visser et al., 2020) amongst others. But the engineering and deployment of systems that involve AM remains a rarity.

With the revolution in NLP ushered in by LLMs, the ability to handle reasoning in language is becoming paramount, and as a result the handling of structures of argumentation is of rapidly increasing importance, as evidenced by the dramatic uptick in papers on the topic in the ACL anthology which returns 7,500 papers for the search "`argument* mining`" at time of writing.

Yet there are several fundamental methodological challenges that face both researchers and developers setting out to build argument mining algorithms and systems.

The all-or-nothing challenge. Reliably extracting the structure of reasoning expressed in natural language remains one of the most challenging open problems in NLP today. Many different architectures and approaches have been applied, and though monolithic end-to-end systems are rather rare (Eger et al., 2017), the more modular approaches very typically have to either engineer end-to-end system componentry, or else release systems that make major I/O assumptions (such as the availability of reliably segmented input data, or the availability of directionality labelling subsystems). Building an entire application system that exploits argument mining is therefore an all-or-nothing affair, requiring system building from user input to user output.

The reusability challenge. Part of the reason for the all-or-nothing challenge is that tools and algorithms released by the community are typically rather shortlived and idiosyncratic, making their reuse difficult in the short term, and all but impossible over the course of a few years. As a result, progress is rarely able to make use of previous work, reusing, for example, techniques for segmentation, where that is not the focus of current work.

The interoperability challenge. The other part of the reason for the all-or-nothing challenge is the lack of well-defined modularity or the ability for subsystems to exchange data in a common representation language. Freeman (Freeman, 1991) has become one of the most expressive underlying reference argumentation theories because of its ability to integrate approaches such as Toulmin (Toulmin, 1958) with simpler pro-con models (Gorur et al., 2025b), and as a result is used in data efforts ranging from monological lab-constructed data of the microtext corpus (Peldszus and Stede, 2016) through to some of the largest manually annotated dialogical corpora (Hautli-Janisz et al., 2022) currently available. Several shared tasks have focused on exploiting this representational adequacy (Ruiz-Dolz et al., 2024), but the sheer creative diversity that has characterised argument mining for more than a decade has also created a rich array of different approaches that effectively stymie interoperability between them.

The evaluation challenge. In both academic and commercial environments, providing unbiased evaluation of techniques and systems is critical, yet reliable measures of different aspects of argument mining performance are difficult to establish beyond the bounds of controlled shared tasks, because of the lack of interoperability and standardisation. Even the very measures that are deployed vary widely from, for example, κ, which fails to account for textual variation, through γ, which is difficult to interpret.

3 Solving challenges in the development of AM work

3.1 Compare against other modules

The `oAMF` allows for easy comparison of approaches on individual argument mining tasks by creating two or more workflows that are identical other than the specific task under consideration. A variety of modules can then be tested on this task, for example comparing a newly developed module against existing state-of-the-art approaches. Importantly, the framework is not bound to any single argumentation model or theory. It is designed to support heterogeneous models and allows components grounded in different frameworks, theories, or representational schemes to interoperate seamlessly. This flexibility ensures that researchers can easily adapt the framework to suit their preferred models or experiment with multiple ones in parallel.

3.2 Fit a single part in to an end-to-end workflow

Although there are an increasing number of AM works which take an 'end-to-end' view (Stab and Gurevych, 2017; Persing and Ng, 2016; Potash et al., 2017), it is still common to focus on specific individual tasks from the identification of argument components, through levels of increasing complexity; considering the role of individual components, considering argumentative relations, and considering more complex argumentative relationships, such as an instance of an argumentation scheme.

The oAMF allows for different implementations to be selected for each of these tasks, creating a unified end-to-end approach that uses the best techniques available along each step of the process.

3.3 Evaluation and Visualisation

Individual oAMF modules and AM pipelines composed of oAMF modules—each responsible for a specific subtask—can be executed, with the output visualised using an oAMF-compatible visualisation tool (see an example of the argument graph visualisation in Figure 1). Additionally, the output can be assessed for performance using another oAMF-compatible module, CASS. The CASS module evaluates oAMF output based on metrics such as Macro F1, Accuracy, Text Similarity, Kappa, and U-Alpha. For example, a pipeline might start with a module for dialog turn segmentation, followed by a module for segmenting text into argumentative discourse units, a module for pre-processing the discourse segments, and finally, a module for argument relation identification. For a list of the modules currently available in oAMF, see Section 4.3.

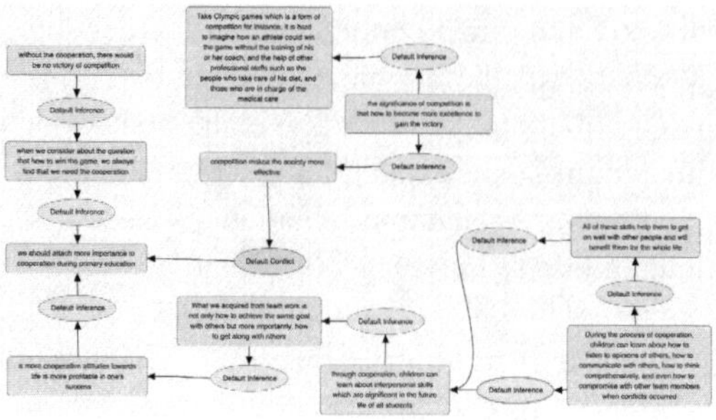

Figure 1: An argument map generated by the visualiser.

```
from xaif import AIF
# Sample xAIF JSON with 2 L nodes and 2 I nodes
aif_data = {"AIF": {"nodes": [
      {"nodeID": 0, "text": "Example L node 1", "type": "L"},
      {"nodeID": 1, "text": "Example L node 2", "type": "L"},
      {"nodeID": 2, "text": "Example I node 1", "type": "I"},
      {"nodeID": 3, "text": "Example I node 2", "type": "I"},
      {"nodeID": 4, "text": "Default Inference", "type": "RA"}
    ],
    "edges": [
      {"edgeID": 0, "fromID": 0, "toID": 2},
      {"edgeID": 1, "fromID": 1, "toID": 3},
      {"edgeID": 2, "fromID": 2, "toID": 4},
      {"edgeID": 4, "fromID": 2, "toID": 3}
    ],
    "locutions": [{"nodeID": 0, "personID": 0}],
    "participants": [{"firstname": "Speaker", "participantID": 0,
          "surname": "Name"}]
  },
   "dialog": True
   }

aif = AIF(aif_data) # Initialise the AIF object with xAIF data
aif.add_component(component_type = "locution", text = "Example L node
      3.", speaker = "Another Speake") # The next ID (5) is assigned
aif.add_component(component_type = "proposition", Lnode_ID = 5,
      proposition = "Example I node 3.") # The L-NodeID is required
aif.add_component(component_type = "argument_relation", relation_type =
      "RA", iNode_ID2=3, iNode_ID1=6) # Requires I-Node IDs and AR type
print(aif.xaif) # Print the generated xAIF data
print(aif.get_csv("argument-relation")) # Exports to tabular format
```

Figure 2: `xaif` package to manipulate xAIF data.

4 Practical Solutions

4.1 How to create an oAMF module

The oAMF allows developers to create new argument mining modules and integrate them with others, simplifying interoperability and reproducibility of AM systems. This section describes the process of creating a new module, covering I/O format constraints, its implementation, the project structure, how to configure the metadata file, the Flask application routes, and a summary of steps for developing oAMF-compatible AM modules.

Input-Output Format: Each module uses xAIF for input and output to ensure interoperability. The *xaif* library provided by the oAMF simplifies xAIF file manipulation (see Figure 2), helping developers in managing argumentative discourse structure in a consistent format. The documentation can be accessed at `https://github.com/arg-tech/xaif/blob/main/docs/tutorial.md`.

Implementation: oAMF modules are implemented as a dockerised web service to ensure portability and scalability. They are implemented using the Flask framework, a lightweight Python web framework for creating RESTful services. A set of endpoints are exposed, allowing users to interact with the module through HTTP requests. Each module takes xAIF as input/output. Developers can build new modules by cloning a template project, updating metadata, implementing module logic, and configuring the service for containerisation. A template to help develop custom modules is available at: `https://github.com/arg-tech/AMF_NOOP/`. A step-by-step summary of module development is provided in Appendix A.

4.2 How to create an oAMF pipeline

The oAMF offers different interfaces for building and executing AM pipelines i.e., multiple modules working sequentially. These components seamlessly integrate by using xAIF as a standardised format for both input and output, ensuring smooth data exchange throughout the pipeline. The available interfaces cover all different levels of technical knowledge, including an API for advanced customisation, a drag-and-drop interface for quick setup, and a web interface for easy execution.

4.2.1 Programming API

The programming API allows defining a pipeline by specifying and connecting modules through their associated tags. The pipeline can then be executed by providing an input file. The script shown in Figure 3 depicts how to build and execute an oAMF pipeline.

```
from oamf import oAMF
# Initialize the library
oamf = oAMF()
# Define pipeline as a graph


pipeline_graph = [
    ("turninator", "segmenter"), # 'turninator' is a module that
        segments dialogue into turns; 'segmenter' segments
        discourse into ADUs
    ("turninator", "segmenter2"), # another segmenter instance for
        parallel processing
    ("segmenter", "bert-te"),   # 'bert-te' is a BERT-based inference
        identifier module
    ("segmenter2", "bert-te2") # another inference module instance
    ]
oamf.pipelineExecutor(pipeline_graph, "input_file.json")
```

Figure 3: Create and execute pipeline with the oAMF API.

4.2.2 Drag-and-Drop Interface

The oAMF integrates with n8n, an open-source workflow automation tool[1], available at `https://n8n.oamf.arg.tech/`, offering a visual, intuitive interface for constructing pipelines. Users can easily drag and drop modules and establish connections. Pipelines can be executed using (1) the n8n interface with user-provided input or (2) the oAMF library by downloading workflow JSON files and running `oamf.pipelineExecutor(pipeline_graph, “input_file.json”, “workflow.json”)`, where `pipeline_graph` can be an empty list, `input_file.json` holds xAIF input data, and `workflow.json` is the n8n workflow.

4.2.3 Web Interface

The oAMF provides a web interface for quickly running AM pipelines, which can be accessed at `https://oAMF.arg.tech`. Users can upload input data (e.g., text or xAIF files), select pre-built pipelines using the n8n interface, and execute them directly on the oAMF server—removing the need for manual pipeline construction.

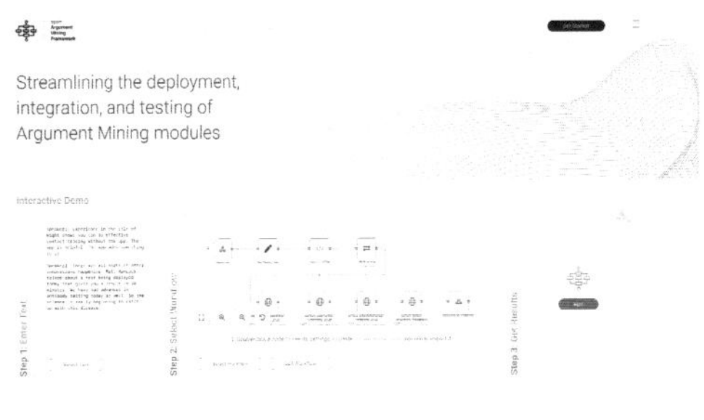

Figure 4: Web interface of oAMF for uploading input data and running pre-built AM pipelines.

4.3 List extant functionality of the oAMF

In addition to providing a complete toolkit to implement new argument mining modules, and different interfaces to connect them and execute pipelines, the oAMF also comes with a set of pre-implemented modules covering basic AM operations such as segmentation, classification, or relation identification. Some of these pre-implemented modules are based on previous AM work. For example, a segmenter based on TARGER (Chernodub et al., 2019), a cascade propositionaliser (Jo et al., 2019), a transformer-based argument relation identifier (Ruiz-Dolz et al., 2021), a decoder-only model

[1] `https://n8n.io`

based on DialoGPT for argument relation identification (Gemechu et al., 2024) or decompositional argument mining (Gemechu and Reed, 2019). By providing this set of pre-implemented modules covering basic AM operations, we make argument mining accessible to a non-technical audience. A list of available modules can be accessed here: `https://github.com/arg-tech/oAMF`.

5 Conclusion

This paper addresses a significant challenge impacting the AM community: the use, development, and evaluation of practical solutions. For that purpose, we provide a complete analysis of the practical problems faced by the AM community, grouped into four major categories. As a solution to these problems, we introduce the `oAMF`: a set of libraries, modules, and interfaces aimed at making AM accessible to users with different technical backgrounds. The `oAMF` allows, at the same time, developers to create new interoperable modules from scratch that can be connected with the existing ones, programmers to implement different AM pipelines connecting different modules and evaluate them fairly, and non-technical users to analyse text in search for argument structures with a codeless interface.

Acknowledgments

This work is funded in part by: the 'AI for Citizen Intelligence Coaching against Disinformation (TITAN)' project, funded by the EU Horizon 2020 research and innovation programme under grant agreement 101070658, and by UK Research and innovation under the UK governments Horizon funding guarantee grant numbers 10040483 and 10055990; the 'Artificial Intelligence for Institutionalised, Multimodal, Gamified, Mass Democratic Deliberations' project, funded by the EU Horizon Europe Framework Programme (HORIZON) under grant agreement 101178806; the 'CLARUS' project, funded by the EU Horizon Europe Framework Programme (HORIZON) under grant agreement 101121182; Volkswagen Stiftung Foundation under grant 98 543, "Deliberation Laboratory"; and the Swiss National Science Foundation under grant 10001FM_200857, "Mining argumentative patterns in context".

References

Jérémie Cabessa, Hugo Hernault, and Umer Mushtaq. 2025. Argument mining with fine-tuned large language models. In *Proceedings of the 31st International Conference on Computational Linguistics*, pages 6624–6635.

Guizhen Chen, Liying Cheng, Luu Anh Tuan, and Lidong Bing. 2024. Exploring the potential of large language models in computational argumentation. In *Proceedings of the 62nd Annual Meeting of the Association for Computational Linguistics (Volume 1: Long Papers)*, pages 2309–2330.

Artem Chernodub, Oleksiy Oliynyk, Philipp Heidenreich, Alexander Bondarenko, Matthias Hagen, Chris Biemann, and Alexander Panchenko. 2019. Targer: Neural argument mining at your fingertips. In *Proceedings of the 57th Annual Meeting of the Association for Computational Linguistics: System Demonstrations*, pages 195–200.

Steffen Eger, Johannes Daxenberger, and Iryna Gurevych. 2017. Neural end-to-end learning for computational argumentation mining. *arXiv preprint arXiv:1704.06104*.

James B. Freeman. 1991. *Dialectics and the Macrostructure of Arguments*. Foris/de Gruyter, Berlin-New York.

Debela Gemechu and Chris Reed. 2019. Decompositional argument mining: A general purpose approach for argument graph construction. In *Proceedings of the 57th Annual Meeting of the Association for Computational Linguistics*, pages 516–526.

Debela Gemechu, Ramon Ruiz-Dolz, and Chris Reed. 2024. Aries: A general benchmark for argument relation identification. In *11th Workshop on Argument Mining, ArgMining 2024*, pages 1–14. Association for Computational Linguistics (ACL).

Deniz Gorur, Antonio Rago, and Francesca Toni. 2025a. Can large language models perform relation-based argument mining? In *Proceedings of the 31st International Conference on Computational Linguistics*, pages 8518–8534.

Deniz Gorur, Antonio Rago, and Francesca Toni. 2025b. Can large language models perform relation-based argument mining? In *Proceedings of the 31st International Conference on Computational Linguistics*, pages 8518–8534, Abu Dhabi, UAE. Association for Computational Linguistics.

Ivan Habernal, Daniel Faber, Nicola Recchia, Sebastian Bretthauer, Iryna Gurevych, Indra Spiecker genannt Döhmann, and Christoph Burchard. 2024. Mining legal arguments in court decisions. *Artificial Intelligence and Law*, 32(3):1–38.

Annette Hautli-Janisz, Zlata Kikteva, Wassiliki Siskou, Kamila Gorska, Ray Becker, and Chris Reed. 2022.

Qt30: A corpus of argument and conflict in broadcast debate. In *Proceedings of the 13th Language Resources and Evaluation Conference*, pages 3291–3300. European Language Resources Association (ELRA).

Yohan Jo, Jacky Visser, Chris Reed, and Eduard Hovy. 2019. A cascade model for proposition extraction in argumentation. In *Proceedings of the 6th Workshop on Argument Mining*, pages 11–24, Florence, Italy. Association for Computational Linguistics.

Masayuki Kawarada, Tsutomu Hirao, Wataru Uchida, and Masaaki Nagata. 2024. Argument mining as a text-to-text generation task. In *Proceedings of the 18th Conference of the European Chapter of the Association for Computational Linguistics (Volume 1: Long Papers)*, pages 2002–2014.

Marie-Francine Moens, Erik Boiy, Raquel M. Palau, and Chris Reed. 2007. Automatic detection of arguments in legal texts. In *Proceedings of the 11th international conference on Artificial intelligence and law*, pages 225–230, Stanford, CA. ACM.

Andreas Peldszus and Manfred Stede. 2016. An annotated corpus of argumentative microtexts. In *Argumentation and Reasoned Action: Proceedings of the 1st European Conference on Argumentation, Lisbon 2015 / Vol. 2*, pages 801–815, London. College Publications.

Isaac Persing and Vincent Ng. 2016. End-to-end argumentation mining in student essays. In *Proceedings of NAACL-HLT*, pages 1384–1394, San Diego, CA.

Peter Potash, Alexey Romanov, and Anna Rumshisky. 2017. Here's my point: Joint pointer architecture for argument mining. In *Proceedings of the 2017 Conference on Empirical Methods in Natural Language Processing*, pages 1364–1373, Copenhagen, Denmark. Association for Computational Linguistics.

Ramon Ruiz-Dolz, Jose Alemany, Stella M Heras Barberá, and Ana García-Fornes. 2021. Transformer-based models for automatic identification of argument relations: A cross-domain evaluation. *IEEE Intelligent Systems*, 36(6):62–70.

Ramon Ruiz-Dolz, John Lawrence, Ella Schad, and Chris Reed. 2024. Overview of dialam-2024: Argument mining in natural language dialogues. In *11th Workshop on Argument Mining, ArgMining 2024*, pages 83–92. Association for Computational Linguistics (ACL).

N. Slonim, Y. Bilu, and C. Alzate. 2021. An autonomous debating system. *Nature*, 591:397–384.

Christian Stab and Iryna Gurevych. 2017. Parsing argumentation structures in persuasive essays. *Computational Linguistics*, 43(3):619–659.

Stephen E. Toulmin. 1958. *The Uses of Argument*. Cambridge University Press.

Jacky Visser, John Lawrence, and Chris Reed. 2020. Reason-checking fake news. *Communications of the ACM*, 63(11):38–40.

Henning Wachsmuth, Martin Potthast, Khalid Al-Khatib, Yamen Ajjour, Jana Puschmann, Jiani Qu, Jonas Dorsch, Viorel Morari, Janek Bevendorff, and Benno Stein. 2017. Building an argument search engine for the web. In *Proceedings of the 4th Workshop on Argument Mining*, pages 49–59, Copenhagen, Denmark. Association for Computational Linguistics.

A Implementation Details

Project Structure The project structure contains the following key components:

- `config/metadata.yaml`: Contains metadata information about the module.
- `project_src_dir/`: Directory with the application code, including Flask routes and logic.
- `boot.sh`: Shell script to activate the environment and launch the app.
- `docker-compose.yaml`: Defines the Docker service and its setup.
- `Dockerfile`: Specifies image configuration and dependencies.
- `requirements.txt`: Python dependencies list.

Metadata Configuration The `metadata.yaml` file provides essential module details:

```
Name: "Name of the Module"
Date: "2024-10-01"
Originator: "Author"
License: "Your License"
AMF_Tag: Your_tag_name
Domain: "Dialog"
Training Data: "Annotated corpus X"
Citation: ""
Variants:
  - name: 0 version: null
  - name: 1 version: null
Requires: text
Outputs: segments
```

Flask Application Routes

- **Index Route** (/): Displays the contents of the `README.md` file.
- **Module Route (customisable)**:
  - `POST` requests process xAIF input and return modified output.
  - `GET` requests return module metadata and documentation.

Steps to Develop a Module

1. Clone the NOOP template from the repository: `https://github.com/arg-tech/AMF_NOOP/`
2. Modify `metadata.yaml` with your module's details.
3. Implement core logic in `routes.py`.
4. Use the `xAIF` library to manipulate xAIF data.
5. Set up `Dockerfile` and `docker-compose.yaml`.
6. Update the `README.md` with documentation.

Argumentative Analysis of Legal Rulings: A Structured Framework Using Bobbitt's Typology

Carlotta Giacchetta[1], Raffaella Bernardi[2], Jacopo Staiano[1], Serena Tomasi[1]
Barbara Montini[3]
[1]University of Trento, [2]Free University of Bozen-Bolzano, [3]University of Brescia
carlotta.giacchetta@studenti.unitn.it, raffaella.bernardi@unibz.it, jacopo.staiano@unitn.it,
serena.tomasi_1@unitn.it, bmontini001@studenti.unibs.it

Abstract

Legal reasoning remains one of the most complex and nuanced domains for AI, with current tools often lacking transparency and domain adaptability. While recent advances in large language models (LLMs) offer new opportunities for legal analysis, their ability to structure and interpret judicial argumentation remains unexplored. We address this gap by proposing a structured framework for AI-assisted legal reasoning, centered on argumentative analysis. In this work, we use GPT-4o for discourse-level and semantic analysis to identify argumentative units and classify them according to Philippe Bobbitt's (Bobbitt, 1984) six constitutional modalities of legal reasoning. We apply this framework to legal rulings from the Italian Court of Cassation. Our experimental findings indicate that LLM-based tools can effectively augment and streamline legal practice, by e.g. preprocessing the legal texts under scrutiny; still, the limited performance of the state-of-the-art generative model tested indicates significant room for progress in human-AI collaboration in the legal domain.

1 Introduction

In this work, our aim is to develop a digital tool based on Argument Mining and Artificial Intelligence to support legal professionals (judges, lawyers, prosecutors, notaries, and legal trainees) in critically analysing and understanding judicial decisions in their full argumentative complexity. The tool is not intended to replace the legal expert, but rather to assist in navigating the often intricate and cognitively demanding task of interpreting judicial texts. A key theoretical premise of this work is that judicial decisions are fundamentally argumentative products, structured through layers of reasoning that go beyond the mere operative part of the ruling or its legal maxim. Traditional approaches, such as relying solely on summaries or syllogistic reduction, risk obscuring the deeper argumentative processes and implicit assumptions embedded in the decision-making. To address this, we draw from argumentation theory and computational linguistics to extract and classify the internal logic of judgments. The proposed system has been developed to perform two primary functions: *i)* to segment the judgment into discrete argumentative units, each representing an independent statement with argumentative value; and *ii)* to semantically label these units by identifying the type of legal reasoning they instantiate, as illustrated in Figure 1.

To this end, we design a classification framework based on Philippe Bobbitt's typology of constitutional argumentation (Bobbitt, 1984): originally developed in the context of U.S. Supreme Court decisions.

Our main contributions are twofold: first, we release the first corpus of Italian judicial decisions (civil and criminal rulings from the Court of Cassation) annotated with argumentative labels based on Bobbitt's constitutional modalities; second, we propose and evaluate a pipeline that integrates large language models with expert annotation to classify argumentative units in legal texts.

We find that GPT-4o, when guided with carefully designed prompts, can capture a significant portion of the argumentative structure, providing a useful framework for assisted legal analysis. However, human input remains essential in identifying subtle distinctions between modalities, especially in complex or ambiguous reasoning contexts. Notably, even junior expert annotators often struggle to reach full agreement, highlighting the intrinsic complexity and subjectivity of the task of argumentative classification in judicial texts.

2 Related Works

Over the past decade, Argument Mining (AM) has become an increasingly prominent area within the

Proceedings of the 12th Argument Mining Workshop, pages 107–115
July 31, 2025

Figure 1: Starting from a legal document, a language model segments the text into paragraphs; then, these are classified by an LLM and domain experts according to Bobbitt's argumentative categories.

intersection of artificial intelligence, computational linguics, and legal informatics.

Our approach builds on a rich body of work by integrating discourse segmentation with semantic classification of legal arguments. Unlike prior studies that focused on broad categories such as premise/conclusion or rhetorical roles(Palau and Moens, 2009), (Santin et al., 2023), (Grundler et al., 2022) we adopt Bobbitt's (Bobbitt, 1984) constitutional modalities as a semantic framework, allowing for a more refined classification of legal reasoning. Further, while much of the previous literature has concentrated on English-language (Chalkidis et al., 2020) decisions from supranational courts (Chlapanis et al., 2024), our work expands the scope by applying the methodology to Italian Court of Cassation rulings. This contributes to the growing interest in multilingual and civil law systems within the AM community, as evidenced by recent shared tasks and datasets, such as the AMELIA (Grundler et al., 2024) challenge for Italian legal texts.

3 Data Collection and Categories

To implement and evaluate our framework, we compiled a custom corpus of Italian judicial decisions and adopted a classification scheme grounded in constitutional legal theory. The process involved selecting representative rulings, curating the textual material, and mapping argumentative content to a set of predefined categories. In what follows, we describe the composition of the dataset and the typology of argumentation used for annotation.

3.1 Corpus Description

The corpus used for this study consists of 20 judgments from the Italian Supreme Court of Cassation, which is the highest judicial authority responsible for ensuring uniform interpretation of the law (a function known as nomofilachy). The selected rulings are among the most significant ones highlighted by the Court's official website[1] and include 10 civil and 10 criminal cases.

All rulings were written in Italian and sourced from the *De Jure* legal database.[2] Civil cases span the years 2018 to 2025, while criminal cases are drawn from 2023 and 2024, reflecting the most recent developments in judicial language and practice.

The rulings vary significantly in length and complexity, ranging from concise decisions of 4 pages to more elaborate ones extending up to 26 pages. This diversity reflects the variability of legal practice and provides a realistic testbed for evaluating both human and model-based annotation of argumentative content.

Prior to annotation, all decisions were preprocessed to extract the full text, removing non-argumentative sections such as headers, metadata, or procedural summaries.[3]

[1] https://www.italgiure.giustizia.it/sncass/

[2] Available at: https://dejure.it/

[3] Preliminary experiments were conducted using the *Demosthenes dataset* (CJEU decisions on fiscal state aid), as it already featured a well-defined argumentative structure. This allowed us to initially focus on the categorization task. However, we later decided to shift our main focus to Italian judicial decisions.

3.2 Categories

To classify the argumentative content of each decision, we adopted Bobbitt's typology of constitutional reasoning. This framework identifies six primary categories (Historical, Textual, Structural, Prudential, Doctrinal, Ethical), each corresponding to a different mode of legal justification.[4]

In addition to these six, we introduced a residual category, `None`, to capture instances where no clear argumentative function could be assigned, either due to lack of information or the presence of purely descriptive or procedural content.

4 Methodology

The core objective of our approach is to transform legal rulings into structured argumentative representations. This involves two main steps: (1) segmenting the ruling into coherent textual units (typically paragraphs), and (2) identifying the role of each segment within the broader argumentative structure of the document.

We operationalize this by first extracting the ruling text and dividing it into paragraphs, which are then labeled based on their argumentative function—either as premises, conclusions, or non-argumentative content. Each paragraph is uniquely identified and embedded in a hierarchical structure that reflects the flow of reasoning. Subsequently, we group semantically related segments and assign them to one of Bobbitt's constitutional categories of argumentation. This process results in a multilayered representation of the ruling that supports both human interpretability and machine processing.

4.1 Text Segmentation into Paragraphs

The tool's primary function is to divide complex legal texts into coherent paragraphs. This is essential as it lays the groundwork for structuring the text, which will later be analyzed at the sentence level. Each paragraph is analyzed and classified into one of the following categories: *premise*, *conclusion* or *null*.

To maintain a structured representation of the argumentation, each paragraph is assigned a unique identifier built via *i)* a single character indicating the argument chain (e.g. A, B..) and *ii)* a progressive number denoting the order within the chain (e.g., A1, A2, B1)[5]. This structured XML representation ensures that the text remains both machine-readable and systematically organized, thereby facilitating downstream processing and analysis. Our pipeline design follows the structure adopted in the Demosthenes dataset proposed by Santin et al. (2023).[6]

4.2 LLM Annotations

The second phase of the pipeline is the annotation process, which is divided into two main steps.

The first step is **semantic grouping**, in which paragraphs are clustered based on their semantic similarity using a GPT-based model. Each group is assigned a unique `group_id` and can include up to eight paragraphs. Paragraphs that do not semantically align with others remain ungrouped and are labeled with `group_id: null` [7] The goal of this phase is to identify groups of argumentative units that address the same topic or rely on a shared line of reasoning. This semantic grouping serves a crucial functional role: it establishes the granularity at which constitutional argumentation categories (as described in Section 3.2) are assigned. Rather than classifying individual paragraphs—which may be too short or context-poor for accurate labeling—we classify entire semantic groups. Each group typically represents a coherent argumentative theme, making it a more suitable unit for the assignment of one of Bobbitt's six categories.

In the categorization step, each semantic group is passed to the LLM, which selects the most appropriate constitutional argument type from the predefined set, or assigns the label `None` if no category applies. The model is instructed to justify its choice with a brief explanation [8].

Both grouping and classification were conducted using a *zero-shot prompt* with structured instructions describing each category, and a temperature setting of 0.2. At the end, each paragraph in the XML file is annotated with three tags: an `<ID>` - corresponding to the paragraph identifier; a `<Group>` – corresponding to the `group_id` assigned to the paragraph and a `<Category>` – representing the classification label of the paragraph.

[4]Details on the description of the Categories are provided in Appendix A.

[5]For details on the prompt's syntactic structure, see Appendix D.

[6]Implemetation details, including file conversions and annotation formatting, are provided in Appendix B.

[7]For details on the prompt's semantic grouping, see Appendix E.

[8]For details on the prompt's categorization, see Appendix F.

4.3 Human Annotation

To validate the output of the automatic annotation pipeline, we collected manual annotations from a panel of five human experts with varying legal backgrounds. The annotators included: Junior experts (one law student, two legal trainees, one PhD candidate), and Senior expert (an university professor of constitutional law).

Each annotator was provided with a structured Excel file containing the paragraphs grouped and labeled with `group_id`, as generated by the model. For each paragraph, they were asked to assign one of Bobbitt's categories using a drop-down menu. To ensure comparability with the model's behavior, all annotators received the exact same prompts used by GPT during the automatic annotation phase. In cases where a semantic group appeared incoherent or internally inconsistent, annotators were instructed to assign the most appropriate category nonetheless—based on the dominant argumentative theme—and to flag the group as "incorrect." They could also provide suggestions for a more appropriate regrouping. This protocol allowed us to both preserve comparability with GPT outputs and collect qualitative feedback on grouping validity.

Each Junior Expert annotated a subset of the rulings, while the Senior Expert annotated the entire corpus. This design allows us to compute both human–AI agreement and human–human agreement, with a focus on the differences between expertise levels and the model's alignment with legal reasoning across varying levels of legal training.[9] Humans took from 30 to 120 minutes per judgment.

5 Experimental Results

To assess the consistency of GPT annotations relative to human judgment, we compute agreement using two complementary strategies: intersection-based and union-based evaluation – Both approaches rely on Cohen's κ (Cohen, 1960). These two perspectives allow us to evaluate GPT both on highly reliable human annotations (intersection) and in more flexible, real-world scenarios (union).

Intersection-based agreement ($\cap$). In this setting, we first construct a subset of the dataset consisting only of those instances where both human annotators independently assigned the same label to a given paragraph. These agreed-upon labels are treated as the gold standard, and GPT's output is compared against them. This provides a high-precision evaluation, focusing only on cases where human consensus exists.

[9]Details on the annotation interface and inter-annotator agreement metrics are provided in Appendix C.

Table 1: **Cohen's Kappa** agreement scores between human annotators (senior and juniors) and GPT for the annotated documents in Criminal and Civil Law.

	Criminal Law	Civil Law
Senior vs Junior	0.17	0.27
Senior vs GPT	0.15	-0.03
Junior vs GPT	0.07	-0.09
Senior $\cap$ Junior vs GPT	0.15	-0.0936
Senior $\cup$ Junior vs GPT	0.46	0.1874

Table 2: Detailed classification report for GPT vs Human (union-based agreement) on annotated documents from Italian Criminal Law.

Categories	Precision	Recall	F1-score	N.
Doctrinal	0.41	0.80	0.54	30
None	0.95	0.87	0.91	212
Prudential	0.00	0.00	0.00	2
Structural	0.00	0.00	0.00	2
Textual	0.00	0.00	0.00	8

Union-based agreement ($\cup$). In the union-based setting, we take a more permissive approach: GPT is considered correct if its predicted label matches either of the two human annotators. This strategy accounts for cases where annotators diverge but GPT still aligns with one of them, thereby capturing partial alignment with human judgment. This formulation is particularly suited for analyzing noisy or ambiguous labels, and reflects the inherent subjectivity of legal interpretation.

Looking at the agreement scores in Table 1, we observe that the Senior Expert achieves consistently higher agreement with GPT than the Junior Expert does, particularly in the Criminal Law domain. This suggests that the model tends to align more closely with interpretations grounded in deeper legal reasoning and experience.

However, when comparing the individual category distributions (Tables 2 and 3), we note that GPT often selects different categories than the experts, especially in cases where legal argumentation is subtle or multi-layered. Moreover, we noticed that GPT captures only a limited subset of argumentative categories, missing the semantic nuances that legal experts can identify thanks to their domain

Table 3: Detailed classification report for GPT vs Human annotators (union-based agreement) on documents from Italian Civil Law.

Categories	Precision	Recall	F1-score	N.
Ethical	0.00	0.00	0.00	1
Doctrinal	0.39	0.76	0.52	66
None	0.77	0.45	0.57	130
Textual	0.50	0.18	0.27	11

knowledge. These findings highlight the complexity of modeling judicial argumentation, where even human annotators often disagree.

Overall, GPT's behavior appears more comparable to that of a Junior Expert: while it demonstrates basic familiarity with argumentative distinctions, it lacks the consistency and depth shown by the Senior Expert, particularly in capturing less frequent or more conceptually demanding categories like Textual, Ethical, and Prudential.

Interestingly, the underlying classification framework shows limitations: Bobbitt's categories, developed for U.S. constitutional contexts, are often too broad or rigid to account for the fact-based and procedural reasoning typical of Italian jurisprudence. This mismatch likely contributes to the observed difficulties in annotation and model prediction, and suggests the need for more refined and context-sensitive taxonomies tailored to the Italian legal system.

Note: In Tables 2 and 3, the last column ("N.") indicates the number of paragraphs in the test set that were assigned to each category according to human annotations. This provides context for interpreting class imbalance and the model's relative performance per category.

6 Conclusion

This project advances the development of epistemically responsible legal AI by addressing the practical and conceptual challenges of Argument Mining in judicial decisions. Through expert-guided annotation, we exposed the limitations of current models in handling complex legal reasoning, particularly in terms of time demands, semantic ambiguity, and segmentation. Yet, the process proved valuable for enhancing legal understanding, with potential applications in education, research, and decision support. By refining classification strategies and prompt design, our work contributes to more transparent and trustworthy AI systems in the legal domain.

Limitations

Our current pipeline relies solely on GPT-4o, a general-purpose model not specifically tuned for legal tasks. This may limit its precision, especially in domains requiring up-to-date legal knowledge or fine-grained distinctions in terminology. Moreover, no systematic comparison has been made with alternative models—either proprietary or open-source.

Future work will benchmark multiple LLMs and investigate domain-adapted models optimized for legal argument classification.

Acknowledgments

References

Philip Bobbitt. 1984. *Constitutional fate: Theory of the Constitution*. Oxford University Press.

Ilias Chalkidis, Manos Fergadiotis, Prodromos Malakasiotis, Nikolaos Aletras, and Ion Androutsopoulos. 2020. Legal-bert: The muppets straight out of law school. *arXiv preprint arXiv:2010.02559*.

Odysseas S Chlapanis, Dimitrios Galanis, and Ion Androutsopoulos. 2024. Lar-echr: A new legal argument reasoning task and dataset for cases of the european court of human rights. *arXiv preprint arXiv:2410.13352*.

Jacob Cohen. 1960. A coefficient of agreement for nominal scales. *Educational and psychological measurement*, 20(1):37–46.

Giulia Grundler, Andrea Galassi, Piera Santin, Alessia Fidelangeli, Federico Galli, Elena Palmieri, Francesca Lagioia, Giovanni Sartor, and Paolo Torroni. 2024. Amelia - argument mining evaluation on legal documents in italian: A calamita challenge. In *CLICIT*.

Giulia Grundler, Piera Santin, Andrea Galassi, Federico Galli, Francesco Godano, Francesca Lagioia, Elena Palmieri, Federico Ruggeri, Giovanni Sartor, and Paolo Torroni. 2022. Detecting arguments in CJEU decisions on fiscal state aid. In *Proceedings of the 9th Workshop on Argument Mining*, pages 143–157, Online and in Gyeongju, Republic of Korea. International Conference on Computational Linguistics.

Raquel Mochales Palau and Marie-Francine Moens. 2009. Argumentation mining: the detection, classification and structure of arguments in text. In *Proceedings of the 12th international conference on artificial intelligence and law*, pages 98–107.

Piera Santin, Giulia Grundler, Andrea Galassi, Federico Galli, Francesca Lagioia, Elena Palmieri, Federico Ruggeri, Giovanni Sartor, and Paolo Torroni. 2023. Argumentation structure prediction in cjeu decisions on fiscal state aid. *Proceedings of the Nineteenth International Conference on Artificial Intelligence and Law*.

A Categories

- `Historical arguments`: refer to reasoning based on the original intentions of lawmakers, often invoking the legislative history or founding principles behind a norm.
- `Textual arguments`: rely on the literal or grammatical meaning of the legal text itself, emphasizing the surface structure of statutory language.
- `Structural arguments`: are concerned with the internal logic and architecture of the legal system, drawing connections between different institutional functions or constitutional provisions.
- `Prudential arguments`: take into account the practical consequences of a legal interpretation, including its potential benefits, risks, or social implications.
- `Doctrinal arguments`: are grounded in legal precedents and established jurisprudential interpretations, aiming to ensure consistency and stability in the application of the law.
- `Ethical arguments`: appeal to moral values or societal ideals, often drawing on broader cultural or philosophical principles.

B Annotation Pipeline and File Formatting

The annotation pipeline consists of a multi-stage process aimed at converting legal rulings in PDF format into structured, machine-readable representations enriched with argumentative annotations. The process includes the following steps:

1. **PDF to XML conversion**: The raw PDF files are preprocessed to extract text, which is then segmented into paragraphs and stored in an XML structure. Each paragraph is enclosed within a `<par>` tag and assigned a unique identifier.
2. **Paragraph classification**: Using a language model, each paragraph is labeled as either a `Premise`, `Conclusion`, or `Null`, and wrapped in corresponding tags (`<prem>`, `<conc>`).
3. **Semantic grouping and categorization**: Related paragraphs are grouped semantically and assigned a `group_id` and a `Category`. A short explanation is generated for each group to justify both the grouping and the assigned category. These elements are stored in a structured JSON file and later used to augment the XML.
4. **XML augmentation**: The JSON-based annotations are reintegrated into the XML as new attributes: `Group` and `Category` are added to each paragraph node, while paragraph identifiers remain embedded as `<ID>` tags.
5. **Export to Excel**: For improved usability, the enriched XML is converted into an Excel spreadsheet in which each row represents a paragraph, and each column corresponds to one of the annotations (e.g., paragraph ID, group ID, argument role, Bobbitt category).

C Human Annotation Protocol

To support training and evaluation, we collect human-annotated data for a subset of legal rulings. The annotation process is carried out by legal experts, who were provided with a structured Excel file to guide and simplify the task. The annotation workflow follows these guidelines:

- **Pre-segmented input**: Annotators receive the ruling already segmented into paragraphs and grouped semantically. Each paragraph is associated with a pre-assigned `group_id`.
- **Category assignment**: For each paragraph, annotators select the most appropriate constitutional argument category from a drop-down menu. The available options correspond to Bobbitt's six constitutional categories: *Historical*, *Textual*, *Structural*, *Prudential*, *Doctrinal*, *Ethical*, or *None*.
- **Group-based validation**: Since all paragraphs belonging to the same group are visually adjacent in the spreadsheet, annotators can easily compare their content and ensure coherent category assignment across the group.

We provide annotators with clear definitions and examples for each label to ensure consistency. This setup reduces annotation ambiguity and improves efficiency. Inter-annotator agreement is evaluated using Cohen's kappa and F1 score. Results are reported in Section 5.

D Prompt syntactic structure

This prompt guides the model in dividing a legal text into coherent paragraphs, each labeled as a "premise", "conclusion", or null. Each paragraph is assigned a unique identifier based on the logic of argument chains. It is used to generate machine-readable XML structures, as described in the main section of the paper.

```
{
    "role": "system",
    "content": (
        "You are an assistant skilled in
        ↪ analyzing and structuring legal
        ↪ texts. "
        "Your task is to divide the given text
        ↪ into coherent paragraphs and
        ↪ annotate each paragraph as either a
        ↪ 'premise' or a 'conclusion', "
        "as part of an argument chain. An
        ↪ argument chain is defined as an
        ↪ argument supporting the final
        ↪ conclusion concerning a specific
        ↪ ground of appeal, "
        "together with all counterarguments
        ↪ considered by the Court. Multiple
        ↪ argument chains may be present in a
        ↪ single decision. "
        "Each premise and conclusion is denoted
        ↪ through a unique identifier (ID),
        ↪ composed of a letter (indicating
        ↪ the argument chain, e.g., A or B) "
        "and a progressive number (indicating
        ↪ the specific premise or conclusion
        ↪ within that chain, e.g., A1, A2, B1,
        ↪ B2).\n\n"
        "**Output Guidelines:**\n"
        "1. **Structure:** Return the output as
        ↪ a JSON array. Each element in the
        ↪ array must have the following
        ↪ structure:\n\n"
        "{\n"
        "  \"ID\": \"A1\",  // A unique ID for
        ↪ the paragraph (e.g., A1, A2, B1,
        ↪ etc.)\n"
        "  \"type\": \"premise\" or
        ↪ \"conclusion\",  // Type of
        ↪ paragraph\n"
        "  \"content\": \"The actual text of the
        ↪ paragraph\"\n"
        "}\n\n"
        "2. **Paragraph Coherence:** Ensure each
        ↪ paragraph represents a single
        ↪ logical unit.\n"
        "3. **Annotation:** Annotate paragraphs
        ↪ accurately as 'premise' or
        ↪ 'conclusion'. "
        "If a paragraph does not fit clearly as
        ↪ a 'premise' or 'conclusion', leave
        ↪ the 'type' field as null.\n"
        "4. **ID Assignment:** Assign IDs using
        ↪ the following pattern:\n"
        "   - Use a letter (e.g., A, B) to
        ↪ indicate the argument chain the
        ↪ paragraph belongs to.\n"
        "   - Use a progressive number (e.g., A1,
        ↪ A2, B1, B2) to denote the order
        ↪ within the chain.\n"
        "5. **Ensure Consistency:** IDs must not
        ↪ restart for each chunk of text.
        ↪ Maintain continuity across all
        ↪ chunks.\n\n"
        "**Example Output:**\n"
        "[\n"
        "  {\"id\": \"A1\", \"type\":
        ↪ \"premise\", \"content\": \"The
        ↪ court finds that...\"},\n"
        "  {\"id\": \"A2\", \"type\":
        ↪ \"conclusion\", \"content\":
        ↪ \"Therefore, the appeal is
        ↪ dismissed.\"},\n"
        "  {\"id\": \"B1\", \"type\":
        ↪ \"premise\", \"content\": \"A
        ↪ counterargument is
        ↪ presented...\"},\n"
        "  {\"id\": \"B2\", \"type\": null,
        ↪ \"content\": \"Background context
        ↪ about the case.\"}\n"
        "]\n\n"
        "Now process the following text
        ↪ according to these guidelines."
    ),
},
{
    "role": "user",
    "content": (
        "Here is the text to process:\n\n"
        f"{text}\n\n"
        "Please divide it into coherent
        ↪ paragraphs, tag them as 'premise',
        ↪ 'conclusion', or null, assign
        ↪ unique IDs, and return the output in
        ↪ JSON format."
        f"PAY ATTENTION: {self.state_message}"
    ),
}
```

This message is dynamically generated and included in the prompt to ensure that the numbering of argument chain IDs (e.g., A1, A2, ...) remains continuous, even when the text is processed in multiple chunks.

```
self.state_message = (
            f"The current chain is '{chain}'.
            ↪ "
            f"Ensure continuity of the chain
            ↪ IDs {self.current_chain}{s⌋
            ↪ elf.current_progressive}."
        )
```

E Prompt semantic grouping

The following is the prompt used to guide the language model in grouping legal sentences based on semantic meaning:

```
{
    "role": "system",
    "content": (
        "You are an assistant skilled in the
        ↪ structural and semantic analysis of
        ↪ legal sentences. "
```

```
        "You will receive sentences annotated
        ↪ with an ID and various attributes. "
        "Your task is to group the sentences
        ↪ that share a common semantic logic
        ↪ or address the same topic.\n\n"
        "Follow these **strict guidelines** when
        ↪ grouping the sentences:\n"
        "1. **Do not exceed 7/8 sentences per
        ↪ group**: Under no circumstances
        ↪ should a group contain more than 8
        ↪ sentences.\n"
        "2. **Group by semantic meaning**:
        ↪ Ignore the IDs and order. Base the
        ↪ grouping purely on the meaning of
        ↪ each sentence.\n"
        "3. **Leave unrelated sentences
        ↪ ungrouped**: Assign them to
        ↪ `group_id: null` with an
        ↪ explanation.\n"
        "4. **Provide clear reasons for
        ↪ grouping**: Explain why sentences
        ↪ are grouped together, focusing on
        ↪ their shared logic or theme.\n\n"
        "Format the response strictly as JSON:\n"
        "{\n"
        "  \"groups\": [\n"
        "    {\n"
        "      \"group_id\": 1,\n"
        "      \"sentence_ids\": [\"ID1\",
        ↪ \"ID2\", \"ID3\"],\n"
        "      \"reason\": \"Explanation for why
        ↪ these sentences are grouped
        ↪ together.\"\n"
        "    },\n"
        "    {\n"
        "      \"group_id\": 2,\n"
        "      \"sentence_ids\": [\"ID4\",
        ↪ \"ID5\"],\n"
        "      \"reason\": \"Explanation for
        ↪ this grouping.\"\n"
        "    },\n"
        "    {\n"
        "      \"group_id\": null,\n"
        "      \"sentence_ids\": [\"ID8\",
        ↪ \"ID20\"],\n"
        "      \"reason\": \"Ungrouped sentences
        ↪ due to lack of thematic
        ↪ connection.\"\n"
        "    }\n"
        "  ]\n"
        "}\n")
},
{
    "role": "user",
    "content": (
        "Here are some legal sentences annotated
        ↪ with IDs:\n\n"
        f"{json.dumps(chunk, indent=2)}\n\n"
        "Please strictly adhere to the
        ↪ guidelines "
        "Group unrelated sentences under
        ↪ `group_id: null`. Provide clear
        ↪ reasons for each group."
        f"{mex}")
}
```

Because the entire text is divided into chunks due to the maximum token length limitation of GPT, it is crucial to maintain the continuity of group assignments across different chunks. To achieve this, the IDs assigned in previous chunks are passed to subsequent chunks. This ensures that sentences that were already grouped together remain in the same group and that no sentence is reassigned to a different group incorrectly. To implement this, the following message (mex) is injected into the prompt, warning the model to preserve the group IDs from previous outputs:

```
mex =   (
        f"PAY ATTENTION:"
        f"The past groups are
        ↪ '{output_file}'. "
        f"Ensure continuity of the groups
        ↪ IDs and don't change groups of
        ↪ senteces that were yet
        ↪ asisigned."
    )
```

F Prompt semantic structure

To systematically categorize supporting arguments in legal texts, we use the following prompt. The goal is to classify a given argument into one of several predefined subcategories, ensuring a structured and interpretable classification process.

```
{
    "role": "system",
    "content": (
        "You are an expert assistant in
        ↪ analyzing legal texts. "
        "Your task is to classify a supporting
        ↪ argument into one of the following
        ↪ subcategories, "
        "or to indicate that none is appropriate:
        ↪ \n"
        "- **Historical Arguments**:
        ↪ Interpretation based on the
        ↪ original intentions of the framers
        ↪ and ratifiers.\n"
        "- **Textual Arguments**: Based solely on
        ↪ the literal meaning of the words.\n"
        "- **Structural Arguments**: Analysis of
        ↪ the overall constitutional system
        ↪ and interactions among its parts.\n"
        "- **Prudential Arguments**: Evaluation
        ↪ of practical pros and cons and
        ↪ social consequences.\n"
        "- **Doctrinal Arguments**: Use of legal
        ↪ precedents to resolve new cases.\n"
        "- **Ethical Arguments**: Based on moral
        ↪ principles and shared societal
        ↪ values.\n\n"
        "If none of the categories is suitable,
        ↪ you may indicate that the text does
        ↪ not fit into any of them.\n\n"
        "Please return the result in the
        ↪ following JSON format:\n\n"
        "{\n"
        f"   \"Group\": \"Group {group}\",\n"
        "   \"Category\": \"[Name of Category or
        ↪ 'None']\",\n"
        "   \"Reason\": \"[Explanation for the
        ↪ classification]\"\n"
```

```
        "}\n"
    )
},
{
    "role": "user",
    "content": (
        f"The following text is a supporting
        ↪ argument: {text}. "
        f"Group: {group}"
        "Analyze the content and identify the
        ↪ most relevant subcategory from the
        ↪ provided options, "
        "or indicate if none of the
        ↪ subcategories is appropriate. "
        "Please ensure the response is formatted
        ↪ strictly as JSON, following the
        ↪ example provided."
    )
}
```

Aspect-Based Opinion Summarization with Argumentation Schemes

Wendi Zhou and **Ameer Saadat-Yazdi** and **Nadin Kökciyan**
School of Informatics,
University of Edinburgh
{wendi.zhou, ameer.saadat, nadin.kokciyan}@ed.ac.uk

Abstract

Reviews are valuable resources for customers making purchase decisions in online shopping. However, it is impractical for customers to go over the vast number of reviews and manually conclude the prominent opinions, which prompts the need for automated opinion summarization systems. Previous approaches, either extractive or abstractive, face challenges in automatically producing grounded aspect-centric summaries. In this paper, we propose a novel summarization system that not only captures predominant opinions from an aspect perspective with supporting evidence, but also adapts to varying domains without relying on a pre-defined set of aspects. Our proposed framework, ASESUM, summarizes viewpoints relevant to the critical aspects of a product by extracting aspect-centric arguments and measuring their *salience* and *validity*. We conduct experiments on a real-world dataset to demonstrate the superiority of our approach in capturing diverse perspectives of the original reviews compared to new and existing methods.

1 Introduction

Online reviews are essential resources for customers to make purchase decisions, as they more authentically reflect the performance of some products or services (Boorugu and Ramesh, 2020; Amplayo et al., 2021). It is very impractical for users to go over most reviews one by one and conclude the prominent opinions discussed themselves. Ideally, users should have access to automated opinion summaries to make informed decisions.

Automatic opinion summarization offers a solution by aggregating all reviews into a concise, easy-to-read summary. Previous methods concerning opinion summarization can be mainly classified as either extractive or abstractive. We see drawbacks with both approaches. Extractive methods select the representative sentences from the input to generate the summary. Although attributable and scalable, they could encounter issues in generating concise and coherent summaries. On the other hand, abstractive methods using neural models to generate fluent and novel summaries may lead to hallucinated content that is challenging to detect without any supporting evidence. Hosking et al. (2023) implement a hybrid summarization system, HERCULES, that produces summaries reflecting the general feedback of all reviewers while abstracting away too many details. Although being abstractive and attributable, their summaries are too general for users interested in certain aspects of the entity.

We argue that an ideal summary should reflect the main opinion expressed in the reviews, be attributable with grounding evidence and include critical aspect information that is essential to assist customers while making their purchase decisions. Many attempts have been made to incorporate aspect information inside the final summary (Amplayo et al., 2021; Tang et al., 2024; Li et al., 2025); however, they either rely on the manually pre-defined aspects or they lose track of the supporting evidence with a fully automated pipeline using large language models (LLMs).

To address these existing limitations, we propose an aspect-centric review summarization framework, ASESUM, to produce high-quality opinion summaries for products. With the help of argumentation schemes and LLMs, ASESUM extracts aspect-centric arguments, where the claim is the user's sentiment towards certain aspects, and the premise is the supporting evidence mentioned by the users in the reviews. This makes the summarization model more generalisable than previous systems as it can easily adapt to new domains, does not require a pre-existing taxonomy of new aspects and can scale up with the number of reviews. By clustering claims supported by similar pieces of evidence, we define a metric to measure the salience and validity of an argument. This metric is used to rank the arguments having the critical aspects

Proceedings of the 12th Argument Mining Workshop, pages 116–125
July 31, 2025

information from which we generate our final summaries. In this paper, our main contributions can be summarized as follows:

- We develop a new automated method that can iteratively induce the aspect taxonomy within the product reviews;
- We introduce a new domain-independent argumentation scheme for aspect-centric argument extraction from customer reviews;
- We propose a novel hybrid review summarization framework (ASESUM)[1] to generate textual summaries. Our model outperforms the current state-of-the-art by 6% on average on a real-world benchmark dataset.

Our paper is organised as follows. We discuss related work on summarization and argumentation in NLP in Section 2. We introduce our review summarization framework (ASESUM) in Section 3, and Section 4 explains our experimental setup before we compare our approach to other models. In Section 5, we show that ASESUM outperforms these models, not only in terms of the amount of semantic information captured by our summaries but also in the diversity of viewpoints presented. We conclude our paper with a discussion in Section 6.

2 Related work

Earlier work on opinion summarization, or review aggregation, is either purely extractive (Mihalcea and Tarau, 2004; Rossiello et al., 2017; Alguliyev et al., 2019; Belwal et al., 2021) or abstractive (Ganesan et al., 2010; Bražinskas et al., 2020). However, both types of methods have their own shortcomings: extractive methods tend to introduce unnecessary details and struggle to cover all topics in multi-topic inputs, while abstractive methods are limited by the input length of neural models or language models and may generate hallucinated content. Hosking et al. (2023) introduce a hybrid approach, where they encode the review sentences as a hierarchy of paths and then decode the most frequent path in the hierarchy structure as the final summary. Though being unsupervised and attributable, their hierarchy encoder is domain-dependent, thus limiting its generalisability. Their approach mainly focuses on the general summary generation, neglecting aspect-relevant information.

[1]All the code is available online at: `https://git.ecdf.ed.ac.uk/s2236454/asesum`

Angelidis et al. (2021) propose an extractive method that generates aspect-specific summaries using the quantized transformer. Similarly, Amplayo et al. (2021) develop an abstractive method where they fine-tune a Pre-trained Language Model with aspect controllers for abstractive summaries generation. However, these methods extract aspects either directly from the sentence or with the assistance of humans. Recently, LLMs have demonstrated great performance across a wide range of natural language understanding tasks. Leveraging this, Tang et al. (2024) propose a fully automated aspect extraction approach through few-shot prompting. They successfully extract aspects together with users' sentiment towards that aspect from reviews; then, after clustering the <aspect, sentiment> pairs, they re-prompt LLMs to generate the aspect-specific keypoints as the final summaries. In this way, they achieve flexible aspect-centric summaries generation at scale, but this iterative prompting pipeline makes their summaries harder to validate without grounding evidence. In contrast, ASESUM framework preserves the same versatility while providing the grounding evidence by considering argumentative structure. In Li et al. (2025), they propose a more explainable and grounded summarization pipeline through prompting LLMs, which separates the tasks of aspect identification, opinion consolidation, and meta-review synthesis. However, their system requires a set of manually pre-defined aspects, while our system incorporates a flexible aspect induce approach.

Argumentation schemes have been widely studied in computational argumentation, aiming to model, extract, and generate human-like arguments. A foundational basis for this theory comes from Walton, where he defines structured patterns of common reasoning used in everyday discourse (Walton et al., 2008). Each scheme is provided with a template for constructing arguments and critical questions for evaluating their validity. More recent approaches incorporate Walton's schemes into neural models to guide argument structure prediction and improve the interpretability of human conversations (Herbets de Sousa et al., 2024).

In the context of product reviews, Wyner Adam et al. (2012) introduce a scheme for product reviews based on customer values for semi-automated review analysis. Similarly, Mumford et al. (2024) use the *Position to Know* scheme and associated critical questions to evaluate the quality of reviews. We find both these approaches limited in that they

Review Argument Scheme (RAS)
Claim: **A** of this product is **S**   *Major Premise*: **X** is a sign that **A** is **S**   *Minor Premise*: The user observes **X** about **A**

Table 1: Proposed argument scheme where **A**, **S**, **X** represent the aspect, sentiment and evidence respectively.

ignore the particular features (aspects) of a product that users are discussing, making the analysis too coarse-grained and the evaluation criteria difficult to apply automatically. In contrast, we base our method on a scheme based on *Argument from Characteristic Sign* which we make specific to our aspect/sentiment framework. Our approach also does not depend on critical questions and instead uses an evidence consistency measure to identify the most salient evidence to provide to a user.

3 ASESUM Framework

In this section, we introduce an aspect-centric review summarization framework, ASESUM. The framework has three stages: (i) aspect-centric argument extraction with a new argumentation scheme, *Review Argument Scheme*, (ii) argument clustering and evidence unification, and (iii) argument scoring guided by aspect-centric argument relations.

3.1 Argument extraction

Inspired by the argumentation schemes defined by Walton et al. (2008), we propose a novel argumentation scheme for product reviews as shown in Table 1. The Review Argument Scheme (RAS) consists of three variables: the aspect (**A**), the sentiment (**S**) and the evidence (**X**). In our framework, **S** takes values from $\{good, bad\}$.

In ASESUM, each argument is defined as an instantiation of RAS, Definition 3.1 provides a formal definition of an argument. Note that Arg_i is used to define the *i*th argument.

Definition 3.1 (Argument). Arg denotes a tuple $\langle a, s, x\rangle$, where a, s, x represent the aspect, sentiment and supporting evidence respectively, as they appear in the instantiated argument scheme Arg.

In order to instantiate RAS, we benefit from LLMs to fill in the scheme variables and generate arguments with provided user reviews. To avoid LLMs generating diverse aspect representations, we first prompt LLMs to initiate the *critical aspects* of the product given the product category information. The critical aspects represent the key evaluation factors of the product, which may greatly influence customers' purchase decisions. Then we feed them as options into the prompt to guide LLM on performing aspect-centric argument extraction (Figure 1a). However, for a small subset of reviews, LLMs fail to generate any valid arguments. As this affects only around 3% of the reviews per domain, it does not have a big influence on the final results. After obtaining all the arguments extracted by LLMs, we further unify the representations of aspects by clustering them and representing each cluster with a symbol $(A_1, A_2...A_n)$. We will provide implementation details in Section 4.2.

3.2 Evidence-based Clustering

Since the evidence for each argument is extracted or slightly summarized by LLMs, it is highly unlikely they will have the same evidence even for arguments sharing the same aspect and sentiment. And so, we cluster arguments sharing semantically close evidence and then select the most representative evidence X_k for each cluster (Figure 1b). We assume the most representative evidence of the cluster is the one that entails the majority of the evidence in the cluster. To achieve this, we build a text graph where the vertices are the semantic embeddings of each sentence, and the edge weights are calculated by the cosine similarity between each node pair. Then we iterate the graph-based ranking algorithm derived from Google's PageRank (Page et al., 1999) as described in TextRank (Mihalcea and Tarau, 2004) until convergence. Finally, we select the vertex with the highest score as the most representative evidence of this cluster.

For each argument Arg_i in a cluster c, we then substitute its original evidence $(Arg_i.x)$ with the representative evidence (X_c) and we rewrite the argument as Arg_i^c. In other words, the evidence of each argument in a cluster is replaced with the most representative evidence. This methodology is depicted in Figure 1b. For example, in *Cluster m*, we see five arguments, where each of them is supported with its unique evidence. X_m would be the representative evidence for *Cluster m*. If Arg_1 is represented as $\langle a_1, s_1, x_1\rangle$, this argument would be rewritten as Arg_1^m=$\langle a_1, s_1, X_m\rangle$. All other arguments could be rewritten similarly.

After unifying similar evidence for every argument, we calculate a score for each argument based on its popularity and its validity in supporting or opposing a claim related to an aspect.

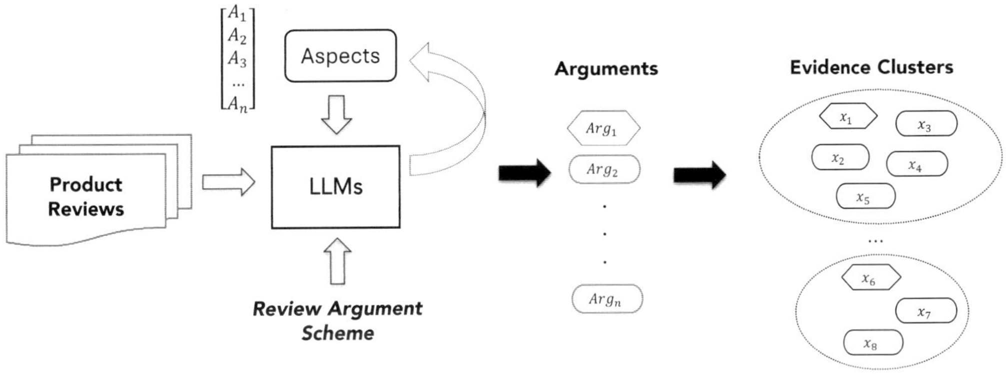

(a) A demonstration of the argument extraction, where we feed the product reviews, the defined Review Argument Scheme together with the set of aspects into LLMs to generate aspect-centric arguments (Definition 3.1). The aspect set is initiated by prompting LLMs, and is updated during the argument extraction. The arguments are then clustered based on their evidence.

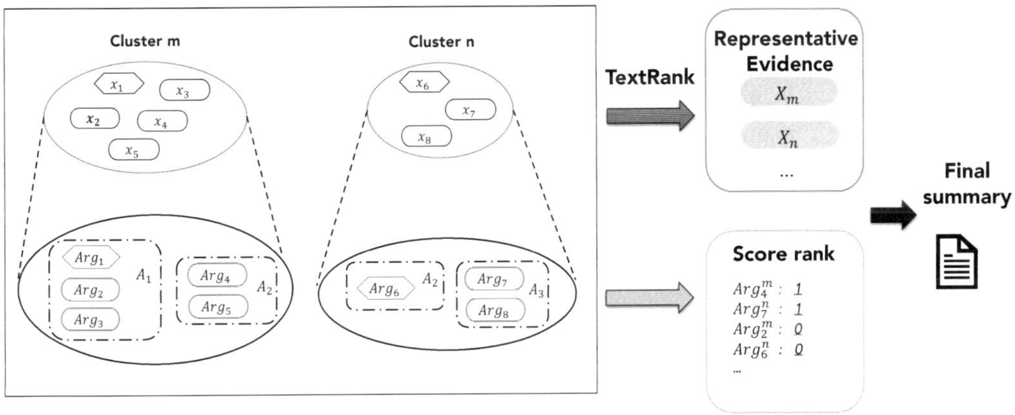

(b) A diagrammatic representation of our methodology starting from clustered arguments. For each clustered argument, ASESUM selects the representative piece of evidence X_k using the TextRank algorithm. This representative evidence is then used to replace the original evidence of each argument in the cluster. Meanwhile, the system builds the relations among arguments within the same cluster based on their aspects, which are used to measure the salience and validity of the argument as defined in Equation 1. Finally, our system selects **N** unique pieces of evidence from the top-ranked arguments to generate the summary.

Figure 1: The Proposed ASESUM Framework

3.3 Aspect-centric Ranking

To quantitatively assess the salience and validity of an argument, we make use of its support and contradiction relations to other arguments in the same cluster (Section 3.2). Firstly, we provide formal definitions of the relations between arguments in Definitions 3.2 and 3.3.

Definition 3.2 (Aspect-centric Support)**.** A support relation between two arguments in the same cluster, Arg_i and Arg_j, exists if and only if both arguments have the same aspect (i.e., $Arg_i.a = Arg_j.a$) and sentiment (i.e., $Arg_i.s = Arg_j.s$).

Definition 3.3 (Aspect-centric Contradiction)**.** A contradiction relation between two arguments in the same cluster, Arg_i and Arg_j, exists if and only if both arguments have the same aspect (i.e., $Arg_i.a = Arg_j.a$) and different sentiment (i.e., $Arg_i.s \neq Arg_j.s$).

Intuitively, we consider an argument to be strengthened when a similar evidence supports the same claim from another argument, and an argument to be weakened if a similar evidence is used to support the opposite claim from another argument. For example, for a pair of shoes, a piece of evidence could be "the shoes are quite wide". If this evidence is used to support both arguments with the claim "The *fit* is good" and the claim "The *fit* is bad"; then for the aspect *fit*, "the shoes are quite wide" is a piece of controversial evidence, thus we should not include it into the final summary.

Based on Definitions 3.2 and 3.3, we measure the global validity of an argument i in a cluster c

by using Equation 1.

$$Score(Arg_i^c) = \sum_{\substack{\forall Arg_j \in c, i \neq j \\ Arg_i.a = Arg_j.a}} \hat{s}_i \times \hat{s}_j, \quad (1)$$

where $\hat{s}_i$ and $\hat{s}_j$ represent the sentiment polarity of Arg_i^c and Arg_j^c, respectively. An argument with a 'good' sentiment is assigned a polarity value of $+1.0$, while an argument with a 'bad' sentiment is assigned a polarity value of -1.0.

In ASESUM, as a final step, we assign each evidence cluster with the highest score achieved by any argument within it. The clusters are then ranked based on their scores, and the top-N representative evidence pieces are selected to generate the final summary.

4 Experimental Setup

In this section, we introduce the datasets used in our experiments (Section 4.1) and discuss the implementation details of ASESUM (Section 4.2). Then we describe other comparison systems (Section 4.3), and explain the automatic metrics for our evaluation (Section 4.4).

4.1 Dataset

We conducted our experiments by using the AmaSum dataset (Bražinskas et al., 2021), the largest abstractive opinion summarization dataset, consisting of more than 33,000 human-written summaries for Amazon products from a wide range of categories. In AmaSum dataset, each product is paired with more than 320 customer reviews and at least one reference summary. Each reference summary includes 'verdict', 'pros' and 'cons', but as the reference summaries are obtained from external resources, they are not grounded in product reviews. Similar to the work of Hosking et al. (2023), we concatenate these three sections together to construct the final reference summary. Moreover, we follow the same setting to build the test set by sampling 50 products per domain for evaluation. Detailed statistics are listed in Table 2.

Test Domain	#Reviews	Avg. Length
Electronic	568	45
Shoes	381	38
Sports & Outdoor	610	44
Home & Kitchen	680	45

Table 2: The statistics of all the domains in our sampled test set. *#Reviews* represents the average number of reviews for all the products, and *Avg. Length* represents the average number of words separated by space in reviews for a particular domain.

4.2 Implementation

In ASESUM framework, we choose one closed-source LLM *GPT-4o-mini* from OpenAI[2]and another open-source LLM *Qwen2.5-7B* (Qwen et al., 2025) as our backbone models. The prompt used for both models is shown in Appendix A.

In order to implement the aspect clustering (Section 3.1) and evidence clustering (Section 3.2), we opt for the Density-based spatial clustering of applications with noise (*DBSCAN*) algorithm (Ester et al., 1996). DBSCAN is the most ideal clustering method for ASESUM as it does not require a predefined number of clusters, thereby enhancing the generalizability of the framework. Based on a series of preliminary trials on the training set, we configure the clustering hyper-parameters as follows: the clustering metric is set to "cosine" similarity, the minimum number of sample per cluster is set to 1, and the ϵ is set to 0.5 and 0.21 for aspect clustering and evidence clustering, respectively. Additionally, we select the top 8 pieces of unique evidence to form our final summary based on our exploratory experiments.

4.3 Other Models for Comparison

As depicted in Figure 1, our proposed ASESUM framework is a hybrid summarization approach that combines *abstractive* methods (by benefiting from LLMs) and *extractive* methods (by selecting the final set of arguments for summarization with clustering and TextRank). According to this, we primarily compare our framework with the previous state-of-the-art hybrid summarization model, HERCULES (Hosking et al., 2023). Since HERCULES is domain-specific, we use their released models for the four domains (*Electronic*, *Shoes*, *Sports & Outdoor*, *Home & Kitchen*) as shown in Table 2. We evaluate the models on these four domains separately using their default configuration settings.

For comparison, we also develop an LLM-based baseline using GPT-4o-mini to evaluate the effectiveness of our ASESUM framework. In this case, we randomly sample 50 reviews (the maximum

[2]https://platform.openai.com/docs/models/gpt-4o-mini

number of reviews that would reliably fit within the context-length of gpt-4o-mini) and pass them to the model along with a simple summarization instruction[3].

4.4 Evaluation Metrics

We use various automatic evaluation metrics to compare ASESUM framework with other models, namely ROUGE-2, ROUGE-L F1 (Lin, 2004), SummaC (Laban et al., 2022). We also propose a new sentence diversity score to measure the sentence-level diversity of a summary.

We calculate the ROUGE-2, ROUGE-L F1 scores against the reference summaries of AmaSum dataset similar to the work of Hosking et al. (2023). SummaC score (Laban et al., 2022) is a popular metric for evaluating how well a summary is entailed by the input document. It segments the input document and reviews into sentences and computes the average entailment score between each pair of the input sentence and the generated summary. We calculate the SummaC score of the generated summaries against the reference (SC_{ref}) and the original input reviews (SC_{in}). Since the reference summary is built independently of the input reviews, the SummaC score computed against original reviews (SC_{in}) provides a more trustworthy indication of the summary quality.

A helpful product review summary should capture the most frequently expressed opinions from the input, but without repeating the same points redundantly. Therefore, we propose a diversity metric that evaluates the sentence-level diversity of the final summary. The idea is to segment a summary into sentences and evaluate the semantic closeness of all the sentences through clustering. As a longer summary having more sentences would result in a higher number of clusters naturally, we normalise the cluster number by the total number of sentences to obtain the final diversity score of a summary. We define this new metric in Equation 2.

$$Diversity(S) = \frac{|Clusters(S)|}{|S|}, \quad (2)$$

where S is the set of sentences in a summary, $|Clusters(S)|$ is the number of clusters and $|S|$ is the number of sentences in S.

In our implementation, we use DBSCAN algorithm with the same parameter settings as the aspect clustering discussed in Section 4.2.

[3]Prompt: `Summarize the following list of reviews. Keep your answer concise while capturing as many diverse points of view as possible.`

5 Evaluation Results

In this section, we analyze the quantitative results based on all automatic evaluation metrics (Section 5.1) and provide a detailed qualitative discussion on the generated summaries for a randomly chosen product (Section 5.2).

5.1 Quantitative Analysis

The evaluation results are shown in Table 3. We observe that ASESUM framework with both closed-source and open-source LLMs consistently outperforms other methods on all four domains across all metrics besides ROUGE-2. Particularly for the SC_{in} score, our ASESUM achieves significantly higher SC_{in} scores across all the domains, indicating that our generated summaries are more representative of the input reviews. Surprisingly, our ASESUM framework paired with Qwen2.5-7B ($ASESUM_{qwen2.5-7B}$) achieves comparable performance with ASESUM paired with GPT-4o-mini ($ASESUM_{gpt-4o-mini}$) across all the domains and evaluation metrics, demonstrating both the robustness and the generalizability of the framework.

Across all models, the big difference between the SC_{in} and SC_{ref} score also suggests that the manually constructed reference summaries do not faithfully entail all the product reviews, as they are built separately. On the other hand, GPT-4o-mini baseline performs the worst on most of the metrics, which can be the result of the limited number of input reviews. However, it achieves higher ROUGE scores and has a smaller difference in SC_{ref} than it has in SC_{in} when compared to other methods. This indicates that summaries generated by GPT-4o-mini are more fluent and closer to manually written summaries.

In terms of the sentence-level diversity, $ASESUM_{qwen2.5-7B}$ even performs better than $ASESUM_{gpt-4o-mini}$ in most domains. Notably, the diversity of summaries generated by our ASESUM framework is greatly dependent on the diversity of unique aspects of products. For domains having products with various aspects, such as *Electronics* (on average 14 aspects per product), the diversity score of our summaries is obviously higher than other domains, such as *Shoes* (on average 10 aspects per product). While ASESUM with LLMs generate less diverse summaries for the *Shoes* and *Sports & Ourdoors* domains, it achieves higher

Models	ROUGE-2	ROUGE-L	SC_{ref}	SC_{in}	Diversity
			Electronics		
GPT-4o-mini	**2.93**	11.38	20.80	43.76	0.55
HERCULES	2.41	12.44	22.87	79.79	0.73
$\text{ASESUM}_{\text{qwen2.5-7B}}$	2.80	12.57	23.91	84.59	**0.81**
$\text{ASESUM}_{\text{gpt-4o-mini}}$	2.68	**12.80**	**24.18**	**85.28**	0.80
			Shoes		
GPT-4o-mini	**3.75**	**13.23**	21.46	42.73	0.47
HERCULES	1.80	12.06	24.35	84.45	0.72
$\text{ASESUM}_{\text{qwen2.5-7B}}$	2.14	11.41	25.30	92.72	**0.75**
$\text{ASESUM}_{\text{gpt-4o-mini}}$	2.01	11.09	**27.09**	**95.28**	0.72
			Sports & Outdoors		
GPT-4o-mini	**2.98**	12.68	20.69	44.68	0.47
HERCULES	1.72	11.45	**24.85**	86.22	**0.86**
$\text{ASESUM}_{\text{qwen2.5-7B}}$	2.20	12.67	24.79	87.27	0.82
$\text{ASESUM}_{\text{gpt-4o-mini}}$	2.65	**12.95**	24.81	**89.15**	**0.86**
			Home & Kitchen		
GPT-4o-mini	**2.74**	12.07	20.62	43.62	0.55
HERCULES	2.26	11.35	23.31	83.24	0.81
$\text{ASESUM}_{\text{qwen2.5-7B}}$	2.45	12.59	**24.10**	87.10	**0.87**
$\text{ASESUM}_{\text{gpt-4o-mini}}$	**2.74**	**12.80**	23.66	**87.38**	0.86
			Average		
GPT-4o-mini	**3.10**	12.34	20.89	44.68	0.51
HERCULES	2.05	11.83	23.85	83.43	0.78
$\text{ASESUM}_{\text{qwen2.5-7B}}$	2.40	12.31	24.53	87.92	0.81
$\text{ASESUM}_{\text{gpt-4o-mini}}$	2.52	**12.41**	**24.94**	**89.27**	**0.81**

Table 3: Results for automatic evaluation on review summarization. ROUGE-2 and ROUGE-L F1 scores are computed against the reference summaries. SC_{ref} and SC_{in} indicate the consistency (measured using SummaC) of generated summaries against reference summaries and input reviews, respectively. Our proposed *Diversity* measures the sentence-level diversity of the final generated summaries. Bold denotes the best score per domain.

SummaC scores on these domains compared to the others. This reveals that a summary could attain a high SummaC score by repeating opinions closely aligned with the input documents, even if such a summary may not be considered helpful in a real-life setting.

5.2 Qualitative Analysis

In addition to the numerical results in Table 3, we randomly select one example product from the *Home & Kitchen* domain to discuss qualitative aspects of our generated summaries. As shown in Figure 2, we notice that our generated results are significantly more faithful to the original reviews. This is because HERCULES decodes the summary from a hierarchical discrete latent embedding space, which strongly relies on its pre-trained codebook that performs the mapping from the discrete code to continuous embeddings (Hosking et al., 2023). However, since the codebook is pre-trained on the training set, for an uncommon product in the training set, their model would struggle to encode the reviews properly and decode the relevant information accordingly. This is also justified by the unsatisfying performance of HERCULES in the *Electronics* domain, where the types of products are more diverse than in other domains. On the contrary, our summaries maintain the topic at hand and minimise the likelihood of hallucination as we only apply abstractive summarization in the

Great Peeler. This product is a joke. Love this *ice crusher*. Not too heavy, not too light. *Easy to peel off. Keeps my coffee hot for hours*. This *ice crusher* works great. The lids fit snug. The plastic is very thin and flimsy. *Crushes ice* very well. *Love this water bottle*!

(a) HERCULES

One tray shattered the first time we used it. I like the fact these have lids. Very easy to pop out the ice cubes. cubes end up being a little small. Lids don't stay closed at all. Lids are nice to help keep the water in the trays when transferring from the sink to the freezer and for stacking while they make ice. Ice cubes are small. trays are very small, not easy to use as ice is hard to remove and there is only enuf ice per tray for one small glass. They stack great.

(b) ASESUM$_{\text{qwen2.5-7B}}$

Very easy to pop out the ice cubes. one tray broke. I like the fact these have lids. the lids do not stay on. the size of the cubes, they seem much smaller than a standard ice cube tray. cubes end up being a little small. Cubes could be a little larger. Each one comes with a lid so it's easy to stack. the silicone bottom makes them pop out with absolutely no effort.

(c) ASESUM$_{\text{gpt-4o-mini}}$

Figure 2: Example generated summaries from HERCULES and ASESUM with LLMs, for a randomly selected product (ice-tray).

initial aspect-centric argument extraction step. In addition, by comparing the textual summary from ASESUM$_{\text{qwen2.5-7B}}$ and ASESUM$_{\text{gpt-4o-mini}}$, we observe that evidence extracted by GPT-4o-mini is summarized to be more concise, which may lead to a lower diversity score for some domains.

6 Conclusion

This paper presents a novel summarization framework that integrates aspect-based sentiment analysis with argument mining to extract aspect-centric arguments for generating diverse yet faithful summaries. Although evaluating arguments based on their controversy level may not be the most ideal solution, our approach obtains strong performance on a benchmark dataset in both numerical and qualitative evaluations. Furthermore, by combining both extractive and abstractive summarization techniques, we demonstrate strong generalisability of our framework through automated aspect generation, the incorporation of multiple LLMs and domain-independent summarization.

Our approach relies on the dynamic extraction of relevant aspects and sentiments towards these aspects. We are planning to use these aspects to generate summaries as part of our future work. We will also conduct user studies to find meaningful ways to present the summary together with this aspect sentiment structure. Future research should also focus on finding ways to automatically evaluate structured summaries, which remains as a challenging problem for the community.

Limitations

ASESUM framework can be easily adapted to other domains and incorporated with other language models; however, we have a number of hyperparameters set to run the clustering algorithm. The consistent performance of our framework across four domains suggests the generalisability of this set of chosen parameters, but it may require more adjustments when adapting to new datasets. Besides, since our summaries are generated by concatenating pieces of evidence from different arguments, they may lack coherence in general.

Acknowledgment

This work was supported by the University of Edinburgh-Huawei Joint Lab grants CIENG4721 and CIENG8329.

References

R. M. Alguliyev, R. M. Aliguliyev, N. R. Isazade, A. Abdi, and N. Idris. 2019. COSUM: Text summarization based on clustering and optimization. *Expert Systems*, 36(1):e12340.

Reinald Kim Amplayo, Stefanos Angelidis, and Mirella Lapata. 2021. Aspect-controllable opinion summarization. In *Proceedings of the 2021 Conference on Empirical Methods in Natural Language Processing*, pages 6578–6593, Online and Punta Cana, Dominican Republic. Association for Computational Linguistics.

Stefanos Angelidis, Reinald Kim Amplayo, Yoshihiko Suhara, Xiaolan Wang, and Mirella Lapata. 2021. Extractive opinion summarization in quantized transformer spaces. *Transactions of the Association for Computational Linguistics*, 9:277–293.

R. C. Belwal, S. Rai, and A. Gupta. 2021. A new graph-based extractive text summarization using keywords or topic modeling. *Journal of Ambient Intelligence and Humanized Computing*, 12:8975–8990.

Ravali Boorugu and G. Ramesh. 2020. A survey on nlp based text summarization for summarizing product reviews. In *2020 Second International Conference on Inventive Research in Computing Applications (ICIRCA)*, pages 352–356.

Arthur Bražinskas, Mirella Lapata, and Ivan Titov. 2020. Unsupervised opinion summarization as copycat-review generation. In *Proceedings of the 58th Annual Meeting of the Association for Computational Linguistics*, pages 5151–5169, Online. Association for Computational Linguistics.

Arthur Bražinskas, Mirella Lapata, and Ivan Titov. 2021. Learning opinion summarizers by selecting informative reviews. In *Proceedings of the 2021 Conference on Empirical Methods in Natural Language Processing*, pages 9424–9442, Online and Punta Cana, Dominican Republic. Association for Computational Linguistics.

Martin Ester, Hans-Peter Kriegel, Jörg Sander, and Xiaowei Xu. 1996. A density-based algorithm for discovering clusters in large spatial databases with noise. In *Proceedings of the Second International Conference on Knowledge Discovery and Data Mining*, KDD'96, page 226–231. AAAI Press.

Kavita Ganesan, ChengXiang Zhai, and Jiawei Han. 2010. Opinosis: A graph based approach to abstractive summarization of highly redundant opinions. In *Proceedings of the 23rd International Conference on Computational Linguistics (Coling 2010)*, pages 340–348, Beijing, China. Coling 2010 Organizing Committee.

Luis Henrique Herbets de Sousa, Guilherme Trajano, Analúcia Schiaffino Morales, Stefan Sarkadi, and Alison R. Panisson. 2024. *Using Chatbot Technologies to Support Argumentation*. SciTePress.

Tom Hosking, Hao Tang, and Mirella Lapata. 2023. Attributable and scalable opinion summarization. *Preprint*, arXiv:2305.11603.

Philippe Laban, Tobias Schnabel, Paul N. Bennett, and Marti A. Hearst. 2022. Summac: Re-visiting nli-based models for inconsistency detection in summarization. *Transactions of the Association for Computational Linguistics*, 10:163–177.

Miao Li, Jey Han Lau, Eduard Hovy, and Mirella Lapata. 2025. Aspect-aware decomposition for opinion summarization. *Preprint*, arXiv:2501.17191.

Chin-Yew Lin. 2004. ROUGE: A package for automatic evaluation of summaries. In *Text Summarization Branches Out*, pages 74–81, Barcelona, Spain. Association for Computational Linguistics.

Rada Mihalcea and Paul Tarau. 2004. TextRank: Bringing order into text. In *Proceedings of the 2004 Conference on Empirical Methods in Natural Language Processing*, pages 404–411, Barcelona, Spain. Association for Computational Linguistics.

Jack Mumford, Stefan Sarkadi, Katie Atkinson, and Trevor Bench-Capon. 2024. Applying Argument Schemes for Simulating Online Review Platforms. In Chris Reed, Matthias Thimm, and Tjitze Rienstra, editors, *Frontiers in Artificial Intelligence and Applications*. IOS Press.

Lawrence Page, Sergey Brin, Rajeev Motwani, and Terry Winograd. 1999. The pagerank citation ranking: Bringing order to the web. Technical Report 1999-66, Stanford InfoLab. Previous number = SIDL-WP-1999-0120.

Qwen, :, An Yang, Baosong Yang, Beichen Zhang, Binyuan Hui, Bo Zheng, Bowen Yu, Chengyuan Li, Dayiheng Liu, Fei Huang, Haoran Wei, Huan Lin, Jian Yang, Jianhong Tu, Jianwei Zhang, Jianxin Yang, Jiaxi Yang, Jingren Zhou, and 25 others. 2025. Qwen2.5 technical report. *Preprint*, arXiv:2412.15115.

Gaetano Rossiello, Pierpaolo Basile, and Giovanni Semeraro. 2017. Centroid-based text summarization through compositionality of word embeddings. In *Proceedings of the MultiLing 2017 Workshop on Summarization and Summary Evaluation Across Source Types and Genres*, pages 12–21, Valencia, Spain. Association for Computational Linguistics.

An Tang, Xiuzhen Zhang, Minh Dinh, and Erik Cambria. 2024. Prompted aspect key point analysis for quantitative review summarization. In *Proceedings of the 62nd Annual Meeting of the Association for Computational Linguistics (Volume 1: Long Papers)*, pages 10691–10708, Bangkok, Thailand. Association for Computational Linguistics.

Douglas Walton, Chris Reed, and Fabrizio Macagno. 2008. *Argumentation Schemes*. Cambridge University Press, Cambridge.

Wyner Adam, Schneider Jodi, Atkinson Katie, and Bench-Capon Trevor. 2012. Semi-Automated Argumentative Analysis of Online Product Reviews. In *Frontiers in Artificial Intelligence and Applications*. IOS Press.

A Appendix A

We provide the prompt used in our paper in Table 4.

Fill the scheme with the provided review. {**Review Argumentation Scheme**} Note: 1. Identify the aspects mentioned in the review. Then provide a new scheme with the relevant evidence for each identified aspect. 2. The most mentioned aspects are {**aspect**}. 3. Only generate a new aspect when there is no matching one above. 4. Do NOT provide scheme having aspect wasn't mentioned in the text. 5. Do NOT include too much details in the evidence. Please return the values in JSON format: [{"aspect": "the property / feature of the product", "sentiment": "positive/negative", "evidence": "support from the argument"}, ...]

Table 4: Prompt provided to $\text{ASESUM}_{\text{gpt-4o-mini}}$ and $\text{ASESUM}_{\text{qwen2.5-7B}}$, where "Review Argumentation Scheme" is the placeholder to fit in the RAS (Table 1) and the "aspect" is the placeholder to interactively input the most popular aspects we have in the current aspect set.

Investigating Subjective Factors of Argument Strength: Storytelling, Emotions, and Hedging

Carlotta Quensel
Leibniz University Hannover
c.quensel@ai.uni-hannover.de

Neele Falk
University of Stuttgart
neele.falk@ims.uni-stuttgart.de

Gabriella Lapesa
Leibniz Institute for the Social Sciences - GESIS & Heinrich Heine University Düsseldorf
gabriella.lapesa@gesis.de

Abstract

In assessing argument strength, the notions of what makes a good argument are manifold. With the broader trend towards treating subjectivity as an asset and not a problem in NLP, new dimensions of argument quality are studied. Although studies on individual subjective features like personal stories exist, there is a lack of large-scale analyses of the relation between these features and argument strength. To address this gap, we conduct regression analysis to quantify the impact of subjective factors – emotions, storytelling, and hedging – on two standard datasets annotated for objective argument quality and subjective persuasion. As such, our contribution is twofold: at the level of contributed resources, as there are no datasets annotated with all studied dimensions, this work compares and evaluates automated annotation methods for each subjective feature. At the level of novel insights, our regression analysis uncovers different patterns of impact of subjective features on the two facets of argument strength encoded in the datasets. Our results show that storytelling and hedging have contrasting effects on objective and subjective argument quality, while the influence of emotions depends on their rhetoric utilization rather than the domain.

1 Introduction

Argument Mining describes the field of detecting arguments and their components, i.e., claims and their premises, and analyzing relationships like support and attack between those (Lawrence and Reed, 2019). This notion of argumentation as primarily reason-giving, paired with the prominent domains of academic writing, student essays, or professional debate, necessitating objectivity for judging and automatic essay scoring, led to a narrow conceptualization of argument quality. Quality assessment, as emerged from argument mining, observes **objective aspects** such as clarity and argument organization (Persing et al., 2010), use of evidence (Rahimi et al., 2014), or a combination of those (Ong et al., 2014). In the past years, however, a clear need for a shift towards a more subjective notion of argument quality has emerged, driven by the entry of laypeople into the debate space through online forums and citizen participation programs, as well as insights contending the link between objective quality and persuasive strength (Benlamine et al., 2017). This paper contributes to a better empirical understanding of the impact of subjectivity on argument quality.

Sports offer a lot more than you'd think... 1) It gives children a sense of being a part of something (crucial for kids without stable families) 2) Sports are a GREAT source of exercise [...] There's **many more** reasons but this is all I **can think** of for now. As for my own experiences, baseball and football has helped me come out of my shell and meet some of the best people I've ever met in my life. I **don't know** where I'd be without these sports. (Δ1, *joy, story, ∅hedges*=0.051)

Table 1: Annotated CORNELL CMV instance with positive labels listed at the end and boldened hedge terms.

More specifically, we focus on three subjective features, namely emotions, storytelling (personal and/or anecdotal narratives), and hedging (terms marking uncertainty, e.g., *probably, I think, likely*). While these aspects have already been investigated individually, i.e., in works investigating the use of personal narratives in argumentation (Falk and Lapesa, 2022), emotional progression (Benlamine et al., 2017), or human values (Kiesel et al., 2022), the crucial element of novelty of this work is the fact that we consider the (joint) impact of such subjective features on argument strength as opposed to previous work that considers them in isolation. Table 1 shows an argument appealing to *joyful* emotions and personal experiences, while recognizing knowledge gaps. The argument originates from the online forum *r/ChangeMyView*, where the user was successful (Δ1) in the forum's goal of persuading the discussion's initiator, showing the importance

Proceedings of the 12th Argument Mining Workshop, pages 126–139
July 31, 2025 ©2025 Association for Computational Linguistics

of investigating these features and their impact on argument quality more rigorously.

Toward this end, we carry out a parallel analysis on two datasets containing argument quality annotations which approximate the diverging conceptualizations of argument strength related to the function of argumentations: for the reason-giving function we selected IBM ArgQ (Toledo et al., 2019), whose annotations encode **objective argument quality**; for the persuasion function, we selected the Cornell CMV dataset (Tan et al., 2016) aggregated from the previously mentioned *r/ChangeMyView* forum, whose metadata (i.e., the presence of a delta indicating that the originator of a discussion changed their opinion following a specific answer) encode **individualized persuasion**. Differing not only in collection method, domain, argument length, and annotation procedure, these two datasets also lend themselves as the perfect pairing for a contrastive analysis of the impact of subjective features.

Our work proceeds in two steps. As a first step, we automatically enrich the two datasets with one annotation layer per subjective feature. To this end, we compare and evaluate alternative annotation methods (cf. Sec. 4) and reflect on their properties and suitability for our domains of interest. In our second step (Sec. 5), we address the main research goal of the paper: the impact of subjective features on argument strength. We employ regression analysis and address two research questions: **RQ1:** Do subjective features impact argument strength? **RQ2:** Do the patterns of their impact differ in the comparison between objective argument quality and individualized persuasion?

The contributions of our work are accordingly twofold. At the level of novel insights on the phenomenon of argument quality, our work is the first one that targets the *joint* impact of storytelling, emotion, and hedging on argument quality. At the level of contributed resources, we release and share with the community the datasets with the new annotation: this will enable further research on the interplay of these phenomena.[1]

2 Related Works

2.1 Argument Strength

The question of what makes a good argument has been studied since Aristotle (2007), who devised three main strategies of *ethos* or appeal to authority (of experience or persona), *pathos* or appeal to emotions, and *logos* or appeal to logic. The latter strategy maps onto the notion of argumentation as *reason-giving*, which has historically been favored in research. In both computational argumentation and the social sciences, a primary view of argumentation as a rational, somewhat mechanistic process of finding the objectively best claim through a combination of premises and evidence narrowed the notion of argument quality into one of successful *logos* rhetoric. In the predominant domains of student essays and professional debate, this is necessary, but limits the features and dimensions investigated in relation to argument quality to the objective and logical. As such, there are several investigations into clarity, use of evidence, or organization (Persing et al., 2010; Persing and Ng, 2013; Rahimi et al., 2014), with multiple argument quality corpora using corresponding definitions: ease of understanding (Swanson et al., 2015) or the general suitability as part of a larger thesis (Toledo et al., 2019; Gretz et al., 2020). These datasets are usually annotated by merging crowdsourcing labels, which further affirms the notion of argument quality as an, if not explicitly objective, then explicitly universal measure.

The inclusion of user-generated arguments in informal online settings shifted this focus at a similar time as the *affective turn* in the political sciences (Hoggett and Thompson, 2012), reorienting argument strength notions toward the persuasion function of argumentation as well as *ethos* and *pathos* strategies. This shift produced multiple studies of features related to *ethos*, mainly codifying meta-information such as prior beliefs, personal characteristics, and human values (Lukin et al., 2017; Al-Khatib et al., 2017; Kiesel et al., 2022), or, only recently, personal narratives as a form of non-traditional expertise (Falk and Lapesa, 2022, 2023). *Ethos*-related works mainly looked at emotional appeal (Benlamine et al., 2017) or fallacious emotions (Ziegenbein et al., 2023). While multiply new datasets were published in parallel to these studies, targeting *convincingness* and *persuasion* (Habernal and Gurevych, 2016; Simpson and Gurevych, 2018; Gleize et al., 2019), or aiming to codify all existing dimensions of argument quality into a cohesive taxonomy and annotation hierarchy (Wachsmuth et al., 2017; Ng et al., 2020), many of these datasets similarly encode argument quality as a universal average of multiple crowdworkers,

[1] Data and code are available at: `https://github.com/CarlottaQuensel/subjective-argument-strength`

thus blurring the distinction between objective and subjective dimensions.

Thus, a gap becomes apparent in the understanding of features relating to *ethos* and *pathos*, such as the establishment of personal authority through *storytelling* or *hedging* and the direct investigation of individual *emotions*. Though these three features hold promise for argument assessment, they are largely understudied in Computational Argumentation.

2.2 Subjective Argument Features

Storytelling Research on personal testimonies or *storytelling* originates from the field of deliberative research, where it has long been recognized as a tool to convey empathy and lived experience (Black, 2008, 2013; Esau, 2018). By establishing personal expertise, personal narratives aid in the construction of *ethos*, though Maia et al. (2020) show how narratives enrich debates in public hearings, incorporating *logos* and *pathos* in complex ways. Thus, storytelling serves as an alternative evidency type for non-experts and allows for disagreements without direct conflicts of facts. These observations, however, stem from small case studies and in Computational Argumentation, storytelling only recently gained attention. El Baff et al. (2020) included the number of anecdote sentences in news editorials, but do not address the feature separately. Falk and Lapesa (2022, 2023) consolidate multiple small social science datasets to allow for computational investigations of the phenomenon and argue that integrating personal narratives into argument mining helps include voices often excluded by logos-centric models. Their exploratory findings suggest that storytelling may positively correlate with several quality dimensions in an annotated corpus, but the effects on overall argument quality remain underexplored in a large scale or systematic analysis.

Emotion There are multiple investigations into the impact of emotions on arguments, though investigations of multiple discrete emotions are scant, small, and very recent. Most Computational Argumentation approaches collapse *emotion* and *emotional appeal* into one feature modeled as stance, polarity (e.g., Grosse et al., 2015; Stede, 2020; El Baff et al., 2020), intensity, or the general presence of any emotion (Fromm et al., 2022). Further, *emotional appeal* is historically seen as a fallacy in rational discourse, leading to multiple works investigating emotions as a negative feature (e.g., toxic emotions, Ziegenbein et al., 2023). The argument quality taxonomy and dataset by Wachsmuth et al. (2017) also includes emotional appeal in its 15 labels. In the deliberative field, Maia and Hauber (2020) observe *anger*, *fear*, *indignation* and *compassion* in political discussions, showing how these emotions are distributed unevenly between different argument directions. Benlamine et al. (2015, 2017) showed the link between emotions and argumentation behavior and found that, from Aristotle's rhetoric strategies, emotional appeal (*pathos*) is most persuasive. Only recently, the first (to our knowledge) small dataset of 1031 German arguments annotated for convincingness and 10 discrete emotions was released by Greschner and Klinger (2024). Despite this encouraging first step, there are, however, neither other (English) datasets nor large-scale analysis of emotions and argument strength available as of yet.

Hedging is one of multiple strategies to verbalize the epistemic modality of a proposition (Lyons, 1977), i.e., convey its degree of certainty (*likely*) or speaker-commitment (*according to* ...). In academic writing, it reflects the precision and caution of the scientific inquiry process, anticipating objections and gaining community acceptance (Hyland, 1998; Martín, 2003). In the fields of medicine and law, hedging serves as a professional face-saver, to build rapport with colleagues, patients, or a jury, and to avoid misinterpretation, thus enhancing speaker credibility (Bryant and Norman, 1979; Prince et al., 1982; Zaitseva, 2023). Informally, hedging is investigated as a strategy of politeness and positive self-image (Ardissono et al., 1999), and as a cooperative strategy to indicate openness to corrections and change (Vasilieva, 2004; Jordan et al., 2012).

Thus, with the rhetoric strategy of *ethos* encompassing recognized expertise, hedging is directly tied to this strategy. Wielded purposely, it appeals to the honest conduct and credibility of a speaker, similar to storytelling, although apparent uncertainty may just as well hamper recognized expertise. Despite this relevance, hedging is rarely studied in Computational Argumentation: Existing works link hedging to debaters' improvement (Luu et al., 2019), predict persuasiveness with paraverbal hesitation cues (Chatterjee et al., 2014) or modal verbs (Wei et al., 2016), but few address the size and direction of any observed effects. Habernal and

Gurevych (2017) show an uneven distribution of hedges skewed toward constructive, nonpolarized discussions. Only Tan et al. (2016) directly observe a positive effect on persuasiveness. The mixed findings highlight a gap: Given its surface-level detectability and interpretive flexibility, hedging is a promising but overlooked feature for capturing subjective argument quality. Hedging might enhance argument strength by boosting credibility, or weaken it by implying doubt – yet no systematic study explores this trade-off.

3 Data

Investigating the link between argument strength and the subjective features of storytelling, emotions, and hedging requires argument data that is annotated not only for argument strength but also for each of these features. As there is currently no such dataset available, a suitable corpus must be aggregated automatically. Multiple corpora are suitable as a base dataset that includes a gold annotation for the target variable (DV) of argument strength. To approximate the diverging conceptualizations of argument strength explicated above, we chose two datasets that differ in collection method, domain, argument length, and annotation procedure, categorized below as objective argument quality and individualized persuasion.

Objective argument quality IBM-ARGQ 5.3k (Toledo et al., 2019) consists of 5.3k short, standalone arguments generated at formal debate events by debate club members of varying skill levels and the general audience. Participants were asked to produce short arguments (max. 36 words) after seeing a professional example argument and choosing one of 11 controversial topics, such as privacy laws, gambling, or vegetarianism with two opposing stances, e.g., *We should adopt vegetarianism* and *We should abandon vegetarianism.* Participants were advised to keep arguments impersonal to avoid privacy concerns in the final dataset.

The argument strength annotation is an average of binary crowd judgments: for each argument, 15-17 annotators judged its adequacy as part of a debate speech,[2] which was averaged for the final score to model the ratio of positive judgments. This procedure attests to a rather unspecific conceptualization of generalized 'overall' argument strength, as the annotators must employ their own concept and hierarchy of relevant features, e.g., topic relevance, linguistic clarity, or sound rhetoric, and the single binary judgment paired with the averaging makes reconstruction of these features impossible. As such, while the utilized notion of argument strength is not explicitly stated 'objective', the domain, style, and annotation process of IBM-ARGQ 5.3k invoke an argument strength conceptualization in line with the traditional *logos* focus of the argument mining field, by removing subjective context and aggregating judgements to approximate a generalized, universal, and thus more objective, argument quality score. Thus, in the following analysis, this dataset is referred to as IBM ARGQ and represents argument strength as conceptualized by the traditional argument mining field.

Individualized persuasion CORNELL CMV was aggregated by Tan et al. (2016) from 11567 comments posted to the Reddit forum *ChangeMyView*[3] between January 2013 and August 2015, where users state their viewpoint with detailed background on their thought process to engage in constructive discussion that aims at changing their view. Thus, in one comment thread, multiple users argue against the same position until the original poster (OP) awards a *delta point* (Δ) to one or more answers that persuade them. The unique setup of the forum provides an inherent annotation and ensures data quality, with the delta point system that denotes the OP's persuasion and posting guidelines that are actively moderated by volunteers both for civility and for maintaining a constructive discussion in which comments must advance the conversation and decisions for delta points must be explained. The resulting label stands in contrast to the score of IBM ARGQ, as it encodes the subjective change in opinion of one person from a specific argument, in the context of a mutual discussion and multiple alternative arguments. The domain properties further make for much longer texts, sometimes containing multiple premises and stances forming a rhetoric argumentative sequence or direct quotes from the OP, which are addressed point by point. In the dataset used here (henceforth CORNELL CMV), the posts are structured as contrasting pairs of comments addressing the same OP, one with and one without a delta point, making for a balanced distribution of the binary persuasiveness label.

Given all the above differences between IBM

[2] *'Disregarding your own opinion on the topic, would you recommend a friend preparing a speech supporting/contesting the topic to use this argument as is in the speech?'*

[3] https://www.reddit.com/r/changemyview/

ArgQ and Cornell CMV, it is apparent that the two datasets conceptualize arguments as well as argument strength in very different ways. Although the number of differences disallows a comparison of pure argument strength conceptualization without any confounding factors, the inclusion of both corpora in the investigation covers idiosyncrasies across the spectrum of the argument mining field on what argument strength means. Tab. 7 shows examples from both datasets. To illustrate the diverging concepts, in the following analysis, argument strength is called *quality* when investigating IBM ArgQ and *persuasiveness* for Cornell CMV.

4 Automatic Annotation of Subjective Features

As the two datasets do not have annotations for the investigated features, it is necessary to enrich the datasets with the corresponding annotation layers as a first step. Thus, an automated annotation model is devised for each of the three features. In what follows, we describe the computational methods we used to achieve this goal separately for each feature. For storytelling and emotions, an ensemble consisting of ten transformer-based classifiers is trained on annotated data. As hedging is a surface feature dependent on individual terms, it is annotated using a simple rule-based algorithm. The following sections 4.1, 4.2, and 4.3 elaborate on the annotation process of each feature and the resulting statistics on the two argument datasets.

4.1 Storytelling

Training Data As most storytelling research is comprised of small case studies from the political sciences, we combine multiple datasets from different sources following the approach of Falk and Lapesa (2022). Falk and Lapesa (2022) use a collection of different datasets and domains covering diverse topics, such as expert-moderated discussions on immigration (Gerber et al., 2018) and consumer debt collection (Park and Cardie, 2018) and a subset of the online debate forum *r/ChangeMyView*. They consolidate different original annotations indicating wether an argument contains a personal experience or story (1) or not.

Training Setup We fine-tune RoBERTa transformers (Liu et al., 2019) using a 10-fold cross-validation ensemble, where the full dataset is split into ten parts and ten separate models are trained, each on a different combination of training and validation folds. This ensemble approach is used to produce more robust and stable predictions, as it mitigates variance due to random initialization and training data fluctuations (cf. e.g., Lakshminarayanan et al., 2017; Mohammed and Kora, 2023). For annotation, we apply the majority vote across the ten ensemble models to assign labels to our two target datasets. This setup follows Falk and Lapesa (2022), both to replicate the results of the original paper and to harness the identification of mixed-domain training as the most robust configuration for cross-domain generalization, making it most suitable for our IBM ArgQ data. As their reported same-domain performance for the *ChangeMyView* subset is on par with the mixed-domain classifier, we additionally train a classifier on only this subset to potentially harness this effect for Cornell CMV.

Results As apparent from the test performance on a heldout dataset (cf. Appendix Tab. 5), the mixed-domain ensemble prevails over the same-domain classifier, both in terms of performance (F_1 =.82 vs. F_1 =.78) and lower variance, which is in line with findings by Falk and Lapesa (2022). Otherwise, the performance is on par with the results of the best-performing models of the original experiments (Falk and Lapesa, 2022) (F_1 between .76 and .92), allowing us to continue with the analysis using the *mixed-domain* annotations. The resulting predictions are, however, very sparse for both corpora (cf. Tab. 2), especially so IBM ArgQ (0.8% positive), which can be attributed in part to the unbalanced distribution in the training data (storytelling is the minority class), but more importantly to the brevity and impersonality of IBM ArgQ instances. To mitigate the sparseness, we follow Lakshminarayanan et al. (2017) and interpret the average classification probability as a certainty measure of the binary annotation, thus introducing a richer source of information in the next step.

4.2 Emotion

Training Data As expanded in section 2, while there are multiple works on *emotionality* (intensity, polarity, etc.) in arguments, there are no works and related datasets modeling discrete emotions in English arguments. As such, our approach has to bridge a gap from the emotion domain to the argument domain. Though recent works showed the capabilities of LLMs in emotion classification (cf. last year's WASSA shared task; Maladry et al.,

Feature	IBM ArgQ #	IBM ArgQ %	IBM ArgQ ∅P	Cornell CMV #	Cornell CMV %	Cornell CMV ∅P
anger	1,814	34.2	.39	6,467	55.9	.43
boredom	116	2.2	.06	538	4.7	.07
disgust	2,920	55.1	.54	5,111	44.2	.37
fear	347	6.6	.14	822	7.1	.11
guilt/shame	107	2.0	.12	631	5.5	.14
joy	47	0.9	.07	208	1.8	.05
pride	80	1.5	.10	615	5.3	.12
relief	64	1.2	.06	256	2.2	.06
sadness	175	3.3	.14	429	3.7	.12
surprise	0	0.0	.03	53	0.5	.04
trust	112	2.1	.07	159	1.4	.04
storytelling	45	0.8	.02	2288	19.8	.22

Table 2: Feature distribution according to the best ensembles for emotion (*masked/aggregated*) and storytelling (*mixed*) on IBM ArgQ and Cornell CMV, including the number (#) and ratio (%) of positive instances, and the corpus-wide average classification probability (∅P).

2024), the zero-shot approach necessitated by our lack of in-domain examples is still outperformed by traditional fine-tuning, given a sufficient amount of high-quality training data (Kazakov et al., 2024). With no emotion-annotated datasets in the argument domain, we selected our training data to best match the register and style of our target data. This precludes both very informal and formal datasets aggregated from Twitter or from novels and news headlines, as well as data collected through emotion-specific emojis, words, hashtags, or forums to avoid surface-level emotion representations with low cross-domain adaptability. Thus, we chose Crowd-enVENT (Troiano et al., 2019) as our training data, a crowdsourced dataset of event descriptions for eleven different emotions,[4] which allows for an implicit emotion representation.

Training Setup In line with the setup for the *storytelling* feature, we employ an ensemble consisting of RoBERTa classifiers (Liu et al., 2019) fine-tuned on a 10-fold data split and aggregate the predictions into a majority vote. The dataset is originally single-label, with 550 event descriptions generated separately for one emotion. For our target data, we cannot assume a single-label distribution. Thus, we trained a separate classifier for each emotion and downsampled 1650 instances from all other emotion instances for a balanced training set with diverse negative instances.[5] Similar to the *storytelling* annotation, we compare two strategies for cross-domain robustness: the event descriptions are available in their original form as well as with salient emotion terms masked. We trained models on both versions to compare the impact of harnessing lexical surface features (*original*) with that of learning more implicit emotion representations (*masked*) and thus gaining more robust performance. As the arguments in Cornell CMV are longer than both the texts in the training data and the model's cutoff token length, we additionally split these instances in half and then aggregate the annotations for both halves.

Results As the test performance from the training process shows, using *masked* training data improves classification performance significantly (avg. F_1 increase: 0.074) and exceeds the benchmark performance reported by Troiano et al. (2023). The resulting label distribution of the best ensemble is reported in Tab. 2. Apart from *anger* and *disgust*, which occur in almost half of all instances, the data – especially IBM ArgQ– emotions are very sparse, with a ratio of positive instances below 10% for all other emotions and *surprise* missing entirely from IBM ArgQ. Thus, we can observe a higher use of emotions in the more subjective Cornell CMV data, together with a general skew towards 'indignation-adjacent' emotions like *anger* and *disgust*. While argument-specific emotion use is further analyzed later on (see Sec. 5), at this point, we observe that very low performance might be related to disuse in argumentation: arguments might intuitively stem from anger or appeal to pride, though arguing from a point of boredom or surprise (our two worst results) might be unusual.

Thus, we continue with annotations from the *masked* and *masked-aggregated* classifiers for our analysis, discarding *surprise* due to its absence in IBM ArgQ and replacing the binary annotation by averaged classification probabilities in further experiments. We thereby combat data sparseness and leverage prediction confidence (to have indications of 'weaker' or 'stronger' signs of emotion), making sure that the statistical model can account for robustness.

4.3 Hedging

As a surface-level feature, hedges can be extracted through a simple lexicon matching approach. We adapt and combine multiple lexicons from approaches outside the argument domain (Islam et al., 2020; Sanchez and Vogel, 2015; Ulinski and

[4] Generated as, e.g., *I felt fear when:* ... and analogously.
[5] The full dataset would result in 8% positive instances.

IV	IBM ArgQ r^2	p		Coef	Cornell CMV pseudo-r^2	p		Odds
storytelling	0.0047	0.0	***	−0.182	0.0004	0.015	*	1.148
anger	0.0011	0.009	**	−0.026	0.0000	0.377		0.928
boredom	0.0006	0.042	*	−0.050	0.0000	0.487		0.897
disgust	0.0022	0.0	***	−0.031	0.0010	0.0	***	0.751
fear	0.0026	0.0	***	0.056	0.0003	0.035	*	1.307
guilt/shame	**0.0097**	0.0	***	−0.139	0.0005	0.006	**	0.640
joy	0.0065	0.0	***	0.173	0.0001	0.149		1.397
pride	0.0003	0.091		0.037	0.0003	0.042	*	1.365
relief	0.0008	0.023	*	0.063	0.0005	0.007	*	1.749
sadness	0.0007	0.031	*	0.044	0.0000	0.470		1.138
trust	0.0067	0.0	***	0.140	0.0000	0.654		0.886
# hedges	0.0027	0.0	***	−0.011	**0.0106**	0.0	***	1.030

Table 3: Individual regression results including the explained variance (adjusted r^2), respectively, pseudo-r^2 for logistic regression, the p-value and significance of the effect (***: $p < 0.001$, **: $p < 0.01$, *: $p < 0.05$) and the coefficient, respectively, the logistic odds.

Hirschberg, 2019), which are targeted toward similar semi-formal domains (i.e., internet forums) and thus include domain-specific abbreviations and colloquialisms like *AFAIK* (*As far as I know*). Our pipeline first tokenizes and parses the arguments, then matches tokens to a hedging lexicon and further disambiguates terms with simple syntax rules, an example of which can be found in table 6. We were thus able to obtain the number of hedges per argument and create different feature variants, i.e., the overall number of hedges in the first and last sentence, versus in the whole argument instance, as well as the hedge-token ratio for each absolute variant. By including multiple, relative variants of the feature, we are able to abstract from the difference in instance length between the two corpora and accurately portray differences in the usage of hedges. Overall, our automated annotation approach proves successful, with increased robustness stemming from our generalization strategies: we find that mixed domain training, masking superficial lexical cues, and employing a deep ensemble is helpful. Although the performance on the argument data is expectably lower than in the training domain, it is nonetheless sufficient for our subsequent analysis and must be seen in relation to the very sparse label distribution in the argument domain.

5 Regression Analysis

Following the successful automated annotation procedure, we implement a regression analysis to investigate the impact of all 16 features (1 *storytelling*, 9 emotions excluding *boredom, surprise*, 6 *hedging*) as independent variables on the dependent variables of *quality* score in IBM ArgQ and *persuasion* label in Cornell CMV. We use the Python *statsmodels* library (Seabold and Perktold, 2010) to implement OLS linear regression with t-testing for significance on the *quality* score of IBM ArgQ and logistic regression with z-testing for significance on the binary *persuasiveness* label of Cornell CMV. To measure how much variance can be explained by individual features and how much additional variance can be explained by combining features, we compare regression models that employ a single feature as IV to richer models with multiple IVs and two-way interactions.

In comparing individual regression results of all features (see Tab. 3), two major divergences between the two corpora emerge. Firstly, both *storytelling* ($\beta = -.182$) and the absolute *hedging* count ($\beta = -.011$, for hedging in all variants, see Appendix Tab. 8) are highly significant negative predictors of argument quality in IBM ArgQ, but significantly improve persuasiveness in Cornell CMV ($\beta_{story} = 0.138$, $\beta_{hedge}) = 0.030$, cf. Fig. 1), with *hedging* constituting the most informative feature for this dataset. Secondly, an overall trend of greater and more frequent significant effects can be observed for IBM ArgQ argument quality than for Cornell CMV persuasion. This trend comes along with a greater predictive power of the IBM ArgQ

There is a difference between a fear of being killed by a terrorist (very small likelihood) and the fear of being *terrorized*. I was in Boston when the marathon bombings happened. Terrorism affected everyone on the streets, even though only 3 people were killed. The scope of an act of terrorism is much greater than the strict number of casualties. It has a psychological and traumatizing effect on people even in its periphery. That being said I am much more afraid of police than an act of terrorism. This is because after the bombings, when Tsarnaev was hiding in a boat about a quarter mile from my apartment at the time, militarized police with bomb dogs searched my house without announcing themselves, came to my door with assault rifles, and kept me locked in my house for a whole day while bomb vans and squad cars raced up and down my street. It was one of the most terrifying days of my life. **I felt** more electric fear answering the door to what looked like a 9-man SWAT team in full tactical gear and AK-47s than I did in the several previous days of news coverage following the bombing. I don't **necessarily** agree that having other things to be afraid of, like the abuse of power by the police, makes being afraid of things like acts of terrorism (which are designed to frighten) unreasonable. Fear is real and you don't always have a choice in the matter when it comes to whether or not it will infiltrate your life. (Δ0, *fear, storytelling, ∅hedges*=0.007)
Don't mean to be harsh, but that thinking is very dumb. There's a fine line between eating other animals, and cannibalism. Cannibalism is morally wrong because you are practical eating yourself. (Δ0, *guilt/shame, disgust, ∅hedges*=0.0)
Social media brings more good than harm. Social media helps reconnect with past friends. I was able to reconnect with a childhood best friend not seen in years shortly before he died. For that I am grateful. (*score*=0.6, *joy, sadness, storytelling, ∅hedge*=0.0)
Social media brings more harm than good. facts are not checked on social media platforms, allowing public shaming of different figures, hurting them and their career immensely even without them doing anything wrong (*score*=0.47, *disgust, anger, ∅hedge*=0.0)
Gambling should be banned. Gambling **can** be addictive and those who become addicted face severe financial and personal consequences such as bankruptcy, jail (from financial crimes as stealing or embezzlement to support the addiction), divorce and suicide. (*score*=1.0, *fear, sadness, ∅hedge*=0.11)
Flu vaccination should not be mandatory. While **I believe** that flu vaccines are beneficial to people, I do not **believe** they **should** be mandatory because I **should** have a right to decide if I want to take a risk with my health.(*score*=0.8, *∅hedge*=0.12)

Table 4: Fully annotated examples from CORNELL CMV and IBM ARGQ, with all positive labels listed below the post text and hedge terms rendered bold.

models,[6] and is continued in the best multiple regression model, which includes more IVs for IBM ARGQ than for CORNELL CMV.

In contrast to these domain differences, the impact of emotions on argument strength is largely domain-independent, with direction and magnitude of effects comparable between IBM ARGQ and CORNELL CMV for all emotions but *trust*. As such, the emotions with the highest impact on argument strength are *guilt/shame* and *disgust*, which both significantly decrease argument strength. For these emotions, as for most others, emotion polarity matches effect direction, including the significant emotions of *relief* (both corpora), *pride* (CORNELL CMV), and *joy* (IBM ARGQ). Two emotions contradict this trend: opposite to their polarity, *fear* (∗∗∗ IBM ARGQ; ∗ CORNELL CMV) and *sadness* (∗ IBM ARGQ) improve argument strength in both corpora.

To further investigate the interplay between different argument features, we implemented two multiple regression analyses with and without interaction. We used stepwise multiple regression, where individual IVs or two-way feature interactions are added incrementally according to their AIC value (predictive improvement relative to model size), while ensuring the significance of added IVs compared to the smaller model through ANOVA (IBM ARGQ) and F-test (CORNELL CMV).

The full models reveal the consistency of most effects on argument strength, as the most informative features of *guilt/shame* retain their salience, and notable observations like the diverging effect of *storytelling* on persuasion vs. quality are present in the full model as well. Interactions show a general trend of same-directed features combining to an effect of greater magnitude, as seen with the individually positive features of *fear* and *sadness* interacting on IBM ARGQ argument quality to form a highly positive combined effect while their individual effects are neutralized (Fig. 2). The full models with interaction further show the persistant importance of *storytelling*, which (in contrast to the individual IBM ARGQ regression) has a positive effect in both datasets. The final explained variance is 3.96% adjusted r^2 for IBM ARGQ and 1.36% pseudo-r^2 for CORNELL CMV. Although generally low, these values are reasonable and expected for a regression on the complex notion of argument strength, considering the exclusion of contextual information (e.g., topic, demographics of the annotators/OPs) and overall low values (and thus error margins) for both independent and target variables (between 0 and 1).

[6]While the adjusted r^2 of the IBM ARGQ models can be interpreted as the percentage of explained variance, this cannot be compared directly to the pseudo-r^2 of the logistic CORNELL CMV models. The general difference in magnitude nonetheless holds.

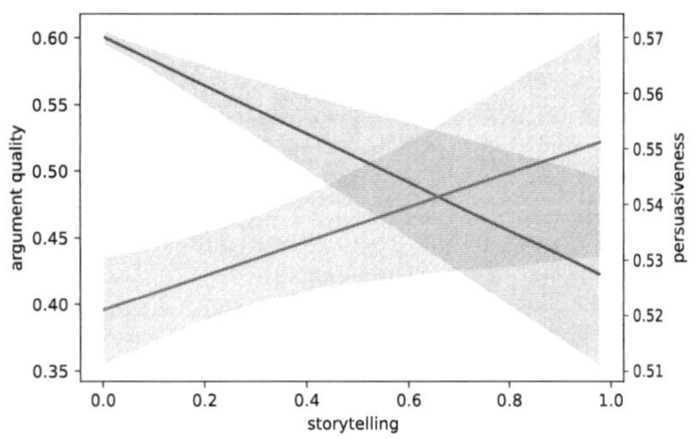

Figure 1: *Storytelling* effect on IBM ARGQ argument quality (teal, left y-axis) and on CORNELL CMV persuasion (blue, right y-axis), with confidence intervals.

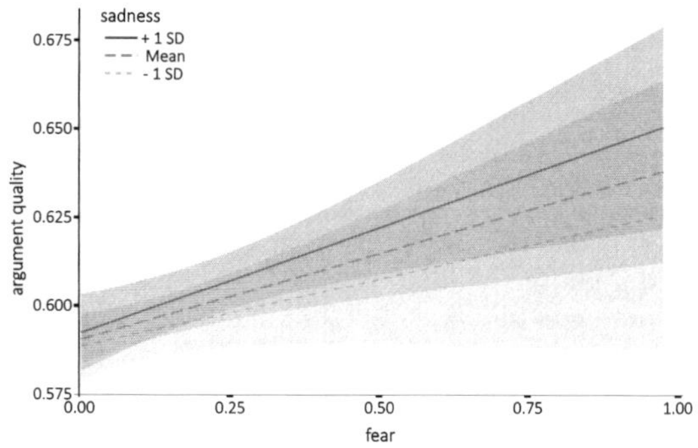

Figure 2: Interaction between *fear* (x-axis) and *sadness* (standard deviations shown through hue and dashing) on IBM ARGQ with confidence intervals.

Discussion The diverging effects of *hedging* and *storytelling* show the importance of domain-aware rhetoric: harnessing such subjective features significantly improves the odds of subjective persuasion, but in the objective domain of IBM ARGQ, they hinder argumentative success (cf. Fig. 1). As all subjective features are infrequent in IBM ARGQ, where arguments were mandated as short and impersonal, their successful use in CORNELL CMV seems intuitive, indicating their importance for non-experts.

When viewing the results of our two steps side by side, it is apparent that emotions are utilized differently in argumentation than in their original context. While *disgust* and *anger* are overrepresented compared to all other features, a qualitative analysis (see Tab. 4) shows their idiosyncratic appearance in arguments. Both emotions seem closer to indignation or 'righteous' anger, and occur, with the similarly impactful *guilt/shame*, almost always explicitly targeted towards either another participant ('*that thinking is very dumb*') or the topic under discussion ('*allowing public shaming*'). The very beneficial emotions of *fear* and *sadness*, on the other hand, seem reframed as an appeal to universal concerns instead of individual experiences, even when combined with personal experiences: '*personal consequences*', '*whether or not it will infiltrate your life*'. Therefore, we hypothesize that discrete emotions are utilized in two diverging strategies of *emotional attacks* and *emotional appeals*. While the latter are highly efficient in persuasion, the former hinder argument strength but are much more frequent in the data.

6 Conclusion

This paper has investigated the impact of a number of subjective features on two diverging facets of argument strength. To that end, we first determined the feasibility of large-scale automated annotation of our subjective features, to then systematically reveal correlations through a regression analysis. We could reveal a significant effect of almost all observed features on argument strength, thus affirming **RQ1**. We moreover demonstrated the importance of argument context for subjective features, as personal anecdotes and uncertainty indicate a lack of rhetoric proficiency in objective settings, but strengthen arguments in the subjective domain, thereby affirming **RQ2**. Further qualitative assessment shows frequent *emotional attacks* with righteous indignation impeding argument strength, while less frequent *emotional appeals* to empathy and universal fears seem to strengthen arguments. This finding reveals an avenue for continuing argument-specific emotion research, a research gap that is further emphasized by the results of our automated modeling. We could successfully model *storytelling* and most emotions automatically due to our robustness strategies of employing a deep ensemble based on training data from mixed-domains and with masked surface lexical cues. Thus, in situations where large-scale gold data is neither available nor easily attainable, these strategies constitute an acceptable alternative. However, the unbalanced and idiosyncratic distribution of emotions also reveals the limits of cross-domain approaches, as some emotions are used extremely seldomly, or appear changed from their original definition. We thus highlight once more the need for emotion data and definitions directed at argumentation, a research gap that has recently been addressed for German text by Greschner and Klinger (2024) and should receive further attention on a larger scale.

Acknowledgments

We would like to thank the anonymous reviewers whose feedback helped us improve this paper. This research has been partially funded by the Bundesministerium für Bildung und Forschung (BMBF) through the project E-DELIB (Powering up e-deliberation: towards AI-supported moderation)

Limitations

Apart from the obvious constraint of English-only modeling, automatically annotating the independent variables bears the risk of modeling the influence of features that differ from the named features. For the features of storytelling and hedging, our success in recreating results from existing works leads us to believe that the annotations are acceptable even on unseen data. For our emotion features, we rely on our strategies of masking salient surface features and aggregating predictions for long instances to lead to an acceptable performance based on the good results on the heldout training data. Thus, we believe our regression to realistically model the influence of the remaining investigated features. This influence is very small, as denoted by the low r^2 and pseudo-r^2 scores of the regression models. However, while this shows that the features investigated here cannot fully explain argument strength, the high significance of most features nonetheless shows their importance for argument strength. As previous research shows, argument strength is a complex and subjective feature. We thus expect that a model regressing argument strength to a higher degree must include context, such as prior beliefs and demographic features of the annotators/OP and the author, topic information, or discussion history. The significance of our results constitutes one step in a growing field of research aiming to explore argument strength as a multi-faceted complex feature.

Ethical Considerations

As always in the analysis of argument strength, our results may potentially be exploited in the persuasion strategies of bad actors. However, we observed significant but very small effects that may be less impactful than demographic and contextual features, which we omitted. Further, features like emotions or uncertainty are likely used intuitively and, as shown elsewhere (cf. e.g., Vasilieva, 2004), used differently depending on demographic factors. While reporting negative influence might discredit argument strategies used by already disadvantaged groups, we believe that our features bear no inherent demographic inclination and understanding such effects is the first step to encourage thoughtful argumentation.

References

Khalid Al-Khatib, Henning Wachsmuth, Matthias Hagen, and Benno Stein. 2017. Patterns of argumentation strategies across topics. In *Proceedings of the 2017 Conference on Empirical Methods in Natural Language Processing*, pages 1351–1357, Copenhagen, Denmark. Association for Computational Linguistics.

Liliana Ardissono, Guido Boella, and Leonardo Lesmo. 1999. Politeness and speech acts. In *Proc. Workshop on Attitude, Personality and Emotions in User-Adapted Interaction*, pages 41–55. Citeseer.

Aristotle. 2007. *On Rhetoric: A Theory of Civic Discourse.* (Kennedy, G.A., translator), Oxford University Press.

Mohamed Sahbi Benlamine, Maher Chaouachi, Serena Villata, Elena Cabrio, Claude Frasson, and Fabien Gandon. 2015. Emotions in argumentation: an empirical evaluation. In *International Joint Conference on Artificial Intelligence, IJCAI 2015*, pages 156–163.

Mohamed Sahbi Benlamine, Serena Villata, Ramla Ghali, Claude Frasson, Fabien Gandon, and Elena Cabrio. 2017. Persuasive argumentation and emotions: An empirical evaluation with users. In *Human-Computer Interaction. User Interface Design, Development and Multimodality*, pages 659–671, Cham. Springer International Publishing.

Laura W. Black. 2008. Deliberation, Storytelling, and Dialogic Moments. *Communication Theory*, 18(1):93–116.

Laura W. Black. 2013. Framing Democracy and Conflict Through Storytelling in Deliberative Groups. *Journal of Public Deliberation*, 9(1):art. 4.

G D Bryant and G R Norman. 1979. The communication of uncertainty. In *Proceedings of the Eighteenth Annual Conference on Research in Medical Education.*

Moitreya Chatterjee, Sunghyun Park, Han Suk Shim, Kenji Sagae, and Louis-Philippe Morency. 2014. Verbal behaviors and persuasiveness in online multimedia content. In *Proceedings of the Second Workshop on Natural Language Processing for Social Media (SocialNLP)*, pages 50–58, Dublin, Ireland. Association for Computational Linguistics and Dublin City University.

Roxanne El Baff, Henning Wachsmuth, Khalid Al Khatib, and Benno Stein. 2020. Analyzing the Persuasive Effect of Style in News Editorial Argumentation. In *Proceedings of the 58th Annual Meeting of the Association for Computational Linguistics*, pages 3154–3160, Online. Association for Computational Linguistics.

Katharina Esau. 2018. Capturing citizens' values: On the role of narratives and emotions in digital participation. *Analyse & Kritik*, 40(1):55–72.

Neele Falk and Gabriella Lapesa. 2022. Reports of personal experiences and stories in argumentation: datasets and analysis. In *Proceedings of the 60th Annual Meeting of the Association for Computational Linguistics (Volume 1: Long Papers)*, pages 5530–5553, Dublin, Ireland. Association for Computational Linguistics.

Neele Falk and Gabriella Lapesa. 2023. StoryARG: a corpus of narratives and personal experiences in argumentative texts. In *Proceedings of the 61st Annual Meeting of the Association for Computational Linguistics (Volume 1: Long Papers)*, pages 2350–2372, Toronto, Canada. Association for Computational Linguistics.

Michael Fromm, Max Berrendorf, Johanna Reiml, Isabelle Mayerhofer, Siddharth Bhargava, Evgeniy Faerman, and Thomas Seidl. 2022. Towards a holistic view on argument quality prediction. *arXiv preprint*.

Marlène Gerber, André Bächtiger, Susumu Shikano, Simon Reber, and Samuel Rohr. 2018. Deliberative abilities and influence in a transnational deliberative poll (europolis). *British Journal of Political Science*, 48(4):1093–1118.

Martin Gleize, Eyal Shnarch, Leshem Choshen, Lena Dankin, Guy Moshkowich, Ranit Aharonov, and Noam Slonim. 2019. Are you convinced? choosing the more convincing evidence with a Siamese network. In *Proceedings of the 57th Annual Meeting of the Association for Computational Linguistics*, pages 967–976, Florence, Italy. Association for Computational Linguistics.

Lynn Greschner and Roman Klinger. 2024. Fearful falcons and angry llamas: Emotion category annotations of arguments by humans and llms. *Preprint*, arXiv:2412.15993.

Shai Gretz, Roni Friedman, Edo Cohen-Karlik, Assaf Toledo, Dan Lahav, Ranit Aharonov, and Noam Slonim. 2020. A large-scale dataset for argument quality ranking: Construction and analysis. In *The Thirty-Fourth AAAI Conference on Artificial Intelligence, (AAAI 2020)*, pages 7805–7813. AAAI Press.

Kathrin Grosse, Maria P Gonzalez, Carlos I Chesnevar, and Ana G Maguitman. 2015. Integrating argumentation and sentiment analysis for mining opinions from twitter. *AI Communications*, 28(3):387–401.

Ivan Habernal and Iryna Gurevych. 2016. Which argument is more convincing? analyzing and predicting convincingness of web arguments using bidirectional LSTM. In *Proceedings of the 54th Annual Meeting of the Association for Computational Linguistics (Volume 1: Long Papers)*, pages 1589–1599, Berlin, Germany. Association for Computational Linguistics.

Ivan Habernal and Iryna Gurevych. 2017. Argumentation mining in user-generated web discourse. *Computational Linguistics*, 43(1):125–179.

Paul Hoggett and Simon Thompson. 2012. *Politics and the Emotions: The Affective Turn in Contemporary Political Studies*. Bloomsbury Publishing.

Ken Hyland. 1998. *Hedging in scientific research articles*. John Benjamins.

Jumayel Islam, Lu Xiao, and Robert E. Mercer. 2020. A lexicon-based approach for detecting hedges in informal text. In *Proceedings of the Twelfth Language Resources and Evaluation Conference*, pages 3109–3113, Marseille, France. European Language Resources Association.

Michelle E. Jordan, Diane L. Schallert, Yangjoo Park, SoonAh Lee, Yueh hui Vanessa Chiang, An-Chih Janne Cheng, Kwangok Song, Hsiang-Ning Rebecca Chu, Taehee Kim, and Haekyung Lee. 2012. Expressing uncertainty in computer-mediated discourse: Language as a marker of intellectual work. *Discourse Processes*, 49(8):660–692.

Roman Kazakov, Kseniia Petukhova, and Ekaterina Kochmar. 2024. PetKaz at SemEval-2024 task 3: Advancing emotion classification with an LLM for emotion-cause pair extraction in conversations. In *Proceedings of the 18th International Workshop on Semantic Evaluation (SemEval-2024)*, pages 1127–1134, Mexico City, Mexico. Association for Computational Linguistics.

Johannes Kiesel, Milad Alshomary, Nicolas Handke, Xiaoni Cai, Henning Wachsmuth, and Benno Stein. 2022. Identifying the human values behind arguments. In *Proceedings of the 60th Annual Meeting of the Association for Computational Linguistics (Volume 1: Long Papers)*, pages 4459–4471, Dublin, Ireland. Association for Computational Linguistics.

Balaji Lakshminarayanan, Alexander Pritzel, and Charles Blundell. 2017. Simple and scalable predictive uncertainty estimation using deep ensembles. In *Advances in Neural Information Processing Systems 30: Annual Conference on Neural Information Processing Systems 2017, December 4-9, 2017, Long Beach, CA, USA*, pages 6402–6413.

John Lawrence and Chris Reed. 2019. Argument mining: A survey. *Computational Linguistics*, 45(4):765–818.

Yinhan Liu, Myle Ott, Naman Goyal, Jingfei Du, Mandar Joshi, Danqi Chen, Omer Levy, Mike Lewis, Luke Zettlemoyer, and Veselin Stoyanov. 2019.

Roberta: A robustly optimized bert pretraining approach. *arXiv preprint*.

Stephanie Lukin, Pranav Anand, Marilyn Walker, and Steve Whittaker. 2017. Argument strength is in the eye of the beholder: Audience effects in persuasion. In *Proceedings of the 15th Conference of the European Chapter of the Association for Computational Linguistics: Volume 1, Long Papers*, pages 742–753, Valencia, Spain. Association for Computational Linguistics.

Kelvin Luu, Chenhao Tan, and Noah A. Smith. 2019. Measuring online debaters' persuasive skill from text over time. *Transactions of the Association for Computational Linguistics*, 7:537–550.

John Lyons. 1977. *Modality*, volume 2, page 787–849. Cambridge University Press.

Rousiley C. M. Maia, Danila Cal, Janine Bargas, and Neylson J. B. Crepalde. 2020. Which types of reason-giving and storytelling are good for deliberation? assessing the discussion dynamics in legislative and citizen forums. *European Political Science Review*, 12(2):113–132.

Rousiley C. M. Maia and Gabriella Hauber. 2020. The emotional dimensions of reason-giving in deliberative forums. *Policy Sciences*, 53:33–59.

Aaron Maladry, Pranaydeep Singh, and Els Lefever. 2024. Findings of the WASSA 2024 EXALT shared task on explainability for cross-lingual emotion in tweets. In *Proceedings of the 14th Workshop on Computational Approaches to Subjectivity, Sentiment, & Social Media Analysis*, pages 454–463, Bangkok, Thailand. Association for Computational Linguistics.

Pedro Martín. 2003. The pragmatic rhetorical strategy of hedging in academic writing. *Vigo International Journal of Applied Linguistics (VIAL)*, 0.

Ammar Mohammed and Rania Kora. 2023. A comprehensive review on ensemble deep learning: Opportunities and challenges. *Journal of King Saud University - Computer and Information Sciences*, 35(2):757–774.

Lily Ng, Anne Lauscher, Joel Tetreault, and Courtney Napoles. 2020. Creating a domain-diverse corpus for theory-based argument quality assessment. In *Proceedings of the 7th Workshop on Argument Mining*, pages 117–126, Online. Association for Computational Linguistics.

Nathan Ong, Diane Litman, and Alexandra Brusilovsky. 2014. Ontology-based argument mining and automatic essay scoring. In *Proceedings of the First Workshop on Argumentation Mining*, pages 24–28, Baltimore, Maryland. Association for Computational Linguistics.

Joonsuk Park and Claire Cardie. 2018. A corpus of eRulemaking user comments for measuring evaluability of arguments. In *Proceedings of the Eleventh International Conference on Language Resources and Evaluation (LREC 2018)*, Miyazaki, Japan. European Language Resources Association (ELRA).

Isaac Persing, Alan Davis, and Vincent Ng. 2010. Modeling organization in student essays. In *Proceedings of the 2010 Conference on Empirical Methods in Natural Language Processing*, pages 229–239, Cambridge, MA. Association for Computational Linguistics.

Isaac Persing and Vincent Ng. 2013. Modeling thesis clarity in student essays. In *Proceedings of the 51st Annual Meeting of the Association for Computational Linguistics (Volume 1: Long Papers)*, pages 260–269, Sofia, Bulgaria. Association for Computational Linguistics.

E.F. Prince, J. Frader, and C. Bosk. 1982. On hedging in physician discourse. *Linguistics and the Professions, Alex Publishing Corporation*, pages 83–97.

Zahra Rahimi, Diane J. Litman, Richard Correnti, Lindsay Clare Matsumura, Elaine Wang, and Zahid Kisa. 2014. Automatic scoring of an analytical response-to-text assessment. In *Intelligent Tutoring Systems*, pages 601–610, Cham. Springer International Publishing.

Liliana Mamani Sanchez and Carl Vogel. 2015. A hedging annotation scheme focused on epistemic phrases for informal language. In *Proceedings of the Workshop on Models for Modality Annotation*, London, UK. Association for Computational Linguistics.

Skipper Seabold and Josef Perktold. 2010. statsmodels: Econometric and statistical modeling with python. In *9th Python in Science Conference*.

Edwin Simpson and Iryna Gurevych. 2018. Finding convincing arguments using scalable Bayesian preference learning. *Transactions of the Association for Computational Linguistics*, 6:357–371.

Manfred Stede. 2020. Automatic argumentation mining and the role of stance and sentiment. *Journal of Argumentation in Context*, 9(1):19–41.

Reid Swanson, Brian Ecker, and Marilyn Walker. 2015. Argument mining: Extracting arguments from online dialogue. In *Proceedings of the 16th Annual Meeting of the Special Interest Group on Discourse and Dialogue*, pages 217–226, Prague, Czech Republic. Association for Computational Linguistics.

Chenhao Tan, Vlad Niculae, Cristian Danescu-Niculescu-Mizil, and Lillian Lee. 2016. Winning arguments: Interaction dynamics and persuasion strategies in good-faith online discussions. *CoRR*, abs/1602.01103.

Assaf Toledo, Shai Gretz, Edo Cohen-Karlik, Roni Friedman, Elad Venezian, Dan Lahav, Michal Jacovi, Ranit Aharonov, and Noam Slonim. 2019. Automatic argument quality assessment - new datasets and methods. In *Proceedings of the 2019 Conference on Empirical Methods in Natural Language Processing and the 9th International Joint Conference on Natural Language Processing (EMNLP-IJCNLP)*, pages 5625–5635, Hong Kong, China. Association for Computational Linguistics.

Enrica Troiano, Laura Oberländer, and Roman Klinger. 2023. Dimensional Modeling of Emotions in Text with Appraisal Theories: Corpus Creation, Annotation Reliability, and Prediction. *Computational Linguistics*, 49(1):1–72.

Enrica Troiano, Sebastian Padó, and Roman Klinger. 2019. Crowdsourcing and validating event-focused emotion corpora for German and English. In *Proceedings of the 57th Annual Meeting of the Association for Computational Linguistics*, pages 4005–4011, Florence, Italy. Association for Computational Linguistics.

Morgan Ulinski and Julia Hirschberg. 2019. Crowdsourced hedge term disambiguation. In *Proceedings of the 13th Linguistic Annotation Workshop*, pages 1–5, Florence, Italy. Association for Computational Linguistics.

I. Vasilieva. 2004. Gender-specific use of boosting and hedging adverbs in english computer-related texts – a corpus-based study. In *International Conference on Language, Politeness and Gender*, pages 2–5.

Henning Wachsmuth, Nona Naderi, Yufang Hou, Yonatan Bilu, Vinodkumar Prabhakaran, Tim Alberdingk Thijm, Graeme Hirst, and Benno Stein. 2017. Computational argumentation quality assessment in natural language. In *Proceedings of the 15th Conference of the European Chapter of the Association for Computational Linguistics: Volume 1, Long Papers*, pages 176–187, Valencia, Spain. Association for Computational Linguistics.

Zhongyu Wei, Yang Liu, and Yi Li. 2016. Is this post persuasive? ranking argumentative comments in online forum. In *Proceedings of the 54th Annual Meeting of the Association for Computational Linguistics (Volume 2: Short Papers)*, pages 195–200, Berlin, Germany. Association for Computational Linguistics.

Margaryta Zaitseva. 2023. Some observations on altering hedging phenomenon in courtroom discourse. *LINGUISTICS*, 1(47):152–162.

Timon Ziegenbein, Shahbaz Syed, Felix Lange, Martin Potthast, and Henning Wachsmuth. 2023. Modeling appropriate language in argumentation. In *Proceedings of the 61st Annual Meeting of the Association for Computational Linguistics (Volume 1: Long Papers)*, pages 4344–4363, Toronto, Canada. Association for Computational Linguistics.

A Supplementary Material

A.1 Data and Annotation

Table 7 shows exemplary instances of the base corpora we used, while tables 5 and 6 explicate the further annotation process.

A.2 Regression Results

Reported below are the regression results for all hedging variants (Tab. 8), the results of full stepwise regression model with interaction (Tab. 9), and two exemplary regression plots (Fig. 1, 2).

Feature	Training variant *masked*	*orig*	Benchmark
anger	0.76(±0.03)	0.69(±0.04)	0.53
boredom	0.88(±0.03)	0.84(±0.02)	0.84
disgust	0.82(±0.03)	0.75(±0.04)	0.66
fear	0.81(±0.03)	0.72(±0.03)	0.65
guilt/shame	0.85(±0.03)	0.80(±0.02)	0.48/0.51
joy	0.77(±0.03)	0.71(±0.02)	0.45
pride	0.83(±0.03)	0.75(±0.03)	0.54
relief	0.82(±0.03)	0.70(±0.25)	0.63
sadness	0.81(±0.04)	0.73(±0.03)	0.59
surprise	0.78(±0.02)	0.67(±0.04)	0.53
trust	0.85(±0.02)	0.80(±0.02)	0.74
	mixed	*one*	
storytelling	0.82(±0.03)	0.78(±0.05)	0.76-0.94

Table 5: F_1 performance of the ensemble classifiers on the heldout test set of their respective training data with standard deviance reported in brackets. The last column lists the originally reported benchmark: Troiano et al.'s (2023 text-based classifier (multilabel versus our single label classifiers) and the best overall approach by Falk and Lapesa (2022, performance is reported separately for three subsets, thus ranging between values).

Term	Rule
about, *around*	If the token is an adjective, it is a non-hedge. **Hedge:** There are *around* 10 million packages in transit right now. **Non-hedge:** We need to talk *about* Mark.
pretty	If the token is used as adverbially, it is a hedge. **Hedge:** I am *pretty* certain about this statistic. **Non-hedge:** She has a really *pretty* cat.
impression	If the token has a 1. person possessive pronoun as dependent or its head has a 1. person nominal subject as a second dependent, it is a hedge. **Hedge:** I get the *impression* that we have to wait longer for official information. **Non-hedge:** The protagonist's performance left a lasting *impression* on everyone.

Table 6: Examplary hedge disambiguation rules, the first of which is lifted from Islam et al. (2020).

IBM ArgQ	
We should ban fossil fuels. fossil fuels are bad for the country because of your country dont have them they have to be in an inferior position to ather countrys. (score=0.18)	*We should ban fossil fuels.* Fossil fuels destabilize the ecosystem which will harm future generations. (score=1.0)
Cornell CMV	
CMV: Driving a car is insanely risky and probably the most dangerous thing you do in your everyday life. I find it difficult to understand how so many people enjoy driving a car or can even relax while doing it. I am almost continually tense while on the road thinking about what's at stake (and I've been driving for almost 20 years). [...]	
By the death rate, eating unhealthy is the most dangerous thing that you can do. Cellular reproduction is up there are well. Then there's realizing your worthless and life is futile, then taking your own life. Looking at the CDC, suicide isn't on there. But breathing shit other than oxygen and nitrogen is up there. So is, the fatty food thing again. (Δ0)	Mortality for drivers in the US is roughly 50 per millions. Death while working in construction in 2006 was 108 per millions. Driving is not the most dangerous thing these workers do in their everyday life. (edit. The more i'm looking into it the more I find that stats regarding this subject varies a lot.) (Δ1)

Table 7: Examples from IBM ArgQ and Cornell CMV of a bad (left) and good (right) argument about the same topic, with the shortened original post from Cornell CMV given above the two answering arguments.

score	sent	r²	Coef	p	
absolute	*first*	**0.0044**	−0.029	**0.0**	***
	final	−0.0002	0.001	0.894	
	all	0.0027	−0.011	0.0	***
ratio	*first*	0.0036	−0.160	0.0	***
	final	0.0007	−0.159	0.026	*
	all	0.0036	−0.296	0.0	***

(a) IBM ArgQ

score	sent	pseudo-r²	Odds	p	
absolute	*first*	0.00005	1.018	0.358	
	final	0.0	0.999	0.947	
	all	**0.01056**	1.030	**0.0**	***
ratio	*first*	0.00002	1.235	0.565	
	final	0.00012	0.579	0.174	
	all	0.00035	0.124	0.018	*

(b) Cornell CMV

Table 8: Individual regression results of each hedging variant as IV on IBM ArgQ argument quality and Cornell CMV persuasiveness. The variants are listed by **score** (absolute or ratio values) and the **sent**ence for which the score is calculated. Reported are the adjusted r^2 percentage, respectively, pseudo-r^2 for logistic regression, the coefficient/odds of the feature variant and the effect's p-value/significance.

IVs	adjusted r^2	sign.
guilt/shame	0.971	x
+ *all hedge×storytelling*	1.723	***
+ *fear×guilt/shame*	2.273	***
+ *joy*	2.602	***
+ *disgust×sadness*	3.082	***
+ *boredom×pride*	3.484	***
+ *pride×relief*	3.579	*
+ *pride×sadness*	3.715	**
+ *disgust×fear*	3.774	*
+ *sadness*	3.845	*
+ *storytelling*	3.904	*
+ *fear×relief*	3.962	*

(a) IBM ArgQ

IVs	pseudo-r^2	sign.
# hedge	0.0106	x
+ *disgust×guilt/shame*	0.0113	***
+ *fear×pride*	0.0119	**
+ *anger×relief*	0.0123	**
+ *# hedge×anger*	0.0128	**
+ *disgust×pride*	0.0132	**
+ *# hedge×guilt/shame*	0.0136	*

(b) Cornell CMV

Table 9: Features and explained variance of the interactive multiple regression on IBM ArgQ and Cornell CMV. The model is built stepwise by adding features/interactions with the highest AIC (Akaike Information Criterion relating predictive power to model size) and stops if no improvement is observed. The significance (***: $p < 0.001$, **: $p < 0.01$, *: $p < 0.05$) of adding each new feature is tested via ANOVA for IBM ArgQ and via F-test for Cornell CMV.

DEBARGVIS: An Interactive Visualisation Tool for Exploring Argumentative Dynamics in Debate

Martin Gruber[1,2] **Zlata Kikteva**[1] **Ignaz Rutter**[1] **Annette Hautli-Janisz**[1]
[1] University of Passau, Germany
[2]University of Tübingen, Germany
martin.gruber@student.uni-tuebingen.de
firstname.lastname@uni-passau.de

Abstract

Television debates play a key role in shaping public opinion, however, the rapid exchange of viewpoints in these settings often makes it difficult to perceive the underlying nature of the discussion. While there exist several debate visualisation techniques, to the best of our knowledge, none of them emphasise the argumentative dynamics in particular. With DEBARGVIS, we present a new interactive debate visualisation tool that leverages data annotated with argumentation structures to demonstrate how speaker interactions unfold over time, enabling users to deepen their comprehension of the debate.

1 Introduction

Broadcast political debates such as BBC1's 'Question Time' in the UK with over a million monthly viewers[1]serve as a cornerstone of political discourse as they provide a compact yet rich source of information that plays a key role in shaping public opinion. However, the rapid exchange of viewpoints in these forums presents a challenge: The wealth of information compressed into a short period of time can make it difficult to parse the underlying dynamics and the connections between speakers' arguments.

One way of representing such dynamics is through an argumentative analysis, which allows us to explore how claims are supported or attacked. Such an analysis is frequently visualised in the form of a graph with nodes containing claims and the relations between them represented in terms of edges. DebateGraph[2] or ArgVis (Karamanou et al., 2011) are, for instance, tools designed for public-facing deliberation analysis; other resources like Araucaria (Reed and Rowe, 2004) and OVA+ (Janier et al., 2014) are more research-oriented, while techniques, such as Reason!Able, target the improvement of critical thinking skills (Van Gelder, 2002). Graph-based representations tend to lack the explicit encoding of the temporal dimension which is crucial for capturing the dynamics of real-time debates. In contrast, visualisation techniques that focus on debate dynamics frequently do so by depicting different layers of the debate, e.g., topics, speaker interactions, and timeline, in distinct infographics (El-Assady et al., 2016b; South et al., 2020), making it difficult to get a holistic understanding of the debate landscape.

In the present paper, we aim to address this gap between argument graph representations and debate visualisations by introducing DEBARGVIS, an interactive tool for visualising argumentative dynamics in debate.[3] As use case we take QT30 (Hautli-Janisz et al., 2022), a corpus of broadcast political debates annotated with argumentative relations using Inference Anchoring Theory (IAT) (Budzynska et al., 2014, 2016). As Fig. 1 depicts, DEBARGVIS interactively combines timeline, debate participants, argumentative relations within and between speaker contributions, video of the debate and debate transcript. This provides users with an overview of the overall debate dynamics, such as how much each speaker contributes and how they interact with each other, while also allowing for a closer inspection of the debate's underlying argumentative structure.

2 Background

A variety of argument visualisation tools have been developed, employing different techniques to represent argumentative relations. One of the well-established approaches is the use of the node-link layout (Lowrance et al., 2000; Van Gelder, 2002; Reed and Rowe, 2004; Van Gelder, 2007; Gordon

[1]https://tinyurl.com/2fkmdyt9
[2]https://debategraph.org
[3]Tool preview (without the original BBC video): zlatakikteva.github.io/DebArgVis-Demo/, video demo: https://youtu.be/ra-RHZ5THN8

Proceedings of the 12th Argument Mining Workshop, pages 140–146

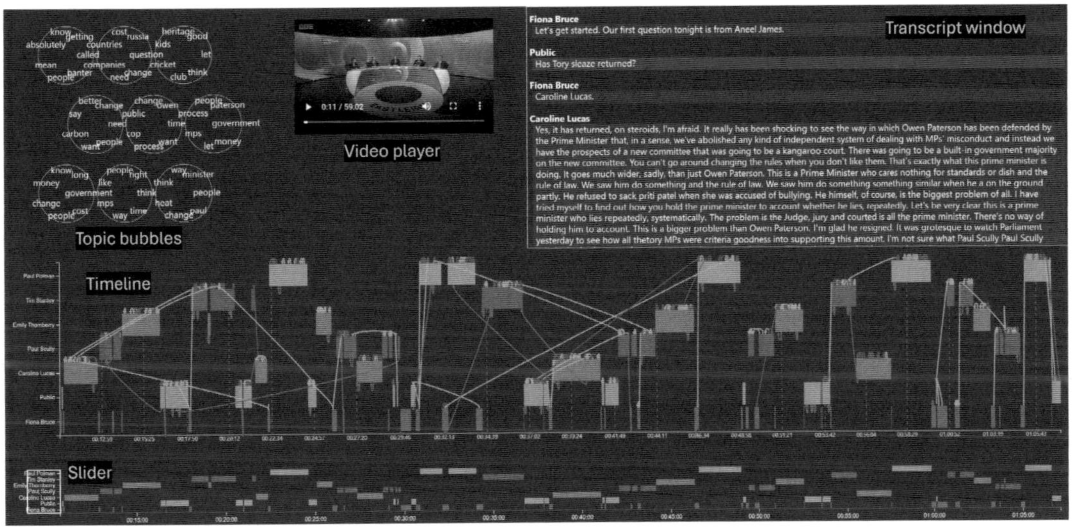

Figure 1: Overview of the DEBARGVIS components.

et al., 2007; Karamanou et al., 2011; Janier et al., 2014), while others visualisation strategies include indentation-based formats (Karacapilidis and Papadias, 2001; Verheij, 2003; Mcalister et al., 2004), and nested layouts (Bell, 1998; Benn and Macintosh, 2012). For the most part, such tools focus on representing reasoning on a smaller scale, where individual arguments are accessible. In contrast, Kiesel et al. (2021) allows to to view and compare larger patterns of reasoning between essays, while Zhou et al. (2019) focus on structures in scientific papers. Hybrid tools, such as DebateGraph, allow for both closer inspection of the data and a general overview of the relations.

Such approaches are not necessarily tailored towards visualising large conversations or spoken debates, for which speaker interactions and temporal progression are important. Approaches that focus on addressing the conversational nature of the discourse include such tools as uVSAT that offers stance visualisation in social media (Kucher et al., 2016), ConToVi that focuses on topic-space in conversations (El-Assady et al., 2016a), and NEREx that provides named-entity based analysis of debates (El-Assady et al., 2017). Furthermore, such tools as VisArgue (El-Assady et al., 2016b) and DebateVis (South et al., 2020) offer sets of visual analytics across several debate dimensions, such as speaker interactions and topic progress along a timeline, while MultiConVis (Hoque and Carenini, 2016) focuses on topics and sentiment in online discussions. Finally, CI dashboard (Ullmann, 2019) includes an argument graph of the node-link layout type among other group discussion analytics in its suite. To the best of our knowledge, however, none of the existing approaches represent debate dynamics through argumentative speaker interactions along a timeline as we are proposing.

3 The QT30 Dataset

The QT30 corpus consists of 30 episodes of 'Question Time' (QT) (Hautli-Janisz et al., 2022), a political talk show in the UK broadcast on BBC1, where the audience challenges a panel of political figures regarding current topics. The panellists then respond and freely discuss the issues with each other. The data is annotated with Inference Anchoring Theory (IAT) (Budzynska et al., 2014, 2016), a framework that captures how arguments evolve and are reacted to in dialogue, anchoring argument structure in dialogue structure by way of illocutionary connections. Data annotated with IAT is split into elementary discourse units (EDUs) between which argumentative relations of support (either between a premise and a conclusion or in a form of agreeing with a statement), attack, and rephrase (either a reformulation of a statement or an answer to a question) are identified. IAT adheres to the AIF+ (Argument Interchange Format variant suitable for dialogue) (Reed et al., 2008), which is a well-established framework for representing argumentation. Therefore, DEBARGVIS can be adapted and used with any debate data in the same format. In addition to the corpus annotations, we separately access the debate transcript and video.

4 Visualisation

With DEBARGVIS we aim to develop a timeline that reflects several dimensions of a debate, including (i) temporal sequence of utterances; (ii) attribution of utterances to speakers; (iii) argumentative relations between utterances; (iv) content of the utterances; (v) debate topics; (vi) additional audio-visual context in video format. The visualisation therefore comprises five components: The *timeline* in Fig. 1 is used to capture (i), (ii), and (iii); the *slider* is used to navigate the *timeline*; the *transcript window* includes (iv); *topic bubbles* contain (v); and a *video player* introduces (vi).

Timeline The timeline is the focal visualisation component. It displays when an utterance is made, who made it, and the argumentative relations between utterances in a diagram with an x-axis representing elapsed time (around one hour in the case of QT debates) and speaker names on the y-axis. The first five names belong to panel members, 'public' represents any member of the audience who is invited to participate in the debate, and Fiona Bruce is the moderator. Speaker contributions are indicated with thin bars in the timeline, where each bar corresponds to an EDU. Thus, each part of a speaker's contribution is usually represented by several consecutive bars. Each individual speaker and the public as a whole are associated with their own colour. Attached to the bars are arrows indicating the argumentative relations based on the IAT annotations. Each relation has a source bar and a target bar. The relations of support (labelled as 'arguing') are in green, of attack ('disagreeing') in red, rephrase ('restating') in purple, and answers to questions ('answering') are in orange.

Slider High density of the utterance bars on the timeline limits the ability to closely examine the data. We mitigate this by introducing a slider in the form of a compressed version of the timeline. When a white transparent rectangle initially located to the left of the diagram is used to move along the slider, a corresponding area in the timeline is expanded.

Transcript Window and Video Player The transcript window displays the text corresponding to the utterance bars in the timeline. It allows the users to examine the content of the speakers' contributions. Each transcript block associated with a different speaker is colour-coded accordingly. The video player adds an audio-visual view of the debate.

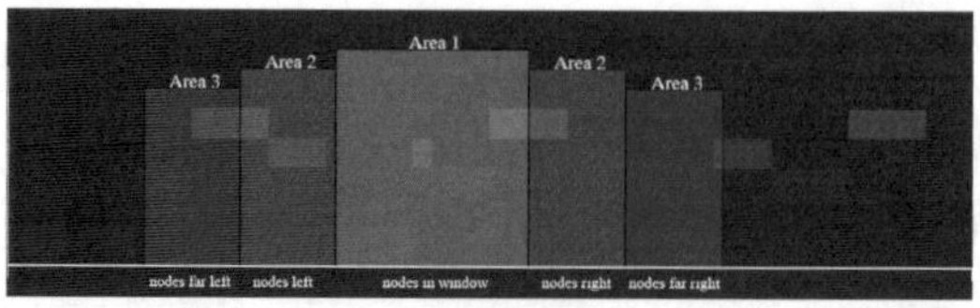

Figure 2: Three areas that are expanded when interacting with the timeline using the slider.

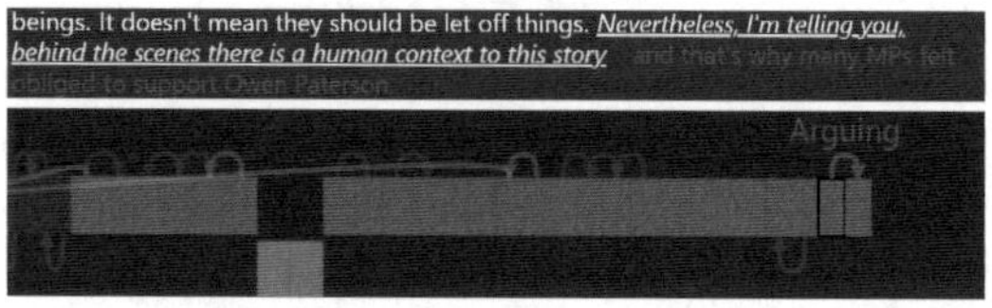

Figure 3: Argumentative relations displayed in the transcript (above) and timeline (below).

Topic Bubbles The purpose of the topic map is to help users gain a deeper understanding of the content by representing the topics covered in the debate. In order to extract topics from the text, Latent Dirichlet Allocation (LDA) (Blei et al., 2001) is used as a 'black box' on the transcript. It returns nine topics, each represented by seven words.

Interaction with the Components The slider can be clicked and dragged and has a major effect on the timeline, transcript, and video player. When the white rectangle is dragged across the slider, the corresponding area on the timeline is enlarged by increasing the width of the bars, while the rest of the timeline gets compressed and dimmed in colour to draw attention to the selected area. Two areas adjacent to the selected section on both sides are enlarged to lesser degrees, which creates a 'fish-eye' effect shown in Fig. 2. Simultaneously, dragging the slider navigates to the text in the transcript window corresponding to the utterance bars in the selected area, along with the corresponding video segment. Starting the video uses the slider functionality by constantly updating the x-value of the center of the sliding window to the current time of the video. Thus, when the video is playing, the sliding window moves automatically.

The users can also interact with the timeline by hovering over the utterance bars. If the utterance bar is a source of an argumentative relation(s), it will be italicised and underlined in the transcript window, while the target(s) of the relation(s) will change their colour to the one of the corresponding relation as shown in Fig. 3. If the target of the relation is outside of the selected area, its text will be displayed over the timeline. Hovering over text in the transcript window will highlight the corresponding utterance bar in the timeline and all potential argumentative relations associated with it both in the timeline and the transcript. In this way, the users are able to closely inspect any arguments in the debate. When hovering over utterance bars outside of the selected area, the corresponding text will be displayed over the timeline.

Topic bubbles can also be interacted with: Hovering over a word in a bubble will highlight all bars in the timeline with a corresponding utterance containing that word, and hovering over the bubble itself highlights the utterances that include the topic. At the same time, text corresponding to the bars is highlighted in the transcript.

Implementation The visualisation is implemented in JavaScript using D3, an open-source visualisation library.[4] The source code is publicly available in the repository at `https://github.com/DarkSilver-1/DebArgVis-Code`.

5 Use Case

In order to showcase how the tool can be used to make meaningful observations regarding the debate dynamics, we use DEBARGVIS to visualise one of the QT30 debates from November 2021 depicted in Fig. 1. At first glance, we notice the general debate structure, where relatively longer panel member turns, indicated by sets of consecutive utterance bars in one colour, are interspersed with public contributions in orange and much shorter input from the moderator in blue. The debate seems balanced as all participants get to contribute to the discussion at various points throughout the debate. Moreover, the length of the speakers' turns suggests that, for the most part, all panel members have relatively equal speaking time, with the exception of Paul Scully, whose turns are on the shorter side.

Further inspection of the visualisation results allows us to make several observations regarding the argumentative patterns within the debate. We find a number of long-distance relations, primarily marked by orange 'answering' arrows between moderator and panel members. The other relation that similarly stands out is 'disagreeing' between the public or moderator and the panel, as well as, in a few instances, between different panel members. Relations of 'arguing' and 'restating' are much rarer between speakers. These patterns indicate that the driving force behind the debate are the moderator and the public with whom the panel members have direct interactions, while exhibiting limited engagement with each other. Relations of 'arguing' and 'rephrase' are significantly more frequent within speaker turns, indicating a general tendency of speakers to support the claims they are making.

We also note how long-distance relations are contained within four separate debate segments. Such behaviour is related to the way 'Question Time' is organised, where the debate is driven by four questions asked by the public at different points in the episode.[5]. This suggests that each question prompts a largely self-contained discussion. Notably, the first two questions appear to be more complex, evidenced by a higher number of long-distance relations within these segments, which together take up about 50 minutes of the episode's total runtime of about one hour.

Finally, we observe that the debate is well moderated as the speaker turns are rarely interrupted. The interruptions are indicated by a gap in the continuous set of utterance bars by one speaker with an utterance by a different participant. One example of such an instance can be found at the 32-minute mark on the timeline when the moderator interrupts Paul Polman with a question. In fact, most of the interruptions are made by the moderator when she invites different audience members to contribute or reiterates questions to the panel to prompt a desirable response. Only in a few rare instances the panel members interrupt each other.

Based on these observations, we conclude that this debate, while giving a relatively equal opportunity for the panel members to respond to the audience members, does not focus on allowing the panel members to interact with each other, who instead have more exchanges with the public and the moderator.

6 Conclusion

With DEBARGVIS we present an interactive tool for the visualisation of argumentative dynamics in debate, with a particular emphasis on the temporal dimension of the data and speaker interaction. We

[4] `https://d3js.org/`

[5] Questions are marked on the timeline in Fig. 4 in the Appendix A.

demonstrate the tool's applicability through a visual analysis of a 'Question Time' episode, which allows insights into several aspects of the debate, such as quality of its moderation, the lack of direct interaction between the invited panel members, and a focus on addressing the audience's questions.

Acknowledgments

The work reported on in this paper was partially funded by the VolkswagenStiftung under grant Az. 98544 'Deliberation Laboratory'.

Limitations

One of the main limitations of our visualisation tool is that currently it is tailored to the data annotated with IAT. While there is more corpora available in this format, such as a corpus of US2016 presidential debates (Visser et al., 2020), this limits the tool's applicability. The decision to use IAT data specifically is based on the fact that the information it offers goes beyond relations of support or attack, to which argument mining corpora are frequently limited. Such information includes, for instance, an indication of when questions are answered, which can provide valuable insights given the nature of the data genre. That being said, it should be possible to adapt the tool to differently annotated corpora, provided a transcript and video are available.

References

Philip Bell. 1998. Using argument representations to make thinking visible for individuals and groups. In *Proceedings of CSCL*, volume 97, pages 10–19.

Neil Benn and Ann Macintosh. 2012. Policy-commons—visualizing arguments in policy consultation. In *Electronic Participation: 4th IFIP WG 8.5 International Conference, ePart 2012, Kristiansand, Norway, September 3-5, 2012. Proceedings 4*, pages 61–72. Springer.

David Blei, Andrew Ng, and Michael Jordan. 2001. Latent dirichlet allocation. In *Advances in Neural Information Processing Systems*, volume 14. MIT Press.

Katarzyna Budzynska, Mathilde Janier, Juyeon Kang, Chris Reed, Patrick Saint-Dizier, Manfred Stede, and Olena Yaskorska. 2014. Towards argument mining from dialogue. In *Proceedings of the Fifth International Conference on Computational Models of Argument (COMMA 2014)*, pages 185–196. IOS Press.

Katarzyna Budzynska, Mathilde Janier, Chris Reed, and Patrick Saint Dizier. 2016. Theoretical foundations for illocutionary structure parsing. *Argument & Computation*, 7(1):91–108.

Mennatallah El-Assady, Valentin Gold, Carmela Acevedo, Christopher Collins, and Daniel Keim. 2016a. Contovi: Multi-party conversation exploration using topic-space views. In *Computer Graphics Forum*, volume 35, pages 431–440. Wiley Online Library.

Mennatallah El-Assady, Valentin Gold, Annette Hautli-Janisz, Wolfgang Jentner, Miriam Butt, Katharina Holzinger, and Daniel A Keim. 2016b. Visargue : A visual text analytics framework for the study of deliberative communication. In *Proc. Int. Conf. Adv. Comput. Anal. Polit. Text*, pages 31–36.

Mennatallah El-Assady, Rita Sevastjanova, Bela Gipp, Daniel Keim, and Christopher Collins. 2017. Nerex: Named-entity relationship exploration in multi-party conversations. In *Computer Graphics Forum*, volume 36, pages 213–225. Wiley Online Library.

Thomas F Gordon, Henry Prakken, and Douglas Walton. 2007. The carneades model of argument and burden of proof. *Artificial intelligence*, 171(10-15):875–896.

Annette Hautli-Janisz, Zlata Kikteva, Wassiliki Siskou, Kamila Gorska, Ray Becker, and Chris Reed. 2022. QT30: A corpus of argument and conflict in broadcast debate. In *Proceedings of the Thirteenth Language Resources and Evaluation Conference*, pages 3291–3300, Marseille, France. European Language Resources Association.

Enamul Hoque and Giuseppe Carenini. 2016. Multiconvis: A visual text analytics system for exploring a collection of online conversations. In *Proceedings of the 21st International Conference on Intelligent User Interfaces*, IUI '16, page 96–107, New York, NY, USA. Association for Computing Machinery.

Mathilde Janier, John Lawrence, and Chris Reed. 2014. Ova+: An argument analysis interface. In *Computational models of argument*, pages 463–464. IOS Press.

Nikos Karacapilidis and Dimitris Papadias. 2001. Computer supported argumentation and collaborative decision making: the hermes system. *Information systems*, 26(4):259–277.

Areti Karamanou, Nikolaos Loutas, and Konstantinos Tarabanis. 2011. Argvis: Structuring political deliberations using innovative visualisation technologies. In *Electronic Participation: Third IFIP WG 8.5 International Conference, ePart 2011, Delft, The Netherlands, August 29–September 1, 2011. Proceedings 3*, pages 87–98. Springer.

Dora Kiesel, Patrick Riehmann, Henning Wachsmuth, Benno Stein, and Bernd Froehlich. 2021. Visual analysis of argumentation in essays. *IEEE Transactions on Visualization and Computer Graphics*, 27(2):1139–1148.

Kostiantyn Kucher, Teri Schamp-Bjerede, Andreas Kerren, Carita Paradis, and Magnus Sahlgren. 2016. Visual analysis of online social media to open up the investigation of stance phenomena. *Information Visualization*, 15(2):93–116.

John D Lowrance, Ian W Harrison, and Andres C Rodriguez. 2000. Structured argumentation for analysis. In *Proceedings of the 12th International Conference on Systems Research, Informatics, and Cybernetics: Focus Symposia on Advances in Computer-Based and Web-Based Collaborative Systems*, pages 47–57.

Simon Mcalister, Andrew Ravenscroft, and Eileen Scanlon. 2004. Combining interaction and context design to support collaborative argumentation using a tool for synchronous cmc. *Journal of Computer Assisted Learning*, 20(3):194–204.

Chris Reed and Glenn Rowe. 2004. Araucaria: Software for argument analysis, diagramming and representation. *International Journal on Artificial Intelligence Tools*, 13(04):961–979.

Chris Reed, Simon Wells, Joseph Devereux, and Glenn Rowe. 2008. Aif+: Dialogue in the argument interchange format. *Frontiers in artificial intelligence and applications*, 172:311.

Laura South, Michail Schwab, Nick Beauchamp, Lu Wang, John Wihbey, and Michelle A Borkin. 2020. Debatevis: Visualizing political debates for non-expert users. In *2020 IEEE Visualization Conference (VIS)*, pages 241–245. IEEE.

Thomas Daniel Ullmann. 2019. A visualisation dashboard for contested collective intelligence. learning analytics to improve sensemaking of group discussion. *RIED: Revista Iboeroamericana de Educación a Distancia (The Ibero-American Journal of Digital Education)*, 22(1):41–80.

Tim Van Gelder. 2002. Argument mapping with reason! able. *The American philosophical association newsletter on philosophy and computers*, 2(1):85–90.

Tim Van Gelder. 2007. The rationale for rationale™. *Law, probability and risk*, 6(1-4):23–42.

Bart Verheij. 2003. Artificial argument assistants for defeasible argumentation. *Artificial intelligence*, 150(1-2):291–324.

Jacky Visser, Barbara Konat, Rory Duthie, Marcin Koszowy, Katarzyna Budzynska, and Chris Reed. 2020. Argumentation in the 2016 us presidential elections: annotated corpora of television debates and social media reaction. *Language Resources and Evaluation*, 54(1):123–154.

Huimin Zhou, Ningyuan Song, Wanli Chang, and Xiaoguang Wang. 2019. Linking the thoughts within scientific papers: Construction and visualization of argumentation graph. *Proceedings of the Association for Information Science and Technology*, 56(1):757–759.

A Four Questions from the Public in the Debate

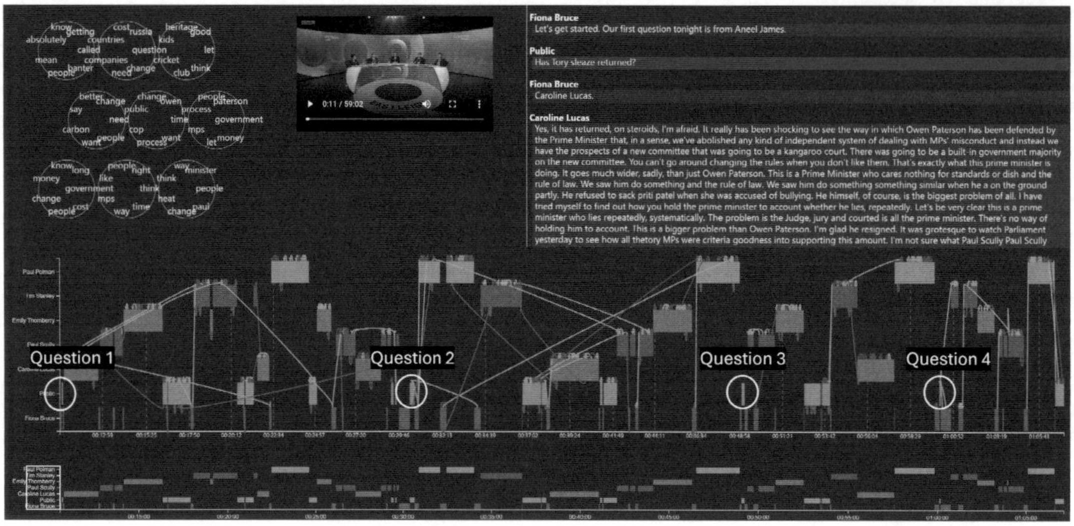

Figure 4: Points in the debate at which the public is invited to introduce new questions for discussion.

Automatic Identification and Naming of Overlapping and Topic-specific Argumentation Frames

Carolin Schindler[1], Annalena Aicher[1], Niklas Rach[2], Wolfgang Minker[1],

[1]Institute of Communications Engineering, Ulm University, Germany
[2]Tensor AI Solutions GmbH, Germany
Correspondence: carolin.schindler@uni-ulm.de

Abstract

Being aware of frames, i. e., the aspect-based grouping of arguments, is crucial in applications that build upon a corpus of arguments, allowing, among others, biases and filter bubbles to be mitigated. However, manually identifying and naming these frames can be time-consuming and therefore not feasible for larger datasets. Within this work, we present a sequential three-step pipeline for automating this task in a data-driven manner. After embedding the arguments, we apply clustering algorithms for identifying the frames and subsequently, utilize methods from the field of cluster labeling to name the frames. The proposed approach is tailored towards the requirements of practical applications where arguments may not be easily split into their argumentative units and hence can belong to more than one frame. Performing a component-wise evaluation, we determine the best-performing configuration of the pipeline. Our results indicate that frames should be identified by performing overlapping and not exclusive clustering and the naming of frames can be accomplished best by extracting aspect terms and weighting them with c-TF-IDF.

1 Introduction

By "select[ing] some aspects of a perceived reality and mak[ing] them more salient in a communicating text" (Entman, 1993, p. 52), framing introduces a bias in the presentation of information. Hence, applications utilizing among others argument mining (Skiera et al., 2022), argument search (Ajjour et al., 2019), discourse analysis (Ruckdeschel and Wiedemann, 2022), summarization (Misra et al., 2016), or argumentative dialogue (Rach et al., 2018; Aicher et al., 2019) need to be aware of the frames that are present in their data.

Within this work, we present a pipeline for automatically identifying and naming such topic-specific frames among a collection of arguments. Thereby, we consider the overlapping nature of the task, i. e., that an argument can belong to more than one frame (Reimers et al., 2019; Dumani et al., 2021; Ruckdeschel and Wiedemann, 2022).

Current works identifying argumentation frames apply an exclusive mapping of arguments to frames and leave the naming of the identified frames to future work. While Reimers et al. (2019) and Daxenberger et al. (2020) directly state these limitations as directions for future work, Dumani et al. (2021) justify the exclusive clustering procedure by assuming that the arguments are provided in elementary parts, i. e. argument units (Trautmann et al., 2020), that belong to exactly one frame. However, this assumption is not always viable for a practical application to arguments "in the wild" since argument unit extraction itself is not an easy task (Stab et al., 2018; Trautmann et al., 2020). Therefore, we focus on creating an overlapping clustering for identifying frames and do not exclude their naming from the task.

Following the conceptual discussion in Schindler (2024), we perform the automatic identification and naming of frames in three sequential steps. First, the arguments need to be embedded in an embedding space that is capable of capturing aspect-based similarity. With this notion of similarity, we then cluster the arguments into frames, thereby considering the overlapping nature of the task. Afterwards, we utilize methods from the field of cluster labeling to name the identified frames. In a component-wise evaluation setup, we identify the best performing approach for each step. In the course of this, we demonstrate that the identification of frames benefits from applying overlapping clustering algorithms on the argument-level and show that the naming performs best when building upon aspect-based candidate extraction.

The remainder is organized as follows: After clarifying the terminology used throughout this work in Section 2, Section 3 gives an overview over

Proceedings of the 12th Argument Mining Workshop, pages 147–159

related work. We detail the individual steps of our pipeline for identifying and naming overlapping, topic-specific argumentation frames in Section 4. The different approaches of performing these steps are evaluated in Section 5 along with a discussion of the results before we conclude in Section 6.

2 Terminology

Following the definition of arguments by Stab and Gurevych (2014), in this work, an *argument* is a sentence that is making a defeasible point and is having a stance towards a debatable topic. Such an argument is built from one or more *argument units* (Trautmann et al., 2020), i. e. indivisible argumentative spans that can be used in different combination in other arguments as well. The *aspects* of an argument "hold the core reason upon which the conclusion/evidence is built" (Schiller et al., 2021, p. 380). The tokens of an argument that are indicative for the aspect(s) addressed by it are *aspect terms* (Trautmann, 2020). When arguments that are addressing similar aspects of the topic are grouped together, the resulting group is a *frame*. In this work, frames are topic-specific, independent of the stance of the arguments, non-redundant, and can be named succinctly in a human-understandable manner by a *frame label*. The grouping of arguments into frames can be also viewed as a grouping of similar aspects into *aspect categories*. Since an argument can address multiple aspects of the topic that not necessarily need to be grouped into the same aspect category, an argumentative sentence can belong to more than one frame (Reimers et al., 2019; Dumani et al., 2021; Ruckdeschel and Wiedemann, 2022).

3 Related Work

Without automation, the identification and naming of frames needs to be performed manually in a time consuming process for every topic individually (Lai et al., 2022; Jurkschat et al., 2022; Ruckdeschel and Wiedemann, 2022). The topic-independent automation, however, is a challenging task. Yet, it is little known about what features are relevant for grouping arguments with respect to the aspects they address (Opitz et al., 2021), but fine-grained semantic nuance might already be crucial (Reimers et al., 2019). Further, there is no general guideline for creating or naming frames, leaving room for subjectivity in the process (Lai et al., 2022; Jurkschat et al., 2022; Ruckdeschel and Wiedemann, 2022).

Identification of Frames When identifying frames with the help of clustering, one performs aspect-based argument clustering. For aspect-based argument clustering, there are no frame labels given and labeling the resulting clusters is often left to future work. By formulating the clustering problem as a similarity scoring task between pairs of arguments, one can perform supervised training; either by regression with a graded scale (Misra et al., 2016) or by classification with a binary labeling scheme (Reimers et al., 2019). Even with little training data, the supervised approach outperforms the unsupervised methods in a cross-topic evaluation setup (Reimers et al., 2019). Moreover, Reimers et al. (2019) point out that exclusive clustering algorithms are a sub-optimal choice since they do not reflect the properties of the data: In 21.9% of the cases the transitivity property induced by exclusive clustering is violated in their dataset. Hence, the overlapping nature of aspect-based argument clustering should be taken into account as in the herein presented work.

Operating on the term-level with an exclusive clustering approach as in Lai et al. (2022) for aspect-based document clustering, was additionally inspired by the following works. Ruckdeschel and Wiedemann (2022) performed an investigation on the level at which frames should be coded. For annotating arguments with a predefined set of frame labels, they found the token-level to be best-suited. In a multi-label argument classification setting, their results suggest that it is beneficial to consider a more granular level than sentence-level. An unsupervised clustering approach proposed by Heinisch and Cimiano (2021) groups fine-granular, topic-specific aspects into more general aspect categories. There, no names are derived for the created categories.

Naming of Frames IBM Project Debater (Slonim et al., 2021; Bar-Haim et al., 2021) makes use of Wikipedia titles that are related to the individual argumentative sentences in order to exclusively cluster and label them. In the summetix API[1], formerly known as ArgumenText API (Daxenberger et al., 2020), a labeling of the clusters is implemented (Skiera et al., 2022) on top of an exclusive clustering with fine-tuned embeddings (Reimers et al., 2019). The label of each cluster is the aspect term with the highest c-TF-IDF (Grootendorst, 2022) score. This

[1] https://api.summetix.com/

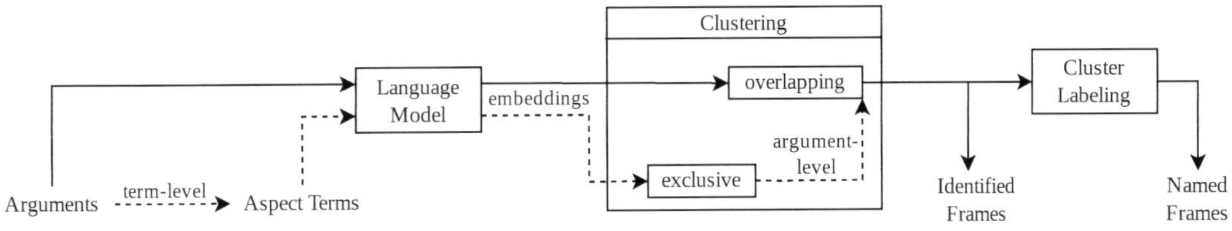

Figure 1: Pipeline for automatic identification and naming of argumentation frames.

is one of the approaches that we are going to test for the naming of overlapping frames.

Topic Modelling Given a collection of texts, *topic modelling* (Churchill and Singh, 2022) aims at structuring these texts by identifying and naming the topics they belong to. Topic modelling is commonly performed on a set of documents, however, it can also be applied to a set of arguments that are belonging to different but unknown topics (Ajjour et al., 2019; Färber and Steyer, 2021). Hence, topic modelling is similar to our task but operating on topics instead of frames. The neural topic model BERTopic (Grootendorst, 2022) is noteworthy in the scope of this work since our steps for identifying and naming frames are similar to theirs for topic modelling and Haddadan et al. (2022) already have applied BERTopic for the qualitative analysis of a dataset into frames. However, our contribution goes beyond the pipeline approach by considering and investigating the overlapping nature of the resulting clustering and providing a quantitative evaluation.

Related Tasks Formally, *frame detection* is a supervised multi-label argument classification task with a predefined set of frame labels (Mou et al., 2022). We, however, do not have any frame labels given and hence we would need to obtain them in a data-driven manner first before performing zero-shot frame detection (Syed et al., 2023; Mou et al., 2022; Ajjour et al., 2018). Moreover, the generalization of classifiers to unseen topics and label sets poses a major challenge for zero-shot approaches. Given a set of arguments, *key point analysis* (Bar-Haim et al., 2020a,b; Friedman et al., 2021) aims at creating a list of prominent key points and then matching the arguments to these key points. This results in every key point being the label for an individual group of arguments. Differently to our task, the groups are stance-dependent and the key points labelling the clusters are argumentative sentences that could be utilized for creating a summary on the topic.

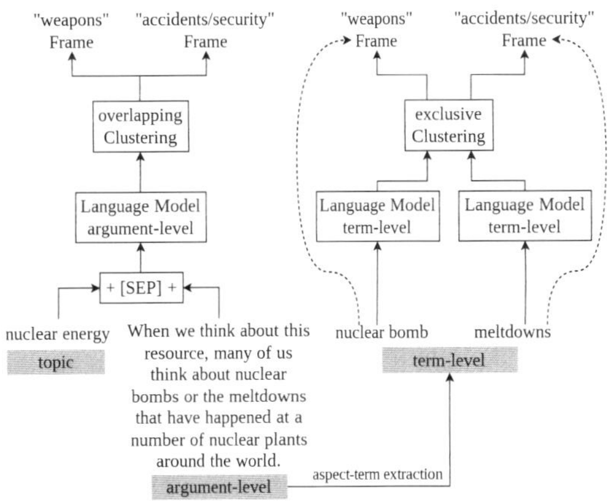

Figure 2: Exemplary processing of an argument from the AAC dataset in our pipeline.

4 Pipeline for Automatic Identification and Naming of Frames

Our pipeline for identifying and naming frames is depicted in Figure 1 and entails three sequential steps, which are described in more detail below. Given a set of n argumentative sentences $\mathcal{S} = \{s_1, ..., s_n\}$ about the topic t, we first require embeddings that capture the notion of aspect-based similarity. Second, we perform a complete clustering $\mathcal{C} = \{c_1, ..., c_k\}$ of the embeddings into k distinct frames with k not being known in advance. Finally, we apply methods from the field of cluster labeling to name the frames with a frame label.

Besides performing the clustering in an overlapping manner on the argument-level, we also experiment with applying exclusive clustering algorithms on the term-level and mapping the resulting clustering back to the argument-level. On the argument-level, the sentential argument itself is treated as the unit to be clustered, while on the term-level we extract the aspect terms from the arguments and utilize these for further processing. An example of performing the frame identification on the argument- and term-level is provided in Figure 2.

4.1 Embeddings for Aspect-based Similarity

To gain embeddings that are suited for aspect-based similarity, it is infeasible to utilize pre-trained language models since they are tailored towards the notion of semantic textual similarity (STS) (Cer et al., 2017). Whereas STS measures the similarity of two texts based on their meaning, we are concerned with the similarity of the aspects addressed by the arguments irrespective of the actual point they are making regarding the aspect (Misra et al., 2016). Hence, when the task involves aspect-based properties, unsupervised models that are pre-trained on semantic properties are outperformed by their fine-tuned counterparts with supervision (Reimers et al., 2019; Dumani et al., 2021).

A task that is utilized for fine-tuning embeddings for aspect-based similarity is aspect-based similarity prediction, where the model has to decide whether two arguments s_1 and s_2 about the same topic t are similar in terms of the aspects they address. In the course of this, every argument is embedded by the model individually and the cosine similarity between the embeddings serves as a measure for aspect-based similarity. The binary classification decision is made by applying a threshold to the predicted similarity score. During fine-tuning, there is also the option to not use a binary but a graded label set, reflecting the circumstance that aspect-based similarity is not a discrete decision (Misra et al., 2016).

In Schindler (2024), the STS-based embeddings of the SBERT (Reimers and Gurevych, 2019) model *all-mpnet-base-v2* were fine-tuned. Following the experimental procedure of Reimers et al. (2019), they performed a four-fold cross-topic validation on the Argument Aspect Similarity (UKP ASPECT) Corpus[2] (Reimers et al., 2019). Depending on the level of granularity that they were operating on, they tested different kinds of information for creating the embeddings.

Here, we employ their respective best performing model in the pipeline. On the argument-level, we utilize their SBERT model fine-tuned on all topics of the UKP ASPECT corpus with the topic t prepended to the argumentative sentence s as an input. With this input configuration, they achieved human-like performance in the four-fold cross-topic validation. On the term-level, the input to the model is a single aspect term AT and no fine-tuning is performed. The aspect terms are extracted from the arguments by querying the summetix API[3] (Schiller et al., 2021).

Their results are confirming that STS is not a good indicator for aspect-based similarity on the argument-level. Nevertheless, STS is performing well on the level of aspect terms. This observation can be explained by the fact that the meaning of terms grouped into an aspect category should be similar. However, for an argumentative sentence, meaning is evaluated on a larger scale than aspects.

4.2 Identification of Frames

We make use of clustering to identify frames, i. e., group the arguments by the aspects they address. The cosine distance between the embeddings of the items serves as the distance measure. To account for the curse of dimensionality that distance measures are prone to (Aggarwal et al., 2001; Steinbach et al., 2004), we apply dimensionality reduction on a per topic basis as a preprocessing step.

For a comparison of overlapping clustering on the argument-level and exclusive clustering on the term-level, which is afterwards mapped back to the argument-level, we select the following equivalent centroid-based clustering algorithms: k-means (MacQueen, 1967) as an exclusive clustering algorithm, which has already been applied for similar frame identification tasks in previous works (e. g., Färber and Steyer (2021); Ajjour et al. (2019); Heinisch and Cimiano (2021)), and fuzzy c-mean (FCM) (Bezdek et al., 1984) as a soft/fuzzy clustering algorithm whose output can be transformed into a hard overlapping clustering. We approach this transformation by assigning every clustered item to the clusters with the highest scores until the cumulative sum of cluster scores that the item is assigned to exceed the threshold θ_{cum}. If multiple clusters are having the same score for an item, we select all of them simultaneously.

4.3 Naming of Frames

For automatically naming the identified frames, we apply a differential cluster labeling strategy that is agnostic of the other frames. This way, the name of the frame label of each frame solely depends on the arguments within the frame and the complete collection of arguments.

First, we generate a set of candidates for each frame. The candidates are either lemmatized as-

[2] `https://tudatalib.ulb.tu-darmstadt.de/handle/tudatalib/1998`

[3] `https://api.summetix.com/`

pect terms *ATs* extracted from the arguments as in Skiera et al. (2022) or terms *FTs* extracted from the lemmatized collection of arguments without stop words based on Luhn's expressiveness of terms assumption (Luhn, 1958). This assumption states that the most important terms are those with mid frequencies, i. e., that neither occur too frequently nor too rarely. To this end, we consider the following approaches, where *frame* and $\neg$*frame* denote that the terms are selected within the frame or among the arguments outside the frame, respectively:

(A) FTs_{frame}

(B) ATs_{frame}

(C) $FTs_{frame} \setminus FTs_{\neg frame}$

(D) $ATs_{frame} \setminus ATs_{\neg frame}$

(E) $FTs_{frame} \cap ATs_{frame}$

(F) $(FTs_{frame} \setminus FTs_{\neg frame}) \cap (ATs_{frame} \setminus ATs_{\neg frame})$

(G) $FTs_{frame} \cup ATs_{frame}$

(H) $(FTs_{frame} \setminus FTs_{\neg frame}) \cup (ATs_{frame} \setminus ATs_{\neg frame})$

For each approach, we optionally remove the topic and the individual words the topic is constituted of from the set of candidates (i. e., $\setminus topic$) and remove the terms *FTs* extracted over the complete collection of arguments (i. e., $\setminus FTs_{corpus}$). Removing the topic and the most frequent terms within the topic, follows the idea of topic-removal for aspect-based argument clustering by Ajjour et al. (2019). Moreover, this way, we can make sure that terms belonging to the topic are not utilized for describing a frame. Afterwards, we weight the candidates per cluster applying class-based TF-IDF (c-TF-IDF) (Grootendorst, 2022). The next step is optional and filters the set of candidates by applying maximal marginal relevance (MMR) (Carbonell and Goldstein, 1998) as in the topic model BERTopic (Grootendorst, 2022) and refines the weighting of the resulting candidates by applying Jensen-Shannon divergence (JSD) as in Carmel et al. (2009). Finally, the name for a frame is either the list of top-i candidates based on the raking by their weight or the name generated by prompting a large language model (LLM) with the task of naming the frame / "subtopic"[4] given the set of all candidates sorted by their weight.

[4]While subtopics and frames are generally distinct concepts, subtopic is a more well-known and well-defined term and due to the limited context, we assume subtopics and frames to be equivalent in the scope of this task.

5 Evaluation

In the following, we individually evaluate the identification and the naming of frames. For each of these subtasks, we detail our experimental setup and subsequently present the results and a discussion of these.

5.1 Dataset and Preprocessing

The Argument Aspect Corpus (AAC)[5] (Ruckdeschel and Wiedemann, 2022) is built for the task of frame detection on the token-level and can thus be viewed as a ground truth dataset for our task. To our knowledge, it is the only dataset containing argumentative sentences and following our definition of overlapping argumentation frames including their naming. The AAC is based on the argumentative sentences written in English of the UKP Sentential Argument Mining Corpus (Stab et al., 2018) regarding the topics abortion, marijuana legalization, minimum wage, and nuclear energy. These topics are not part of the UKP ASPECT Corpus (Reimers et al., 2019) that was used for fine-tuning the embeddings. Per topic, there are $1,118$ to $1,502$ arguments and 12 to 15 frames excluding the frame with the label *Other*. Note, that the definition of frames utilized in this work precludes the usage of an *Other* category, which is a grouping of multiple unrelated aspects. Hence, we include all arguments of the AAC for identifying frames but ignore the *Other* label and arguments solely belonging to it during evaluation and for naming the frames. The overlap size of the frames in the AAC dataset is 1.2261, meaning that approximately every fifth argument belongs not only to one frame but to two frames.

5.2 Identification of Frames

Experimental Procedure Based on the results in Schindler (2024), we apply the following dimensionality reduction prior to the clustering: Principal component analysis (PCA) (Pearson, 1901) with 75 components on the term-level and uniform manifold approximation and projection (UMAP) (McInnes and Healy, 2018) with 50 output dimensions and a local neighborhood of 30 on the argument-level.

We perform the topic-wise grouping of arguments into frames by applying the overlapping clustering algorithm (i. e., FCM) on the argument-level and the exclusive clustering algorithm (i. e., k-

[5]`https://doi.org/10.5281/zenodo.7525183`

means) on the term-level. The clustering on the term-level is mapped back to the argument-level based on the association of the terms to the arguments. To compare against the so-far common procedure, we additionally apply exclusive clustering with k-means to the argument-level.

Building upon the PyClustering library (Novikov, 2019), we transform the results of FCM into a hard overlapping clustering by either setting $\theta_{\text{cum}} = 0$, which equals selecting the cluster(s) with the highest score, or $\theta_{\text{cum}} = 0.5$. The initial points for the clustering are selected by the k-means++ algorithm (Arthur and Vassilvitskii, 2007) utilizing the farthest points as centers. Since the amount k of frames is not known in advance, we test different values between 6 and 21. Based on previous works (Boydstun et al., 2014; Dumani et al., 2021; Jurkschat et al., 2022; Ruckdeschel and Wiedemann, 2022; Aicher et al., 2022), where frames and generic aspect-based categories were defined manually, this is a reasonable range. We are not aware of a common method to automatically determine the amount of clusters for an overlapping clustering without accessing the ground truth. Therefore, we report our results averaged over all k to get an insight on the overall performance independent of the selection of k.

Since we evaluate the identification of frames on the argument-level, where overlapping clusters are formed, we apply measures suited for this kind of clustering. Following (N'Cir et al., 2015), we report the extrinsic measures P_{sim}, R_{sim}, $F1_{sim}$, $BCubed\text{-}P_{sim}$, $BCubed\text{-}R_{sim}$, and $BCubed\text{-}F1_{sim}$ and the intrinsic measure *overlap size*. The $BCubed$- variants are calculated with a re-implementation[6] of the work by (Amigó et al., 2009), extending the measures from the domain of exclusive to overlapping clustering. An advantage of the $BCubed$- measures over the regular ones is that they additionally consider the amount of predicted and ground truth clusters shared between the pairs of arguments. For consistency with formerly reported measures on the task of aspect-based argument similarity prediction (Reimers et al., 2019), we additionally calculate P_{dissim}, R_{dissim}, $F1_{dissim}$ and $F1_{marco}$. Moreover, we report *OmegaSoft*[7] (Lutov et al., 2019), which is a generalization of the adjusted Rand index (ARI) for overlapping clusters, and *GNMI*[8] (Lutov et al., 2019), which is the respective generalization of normalized mutual information (NMI). To determine the best approach for identifying frames, we focus on the measures $F1_{marco}$, $BCubed\text{-}F1_{sim}$, *OmegaSoft*, *GNMI*, and *overlap size*.

[6]https://github.com/hhromic/python-bcubed

[7]https://github.com/eXascaleInfolab/xmeasures

[8]https://github.com/eXascaleInfolab/GenConvNMI

clustering	term-level k-means	argument-level k-means	argument-level $\text{FCM}_{(\theta_{\text{cum}}=0)}$	argument-level $\text{FCM}_{(\theta_{\text{cum}}=0.5)}$
$\mathbf{F1_{macro}}$	0.5712	0.6060	0.6075	**0.6185**
$F1_{sim}$	0.3500	0.3261	0.3284	**0.3625**
P_{sim}	0.2930	0.4843	**0.4872**	0.4378
R_{sim}	**0.4593**	0.2608	0.2627	0.3281
$F1_{dissim}$	0.7925	0.8860	**0.8865**	0.8744
P_{dissim}	**0.8566**	0.8456	0.8460	0.8531
R_{dissim}	0.7421	0.9323	**0.9330**	0.8991
$\mathbf{BCubed\text{-}F1_{sim}}$	0.3564	0.3735	0.3738	**0.4115**
$BCubed\text{-}P_{sim}$	0.2931	0.4969	**0.4981**	0.4691
$BCubed\text{-}R_{sim}$	**0.4766**	0.3109	0.3108	0.3804
OmegaSoft	0.1467	0.2255	0.2283	**0.2377**
GNMI	0.2316	0.3941	0.3951	**0.4158**
overlap size	1.8960	1.000	1.0000	**1.2133**

Table 1: Results for identifying frames averaged over five random seeds, 16 different k, and the four topics of the AAC. The highest standard errors for the individual averaging steps are 0.0361 for the seeds, 0.0244 for k, and 0.0264 for the topics. The ground truth overlap size is 1.2261.

Results and Discussion The results averaged over five random seeds, the 16 different values of k, and the four topics of the AAC are presented in Table 1. Performing the clustering on the term-level leads to worse results than following the so-far common approach of exclusively clustering on the argument-level. The higher $(BCubed\text{-})R_{sim}$ and P_{dissim} on the term-level show that more arguments are regarded as similar on the term-level than on the argument-level. On the argument-level, $\text{FCM}_{(\theta_{\text{cum}}=0.5)}$ is performing slightly better than $\text{FCM}_{(\theta_{\text{cum}}=0)}$ by 0.94 up to 3.77 percent points, while $\text{FCM}_{(\theta_{\text{cum}}=0)}$ and k-means are performing equally well. Moreover, we can observe the following relationship between the performance of the approaches and their *overlap size*: The closer the *overlap size* is to the ground truth, the better the performance of the approach.

This observation can be explained by the indicative role of the overlap size for the amount of argument pairs that are regarded as similar or dissimilar. The higher the overlap in the clustering, the more arguments are predicted to be similar in terms of the aspects they address. Thus, it is not surprising that the algorithms show a better performance, the more this property is in line with the data that we compare against. A reason why the term-level is not performing as well as the argument-level, could be the fewer amount of context that is provided by aspect terms compared to a whole sentence. Moreover, it is possible that we identified valid frames which are differing from the ones in the dataset. Hence, our evaluation procedure comparing against the frames in the AAC, which were created with a single topic-wise pre-defined set of frame labels, might underestimate the performance. Deep clustering algorithms (Zhou et al., 2022), which are learning the embedding and the clustering of the arguments jointly, are an interesting direction for future work. While different embeddings and clustering algorithms could have been employed in this work to gain even better results, note that this was not the goal of our evaluation. Instead, we have shown that clustering arguments in an overlapping manner can overcome limitations of and improve upon the so-far common procedure of exclusively clustering arguments into frames. To this end, we utilized embeddings with human-like performance in the task of aspect-based similarity detection and a well-known centroid based clustering algorithm which is used in its exclusive formulation in related work as well.

5.3 Naming of Frames

Experimental Procedure We evaluate the automatic naming of frames by applying our set of methods topic-wise to the ground truth frames of the AAC. The aspect terms (ATs) are extracted by the summetix API[9] (Schiller et al., 2021). For the terms *FTs*, we consider 1- to 4-grams (Hoppe, 2010) with a document frequency between 0.1 and 0.9. The implementation of c-TF-IDF, MMR, and the name generation with the LLM *flan-T5-base* (Chung et al., 2022) follow the one in BERTopic (Grootendorst, 2022).

Since automatically evaluating the naming against the ground truth with exact matching is too restrictive and collecting any possible equally correct frame labels is not feasible, we conduct an annotation study. To reduce the set of approaches to a reasonable amount for the human, quantitative evaluation, we first perform a qualitative evaluation with the following criteria based on the top-1 candidate: Every frame should have a different name, otherwise the frames would be describing the same aspect category and hence could be merged. We refer to this criterion as the *diff-criterion*. Moreover, no frame must be named with (a) the name of another frame as this name is definitely wrong, (b) the topic of the arguments as this is the wrong level of granularity, or (c) with no name in case the set of candidate terms is empty. Approaches that are not fulfilling this criterion are viewed as invalid.

In the subsequent human annotation, we ask seven participants the following four questions per frame / "subtopic"[10] in the light of the broader main topic, where question (2) and (4) are rated on a seven-point Likert scale from 1 (totally disagree) to 7 (totally agree):

(1) Which of the following lists of terms describes the subtopic <*frame label*> the best?

(2) The list of terms I have selected in the previous question describes the subtopic <*frame label*> well.

(3) Which of the following lists of terms describes the subtopic <*frame label*> the worst?

(4) The list of terms I have selected in the previous question describes the subtopic <*frame label*> well.

Additionally, the participants were instructed to take the order of the list of terms into account when choosing the best and worst one. To avoid bias in the single choice questions due the order in which the lists of terms of the different approaches are presented, we randomize their sequence for every participant. We perform two plausibility checks on the annotations, more precisely per frame (a) the selected list of terms has to be different for question (1) and question (3) and (b) the rating in question (4) must not be higher than the rating in question (2). Among the plausible annotations, we select the three most agreeing ones for evaluation based on the inter-rater reliability assessed through Krippendorff's alpha (Krippendorff, 2019) for ordinal data. Therewith, we gain a result that is as objective as possible by eliminating outliers (Wachsmuth et al., 2017). For questions (1) and (3), we perform the majority vote and report the percentage of best and worst rated namings per approach. In case the majority vote is inconclusive, we do not consider any of the lists of terms as best or worst, respectively. For questions (2) and (4), we report the mean based on the averaged rating per question.

[9] https://api.summetix.com/

[10] While subtopics and frames are generally distinct concepts, subtopic is a more well-known and well-defined term and due to the limited context, we assume subtopics and frames to be equivalent in the scope of this task.

Results and Discussion Any approach building upon candidate set (F), applying JSD, or utilizing the generative approach in the last step, were not able to fulfill the diff-criterion for any topic, i. e., they were not able to produce a naming without giving at least one name to more than one frame. The approaches including JSD or the generative approach are also the only approaches producing certainly wrong names for the frames by suggesting frame labels that belong to other frames. Additionally, set (E) and (F) are prone to producing empty candidate lists. Continuing with the remaining approaches, there is no difference in our criteria for applying MMR or not. Applying both $\setminus$*topic* and $\setminus FTs_{corpus}$ has the same effect as performing $\setminus$*topic* or $\setminus FTs_{corpus}$ on its own, except for the topic *nuclear energy* in case of the latter. To make sure that the topic cannot be utilized as a name for a frame, we therefore propose to apply $\setminus$*topic* and if the topic was not known, $\setminus FTs_{corpus}$ as an approximation of the same. With this configuration, candidate set (B) violates the diff-criterion one time and candidate set (D) three times over all topics, while candidate sets (A), (C), (G), and (H) never violate the diff-criterion.

Since it might be hard to grasp the concept of a frame by just having a look at the candidate with the highest weight, we perform the annotation study with the top-3 ranked candidates and thus include all of the six remaining sets. Therewith, our annotation study reduces to identifying the best set of candidate terms when applying $\setminus$*topic* and weighting with c-TF-IDF. Our plausibility checks lead to the exclusion of two study participants. The remaining five participants have an inter-rater agreement of 0.39 for questions (1) and (3), and of 0.56 for the questions with Likert scales. The three most agreeing annotators are the same for both kinds of questions and have an agreement of 0.59 and 0.70, respectively. For the lists of terms, the descriptive fit with respect to the frame label is rated on average with 5.94 for the best and 3.33 for the worst one. This indicates that the approaches are in general able to produce a naming that is describing the frame very well, while at the same time the worst namings have a rather bad descriptiveness. Based on the evaluation of the single choice questions, which is provided in Table 2, set (B) is performing the best and set (D) is by far the worst. Thus, we can conclude that for the top-3 terms as a naming, the best configuration among our approaches is to extract the aspect terms ATs_{frame} of the frame, apply topic-removal $\setminus$*topic*, and weight the terms with the c-TF-IDF procedure. The naming generated with this approach and set (A) is exemplarily shown in Table 3 in the appendix.

set	A	B	C	D	G	H
best	0.44	**0.65**	0.44	0.12	0.56	0.50
worst	0.19	0.17	0.19	**0.71**	0.12	0.13

Table 2: Results for naming the frames. We report the ratio of best and worst rated list of terms over all topics for the respective approaches. Set (A) and (C) are based on frequent terms, set (B) and (D) on aspect terms, and set (G) and (H) on the union of both kind of terms.

The results indicate that the approaches with JSD or the generative naming approach are performing on the wrong level of granularity since the predicted names are more related to the general concept of the topic. For MMR, we did not observe a difference even within the top-10 since for the valid approaches, the amount of extracted candidates either is already below the 10 candidates that MMR is filtering for or MMR removed candidates that are not within the top-10 anyways. The differences in inter-coder agreement in the annotation study shows that there is still subjectivity in the ratings. However, by performing the evaluation with the three best agreeing participants, we were able to substantially improve the reliability of our results. Interestingly, the best (ATs_{frame}) as well as the worst ($ATs_{frame} \setminus ATs_{\neg frame}$) performing set are based on aspect terms. This observation allows to conclude that the aspect terms shared among different frames are highly relevant to the success of naming the frames. While this might be surprising in the first place, the context provided by the other aspect terms of the frame can lead to a different interpretation of the same aspect terms and therefore give rise to a different frame label. In future work, the approaches for naming the frames could benefit from utilizing external sources that are not generative as in this work to group the candidate terms into the underlying concept they are describing.

6 Conclusion and Future Work

We introduced a sequential three-step pipeline that not only identifies but also names frames while considering the fact that an argument can belong to more than one frame. Through evaluating each step of the pipeline individually, we obtain the following configuration: The pipeline operates on the argument-level, where the arguments are embedded together with their topic by an SBERT model that is fine-tuned for aspect-based similarity. Afterwards, we apply fuzzy c-means clustering and perform a transformation to a hard overlapping clustering such that the *overlap size* of the resulting frames is close to 1.2. Our alternative approach performing the clustering on the term-level with k-means and mapping the results back to the argument-level is performing worse than the so-far common procedure of exclusive clustering on the argument-level. The naming of the frames, which is the last step in the pipeline, is performed for each frame individually. Per frame, we select the candidates with the highest c-TF-IDF scores from a set of candidates obtained through aspect term extraction and removing any terms that are part of the topic.

The next step with respect to evaluation is to investigate the pipeline in its entirety since there is an interaction between identifying and naming frames. The data-driven identification of frames, as performed in the herein work, poses the risk of resulting in an infeasibly large amount of clusters or clusters not representing meaningful and well-defined frames (Jurkschat et al., 2022; Ruckdeschel and Wiedemann, 2022). Nevertheless, the latter is a general risk when not defining the frame labels by hand and the amount of clusters can be defined by setting the hyperparameters respectively. Though, the question remains how many frames to create. To this end, we propose to either investigate internal clustering measures or to perform a selection with a human-in-the-loop setting based on the predicted frame labels of the frames. Moreover, it would be interesting to investigate deductive approaches to frame identification as a post-processing step once the respective names of the frames are known.

Limitations

In our experiments, we did not select the amount of frames and instead averaged over all tested k. For exclusive clustering algorithms, k can be selected by applying the elbow method, average silhouette approach, Hartigan statistics, or gap static, for example (Yang et al., 2019). Though, these selection methods are still having weaknesses that need to be overcome, making the problem relevant to active research (Yang et al., 2019). Overlapping clustering algorithms, additionally, are lacking intrinsic evaluation metrics that go beyond the measure of *overlap size*. Due to this, it is not clear how to perform the selection of k without having access to the ground truth. Since an investigation of strategies for automatically determining the amount of clusters in overlapping clustering goes beyond the scope of this work, we performed an evaluation that remains agnostic to the ground truth in the dataset by treating k as a factor to be averaged out. Moreover, not selecting k based on intrinsic cluster evaluation metrics also provides the chance to have the user decide on the amount and hence the granularity of the frames that is best suited to their application. Such a decision could be guided by the respective naming of the frames for different k.

To evaluate the automatic naming of frames, we performed a qualitative evaluation on the identified ground-truth frames. Though, it would be interesting to apply the naming to the frames identified by our approach and therewith go a step towards evaluating the pipeline end-to-end. Additionally, instead of selecting the three top-ranked terms from the weighted list of candidates as the herein work, one could also investigate other heuristics for choosing the terms, assuring that the frame is well described and potentially can be transformed into a single-term description for the frame label.

Throughout the work, we based our experiments on a single dataset since to the best of our knowledge this is the only one suiting our task with topic-specific overlapping argumentation frames including ground truth labels for their naming. However, since the dataset is covering four different topics, our results should be generalizable with respect to the topic of the arguments.

Ethical Considerations

Consideration of ethics is essential for applications that work with arguments. Our proposed automation of identifying and naming frames, is a generic approach that allows to further structure collections of topic-related arguments based on the aspects they address. Employed in combination with argument search, for example, this will make discussions and their arguments more intuitively accessible to humans. Moreover, by creating awareness of frames, our work allows to, among others, discover biases and filter bubbles (Pariser, 2011; Ekström et al., 2022) in the data and thus paves the path for approaches to mitigate these. While our work could be misused to influence people, e. g., by reinforcing such biases and filter bubbles, we see the positives of our work prevailing, namely being a tool providing transparency about the frames that are existing in the data. As such, it could also be utilized in the process of discovering such malicious intentions.

Acknowledgments

This work has been funded by the DFG within the project "BEA - Building Engaging Argumentation", Grant no. 313723125, as part of the Priority Program "Robust Argumentation Machines (RATIO)" (SPP-1999). We thank summetix GmbH for supporting our research with access to their Aspect API.

References

Charu C. Aggarwal, Alexander Hinneburg, and Daniel A. Keim. 2001. On the surprising behavior of distance metrics in high dimensional spaces. In *Database Theory - ICDT 2001, 8th International Conference, London, UK, January 4-6, 2001, Proceedings*, volume 1973 of *Lecture Notes in Computer Science*, pages 420–434. Springer.

Annalena Aicher, Nadine Gerstenlauer, Isabel Feustel, Wolfgang Minker, and Stefan Ultes. 2022. Towards building a spoken dialogue system for argument exploration. In *Proceedings of the Thirteenth Language Resources and Evaluation Conference*, pages 1234–1241, Marseille, France. European Language Resources Association.

Annalena Aicher, Niklas Rach, Wolfgang Minker, and Stefan Ultes. 2019. Opinion building based on the argumentative dialogue system BEA. In *Increasing Naturalness and Flexibility in Spoken Dialogue Interaction - 10th International Workshop on Spoken Dialogue Systems, IWSDS 2019, Syracuse, Sicily, Italy, 24-26 April 2019*, volume 714 of *Lecture Notes in Electrical Engineering*, pages 307–318. Springer.

Yamen Ajjour, Milad Alshomary, Henning Wachsmuth, and Benno Stein. 2019. Modeling frames in argumentation. In *Proceedings of the 2019 Conference on Empirical Methods in Natural Language Processing and the 9th International Joint Conference on Natural Language Processing (EMNLP-IJCNLP)*, pages 2922–2932, Hong Kong, China. Association for Computational Linguistics.

Yamen Ajjour, Henning Wachsmuth, Dora Kiesel, Patrick Riehmann, Fan Fan, Giuliano Castiglia, Rosemary Adejoh, Bernd Fröhlich, and Benno Stein. 2018. Visualization of the topic space of argument search results in args.me. In *Proceedings of the 2018 Conference on Empirical Methods in Natural Language Processing: System Demonstrations*, pages 60–65, Brussels, Belgium. Association for Computational Linguistics.

Enrique Amigó, Julio Gonzalo, Javier Artiles, and Felisa Verdejo. 2009. A comparison of extrinsic clustering evaluation metrics based on formal constraints. *Inf. Retr.*, 12(4):461–486.

David Arthur and Sergei Vassilvitskii. 2007. k-means++: the advantages of careful seeding. In *Proceedings of the Eighteenth Annual ACM-SIAM Symposium on Discrete Algorithms, SODA 2007, New Orleans, Louisiana, USA, January 7-9, 2007*, pages 1027–1035. SIAM.

Roy Bar-Haim, Lilach Eden, Roni Friedman, Yoav Kantor, Dan Lahav, and Noam Slonim. 2020a. From arguments to key points: Towards automatic argument summarization. In *Proceedings of the 58th Annual Meeting of the Association for Computational Linguistics*, pages 4029–4039, Online. Association for Computational Linguistics.

Roy Bar-Haim, Yoav Kantor, Lilach Eden, Roni Friedman, Dan Lahav, and Noam Slonim. 2020b. Quantitative argument summarization and beyond: Cross-domain key point analysis. In *Proceedings of the 2020 Conference on Empirical Methods in Natural Language Processing (EMNLP)*, pages 39–49, Online. Association for Computational Linguistics.

Roy Bar-Haim, Yoav Kantor, Elad Venezian, Yoav Katz, and Noam Slonim. 2021. Project Debater APIs: Decomposing the AI grand challenge. In *Proceedings of the 2021 Conference on Empirical Methods in Natural Language Processing: System Demonstrations*, pages 267–274, Online and Punta Cana, Dominican Republic. Association for Computational Linguistics.

James C. Bezdek, Robert Ehrlich, and William Full. 1984. FCM: The fuzzy c-means clustering algorithm. *Computers & Geosciences*, 10(2-3):191–203.

Amber E. Boydstun, Dallas Card, Justin Gross, Paul Resnick, and Noah A. Smith. 2014. Tracking the Development of Media Frames within and across Policy Issues.

Jaime G. Carbonell and Jade Goldstein. 1998. The use of mmr, diversity-based reranking for reordering documents and producing summaries. In *SIGIR '98: Proceedings of the 21st Annual International ACM SIGIR Conference on Research and Development in Information Retrieval, August 24-28 1998, Melbourne, Australia*, pages 335–336. ACM.

David Carmel, Haggai Roitman, and Naama Zwerdling. 2009. Enhancing cluster labeling using wikipedia. In *Proceedings of the 32nd International ACM SIGIR Conference on Research and Development in Information Retrieval*, SIGIR '09, page 139–146, New York, NY, USA. Association for Computing Machinery.

Daniel Cer, Mona Diab, Eneko Agirre, Iñigo Lopez-Gazpio, and Lucia Specia. 2017. SemEval-2017 task 1: Semantic textual similarity multilingual and crosslingual focused evaluation. In *Proceedings of the 11th International Workshop on Semantic Evaluation (SemEval-2017)*, pages 1–14, Vancouver, Canada. Association for Computational Linguistics.

Hyung Won Chung, Le Hou, Shayne Longpre, Barret Zoph, Yi Tay, William Fedus, Eric Li, Xuezhi Wang, Mostafa Dehghani, Siddhartha Brahma, Albert Webson, Shixiang Shane Gu, Zhuyun Dai, Mirac Suzgun, Xinyun Chen, Aakanksha Chowdhery, Sharan Narang, Gaurav Mishra, Adams Yu, and 12 others. 2022. Scaling instruction-finetuned language models. *CoRR*, abs/2210.11416.

Rob Churchill and Lisa Singh. 2022. The evolution of topic modeling. *ACM Comput. Surv.*, 54(10s):215:1–215:35.

Johannes Daxenberger, Benjamin Schiller, Chris Stahlhut, Erik Kaiser, and Iryna Gurevych. 2020. Argumentext: Argument classification and clustering in a generalized search scenario. *Datenbank-Spektrum*, 20(2):115–121.

Lorik Dumani, Tobias Wiesenfeldt, and Ralf Schenkel. 2021. Fine and coarse granular argument classification before clustering. In *CIKM '21: The 30th ACM International Conference on Information and Knowledge Management, Virtual Event, Queensland, Australia, November 1 - 5, 2021*, pages 422–432. ACM.

Axel G. Ekström, Diederick C. Niehorster, and Erik J. Olsson. 2022. Self-imposed filter bubbles: Selective attention and exposure in online search. *Computers in Human Behavior Reports*, 7:100226.

Robert M. Entman. 1993. Framing: Toward Clarification of a Fractured Paradigm. *Journal of Communication*, 43(4):51–58.

Michael Färber and Anna Steyer. 2021. Towards full-fledged argument search: A framework for extracting and clustering arguments from unstructured text. *CoRR*, abs/2112.00160.

Roni Friedman, Lena Dankin, Yufang Hou, Ranit Aharonov, Yoav Katz, and Noam Slonim. 2021. Overview of the 2021 key point analysis shared task. In *Proceedings of the 8th Workshop on Argument Mining*, pages 154–164, Punta Cana, Dominican Republic. Association for Computational Linguistics.

Maarten Grootendorst. 2022. Bertopic: Neural topic modeling with a class-based TF-IDF procedure. *CoRR*, abs/2203.05794.

Shohreh Haddadan, Elena Cabrio, Axel J. Soto, and Serena Villata. 2022. Topic modelling and frame identification for political arguments. In *AIxIA 2022 - Advances in Artificial Intelligence - XXIst International Conference of the Italian Association for Artificial Intelligence, AIxIA 2022, Udine, Italy, November 28 - December 2, 2022, Proceedings*, volume 13796 of *Lecture Notes in Computer Science*, pages 268–281. Springer.

Philipp Heinisch and Philipp Cimiano. 2021. A multitask approach to argument frame classification at variable granularity levels. *it Inf. Technol.*, 63(1):59–72.

Dennis Hoppe. 2010. Cluster-labeling: Paradigmen und validierung. Master's thesis, Bauhaus-Universität Weimar, Fakultät Medien, Medieninformatik.

Lena Jurkschat, Gregor Wiedemann, Maximilian Heinrich, Mattes Ruckdeschel, and Sunna Torge. 2022. Few-shot learning for argument aspects of the nuclear energy debate. In *Proceedings of the Thirteenth Language Resources and Evaluation Conference*, pages 663–672, Marseille, France. European Language Resources Association.

Klaus Krippendorff. 2019. *Content Analysis: An Introduction to Its Methodology*, 4 edition. SAGE Publications, Inc.

Sha Lai, Yanru Jiang, Lei Guo, Margrit Betke, Prakash Ishwar, and Derry Tanti Wijaya. 2022. An unsupervised approach to discover media frames. In *Proceedings of the LREC 2022 workshop on Natural Language Processing for Political Sciences*, pages 22–31, Marseille, France. European Language Resources Association.

Hans Peter Luhn. 1958. The automatic creation of literature abstracts. *IBM J. Res. Dev.*, 2(2):159–165.

Artem Lutov, Mourad Khayati, and Philippe Cudré-Mauroux. 2019. Accuracy evaluation of overlapping and multi-resolution clustering algorithms on large datasets. In *IEEE International Conference on Big Data and Smart Computing, BigComp 2019, Kyoto, Japan, February 27 - March 2, 2019*, pages 1–8. IEEE.

James MacQueen. 1967. Some methods for classification and analysis of multivariate observations. In *Proceedings of the Fifth Berkeley Symposium on Mathematical Statistics and Probability*, volume 1, pages 281–297. University of California Press.

Leland McInnes and John Healy. 2018. UMAP: uniform manifold approximation and projection for dimension reduction. *CoRR*, abs/1802.03426.

Amita Misra, Brian Ecker, and Marilyn Walker. 2016. Measuring the similarity of sentential arguments in dialogue. In *Proceedings of the 17th Annual Meeting of the Special Interest Group on Discourse and Dialogue*, pages 276–287, Los Angeles. Association for Computational Linguistics.

Xinyi Mou, Zhongyu Wei, Changjian Jiang, and Jiajie Peng. 2022. A two stage adaptation framework for frame detection via prompt learning. In *Proceedings of the 29th International Conference on Computational Linguistics*, pages 2968–2978, Gyeongju, Republic of Korea. International Committee on Computational Linguistics.

Chiheb-Eddine Ben N'Cir, Guillaume Cleuziou, and Nadia Essoussi. 2015. *Overview of Overlapping Partitional Clustering Methods*, pages 245–275. Springer International Publishing, Cham.

Andrei Novikov. 2019. PyClustering: Data mining library. *Journal of Open Source Software*, 4(36):1230.

Juri Opitz, Philipp Heinisch, Philipp Wiesenbach, Philipp Cimiano, and Anette Frank. 2021. Explainable unsupervised argument similarity rating with Abstract Meaning Representation and conclusion generation. In *Proceedings of the 8th Workshop on Argument Mining*, pages 24–35, Punta Cana, Dominican Republic. Association for Computational Linguistics.

E. Pariser. 2011. *The Filter Bubble: How the New Personalized Web Is Changing What We Read and How We Think*. Penguin Publishing Group.

Karl Pearson. 1901. LIII. On lines and planes of closest fit to systems of points in space. *The London, Edinburgh, and Dublin Philosophical Magazine and Journal of Science*, 2(11):559–572.

Niklas Rach, Klaus Weber, Louisa Pragst, Elisabeth André, Wolfgang Minker, and Stefan Ultes. 2018. EVA: A multimodal argumentative dialogue system. In *Proceedings of the 2018 on International Conference on Multimodal Interaction, ICMI 2018, Boulder, CO, USA, October 16-20, 2018*, pages 551–552. ACM.

Nils Reimers and Iryna Gurevych. 2019. Sentence-BERT: Sentence embeddings using Siamese BERT-networks. In *Proceedings of the 2019 Conference on Empirical Methods in Natural Language Processing and the 9th International Joint Conference on Natural Language Processing (EMNLP-IJCNLP)*, pages 3982–3992, Hong Kong, China. Association for Computational Linguistics.

Nils Reimers, Benjamin Schiller, Tilman Beck, Johannes Daxenberger, Christian Stab, and Iryna Gurevych. 2019. Classification and clustering of arguments with contextualized word embeddings. In *Proceedings of the 57th Annual Meeting of the Association for Computational Linguistics*, pages 567–578, Florence, Italy. Association for Computational Linguistics.

Mattes Ruckdeschel and Gregor Wiedemann. 2022. Boundary detection and categorization of argument aspects via supervised learning. In *Proceedings of the 9th Workshop on Argument Mining*, pages 126–136, Online and in Gyeongju, Republic of Korea. International Conference on Computational Linguistics.

Benjamin Schiller, Johannes Daxenberger, and Iryna Gurevych. 2021. Aspect-controlled neural argument generation. In *Proceedings of the 2021 Conference of the North American Chapter of the Association for Computational Linguistics: Human Language Technologies*, pages 380–396, Online. Association for Computational Linguistics.

Carolin Schindler. 2024. Overlapping aspect-based argument cluster analysis including cluster labelling for opinion formation with argumentative dialogue systems. Master's thesis, Institute of Communications Engineering, University of Ulm.

Bernd Skiera, Shunyao Yan, Johannes Daxenberger, Marcus Dombois, and Iryna Gurevych. 2022. Using information-seeking argument mining to improve service. *Journal of Service Research*, 25(4):537–548.

Noam Slonim, Yonatan Bilu, Carlos Alzate, Roy Bar-Haim, Ben Bogin, Francesca Bonin, Leshem Choshen, Edo Cohen-Karlik, Lena Dankin, Lilach Edelstein, Liat Ein-Dor, Roni Friedman-Melamed, Assaf Gavron, Ariel Gera, Martin Gleize, Shai Gretz, Dan Gutfreund, Alon Halfon, Daniel Hershcovich, and 34 others. 2021. An autonomous debating system. *Nat.*, 591(7850):379–384.

Christian Stab and Iryna Gurevych. 2014. Annotating argument components and relations in persuasive essays. In *Proceedings of COLING 2014, the 25th International Conference on Computational Linguistics: Technical Papers*, pages 1501–1510, Dublin, Ireland. Dublin City University and Association for Computational Linguistics.

Christian Stab, Tristan Miller, Benjamin Schiller, Pranav Rai, and Iryna Gurevych. 2018. Cross-topic argument mining from heterogeneous sources. In *Proceedings of the 2018 Conference on Empirical Methods in Natural Language Processing*, pages 3664–3674, Brussels, Belgium. Association for Computational Linguistics.

Michael Steinbach, Levent Ertöz, and Vipin Kumar. 2004. *The Challenges of Clustering High Dimensional Data*, pages 273–309. Springer Berlin Heidelberg, Berlin, Heidelberg.

Shahbaz Syed, Timon Ziegenbein, Philipp Heinisch, Henning Wachsmuth, and Martin Potthast. 2023. Frame-oriented summarization of argumentative discussions. In *Proceedings of the 24th Annual Meeting of the Special Interest Group on Discourse and Dialogue*, pages 114–129, Prague, Czechia. Association for Computational Linguistics.

Dietrich Trautmann. 2020. Aspect-based argument mining. In *Proceedings of the 7th Workshop on Argument Mining*, pages 41–52, Online. Association for Computational Linguistics.

Dietrich Trautmann, Johannes Daxenberger, Christian Stab, Hinrich Schütze, and Iryna Gurevych. 2020. Fine-grained argument unit recognition and classification. In *The Thirty-Fourth AAAI Conference on Artificial Intelligence, AAAI 2020, The Thirty-Second Innovative Applications of Artificial Intelligence Conference, IAAI 2020, The Tenth AAAI Symposium on Educational Advances in Artificial Intelligence, EAAI 2020, New York, NY, USA, February 7-12, 2020*, pages 9048–9056. AAAI Press.

Henning Wachsmuth, Nona Naderi, Yufang Hou, Yonatan Bilu, Vinodkumar Prabhakaran, Tim Alberdingk Thijm, Graeme Hirst, and Benno Stein. 2017. Computational argumentation quality assessment in natural language. In *Proceedings of the 15th Conference of the European Chapter of the Association for Computational Linguistics: Volume 1, Long Papers*, pages 176–187, Valencia, Spain. Association for Computational Linguistics.

Jaekyung Yang, Jong-Yeong Lee, Myoungjin Choi, and Yeongin Joo. 2019. A new approach to determine the optimal number of clusters based on the gap statistic. In *Machine Learning for Networking - Second IFIP TC 6 International Conference, MLN 2019, Paris, France, December 3-5, 2019, Revised Selected Papers*, volume 12081 of *Lecture Notes in Computer Science*, pages 227–239. Springer.

Sheng Zhou, Hongjia Xu, Zhuonan Zheng, Jiawei Chen, Zhao Li, Jiajun Bu, Jia Wu, Xin Wang, Wenwu Zhu, and Martin Ester. 2022. A comprehensive survey on deep clustering: Taxonomy, challenges, and future directions. *CoRR*, abs/2206.07579.

A Example for Naming of Frames

Table 3 shows the lists of top-3 candidate terms for set (A) and (B) as utilized in the annotation study for the topics *abortion* and *minimum wage*. The configuration with set (B) was identified as the best performing one for naming the frames.

ground truth	set (A): FTs_{frame}	set (B): ATs_{frame}
abortion		
abortion industry	industry, profit, consistent	industry, profit, dirty
adoption	adoption, couple, adopt	adoption, baby, kid
bodily autonomy/women's rights	choice, body, make	choice, body, decision
consequences of childbirth	welfare, unwanted, care	raise, unwanted, poverty
fetal defects/disabilities	defect, syndrome, fetal	syndrome, health, pregnancy
fetal/newborn rights	fetus, person, unborn	fetus, person, unborn
funding of abortion	poor, medicaid, funding	poor, medicaid, funding
health effects of pregnancy/childbirth	pregnancy, mother, risk	pregnancy, mother, risk
illegal abortions	illegal, unsafe, 000	illegal, unsafe, alley
moral/ethical values	god, moral, immoral	moral, religious, catholic
parental consent	parental, minor, parent	minor, parent, consent
psychological effects of abortion	regret, mental, psychological	regret, mental, psychological
rape	rape, incest, raped	rape, incest, raped
responsibility	contraception, control, use	control, contraception, contraceptive
safety/health effects of legal abortion	cancer, breast, risk	cancer, risk, medical
minimum wage		
capital vs labor	power, sweatshop, bargaining	market, labor, monopsony
competition/business challenges	small, company, owner	small, profit, hotel
economic impact	economy, spend, money	economy, spend, money
government	government, market, free	government, market, state
low-skilled	skilled, unskilled, employment	employment, young, skill
motivation/chances	school, opportunity, skill	school, opportunity, skill
prices	price, consumer, raise	price, consumer, raise
social justice/injustice	poverty, living, income	poverty, income, inflation
turnover	turnover, training, employee	turnover, productivity, reduce
un/employment rate	employment, unemployment, effect	employment, unemployment, labor
welfare	tax, program, assistance	tax, government, income
youth and secondary wage earners	household, family, teenager	household, family, teenager

Table 3: Frame labels as predicted by the automated naming approaches selecting the top-3 candidates ranked by their c-TF-IDF weight from the respective candidate set with topic-removal.

A Simple but Effective Context Retrieval for Sequential Sentence Classification in Long Legal Documents

Anas Belfathi, Nicolas Hernandez, Laura Monceaux, Richard Dufour
Nantes Université, École Centrale Nantes, CNRS, LS2N, UMR 6004, F-44000, France
firstname.lastname@univ-nantes.fr

Abstract

Sequential sentence classification extends traditional classification, especially useful when dealing with long documents. However, state-of-the-art approaches face two major challenges: pre-trained language models struggle with input-length constraints, while proposed hierarchical models often introduce irrelevant content. To address these limitations, we propose a simple and effective document-level retrieval approach that extracts only the most relevant context. Specifically, we introduce two heuristic strategies: **Sequential**, which captures local information, and **Selective**, which retrieves the semantically similar sentences. Experiments on legal domain datasets show that both heuristics lead to consistent improvements over the baseline, with an average increase of $\sim$5.5 weighted-F1 points. Sequential heuristics outperform hierarchical models on two out of three datasets, with gains of up to $\sim$1.5, demonstrating the benefits of targeted context.

1 Introduction

Sequential sentence classification (SSC) is the task of classifying each sentence based on its semantic role within a document. Since a sentence's meaning is often shaped by its surrounding context, SSC is particularly useful in structured texts such as legal cases. Identifying key rhetorical components (e.g., preamble, issue, or analysis; see Figure 1) benefits downstream tasks such as information retrieval (Neves et al., 2019; Safder and Hassan, 2019) and document summarization (Kalamkar et al., 2022; Muhammed et al., 2024).

Recent SSC approaches rely on hierarchical models that process full-document sequences to capture broader context (Jin and Szolovits, 2018; Brack et al., 2021; Kalamkar et al., 2022). However, processing all sentences is not always beneficial, as it may introduce noise from irrelevant content (Shi et al., 2023). This issue is compounded by the fact that pre-trained language models (PLMs) remain constrained by input-length limitations (Warner et al., 2024), even with advances in large language models (LLMs) (BehnamGhader et al., 2024). Overcoming these limitations by retrieving only the most relevant context offers a way to both reduce noise and improve the efficiency of SSC models, particularly when using PLMs.

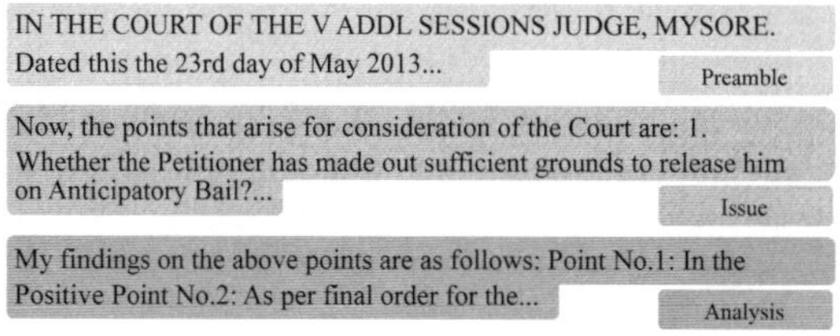

Figure 1: A segment of a legal document with sentences labeled by their function.

Several studies have begun exploring strategies for retrieving relevant informations (Amalvy et al., 2023; Lan et al., 2024). However, to our knowledge, no prior work has specifically addressed how to retrieve the most relevant sentence-level context to optimize PLMs performance for the SSC task. We focus only on encoder-only models, which currently combine effectiveness with low computational cost compared to LLMs for classification tasks (Roccabruna et al., 2024).

In this paper, our contributions are twofold: (1) we analyze the role of context in SSC by introducing two heuristic retrieval strategies—*Sequential*, which assumes that the most informative context lies in positional proximity, and *Selective*, which retrieves semantically similar sentences regardless of their position in the document; and (2) we demonstrate that these strategies enhance PLM performance by providing more relevant context and can outperform state-of-the-art hierarchical models.

We evaluate on document-level datasets in the legal domain, the primary benchmark for SSC task. To foster transparency and reproducibility, we release our code under an open-source license[1].

[1] https://github.com/AnasBelfathi/ACL-2025

Proceedings of the 12th Argument Mining Workshop, pages 160–167
July 31, 2025 ©2025 Association for Computational Linguistics

2 Related Work

2.1 Input Sequence Constraints in PLMs

Encoder-only models such as BERT (Devlin et al., 2019) offer a strong tradeoff between size and performance, making them a compelling alternative to larger generative models for classification tasks. However, the quadratic complexity of self-attention in vanilla Transformer models limits their effective input length, posing challenges for processing long documents. To mitigate this, sparse attention mechanisms have been introduced to reduce computational costs (Zaheer et al., 2020; Wang et al., 2020; Beltagy et al., 2020). While these methods extend the range of accessible context, they still struggle to effectively aggregate the task-relevant information needed for fine-grained sentence classification in long-document settings (Warner et al., 2024; Nussbaum et al., 2025).

2.2 SSC for Long Documents

Early work on SSC focused on hierarchical models to incorporate broader context into sentence representations. Hierarchical Sequential Labeling Network (HSLN) was among the first to process full-document sequences for contextualized representations (Jin and Szolovits, 2018; Brack et al., 2021; Kalamkar et al., 2022). More recent studies have explored refined learning strategies: T.y.s.s. et al. (2024) applied contrastive and prototypical learning to enhance sentence representations by leveraging semantic similarities, while Santosh et al. (2024) introduced a hierarchical curriculum learning framework to progressively improve the model's ability to distinguish rhetorical labels at different levels of granularity.

While these studies have primarily focused on improving HSLN, our work addresses a different challenge: overcoming PLM input-length constraints by retrieving only the relevant context, thus reducing noise and improving efficiency in SSC.

3 Context Retrieval

We propose a simple yet effective set of heuristics to enhance SSC in long documents. The motivation for introducing the two types—**Sequential** and **Selective**—is to explore complementary definitions of contextual relevance. Sequential heuristics are based on the assumption that the most useful context comes from nearby sentences, leveraging **positional proximity**. In contrast, Selective heuristics test whether **semantically similar** sentences, regardless of their position, provide better context, particularly in long structured documents.

Sequential Heuristics extract context from sentences adjacent to the target sentence within the same document. We consider three widely adopted strategies:

- Before: Selects the k sentences immediately preceding the target sentence.
- After: Selects the k sentences immediately following the target sentence.
- Surrounding: Selects $\frac{k}{2}$ sentences before and after the target sentence.

Selective Heuristics , unlike sequential strategies, retrieve sentences from anywhere in the document, independent of their position relative to the target sentence. We explore three selection techniques:

- Random: Randomly selects k sentences from the entire document.
- BM25: Retrieves the k most relevant sentences using a ranking function based on term frequency-inverse document frequency (TF-IDF) weighting (Trotman et al., 2014), widely used in information retrieval for lexical relevance scoring.
- Sentence-BERT: Selects the k semantically closest sentences to the target sentence using embeddings that capture sentence-level similarity via a siamese BERT network (Reimers and Gurevych, 2019).

Given computational constraints, we limit our analysis to $k = 6$. Table 2 in the Appendix provides illustrative examples.

Sentence Ordering We further investigate whether the order of retrieved sentences impacts SSC performance. Inspired by NAREOR (Gangal et al., 2022), which explores sentence reordering to analyze narrative coherence in storytelling, we examine whether maintaining full document sentences ($k = N$) while altering their order affects performance.

To evaluate this, we use our heuristics. In Sequential, we retain the original human-written order to preserve logical flow. In Selective, we reorder sentences based on their relevance to the target sentence while ensuring that all remain included for a fair comparison.

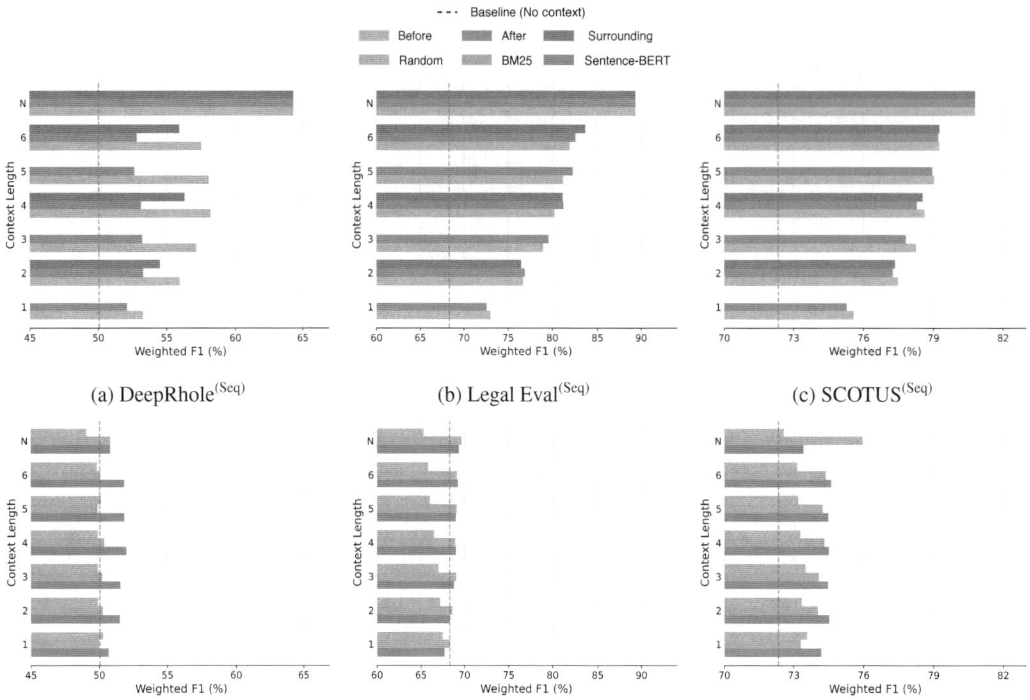

(a) DeepRhole$^{(Seq)}$ (b) Legal Eval$^{(Seq)}$ (c) SCOTUS$^{(Seq)}$

(d) DeepRhole$^{(Sel)}$ (e) Legal Eval$^{(Sel)}$ (f) SCOTUS$^{(Sel)}$

Figure 2: Weighted F1 scores for different context lengths k across three datasets. The top row (a, b, c) presents results using Sequential context$^{(Seq)}$, while the bottom row (d, e, f) represents Selective context$^{(Sel)}$. $k = N$ indicates that the full document is used to address the sentence ordering question. We set k as an even number for Surrounding heuristic to ensure comparability in context length with other ones.

4 Experimental protocol

4.1 Datasets

Our experiments focus on the legal domain, as it is the only domain with datasets annotated at the document level in english. We utilize three datasets: (i) DeepRhole (Bhattacharya et al., 2023), (ii) LegalEval (Kalamkar et al., 2022), and (iii) SCOTUS (Lavissière and Bonnard, 2024), derived from Indian and U.S. legal judgments. DeepRhole contains 7 rhetorical role labels, while the others have 13 each. For evaluation, we report the weighted F1-score[2].

4.2 SSC Model for Context Analysis

To ensure that our analysis covers all sentences in a document, we build upon the hierarchical HSLN model (Brack et al., 2021), with two minor modifications: (1) Motivated by ablation studies (Jin and Szolovits, 2018; Chen et al., 2023), which identified the contextual sentence enrichment layer as HSLN's primary driver of effectiveness, we removed the conditional random field (CRF) layer, and (2) We optimize only over the target sentence, enriched with context selected by our heuristics.

Further architectural details, including our refinements, are provided in Appendix A. All results are averaged over three runs for robustness.

5 Results

5.1 Context Analysis

Figure 2 shows that Sequential Heuristics systematically improve classification as more sentences are included. In LegalEval and SCOTUS, the *Surrounding* heuristic achieves the highest F1 score (83.6% and 79.2% at $k = 6$, respectively). This indicates that rhetorical signals are distributed in both directions, and that accessing context from both sides helps to more accurately situate the current sentence within its transitional flow. However, in DeepRhole, the *Before* heuristic performs best, reaching 58.2%. This suggests that this dataset follows a progressive narrative and argumentative thread, where the meaning of each sentence is fun-

[2]All datasets were split at the document level into 80% training, 10% validation, and 10% test sets.

Model	Seq	DeepRhole	Legal Eval	SCOTUS
BERT (baseline)	512	52.23	69.74	75.58
+ Before		**67.18**†	<u>78.41</u>†	<u>79.74</u>†
+ After		56.72†	**79.74**†	**81.34**†
+ Surrounding		<u>62.87</u>†	77.27†	75.47
+ Random		46.86	67.05	74.70
+ BM25		51.59	69.43	75.96
+ Sentence-BERT		52.23	68.98	76.24
Nomic-BERT (baseline)	2048	50.32	68.90	75.50
+ Before		**67.89**†	<u>80.54</u>†	<u>81.12</u>†
+ After		57.75†	**81.11**†	**81.32**†
+ Surrounding		<u>65.51</u>†	78.20†	80.81†
+ Random		51.61	68.43	75.73
+ BM25		53.90	70.82‡	77.06†
+ Sentence-BERT		54.02‡	70.76‡	77.17‡
BERT-HSLN (SOTA)	$512 \times N$	54.45	93.06	79.66

Table 1: Performance of PLMs using the best configuration observed in context analysis for $k \leq 6$ for each heuristic. Bold values represent the best improvement over the baseline (w/o context), while underlined values indicate the second-best. BERT-HSLN is the SOTA for the SSC task. Markers † and ‡ denote statistical significance over the baseline at $p = 0.05$ and $p = 0.01$, respectively.

damentally built upon what has been previously developed.

In contrast, Selective Heuristics yield marginal gains, with *BM25* being the most effective, reaching $\approx 74\%$ F1 in SCOTUS when $k \leq 6$.
The limited effectiveness of those heuristics could be attributed to two factors: (1) When documents lack semantically similar sentences, heuristics retrieve unrelated ones, adding noise (as observed in DeepRhole), and (2) The rhetorical function of a sentence often depends on its placement within the overall argumentative structure, rather than on its intrinsic semantics alone.

At $k = N$, the Sentence Ordering experiment confirms that SSC is sensitive to how context is structured—with the highest scores observed when the document's logical flow is preserved. Conversely, reordering sentences using Selective heuristics suggests that taking the full document may not be necessary; instead, prioritizing only the most relevant ones yields competitive performance.

5.2 Context Enrichment for PLMs

To examine how PLMs benefit from contextual enrichment[3], we conduct experiments with BERT (Devlin et al., 2019) and the recently introduced model Nomic-BERT (Nussbaum et al., 2025), as shown in Table 1.

[3]Context sentences were integrated with the target sentence into the PLM input while maintaining the natural human order for sequential heuristics.

Our results indicate that Sequential heuristics typically yield the largest improvements, significantly outperforming both the no-context baseline and state-of-the-art BERT-HSLN[4]. We attribute the substantial improvement observed, particularly in DeepRhole, to a statistical property of the dataset: on average, a rhetorical label persists across approximately 8.56 consecutive sentences before shifting to another[5][6]. Consequently, fully hierarchical models like BERT-HSLN, which process entire document sequences, may dilute the relevant signal by incorporating structurally irrelevant or conflicting content. In contrast, a simpler PLM guided by a well-targeted *Before* context can focus more effectively on the most informative local cues, resulting in more accurate and efficient predictions.

However, LegalEval remains challenging, as these PLMs have not yet matched SOTA performance. A plausible explanation is its higher label complexity, making it difficult for small models like BERT to achieve strong discrimination, as noted in SCOTUS annotation guidelines (Lavissière and Bonnard, 2024).

Finally, our retrieval-based models offer substantial efficiency gains compared to BERT-HSLN. With $k = 6$, our models typically process around 500 tokens per example using BERT as the backbone, whereas BERT-HSLN requires additional components for enriching representations and processes entire document sequences. This results in a $\sim 3\times$ to $5\times$ reduction in GPU memory usage and $\sim 2\times$ to $4\times$ faster training and inference time, depending on batch size and model configuration (see Appendix A for details).
Additional results with RoBERTa (Liu et al., 2019), LegalBERT (Chalkidis et al., 2020), and Longformer (Beltagy et al., 2020) are provided in Appendix B.

6 Conclusion and Future Work

In this study, we investigated how the role of context affects the SSC task in long legal documents. Our findings reveal that sequential heuristics, which preserve the natural flow of discourse, systematically lead to stronger performance gains than selective heuristics. An important insight is

[4]For a fair comparison, we compare against the original model, which does not include our modifications introduced in context analysis.

[5]Segment refers to consecutive annotation units (sentences) that share the same label within a document.

[6]The statistics are based on our corpus analysis.

that similarity alone is not enough—what matters more is where the sentence appears and whether the extracted relevant context forms a coherent unit. Moreover, enriching PLMs such as BERT with useful context yielded significant improvements over hierarchical models that process entire documents. Future work should give priority to (1) expanding the study to the corpus level, where multi-document signals will be explored, and (2) refining selective heuristics to extract high-quality context without increasing noise.

7 Limitations

While this study demonstrates the benefits of contextual information for SSC, a few limitations must be considered:

- We purposefully kept the heuristics basic, as our focus is not on peak performance. Nonetheless, more sophisticated approaches may yield higher scores than what we present.
- We have focused our experiments on a single document. In practice, integrating the context of several documents could potentially offer richer information for selective heuristics.
- We cannot reject the hypothesis that our findings about the utility of context may not be universally generalizable across other tasks. Our analysis centered on legal datasets, and thus further research is needed to determine whether similar gains would arise in other settings.

8 Ethical Statement

This work fully complies with the ACL Ethics Policy. To the best of our knowledge, we declare that there are no ethical issues in this paper.

9 Acknowledgments

This research was funded, in whole or in part, by l'Agence Nationale de la Recherche (ANR), project ANR-22-CE38-0004.

References

Arthur Amalvy, Vincent Labatut, and Richard Dufour. 2023. The role of global and local context in named entity recognition. In *Proceedings of the 61st Annual Meeting of the Association for Computational Linguistics (Volume 2: Short Papers)*, pages 714–722, Toronto, Canada. Association for Computational Linguistics.

Parishad BehnamGhader, Vaibhav Adlakha, Marius Mosbach, Dzmitry Bahdanau, Nicolas Chapados, and Siva Reddy. 2024. LLM2Vec: Large language models are secretly powerful text encoders. In *First Conference on Language Modeling*.

Iz Beltagy, Matthew E Peters, and Arman Cohan. 2020. Longformer: The long-document transformer. *arXiv preprint arXiv:2004.05150*.

Paheli Bhattacharya, Shounak Paul, Kripabandhu Ghosh, Saptarshi Ghosh, and Adam Wyner. 2023. Deeprhole: deep learning for rhetorical role labeling of sentences in legal case documents. *Artificial Intelligence and Law*, pages 1–38.

A Brack, A Hoppe, P Buschermöhle, and R Ewerth. 2021. Sequential sentence classification in research papers using cross-domain multi-task learning. corr. *arXiv preprint arXiv:2102.06008*.

Ilias Chalkidis, Manos Fergadiotis, Prodromos Malakasiotis, Nikolaos Aletras, and Ion Androutsopoulos. 2020. LEGAL-BERT: The muppets straight out of law school. In *Findings of the Association for Computational Linguistics: EMNLP 2020*, pages 2898–2904, Online. Association for Computational Linguistics.

Yu Chen, You Zhang, Jin Wang, and Xuejie Zhang. 2023. YNU-HPCC at SemEval-2023 task 6: LEGAL-BERT based hierarchical BiLSTM with CRF for rhetorical roles prediction. In *Proceedings of the 17th International Workshop on Semantic Evaluation (SemEval-2023)*, pages 2075–2081, Toronto, Canada. Association for Computational Linguistics.

Jacob Devlin, Ming-Wei Chang, Kenton Lee, and Kristina Toutanova. 2019. BERT: Pre-training of deep bidirectional transformers for language understanding. In *Proceedings of the 2019 Conference of the North American Chapter of the Association for Computational Linguistics: Human Language Technologies, Volume 1 (Long and Short Papers)*, pages 4171–4186, Minneapolis, Minnesota. Association for Computational Linguistics.

Varun Gangal, Steven Y. Feng, Malihe Alikhani, Teruko Mitamura, and Eduard Hovy. 2022. Nareor: The narrative reordering problem. *Proceedings of the AAAI Conference on Artificial Intelligence*, 36(10):10645–10653.

S Hochreiter. 1997. Long short-term memory. *Neural Computation MIT-Press*.

Di Jin and Peter Szolovits. 2018. Hierarchical neural networks for sequential sentence classification in medical scientific abstracts. In *Proceedings of the 2018 Conference on Empirical Methods in Natural Language Processing*, pages 3100–3109, Brussels, Belgium. Association for Computational Linguistics.

Prathamesh Kalamkar, Aman Tiwari, Astha Agarwal, Saurabh Karn, Smita Gupta, Vivek Raghavan, and

Ashutosh Modi. 2022. Corpus for automatic structuring of legal documents. In *Proceedings of the Thirteenth Language Resources and Evaluation Conference*, pages 4420–4429, Marseille, France. European Language Resources Association.

Mengfei Lan, Lecheng Zheng, Shufan Ming, and Halil Kilicoglu. 2024. Multi-label sequential sentence classification via large language model. In *Findings of the Association for Computational Linguistics: EMNLP 2024*, pages 16086–16104, Miami, Florida, USA. Association for Computational Linguistics.

Mary C. Lavissière and Warren Bonnard. 2024. Who's really got the right moves? analyzing recommendations for writing american judicial opinions. *Languages*, 9(4).

Yinhan Liu, Myle Ott, Naman Goyal, Jingfei Du, Mandar Joshi, Danqi Chen, Omer Levy, Mike Lewis, Luke Zettlemoyer, and Veselin Stoyanov. 2019. Roberta: A robustly optimized bert pretraining approach.

Akheel Muhammed, Hamna Muslihuddeen, Shalaka Sankar, and M Anand Kumar. 2024. Impact of rhetorical roles in abstractive legal document summarization. In *2024 5th International Conference on Innovative Trends in Information Technology (ICITIIT)*, pages 1–6. IEEE.

Mariana Neves, Daniel Butzke, and Barbara Grune. 2019. Evaluation of scientific elements for text similarity in biomedical publications. In *Proceedings of the 6th Workshop on Argument Mining*, pages 124–135, Florence, Italy. Association for Computational Linguistics.

Zach Nussbaum, John X. Morris, Brandon Duderstadt, and Andriy Mulyar. 2025. Nomic embed: Training a reproducible long context text embedder.

Nils Reimers and Iryna Gurevych. 2019. Sentence-BERT: Sentence embeddings using Siamese BERT-networks. In *Proceedings of the 2019 Conference on Empirical Methods in Natural Language Processing and the 9th International Joint Conference on Natural Language Processing (EMNLP-IJCNLP)*, pages 3982–3992, Hong Kong, China. Association for Computational Linguistics.

Gabriel Roccabruna, Massimo Rizzoli, and Giuseppe Riccardi. 2024. Will LLMs replace the encoder-only models in temporal relation classification? In *Proceedings of the 2024 Conference on Empirical Methods in Natural Language Processing*, pages 20402–20415, Miami, Florida, USA. Association for Computational Linguistics.

Iqra Safder and Saeed-Ul Hassan. 2019. Bibliometric-enhanced information retrieval: a novel deep feature engineering approach for algorithm searching from full-text publications. *Scientometrics*, 119:257–277.

T.y.s.s Santosh, Apolline Isaia, Shiyu Hong, and Matthias Grabmair. 2024. HiCuLR: Hierarchical curriculum learning for rhetorical role labeling of legal documents. In *Findings of the Association for Computational Linguistics: EMNLP 2024*, pages 7357–7364, Miami, Florida, USA. Association for Computational Linguistics.

Freda Shi, Xinyun Chen, Kanishka Misra, Nathan Scales, David Dohan, Ed H. Chi, Nathanael Schärli, and Denny Zhou. 2023. Large language models can be easily distracted by irrelevant context. In *Proceedings of the 40th International Conference on Machine Learning*, volume 202 of *Proceedings of Machine Learning Research*, pages 31210–31227. PMLR.

Andrew Trotman, Antti Puurula, and Blake Burgess. 2014. Improvements to bm25 and language models examined. In *Proceedings of the 19th Australasian Document Computing Symposium*, ADCS '14, page 58–65, New York, NY, USA. Association for Computing Machinery.

Santosh T.y.s.s., Hassan Sarwat, Ahmed Mohamed Abdelaal Abdou, and Matthias Grabmair. 2024. Mind your neighbours: Leveraging analogous instances for rhetorical role labeling for legal documents. In *Proceedings of the 2024 Joint International Conference on Computational Linguistics, Language Resources and Evaluation (LREC-COLING 2024)*, pages 11296–11306, Torino, Italia. ELRA and ICCL.

Sinong Wang, Belinda Z. Li, Madian Khabsa, Han Fang, and Hao Ma. 2020. Linformer: Self-attention with linear complexity. *CoRR*, abs/2006.04768.

Benjamin Warner, Antoine Chaffin, Benjamin Clavié, Orion Weller, Oskar Hallström, Said Taghadouini, Alexis Gallagher, Raja Biswas, Faisal Ladhak, Tom Aarsen, Nathan Cooper, Griffin Adams, Jeremy Howard, and Iacopo Poli. 2024. Smarter, better, faster, longer: A modern bidirectional encoder for fast, memory efficient, and long context finetuning and inference.

Manzil Zaheer, Guru Guruganesh, Kumar Avinava Dubey, Joshua Ainslie, Chris Alberti, Santiago Ontanon, Philip Pham, Anirudh Ravula, Qifan Wang, Li Yang, and Amr Ahmed. 2020. Big bird: Transformers for longer sequences. In *Advances in Neural Information Processing Systems*, volume 33, pages 17283–17297. Curran Associates, Inc.

A Model Overview for Context Analysis

The model consists of four key components:

- **Word Embedding:** The target sentence and its retrieved context are encoded using BERT (Devlin et al., 2019), generating word-level embeddings.
- **Sentence Encoding:** A Bi-LSTM (Hochreiter, 1997) processes these embeddings, followed by attention-based pooling to obtain sentence representations.
- **Context Enrichment:** This layer models inter-sentence relationships to refine contextualized embeddings.
- **Output Layer:** A linear transformation maps the target sentence representation to logits, with labels predicted via softmax[7].

Model	Seq	DeepRhole	Legal Eval	SCOTUS
Roberta-base (baseline)	512	52.63	72.43	76.28
+ Before		**68.29**†	78.3†	**81.75**†
+ After		60.3†	**80.12**†	81.43†
+ Surrounding		63.86†	78.40†	80.10†
+ Random		50.04	72.35	75.79
+ BM25		53.54	72.79	77.78‡
+ Sentence-BERT		53.33	73.25‡	77.84‡
Legal-BERT (baseline)	512	54.06	69.43	76.85
+ Before		**69.10**†	79.65†	81.40†
+ After		63.19†	**80.99**†	**82.81**†
+ Surrounding		67.15†	78.55†	78.72
+ Random		50.32	68.55	76.56
+ BM25		54.59	70.77‡	77.06
+ Sentence-BERT		56.30	70.55	77.47
Longformer (baseline)	4096	53.83	72.57	76.26
+ Before		**67.62**†	79.89†	**81.58**†
+ After		61.16†	**80.09**†	81.09†
+ Surrounding		64.83†	73.09†	81.35†
+ Random		52.55	72.54	75.78
+ BM25		54.82	73.22	77.44†
+ Sentence-BERT		54.3	77.95‡	77.47‡

Table 3: Performance of PLMs using the best configuration observed in context analysis for $k \leq 6$ for each heuristic. Bold values represent the best improvement over the baseline (w/o context), while underlined values indicate the second-best. Markers † and ‡ denote statistical significance over the baseline at $p = 0.05$ and $p = 0.01$, respectively.

[7]We optimize for the target sentence, eliminating the CRF layer, as supported by the ablation study in Jin and Szolovits (2018).

Dataset	Source	Sub-domain	Targets
DeepRhole	(Bhattacharya et al., 2023)	Indian law	7 classes
Legal Eval	(Kalamkar et al., 2022)	Indian law	13 classes
SCOTUS	(Lavissière and Bonnard, 2024)	U.S. law	13 classes

Table 4: Statistics of the datasets used for evaluation.

B Additional Results

We report additional results with enriching PLMs: RoBERTa (Liu et al., 2019), LegalBERT (Chalkidis et al., 2020), and Longformer (Beltagy et al., 2020) in Table 3.

Target Sentence: *"This case focuses upon the requirement of 'fair presentation.'"*

Heuristic	Extracted Sentence
Before	*"O'Sullivan v. Boerckel, 526 U.S. 838, 845 (1999)."*
After	*"Michael Reese, the respondent, appealed his state-court kidnapping and attempted sodomy convictions and sentences through Oregon's state court system."*
Surrounding	*"O'Sullivan v. Boerckel, 526 U.S. 838, 845 (1999)."* *"Michael Reese, the respondent, appealed his state-court kidnapping and attempted sodomy convictions and sentences through Oregon's state court system."*
Random	*"In such instances, the nature of the issue may matter more than does the legal validity of the lower court decision."*
BM25	*"For another thing, the opinion-reading requirement would impose a serious burden upon judges of state appellate courts, particularly those with discretionary review powers."*
Sentence-BERT	*"The petition provides no citation of any case that might have alerted the court to the alleged federal nature of the claim."*

Table 2: Examples of sentences extracted using different heuristics from the SCOTUS dataset.

Stance-aware Definition Generation for Argumentative Texts

Natalia Evgrafova and **Loic De Langhe** and **Véronique Hoste** and **Els Lefever**
LT3, Ghent University, Belgium
{natalia.evgrafova,loic.delanghe,veronique.hoste,els.lefever}@ugent.be

Abstract

Definition generation models trained on dictionary data are generally expected to produce neutral and unbiased output while capturing the contextual nuances. However, previous studies have shown that generated definitions can inherit biases from both the underlying models and the input context. This paper examines the extent to which stance-related bias in argumentative data influences the generated definitions. In particular, we train a model on a slang-based dictionary to explore the feasibility of generating persuasive definitions that concisely reflect opposing parties' understandings of contested terms. Through this study, we provide new insights into bias propagation in definition generation and its implications for definition generation applications and argument mining.

1 Introduction

The task of definition generation has been explored in the context of lexical semantic change analysis (Giulianelli et al., 2023), automated generation of definitions for unfamiliar terms in scientific contexts (August et al., 2022), and assisted language learning and reading (Huang et al., 2022).

Definition generation can be framed as a sequence-to-sequence problem: "Given an input sequence *C* containing a term *T*, generate a contextually appropriate, neutral definition *D* for *T*" (Giulianelli et al., 2023). As illustrated in Table 1, the model receives an input sequence — in this case, an argumentative usage example — and is prompted to define the term *death penalty* as used in context. The generated output is the corresponding definition.

Models fine-tuned on dictionary data are generally expected to produce neutral and unbiased output. However, previous research on definition generation has shown that generated definitions can exhibit bias or reflect stereotypes inherited from the underlying models (Giulianelli et al., 2023). Since definition generation relies on contextual embeddings of input sequences, we hypothesize that stance-related bias in the argumentative input sequence can also propagate into the generated definitions.

Not all bias in natural language is inherently negative (Shah et al., 2020). Some forms of bias reflect diverse cultural perspectives, values, and stances on a given topic. In argumentation, for instance, one group may define abortion as murder, while another may describe it as a right of a woman to choose to terminate her pregnancy. While both groups agree that murder is immoral, they differ in how they interpret and categorize abortion. As a result, their definitions carry distinct emotive connotations aligned with their stance. Reflecting such subjectivity could be leveraged in argument mining to generate persuasive definitions that capture differing perspectives and understandings of the contested terms. This can aid in clustering arguments by perspective, summarizing key points of contention, and enhancing the understanding of diverse viewpoints within debates.

This paper examines how biased training data and biased input sequences influence the presence of bias in the generated definitions. It also explores the intentional generation of contextually biased, or persuasive, definitions that express an opinion about the target word based on usage examples from argumentative texts.

This study **contributes** the following:

- We demonstrate that stance-related bias from argumentative data can propagate to varying degrees into definitions generated by dictionary-trained models, resulting in outputs such as *"abortion is the act of deliberately killing a fetus"* produced by Llama-3-8b-Instruct[1] trained on three standard English

[1] https://github.com/meta-llama/llama3/blob/main/MODEL_CARD.md

Proceedings of the 12th Argument Mining Workshop, pages 168–180

Usage Example	Target Word	Definition
As long as death penalty is kept, this confirms that our society is founded on violence.	**death penalty**	The punishment of death by a state or other legal system for a crime or offence.

Table 1: An example of a definition generated by Flan-T5 Base (Giulianelli et al., 2023) on an instance of the IBM argument corpus (Friedman et al., 2021).

dictionaries.

- Our findings confirm that a model fine-tuned on more expressive and loaded language, such as Llama-3-8b-Instruct fine-tuned on the Urban Dictionary (Ni and Wang, 2017), which is usually avoided (Periti et al., 2024), is more likely to capture and reproduce stance-related bias with examples as follows: "a punishment for someone who has committed a crime that is so bad that it should result in death", "assisted suicide is a euphemism for murder". This model exhibits the biggest overlap between stances of the generated definitions and those of the corresponding argument.

- We show that inference-time prompts can influence the degree of propagated stance-related bias in generated definitions.

- We provide (1) a manually annotated dataset evaluating the stance and plausibility of generated definitions, which can be used for neutral plausible definition detection or persuasive definition detection tasks; (2) a series of Llama-3-8b-Instruct definition generation models trained on dictionaries and combinations of dictionaries (including and excluding the Urban Dictionary) that have comparable performance to the state of the art[2].

2 Related work

2.1 Definition generation

In recent years, a number of studies have focused on generating contextual definitions, based on an input sequence and a target word (Giulianelli et al., 2023; Periti et al., 2024; Mickus et al., 2022). The generation of definitions has been successfully applied to a variety of tasks, such as interpretability of static embeddings (Gadetsky et al., 2018), learning and reading assistance (Ni and Wang, 2017; Zhang et al., 2022), and semantic change analysis (Giulianelli et al., 2023; Fedorova et al., 2024). Notably, Giulianelli et al. (2023) show that generated definitions, derived from word usage examples, enhance the interpretability of semantic change analysis, making it easier for lexicographers and other researchers to track diachronic shifts in meaning.

Most English training data are sourced from traditional lexical resources such as the Oxford English Dictionary (Gadetsky et al., 2018), WordNet (Noraset et al., 2017), Wikipedia (Ishiwatari et al., 2019), and Wiktionary (Mickus et al., 2022), while the Urban Dictionary is generally avoided unless non-standard English is specifically targeted, as in the work of Ni and Wang (2017).

Recent methods approach the task as a language modeling problem, where transformer-based large language models are instruction-tuned (Zhang et al., 2023) to generate contextually appropriate definitions, as illustrated in Table 1. Several models have been explored in this setup, including sequence-to-sequence transformers like Flan-T5 (Giulianelli et al., 2023) and decoder-only architectures such as Llama2-Chat and Llama3-Instruct (Periti et al., 2024). These models are typically fine-tuned and evaluated on a combination of different dictionaries to assess their generalization ability.

In addition to instruction tuning, methods have been developed to enhance the quality of generated definitions, such as adjusting their specificity (Huang et al., 2021) and complexity (August et al., 2022). These adjustments help tailor definitions to different contexts, making them more informative and interpretable across various applications.

The quality of generated definitions is typically assessed using standard natural language generation (NLG) metrics that measure overlaps with reference texts, such as BLEU (Papineni et al., 2002), SACREBLEU (Post, 2018) NIST (Doddington, 2002), ROUGE-L (Lin, 2004), and METEOR (Banerjee and Lavie, 2005), alongside semantic similarity measures such as BERTScore (Zhang et al., 2020). Additionally, hu-

[2]The models, their training parameters, and data are available at huggingface.co/collections/LT3/stance-aware-definition-generation-for-argumentative-texts-6841456cadeec0116d0bad24.

man evaluations are conducted to assess the quality of the generated output, addressing, for example, 'truthfulness' and 'fluency', with inter-annotator agreement between 0.35 and 0.45 Krippendorff's alpha (Giulianelli et al., 2023). Human annotations play a crucial role in evaluating the plausibility, or soundness, of generated definitions, offering insights into how well they align with intended meanings based on specific evaluation criteria. Combining NLG metrics with human judgments ensures a more comprehensive and balanced evaluation, leveraging both quantitative and qualitative perspectives.

Generally, definition generation models have demonstrated the ability to capture fine-grained semantic nuances of target words depending on the context, highlighting their potential for broader applications in Natural Language Processing.

2.2 Definitions in argumentation

Work on argumentation theory has stated that many argumentative discussions stem from or involve a debate about how to define particular terms (Walton, 2005). The notions of persuasive definitions and quasi-definitions were introduced by Stevenson (1938, 1944). They often include loaded terms and rely on pathos, or emotive meaning, to make an argument about a topic: "Abortion is a murder of a human being". A pro-choice definition of abortion could then be "Abortion is the right of every woman to decide to have a child or not".

Formally, these statements function as definitions. However, they also serve as implicit arguments because they convey a stance. This contrasts with standard dictionary definitions, which aim to be objective and do not typically reflect an opinion. Dictionary definitions rely on common knowledge — accepted propositions that are not subject to dispute (Macagno and Walton, 2008) — whereas persuasive definitions act as implicit arguments, often reflecting the values and priorities of a particular group advocating for or against a topic, and implying a conclusion (Walton, 2005, p. 224).

Macagno and Walton (2008) describe persuasive definitions as those that align with two key argumentative schemes: argument from classification and argument from values. Stevenson (1938, 1944) identified two main strategies: altering the denotative meaning of a term by including or excluding specific objects (e.g., "Graffiti is art," redefining art to include graffiti), or modifying its emotive connotation without changing its meaning (e.g., "The death penalty is murder," framing the death penalty in morally charged terms). According to Macagno and Walton (2008), argument from classification involves redefining a term's denotation, while argument from values shifts its emotional connotation.

While exploring the shifting boundaries of such terms as art, justice, democracy, etc. using NLP techniques presents an intriguing area for exploration, this paper focuses on analyzing definitions as potential arguments from values. Specifically, we aim to examine whether models trained on biased or unbiased data capture stance-related emotive connotations in the generated definitions.

Similarly, as stated by (Walton, 2005), defining a term using loaded language constitutes an argument. While such definitions may not always be considered high-quality arguments, they provide a stance-specific interpretation of a concept, highlighting the value-based aspects that are most relevant to a given perspective — an approach also referred to as framing (Eemeren and Houtlosser, 1999; Ajjour et al., 2019a).

In argument mining, the subjective and values-related nature of arguments has recently gained increased attention, leading to the adaptation of value taxonomies and the annotation of argumentative data for values (Kiesel et al., 2022), as well as the generation of arguments tailored to specific sets of morals (Alshomary et al., 2022). In this context, we investigate whether value-based information about opposing groups can be retrieved by generating context-dependent definitions that capture differing moral perspectives on a given topic.

3 Methodology

As we have demonstrated above, definition generation has the potential to move beyond neutrality, offering a means to explore and represent stance-based perspectives in argumentative contexts.

Based on these considerations, this paper investigates the following hypotheses:

1. H1: The stance-related bias in argumentative data will seep into definitions generated by dictionary-trained models that are expected to produce neutral definitions.

2. H2: A model fine-tuned on more expressive and loaded language will capture stance-related bias more accurately.

3. H3: In instruction fine-tuned models, prompts for zero-shot inference can be used to control

the degree of persuasiveness (and/or bias) in the generated definitions.

To explore these hypotheses, we instruction-tune Llama-3-8b-Instruct on the same dictionary data as in (Giulianelli et al., 2023; Periti et al., 2024): WordNet (Ishiwatari et al., 2019), Oxford (Gadetsky et al., 2018), as well as Wiktionary (Mickus et al., 2022), the standard English dictionaries. In addition to that, we include the online Urban Dictionary (Ni and Wang, 2017) in our training data. This crowd-sourced dictionary defines slang words, phrases, and cultural expressions. Previously, researchers abstained from using the Urban Dictionary as training data for non-slang applications to avoid unnecessary bias or possible errors (Periti et al., 2024). The train, validation, and test splits are used as in Ishiwatari et al. (2019)[3].

We adhere to the Alpaca template (Taori et al., 2023) for instruction-tuning our dictionary models. This involves providing the model with a prompt consisting of an instruction and an input context sequence. The model is instructed to answer the following prompt: `What is the definition of {keyword} in the following text: {usage example}?`

The fine-tuned dictionary models are then used to generate definitions for a target word in an argumentative input sequence. The target word is the topic of the argument, the input sequence is the argumentative sentence containing the target word. Each input sequence thus expresses a stance towards the target word — pro or contra; see Table 1 for an example.

The argumentative dataset comprises stance-annotated arguments on abortion, gay marriage, and the death penalty from the Webis args.me corpus (Ajjour et al., 2019b), as well as arguments on assisted suicide and capital punishment from the IBM Keypoint Dataset (Friedman et al., 2021), sourced from a debate platform described by Bar-Haim et al. (2020). The topics were selected based on the high number of available arguments and their contested nature, as agreed upon in discussions among the authors. We preprocess the datasets by retaining only the sentences that contain the target word: arguments are first split into sentences, and only those in which the target word appears are kept. Corpus statistics are shown in Table 2, with abortion being the most represented topic.

[3]`https://github.com/shonosuke/ishiwatari-naacl2019`

Dataset	Topic	PRO	CON
Webis	Abortion	3773	3560
	Gay marriage	960	871
	Death penalty	947	1144
IBM	Assisted suicide	121	125
	Capital punishment	110	126

Table 2: Number of argumentative sentences per stance and topic

The generated definitions are evaluated using standard NLG metrics mentioned above, followed by a qualitative analysis assessing the stance (pro, con, neutral) and plausibility — a clear and accurate explanation of the term — in the generated definitions.

4 Results

4.1 Language Model Evaluation

We train unsloth/llama-3-8b-Instruct[4] on Oxford, Wordnet, and Urban dictionaries separately, in combination "All" — all dictionaries including Urban, and "NoSlang" — all dictionaries excluding the Urban Dictionary.

We evaluate the fine-tuned models' performance on dictionary test sets as in Ishiwatari et al. (2019), reporting the above-mentioned standard NLG metrics for comparison with previous work, including BERTScore (BERT-F1), ROUGE-L, BLEU, NIST, SacreBLEU, METEOR, and EXACT MATCH: these metrics demonstrate both exact lexical overlap between the generated output and the reference as well as semantic similarity (BERT-F1).

Table 3 presents the evaluation results of our trained Llama models compared to the recent state-of-the-art Flan-T5[5] (Giulianelli et al., 2023) and Llama[6] (Periti et al., 2024) models.

The performance of our models trained with the Unsloth framework[7] is comparable to state-of-the-art results but does not significantly exceed established benchmarks due to lightweight training and reduced training parameters, but it demonstrates the highest semantic similarity score for the Oxford-trained model and higher overlap rates for "NoSlang" combination.

[4]Llama-3-70b was also fine-tuned but showed only marginal improvement with the average BERT-F1 of 88.19 on test splits

[5]`https://huggingface.co/ltg/flan-t5-definition-en-xl`

[6]`https://huggingface.co/FrancescoPeriti/Llama3Dictionary`

[7]`https://huggingface.co/unsloth`

Model	BERTScore-F1	ROUGE-L	BLEU	NIST	SACREBLEU	METEOR	EX. MATCH
Oxford	**0.882**	0.293	0.091	0.498	9.200	0.259	13.650
WordNet	0.870	0.225	0.058	0.411	5.900	0.185	10.350
All	0.865	0.312	0.101	0.325	10.100	0.269	**49.800**
Slang	0.868	0.155	0.028	0.365	2.800	0.112	4.367
NoSlang	0.860	**0.426**	0.132	0.327	13.200	**0.381**	49.700
Flan-T5 XL	0.867	0.268	0.180	0.583	12.010	0.249	0.110*
Llama3 Dict	0.869	0.292	**0.191**	**0.680**	**13.729**	0.305	**50.093***

Table 3: Comparison of definition generation models across training data sources. The table presents average scores across all test sets (Oxford, WordNet, Wiki, Urban). Notably, the "Oxford" model achieves the highest BERTScore-F1, indicating superior semantic similarity, while the "NoSlang" model excels in ROUGE-L and METEOR scores, reflecting its effectiveness in capturing content overlap. Averages for the Flan-T5 XL (Giulianelli et al., 2023) and Llama3 Dict (Periti et al., 2024) baselines are based on results reported in Periti et al. (2024). *On seen data.

4.2 Bias evaluation

As part of our preliminary analysis, we apply a sentiment classification model[8] to pre-annotate the sentiment of definitions on the three largest topics of our argumentative data — Abortion, Death Penalty, and Gay Marriage. Initially, we expected Llama-Slang to produce a consistently more negative output, however, that was not confirmed: our results did not show any particular pattern for the models; what we observed was a general negative sentiment (-0.4) associated with the topics. We attribute this mostly to the negatively associated vocabulary in the chosen topics.

Next, we automatically annotated the stance of the generated definitions for the three topics of the preprocessed Webis args.me dataset. To do so, we fine-tuned microsoft/deberta-v3-base[9] models. The training utilized argumentative sentences containing target words from the Webis args.me corpus, with train, validation, and test splits as detailed in Table 4. The model's performance was evaluated on the test split, yielding the following results: for *gay marriage*, Macro-F1: 0.747 and Accuracy: 0.755; for *death penalty*, Macro-F1: 0.754 and Accuracy: 0.755; and for *abortion*, Macro-F1: 0.707 and Accuracy: 0.707.

This setup allowed us to compare the pro and contra stance detected in each generated definition with the gold-standard stance of the corresponding argument. The results (see Figure 1) show the percentage of stance overlap for each Llama model

Topic	Train	Dev	Test
Abortion	3480	1160	1160
Gay Marriage	1005	335	336
Death Penalty	1397	466	466

Table 4: Dataset splits illustrating the number of sentences containing the target word used for training topic-based stance-detection deberta-v3-base models.

and prompt: a neutral Prompt 0, context-sensitive Prompts 1-2, persuasive Prompt 3, and emotionally charged Prompt 4, as shown in Table 5. The highest proportion of stance-aligned definitions — those that expressed the same stance as the argument in the original corpus — was observed for the model trained on Urban Dictionary data (Llama-Slang), followed by the model trained on all dictionaries (Llama-All). The WordNet-trained model also achieved relatively high stance alignment in the *abortion* topic, likely due to its broad lexical coverage and usage examples. Prompts 1 and 4 consistently resulted in slightly higher stance alignment rates, while Prompts 3 and 4 tended to produce longer definitions — by approximately 5–10 tokens on average.

In addition, we computed how often Llama-Slang's higher proportion of stances overlap was statistically significant compared to other models using a two-proportion z-test (see Table 10 in the Appendix for the detailed scores). As summarized in Figure 6, Llama-Slang showed statistically significant results in seven comparisons against Llama-NoSlang, four against Llama-WordNet, and nine against Llama-Oxford. These effects were most prominent for Prompt 1 and Prompt 4, which

[8]https://huggingface.co/tabularisai/multilingual-sentiment-analysis

[9]https://huggingface.co/microsoft/deberta-v3-base

explicitly encouraged contextually or emotionally framed definitions (see Figure 7).

#	Prompt Text
0	What is the definition of {keyword} in the following text?
1	What is the contextual definition of {keyword} in this text?
2	In what sense is the {keyword} used in the following text?
3	What is the persuasive definition of {keyword} in the following text?
4	What is the emotionally charged definition of {keyword} in the following text?

Table 5: Prompts used for definition generation.

4.3 Definitions Topic Modeling

Previous research has explored clustering methods for retrieving various word senses (Giulianelli et al., 2023). In this study, we investigate whether soft clusters obtained through unsupervised topic models exhibit stance-related bias. To this end, we apply a BERTopic model (Grootendorst, 2022) on definitions of the term "abortion" generated by both the Llama-Slang — which is expected to produce stance-related clusters — and Llama-Oxford — which showed best results for the definition generation similarity to dictionary gold standards — models on the same dataset.

Our results (see Appendix for visualizations) indicate that Llama-Slang, in addition to using more loaded and emotive language, tends to produce topics that reflect opposing perspectives on abortion. Interestingly, both sides of the argument are reflected in the output, with some clusters focusing on keywords "right to choose" while others contain negatively associated words such as "killing unborn baby" or "innocent/killing/murder". This is in contrast to Llama-Oxford where topics tend to be fairly uniform and lack the more charged language of the context sentences.

These findings lead us to believe that contextual bias from the test data seeps into the generated definitions, primarily when the model is trained on emotionally charged data. The model's awareness of bias can help better reflect varying perspectives, making it a potential tool for analyzing how different ideological groups use and frame a particular term. In contrast, we find Llama-Oxford to be much more robust with most clusters corresponding to what one would intuitively consider a neutral and plausible definition. A thorough analysis of the generated definitions shows, however, that a "neutral" model might still generate biased output based on the input: "abortion is the act of deliberately killing a fetus", "death penalty is the judicial killing of a human", "assisted suicide is a deliberate act of self-destruction that is facilitated by another person" — these definitions are generated by one of our most robust models — Llama-NoSlang.

4.4 Annotated stance and plausibility across models

Evaluation of generated definitions is often supplemented by qualitative analysis and human annotations. Despite a decent BERTScore-F1 (0.87) across models as shown in Table 3, generated definitions might not be plausible because they are too general, subjective (Huang et al., 2021), or not meaningful.

In order to provide a thorough assessment of the generated definitions, we set up an annotation task where we analyze the presence of stance in the definition — pro, contra, and neutral — and assess the general plausibility of the generated definitions. In this setup, plausibility is understood as clarity and accuracy of the definition. The annotations were performed by two human annotators, both graduate-level NLP researchers, authors of this paper. In the task, annotators were presented with a target word, its corresponding generated definition, and were asked to evaluate:

- **Stance:** What stance is expressed in the definition towards the topic?
(Options: Pro, Contra, Neutral)
- **Plausibility:** Does the generated text function as a proper definition by providing a clear and accurate explanation of the term?
(Options: Yes, No)

In total, 1000 definitions were annotated. First, we selected random samples of 100 definitions generated by each of the following models: Llama-Slang, Llama-NoSlang, Llama-All; Flan-T5-Base and Flan-T5-XL (Giulianelli et al., 2023) to explore stance-related bias in both Llama and Flan-T5 model outputs. In addition, we took a closer look at all five Llama models trained on Oxford, Wordnet, Slang, All and NoSlang data — specifically for the topic of abortion — to assess how training data influences the stance-related bias in generated definitions.

Both stance and plausibility judgments involve a degree of subjectivity, with agreement scores in-

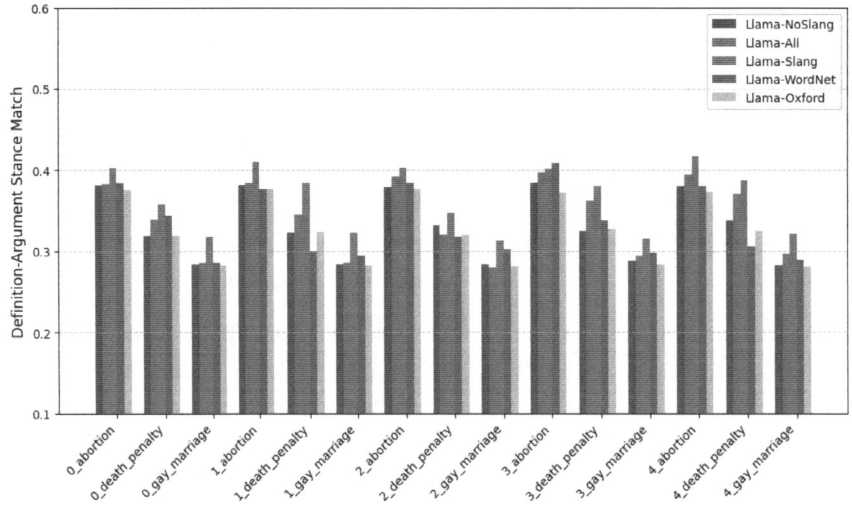

Figure 1: The overlap between the stance detected in the generated definitions and the gold-standard stance of the arguments used as context during generation.

Baseline Model	↑ Accuracy	p < 0.05
Llama-NoSlang	15/15	7/15
Llama-WordNet	14/15	4/15
Llama-Oxford	15/15	9/15

Table 6: Llama-Slang vs. baselines across 15 prompts. Columns show how often Llama-Slang outperformed each model in stance accuracy and in how many cases the difference was statistically significant ($p < 0.05$).

Prompt 0	Prompt 1	Prompt 2	Prompt 3	Prompt 4
0.1334	**0.0250**	0.2172	0.1720	**0.0184**

Table 7: Average p-values across model comparisons per prompt for Llama-Slang. Prompts 1 and 4 showed significant differences ($p < 0.05$), indicating stronger stance alignment under subjectively framed instructions.

fluenced not only by individual annotator interpretations but also by the diversity and distribution of annotated instances. In Table 8, we report both the percentage of agreement between the two annotators and Cohen's Kappa (κ) to assess inter-annotator reliability for stance and plausibility annotations. Although the overall agreement is moderate, the highest inter-annotator agreement is observed for Llama-Slang in stance annotation (84%, $\kappa = 0.688$), which corresponds to the model with the largest proportion of biased definitions. This suggests that Llama-Slang produced more polarized definitions that facilitated stronger annotator agreement.

The polarized definitions were not marked as plausible in most cases, as they were too subjective for a standard definition. For other models, annotators often detected slight biases that were insufficient to be annotated as pro or contra stance; thus, they were marked *neutral*. Higher percentages and low κ in Table 8 indicate cases where most stances were annotated as *neutral*.

For example, Llama-NoSlang, which was expected to generate more neutral definitions, showed the highest percentage of agreement for stance (94%), but worse-than-chance Kappa score ($\kappa = -0.017$), which was the result of most generated definitions being neutral, suggesting that Llama-NoSlang is generally successful in generating neutral, dictionary-like definitions.

Models	Stance (%)	Plaus. (%)	Stance (κ)	Plaus. (κ)
Llama-Slang	84	72	**0.688**	0.440
Llama-All	85	71	0.454	0.430
Llama-NoSlang	94	66	-0.017	0.222
Flan-T5-Base	95	82	0.519	0.572
Flan-T5-XL	**97**	76	0.652	0.465
Llama-Wordnet: abortion	78	74	0.541	0.470
Llama-Oxford: abortion	91	81	0.469	0.313
Llama-NoSlang: abortion	94	**93**	0.603	0.682
Llama-All: abortion	82	84	0.621	**0.684**
Llama-Slang: abortion	76	85	0.574	0.676

Table 8: Inter-Annotator Agreement for Llama and Flan-T5 definition annotations for stance and plausibility.

For plausibility judgments, agreement scores are generally lower than for stance, with Llama-Slang reaching $\kappa = 0.440$ and Llama-NoSlang showing the lowest reliability ($\kappa = 0.222$) with most ex-

Model	% Stance-Taking	Match Rate (if stance)	Overall Match Rate	Avg. Plausibility (%)
Llama-Slang	**38.75**	76.84	**29.75**	37.25
Llama-All	24.00	75.27	17.75	53.25
Llama-WordNet	35.00	49.66	17.50	43.00
Llama-Oxford	9.00	54.17	5.50	**84.50**
Llama-NoSlang	5.50	35.42	2.00	79.75
Flan-T5-Base	5.50	81.67	4.50	70.00
Flan-T5-XL	4.50	75.00	3.50	66.00

Table 9: Comparison of stance sensitivity and definition plausibility across models. Llama-Slang produced the highest number of stance-aligned definitions, while Llama-Oxford and Flan models received the highest plausibility ratings.

amples being *neutral* and plausible; a larger-scale plausibility annotation might help evaluate the models better.

While for all the Llama models neutral stance would be associated with plausibility, annotators observed that Flan-T5 had cases of neutral definitions that are not plausible, like: "Gay marriage is the practice of marrying people who are not your mate" (Flan-T5-XL). These models would also reproduce bias from the input sequence as in this definition of death penalty: "The infliction of the death penalty, in particular, the killing of an innocent person as a form of punishment".

The moderate and substantial inter-annotator agreement suggests that while stance annotation involves some interpretative variation, annotators were largely consistent in their judgments when evaluating biased definitions.

Table 9 presents a comparison of models based on their stance sensitivity (both pro and con) and definition plausibility. Llama-Slang stands out with the highest percentage of stance-taking definitions (38.75%) and the highest overall stance match rate between definitions and original arguments (29.75%), indicating that training on informal or biased data (like slang) can steer models to produce more context-sensitive outputs. However, these benefits come at the cost of plausibility: LLama-Slang received the lowest average plausibility rating (37.25%), mostly because annotators would not perceive biased definitions as plausible. In contrast, models like LLama-Oxford and Flan-T5-Base produced significantly fewer stance-taking definitions but were rated as more plausible, with Oxford achieving the highest plausibility score (84.5%). The model choice should therefore be guided by the specific goals of the application, whether to prioritize contextual and/or stance- sensitivity or definitional neutrality.

5 Conclusions and Future Work

This study explored how stance-related bias in argumentative data is reflected in the definitions generated by models trained on dictionary data. Our findings confirm key hypotheses regarding bias propagation, demonstrating how both training data and prompts influence models to produce more context-sensitive and stance-aware definitions.

H1: Stance-related bias in argumentative data seeps into definitions generated by dictionary-trained models. Our results demonstrate that Llama and Flan-T5 models trained on neutral dictionary data might be influenced by bias present in the input sequence to a different extent. The best results in terms of neutrality were demonstrated by Llama-NoSlang trained on a few standard dictionaries and Llama-Oxford that shows the least changes when prompted to generate more contextually sensitive definitions.

H2: Models fine-tuned on more expressive and loaded language capture stance-related bias more accurately. We demonstrated that Llama-Slang, fine-tuned on the Urban Dictionary, had the highest degree of definition stance alignment with the corresponding argument sentence. Llama-All, trained on all the dictionaries including Urban, showed second-best sensitivity to stance-related bias in the input sequence among Llama models.

H3: Instruction fine-tuned models allow for prompt-based control over persuasiveness. We observed a statistically significant improvement in stance match accuracy for the model trained on slang data when prompts encouraged contextually or emotionally framed definitions. These prompts also resulted in longer definitions, indicating that explicitly requesting more context led to more elaborate and persuasive outputs.

Overall, our study provides insights into how stance-related biases of the argumentative data manifest in automated definition generation of the words that represent a topic of an argument across Llama and Flan-T5 models. The results highlight opportunities for refining models to better balance neutrality and context awareness. Additionally, leveraging context-dependent bias can offer valuable insights into underlying opinions and perspectives in argumentative discourse. Future work may focus on developing robust methods for controlling the degree of contextual bias in generated output and fine-tuning models specifically tailored for persuasive definition generation.

Limitations

The limitations of this study are the following. First, the study is limited to English-language data and perspective only: what is plausible may differ across languages and countries depending on, for example, whether the death penalty, abortion, gay marriage, etc. is a legal practice or not. Second, we only trained and evaluated a series of comparatively smaller generative Llama models (Llama-8b), and only marginally touched upon other models, like Flan-T5. It is possible that our observations of stance and bias do not fully generalize to other models. Here, we anticipate two key possibilities: different or larger models could potentially be more robust against contextual variation in the input prompt, or they might become more reliant on their original training data, potentially reinforcing certain biases and failing to capture context entirely. Third, we only annotated a limited number of the generated definitions for the stance dataset. As a result, the analysis presented in the paper only provides a snapshot of the broader picture. While our sample size is sufficient for initial insights, future work should aim to extend the annotation process and provide a more complete human evaluation of the generated data. Fourth, we limited ourselves to target words that corresponded to topics of arguments, however, the arguments might have other interesting target words that can be defined persuasively e.g. fetus in a debate on abortion. Finally, there is a lot of room to explore not only arguments from values but also arguments from classification: understanding the boundaries of abstract concepts that are commonly used in arguments is an exciting area for further research that could provide insights into questions like "What is understood with terms like extremism, terrorism, justice, democracy across languages and cultures?".

Acknowledgements

This work was supported by the Research Foundation — Flanders (FWO) under grant FWO.OPR.2023.0004.01 (G019823N).

References

Yamen Ajjour, Milad Alshomary, Henning Wachsmuth, and Benno Stein. 2019a. Modeling frames in argumentation. In *Proceedings of the 2019 Conference on Empirical Methods in Natural Language Processing and the 9th International Joint Conference on Natural Language Processing (EMNLP-IJCNLP)*, pages 2922–2932, Hong Kong, China. Association for Computational Linguistics.

Yamen Ajjour, Henning Wachsmuth, Johannes Kiesel, Martin Potthast, Matthias Hagen, and Benno Stein. 2019b. Data acquisition for argument search: The args.me corpus. In *KI 2019: Advances in Artificial Intelligence*, pages 48–59, Cham. Springer International Publishing.

Milad Alshomary, Roxanne El Baff, Timon Gurcke, and Henning Wachsmuth. 2022. The moral debater: A study on the computational generation of morally framed arguments. In *Proceedings of the 60th Annual Meeting of the Association for Computational Linguistics (Volume 1: Long Papers)*, pages 8782–8797, Dublin, Ireland. Association for Computational Linguistics.

Tal August, Katharina Reinecke, and Noah A. Smith. 2022. Generating scientific definitions with controllable complexity. In *Proceedings of the 60th Annual Meeting of the Association for Computational Linguistics (Volume 1: Long Papers)*, pages 8298–8317, Dublin, Ireland. Association for Computational Linguistics.

Satanjeev Banerjee and Alon Lavie. 2005. Meteor: An automatic metric for mt evaluation with improved correlation with human judgments. In *Proceedings of the ACL Workshop on Intrinsic and Extrinsic Evaluation Measures for Machine Translation and/or Summarization*, pages 65–72.

Roy Bar-Haim, Lilach Eden, Roni Friedman, Yoav Kantor, Dan Lahav, and Noam Slonim. 2020. From arguments to key points: Towards automatic argument summarization. In *Proceedings of the 58th Annual Meeting of the Association for Computational Linguistics*, pages 4029–4039, Online. Association for Computational Linguistics.

George Doddington. 2002. Automatic evaluation of machine translation quality using n-gram co-occurrence statistics. In *Proceedings of the Second International Conference on Human Language Technology Research (HLT 2002)*, pages 138–145.

Frans Van Eemeren and Peter Houtlosser. 1999. Strategic manoeuvring in argumentative discourse. *Discourse Studies*, 1(4):479–497.

Mariia Fedorova, Andrey Kutuzov, and Yves Scherrer. 2024. Definition generation for lexical semantic change detection. In *Findings of the Association for Computational Linguistics: ACL 2024*, pages 5712–5724, Bangkok, Thailand. Association for Computational Linguistics.

Roni Friedman, Lena Dankin, Yufang Hou, Ranit Aharonov, Yoav Katz, and Noam Slonim. 2021. Overview of the 2021 key point analysis shared task. In *Proceedings of the 8th Workshop on Argument Mining*, pages 154–164, Punta Cana, Dominican Republic. Association for Computational Linguistics.

Artyom Gadetsky, Ilya Yakubovskiy, and Dmitry Vetrov. 2018. Conditional generators of words definitions. In *Proceedings of the 56th Annual Meeting of the Association for Computational Linguistics (Volume 2: Short Papers)*, pages 266–271, Melbourne, Australia. Association for Computational Linguistics.

Mario Giulianelli, Iris Luden, Raquel Fernandez, and Andrey Kutuzov. 2023. Interpretable word sense representations via definition generation: The case of semantic change analysis. In *Proceedings of the 61st Annual Meeting of the Association for Computational Linguistics (Volume 1: Long Papers)*, pages 3130–3148, Toronto, Canada. Association for Computational Linguistics.

Maarten Grootendorst. 2022. Bertopic: Neural topic modeling with a class-based tf-idf procedure. *arXiv preprint arXiv:2203.05794*.

Han Huang, Tomoyuki Kajiwara, and Yuki Arase. 2021. Definition modelling for appropriate specificity. In *Proceedings of the 2021 Conference on Empirical Methods in Natural Language Processing*, pages 2499–2509, Online and Punta Cana, Dominican Republic. Association for Computational Linguistics.

Han Huang, Tomoyuki Kajiwara, and Yuki Arase. 2022. JADE: Corpus for Japanese definition modelling. In *Proceedings of the Thirteenth Language Resources and Evaluation Conference*, pages 6884–6888, Marseille, France. European Language Resources Association.

Shonosuke Ishiwatari, Hiroaki Hayashi, Naoki Yoshinaga, Graham Neubig, Shoetsu Sato, Masashi Toyoda, and Masaru Kitsuregawa. 2019. Learning to describe unknown phrases with local and global contexts. In *Proceedings of the 2019 Conference of the North American Chapter of the Association for Computational Linguistics: Human Language Technologies, Volume 1 (Long and Short Papers)*, pages 3467–3476, Minneapolis, Minnesota. Association for Computational Linguistics.

Johannes Kiesel, Milad Alshomary, Nicolas Handke, Xiaoni Cai, Henning Wachsmuth, and Benno Stein. 2022. Identifying the human values behind arguments. In *Proceedings of the 60th Annual Meeting of the Association for Computational Linguistics (Volume 1: Long Papers)*, pages 4459–4471, Dublin, Ireland. Association for Computational Linguistics.

Chin-Yew Lin. 2004. Rouge: A package for automatic evaluation of summaries. In *Text Summarization Branches Out*, pages 74–81.

Fabrizio Macagno and Douglas Walton. 2008. Persuasive definitions: Values, meanings and implicit disagreements. *Informal Logic*, 28(3):203–228. 26 Pages, Posted: 23 Jan 2011.

Timothee Mickus, Kees Van Deemter, Mathieu Constant, and Denis Paperno. 2022. Semeval-2022 task 1: CODWOE – comparing dictionaries and word embeddings. In *Proceedings of the 16th International Workshop on Semantic Evaluation (SemEval-2022)*, pages 1–14, Seattle, United States. Association for Computational Linguistics.

Ke Ni and William Yang Wang. 2017. Learning to explain non-standard English words and phrases. In *Proceedings of the Eighth International Joint Conference on Natural Language Processing (Volume 2: Short Papers)*, pages 413–417, Taipei, Taiwan. Asian Federation of Natural Language Processing.

Thanapon Noraset, Chen Liang, Larry Birnbaum, and Doug Downey. 2017. Definition modeling: Learning to define word embeddings in natural language. In *Proceedings of the 31st AAAI Conference on Artificial Intelligence (AAAI)*, pages 3259–3266.

Kishore Papineni, Salim Roukos, Todd Ward, and Wei-Jing Zhu. 2002. Bleu: a method for automatic evaluation of machine translation. In *Proceedings of the 40th Annual Meeting of the Association for Computational Linguistics (ACL)*, pages 311–318.

Francesco Periti, David Alfter, and Nina Tahmasebi. 2024. Automatically generated definitions and their utility for modeling word meaning. In *Proceedings of the 2024 Conference on Empirical Methods in Natural Language Processing*, pages 14008–14026, Miami, Florida, USA. Association for Computational Linguistics.

Matt Post. 2018. A call for clarity in reporting bleu scores. In *Proceedings of the Third Conference on Machine Translation: Research Papers*, pages 186–191.

Deven Santosh Shah, H. Andrew Schwartz, and Dirk Hovy. 2020. Predictive biases in natural language processing models: A conceptual framework and overview. In *Proceedings of the 58th Annual Meeting of the Association for Computational Linguistics*, pages 5248–5264, Online. Association for Computational Linguistics.

Charles L. Stevenson. 1938. Persuasive definitions. *Mind*, 47:331–350.

Charles L. Stevenson. 1944. *Ethics and Language*. Yale University Press, New Haven.

Rohan Taori, Ishaan Gulrajani, Tianyi Zhang, Yann Dubois, Xuechen Li, Carlos Guestrin, Percy Liang, and Tatsunori B. Hashimoto. 2023. Stanford alpaca:

An instruction-following llama model. `https://github.com/tatsu-lab/stanford_alpaca`.

Douglas Walton. 2005. *Fundamentals of Critical Argumentation*. Cambridge University Press.

Hengyuan Zhang, Dawei Li, Shiping Yang, and Yanran Li. 2022. Fine-grained contrastive learning for definition generation. In *Proceedings of the 2nd Conference of the Asia-Pacific Chapter of the Association for Computational Linguistics and the 12th International Joint Conference on Natural Language Processing (Volume 1: Long Papers)*, pages 1001–1012, Online only. Association for Computational Linguistics.

Shengyu Zhang, Linfeng Dong, Xiaoya Li, Sen Zhang, Xiaofei Sun, Shuhe Wang, Jiwei Li, Runyi Hu, Tianwei Zhang, Fei Wu, et al. 2023. Instruction tuning for large language models: A survey. *arXiv preprint arXiv:2308.10792*.

Tianyi Zhang, Varsha Kishore, Felix Wu, Kilian Q. Weinberger, and Yoav Artzi. 2020. BERTScore: Evaluating text generation with BERT. In *Proceedings of the 8th International Conference on Learning Representations (ICLR)*.

Appendix

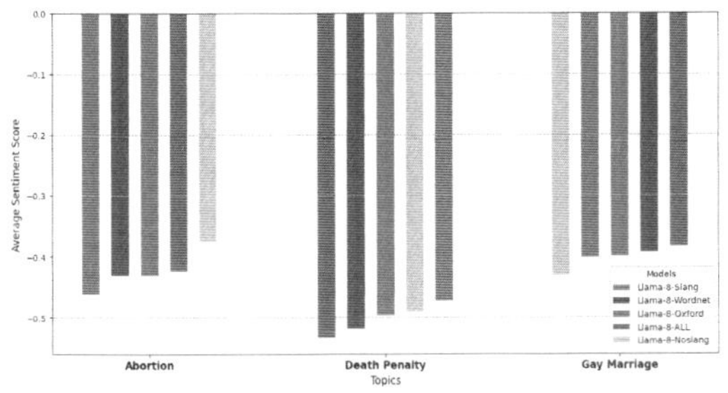

Figure 2: Average sentiment score per model across topics.

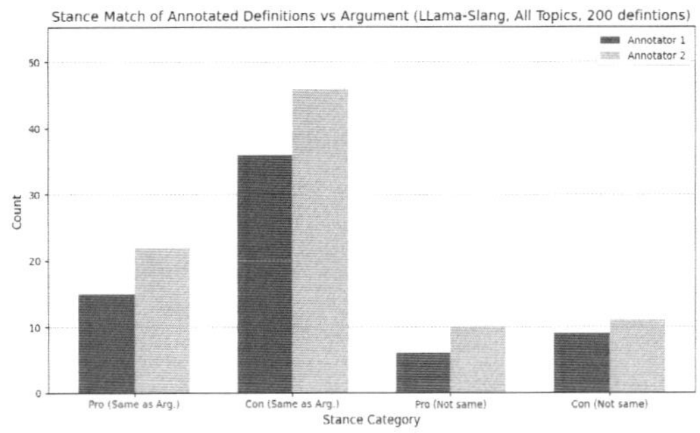

Figure 3: Llama-Slang: overlap between annotated stance of definitions and their corresponding argument stances.

Topic	Definition	Model B	Acc A (%)	Acc B (%)	Z	p-value
Death	definition_1_death_penalty	Llama-WordNet	38.41	29.98	3.673	0.0002
Death	definition_4_death_penalty	Llama-WordNet	38.76	30.56	3.559	0.0004
Abortion	definition_4_abortion	Llama-Oxford	41.62	37.33	3.096	0.0020
Death	definition_4_death_penalty	Llama-Oxford	38.76	32.44	2.729	0.0064
Death	definition_1_death_penalty	Llama-NoSlang	38.41	32.20	2.683	0.0073
Abortion	definition_4_abortion	Llama-WordNet	41.62	37.98	2.630	0.0085
Death	definition_1_death_penalty	Llama-Oxford	38.41	32.32	2.632	0.0085
Abortion	definition_4_abortion	Llama-NoSlang	41.62	38.02	2.601	0.0093
Abortion	definition_1_abortion	Llama-Oxford	41.06	37.62	2.490	0.0128
Abortion	definition_1_abortion	Llama-WordNet	41.06	37.62	2.490	0.0128
Death	definition_3_death_penalty	Llama-NoSlang	37.94	32.44	2.381	0.0172
Gay Marriage	definition_4_gay_marriage	Llama-Oxford	32.19	28.18	2.289	0.0221
Gay Marriage	definition_1_gay_marriage	Llama-Oxford	32.26	28.25	2.287	0.0222
Death	definition_3_death_penalty	Llama-Oxford	37.94	32.67	2.278	0.0227
Gay Marriage	definition_4_gay_marriage	Llama-NoSlang	32.19	28.25	2.247	0.0247
Gay Marriage	definition_1_gay_marriage	Llama-NoSlang	32.26	28.32	2.245	0.0248
Abortion	definition_1_abortion	Llama-NoSlang	41.06	38.06	2.170	0.0300
Death	definition_4_death_penalty	Llama-NoSlang	38.76	33.72	2.164	0.0304
Abortion	definition_3_abortion	Llama-Oxford	40.14	37.21	2.120	0.0340
Gay Marriage	definition_0_gay_marriage	Llama-Oxford	31.75	28.25	2.001	0.0454

Table 10: Results of z-tests comparing stance-match accuracy between Llama-Slang and baseline models. Only definition-topic pairs with statistically significant differences ($p < 0.05$) are shown.

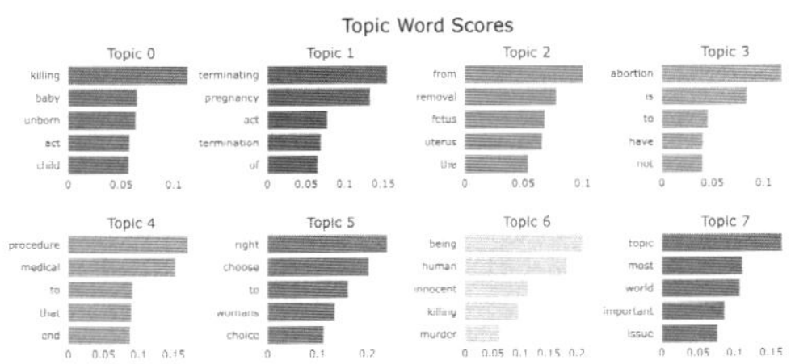

Figure 4: Llama-Slang abortion definitions

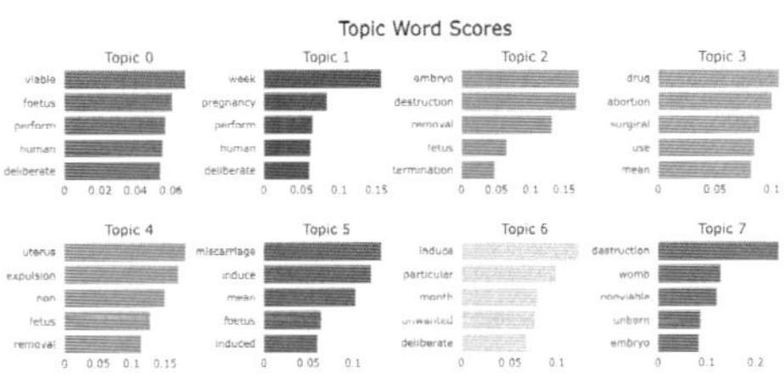

Figure 5: Llama-Oxford abortion definitions

Model	Topic	Stance	Generated Definition
Llama-Slang	Abortion	neutral	the act of a woman to remove an unwanted fetus from her uterus
Llama-Slang	Abortion	pro	a medical procedure that is both a right and a responsibility of women, and should not be illegal
Llama-Slang	Abortion	contra	the act of a woman killing a fetus with her body
Llama-All	assisted suicide	neutral	a method of suicide in which a person deliberately ends their own life with the assistance of another person or a device
Llama-All	assisted suicide	contra	the act of killing another human
Llama-All	assisted suicide	pro	the right to choose to end one's life
Llama-NoSlang	Abortion	neutral	the deliberate termination of a human pregnancy, most commonly performed as a surgical procedure by a qualified health professional
Llama-NoSlang	Abortion	pro	the deliberate termination of a human pregnancy, as a means of birth control, or because it poses health risks to the mother; the induced expulsion of a fetus or embryo from the uterus before the viability of birth.
Llama-NoSlang	Abortion	contra	the act of deliberately killing a human fetus
Llama-Oxford	Abortion	contra	a violent or illegal termination of pregnancy
Llama-Oxford	Abortion	neutral	the termination of a pregnancy by the removal or expulsion from the uterus of a non-viable fetus, or a fetus that does not stand a viable chance of survival after birth
Llama-Oxford	Abortion	neutral	the deliberate termination of a human pregnancy, most often performed before the fetus is viable, by various medical means, in order to remove a fetus that has serious abnormalities or is otherwise unsuitable for delivery or would otherwise produce a child that would suffer.
Flan-T5-Base	Death penalty	neutral	The punishment of death, in particular the execution of a condemned person by hanging
Flan-T5-Base	Gay marriage	contra	The practice of marrying people who are not your mate
Flan-T5-Base	Abortion	neutral	The act of terminating a pregnancy, either naturally or by artificial means
Flan-T5-Base	Death penalty	contra	The infliction of the death penalty, in particular the killing of an innocent person as a form of punishment
Flan-T5-Base	Death penalty	neutral	The punishment of death, especially as a legally mandated part of a state's criminal code
Flan-T5-XL	Gay marriage	neutral	The practice of marrying people who are not your mate
Flan-T5-XL	Abortion	neutral	The act of terminating a pregnancy, either naturally or by artificial means
Flan-T5-XL	Death penalty	contra	The infliction of the death penalty, in particular the killing of an innocent person as a form of punishment

Table 11: Generated definitions across models and stances for contested topics. Each definition reflects a perspective that aligns with a stance (pro, contra, neutral) as annotated by human annotators.

Reproducing the Argument Quality Prediction of Project Debater

Ines Zelch[1,2] **Matthias Hagen**[1] **Benno Stein**[3] **Johannes Kiesel**[4]

[1]Friedrich-Schiller-Universität Jena [2]Leipzig University [3]Bauhaus-Universität Weimar
[4]GESIS – Leibniz Institute for the Social Sciences

Abstract

A crucial task when analyzing arguments is to determine their quality. Especially when you have to choose from a large number of suitable arguments, the determination of a reliable argument quality value is of great benefit. Probably the best-known model for determining such an argument quality value was developed in IBM's Project Debater and made available to the research community free of charge via an API. In fact, the model was never open and the API is no longer available. In this paper, IBM's model is reproduced using the freely available training data and the description in the corresponding publication. Our reproduction achieves similar results on the test data as described in the original publication. Further, the predicted quality scores of reproduction and original show a very high correlation (Pearson's $r = 0.9$) on external data.

1 Introduction

When developing large datasets of arguments, the automatic assessment of the arguments' quality is crucial in order to provide arguments of sufficient quality for applications like a searchable argument index (Dumani and Schenkel, 2020; Wachsmuth et al., 2017b). A commonly used model for argument quality prediction was developed as part of the IBM argumentation system Project Debater (Bar-Haim et al., 2021; Slonim et al., 2021) and was made available for researchers via an API (Bar-Haim et al., 2021). The model was used, for example, by Bar-Haim et al. (2020) to select high quality arguments for the generation of key points, and by Alshomary and Wachsmuth (2023) for the generation of counter-arguments. However, as the API was closed in May 2024 (and the model is no longer available on request from the authors), this high-quality resource is no longer accessible to researchers; i.e., research based on this model cannot be applied to new datasets.

This paper contributes to an open reproduction of IBM's original model in order to make this important resource available again.[1] We follow the specifications of the original publication (Gretz et al., 2019) to finetune a BERT regression model on the publicly available original dataset of crowd-sourced arguments and quality ratings.[2] As shown in this paper, our model achieves a very high correlation in terms of predicted quality scores with the IBM model: In a test with a subset of the third-party args.me corpus, the Pearson's r is 0.9.

The paper in hand outlines the retraining process and presents an analysis of the predictions of the trained models and a comparison with the original model. Section 2 provides an overview of the concept of argument quality in general and the IBM model of Gretz et al. (2019) in particular. Section 3 describes the reproduction of the IBM model in the detail. Section 4 reports on two evaluation studies on our reproduced model: (1) Using the original test data, we calculate the Pearson and Spearman correlation coefficients between the predictions of our model and the real annotations and compare these with the numbers given in the original paper (Gretz et al., 2019). (2) Using the args.me corpus (Ajjour et al., 2019), we calculate the same coefficients, but between the predictions of our model and the IBM model. For this purpose, we had acquired the necessary predictions of the IBM model before the API shut down. Interestingly, we find considerable differences in predictions for argumentative texts from the args.me corpus, although we achieve similar effectiveness with the original test set. This observation implies that the score achieved on a particular test set does not necessarily reflect the ability of the model to generalize to external data.

In order to keep the reproduced model lean and

[1] github.com/webis-de/argmining25-reproducing-ibm-arg-quality-api

[2] https://research.ibm.com/debating_data.shtml#Argument_Quality

Proceedings of the 12th Argument Mining Workshop, pages 181–188
July 31, 2025

to make it usable in downstream applications without further dependencies on external models, we deliberately refrained from extending the IBM model by integrating LLMs.

2 Related Work

Argument quality can be assessed considering various quality dimensions. An overview of these dimensions is compiled in Wachsmuth et al. (2017a) and extended by Ivanova et al. (2024). They include logical dimensions that affect the cogency of an argument, dialectic dimensions that influence the reasonableness of arguments, and rhetoric dimensions that are important for an argument's effectiveness. Different quality dimensions are considered in existent datasets, mainly annotated in an absolute manner where each argument is labeled individually (Toledo et al., 2019; Ivanova et al., 2024). Other works approach argument quality analysis in a relative way, processing arguments in pairs and choosing the one of higher quality (Toledo et al., 2019). The latter approach has the advantage of being less complex (Ivanova et al., 2024), resulting in potentially more consistent annotations. Additionally, the various approaches applying absolute annotations often use different annotation scales that are not necessarily transferable to each other (Ivanova et al., 2024).

The argument quality model of the Project Debater was trained on the IBM-Rank-30k dataset (Gretz et al., 2019). In order to avoid subjective scales, it was labeled in a relative manner, comparing pairs of arguments (independent of the personal opinion) on 71 controversial topics that were created by crowd-workers. Each argument was annotated by ten different annotators. To derive continuous argument quality scores from the binary annotations, the authors calculate the likelihood of a positive label between 0 and 1, using MACE probability (MACE-P) (Hovy et al., 2013; Habernal and Gurevych, 2016) and Weighted-Average (WA). Both scores inherently incorporate the annotator reliability in the final label. A comparison of the two scoring functions reveals that WA tends to produce a gradual continuous scale, while MACE-P tends to binary labels (i.e., it produces more extreme values close to 0 and 1).

Based on these continuous scores, Gretz et al. (2019) train different models on both WA and MACE-P scores. We focus on the model with the best effectiveness, which is a pre-trained BERT model (Devlin et al., 2019), finetuned in a regression task to predict quality scores given an argument and the corresponding topic. The model is evaluated using Pearson (r) and Spearman (ρ) correlations on the test set (Gretz et al., 2019). Using BERT as contextual language model, Gretz et al. (2019) aim to create an argument quality model that is able to consider quality dimensions such as clarity, relevance and impact of an argument.

Recent works addressing the assessment of argument quality rely on BERT models as well as on "traditional" approaches such as interpreting the sentence lengths (Skitalinskaya et al., 2021; Joshi et al., 2023). An evaluation of the usefulness of large language models for automated argument quality assessment shows a moderate agreement with human annotations, but also demonstrates the potential for improving agreement between annotators (Mirzakhmedova et al., 2024).

3 Reproducing the IBM Model

The original model training process is described in Gretz et al. (2019); we here add missing details and outline how we dealt with these. The authors also referred us to the paper and the original dataset when we asked them for access to the model.

For the pre-trained model on which the IBM model is built, Gretz et al. (2019) link to the official BERT repository,[3] but do not specify which of the various models listed on this page it refers to, except for that is has an output dimensionality of 768. We use the BERT-Base model in the uncased variant, as we assume this is the most frequently used one that matches the description. Following Gretz et al. (2019), we add a linear layer to this pre-trained model and use a sigmoid activation function for the output; the loss is calculated as the mean squared error (MSE). Inspired by Hugginface's BertForSequenceClassification model, we also add a dropout level (with a probability of 0.1), although this is not specified in the paper for the original model, which improves the predictions of our model in preliminary tests. A detailed overview of all training parameters can be found in Table 3 as well as in our public repository (linked in Section 1).

Gretz et al. (2019) do not report the number of training epochs used, nor whether the final model was trained on the WA or MACE-P scores in the dataset (see Section 2). For this reason, we report

[3]https://github.com/google-research/bert

the results for different models trained, based on the WA and MACE-P scores and with a different number of epochs for evaluation on the test set.

The models with the highest scores that achieve similar results in the test set to the original model reported in Gretz et al. (2019) are applied to "external" data as an additional assessment. This data comes from the args.me corpus (Ajjour et al., 2019). This corpus contains argumentative texts on controversial topics that were crawled from various debate portals. In another work of ours (Zelch et al., 2025), we extracted 50 sample texts on different topics from this corpus and split them into sentences (resulting in about 1,100 sentences). While the API of the Project Debater was still available, we predicted the argumentative quality of these sentences using the Debater API to filter out non-argumentative sentences. To evaluate the newly trained models, we compare their predictions on sentences from the args.me corpus with the predictions of the IBM model by calculating the Pearson (r) and Spearman (ρ) correlation coefficients, similar to the evaluation of the original test set.

4 Evaluating the Reproduced Model

We compare the predictions of the reproduced argumentation quality models with the predictins of the IBM model both with the original test dataset and with an "external dataset" that was not used during training.

4.1 Evaluation on the Original Test Set

In a first step, we evaluate our reproduced models similarly to the original IBM model as described in Gretz et al. (2019). Table 1 shows the effectiveness of the reproduced models on the original test data in terms of correlation with the two types of ground truth scores (WA and MACE-P). As the table shows, the original effectiveness on the test set can be achieved within one or two training epochs. With longer training, the model quickly overfits. On average, the models that are trained for two epochs achieve the highest values. For this reason, we use these two models in the following evaluations, one that is trained for two epochs on the MACE-P scores (referred to as MACE-P2), the other that is trained for two epochs on the weighted average scores (referred to as WA2).

4.2 Evaluation on External Data

In addition to the comparison on the original test set, we evaluate the generalization ability of our models on an external dataset. For this, we compare the predictions of the reproduced models and the original IBM model, reporting the deviation between their predictions and fitting a simple linear regression between the original and reproduced models' scores. As described in Section 3, the external dataset consists of roughly 1,100 sentences from 50 texts on various topics from the args.me corpus (Ajjour et al., 2019) that were labeled while the IBM Project Debater API was still available.

To evaluate our reproduced models, we compare their predictions on the args.me sentences with the predictions of the IBM model in Table 2, calculating the Pearson r and Spearman ρ correlation coefficient between the predictions. The results show a high correlation between the predictions of the reproduced models and the predictions of the original model as ground truth. The RMSE is low for the model trained on the basis of the weighted average values (WA2), which indicates that the predictions are close to those of the original model. The number of predictions that are lower and higher than the original values is more or less balanced. In contrast, the MACE-P2 model (trained on the MACE-P scores of the dataset) produces consis-

Model	**Correlation with Ground-Truth**			
	MACE-P		**WA**	
	r	ρ	r	ρ
Original	0.53	0.52	0.52	0.48
Reproduced				
1 epoch	0.537	0.523	0.532	0.482
2 epochs	0.533	0.522	0.536	0.487
3 epochs	0.485	0.480	0.494	0.441

Table 1: Effectiveness of the reproduced models on the testset, compared to the results reported for the original model by Gretz et al. (2019) in terms of correlation (Pearson's r and Spearman's ρ) with the ground-truth.

Model	**RMSE**	#$\searrow$	$\searrow$	#$\nearrow$	$\nearrow$	r	ρ
MACE-P2	0.359	1132	0.34	1	0.03	0.816	0.823
WA2	0.080	428	0.05	705	0.07	0.901	0.889

Table 2: Correlation between the quality scores of the retrained models and the original IBM scores on args.me arguments; reporting the RMSE, the number of arguments for which the reproduced model predicts a lower score (#$\nearrow$) or a higher score (#$\searrow$), the average distance to the original score for the lower and higher predictions($\nearrow$ and $\searrow$), and the Pearson (r) and Spearman (ρ) correlation coefficient.

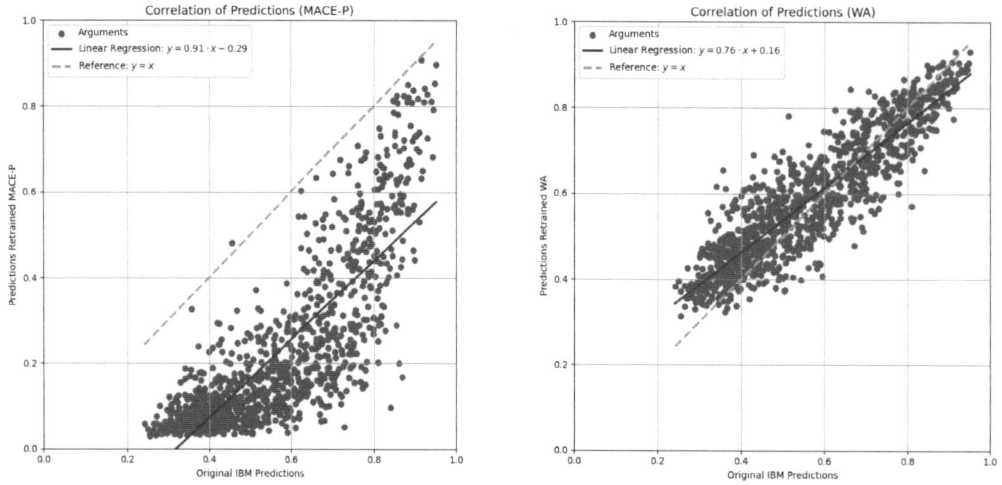

Figure 1: Correlations of the reproduced models' predictions and the original IBM model's predictions on external data (sentences from the args.me corpus). The models are trained on the MACE-P (left) and the WA scores (right).

tently lower scores than the IBM model, which also have a higher deviation (see the higher RMSE). This is consistent with the observation by Gretz et al. (2019) that the models trained on MACE-P scores tend to produce more extreme values close to 0 and 1, while the WA scoring function leads to graduated values.

For the WA2 model, only 12 of 1133 predictions deviate more than 0.2 (but all less than 0.3) from the original IBM predictions. About 20% of the WA2 predictions deviate more than 0.1 from the IBM predictions (223 of 1133), for only 64 of them the difference is greater than 0.15. About half of the WA2 predictions deviate less than 0.05 from the IBM predictions (536 of 1133), 102 of them less than 0.01.

The results in Table 2 are complemented by two scatter plots in Figure 1, which illustrate the correlation between the reproduced models' predictions and the original IBM model for each of the arguments (sentences) from 50 args.me texts. For both models, we show the least squares linear regression ($y = ax + b$) for the given data (red line) and the optimal linear reference (dashed yellow line). For model WA2 (graph on the right), the regression line is close to the optimum, but has a steeper slope (regression coefficients: $a = 0.76$ and $b = 0.16$). The variance is slightly lower at the upper and lower end of the scale. This makes sense, as arguments that are clearly of high or low quality should be easier to identify than arguments of medium quality. Overall, the predictions are roughly in the same range as the original predictions, deviating on average by about 0.05 to 0.07 from the IBM predictions. The scatter plot for the MACE-P2 model (left) looks completely different. The predictions show a strong bias towards lower values and also a significantly higher variance. The regression line has a similar slope to the reference line (regression coefficients: $a = 0.91$ and $b = -0.29$), but is shifted downwards by around 0.3, corresponding to the RMSE in Table 2. The variance of the predictions increases with the improved quality of the arguments, indicating that the models have problems identifying high quality arguments. Based on our evaluation, we therefore assume that the original model was trained on weighted averages with two epochs.

Qualitative Evaluation Table 4 shows exemplary sentences and corresponding quality scores from the second evaluation scenario using args.me texts. The consistently low scores of MACE-P2 are reflected in these examples. There are several cases for which the low predictions are adequate (sentences 6, 7 and 8), however, this cannot be attributed to a good discrimination ability of the model, since most of its predictions are similarly low. The WA2 model predicts similar scores as the IBM model for the examples 2, 3 and 5. In some cases the WA2 predictions appear more reasonable than the IBM scores, such as the higher quality score for sentence 1, as well as the lower score for sentence 6. It is interesting to investigate this in more detail in a follow-up work, to analyze whether one of the two models is consistently better than the other on external data. Both IBM and WA2 seem to have difficulties to recognize non-argumentative sequences, such as the examples 6, 7 and 8 (probably because this kind of data is not present in the training data). However, this is not necessarily problematic as it can be taken into account with an appropriate filtering threshold.

We additionally list the sentences for which the WA2 predictions deviate more than 0.2 from the original IBM predictions in Table 5 (upper half). Interestingly, for these sentences, the reproduced models predictions are all higher than the IBM predictions, except for one (sentence 6). A shared feature of many of these sentences is that they are potentially argumentative for the respective topic when considered together with one or more neighboring sentences—however, they are difficult to interpret without their context. This might also explain the larger deviations in the predictions of the models. The lower half of Table 5 shows the nine sentences with the most similar predictions of WA2 and the IBM model (difference <= 0.001). Several of these sentences with medium scores would not be considered to be very argumentative by humans (e.g., sentence 1132 or 1128), it is interesting that the predicted scores are so similar nevertheless.

5 Conclusion

The paper reports on the reproduction of a model for argument quality prediction that was provided as part of IBM's Project Debater. The original IBM model is not available any longer. With our reproduced models,[4] which follow the training instructions given in Gretz et al. (2019), we achieve similar results on the original test set as reported for the IBM model. On external texts from the args.me corpus, we reach a Pearson's r of 0.9 for the predictions of our best model and the original IBM predictions as ground truth. It is not clear whether this means that the predictions of our reproduced model are worse on the external data, or even better than the predictions of the IBM model. We will address this question in a future work, together with a comparison of our models with more recent approaches.

[4]Repository and models are made available to the public.

Limitations

Our reproduced model achieves similar results as the original model on the original test data, and a high correlation with the IBM predictions on foreign data. Nevertheless, the question remains as to where the remaining gap in this correlation and also the partially high variance of the predictions come from. Although we follow the training instructions provided in the paper as good as possible for the reconstruction of the model, some information are not available which might cause small deviations in the training process.

Acknowledgments

This publication has been partially supported by the European Union's Horizon Europe research and innovation programme under grant agreement No 101070014 (OpenWebSearch.EU), and by the German Federal Ministry of Education and Research (BMBF) through the project "DIALOKIA: Überprüfung von LLM-generierter Argumentation mittels dialektischem Sprachmodell" (01IS24084A-B).

References

Yamen Ajjour, Henning Wachsmuth, Johannes Kiesel, Martin Potthast, Matthias Hagen, and Benno Stein. 2019. Data Acquisition for Argument Search: The args.me Corpus. In *42nd German Conference on Artificial Intelligence (KI 2019)*, pages 48–59.

Milad Alshomary and Henning Wachsmuth. 2023. Conclusion-based counter-argument generation. In *Proceedings of EACL 2023*, pages 957–967.

Roy Bar-Haim, Yoav Kantor, Lilach Eden, Roni Friedman, Dan Lahav, and Noam Slonim. 2020. Quantitative Argument Summarization and Beyond: Cross-Domain Key Point Analysis. In *Proceedings of EMNLP 2020*.

Roy Bar-Haim, Yoav Kantor, Elad Venezian, Yoav Katz, and Noam Slonim. 2021. Project Debater APIs: Decomposing the AI Grand Challenge. In *Proceedings of EMNLP 2021*, pages 267–274.

Jacob Devlin, Ming-Wei Chang, Kenton Lee, and Kristina Toutanova. 2019. BERT: Pre-training of Deep Bidirectional Transformers for Language Understanding. In *Proceedings of NAACL-HLT 2019*, pages 4171–4186.

Lorik Dumani and Ralf Schenkel. 2020. Quality-Aware Ranking of Arguments. In *Proceedings of CIKM 2020*, pages 335–344. ACM.

Shai Gretz, Roni Friedman, Edo Cohen-Karlik, Assaf Toledo, Dan Lahav, Ranit Aharonov, and Noam Slonim. 2019. A Large-scale Dataset for Argument Quality Ranking: Construction and Analysis. arXiv/1911.11408.

Ivan Habernal and Iryna Gurevych. 2016. Which argument is more convincing? Analyzing and predicting convincingness of Web arguments using bidirectional LSTM. In *Proceedings of ACL 2016*.

Dirk Hovy, Taylor Berg-Kirkpatrick, Ashish Vaswani, and Eduard H. Hovy. 2013. Learning Whom to Trust with MACE. In *Proceedings of NAACL-HLT 2013*, pages 1120–1130.

Rositsa V. Ivanova, Thomas Huber, and Christina Niklaus. 2024. Let's discuss! Quality Dimensions and Annotated Datasets for Computational Argument Quality Assessment. In *Proceedings of EMNLP 2024*, pages 20749–20779.

Omkar Joshi, Priya Pitre, and Yashodhara Haribhakta. 2023. ArgAnalysis35K : A large-scale dataset for Argument Quality Analysis. In *Proceedings of ACL 2023*, pages 13916–13931.

Nailia Mirzakhmedova, Marcel Gohsen, Chia-Hao Chang, and Benno Stein. 2024. Are Large Language Models Reliable Argument Quality Annotators? In *Proceedings of RATIO 2024*, volume 14638 of *Lecture Notes in Computer Science*, pages 129–146.

Gabriella Skitalinskaya, Jonas Klaff, and Henning Wachsmuth. 2021. Learning From Revisions: Quality Assessment of Claims in Argumentation at Scale. In *Proceedings of EACL 2021*, pages 1718–1729.

Noam Slonim, Yonatan Bilu, Carlos Alzate, Roy Bar-Haim, Ben Bogin, Francesca Bonin, Leshem Choshen, Edo Cohen-Karlik, Lena Dankin, Lilach Edelstein, Liat Ein-Dor, Roni Friedman-Melamed, Assaf Gavron, Ariel Gera, Martin Gleize, Shai Gretz, Dan Gutfreund, Alon Halfon, Daniel Hershcovich, Ron Hoory, Yufang Hou, Shay Hummel, Michal Jacovi, Charles Jochim, Yoav Kantor, Yoav Katz, David Konopnicki, Zvi Kons, Lili Kotlerman, Dalia Krieger, Dan Lahav, Tamar Lavee, Ran Levy, Naftali Liberman, Yosi Mass, Amir Menczel, Shachar Mirkin, Guy Moshkowich, Shila Ofek-Koifman, Matan Orbach, Ella Rabinovich, Ruty Rinott, Slava Shechtman, Dafna Sheinwald, Eyal Shnarch, Ilya Shnayderman, Aya Soffer, Artem Spector, Benjamin Sznajder, Assaf Toledo, Orith Toledo-Ronen, Elad Venezian, and Ranit Aharonov. 2021. An Autonomous Debating System. *Nat.*, 591(7850):379–384.

Assaf Toledo, Shai Gretz, Edo Cohen-Karlik, Roni Friedman, Elad Venezian, Dan Lahav, Michal Jacovi, Ranit Aharonov, and Noam Slonim. 2019. Automatic Argument Quality Assessment - New Datasets and Methods. In *Proceedings of EMNLP-IJCNLP 2019*, pages 5624–5634.

Henning Wachsmuth, Nona Naderi, Yufang Hou, Yonatan Bilu, Vinodkumar Prabhakaran, Tim Alberdingk Thijm, Graeme Hirst, and Benno Stein. 2017a. Computational Argumentation Quality Assessment in Natural Language. In *Proceedings of EACL 2017*, pages 176–187.

Henning Wachsmuth, Martin Potthast, Khalid Al-Khatib, Yamen Ajjour, Jana Puschmann, Jiani Qu, Jonas Dorsch, Viorel Morari, Janek Bevendorff, and Benno Stein. 2017b. Building an Argument Search Engine for the Web. In *Proceedings of ArgMining 2017*, pages 49–59.

Ines Zelch, Matthias Hagen, Benno Stein, and Johannes Kiesel. 2025. Segmentation of Argumentative Texts by Key Statements for Argument Mining from the Web. In *Proceedings of ArgMining 2025*.

A Appendix

Parameter	Value
Base model	bert-base-uncased
Seed	42
Epochs	2
Batch size	32
Dropout	0.1
Learning rate	2e-5
Epsilon	1e-8
Optimizer	AdamW
Early stopping	no
Added layers	dropout, linear, sigmoid

Table 3: Training parameters for the reproduced argument quality model.

	Sentence	Quality Scores		
		IBM Model	MACE-P2	WA2
(1)	The military is in no obligation to let women into the frontlines just because they hold 95% of the Armies positions, just like why Hooters as no obligation to let men in.	0.52	0.18	0.65
(2)	1) Women already hold just about every kind of post/job in the military and make up a substantial portion of the military My problem with this argument is that it doesn't actually say why the Army should allow women in the frontlines.	0.75	0.48	0.75
(3)	Evidence show the DP is more expensive.	0.45	0.08	0.48
(4)	So there are undoubtedly instances in the past where we have executed an innocent man but did not know so, and still do not know.	0.82	0.29	0.69
(5)	But does this make it right to kill them back?.	0.43	0.06	0.47
(6)	In these cases I made it clear that I could not properly refute my opponent without proper sources.	0.71	0.18	0.56
(7)	Now as for the definition.	0.39	0.14	0.48
(8)	[1] http://www.military.com... [2] http://www.healthline.com... [3] Stuart A. Cohen Israel and Its Army: From Cohesion to Confusion, pg.	0.37	0.24	0.54

Table 4: Example sentences from the args.me corpus on various topics ("We should prohibit women in combat", "We should abolish capital punishment", etc.), along with the quality predictions of the original IBM model and the two reproduced models.

	Sentence	Quality Scores	
		IBM Model	WA2
(1)	Being locked in a single small room in solitary confinement for years on end is certainly not very pleasant.	0.36	0.65
(2)	Just because there are movements for something doesn't mean we should be worried about it.	0.34	0.62
(3)	That's what will soon happen if we can clone, if we can just donor this for that, saving people's lives, people got cured, got strong again, maybe they won't be immortal, but the point is that the increasing of human will soon beyond the balance, causes the disrupt of nature and it's balance, human cloning as you say that is "ethical" can also create tons more of human, also add fuel to that big problem.	0.51	0.78
(4)	(imagine [...] they suddenly see that ring on their finger and it sends a flood of guilt through them) In polygamy a very unfair 'status' system will form where only the offspring of the alpha male of the previous generation will be able to compete for the next because all women will think "OOH!	0.43	0.69
(5)	-When people give up all their rights to be protected their is a problem.	0.36	0.61
(6)	It was reported that 0.5% of inmates escaped.	0.81	0.57
(7)	... 2)All the ways that nature preserves that God preserves to help decreasing human population(old age, sickness.	0.32	0.55
(8)	However, when that present is a grenade with the pin pulled out, THEN it becomes immoral.	0.35	0.57
(9)	There are two parts of the act: Giving, and the danger of the grenade" _ So my opponent here believe it is ok to give thee grenade for the present, just don't pull the pin, ok here are the problems with that analogy: 1) How can you give a grenade, a dangerous present to a person whom you loved?	0.33	0.54
(10)	You don't have to learn golf, study it, know the rules and own clubs to be a non-golf player!	0.43	0.64
(11)	More simply, she's protecting rights by protecting rights.	0.48	0.69
(12)	Violating anothers rights does not deprive you of your own: John Stuart Mill is essentially saying the "eye for eye tooth for tooth" concept is right.	0.41	0.61
(1133)	Whether it is or isn't morally correct?	0.47	0.47
(1132)	The goal of debate is to find objective truth.	0.65	0.65
(1131)	First of I would like to say that prostitution is somewhat legal in the U. S. (since only two states allow it, Nevada and Rhode Island).	0.41	0.41
(1130)	Immigration Actually, application for citizenship is still a necessity, as well as a very rigorous INS process which requires applicants to display some sort of evidence of a pre-existing relationship prior to entering the country.	0.64	0.64
(1129)	You might say women have no issue with this, but I will explain.	0.41	0.41
(1128)	My opponent has clearly adopted a strategy based in deception and omission.	0.64	0.64
(1127)	In 2003, Terri Schiavo recovered from a vegetative state that she had been in for 13 years.	0.82	0.82
(1126)	Sure, I'll grant my opponent that there's a correlation; however, we all know that correlation doesn't imply causation, especially considering the maelstrom of recent evidence that I provided in Round 1 suggesting the opposite of Pro's claims.	0.66	0.66
(1125)	Arson is an essential tool in the quest for reform.	0.82	0.82

Table 5: Sentences from the args.me corpus for which the WA2 model's predictions deviate most (> 0.2, upper half) and least (≤ 0.001, lower half) from the original IBM predictions.

Reasoning Under Distress: Mining Claims and Evidence in Mental Health Narratives

Jannis Köckritz[1,2], Bahar İlgen[1], Georges Hattab[1,2]
[1] Center for Artificial Intelligence in Public Health Research (ZKI-PH), Robert Koch Institute, Berlin, 13353, Germany
[2] Department of Mathematics and Computer Science, Freie Universität Berlin, Berlin, 14195, Germany
Correspondence: KoeckritzJ@rki.de

Abstract

This paper explores the application of argument mining to mental health narratives using zero-shot transfer learning. We fine-tune a BERT-based sentence classifier on ~15k essays from the Persuade dataset—achieving 69.1% macro-F1 on its test set—and apply it without domain adaptation to the CAMS dataset, which consists of anonymized mental health–related Reddit posts. On a manually annotated gold-standard set of 150 CAMS sentences, our model attains 54.7% accuracy and 48.9% macro-F1, with evidence detection (F1 = 63.4%) transferring more effectively than claim identification (F1 = 32.0%). Analysis across expert-annotated causal factors of distress shows that personal narratives heavily favor experiential evidence (65–77% of sentences) compared to academic writing. The prevalence of evidence sentences, many of which appear to be grounded in lived experiences, such as descriptions of emotional states or personal events, suggests that personal narratives favor descriptive recollection over formal, argumentative reasoning. These findings underscore the unique challenges of argument mining in affective contexts and offer recommendations for enhancing argument mining tools within clinical and digital mental health support systems.

1 Introduction

Argument mining (AM) has produced strong results with structured texts, such as persuasive essays and legal documents (Stab and Gurevych, 2017; Habernal et al., 2023; Lippi and Torroni, 2016). Recent approaches have expanded the scope of AM to include less formal domains, such as online forums and social media (Schaefer and Stede, 2020). However, mental health narratives—personal accounts of psychological distress shared on peer support platforms—remain understudied despite their potential to reveal how individuals think about their mental state (Iskender et al., 2021).

This paper investigates whether models trained on structured, formal-domain texts can be used to analyze mental health narratives in a zero-shot transfer setting. Additionally, we examine how argumentative structures vary across expert-annotated causal factors of distress in mental health–related posts. Our approach involves fine-tuning BERT on the Persuade corpus of argumentative essays (Crossley et al., 2022), applying it without adaptation to the CAMS dataset of Reddit posts about mental health (Garg et al., 2022), and evaluating both transfer performance and shifts in argumentative patterns[1].

Our contributions are:

1. **An empirical evaluation of zero-shot AM across domains** was conducted, demonstrating a decrease in macro-F1 scores from 69.1% in the source domain to 48.9% in mental health narratives and quantifying transfer limitations.

2. **The analysis of argumentative structures in mental health discourse** revealed that personal narratives predominantly consist of experiential evidence (65-77%), with minimal explicit claims. This contrasts sharply with academic writing.

This study deepens our understanding of how argumentation occurs under psychological distress. It also paves the way for the development of domain-specific argumentation management (AM) tools for affective contexts, such as clinical and digital mental health applications.

[1] All code and datasets used in this study are publicly available at `https://github.com/JannisKoeckritz/ReasoningUnderDistress`

Proceedings of the 12th Argument Mining Workshop, pages 189–194
July 31, 2025 ©2025 Association for Computational Linguistics

2 Related Work

Argument mining identifies components such as claims and premises within a text (Lawrence and Reed, 2020). Earlier work demonstrated strong performance in formal domains—persuasive essays (Wachsmuth et al., 2016; Stab and Gurevych, 2017), legal reasoning (Habernal et al., 2023), and debates (Lippi and Torroni, 2016)—where arguments align with clear schemas (Lauscher et al., 2018; Cohan et al., 2019). More recent research has extended AM to informal genres, including online discussions and social media, where models confront implicit argumentation and emotionally charged content (Dusmanu et al., 2017; Vecchi et al., 2021; Cabessa et al., 2024; Mezza et al., 2024). Some studies such as Gupta et al. (2024) propose novel zero-shot methods for argument explication using large language models (LLMs). These LLMs decompose informal arguments into structured components, such as claims, reasons, and warrants.

Research in mental health NLP has focused on diagnostics, such as identifying depression and suicide risk, using lexical and affective features (Malgaroli et al., 2023; Montejo-Ráez et al., 2024), with little attention to argumentative structure. A small number of studies have applied AM to subjective or health-related narratives (Mayer et al., 2020), but cross-domain transfer remains largely unexplored.

This work bridges the fields of argumentation mining (AM) and mental health by applying a formal-domain AM model to CAMS. This reveals the challenges of mining arguments in affect-laden, informal texts. Building on this research, we explore whether formal-domain AM models can be applied to mental health discourse in a zero-shot setting.

3 Data & Methodology

3.1 Datasets

We use two datasets. The Persuade dataset is used to train argument mining models, and the CAMS dataset is used for zero-shot evaluation in the mental health domain.

The **Persuade dataset** (Crossley et al., 2022) contains argumentative essays from U.S. students in grades 6-12 with professional annotations across seven categories: Lead, Position, Claim, Counterclaim, Rebuttal, Evidence, and Concluding Statement. We have consolidated these into three categories: (1) *Claim* (combining original Claim, Counterclaim, and Rebuttal), (2) *Evidence*, and (3) *Other* (consolidating Lead, Position, Concluding Statement, and unannotated text). This simplified taxonomy makes it easier to transfer to informal contexts while preserving the core argumentative distinctions. The dataset consists of approximately 25,000 documents. For training our sentence-level classification model, we used only 15,000 of these documents, corresponding to around 300,000 sentences.

The **CAMS dataset** (Garg et al., 2022) comprises 5,051 Reddit posts that have been annotated for an interpretable causal analysis of mental health issues. It includes 3,155 posts that were crawled from the *r/depression* subreddit, as well as 1,896 reannotated posts from the existing SDCNL dataset. Each post is labeled with one of six categories reflecting psychological distress: (i) no reason, (ii) bias or abuse, (iii) jobs and careers, (iv) medication, (v) relationships, and (vi) alienation. The distribution of posts across causal categories is shown in Figure 1. Trained student annotators performed the annotations following expert-developed guidelines, and a clinical psychologist and a rehabilitation counselor later verified them. Posts were selected using keyword filtering and language criteria to ensure relevance and consistency.

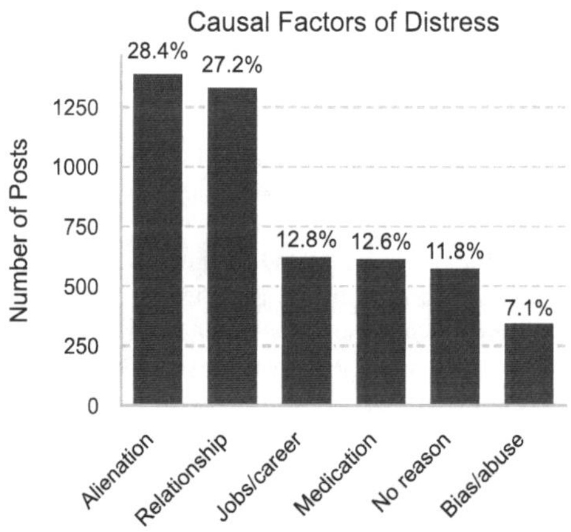

Figure 1: Distribution of Causal Factors in Mental Health Distress This figure shows how 4,963 social media posts are distributed across six categories of causal factors of mental health distress. Alienation (28.4%) and relationship issues (27.2%) collectively account for over half of all posts, highlighting the predominance of social and existential concerns. The remaining categories—jobs/career (12.8%), medication (12.6%), no identified reason (11.8%), and bias/abuse (7.1%)—represent a more diverse set of external stressors and unexplained distress.

3.2 Model Architecture and Training

We fine-tuned a sentence-level classification model based on BERT-base, treating each sentence as a discrete argumentative unit. The preprocessing pipeline involves sentence segmentation using spaCy, followed by BERT tokenization. The model architecture consists of a classification head that receives the token representation from BERT, applies dropout with a probability of 0.1, and passes it through a linear layer with softmax activation to produce the final classification. We use cross-entropy loss with class weighting based on inverse frequency to address class imbalance for training. We also use a batch size of 32, and a learning rate of 5e-4 with linear decay. We employed early stopping based on the validation F1 score with a patience of 20 epochs. The trained model achieves 69.0% accuracy and 69.1% macro F1 on the Persuade test set, performing best on *Evidence* identification (F1: 76.9%).

3.3 Evaluation Methodology

To establish a reliable evaluation baseline for the mental health domain, we manually annotated 150 sentences, randomly sampled from 30 CAMS posts and balanced across six causal-factor categories. Although this subset is a small part of the full CAMS corpus, it was carefully chosen to include a variety of distress sources, making it a good sample for our analysis. Two annotators, both experts in argument mining and mental health discourse, independently labeled each sentence in the CAMS sample as *Claim*, *Evidence*, or *Other*, based on our consolidated taxonomy. The six causal factors were pre-existing annotations in the CAMS dataset; however, the argumentative role labels introduced in this study were newly assigned by the annotators. The annotation process achieved an inter-annotator agreement of Cohen's $\kappa = 0.71$. Disagreements resolved through discussion to create the final gold standard.

We evaluated zero-shot transfer by applying the Persuade-trained model directly to the CAMS dataset without additional training. For the quantitative evaluation, we report the accuracy and F1 scores on the gold-standard subset. Then, to analyze domain-specific patterns, we apply the model to the full CAMS dataset and examine the distribution of argumentative elements across causal factors. Finally, we compare these patterns to those observed in the Persuade corpus.

4 Results

We consolidated the original Persuade annotation scheme by mapping Claim, Counterclaim, and Rebuttal into a single *Claim* category, maintaining *Evidence* as a separate category, and grouping Lead, Position, Concluding Statement, and unannotated text as *Other*.

Our BERT-based sentence classification model achieved an overall accuracy of 69.0% and a macro-averaged F1 score of 69.1% on the Persuade test set. Performance varied across argument categories, with *Evidence* sentences achieving the highest F1 score (76.9%), while Claims proved more challenging (F1: 53.1%). Table 2 presents the detailed performance metrics.

Category	Precision	Recall	F1 Score
Other	0.686	0.642	0.663
Claim	0.578	0.491	0.531
Evidence	0.736	0.806	0.769
Accuracy		0.690	
Avg F1		0.691	

Table 1: Classification performance metrics for the BERT sentence classification model on the Persuade test set.

The confusion matrix (Figure 2) reveals that the model most frequently confused *Claims* with *Evidence* (2,185 instances), indicating the challenge of distinguishing between these categories. *Claims* were also frequently misclassified as *Other* (1,029 instances). The model demonstrated strongest performance in identifying *Evidence*, correctly classifying 13,239 instances.

4.1 Zero-Shot Domain Transfer Evaluation

To evaluate cross-domain generalization, we manually annotated a gold-standard subset of 150 sentences from the CAMS dataset using our three-category scheme. When evaluated against this standard, our model achieved an accuracy of 54.7% and a macro F1 score of 48.9%. Performance varied across categories, with *Evidence* again being most reliably identified (F1: 63.4%), followed by *Other* (F1: 51.3%), while *Claim* classification remained challenging (F1: 32.0%). Compared to the source domain, this represents a 14.3-percentage-point drop in accuracy and a 20.2-point drop in macro F1, highlighting the challenges of cross-domain transfer to mental health narratives. These scores are informative but should be interpreted cautiously

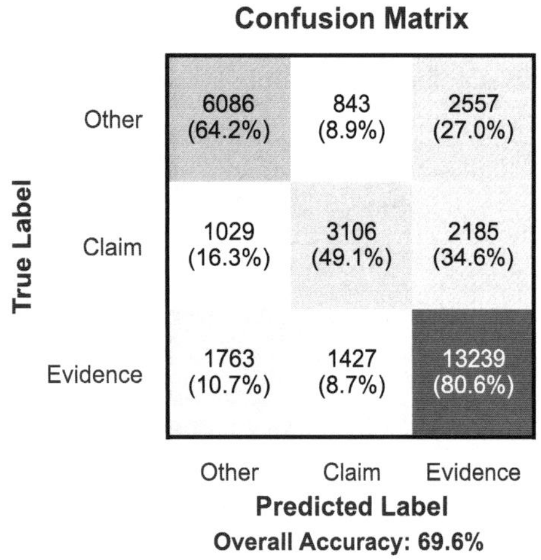

Figure 2: Confusion matrix for the BERT sentence classification model on the Persuade test set, showing the distribution of predicted vs. true labels.

due to the small evaluation sample size and the very low number of claim-labeled sentences. Larger annotated samples are needed to reliably estimate cross-domain generalization, particularly for underrepresented argument types.

Category	Precision	Recall	F1 Score
Other	0.547	0.482	0.513
Claim	0.376	0.279	0.320
Evidence	0.618	0.651	0.634
Accuracy		0.547	
Avg F1		0.489	

Table 2: Zero-shot transfer performance on the gold standard CAMS dataset.

The prevalence of evidence sentences, many of which appear to be grounded in lived experiences, such as descriptions of emotional states or personal events, suggests that personal narratives favor descriptive recollection over formal argumentative reasoning. During the annotation process, sentences were labeled as evidence if they served a justifying function, typically through descriptions of lived experiences, emotional states, or contextual details, even if they lacked external citations. This differs from academic domains, where evidence often consists of formally structured reasoning or references to facts.

A comparative analysis revealed that *Evidence* identification transferred relatively well across domains, while *Claim* recognition showed more significant degradation. This pattern aligns with our hypothesis that personal narratives express claims differently than academic writing does, while the presentation of evidence (often through personal experiences or references to external sources) shows more structural consistency across domains.

4.2 Distribution of Argumentative Elements by Causal Factors of Distress

We used our model to analyze how argumentative elements are distributed across different mental health categories in the CAMS dataset (Figure 3). The analysis reveals distinct patterns across categories. *Evidence* represents the most significant proportion in most categories, accounting for approximately 42-75% of sentences. In contrast, *Claims* remain consistently low across all categories (under 2%). This differs markedly from the Persuade corpus, where *Claims* represent approximately 28% of sentences.

The *Other* class is also well-represented, especially in the "No reason" and "Alienation" categories, where it accounts for about 40-55% of the sentences.

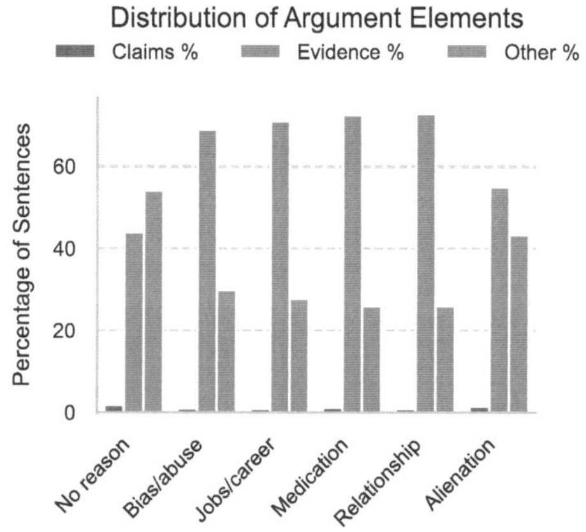

Figure 3: Distribution of argumentative elements (*Claims*, *Evidence*, *Other*) across the expert-annotated causal factors of distress in the CAMS dataset. Evidence statements are prevalent across most categories, while claims are rare.

The prevalence of *Evidence* across all causal factors suggests that personal narratives prioritize experiential descriptions over explicit claims or conclusions. Distress attributed to "Bias/abuse," "Jobs/career," "Medication," and "Relationship" shows the highest proportion of *Evidence* (>60%), indicating a greater focus on descriptive content. The "No reason" and "Alienation" categories exhibit slightly lower *Evidence* proportions and higher *Other* content, potentially reflecting more abstract or emotional expressions that fall outside our argumentative framework.

5 Discussion

Our results demonstrate the challenges and insights gained from applying argument mining to mental health narratives. The uneven transfer of argumentative components—with *Evidence* transferring more successfully than *Claims*—reveals fundamental differences in how arguments manifest across domains. This asymmetry, coupled with the substantial performance degradation in zero-shot transfer (20.2 point drop in macro F1), highlights the domain-specific nature of argumentative structures.

Mental health narratives exhibit a distinctive argumentative profile: *Evidence* statements (65-77%) dominate across all causal factors of distress. In contrast, *Claims* represent only 1-2% of the content, which is dramatically different from academic writing where claims form the backbone of argumentation. This suggests that, when explaining psychological distress, individuals prioritize experiential descriptions over explicit claim-making, regardless of the attributed cause. The boundary between personal experience (*Evidence*) and interpretation (*Claim*) often blurs in mental health narratives, creating inherent ambiguity. For example, a sentence such as "I stopped going to work because I couldn't get out of bed" can be both a factual recounting and an implied assertion of a causal link. This interpretive ambiguity suggests the need for more nuanced annotation schemes in emotionally charged contexts. These challenges highlight the potential benefits of redefining argumentation categories for mental health discourse.

Although zero-shot classification is simple to implement, it fails to account for domain-specific patterns. More promising approaches include few-shot learning with minimal in-domain data and domain-adversarial training, which explicitly models cross-domain differences. This work contributes valuable insights into cross-domain argument mining for mental health narratives; however, certain limitations should be acknowledged. First, the annotated CAMS subset is relatively small, which may affect generalizability. Additionally, although BERT provides a robust and well-established baseline, future studies could examine more recent transformer models, such as DeBERTa and RoBERTa, as well as instruction-tuned LLMs. Other promising directions include few-shot adaptation, discourse-level modeling, and developing domain-specific taxonomies suited to affective contexts.

Future research should develop argumentation schemes specific to mental health and expand beyond sentence-level classification to capture multi-sentence argumentative structures. Dialog-based systems that integrate interaction and explanation could provide additional value. For instance, Castagna et al. (2023) propose EQRbot, a chatbot that uses expert knowledge to provide argument-based explanations and critical questions. Such systems not only classify argument types but also clarify reasoning—particularly valuable in emotionally charged, ambiguous contexts like mental health discourse. Integrating dialogic and explanatory elements into future AM models could better align computational processing with real-world needs in digital mental health, enhancing clinical applications, peer support, content moderation, and research

6 Conclusion

This study examined the zero-shot transfer of argument mining from structured essays to mental health narratives. Our results show that evidence transfers reasonably well across domains, but claims are more difficult due to how they manifest in emotional contexts. The 20.2-point drop in macro F1 score between domains underscores the need for argument mining techniques tailored to mental health discourse. Promising directions include few-shot learning and domain-adaptive approaches to better capture argumentative structures in narratives about psychological distress. Recent work has emphasized the growing role of AI in public health infrastructure and decision support systems, particularly through explainable and human-in-the-loop approaches to foster trust and transparency (Hattab et al., 2025). Our findings underscore the importance of domain-specific natural language processing (NLP) techniques for understanding patient-generated narratives in digital health contexts.

References

Jérémie Cabessa, Hugo Hernault, and Umer Mushtaq. 2024. Argument mining in BioMedicine: Zero-shot, in-context learning and fine-tuning with LLMs. In *Proceedings of the 10th Italian Conference on Com-*

putational Linguistics (CLiC-it 2024), pages 122–131, Pisa, Italy. CEUR Workshop Proceedings.

Federico Castagna, Alexandra Garton, Peter McBurney, Simon Parsons, Isabel Sassoon, and Elizabeth I. Sklar. 2023. Eqrbot: A chatbot delivering eqr argument-based explanations. *Frontiers in Artificial Intelligence*, 6.

Arman Cohan, Iz Beltagy, Daniel King, Bhavana Dalvi, and Dan Weld. 2019. Pretrained language models for sequential sentence classification. In *Proceedings of the 2019 Conference on Empirical Methods in Natural Language Processing and the 9th International Joint Conference on Natural Language Processing (EMNLP-IJCNLP)*. Association for Computational Linguistics.

Scott A. Crossley, Perpetual Baffour, Yu Tian, Aigner Picou, Meg Benner, and Ulrich Boser. 2022. The persuasive essays for rating, selecting, and understanding argumentative and discourse elements (persuade) corpus 1.0. *Assessing Writing*, 54:100667.

Mihai Dusmanu, Elena Cabrio, and Serena Villata. 2017. Argument mining on twitter: Arguments, facts and sources. In *Proceedings of the 2017 Conference on Empirical Methods in Natural Language Processing*, pages 2317–2322.

Muskan Garg, Chandni Saxena, Sriparna Saha, Veena Krishnan, Ruchi Joshi, and Vijay Mago. 2022. CAMS: An Annotated Corpus for Causal Analysis of Mental Health Issues in Social Media Posts. In *Proceedings of the Thirteenth Language Resources and Evaluation Conference*, pages 6387–6396, Marseille, France. European Language Resources Association.

Ankita Gupta, Ethan Zuckerman, and Brendan O'Connor. 2024. Harnessing toulmin's theory for zero-shot argument explication. In *Proceedings of the 62nd Annual Meeting of the Association for Computational Linguistics (Volume 1: Long Papers)*, pages 10259–10276, Bangkok, Thailand. Association for Computational Linguistics.

Ivan Habernal, Daniel Faber, Nicola Recchia, Sebastian Bretthauer, Iryna Gurevych, Indra Spiecker genannt Döhmann, and Christoph Burchard. 2023. Mining legal arguments in court decisions. *Artificial Intelligence and Law*, 32(3):1–38.

Georges Hattab, Christopher Irrgang, Nils Körber, Denise Kühnert, and Katharina Ladewig. 2025. The way forward to embrace artificial intelligence in public health. *American Journal of Public Health*, 115(2):123–128.

Neslihan Iskender, Robin Schaefer, Tim Polzehl, and Sebastian Möller. 2021. *Argument Mining in Tweets: Comparing Crowd and Expert Annotations for Automated Claim and Evidence Detection*, page 275–288. Springer International Publishing.

Anne Lauscher, Goran Glavaš, and Simone Paolo Ponzetto. 2018. An argument-annotated corpus of scientific publications. In *Proceedings of the 5th Workshop on Argument Mining*, page 40–46. Association for Computational Linguistics.

John Lawrence and Chris Reed. 2020. Argument mining: A survey. *Computational Linguistics*, 45(4):765–818.

Marco Lippi and Paolo Torroni. 2016. Argument mining from speech: Detecting claims in political debates. In *Proceedings of the AAAI conference on artificial intelligence*, volume 30.

Matteo Malgaroli, Thomas D. Hull, James M. Zech, and Tim Althoff. 2023. Natural language processing for mental health interventions: a systematic review and research framework. *Translational Psychiatry*, 13(1).

Tobias Mayer, Elena Cabrio, and Serena Villata. 2020. Transformer-based argument mining for healthcare applications. In *ECAI 2020*, pages 2108–2115. IOS Press.

Stefano Mezza, Wayne Wobcke, and Alan Blair. 2024. Exploiting dialogue acts and context to identify argumentative relations in online debates. In *Proceedings of the 11th Workshop on Argument Mining (ArgMining 2024)*, pages 36–45, Bangkok, Thailand. Association for Computational Linguistics.

Arturo Montejo-Ráez, M. Dolores Molina-González, Salud María Jiménez-Zafra, Miguel Ángel García-Cumbreras, and Luis Joaquín García-López. 2024. A survey on detecting mental disorders with natural language processing: Literature review, trends and challenges. *Computer Science Review*, 53:100654.

Robin Schaefer and Manfred Stede. 2020. Annotation and detection of arguments in tweets. In *Proceedings of the 7th Workshop on Argument Mining*, pages 53–58, Online. Association for Computational Linguistics.

Christian Stab and Iryna Gurevych. 2017. Parsing argumentation structures in persuasive essays. *Computational Linguistics*, 43(3):619–659.

Eva Maria Vecchi, Neele Falk, Iman Jundi, and Gabriella Lapesa. 2021. Towards argument mining for social good: A survey. In *Proceedings of the 59th Annual Meeting of the Association for Computational Linguistics and the 11th International Joint Conference on Natural Language Processing (Volume 1: Long Papers)*, pages 1338–1352.

Henning Wachsmuth, Khalid Al-Khatib, and Benno Stein. 2016. Using argument mining to assess the argumentation quality of essays. In *Proceedings of COLING 2016, the 26th International Conference on Computational Linguistics: Technical Papers*, pages 1680–1691, Osaka, Japan. The COLING 2016 Organizing Committee.

Multi-Class versus Means-End: Assessing Classification Approaches for Argument Patterns

Maximilian Heinrich
Bauhaus-Universität Weimar

Khalid Al-Khatib
University of Groningen

Benno Stein
Bauhaus-Universität Weimar

Abstract

In the study of argumentation, the schemes introduced by Walton et al. (2008) represent a significant advancement in understanding and analyzing the structure and function of arguments. Walton's framework is particularly valuable for computational reasoning, as it facilitates the identification of argument patterns and the reconstruction of enthymemes. Despite its practical utility, automatically identifying these schemes remains a challenging problem. To aid human annotators, Visser et al. (2021) developed a decision tree for scheme classification. Building on this foundation, we propose a means-end approach to argument scheme classification that systematically leverages expert knowledge—encoded in a decision tree—to guide language models through a complex classification task. We assess the effectiveness of the means-end approach by conducting a comprehensive comparison with a standard multi-class approach across two datasets, applying both prompting and supervised learning methods to each approach. Our results indicate that the means-end approach, when combined with supervised learning, achieves scores only slightly lower than those of the multi-class classification approach. At the same time, the means-end approach enhances explainability by identifying the specific steps in the decision tree that pose the greatest challenges for each scheme—offering valuable insights for refining the overall means-end classification process.

1 Introduction

Argumentation is a crucial process in shaping our understanding of the world and fostering critical thinking. It plays a vital role in a range of contexts, including debate, decision-making, and the process of informing or changing beliefs. To classify common patterns of argumentation, the schemes developed by Walton et al. (2008) are of particular interest, as these schemes are extremely versatile and allow for a range of use cases. They can identify reasoning patterns within specific domains, such as legal reasoning (Verheij, 2003), help in the selection of argumentation strategies (Wachsmuth et al., 2018), and also uncover patterns in reasoning synthesis applications (Baff et al., 2019). In addition, the schemes can be used to reconstruct missing parts of arguments (Feng and Hirst, 2011), to train argumentation skills, or to enhance existing debate systems such as those described by Rakshit et al. (2017); Le et al. (2018); Slonim et al. (2021). Table 1 illustrates an example of such a scheme, namely the 'Cause to Effect' scheme.[1] Due to their fine nuances, the classification of Walton schemes is very challenging, even for people with a background in linguistics (Macagno et al., 2017). In addition, in a real life argumentation scenario, many parts of the schemes are only hinted and not explicitly mentioned (Dumani et al., 2021). To help people classify arguments based on Walton schemes, Visser et al. (2021) has developed the Argument Scheme Key (ASK) - a decision tree that guides users step by step through the annotation process. This raises the question of whether such a decision tree approach could be applied to language models to improve argument classification.

In this paper, we explore how the ASK decision tree can enhance the effectiveness of argument scheme classification. We refer to this approach as means-end classification. Rather than requiring the model to perform the complex task of scheme detection in a single step, the means-end approach decomposes the process into a guided sequence of simpler subtasks. At each stage, the model executes a straightforward task, such as identifying the presence of a specific argument property. In addition to potentially improving classification scores, this approach also boosts explainability: it enables the analysis of each decision made during the pro-

[1] In Walton's compendium (Walton et al., 2008), scheme names frequently begin with the prefix 'Argument from'. For brevity, we omit this prefix throughout this work.

Proceedings of the 12th Argument Mining Workshop, pages 195–204
July 31, 2025 ©2025 Association for Computational Linguistics

	Cause to Effect
Definition	
Premise 1	Generally, if A occurs, then B will (might) occur.
Premise 2	In this case, A occurs (might occur).
Conclusion	Therefore, in this case, B will (might) occur.
Examples	
Dataset	EthiX
Example 1	If entropy leads to universal randomness and randomness is the lack of all deterministic forces, then at least one part of a wholly deterministic universe is false, meaning there must be something else influencing the universe outside of determinism.
Example 2	The sensations felt when consuming marijuana and alcohol are very different. As such, they are not interchangeable, meaning that people may use both.
Dataset	USTV
Example 1	USA is in deep trouble. These countries, especially China, are giving incentives.
Example 2	NRA is protecting the Second Amendment. NRA are very, very good people. TRUMP is very proud of the endorsement of the NRA.

Table 1: Definition of the Cause to Effect' scheme, accompanied by examples from the EthiX (Bezou-Vrakatseli et al., 2024) and USTV (Visser et al., 2021) datasets. The definition used follows the version in Bezou-Vrakatseli et al., which slightly adapts the original formulation by Walton et al. (2008). As shown, most of the arguments are enthymemes, lacking a direct correspondence to the scheme definitions, and the two datasets display distinct styles of argumentation.

cess, making it possible to identify where and why the model's classification succeeds or fails. The contributions of this paper are:

(1) We conduct a comprehensive evaluation of argument scheme classification by comparing the traditional multi-class classification approach with the means-end approach on two separate datasets. Each approach is evaluated using both prompting-based and supervised learning methods. Our results highlight the key strengths and weaknesses of each approach and offer insights into how the means-end approach can be effectively applied to scheme classification tasks.

(2) We assess the effectiveness of ASK decision tree nodes using both prompting-based and supervised learning models. This novel analysis yields valuable insights into the utility—and limitations—of individual nodes in argument scheme classification. It also reveals which schemes can be reliably identified and to what extent. These findings offer a deeper understanding of the classification process, surpassing the explanatory power of traditional multi-class classification approaches.

2 Related Work

This section provides an overview of the diverse applications and methodological approaches to argument schemes within computational argumentation. We explore the classification and analysis of these schemes, their incorporation into datasets, and the challenges in their annotation and automated generation. The concept of argument schemes suggests that arguments can be organized based on diverse characteristics, reflecting commonly used patterns of argumentative reasoning (Macagno and Walton, 2015). This idea has ancient roots, tracing back to the works of Aristotle, as discussed in (Macagno et al., 2017). One of the most debated issues in this context is how such schemes should be appropriately classified, leading to the development of multiple approaches. The dialectical approach, highlighted by van Eemeren and Grootendorst (2003), focuses on the abstract representation of arguments within debates, while Wagemans (2016) organizes arguments into three main distinctions, culminating in the periodic table of arguments. Other approaches, such as those by Kienpointner (1992) and Grennan (1997), aimed to identify common argumentative features. In this tradition, Walton schemes are empirically developed in a bottom-up manner (Walton, 1996; Walton et al., 2008), involving the selection and analysis of arguments from varied domains. This method has led to the documentation of over 60 primary schemes and more than 100 sub-schemes (Walton et al., 2008). An initial approach to grouping schemes together was

ID	Which option applies to the argument?
ID-17	A: Conclusion is about a course of action B: Conclusion is not specifically action-oriented
ID-32	A: Argument explicitly mentions values B: Argument is not specifically value-based
ID-47	A: Argument relies on a causal relation B: Argument does not specifically rely on causality

Table 2: Dichotomous questions from the ASK decision tree.

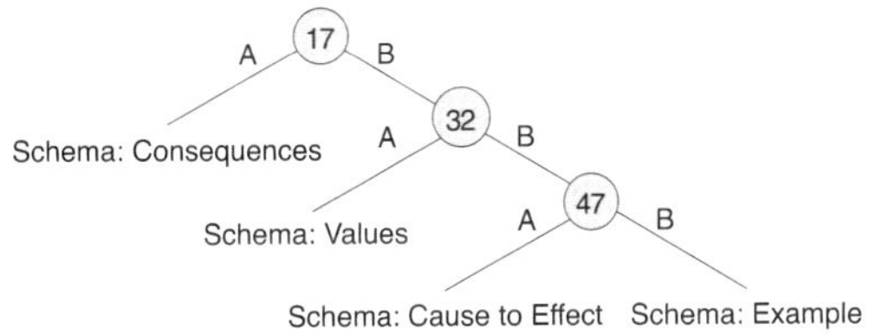

Figure 1: Trimmed ASK decision tree for classifying four argumentation schemes. Classification starts at the root node (ID-17), where the user selects the option that best matches the argument under analysis. Each response directs the user to the next relevant question, guiding them through the tree until the correct scheme is identified. The options for each node are listed in Table 2. The ID number assigned to each node corresponds to the original node IDs in the ASK decision tree from Visser et al. (2021). To correctly identify a scheme as 'Cause to Effect' (see Table 1 for examples), one must answer node ID-17 with 'B', node ID-32 with 'B', and node ID-47 with 'A'.

first proposed by Walton et al. (2008) and later refined by Walton and Macagno (2015).

Various datasets have been created to support research on Walton schemes. The Araucaria dataset, for instance, includes arguments from various media and institutional sources (Katzav et al., 2004; Reed, 2006; Moens et al., 2007). The dataset by Visser et al. captures the dynamics of the 2016 presidential debates (Visser et al., 2021), while the ReCAP dataset focuses on German education policy (Dumani et al., 2021). Further, datasets like those curated by Macagno (2022) and Bezou-Vrakatseli et al. (2024) expand the scope to argumentative tweets and ethical debates, respectively. A significant challenge in this field is achieving high levels of annotator agreement. Studies such as those by Lindahl et al. (2019) have revealed inconsistencies in annotation, underscoring the need for clearer guidelines. The use of decision trees for scheme annotation has been shown to significantly improve annotator agreement (Visser et al., 2021; Macagno, 2015, 2022).

Walton schemes are used to analyze various areas, such as newspapers (Lindahl et al., 2019), elections (Hansen and Walton, 2013) or student work (Duschl, 2007). They are also used to analyze paralogisms in student work (Rapanta and Walton, 2016a). Automated generation of arguments aligned with specific schemes has been explored in works like those by Saha and Srihari (2023) and the NLAS-multi corpus (Ruiz-Dolz et al., 2024a), showcasing the potential for synthetic argument generation. Several methods have been developed to classify schemes in texts (Bezou-Vrakatseli et al., 2024). Feng and Hirst (2011) analyze the five most common arguments from the Araucaria dataset to construct decision trees based on argumentative structural and linguistic features. The approach of Moens et al. (2007) leverages the same dataset to detect arguments using a multinomial naive Bayes classifier and a maximum entropy model. Song et al. (2014) develop protocols for annotating Walton schemes and their associated critical questions. Furthermore, Bezou-Vrakatseli et al. (2024) utilizes a range of BERT-based classifiers for automated scheme classification, while Lawrence and Reed (2016) leverages argumentation schemes to identify argumentative structures. Similarly, Green (2018) utilizes logic programs and schemes to mine arguments in biomedical research articles, building on earlier work (Green, 2015). Walton schemes are utilized across various domains to analyze content from newspapers, election campaigns, and educational settings, highlighting their adaptability and relevance in real-world applications (Lindahl et al., 2019; Hansen and Walton, 2013; Duschl, 2007; Rapanta and Walton, 2016a).

3 Multi-Class and Means-End Approaches

Humans often struggle with annotating argumentation schemes, partly because many schemes rely on implicit assumptions (enthymemes), and some schemes such as consequences require multiple steps of reasoning (Macagno and Walton, 2015). To simplify the annotation process for schemes, Visser et al. (2021) developed a binary decision tree that systematically guides annotators through the annotation task. Rather than classifying the argument directly, annotators make a series of choices between two characteristics of the argument at each step. For instance, one choice might involve determining whether the conclusion of the argument is about a course of action. Each decision narrows down the classification path by determining the next characteristic to be evaluated. An illustration of this classification procedure is provided in Figure 1.

Instead of relying on a human annotator, a language model can follow the steps outlined in the decision tree—a method we refer to as the means-end approach for argument classification. In contrast, traditional multi-class classification presents the model with an argument—optionally enriched with contextual information—and requires it to select the appropriate argumentation scheme from a predefined set. The means-end approach, by contrast, decomposes the classification task into a sequence of smaller, more manageable decisions. At each step, the model identifies a specific characteristic of the argument, which then determines the subsequent step in the classification sequence. This procedure is guided by external expert knowledge structures, such as decision trees. The approach is inspired by the *means-end analysis* problem-solving technique, in which an agent incrementally selects and applies actions to achieve a goal, based on an information gain heuristic (Newell and Simon, 1995). Note that this approach is different from merely breaking a problem into smaller steps; it also encodes a specific sequence for how the classification should be performed. The correctness of this sequence is ensured by the expert knowledge employed.

A key advantage of the employed step-wise decomposition is enhanced explainability: unlike the multi-class approach, which often operates as a black box, the means-end method allows for detailed analysis of each individual decision. This not only helps identify sources of classification errors but also makes it easier to refine specific steps within the classification process. Moreover, this approach is not limited to the domain of argumentation and can be applied to other complex classification tasks that benefit from codified expert knowledge.

4 Experiments and Evaluation

Our experiments are designed to address two primary objectives. First, we evaluate whether the means-end approach—guided by the ASK decision tree—offers improved results over the traditional multi-class classification approach for argument scheme classification. Second, we conduct a detailed analysis of the means-end approach to determine which decision points are most effective and where the classification process is most susceptible to errors, all while providing a high level of explainability.[2]

4.1 Dataset and Decision Tree

For argument scheme classification, we utilize two datasets: EthiX (Bezou-Vrakatseli et al., 2024) and the US2016G1tvWALTON dataset (referred to as USTV) (Visser et al., 2021). The EthiX dataset consists of 686 arguments extracted from ethical debates on Kialo[3], spanning 22 topics and covering eight distinct argumentation schemes. The USTV dataset includes 505 arguments in total, spanning 38 argumentation schemes. Its content is sourced from the first head-to-head debate of the 2016 U.S. general election and was transformed into the Argument Interchange Format (Chesñevar et al., 2006). A key advantage of these two datasets is that the human annotators applied the same ASK decision tree logic from Visser et al. (2021) that we utilize for the means-end classification approach. To facilitate the classification process and ensure a sufficient amount of training data, we focus on four schemes that are included in both the EthiX and USTV datasets. For the means-end approach, we simplify the original ASK decision tree by retaining only the three nodes necessary to differentiate between the four considered schemes. This refinement removes questions related to not-considered schemes while preserving the consistency and integrity of the remaining ones. Although the original annotators had to answer a greater number of questions, those included in the reduced tree are answered identically to the original process, allowing for a meaningful comparison between human and machine judgment. Figure 1 presents the modified decision tree, used in our means-end experiments. A summary of the refined dataset, along with key statistics, is provided in Table 3. We split the datasets in a 70/10/20 ratio for training, validation and testing, respectively. Minor adjustments were made to ensure that each scheme was represented in every split. For the EthiX dataset specifically, we ensured that every combination of scheme and topic appeared in each split. Additionally, we made sure that the test set for each dataset contained at least 11 distinct arguments for each scheme.

[2]All our code is available at: `https://github.com/webis-de/Argmining-25`

[3]`https://www.kialo.com/`

Argument Schemes			Datasets					
			EthiX		USTV		Σ	
Name	Walton-ID	DT-Depth	#	%	#	%	#	%
Example	6	3	120	24.0	81	44.0	201	29.4
Values	19	2	118	23.6	15	8.2	133	19.5
Cause to Effect	28	3	87	17.4	48	26.1	135	19.8
Consequences	33	1	174	34.9	40	21.7	214	31.3
Σ			499		184		683	

Table 3: Overview of the four schemes and their frequency in the EthiX (Bezou-Vrakatseli et al., 2024) and USTV (Visser et al., 2021) datasets. The second column, labeled 'Walton-ID', shows the canonical scheme numbers as defined by Walton et al. (2008). The 'DT-depth' column (Decision Tree Depth) indicates the number of decisions required in the trimmed ASK decision tree to correctly identify each scheme (see Figure 1).

	Multi-Class				Means-End			
	EthiX		USTV		EthiX		USTV	
	PR	SV	PR	SV	PR	SV	PR	SV
Macro F_1	0.63	0.72	0.44	0.44	0.44	0.68	0.33	0.38
Micro F_1	0.65	0.72	0.48	0.50	0.45	0.68	0.35	0.45

Table 4: Macro and Micro F_1 scores are reported for multi-class and means-end approaches using two classification methods: few-shot prompting (PR) with GPT-4o-mini and a supervised training approach (SV) with BERT. Results are presented for the EthiX and USTV datasets.

4.2 Experiments Overview

For each classification approach, we employ two distinct methods. The first is prompting, which leverages a large language model—specifically, GPT-4o-mini (2024-07-18) (OpenAI, 2023). Prompting enables us to provide the model with the same natural language instructions used by human annotators, making it particularly suitable for executing decision trees designed for human reasoning. The second method is supervised learning, in which we fine-tune a conventional BERT-based classifier (Devlin et al., 2019) on the training data. These two methods also incorporate different model architectures. GPT-4o-mini processes text unidirectionally, from left to right, predicting each token based solely on the preceding tokens. In contrast, BERT's bidirectional architecture allows it to consider both the preceding and following context around every token simultaneously, enabling a holistic understanding of the text.

In the multi-class approach using prompting, the model receives an argument along with a list of argumentation schemes and is tasked with selecting the most appropriate scheme. The prompt also includes definitions of all the schemes (for an example, see Table 1), adapted from Bezou-Vrakatseli et al. (2024) and based on the original formulations in Walton et al. (2008). Similarly, the means-end approach combined with prompting provides the model with an argument paired with a characterization derived from the ASK decision tree, where the model's task is to determine which characterization best applies to the argument. In all prompting-based methods, we employ a few-shot learning strategy by including example instances. To minimize randomness and encourage precise, controlled outputs, we set the temperature to 0.2 and the top-p value to 0.1 across all tasks. In the multi-class approach using supervised learning, a single classifier is trained to differentiate among the four argumentation schemes. In contrast, the supervised learning means-end approach trains a separate binary classifier for each of the three nodes in the decision tree. As a result, nodes deeper in the tree receive fewer training examples, since each node—except the root—handles only a subset of the full set of arguments. Table 4 presents the macro and micro F_1 scores for both the multi-class and means-end classification approaches. The detailed results for the multi-class classification methods are shown in Table 5. Table 6 reports the scores for the means-end approach, along with the accuracy of the corresponding decision tree nodes. To ensure consistent evaluation across argument schemes, classification approaches, and datasets, we sample 10 arguments per scheme from each dataset. The same set of arguments is used across all experiments to compute the reported scores.

5 Discussion

Classifying arguments remains a particularly challenging task, as reflected in our results. First, we

	Multi-Class											
	EthiX						USTV					
	Prompting			Supervised			Prompting			Supervised		
Scheme	Pre.	Rec.	F_1	Pre.	Rec.	F_1	Pre.	Rec.	F_1	Pre.	Rec.	F_1
Example	1.00	0.40	0.57	0.75	0.60	0.67	0.33	0.10	0.15	0.67	0.60	0.63
Values	0.64	0.70	0.67	0.73	0.80	0.76	0.73	0.80	0.76	0.0	0.0	0.0
Cause to Effect	0.62	0.50	0.56	0.78	0.70	0.74	0.40	0.40	0.40	0.36	0.80	0.50
Consequences	0.59	1.00	0.74	0.67	0.80	0.73	0.38	0.60	0.46	0.67	0.60	0.63

Table 5: Overview of multi-class classification results for Precision ('Pre.'), Recall ('Rec.'), and F_1 on the EthiX and USTV datasets. 'Prompting' refers to the few-shot approach using the GPT-4o-mini model, while 'Supervised' denotes the fine-tuned BERT-based classifier.

		Means-End											
		Prompting						Supervised					
		DT-Nodes						DT-Nodes					
		ID-17	ID-32	ID-47	Scheme classification			ID-17	ID-32	ID-47	Scheme classification		
Dataset	**Scheme**	Acc.	Acc.	Acc.	Pre.	Rec.	F_1	Acc	Acc	Acc	Pre.	Rec.	F_1
EthiX	Example	0.80	0.80	0.70	0.43	0.60	0.50	0.90	0.90	0.60	0.55	0.60	0.57
	Values	0.80	0.60		0.44	0.40	0.42	0.90	0.70		0.70	0.70	0.70
	Cause to Effect	1.00	0.80	0.60	0.50	0.50	0.50	1.00	0.90	0.70	0.67	0.60	0.63
	Consequences	0.30			0.43	0.30	0.35	0.80			0.80	0.80	0.80
USTV	Example	0.60	0.60	0.60	0.22	0.20	0.21	1.00	1.00	0.90	0.36	0.90	0.51
	Values	0.40	0.50		0.33	0.20	0.25	1.00	0.0		0.0	0.0	0.0
	Cause to Effect	0.90	0.80	0.50	0.50	0.30	0.38	1.00	1.00	0.60	0.50	0.60	0.55
	Consequences	0.70			0.37	0.70	0.48	0.30			1.00	0.30	0.46

Table 6: Overview of two classification method for the Means-End approach. 'Prompting' refers to the few-shot prompting method using the GPT-4o-mini model, while 'Supervised' denotes the fine-tuned BERT-based classifier. 'DT-Nodes' represents the nodes in the ASK decision tree that an argument must pass through to be correctly classified. The node IDs correspond to those listed in Table 2. The Accuracy ('Acc.') columns indicate the proportion of the 10 arguments per scheme that were correctly identified at the respective decision nodes. Accuracy is computed by tracing each argument's correct path through the decision tree and recording the decision at each node. The Precision ('Pre.'), Recall ('Rec.'), and F_1 columns represent overall classification performance, with each argument's scheme determined by following the decision tree logic. The evaluation is conducted on the EthiX and USTV datasets.

observe that the supervised learning method consistently outperforms LLM prompting. The limitations of large language models in classification tasks stem from the nature of their pretraining, which often does not sufficiently prepare them for domain-specific or fine-grained distinctions without additional adaptation. It is unlikely that an LLM has encountered highly specialized tasks—such as argument scheme classification using a means-end approach—during its training, which limits its effectiveness in this context. In contrast, the supervised learning approach benefits from explicit fine-tuning on the relevant argument schemes and datasets, resulting in substantially improved scores. Classification scores on the EthiX dataset are consistently higher than those on the USTV dataset, regardless of the approach or methods used. This disparity can be attributed to the nature of the USTV arguments, which are especially difficult to interpret without a clear understanding of the specific speech context in which they were made. In particular, the notably weak scores of the supervised method on the 'Values' scheme in the USTV dataset can be attributed to the extremely limited number of training examples available for that category. In contrast, the prompting method achieves better results for this scheme, leveraging the extensive pre-training of large language models. However, due to the high complexity of the arguments in the datasets and the small sample size used for the comparison, these results should be interpreted with caution.

As shown in Table 4, a comparison of the multi-class and means-end approaches indicates that, despite comparable overall F_1 scores, the multi-class approach achieves marginally higher results. Nonetheless, the scores for the means-end approach remain solid, especially given the reduced amount of training data available for nodes deeper in the classification tree. Examining the scores for individual schemes reveals varying results. For the Ethix and 'Consequences' schemes, the supervised means-end approach achieves the highest F_1 score among all compared configurations (Table 6). In the same configuration, the 'Example' scheme produces the lowest F_1 score. A similar variation in scheme scores is observed in the multi-class approach (Table 5). This suggests that some argument schemes (e.g., 'Consequences') are easier to classify than others. A key challenge in classification arises from the nature of the arguments themselves: they are often highly enthymematic, containing implicit or omitted components. In contrast, arguments associated with certain schemes may be more explicit, leading to higher classification scores.

One of the key advantages of the means-end approach is its explainability, as illustrated in Table 6. Here, differences appear notably at the root node ID-17. For most schemes—except 'Consequences'—the prompting method classifies this node correctly. However, since this node is intended to distinguish 'Consequences' from other schemes, it is not an appropriate choice at this point. In contrast, the supervised learning method shows better accuracy in detecting 'Consequences' arguments. We also observe that node ID-47 consistently struggles to differentiate between the 'Example' and 'Cause to Effect' schemes across both prompting and supervised learning methods in both datasets. This kind of insight underscores a key advantage of the means-end approach: when specific decision points in the tree underperform, human experts can intervene to refine the relevant nodes, thereby enhancing the overall system (Visser et al., 2021). Additionally, the means-end approach offers flexibility by allowing adaptation to the granularity of the classification task. If the objective is to classify broader categories of argument schemes rather than individual ones, the decision tree can be truncated at a desired depth—for example, by omitting node ID-47. In doing so, the classification process can be adjusted dynamically without requiring further training.

6 Conclusion

There are several compelling reasons why automated classification of Walton schemes is valuable. First, an automated classifier enables large-scale analysis of argumentation patterns across diverse domains, such as legal reasoning, online debates, and news articles. Second, once a scheme is classified, it becomes possible to identify corresponding critical questions as provided by Walton et al. (2008), facilitating the detection of errors in argumentation. These critical questions can also serve as commonplace arguments (Bilu et al., 2019). Third, schemes support enthymeme reconstruction, the training of argumentation skills and critical thinking (Figueras and Agerri, 2024), and the enhancement of existing debate systems (Rapanta and Walton, 2016b). Reliable scheme identification poses a significant challenge for human annotators due to the high cognitive load involved (Bezou-Vrakatseli et al., 2024). Additionally, while multi-class classification proves more effective for scheme detection, the means-end approach delivers comparable results with only a slight decrease in scores. To this end, the means-end approach offers significant advantages by providing valuable insights into the classification process, highlighting potential sources of error, and clearly identifying which specific argument characteristic are inconsistently recognized. Our findings confirm that automatically detecting argument schemes continues to be a challenging task. Additionally, our results show that the supervised training approach leveraging BERT surpasses the prompting method in performance across both multi-class and means-end approaches.

For future work, several directions are promising. One avenue is to further fine-tune the decision tree nodes, particularly those deeper in the tree that have fewer training examples. In this context, supplementary datasets—including synthetically generated arguments—may prove valuable. Another promising direction is the exploration of alternative datasets that feature more formal argumentation (Saha and Srihari, 2023; Ruiz-Dolz et al., 2024a). Hybrid methods for argument scheme classification deserve further investigation. For example, the vast knowledge contained in large language models might be used to create contextual information that enhances a fine-tuned classifier based on the means-end framework—thus effectively merging the advantages of prompting and supervised learning techniques. Additionally, alternative decision tree structures—such as those proposed by Macagno (2015) and Macagno (2022)—or other classification frameworks could be employed to further improve classification scores within the means-end approach.

7 Limitations

The effectiveness of the means-end approach depends on the quality of the underlying decision tree. For the approach to be practical, each node's task must be clearly defined, precise, and easily interpretable. This enables annotators or language models to make accurate decisions without relying on extensive prior knowledge. However, when tasks are overly complex or ambiguous, the overall effectiveness of the approach declines. As a result, designing an effective decision tree poses a significant challenge, even for experts.

Ideally, a well-optimized decision tree would position nodes that classify frequently used schemes closer to the root, reducing the expected external path length. However, the ASK decision tree is imbalanced. For example, identifying an argument as the frequently used 'Example' scheme (see Table 3) requires correctly answering three successive decisions. The more decisions that must be made, the higher the risk of misclassification. This structural imbalance is also evident in the original ASK tree presented by Visser et al. (2021).

Both datasets largely consist of enthymemes, containing implicit premises or conclusions. In the EthiX dataset, arguments are drawn from Kialo debates; however, the specific context—such as whether an argument supports or attacks another—is not explicitly provided. In the USTV dataset, arguments originate from a televised debate, where many points rely on prior context and earlier topics that are not directly present within the arguments themselves. In such cases, contextual understanding and enthymeme reconstruction are essential for accurate classification by both human annotators and language models. This absence of explicit context makes the classification task particularly challenging. A markedly improved outcome is observed when classifying arguments that strictly follow the semi-formal Walton scheme definitions, as demonstrated by Ruiz-Dolz et al. (2024b), with near perfect F_1 scores. Lastly, it should also be considered that, due to the limited available data, only 10 arguments could be tested per scheme and dataset, which restricts the generalizability of the results.

Acknowledgments

This work was supported by the German Federal Ministry of Education and Research (BMBF) through the project "DIALOKIA: Überprüfung von LLM-generierter Argumentation mittels dialektischem Sprachmodell" (01IS24084A-B).

References

Roxanne El Baff, Henning Wachsmuth, Khalid Al Khatib, Manfred Stede, and Benno Stein. 2019. Computational argumentation synthesis as a language modeling task. In *Proceedings of the 12th International Conference on Natural Language Generation, INLG 2019, Tokyo, Japan, October 29 - November 1, 2019*, pages 54–64. Association for Computational Linguistics.

Elfia Bezou-Vrakatseli, Oana Cocarascu, and Sanjay Modgil. 2024. Ethix: A dataset for argument scheme classification in ethical debates. In *ECAI 2024 - 27th European Conference on Artificial Intelligence, 19-24 October 2024, Santiago de Compostela, Spain - Including 13th Conference on Prestigious Applications of Intelligent Systems (PAIS 2024)*, volume 392 of *Frontiers in Artificial Intelligence and Applications*, pages 3628–3635. IOS Press.

Yonatan Bilu, Ariel Gera, Daniel Hershcovich, Benjamin Sznajder, Dan Lahav, Guy Moshkowich, Anael Malet, Assaf Gavron, and Noam Slonim. 2019. Argument invention from first principles. In *Proceedings of the 57th Conference of the Association for Computational Linguistics, ACL 2019, Florence, Italy, July 28- August 2, 2019, Volume 1: Long Papers*, pages 1013–1026. Association for Computational Linguistics.

Carlos I. Chesñevar, Jarred McGinnis, Sanjay Modgil, Iyad Rahwan, Chris Reed, Guillermo R. Simari, Matthew South, Gerard Vreeswijk, and Steven Willmott. 2006. Towards an argument interchange format. *Knowl. Eng. Rev.*, 21(4):293–316.

Jacob Devlin, Ming-Wei Chang, Kenton Lee, and Kristina Toutanova. 2019. BERT: pre-training of deep bidirectional transformers for language understanding. In *Proceedings of the 2019 Conference of the North American Chapter of the Association for Computational Linguistics: Human Language Technologies, NAACL-HLT 2019, Minneapolis, MN, USA, June 2-7, 2019, Volume 1 (Long and Short Papers)*, pages 4171–4186. Association for Computational Linguistics.

Lorik Dumani, Manuel Biertz, Alex Witry, Anna-Katharina Ludwig, Mirko Lenz, Stefan Ollinger, Ralph Bergmann, and Ralf Schenkel. 2021. The recap corpus: A corpus of complex argument graphs on german education politics. In *15th IEEE International Conference on Semantic Computing, ICSC 2021, Laguna Hills, CA, USA, January 27-29, 2021*, pages 248–255. IEEE.

Richard A. Duschl. 2007. Quality argumentation and epistemic criteria. In Sibel Erduran and María P. Jiménez-Aleixandre, editors, *Argumentation in Science Education*, volume 35, pages 159–175. Springer Netherlands, Dordrecht.

Vanessa W. Feng and Graeme Hirst. 2011. Classifying arguments by scheme. In *The 49th Annual Meeting of the Association for Computational Linguistics: Human Language Technologies, Proceedings of the Conference, 19-24 June, 2011, Portland, Oregon, USA*, pages 987–996. The Association for Computer Linguistics.

Blanca C. Figueras and Rodrigo Agerri. 2024. Critical questions generation: Motivation and challenges. In *Proceedings of the 28th Conference on Computational Natural Language Learning*, pages 105–116, Miami, FL, USA. Association for Computational Linguistics.

Nancy L. Green. 2015. Annotating evidence-based argumentation in biomedical text. In *2015 IEEE International Conference on Bioinformatics and Biomedicine, BIBM 2015, Washington, DC, USA, November 9-12, 2015*, pages 922–929. IEEE Computer Society.

Nancy L. Green. 2018. Towards mining scientific discourse using argumentation schemes. *Argument Comput.*, 9(2):121–135.

Wayne Grennan. 1997. *Informal Logic: Issues and Techniques*. McGill-Queen's University Press, Montreal; Buffalo.

Hans V. Hansen and Douglas N. Walton. 2013. Argument kinds and argument roles in the ontario provincial election, 2011. *Journal of Argumentation in Context*, 2(2):226–258.

Joel Katzav, Chris Reed, and Glenn Rowe. 2004. Argument research corpus. In *Proceedings of Practical Applications in Language and Computers (PALC 2003): 4th Biennial International Conference on Practical Applications in Language Corpora, 4–6 April 2003, Łódź*. Peter Lang.

Manfred Kienpointner. 1992. *Alltagslogik: Struktur und Funktion von Argumentationsmustern*. Number 126 in Problemata. Frommann-Holzboog, Stuttgart-Bad Cannstatt.

John Lawrence and Chris Reed. 2016. Argument mining using argumentation scheme structures. In *Computational Models of Argument - Proceedings of COMMA 2016, Potsdam, Germany, 12-16 September, 2016*, volume 287 of *Frontiers in Artificial Intelligence and Applications*, pages 379–390. IOS Press.

Dieu-Thu Le, Cam-Tu Nguyen, and Kim A. Nguyen. 2018. Dave the debater: a retrieval-based and generative argumentative dialogue agent. In *Proceedings of the 5th Workshop on Argument Mining, ArgMining@EMNLP 2018, Brussels, Belgium, November 1, 2018*, pages 121–130. Association for Computational Linguistics.

Anna Lindahl, Lars Borin, and Jacobo Rouces. 2019. Towards assessing argumentation annotation - A first step. In *Proceedings of the 6th Workshop on Argument Mining, ArgMining@ACL 2019, Florence, Italy, August 1, 2019*, pages 177–186. Association for Computational Linguistics.

Fabrizio Macagno. 2015. A means-end classification of argumentation schemes. In Frans H. van Eemeren and Bart Garssen, editors, *Reflections on Theoretical Issues in Argumentation Theory*, pages 183–201. Springer International Publishing.

Fabrizio Macagno. 2022. Argumentation profiles and the manipulation of common ground. the arguments of populist leaders on twitter. *Journal of Pragmatics*, 191:67–82.

Fabrizio Macagno, Douglas Walton, and Chris Reed. 2017. Argumentation schemes. history, classifications, and computational applications. *IfCoLog Journal of Logics and Their Applications*, 8(4):2493–2556.

Fabrizio Macagno and Douglas N. Walton. 2015. Classifying the patterns of natural arguments. *Philosophy & Rhetoric*, 48(1):26–53.

Marie-Francine Moens, Erik Boiy, Raquel M. Palau, and Chris Reed. 2007. Automatic detection of arguments in legal texts. In *The Eleventh International Conference on Artificial Intelligence and Law, Proceedings of the Conference, June 4-8, 2007, Stanford Law School, Stanford, California, USA*, pages 225–230. ACM.

Allen Newell and Herbert A. Simon. 1995. *GPS, a Program that Simulates Human Thought*, pages 415–428. American Association for Artificial Intelligence, USA.

OpenAI. 2023. GPT-4 technical report. *CoRR*, abs/2303.08774.

Geetanjali Rakshit, Kevin K. Bowden, Lena Reed, Amita Misra, and Marilyn A. Walker. 2017. Debbie, the debate bot of the future. In *Advanced Social Interaction with Agents - 8th International Workshop on Spoken Dialog Systems, IWSDS 2017, Farmington, PA, USA, 6-9 June 2017, revised selected papers*, volume 510 of *Lecture Notes in Electrical Engineering*, pages 45–52. Springer.

Chrysi Rapanta and Douglas N. Walton. 2016a. Identifying paralogisms in two ethnically different contexts at university level / identificación de paralogismos en dos contextos universitarios diferenciados étnicamente. *Journal for the Study of Education and Development*, 39(1):119–149.

Chrysi Rapanta and Douglas N. Walton. 2016b. The use of argument maps as an assessment tool in higher education. *International Journal of Educational Research*, 79:211–221.

Chris Reed. 2006. Preliminary results from an argument corpus. In *Linguistics in the Twenty First Century*, pages 185–195. Cambridge Scholar Press, Newcastle, UK.

Ramon Ruiz-Dolz, Joaquín Taverner, John Lawrence, and Chris Reed. 2024a. Nlas-multi: A multilingual corpus of automatically generated natural language argumentation schemes. *Data in Brief*, 57:111087.

Ramon Ruiz-Dolz, Joaquín Taverner, John Lawrence, and Chris Reed. 2024b. Nlas-multi: A multilingual corpus of automatically generated natural language argumentation schemes. *CoRR*, arXiv:2402.14458.

Sougata Saha and Rohini K. Srihari. 2023. Argu: A controllable factual argument generator. In *Proceedings of the 61st Annual Meeting of the Association for Computational Linguistics (Volume 1: Long Papers), ACL 2023, Toronto, Canada, July 9-14, 2023*, pages 8373–8388. Association for Computational Linguistics.

Noam Slonim, Yonatan Bilu, Carlos Alzate, Roy Bar-Haim, Ben Bogin, Francesca Bonin, Leshem Choshen, Edo Cohen-Karlik, Lena Dankin, Lilach Edelstein, Liat Ein-Dor, Roni Friedman-Melamed, Assaf Gavron, Ariel Gera, Martin Gleize, Shai Gretz, Dan Gutfreund, Alon Halfon, Daniel Hershcovich, and 34 others. 2021. An autonomous debating system. *Nat.*, 591(7850):379–384.

Yi Song, Michael Heilman, Beata B. Klebanov, and Paul Deane. 2014. Applying argumentation schemes for essay scoring. In *Proceedings of the First Workshop on Argument Mining, hosted by the 52nd Annual Meeting of the Association for Computational Linguistics, ArgMining@ACL 2014, June 26, 2014, Baltimore, Maryland, USA*, pages 69–78. The Association for Computer Linguistics.

Frans H. van Eemeren and Rob Grootendorst. 2003. *A Systematic Theory of Argumentation: The Pragma-Dialectical Approach*. Cambridge University Press, Cambridge.

Bart Verheij. 2003. Dialectical argumentation with argumentation schemes: An approach to legal logic. *Artificial Intelligence and Law*, 11(2/3):167–195.

Jacky Visser, John Lawrence, Chris Reed, Jean H. M. Wagemans, and Douglas N. Walton. 2021. Annotating argument schemes. *Argumentation*, 35(1):101–139.

Henning Wachsmuth, Manfred Stede, Roxanne El Baff, Khalid Al Khatib, Maria Skeppstedt, and Benno Stein. 2018. Argumentation synthesis following rhetorical strategies. In *Proceedings of the 27th International Conference on Computational Linguistics, COLING 2018, Santa Fe, New Mexico, USA, August 20-26, 2018*, pages 3753–3765. Association for Computational Linguistics.

Jean H. M. Wagemans. 2016. Constructing a periodic table of arguments. In P. Bondy and L. Benacquista, editors, *Argumentation, Objectivity, and Bias: Proceedings of the 11th International Conference of the Ontario Society for the Study of Argumentation (OSSA)*, pages 1–12, 18–21. OSSA.

Douglas N. Walton. 1996. *Argumentation Schemes for Presumptive Reasoning*. L. Erlbaum Associates, Mahwah, N.J.

Douglas N. Walton and Fabrizio Macagno. 2015. A classification system for argumentation schemes. *Argument & Computation*, 6(3):219–245.

Douglas N. Walton, Chris Reed, and Fabrizio Macagno. 2008. *Argumentation Schemes*. Cambridge University Press.

From Debates to Diplomacy: Argument Mining Across Political Registers

Maria Poiaganova
Marketing for Social Impact
University of Zürich
Zürich, Switzerland
maria.poiaganova@business.uzh.ch

Manfred Stede
Applied Computational Linguistics
University of Potsdam
Potsdam, Germany
stede@uni-potsdam.de

Abstract

This paper addresses the problem of cross-register generalization in argument mining within political discourse. We examine whether models trained on adversarial, spontaneous U.S. presidential debates can generalize to the more diplomatic and prepared register of UN Security Council (UNSC) speeches. To this end, we conduct a comprehensive evaluation across four core argument mining tasks. Our experiments show that the tasks of detecting and classifying argumentative units transfer well across registers, while identifying and labeling argumentative relations remains notably challenging, likely due to register-specific differences in how argumentative relations are structured and expressed. As part of this work, we introduce *ArgUNSC*, a new corpus of 144 UNSC speeches manually annotated with claims, premises, and their argumentative links. It provides a resource for future in- and cross-domain studies and novel research directions at the intersection of argument mining and political science.

1 Introduction

Argumentation is integral to human communication, enabling individuals to express opinions, persuade others, and collaboratively reason about the world. As artificial intelligence systems increasingly assist humans, both in everyday interactions and in high-stakes decision-making scenarios, their ability to detect and interpret arguments is more critical than ever. Therefore, Argumentation Mining (AM) plays a central role in such systems, enabling them to identify and structure argumentative content across a variety of domains, spanning legal decision support (Habernal et al., 2024), educational tools for developing students' reasoning skills (Wambsganss et al., 2021), social media analysis (Feger and Dietze, 2024; Chakrabarty et al., 2019), and even autonomous debating technologies (Slonim et al., 2021).

Building robust AM systems is tightly connected to high-quality annotated data. However, creating such datasets across all potential domains and contexts is time-consuming, costly, and intellectually demanding. To address this challenge, *cross-domain* generalization—a strategy where models trained in one domain (e.g., legal) are evaluated in another (e.g., medical)—has emerged (Daxenberger et al., 2017; Schaefer et al., 2022; Gemechu et al., 2024). At the same time, relatively little attention has been paid to *cross-register* generalization—a special case of domain transfer where the broader discourse remains consistent but the rhetorical style, structure, or communicative setting varies. This scenario appears promising and challenging at the same time, as, on the one hand, registers within the same domain often share core argumentative structures, allowing for potential knowledge transfer, particularly when communicative goals such as persuasion or justification are preserved. On the other hand, even subtle differences in style, lexical choices, or discourse organization can hinder generalization.

To address this open question, our paper focuses on the challenge of cross-register generalization in AM within the domain of political discourse. We contrast U.S. presidential debates and United Nations Security Council (UNSC) speeches, which represent markedly different registers. Presidential debate discourse is often spontaneous, and aimed at persuading a public audience. In contrast, UNSC speeches are mostly prepared, and delivered in formal institutional settings to articulate national positions.

Our goal is to investigate whether argumentation models trained on political speech of one register can generalize to a speech with a different register. We evaluate this across four core AM tasks: (1) Argumentative Component Segmentation (ACS) – detecting argumentative components (*claims* and *premises*); (2) Argumentative Component Classifi-

Proceedings of the 12th Argument Mining Workshop, pages 205–216
July 31, 2025 ©2025 Association for Computational Linguistics

cation (ACC) – distinguishing between claims and premises; (3) Argumentative Relation Identification (ARI) – determining whether a claim and a premise are argumentatively related; and (4) Argumentative Relation Classification (ARC) – identifying whether the relation is *support* or *attack*. For language modeling, we use encoder-based architectures (BERT and RoBERTa) and evaluate performance in both in-register and cross-register settings. Additionally, we prompt GPT-4 in zero- and few-shot setups and compare its performance to that of fine-tuned models.

Beyond this systematic cross-task and cross-model evaluation, a major part of our contribution lies in releasing a novel corpus of 144 UNSC speeches, annotated with claims, premises, and the relations between them.

Our results reveal that ACS and ACC tasks generalize well across registers, whereas ARI and ARC do not, highlighting the greater complexity of relation-level tasks and their sensitivity to register variation. Additionally, LLMs consistently underperform compared to encoder models fine-tuned both in in- and cross-register scenarios, with particularly large performance gaps on ACS and ACC tasks.

2 Related Work

2.1 Political Argument Mining

Our work contributes to the literature on political argument mining, motivating a review of existing political corpora and the specific AM tasks they support. For example, Menini et al. (2018) introduce a corpus of 1,462 manually annotated argument pairs drawn from Nixon and Kennedy's 1960 presidential campaign speeches. The pairs are labeled with support and attack relations across five major political topics.

Similarly, Visser et al. (2020) present the $US2016$ corpus, which includes transcriptions of televised debates leading up to the 2016 US presidential election, as well as audience reactions collected from Reddit.[1]

Lippi and Torroni (2016a) compile an original dataset based on the 2015 UK political election debates, combining textual and audio features and test whether spoken language cues improve claim detection.

Another multimodal corpus is presented by Mestre et al. (2021). Their *M-Arg* dataset is based on the US 2020 presidential debates and includes both audio and transcripts, annotated with claims and premises and the argumentative relationship between them across 4,104 sentence pairs.

Haddadan et al. (2019) present a large-scale corpus of 39 U.S. presidential debates spanning from 1960 to 2016, annotated with claims and premises. They further explore argument filtering and argument component classification. A recent extension enriches the corpus with relation annotations and labels for argumentative fallacy types (Goffredo et al., 2022). We select this corpus to represent the presidential debates register in our study.

2.2 Argument Mining under Low-Resource Conditions

2.2.1 Cross-Domain Generalization

The challenge of transferring models across domains or text genres has been widely studied in NLP more broadly (Hupkes et al., 2023), and remains particularly difficult in the context of AM. In an early study, Ajjour et al. (2017) demonstrate significant generalizability issues for the argument unit segmentation task across three datasets. Daxenberger et al. (2017) undertake systematic experiments in cross-domain claim classification in six different datasets, and find generally high degradation compared to in-domain performance. Using qualitative analysis, they show that the underlying notions of claim in the datasets vary significantly. Similarly, Schaefer et al. (2022) use four corpora of varying genres and sizes and conclude that large training sets, homogeneous claim ratios, and less formal language tend to improve generalization. In a series of relation identification tasks, Gemechu et al. (2024) propose a benchmark architecture encompassing three approaches and conduct experiments on—and across—eight datasets. In line with previous cross-domain studies, they observe consistently poor performance when detecting support and attack relations in corpora unseen during training.

Turning from cross-domain to cross-register setups closer to ours, Blokker et al. (2020) examine the generalizability of claim detection models by training on newspaper data and testing on political party manifestos. Despite linguistic and conceptual differences between formats, their BERT-based model shows strong cross-text performance and strong overlap in party positions across registers.

[1]https://www.reddit.com/

2.2.2 Large Language Models in AM

A rapidly growing body of literature highlights the remarkable capabilities of Large Language Models (LLMs) in argument mining (Chen et al., 2024; Favero et al., 2025; Cabessa et al., 2025; Sviridova et al., 2024). LLMs are particularly well-suited for low-resource settings, showing strong performance even with simple instruction prompts. However, given their recent emergence, research remains limited and evidence mixed regarding their performance on AM tasks compared to other state-of-the-art models. For instance, Gorur et al. (2025) examine argument relation identification and find that prompted LLMs significantly outperform RoBERTa across 11 datasets. On the other hand, Ruiz-Dolz and Lawrence (2023) find that fine-tuned RoBERTa outperforms GPT-4 in most cases in the context of argumentative fallacy detection.

3 Data

3.1 US Presidential Debates

As a starting point for our register transfer experiments, we focus on presidential debates discourse. We adopt the large-scale US-ElecDeb16To60 v.01 corpus (hereafter, USElecDeb), introduced by Haddadan et al. (2019). The corpus comprises transcripts from 39 U.S. presidential and vice-presidential debates spanning from 1960 to 2016. These transcripts were originally obtained from the Commission on Presidential Debates[2].

The USElecDeb corpus contains annotations of argumentative components, namely claims and premises. According to Haddadan et al. (2019), in political debate discourse, a claim may take the form of an advocated policy, a candidate's stance on a policy, an opinion on a particular issue, or their personal judgment. To justify their claims, politicians provide premises (sometimes referred to as evidence in the AM literature (e.g., Cheng et al. (2022); Lippi and Torroni (2016b)), which may include references to specific events, data, outcomes of past policies, etc.

Importantly, annotations in the original corpus are made on the component level, with components defined as the minimal discourse units that independently convey argumentative meaning. Such units can span the entire sentence or be more granular, e.g., take the form of a clause. For modeling purposes, the authors map the component-level annotations to the sentence level, a setup we adopt in our experiments as well. Table 1 provides the sentence-level distribution of claims and premises in the USElecDeb corpus.

Level	Total	Arg	Non-Arg	Claim	Premise
Sent.	29.621	22.280	7.252	11.964	10.316

Table 1: Distribution of argumentative sentence types in the USElecDeb.

While the original dataset did not include relation annotations, these were later introduced by Goffredo et al. (2022) as part of a study on fallacy detection. In addition to augmenting the corpus with relational links (support or attack) between components, this extended version also includes transcripts from Biden-Trump debates held in 2020.[3] We use this enhanced version for our experiments on Argumentative Relation Identification (ARI) and Argumentative Relation Classification (ARC). The summary statistics on support vs. attack sentence pairs is presented in Table 2.

Level	Total	Support	Attack
Sent.	25.524	21.689	3.835

Table 2: Distribution of support/attack sentence-pairs in the USElecDeb.

Example (1) represents an argumentative structure in USElecDeb. Claims are marked in **bold**, premises in *Italics*, and the component boundaries are additionally indicated by [square brackets]. In this example, both premises support the claim.

(1) Nixon-Kennedy, September 26, 1960:

NIXON: We often hear gross national product discussed, and in that respect may I say that [*when we compare the growth in this Administration with that of the previous Administration that then there was a total growth of eleven percent over seven years*]$_{\text{Premise}_1}$; [*in this Administration there has been a total growth of nineteen percent over seven years*]$_{\text{Premise}_2}$. **[That shows that there's been more growth in this Administration than in its predecessor]**$_{\text{Claim}}$.

[2] https://www.debates.org/

[3] https://github.com/pierpaologoffredo/ElecDeb60to20/tree/main

3.2 UN Security Council Speeches

The United Nations Security Council (UNSC) is a principal body responsible for maintaining international peace and security; it convenes when global conflicts, crises, or threats to peace require collective diplomatic response. The UNSC discourse was selected as a contrasting register to presidential debates in our cross-register experiments. Its largely formal and pre-written language differs markedly from the spontaneous and often emotionally charged language of debates. Beyond this stylistic divergence, it also holds intrinsic value for argument mining due to its high-stakes discourse in which nations articulate their positions through structured and strategic reasoning.

To collect the data, we use the raw corpus of UNSC speeches published by Schönfeld et al. (2019). We select speeches from the years 2014 to 2018, a period marked by the onset of the Russia-Ukraine conflict—a topic that prompted diverse and rich argumentative positions from various countries. In addition to discussions of this conflict, a few speeches address issues related to the UNSC's Women, Peace, and Security (WPS) agenda. The final dataset includes 144 speeches delivered by representatives from 24 different nations. Appendix A details the distribution of speeches by country and year. Notably, our corpus was developed in parallel with UNSCon (Zaczynska et al., 2024) and contains 44 overlapping speeches, enabling joint analyses of argumentation structures and conflict discourse in diplomatic setting in future work.

Level	Total	Arg	Non-Arg	Claim	Premise
Sent.	4.765	4.105	660	2.081	2.024

Table 3: Distribution of argumentative types across sentences in the ArgUNSC.

Level	Total	Claim	Premise
Component	4.584	2.328	2.256

Table 4: Distribution of claim and premise components in the ArgUNSC.

During annotation, claims and premises were marked on a component level, following Haddadan et al. (2019). To identify and distinguish argument components, we initially relied on the guidelines provided by the authors of USElecDeb. We note that, as the genres are slightly different, we met several types of arguments that are specific to our data, which resulted in some annotation guideline extensions. In particular, diplomatic speeches focusing on military conflict often include *claims* that express the speaker nation's interpretation or evaluation of the current situation, their position on the actions of other parties, or proposals for conflict mitigation. Typical *premises* in this context involve references to concrete events or official documents. These statements frequently include details such as dates, actors involved, actions taken, and consequences observed, as illustrated in Example (2).

Level	Total	Support	Attack
Component	2.973	2.623	350

Table 5: Distribution of support/attack argumentative-component pairs in the ArgUNSC.

N premises	N components
no premise	640
one premise	1007
two premises	381
three premises	156
> three premises	144

Table 6: Distribution of the number of premises per one claim in the ArgUNSC corpus.

A *support* relation indicates that the premise provides a reason to believe the claim, as in Example (2), while an *attack* relation represents an opposing position—typically anticipating or addressing potential objections a hearer might raise, as shown in Example (3).

(2) United Kingdom, 2014:

[The situation in eastern Ukraine has continued to deteriorate]$_{\text{Claim}}$. [*Armed groups stormed the Prosecutor's office in Donetsk yesterday, further increasing the number of Government buildings occupied since the 17 April Geneva agreement*]$_{\text{Premise}}$

(3) China, 2014:

China notes that, [*since the signing of the Minsk agreements between the Ukrainian Government and eastern militias at the beginning of September, there have been no large-scale armed clashes in eastern Ukraine*]$_{\text{Premise}}$. However, **[the security situation on the ground still remains fragile with sporadic violent attacks in violation of the ceasefire agreement, causing casualties and damage**

to infrastructure]$_{\text{Claim}}$

We report statistics of the dataset for both sentence- and component levels. (Tables 3 and 4). Like in the USElecDeb corpus, we observe that claims slightly outnumber premises, which is not rare in political discourse, where speakers do not always provide premises to justify their claims.

We also note that, according to our guidelines, claims can relate to more than one premise at a time. Similarly, one premise may relate to one or more claims. In our corpus, we observe considerable variation in the number of premises per claim, ranging from none to more than three, as shown in Table 6. Regarding relations, as seen from the tables 2 and 5, in both UNSC speeches and presidential debates, premises predominantly support rather than attack claims, reflecting speakers' tendency to reinforce their position, no matter if one is speaking on behalf of a country or campaigning for the presidency.

Three annotators with backgrounds in computational linguistics participated in the annotation process. First, A1 and A2 collaboratively developed the annotation guidelines, using several test speeches to explore the intricacies of the corpus and iteratively refine the guidelines. After this pilot phase, A1 completed the full annotation of the corpus. Subsequently, A2 independently annotated 29 documents (excluding the test set), representing 20% of the corpus), labeling argumentative components as claims or premises. The annotation of argumentative relations (support/attack) was then performed by a third annotator (A3), who had access to the existing fixed component boundaries established by A2. The annotation process was carried out using the INCEpTION software (Klie et al., 2018).

Inter-annotator agreement (IAA) was measured using Cohen's κ statistic, calculated at the sentence level. First, we assessed whether annotators agreed on the sentence's argumentative status ($\kappa = 0.69$). Next, considering only sentences both annotators identified as argumentative, we measured agreement on whether the sentence contained a claim or a premise ($\kappa = 0.77$). To compute IAA for relations, we considered the sentence-pair level. Within each speech, we generated the set of all possible claim-premise pairs of sentences and calculate agreement on whether each pair is labeled as support, attack, or no relation ($\kappa = 0.68$). Thus, we report overall *substantial* agreement on argument component and relation annotation tasks (Artstein and Poesio, 2008). A1's labels serve as gold standard.

4 Methodology

4.1 Argument Mining Pipeline

Following Liu et al. (2023), we divide argumentation mining into the following four steps. We approach each step as a binary classification task, precisely formulated as follows.

Argumentative Component Segmentation (ACS). Given a sentence X, predict whether it *contains* an argumentative component (can be either a claim or a premise) or not.

Argumentative Component Classification (ACC). Given an argumentative sentence X, predict whether it *contains* a claim or a premise.

Argumentative Relation Identification (ARI). Given a pair of sentences (or components) (X, Y), the task is to predict whether X is argumentatively related to Y (as either support or attack), or not. For training, we randomly generate an equal number of unrelated pairs by sampling sentences (or components) from speeches in close temporal proximity—specifically, within eight speeches before or after the given speech—thereby ensuring comparable contextual conditions.

Argumentative Relation Classification (ARC). Given a pair of argumentatively related sentences *(or components)* (X, Y), predict whether X and Y are in a support or attack relationship.

All tasks are first performed at the sentence level. For ACS, a sentence is labeled argumentative if it contains at least one argumentative component—claim or premise. For ACC, since a sentence may contain both a claim and a premise, we follow Haddadan et al. (2019) and assign the label based on the longer component. For ARI and ARC, we consider a sentence pair (X, Y) as related if a component in X is linked to a component in Y. While the sentence-level setup is straightforward, we acknowledge that it may obscure information when multiple components appear in the same sentence. In our corpus, this happens in about 7% of cases, which poses particular challenges for relation-based tasks. Therefore, we also report component-level results for ARI and ARC.

4.2 Experimental Setup

We treat all tasks as sequence classification and fine-tune transformer-based encoders using the *bert-for-*

Evaluation	Label	Majority Vote F1	BERT P	BERT R	BERT F1	RoBERTa P	RoBERTa R	RoBERTa F1
IR–USElecDeb$_{sentence}$	Argument	0.810	0.877	0.939	0.907	0.883	0.945	0.913
	Not Argument	0.000	0.717	0.541	0.617	0.745	0.563	0.641
	Avg Macro	0.551	0.797	0.740	0.762	0.814	0.754	0.777
IR–ArgUNSC$_{sentence}$	Argument	0.926	0.936 ± 0.008	0.973 ± 0.008	0.954 ± 0.004	0.937 ± 0.008	0.978 ± 0.005	0.957 ± 0.004
	Not Argument	0.000	0.778 ± 0.043	0.586 ± 0.055	0.667 ± 0.038	0.810 ± 0.029	0.591 ± 0.056	0.682 ± 0.039
	Avg Macro	0.463	0.857 ± 0.022	0.780 ± 0.026	0.810 ± 0.021	0.874 ± 0.015	0.784 ± 0.027	0.819 ± 0.021
CR$_{sentence}$	Argument	0.926	0.916	0.980	0.947	0.930	0.965	0.947
	Not Argument	0.000	0.776	0.441	0.562	0.713	0.547	0.619
	Avg Macro	0.463	0.846	0.710	0.754	0.822	0.756	0.783

Table 7: F1-score for the majority vote baseline and Precision (P), Recall (R), and F1-scores for BERT and RoBERTa. Task: **Argumentative Component Segmentation (ACS)** in in-register and cross-register settings.

Evaluation	Label	Majority Vote F1	BERT P	BERT R	BERT F1	RoBERTa P	RoBERTa R	RoBERTa F1
IR–USElecDeb$_{sentence}$	Claim	0.677	0.671	0.754	0.710	0.660	0.806	0.726
	Premise	0.000	0.705	0.614	0.656	0.736	0.567	0.640
	Avg Weighted	0.346	0.688	0.685	0.684	0.698	0.689	0.684
IR–ArgUNSC$_{sentence}$	Claim	0.673	0.716 ± 0.006	0.850 ± 0.019	0.777 ± 0.006	0.757 ± 0.029	0.766 ± 0.027	0.761 ± 0.009
	Premise	0.000	0.809 ± 0.014	0.653 ± 0.028	0.722 ± 0.014	0.756 ± 0.014	0.745 ± 0.045	0.750 ± 0.020
	Avg Weighted	0.341	0.762 ± 0.006	0.753 ± 0.007	0.750 ± 0.008	0.757 ± 0.014	0.755 ± 0.014	0.755 ± 0.013
CR$_{sentence}$	Claim	0.673	0.698	0.801	0.746	0.719	0.772	0.745
	Premise	0.000	0.759	0.643	0.696	0.747	0.690	0.717
	Avg Weighted	0.341	0.728	0.723	0.721	0.733	0.732	0.731

Table 8: F1-score for the majority vote baseline and Precision (P), Recall (R), and F1-scores for BERT and RoBERTa. Task: **Argumentative Component Classification (ACC)** in in-register and cross-register settings.

sequence-classification framework[4], which builds on HuggingFace Transformers (Wolf et al., 2020). We use *bert-base-uncased* (Devlin et al., 2019) and *roberta-base* (Liu et al., 2019), both comprising 12 transformer layers with 12 attention heads each. A linear classification head is placed on top of the final hidden state. Models are trained using the Adam optimizer (Kingma and Ba, 2014) and negative log-likelihood loss. We compare performances of BERT and RoBERTa against a majority vote baseline, which always predicts the most frequent class.

Regarding training, we find that two epochs are optimal for fine-tuning on the large USElecDeb corpus across all tasks. In contrast, the smaller size of ArgUNSC benefits from longer training, and we fix the number of epochs between 6 and 8 for all cross-validation runs.

[4]`https://pypi.org/project/bert-for-sequence-classification/`

In addition to experimenting with encoder-only models like BERT and RoBERTa, we evaluate a GPT-4 LLM developed by OpenAI (OpenAI, 2023). We prompt GPT-4 under two conditions: zero-shot and few-shot. In the zero-shot setup, the model is given only task instructions without any labeled examples. In the few-shot setup, the prompt is augmented with three labeled examples per class. For instance, in the ACS task, the prompt includes three sentences labeled as arguments and three labeled as non-arguments to guide the model's classification.

4.3 Evaluation Setup

Our experiments are designed to evaluate model performance both within and across two corpora. We consider three main scenarios: (a) fine-tuning and testing on the large-scale USElecDeb corpus (serving as an in-register baseline), (b) fine-tuning and testing on the smaller ArgUNSC corpus, and (c) fine-tuning on USElecDeb and testing on Ar-

Evaluation	Label	Majority Vote F1	BERT P	BERT R	BERT F1	RoBERTa P	RoBERTa R	RoBERTa F1
IR–USElecDeb$_{sentence}$	Relation	0.666	0.696	0.824	0.755	0.754	0.876	0.810
	No Relation	0.000	0.785	0.640	0.705	0.852	0.714	0.777
	Avg Weighted	0.333	0.741	0.732	0.730	0.803	0.795	0.794
IR–ArgUNSC$_{sentence}$	Relation	0.667	0.664 ± 0.023	0.738 ± 0.048	0.697 ± 0.011	0.698 ± 0.022	0.774 ± 0.031	0.733 ± 0.007
	No Relation	0.000	0.706 ± 0.020	0.623 ± 0.061	0.659 ± 0.028	0.747 ± 0.013	0.662 ± 0.048	0.700 ± 0.023
	Avg Weighted	0.333	0.685 ± 0.008	0.680 ± 0.009	0.678 ± 0.011	0.722 ± 0.008	0.718 ± 0.011	0.717 ± 0.012
IR–ArgUNSC$_{component}$	Relation	0.670	0.642 ± 0.009	0.712 ± 0.040	0.675 ± 0.019	0.708 ± 0.009	0.741 ± 0.062	0.723 ± 0.025
	No Relation	0.000	0.678 ± 0.024	0.603 ± 0.027	0.637 ± 0.011	0.732 ± 0.043	0.693 ± 0.036	0.710 ± 0.006
	Avg Weighted	0.335	0.660 ± 0.014	0.657 ± 0.012	0.656 ± 0.011	0.720 ± 0.019	0.717 ± 0.014	0.717 ± 0.013
CR$_{sentence}$	Relation	0.667	0.541	0.922	0.682	0.536	0.960	0.688
	No Relation	0.000	0.738	0.219	0.338	0.808	0.169	0.279
	Avg Weighted	0.333	0.640	0.571	0.510	0.672	0.564	0.484

Table 9: F1-score for the majority vote baseline and Precision (P), Recall (R), and F1-scores for BERT and RoBERTa. Task: **Argumentative Relation Identification (ARI)** in in-register and cross-register settings on both sentence and component levels.

gUNSC to evaluate cross-register generalization ability of models. Hereinafter, we adopt the **IR** abbreviation for the *in-register* experiments and **CR** for the *cross-register* ones.

For all experiments involving USElecDeb, we use the official training and testing splits provided by the authors. In the CR setting, we fine-tune the models on the USElecDeb training set and evaluate on the full ArgUNSC corpus. For IR experiments on ArgUNSC, we follow a 5-fold stratified cross-validation protocol and report mean and standard deviation. GPT-4 setups are evaluated using the entire ArgUNSC.

Across all IR and CR settings, and for both encoder-based models and LLMs, each of the four stages in the argument mining pipeline is evaluated using gold standard labels, without propagating errors from one step to the next.

5 Results and Discussion

5.1 In- and Cross-Register Performance

Table 7 presents IR and CR results on the **Argumentative Component Segmentation (ACS)** task. First, we observe that in-register (IR) performance for both ArgUNSC and USElecDeb is moderately high, with RoBERTa approaching an F1 score of 0.8, indicating that argument segmentation (ACS) is a fairly solvable task in both corpora, even with class imbalance. We also note that, with per-class F1 scores of 0.913 and 0.641, our RoBERTa model performs competitively compared to the LSTM predictions reported in Haddadan et al. (2019), which are 0.913 and 0.547, respectively. In the cross-register (CR) setting, RoBERTa achieves an F1 score of 0.783, which—when compared to the strong majority vote baselines in IR and CR—suggests robust generalization, both overall and at the class level. BERT follows a similar pattern, showing solid cross-register performance, although RoBERTa consistently outperforms it across all setups.

Results for the **Argumentative Component Classification (ACC)** task are shown in Table 8. First, we again note a competitive performance of our RoBERTa (0.684) compared to Haddadan et al. (2019)'s LSTM (0.673). Generally, while performance in both IR and CR settings hovers around the 0.7 F1 mark, there is a consistent drop compared to ACS, reflecting the higher complexity of component type classification. Nevertheless, both BERT and RoBERTa generalize remarkably well: in the CR setup, they achieve F1 scores of 0.721 and 0.731 accordingly, surpassing even their IR performance on USElecDeb. This suggests that the conceptual distinction between claims and premises is relatively stable across the two political speech genres.

Argumentative Relation Identification (ARI) results are summarized in Table 9. In the IR set-

Evaluation	Label	Majority Vote F1	BERT P	BERT R	BERT F1	RoBERTa P	RoBERTa R	RoBERTa F1
IR–USElecDeb$_{\text{sentence}}$	Support	0.919	0.890	0.970	0.929	0.908	0.954	0.931
	Attack	0.000	0.658	0.326	0.436	0.639	0.456	0.532
	Avg Macro	0.459	0.774	0.648	0.682	0.773	0.705	0.731
IR–ArgUNSC$_{\text{sentence}}$	Support	0.937	0.918 ± 0.008	0.973 ± 0.006	0.944 ± 0.003	0.937 ± 0.014	0.958 ± 0.016	0.947 ± 0.005
	Attack	0.000	0.628 ± 0.039	0.349 ± 0.075	0.444 ± 0.068	0.630 ± 0.047	0.511 ± 0.126	0.551 ± 0.049
	Avg Macro	0.469	0.773 ± 0.022	0.661 ± 0.035	0.694 ± 0.035	0.783 ± 0.021	0.735 ± 0.057	0.749 ± 0.031
IR–ArgUNSC$_{\text{component}}$	Support	0.936	0.925 ± 0.006	0.974 ± 0.007	0.949 ± 0.003	0.943 ± 0.009	0.973 ± 0.010	0.958 ± 0.003
	Attack	0.000	0.673 ± 0.060	0.399 ± 0.055	0.497 ± 0.044	0.741 ± 0.065	0.548 ± 0.075	0.624 ± 0.040
	Avg Macro	0.468	0.799 ± 0.029	0.686 ± 0.026	0.723 ± 0.023	0.842 ± 0.030	0.761 ± 0.034	0.791 ± 0.021
CR$_{\text{sentence}}$	Support	0.937	0.884	0.994	0.936	0.895	0.982	0.937
	Attack	0.000	0.320	0.023	0.043	0.511	0.137	0.216
	Avg Macro	0.469	0.602	0.508	0.489	0.703	0.560	0.576

Table 10: F1-score for the majority vote baseline and Precision (P), Recall (R), and F1-scores for BERT and RoBERTa. Task: **Argumentative Relation Classification (ARC)** in in-register and cross-register settings on both sentence and component levels.

tings, models perform reasonably well, with F1 scores surpassing 0.79 on RoBERTa—comparable to or even exceeding results from ACC, despite ARI typically being considered the more complex task.

In contrast, cross-register generalization (CR) reveals a substantial performance drop: the weighted F1 score decreases to 0.484 for RoBERTa and 0.510 for BERT. Notably, the model barely improves over the majority vote baseline for the Relation class. A likely explanation lies in the structural differences between corpora. In the USElecDeb corpus, argumentative relations are annotated not only between premises and claims but also between claims and between premises. This variation likely introduces noise and confuses the model at inference time.

We also report component-level results for ARI, where we expected a performance gain due to more granular inputs. However, the results remain on par with the sentence-level setting.

Argumentative Relation Classification (ARC) results are reported in Table 10. In the IR settings, both models perform well, but RoBERTa proves to be more competitive. We note that Attack relations remain substantially harder than Support relations, consistently showing F1 scores below 0.65 – even IR.

The CR scenario further highlights this difficulty. While Support generalizes well (0.937 F1 with RoBERTa), Attack F1 drops to 0.216, pulling the macro average down to 0.576 on RoBERTa. These results suggest that although positive argumentative relations transfer reliably across registers, adversarial patterns (e.g., attacks) are less stable.

Component-level results show slightly improved performance compared to sentence-level, with a more pronounced benefit for ARC than ARI. This is likely because fine-grained component boundaries benefit the task of distinguishing relation polarity (support vs. attack) more than the task of relation existence detection.

General findings can be summarized as follows. First, RoBERTa consistently outperforms BERT across all tasks and evaluation settings (with the only notable exception of ARI in cross-register setting), confirming its superior contextual representation capabilities for argumentative language. Second, among the four tasks, ACS emerges as the easiest in the IR setting, likely due to the presence of clear lexical markers. In contrast, ARC proves to be the most challenging, as it demands nuanced modeling of argument polarity. Third, for ARC, moving from sentence- to component-level modeling substantially improves performance, particularly in the ArgUNSC IR setting. RoBERTa achieves near 0.80 F1, underscoring the value of increased granularity in argumentative polarity classification. Finally, regarding generalization, the best transfer is observed for ACC and ACS. ARC ex-

Task	IR	CR	GPT-4 zero	GPT-4 few
ACS	0.819	0.783	0.652	0.767
ACC	0.755	0.733	0.683	0.706
ARI	0.717	0.484	0.594	0.562
ARC	0.749	0.576	0.636	0.639

Table 11: F1 scores (average macro for tasks ACS and ARC and average weighted for tasks ACC and ARI) for GPT-4-prompting methods compared with the IR and CR predictions (RoBERTa).

hibits moderate robustness, suggesting that relation polarity (e.g., support vs. attack) transfers more reliably than the identification of whether a relation exists at all. ARI remains the most difficult to generalize, potentially due to cross-register differences in density, directionality, and linking strategies in underlying argument structure graphs.

5.2 Comparison to GPT-4 models

Table 11 presents the results of zero-shot and few-shot prompting using the GPT-4 model across the four core argument mining tasks on ArgUNSC dataset. Overall, GPT-4 underperforms compared to fine-tuned RoBERTa models in all IR and half of the CR scenarios. The gap is particularly pronounced in tasks ACS (0.819 IR and 0.783 CR vs. 0.767 few-shot) and ACC (0.755 IR and 0.733 CR vs 0.706 few-shot). On ARI and ARC, zero- and few-shot prompting outperforms the CR setup, but it still falls short of IR-fine-tuned RoBERTa on these tasks with.

This may be because fine-tuned BERT-based models are directly adapted to the domain, register and context intricacies of the dataset, while prompting alone often fails to capture such subtleties—especially for complex discourse tasks like argumentative relation detection in political speech. Fine-tuning large open-weight models such as LLaMA (Touvron et al., 2023) or Mistral (Jiang et al., 2023) could address this gap.

6 Conclusion

Our work presents a comprehensive study of cross-register generalization in argument mining within political discourse. We introduce ArgUNSC, a new manually annotated corpus of UN Security Council speeches, and benchmark four core AM tasks.

We acknowledge several limitations. The study is restricted to the English language and two political registers. Further, our sentence-level setup simplifies structures in multi-component sentences,—future work may explore more fine-grained approaches, such as token-level prediction.

In the future, we plan to conduct a qualitative error analysis to identify which register-specific differences contribute to model failures in ARI and ARC.

Beyond its value for argument mining pipelines, ArgUNSC also opens new avenues for political science research, such as analyzing how nations justify their own or foreign policies and rhetorically align with allies or opponents.

Reproducibility

The new ArgUNSC dataset, annotation guidelines and Python scripts can be found at: `https://github.com/mpoiaganova/political-argument-mining`

Acknowledgements

The work was supported by the Deutsche Forschungsgemeinschaft (DFG), project (448421482) "Trajectories of Conflict: The Dynamics of Argumentation in the UN Security Council“.

We thank Costanza Rasi, Dietmar Benndorf, and Karolina Zaczynska for their support with data annotation and corpus preparation.

References

Yamen Ajjour, Wei-Fan Chen, Johannes Kiesel, Henning Wachsmuth, and Benno Stein. 2017. Unit segmentation of argumentative texts. In *4th Workshop on Argumentation Mining*, pages 118–128.

Ron Artstein and Massimo Poesio. 2008. Inter-coder agreement for computational linguistics. *Computational linguistics*, 34(4):555–596.

Nico Blokker, Erenay Dayanik, Gabriella Lapesa, and Sebastian Padó. 2020. Swimming with the tide? positional claim detection across political text types. In *Proceedings of the Fourth Workshop on Natural Language Processing and Computational Social Science*, pages 24–34, Online. Association for Computational Linguistics.

Jérémie Cabessa, Hugo Hernault, and Umer Mushtaq. 2025. Argument mining with fine-tuned large language models. In *Proceedings of the 31st International Conference on Computational Linguistics*, pages 6624–6635, Abu Dhabi, UAE. Association for Computational Linguistics.

Tuhin Chakrabarty, Christopher Hidey, Smaranda Muresan, Kathy McKeown, and Alyssa Hwang. 2019. AMPERSAND: Argument mining for PERSuAsive oNline discussions. In *Proceedings of the 2019 Conference on Empirical Methods in Natural Language Processing and the 9th International Joint Conference on Natural Language Processing (EMNLP-IJCNLP)*, pages 2933–2943, Hong Kong, China. Association for Computational Linguistics.

Guizhen Chen, Liying Cheng, Anh Tuan Luu, and Lidong Bing. 2024. Exploring the potential of large language models in computational argumentation. In *Proceedings of the 62nd Annual Meeting of the Association for Computational Linguistics (Volume 1: Long Papers)*, pages 2309–2330, Bangkok, Thailand. Association for Computational Linguistics.

Liying Cheng, Lidong Bing, Ruidan He, Qian Yu, Yan Zhang, and Luo Si. 2022. IAM: A comprehensive and large-scale dataset for integrated argument mining tasks. In *Proceedings of the 60th Annual Meeting of the Association for Computational Linguistics (Volume 1: Long Papers)*, pages 2277–2287, Dublin, Ireland. Association for Computational Linguistics.

Johannes Daxenberger, Steffen Eger, Ivan Habernal, Christian Stab, and Iryna Gurevych. 2017. What is the essence of a claim? cross-domain claim identification. In *Proceedings of the 2017 Conference on Empirical Methods in Natural Language Processing*, pages 2055–2066, Copenhagen, Denmark. Association for Computational Linguistics.

Jacob Devlin, Ming-Wei Chang, Kenton Lee, and Kristina Toutanova. 2019. Bert: Pre-training of deep bidirectional transformers for language understanding. In *Proceedings of the 2019 conference of the North American chapter of the association for computational linguistics: human language technologies, volume 1 (long and short papers)*, pages 4171–4186.

Lucile Favero, Juan Antonio Pérez-Ortiz, Tanja Käser, and Nuria Oliver. 2025. Leveraging small llms for argument mining in education: Argument component identification, classification, and assessment. *arXiv preprint arXiv:2502.14389*.

Marc Feger and Stefan Dietze. 2024. TACO – Twitter arguments from COnversations. In *Proceedings of the 2024 Joint International Conference on Computational Linguistics, Language Resources and Evaluation (LREC-COLING 2024)*, pages 15522–15529, Torino, Italia. ELRA and ICCL.

Debela Gemechu, Ramon Ruiz-Dolz, and Chris Reed. 2024. Aries: A general benchmark for argument relation identification. In *11th Workshop on Argument Mining, ArgMining 2024*, pages 1–14. Association for Computational Linguistics (ACL).

Pierpaolo Goffredo, Shohreh Haddadan, Vorakit Vorakitphan, Elena Cabrio, and Serena Villata. 2022. Fallacious argument classification in political debates. In *Thirty-First International Joint Conference on Artificial Intelligence {IJCAI-22}*, pages 4143–4149. International Joint Conferences on Artificial Intelligence Organization.

Deniz Gorur, Antonio Rago, and Francesca Toni. 2025. Can large language models perform relation-based argument mining? In *Proceedings of the 31st International Conference on Computational Linguistics*, pages 8518–8534, Abu Dhabi, UAE. Association for Computational Linguistics.

Ivan Habernal, Daniel Faber, Nicola Recchia, Sebastian Bretthauer, Iryna Gurevych, Indra Spiecker genannt Döhmann, and Christoph Burchard. 2024. Mining legal arguments in court decisions. *Artificial Intelligence and Law*, 32(3):1–38.

Shohreh Haddadan, Elena Cabrio, and Serena Villata. 2019. Yes, we can! mining arguments in 50 years of US presidential campaign debates. In *Proceedings of the 57th Annual Meeting of the Association for Computational Linguistics*, pages 4684–4690, Florence, Italy. Association for Computational Linguistics.

Dieuwke Hupkes, Mario Giulianelli, Verna Dankers, Mikel Artetxe, Yanai Elazar, Tiago Pimentel, Christos Christodoulopoulos, Karim Lasri, Naomi Saphra, Arabella Sinclair, et al. 2023. A taxonomy and review of generalization research in nlp. *Nature Machine Intelligence*, 5(10):1161–1174.

Albert Q. Jiang, Alexandre Sablayrolles, Arthur Mensch, Chris Bamford, Devendra Singh Chaplot, Diego de las Casas, Florian Bressand, Gianna Lengyel, Guillaume Lample, Lucile Saulnier, Lélio Renard Lavaud, Marie-Anne Lachaux, Pierre Stock, Teven Le Scao, Thibaut Lavril, Thomas Wang, Timothée Lacroix, and William El Sayed. 2023. Mistral 7b. *Preprint*, arXiv:2310.06825.

Diederik P Kingma and Jimmy Ba. 2014. Adam: A method for stochastic optimization. *arXiv preprint arXiv:1412.6980*.

Jan-Christoph Klie, Michael Bugert, Beto Boullosa, Richard Eckart De Castilho, and Iryna Gurevych. 2018. The inception platform: Machine-assisted and knowledge-oriented interactive annotation. In *Proceedings of the 27th international conference on computational linguistics: system demonstrations*, pages 5–9.

Marco Lippi and Paolo Torroni. 2016a. Argument mining from speech: Detecting claims in political debates. In *Proceedings of the AAAI conference on artificial intelligence*, volume 30.

Marco Lippi and Paolo Torroni. 2016b. Margot: A web server for argumentation mining. *Expert Systems with Applications*, 65:292–303.

Boyang Liu, Viktor Schlegel, Riza Batista-Navarro, and Sophia Ananiadou. 2023. Argument mining as a multi-hop generative machine reading comprehension task. In *Findings of the Association for Computational Linguistics: EMNLP 2023*, pages 10846–10858, Singapore. Association for Computational Linguistics.

Yinhan Liu, Myle Ott, Naman Goyal, Jingfei Du, Mandar Joshi, Danqi Chen, Omer Levy, Mike Lewis, Luke Zettlemoyer, and Veselin Stoyanov. 2019. Roberta: A robustly optimized bert pretraining approach. *arXiv preprint arXiv:1907.11692*.

Stefano Menini, Elena Cabrio, Sara Tonelli, and Serena Villata. 2018. Never retreat, never retract: Argumentation analysis for political speeches. In *Proceedings of the AAAI Conference on Artificial Intelligence*, volume 32.

Rafael Mestre, Razvan Milicin, Stuart E. Middleton, Matt Ryan, Jiatong Zhu, and Timothy J. Norman. 2021. M-arg: Multimodal argument mining dataset for political debates with audio and transcripts. In *Proceedings of the 8th Workshop on Argument Mining*, pages 78–88, Punta Cana, Dominican Republic. Association for Computational Linguistics.

OpenAI. 2023. Gpt-4 technical report.

Ramon Ruiz-Dolz and John Lawrence. 2023. Detecting argumentative fallacies in the wild: Problems and limitations of large language models. In *Proceedings of the 10th Workshop on Argument Mining*. Association for Computational Linguistics.

Robin Schaefer, René Knaebel, and Manfred Stede. 2022. On selecting training corpora for cross-domain claim detection. In *Proceedings of the 9th workshop on argument mining*, pages 181–186.

Mirco Schönfeld, Steffen Eckhard, Ronny Patz, and Hilde Van Meegdenburg. 2019. The un security council debates 1995-2017. *arXiv preprint arXiv:1906.10969*.

Noam Slonim, Yonatan Bilu, Carlos Alzate, Roy Bar-Haim, Ben Bogin, Francesca Bonin, Leshem Choshen, Edo Cohen-Karlik, Lena Dankin, Lilach Edelstein, et al. 2021. An autonomous debating system. *Nature*, 591(7850):379–384.

Ekaterina Sviridova, Anar Yeginbergen, Ainara Estarrona, Elena Cabrio, Serena Villata, and Rodrigo Agerri. 2024. CasiMedicos-arg: A medical question answering dataset annotated with explanatory argumentative structures. In *Proceedings of the 2024 Conference on Empirical Methods in Natural Language Processing*, pages 18463–18475, Miami, Florida, USA. Association for Computational Linguistics.

Hugo Touvron, Louis Martin, Kevin Stone, Peter Albert, Amjad Almahairi, Yasmine Babaei, Nikolay Bashlykov, Soumya Batra, Prajjwal Bhargava, Shruti Bhosale, et al. 2023. Llama 2: Open foundation and fine-tuned chat models. *arXiv preprint arXiv:2307.09288*.

Jacky Visser, Barbara Konat, Rory Duthie, Marcin Koszowy, Katarzyna Budzynska, and Chris Reed. 2020. Argumentation in the 2016 us presidential elections: annotated corpora of television debates and social media reaction. *Language Resources and Evaluation*, 54(1):123–154.

Thiemo Wambsganss, Tobias Kueng, Matthias Soellner, and Jan Marco Leimeister. 2021. Arguetutor: An adaptive dialog-based learning system for argumentation skills. In *Proceedings of the 2021 CHI conference on human factors in computing systems*, pages 1–13.

Thomas Wolf, Lysandre Debut, Victor Sanh, Julien Chaumond, Clement Delangue, Anthony Moi, Pierric Cistac, Tim Rault, Remi Louf, Morgan Funtowicz, Joe Davison, Sam Shleifer, Patrick von Platen, Clara Ma, Yacine Jernite, Julien Plu, Canwen Xu, Teven Le Scao, Sylvain Gugger, Mariama Drame, Quentin Lhoest, and Alexander Rush. 2020. Transformers: State-of-the-art natural language processing. In *Proceedings of the 2020 Conference on Empirical Methods in Natural Language Processing: System Demonstrations*, pages 38–45, Online. Association for Computational Linguistics.

Karolina Zaczynska, Peter Bourgonje, and Manfred Stede. 2024. How diplomats dispute: The un security council conflict corpus. In *Proceedings of the 2024 Joint International Conference on Computational Linguistics, Language Resources and Evaluation (LREC-COLING 2024)*, pages 8173–8183.

A ArgUNSC Descriptive Statistics

Year	Speeches
2014	93
2015	27
2016	11
2017	7
2018	6

Table 12: Number of speeches per year

Country	Speeches
Russia	25
Ukraine	16
United States	15
United Kingdom	11
France	11
China	11
Lithuania	8
Australia	7
Rwanda	6
The Republic of Korea	6
Luxembourg	5
Argentina	4
Chile	4
Nigeria	3
Jordan	2
Sweden	1
Ethiopia	1
Angola	1
Belgium	1
New Zealand	1
Venezuela	1
Spain	1
Chad	1
Indonesia	1
UNSC Briefing	1

Table 13: Number of speeches per country

Storytelling in Argumentative Discussions: Exploring the Use of Narratives in ChangeMyView

Sara Nabhani **Khalid Al-Khatib** **Federico Pianzola** **Malvina Nissim**

University of Groningen
{s.nabhani,khalid.alkhatib,f.pianzola,m.nissim}@rug.nl

Abstract

Psychological research has long suggested that storytelling can shape beliefs and behaviors by fostering emotional engagement and narrative transportation. However, it remains unclear whether these effects extend to online argumentative discourse. In this paper, we examine the role of narrative in real-world argumentation using discussions from the *ChangeMyView* subreddit. Leveraging an automatic story detection model, we analyze how narrative use varies across persuasive comments, user types, discussion outcomes, and the kinds of change being sought. While narrative appears more frequently in some contexts, it is not consistently linked to successful persuasion. Notably, highly persuasive users tend to use narrative less, and storytelling does not demonstrate increased effectiveness for any specific type of persuasive goals. These findings suggest that narrative may play a limited and context-dependent role in online discussions, highlighting the need for computational models of argumentation to account for rhetorical diversity.

1 Introduction

Argumentation is a key form of communication in online spaces, where people often try to justify their beliefs, challenge others' opinions, or persuade readers to reconsider their views. Research in computational argumentation has predominantly focused on identifying argumentative components (Lawrence and Reed, 2019), evaluating argument quality (Wachsmuth et al., 2024), and generating arguments automatically (Saha and Srihari, 2023). However, effective persuasion, arguably one of the primary goals of argumentation, often extends beyond logical structure, relying on rhetorical strategies such as framing, emotional appeal, and narrative (Nabi and Green, 2015). Among these strategies, narrative remains relatively underexplored in existing computational approaches.

In social sciences, narrative has been extensively studied as a persuasive strategy. A substantial body of research highlights the role of narrative transportation in enhancing persuasive effects (Fitzgerald and Green, 2017). Narrative transportation refers to the psychological process through which individuals become deeply immersed in a story, experiencing it as if it were unfolding around them. This immersion has been shown to reduce counterarguing, increase identification with characters, and render arguments more natural and emotionally resonant. As a result, narrative emerges as a powerful tool for influencing beliefs, attitudes, intentions, and behaviors. While these effects are well-documented in controlled experimental settings (de Graaf et al., 2016; van Laer et al., 2013) and across applied domains such as education (Green, 2004), law (Mazzocco, 2011), and public health (Huang and Green, 2022; de Graaf et al., 2016), it remains unclear whether similar persuasive mechanisms operate in everyday online discourse, where users engage in informal and often unstructured debates across a wide range of topics.

Building on these insights from the social sciences, this paper investigates the role of *narrative* in online argumentation through a large-scale empirical analysis of discussions from the *ChangeMyView* (CMV) subreddit. Our goal is to examine whether the use of narrative in this context reflects the persuasive patterns established in prior research, and to better understand its association with successful persuasion. We adopt a computational approach, leveraging predictions from a story detection model trained on Reddit data to identify narrative across thousands of CMV discussions. We then conduct a series of analyses to explore how narrative presence correlates with *persuasion outcomes* (e.g., successful), *user argumentation skill* (e.g., average), and *targeted change type* (e.g., attitude). The analyses showed that while narrative is not strongly predictive of persuasive success at

Proceedings of the 12th Argument Mining Workshop, pages 217–227
July 31, 2025 ©2025 Association for Computational Linguistics

the comment or user level, its frequent appearance suggests that it still plays a meaningful role in how users frame and express arguments.

This type of analysis is important for bridging theoretical and applied perspectives on narrative persuasion. It enables us to empirically test assumptions from narrative theory within real-world, user-generated discourse, offering insights into how storytelling functions as a rhetorical strategy in everyday argumentative practice. More broadly, this work contributes to the advancement of argument mining by extending its scope beyond logical structure to include richer rhetorical dimensions, such as narrative, that shape how arguments are constructed and received.

2 Related Work

Narratives have been widely studied in social science as a tool for persuasion, but their role in computational models of argumentation has received less attention. Recent efforts, however, have begun to bridge this gap by modeling narrative in argumentative contexts.

Falk and Lapesa (2023) introduce *StoryARG*, a multi-layer annotated corpus that captures both narrative and argumentative dimensions of stories. The corpus includes annotations for narrative elements (e.g., protagonist type, narrative proximity) and argumentative properties (e.g., claim, stance, effectiveness). Stories were collected from *ChangeMyView* (Egawa et al., 2019), *RegulatingRooms* (Park and Cardie, 2018), *Europolis* (Gerber et al., 2018), and *NYT* comments. The argumentative effectiveness of the stories was evaluated through four annotators' ratings of how persuasive each story was. Their findings suggest that stories proposing solutions tend to be rated as more effective, and that narratives with certain structural properties (e.g. longer text, first-person perspective) are perceived as more persuasive. However, the persuasiveness here is measured via the annotators' perception rather than real-world behavioral outcomes, and the dataset remains relatively small.

In a follow-up to their earlier work, Falk and Lapesa (2024) study the role of storytelling in online discourse during the COVID-19 pandemic, focusing on how users use personal experiences and narratives in socially tense discussions. Using Reddit data from multiple subreddits, including *ChangeMyView*, they apply the *StoryARG* framework to automatically detect storytelling spans and classify them by narrative type and argumentative function. The study finds that different types of stories are used in distinct argumentative contexts: personal narratives are common in discussions around social distancing, harm disclosure stories often appear in environmental and social issues threads, solution-oriented stories dominate in homeschooling debates, and background-setting narratives are especially prevalent in conversations involving conspiracy theories. However, their study does not evaluate the persuasive impact of the stories.

Antoniak et al. (2024) present *StorySeeker*, a toolkit and classifer for detecting narrative spans in online dicourse. Using a RoBERTa-based model (Liu et al., 2019) fine-tuned on Reddit data, they predict storytelling presence across 1,000 samples from 291 subreddits, showing that narrative is a widespread communicative strategy with over 50% of texts containing stories, with higher prevalence in subreddits centered on personal experience and lower rates in abstract or analytical domains. In a focused case study on ChangeMyView, they apply their model alongside topic modeling to examine where and how stories are used in persuasive discourse. They find that topics related to lifestyle and personal decisions tend to receive more storytelling, while abstract topics such as economics receive less. However, they also observe that the presence of narrative does not strongly correlate with persuasive success across topics. Our work complements these studies by taking a broader perspective, examining how narrative use relates to persuasion outcomes at scale using behavioral signals like CMV delta awards.

3 Data

Exploring the role of narrative in argumentation requires a source where narrative use is both likely and observable within argumentative discourse. One prominent source of publicly available data for such analysis is the *ChangeMyView* (CMV) subreddit.[1] CMV is an online discussion forum where users post a viewpoint on a given topic and invite others to challenge it. CMV is designed to promote open, thoughtful conversations in which participants are encouraged to reconsider their stances in response to sound counterarguments.

To indicate when persuasion has occurred, CMV employs a delta system. When a commenter successfully changes the mind of the original poster

[1] `https://www.reddit.com/r/changemyview`

Statistic	Value
Total posts	20,436
Unique original posters (OPs)	13,704
Total comments	1,017,724
Awarded deltas	11,643
Avg. deltas per post	0.5697
Avg. comments per post	49.9619
Avg. unique participants per post	23.7417

Table 1: Summary statistics of the *ChangeMyView* dataset after preprocessing.

(OP) or another participant, the person whose view was changed responds with a delta symbol (Δ). We treat the presence of a delta as an explicit signal that a comment was persuasive. An example of a CMV thread and delta interaction is shown in Figure 1.

CMV hosts a diverse range of discussion topics from everyday issues and personal decisions to political, ethical, and philosophical debates. This diversity makes it a valuable resource for studying how people, often without formal training in debate, engage in argumentation, persuasion, and opinion expression through various rhetorical strategies, including the use of narrative.

For this study, we use the CMV corpus built by Tan et al. (2016), which comprises all CMV threads posted between January 2013 and August 2015. Although the corpus is split into training and held-out subsets, we include both in our analysis.

Prior to the analysis (see Section 5), we applied several preprocessing steps to clean the dataset. We removed all empty comments and those marked as deleted by the system, as they lack textual content. We also excluded threads created by moderators or system accounts, which typically serve administrative or community-oriented purposes such as gathering feedback, announcing new features, or outlining policy changes, and do not represent authentic attempts to present or defend a personal view. Summary statistics of the final dataset are provided in Table1.

4 Analysis Method

We conduct our study to analyze the use of narrative in CMV discussions by following a structured methodology. First, we employ a computational model to detect the presence of narrative elements in CMV posts and comments. Next, we categorize these texts based on key criteria such as persuasion outcome, the argumentation skills of the author, and the type of change being targeted. We then apply our identification model to each group to examine the presence, frequency, and intensity of narrative use across these different contexts. Finally, we synthesize our findings to draw informed conclusions about the role and patterns of narrative in CMV interactions.

4.1 Narrative Identification Method

To identify the presence of narrative in CMV posts and comments, we use the story detection model introduced as part of the *StorySeeker* toolkit[2] by Antoniak et al. (2024).

The model is based on a RoBERTa-base language model (Liu et al., 2019), fine-tuned on a dataset of Reddit posts sampled from the Webis-TLDR-17 Reddit corpus (Völske et al., 2017). The training data was annotated by two expert annotators, who labeled whether each post contained storytelling, as well as the specific spans that formed the narrative, using the definition of a story as "a sequence of events involving one or more people" provided in the annotation guideline (Antoniak et al., 2024).

The model was trained as a binary classifier to distinguish between texts that contain storytelling and those that do not. On the expert-annotated test set, it achieved strong performance: an F1 score of 0.86 for the *story* class and 0.88 for the *non-story* class. These scores were averaged across five cross-validation folds and demonstrated low variance, indicating the model's stability and reliability. In addition to Reddit-based evaluation, the model was tested on several non-Reddit datasets. Despite domain differences, it maintained strong performance, showing good generalizability across various text types and topics.

We selected this model due to its high performance and close alignment with our data domain. Since both the training corpus and our target dataset for analysis are drawn from Reddit, the language style, tone, and structure are closely matched. This domain similarity, combined with the model's demonstrated effectiveness, makes it particularly well-suited for detecting narrative content in *ChangeMyView* arguments.

[2]https://huggingface.co/mariaantoniak/storyseeker

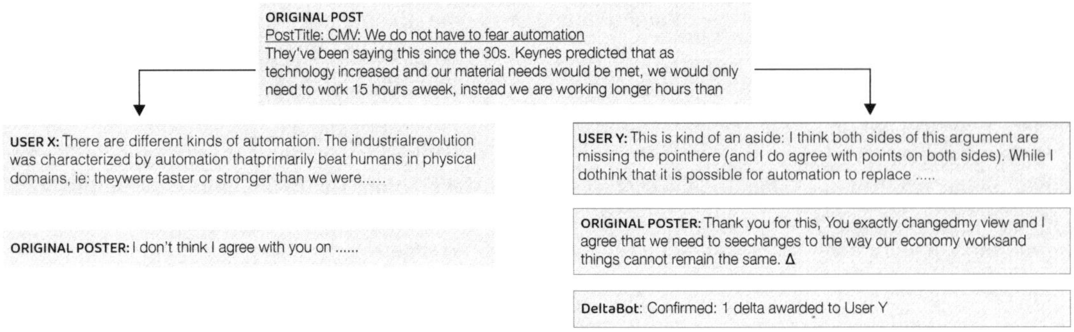

Figure 1: An example CMV discussion thread. The original poster (OP) expresses a belief, and other users respond. The green comment is the one that received a delta, indicating it successfully changed the OP's view. The red comment is the OP's response awarding the delta. The blue comment is an automatic confirmation from DeltaBot, Reddit's system for tracking awarded deltas.

5 Analyses and Results

Using the narrative predictions generated by the *StorySeeker* model, we conduct an analysis of how narrative is employed in argumentation on *ChangeMyView*. Our investigation spans multiple levels including the comment level, user level, and discussion level to uncover broader patterns in narrative usage. Specifically, we examine: (1) the relationship between narrative and comment-level persuasiveness, (2) variations in narrative use based on debater effectiveness, and (3) shifts in narrative use across different types of targeted change. The following subsections detail our analytical approach and provide a discussion of the findings.

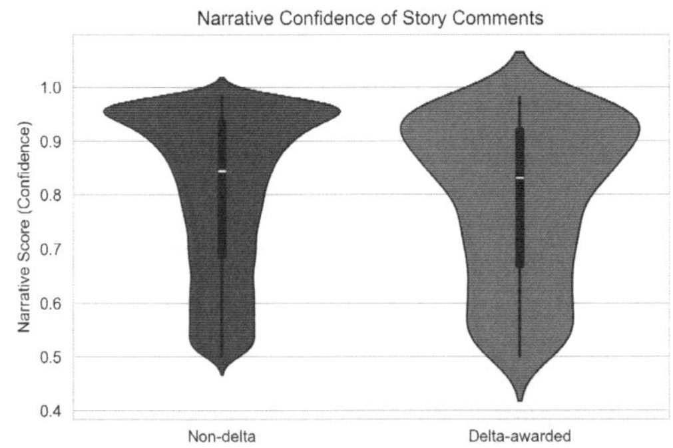

Figure 2: Narrative confidence scores for comments labeled as *story*, grouped by whether the comment received a delta.

5.1 Narrative Use in Persuasive Comments

Our first analysis is conducted at the comment level, investigating whether persuasive comments (i.e., those that received a delta) are more likely to contain narrative elements than non-persuasive ones. This provides a direct means of assessing the potential relationship between storytelling and persuasive success in CMV argumentation. To address this question, we employ the binary predictions of the *StorySeeker* model to classify each comment in the CMV discussions as either narrative or non-narrative. We then compare the proportion of narrative comments between two groups: those that received a delta and those that did not. In addition, we examine the degree of narrativity among comments labeled as *story*, using the model's confidence scores as a proxy for narrative strength.

Results: Our findings reveal that 5.06% of delta-awarded comments are labeled as narrative, compared to 4.63% of non-delta comments. This indicates that storytelling is slightly more prevalent in persuasive arguments. To assess the significance of this difference, we conduct a chi-square test of independence, which yields a statistically significant result ($p = 0.0384 < 0.05$). However, the effect size, measured using Cramér's V, is very small ($V = 0.0025$), suggesting a weak association between narrative presence and persuasive outcome. Table 2 presents the distribution of both groups across the full dataset.

The results also show that non-delta comments have a slightly higher average narrative score ($M = 0.8048$, $SD = 0.1444$) than delta-awarded comments ($M = 0.7914$, $SD = 0.1459$). A Mann–Whitney U test indicated that this difference is statistically significant ($p = 0.0183 < 0.05$), with a very small effect size ($Rank - Biserial\ Correlation = 0.0598$). Figure 2 shows the distribution of narrative confidence scores across the two groups.

Comment Type	Narrative		Non-narrative		Total	
	Count	%	Count	%	Count	%
Delta-awarded	525	0.05%	9,844	0.97%	10,369	1.02%
Non-delta	46,628	4.58%	960,727	94.40%	1,007,355	98.98%
Total	47,153	4.63%	970,571	95.37%	1,017,724	100.00%

Table 2: Distribution of narrative and non-narrative comments across delta-awarded and non-delta comments. Percentages reflect proportions of the full dataset.

5.2 Narrative Use in Delta-Awarded Discussions

For this analysis, we move beyond individual comments to the level of full discussion threads, aiming to assess whether narrative use is more prevalent in persuasive conversations overall. Specifically, we compare threads where at least one delta was awarded (*delta threads*) to those without any deltas (*non-delta threads*) in terms of both narrative density and narrativity degree. For each thread, we compute the following metrics:

- **Narrative density**: the proportion of comments within the thread classified as *story* by the *StorySeeker* model.
- **Average degree of narrativity**: the mean narrative confidence score across all comments labeled as *story* within the thread (Steg et al., 2022).

Results: Threads that received deltas exhibit a higher average narrative density (0.0486) than those that did not (0.0407), and this difference is statistically significant ($p < 0.001, Rank - Biserial\ Correlation = 0.1340$). Figure 3 shows the distribution of narrative density across both groups, highlighting a greater concentration of narrative-heavy threads among delta threads.

As for the degree of narrativity, delta threads also display a slightly higher average confidence score (0.7900) compared to non-delta threads (0.7884). However, this difference is not statistically significant ($p > 0.05$). The distribution of narrativity degree across groups is illustrated in Figure 4.

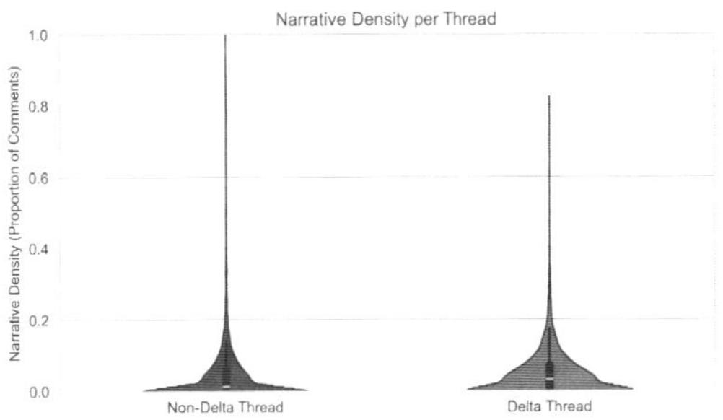

Figure 3: Narrative density per thread, grouped by whether a delta was awarded in the thread.

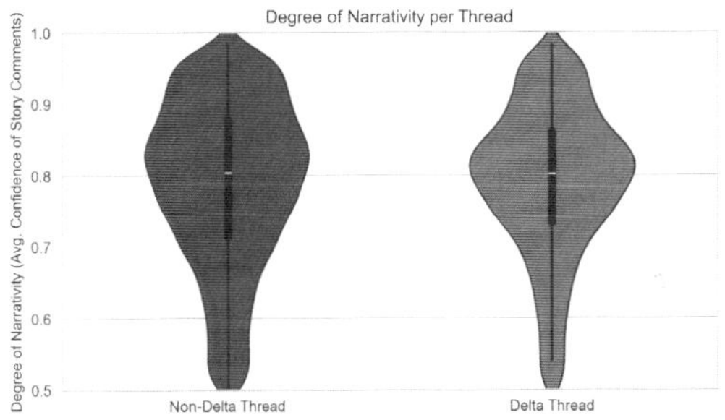

Figure 4: Degree of narrativity per thread, measured as the average confidence score for comments labeled as *story*, grouped by whether a delta was awarded in the thread.

5.3 Narrative Use by Delta-Awarded vs. Other Participants

In this analysis, we investigate whether users who successfully persuaded someone in a thread (i.e., those who received a delta) tend to use more narrative than other participants within the same discussion. Focusing exclusively on delta-awarded threads, we compute two metrics for each user per thread: narrative density and degree of narrativity. We then compare these metrics between delta recipients and non-recipients within each thread.

Results: Interestingly, users who received a delta used slightly less narrative than their peers in the same persuasive threads. The average narrative density for delta recipients was 0.0544 ($SD = 0.1703$), compared to 0.0560 ($SD = 0.2064$) for non-recipients. This difference is statistically significant ($p < 0.001, Rank - Biserial\ Correlation = 0.0474$).

Similarly, the degree of narrativity was lower

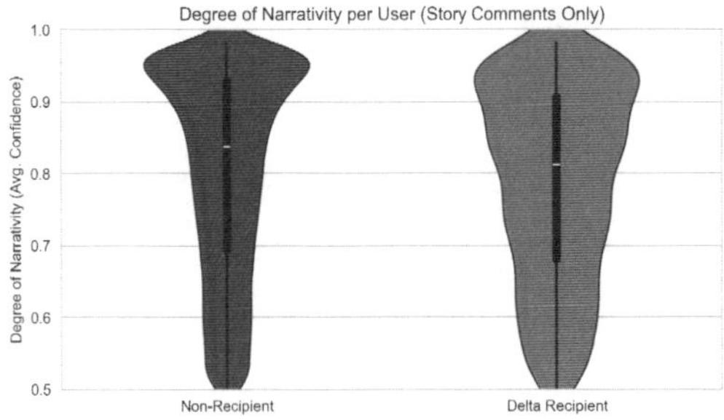

Figure 5: Degree of narrativity per user in delta-awarded threads, among users who wrote at least one narrative comment, grouped by whether a user was awarded a delta in the post

for delta recipients ($M = 0.7866$) than for non-recipients ($M = 0.8037$), and this difference was also statistically significant ($p < 0.001, Rank - Biserial\ Correlation = 0.0862$). Figure 5 shows the distribution of narrativity degree across both user groups.

5.4 Narrative and User Persuasiveness

Prior work on persuasion in *ChangeMyView* has categorized users based on their overall effectiveness in persuasion, measured by the frequency with which their comments receive deltas (Wiegmann et al., 2022). Following this classification, we examine the relationship between a user's persuasive skill and their use of narrative. Users are grouped into three categories:

- **Good debaters**: at least 5% of their comments received deltas.
- **Average debaters**: between 0% and 5%.
- **Poor debaters**: 0% of their comments received deltas.

For each user, we compute two metrics: narrative density and degree of narrativity. These metrics are then compared across the debater categories.

Results: Narrative density varies significantly across debater groups, as indicated by a Kruskal–Wallis H test ($p < 0.001, \epsilon^2 = 0.0487$). As shown in Table 3, poor debaters exhibit the highest average narrative density (0.0714), followed by good debaters (0.0673), and average debaters (0.0445). All pairwise differences are statistically significant ($p < 0.001$). However, the distributional patterns point to a more nuanced interpretation: the median narrative density for both good and poor debaters

Debater Type	Count	Density	Narr. Deg.
Good	2063	0.0673	0.7915
Average	2373	0.0445	0.7921
Poor	68040	0.0714	0.8081

Table 3: Narrative use statistics by debater quality.

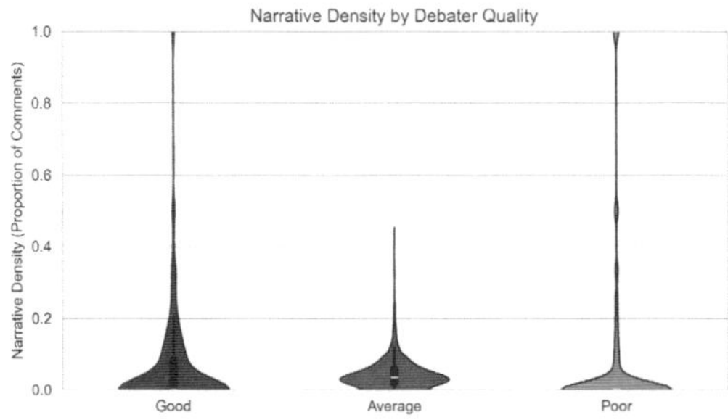

Figure 6: Narrative density by debater quality.

is 0.0, suggesting that many users in both groups rarely employ narrative. Poor debaters also show the greatest variability ($SD = 0.2058$), with a long tail of users who employ narrative heavily, thereby skewing the group mean upward. These patterns are visualized in Figure 6, which highlights the presence of heavy tails and outliers, particularly among poor debaters.

Narrativity degree also differs significantly among debater groups, again confirmed by a Kruskal–Wallis H test ($p < 0.001, \epsilon^2 = 0.0071$). Poor debaters have the highest average narrativity degree (0.8081), followed by average debaters (0.7921), and good debaters (0.7915). Pairwise comparisons show that poor debaters use significantly stronger narrative than both good and average debaters ($p < 0.001$), while the difference between good and average debaters is not statistically significant ($p = 0.019$). Figure 7 illustrates the distribution of narrativity degree across the three groups.

5.5 Narrative Use and Effectiveness Across Persuasion Goals

Prior work in narrative persuasion suggests that the effectiveness of storytelling may vary based on the type of change being targeted, such as shifts in beliefs, attitudes, intentions, and behaviors (Zebregs et al., 2015; Green and Appel, 2024). To investigate whether similar patterns hold in the context of *ChangeMyView*, we analyze narrative use across different persuasion goals. We begin by classifying each original post according to the type of change

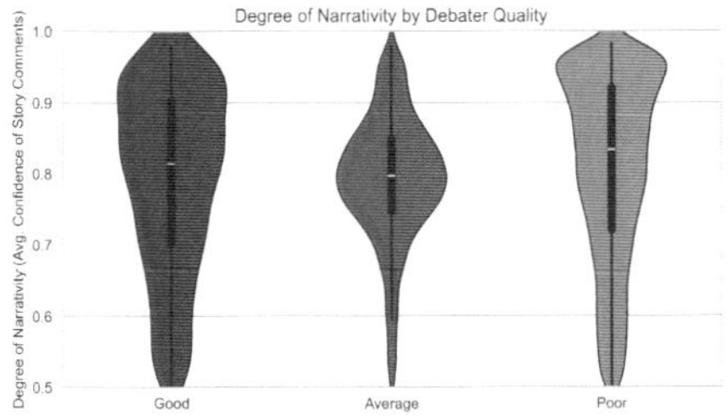

Figure 7: Narrativity degree by debater quality. Poor debaters show higher narrative confidence scores overall.

it aims to achieve: *belief*, *attitude*, *intention*, or *behavior*. For each post, we compute two key metrics: narrative density and degree of narrativity. These values are compared across the four goal types to examine how narrative use differs by persuasion context. Finally, to assess the effectiveness of narrative in each goal category, we compare its usage in persuasive (delta-awarded) versus non-persuasive (non-delta) comments within each group.

For the classification task, we employ a zero-shot classifier[3] (Laurer et al., 2024), trained as a universal classifier using Natural Language Inference (NLI). The model evaluates whether a given post (the premise) entails a hypothesis representing each potential goal type. We use the hypothesis template: "This post is primarily about changing someone's [LABEL]", with the placeholder replaced by one of the candidate labels. The label with the highest entailment score is assigned as the persuasive goal for the post. To ensure label reliability, we include only posts where the top prediction exceeds a confidence threshold of 0.7. Appendix A presents two *ChangeMyView* posts after classification, including the persuasive goals assigned by the model and example comments from the discussions.

Results: Narrative density varies significantly across persuasion goals ($p < 0.001, \epsilon^2 = 0.0167$). Posts targeting behavior and belief change exhibit the highest average narrative density (0.0549 and 0.0532, respectively), while posts targeting attitude and intention show lower values (0.0341 and 0.0405, respectively). Pairwise comparisons confirm that behavior and belief posts include significantly more narrative than intention posts ($p < 0.001$); no other pairwise differences are statistically significant.

By contrast, narrativity degree does not differ

[3]https://huggingface.co/MoritzLaurer/deberta-v3-base-zeroshot-v1.1-all-33

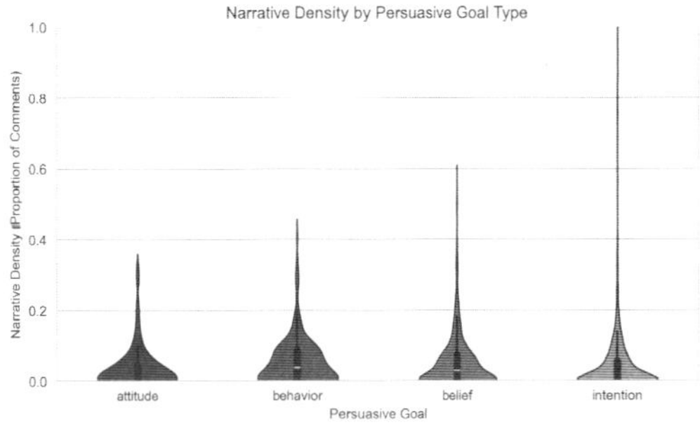

Figure 8: Narrative density by persuasive goal type.

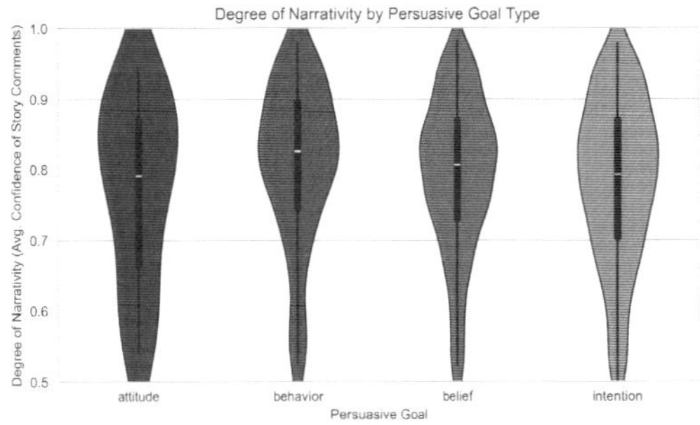

Figure 9: Narrativity degree by persuasive goal type.

significantly across persuasion goals ($p > 0.05$), and none of the pairwise comparisons reach significance. Figures 8 and 9 show the distributions of narrative density and degree of narrativity, respectively. Summary statistics for narrative use across persuasion goal types are shown in Table 4.

Regarding narrative effectiveness, we find no significant differences in the proportion of narrative use between delta-awarded and non-delta comments within any of the goal categories ($p > 0.05$). Likewise, the degree of narrativity does not differ significantly between persuasive and non-persuasive comments across all goal types. Full results are presented in Tables 5 and 6.

6 Discussion

The results of our analysis show that while narrative is present in online persuasive discourse, its association with success is weak and more limited than found in prior theory. We find a small but statistically significant increase in the proportion of narrative comments among delta-awarded comments, yet the effect size is negligible. Also, delta-awarded comments tend to have a slightly lower narrativity degree than the non-delta ones, suggesting that stronger storytelling, measured by model

Goal	Count	Density	Narrativity
Attitude	44	0.0341	0.7733
Behavior	212	0.0549	0.8073
Belief	1157	0.0532	0.7920
Intention	1149	0.0405	0.7826

Table 4: Narrative use by persuasive goal type.

Goal	Delta%	Non-Delta%
Attitude	0	0.0401
Behavior	0.0667	0.0625
Belief	0.0610	0.0550
Intention	0.0377	0.0432

Table 5: Proportion of narrative comments in *Delta* vs. *Non-delta* comments across goal types

Goal	Delta	Non-Delta
Attitude	-	0.7761
Behavior	0.7435	0.8189
Belief	0.8220	0.8160
Intention	0.7903	0.7981

Table 6: Narrativity degree of comments in *Delta* vs. *Non-delta* comments across goal types

confidence, does not guarantee persuasiveness.

At the thread level, posts where a delta was awarded tend to contain more narrative overall. However, when we zoom in to the user level within the same discussions, we find that users who received deltas used slightly less narrative than other participants. This finding is counterintuitive if narrative was a consistent indicator of persuasion success, and suggests that successful arguers may rely more on other rhetorical techniques, or that narrative alone is not sufficient to persuade.

The patterns observed at the user level support this idea. We found that poor debaters use narrative more than good ones, and use stories with higher narrativity. A potential explanation for this could be that relying on narrative may be a fallback strategy for users who struggle to persuade with reasoning, but this needs to be confirmed by additional research.

The analysis of the narrative use across different types of persuasive goals showed that stories are more frequently used in posts aiming to change beliefs or behaviors. Yet, this difference in usage does not translate into effectiveness: narrative comments are not more likely to succeed within any goal type, and narrativity degree does not differ between persuasive and non-persuasive comments in these contexts.

Overall, these findings suggest that narrative is a visible but not consistently persuasive part of online argumentation. Its effectiveness likely depends on how it is used, who the audience is, and what norms govern the discussion space.

Several limitations should be taken into account when interpreting these findings. First, our analysis depends on the predictions of an automatic story detection model. Although the model was trained on Reddit data and demonstrates strong performance on held-out benchmarks, it may still overlook more subtle or implicit forms of storytelling. Second, the classification of persuasion goals relies on zero-shot predictions from an NLI-based model. To enhance reliability, we included only posts with high-confidence predictions; however, the absence of human validation may introduce noise. Third, we operationalize persuasion success through delta awards. While deltas serve as a useful community-driven signal of agreement, they do not capture all forms of influence. Some persuasive comments may go unrecognized, while others may receive deltas for reasons unrelated to argumentation quality. Finally, our findings are specific to the *ChangeMyView* (CMV) platform, which has distinct rules, cultural norms, and moderation practices. These factors influence how arguments are constructed and what is considered persuasive. As such, the generalizability of our results to other platforms or domains remains an open question.

7 Conclusion

In this paper, we have examined the role of narrative in online argumentation through a large-scale analysis of persuasive interactions on *ChangeMyView*. By applying an automatic story detection model to user comments, we have explored how narrative has been employed in argumentative contexts and whether it contributes to persuasive success. Our findings have shown that narrative is indeed used in argumentative discourse. However, its presence alone has not consistently predicted successful persuasion. These results suggest a more complex relationship between storytelling and persuasion than what has often been assumed in theoretical or experimental work.

Future research could build on these insights by examining how narrative interacts with other rhetorical strategies. Also, distinguishing between types of stories, such as personal experiences versus hypothetical scenarios, and analyzing how they are integrated into arguments may offer a deeper understanding of when and how narrative enhances persuasion. Extending this analysis to other platforms may also help identify the broader conditions under which storytelling supports persuasiveness.

References

Maria Antoniak, Joel Mire, Maarten Sap, Elliott Ash, and Andrew Piper. 2024. Where do people tell stories online? story detection across online communities. In *Proceedings of the 62nd Annual Meeting of the Association for Computational Linguistics (Volume 1: Long Papers)*, pages 7104–7130, Bangkok, Thailand. Association for Computational Linguistics.

Anneke de Graaf, José Sanders, and J.A.L. Hoeken. 2016. Characteristics of narrative interventions and health effects: A review of the content, form, and context of narratives in health-related narrative persuasion research. *Review of Communication Research*, 4:88–131.

Ryo Egawa, Gaku Morio, and Katsuhide Fujita. 2019. Annotating and analyzing semantic role of elementary units and relations in online persuasive arguments. In *Proceedings of the 57th Annual Meeting of the Association for Computational Linguistics: Student Research Workshop*, pages 422–428, Florence, Italy. Association for Computational Linguistics.

Neele Falk and Gabriella Lapesa. 2023. StoryARG: a corpus of narratives and personal experiences in argumentative texts. In *Proceedings of the 61st Annual Meeting of the Association for Computational Linguistics (Volume 1: Long Papers)*, pages 2350–2372, Toronto, Canada. Association for Computational Linguistics.

Neele Falk and Gabriella Lapesa. 2024. Stories and personal experiences in the COVID-19 discourse. In *Proceedings of the 2024 Joint International Conference on Computational Linguistics, Language Resources and Evaluation (LREC-COLING 2024)*, pages 15320–15340, Torino, Italia. ELRA and ICCL.

Kaitlin S. Fitzgerald and Melanie C. Green. 2017. *Chapter 3. Narrative persuasion: Effects of transporting stories on attitudes, beliefs, and behaviors*, pages 49–67. John Benjamins Publishing Company.

Marlène Gerber, André Bächtiger, Susumu Shikano, Simon Reber, and Samuel Rohr. 2018. Deliberative abilities and influence in a transnational deliberative poll (europolis). *British Journal of Political Science*, 48(4):1093–1118.

Melanie C. Green. 2004. Storytelling in teaching. *APS observer*, 17.

Melanie C. Green and Markus Appel. 2024. Chapter one - narrative transportation: How stories shape how we see ourselves and the world. volume 70 of *Advances in Experimental Social Psychology*, pages 1–82. Academic Press.

Yan Huang and Melanie Green. 2022. Reducing covid-19 vaccine hesitancy among african americans: The effects of narratives, character's self-persuasion, and trust in science. *Journal of Behavioral Medicine*, 46.

Moritz Laurer, Wouter van Atteveldt, Andreu Casas, and Kasper Welbers. 2024. Building efficient universal classifiers with natural language inference. *Preprint*, arXiv:2312.17543.

John Lawrence and Chris Reed. 2019. Argument mining: A survey. *Computational Linguistics*, 45(4):765–818.

Yinhan Liu, Myle Ott, Naman Goyal, Jingfei Du, Mandar Joshi, Danqi Chen, Omer Levy, Mike Lewis, Luke Zettlemoyer, and Veselin Stoyanov. 2019. Roberta: A robustly optimized bert pretraining approach. *Preprint*, arXiv:1907.11692.

Philip J. Mazzocco. 2011. Narrative persuasion in legal settings: What's the story?

Robin L. Nabi and Melanie C. Green. 2015. The role of a narrative's emotional flow in promoting persuasive outcomes. *Media Psychology*, 18(2):137–162.

Joonsuk Park and Claire Cardie. 2018. A corpus of eRulemaking user comments for measuring evaluability of arguments. In *Proceedings of the Eleventh International Conference on Language Resources and Evaluation (LREC 2018)*, Miyazaki, Japan. European Language Resources Association (ELRA).

Sougata Saha and Rohini Srihari. 2023. ArgU: A controllable factual argument generator. In *Proceedings of the 61st Annual Meeting of the Association for Computational Linguistics (Volume 1: Long Papers)*, pages 8373–8388, Toronto, Canada. Association for Computational Linguistics.

Max Steg, Karlo Slot, and Federico Pianzola. 2022. Computational detection of narrativity: A comparison using textual features and reader response. In *Proceedings of the 6th Joint SIGHUM Workshop on Computational Linguistics for Cultural Heritage, Social Sciences, Humanities and Literature*, pages 105–114, Gyeongju, Republic of Korea. International Conference on Computational Linguistics.

Chenhao Tan, Vlad Niculae, Cristian Danescu-Niculescu-Mizil, and Lillian Lee. 2016. Winning arguments: Interaction dynamics and persuasion strategies in good-faith online discussions. In *Proceedings of WWW*.

Tom van Laer, Ko de Ruyter, Luca M. Visconti, and Martin Wetzels. 2013. The extended transportation-imagery model: A meta-analysis of the antecedents and consequences of consumers' narrative transportation. *Journal of Consumer Research*, 40(5):797–817.

Michael Völske, Martin Potthast, Shahbaz Syed, and Benno Stein. 2017. TL;DR: Mining Reddit to learn automatic summarization. In *Proceedings of the Workshop on New Frontiers in Summarization*, pages 59–63, Copenhagen, Denmark. Association for Computational Linguistics.

Henning Wachsmuth, Gabriella Lapesa, Elena Cabrio, Anne Lauscher, Joonsuk Park, Eva Maria Vecchi, Serena Villata, and Timon Ziegenbein. 2024. Argument quality assessment in the age of instruction-following large language models. In *Proceedings of the 2024 Joint International Conference on Computational Linguistics, Language Resources and Evaluation (LREC-COLING 2024)*, pages 1519–1538, Torino, Italia. ELRA and ICCL.

Matti Wiegmann, Khalid Al Khatib, Vishal Khanna, and Benno Stein. 2022. Analyzing persuasion strategies of debaters on social media. In *Proceedings of the 29th International Conference on Computational Linguistics*, pages 6897–6905, Gyeongju, Republic of Korea. International Committee on Computational Linguistics.

Simon Zebregs, Bas van den Putte, Peter Neijens, and Anneke de Graaf and. 2015. The differential impact of statistical and narrative evidence on beliefs, attitude, and intention: A meta-analysis. *Health Communication*, 30(3):282–289. PMID: 24836931.

A Example CMV Threads

Table 7 presents examples of *ChangeMyView* (CMV) threads targeting different persuasive goals, with comments annotated for narrative presence and persuasive success (delta).

Type	Content
Title	I'm financially stable, but I don't intend to give to charity until I'm older and have gathered even more money. CMV.
Post	I could: - Never give any money to charity - Give lots of my money to charity right now (i.e., give up my worldly possessions so that others may thrive) - Give a small amount of money now, and on a regular, continuing basis (e.g., every Christmas give out X% of my current net worth) - Invest now, and give lots of my money later (perhaps all of it, donated via my will) The last option appears wisest to me. It seems like it will get the most money out to charity in the long term. It also allows me a cushion in case hard times happen to hit me, which is likely enough. I think that people seem to encourage the 3rd option (continue giving, regularly). Why is my choice not the best? Is there a better choice, and I just didn't think of it to list here?
Comment 1 *Delta* *Non-Story*	Charity works both ways. It helps the people you give it to, and it also helps you by changing your heart and making you more caring. Every time you put off good deeds, you are not just delaying the receipt of those good deeds, you are also becoming a less caring person. You are developing habits that make you less likely to help others around you as well as less likely to give to charity later. If you genuinely believe that your investment strategies are so much better than the strategies of any other charitable foundations (are you Warren Buffett?) then by all means invest your donations. Create a separate bank account (or foundation - if you're that good you'll need one) and donate to that account/foundation, acting as custodian of that money in terms of investment choices but knowing that you've already set it aside for others and that it is no longer yours. And by all means, recognize that most charity is not money. It is good deeds.
Comment 2 *Non-Delta* *Non-Story*	I can give a defense of option 3, which is potentially the best one. Think of it this way- nonprofits have budgets, and they have to try and stay within them, like everyone else. Charities have a chronic problem of being unsure about what their budget will look like. Giving money regularly gives those charities budgeting power, meaning not only will they have more money, but they can use that money more effectively and consistently because they'll have a better understanding of what their finances will look like next month or next year. Big one-time donations are great, don't get me wrong, and it certainly helps, but it doesn't give them the same kind of budgetary power.

(a) Example of a thread targeting **intention change**

Type	Content
Title	CMV: 'Be yourself' is a totally useless piece of advice.
Post	What does it even mean? How can one not be one-self? Now I'm mostly talking about the everyday use of the phrase – where it is typically offered moments before an uncomfortable or unfamiliar social interaction, like a date. And in this scenario, I assume it means something like 'be yourself but without any of the debilitating neurosis and subsequent façade'. But this is just as useless. Don't you think if people could magically wish away such impediments, they would have already done so? It's possible that some people are able to do this – but then they presumably wouldn't be in need of such banal advice. But even if you are held back by anxiety / hiding behind a façade etc. – are these things not an integral part of the ego that constitutes the 'self'? ...
Comment 1 *Delta* *Story*	So how can we change your view about this? You don't think there are people who need this advice, but I can anecdotally tell you that it took *several* people telling me *this exact advice* before it finally 'clicked' and I started acting more like my usual self on dates. For a long time I would take a girl out and then try to act like the person I thought she wanted me to be. It took my mother, father, and a few close friends, and then finally an actual **date** of mine, before I finally got the message that I really should just "be myself".
Comment 2 *Non-Delta* *Story*	Oh sure, it's plainly obvious. Simply stating it in a nonchalant manner probably won't do anything. But I had a friend who was the opposite of me. We were very similar (humor, likes, dislikes, what we like to do for fun) except I would get anxious and this guy was fearless. By a kind of lead by example "be yourself" philosophy he lived by, he rubbed off on me slowly over time and I became less anxious. So yeah, I guess a simple statement won't do much, or maybe it's the slap on the face someone needs to get motivated. But the philosophy behind it definitely helped me personally gravitate towards confidence and normalcy.

(b) Example of a thread targeting **belief change**

Table 7: Examples of CMV threads targeting **intention change** and **belief change**.

Segmentation of Argumentative Texts by Key Statements for Argument Mining from the Web

Ines Zelch[1,2] **Matthias Hagen**[1] **Benno Stein**[3] **Johannes Kiesel**[4]

[1]Friedrich-Schiller-Universität Jena [2]Leipzig University [3]Bauhaus-Universität Weimar
[4]GESIS – Leibniz Institute for the Social Sciences

Abstract

Argument mining is the task of identifying the argument structure of a text: claims, premises, support/attack relations, etc. However, determining the complete argument structure can be quite involved, especially for unpolished texts from online forums, while for many applications the identification of argumentative key statements would suffice (e.g., for argument search). To this end, we introduce and investigate the new task of segmenting an argumentative text by its key statements. We formalize the task, create a first dataset from online communities, propose an evaluation scheme, and conduct a pilot study with several approaches. Interestingly, our experimental results indicate that none of the tested approaches (even LLM-based ones) can actually satisfactorily solve key statement segmentation yet.

> Thanks for the timely response. To address my opponents argument, I want to emphasize that eating meat isn't necessary for maximum physical development. All of the vitamins, minerals etc. in meat can also be found in other foods. And does the taste of meat really outweigh the costs of killing? My conclusion: Vegetarianism is a good thing because it saves animals' lives, improves one's health and helps the environment. I didn't bring religion into this debate but almost all of the major religions (even the ones that allow meat eating) agree that vegetarianism is better than eating meat.

Figure 1: Argumentative text on *vegetarianism*, highlighting key statements (underlined) and optional supplements of segments (colored).

1 Introduction

The field of argument mining deals with the identification and extraction of arguments from a text. A fundamental step in argument mining is text segmentation, which deals with the separation of different statements (argumentative discourse units) from each other (Stede and Schneider, 2019). When placed in relation to each other, the statements form a tree structure in which the root node represents the topic statement of the text and the nodes of the first level correspond to the main statements on this topic (Lawrence et al., 2014). Other nodes in the tree are, for example, explanations and examples that support their parent node.

But identifying the segments within a text is challenging, mainly because the exact segment boundaries are often up for debate (Pevzner and Hearst, 2002; Ghosh et al., 2014). Natural language texts, especially in debate forums and other argumentation-rich media, are rarely comprised of clear-cut and well arranged statements. Ambiguities, interjections, digressions and other factors prevent the establishment of general rules for the delimitation of segments. However, many argument analysis tasks do not require to identify the fine-grained argument structure of a text. To know what an argumentative text is about, it is usually sufficient to know its main points, which are thus typically the elements of interest in applications such as key point generation (Bar-Haim et al., 2020a,b), argumentation summarization (Syed et al., 2020) or argument search (Wachsmuth et al., 2017).

So far, main points have mostly been gathered by crowdsourcing (e.g., Misra et al. (2015); Friedman et al. (2021)). For an automated extraction of the main points of a text, we propose an alternative and coarser-grained segmentation task that aims to separate the *key statements*—the level-one nodes in the argument tree—from each other. To model the ambiguity of boundaries, we only require a segment to (1) completely cover a single key statement and (2) not overlap with other key statements. Other contents can be included in the segment, but do not have to be. To illustrate the segmentation goal, Figure 1 shows examples of key statements (underlined) and text passages that could be included in a segment (colored text without underlining). To address this new task on realistic web data, we

Proceedings of the 12th Argument Mining Workshop, pages 228–242
July 31, 2025

use the args.me corpus, which provides texts on different controversial topics crawled from four different debate portals (Ajjour et al., 2019b). We apply a range of segmentation approaches, including simple sentence and paragraph segmenters, two previous models for argument unit segmentation, and two different LLMs.[1]

Section 2 provides an overview of the challenges of the segmentation task and presents previous segment approaches. Section 3 defines key statements against the background of different terms of argumentative text units and formalizes the coarse-grained segmentation task. Section 4 outlines the evaluation procedure and Section 5 presents the corresponding results. Amongst others, we find that a segmentation by paragraphs provides a good baseline and LLMs achieve the best results. The predictions of the previous argument unit segmentation approaches are often too short to be useful.

2 Background

This section outlines various challenges of argument segmentation and introduces a selection of approaches that tackle this task.

Challenges Some challenges arise due to the overall distribution of arguments in texts. A segmentation at sentence boundaries is usually not sufficient, as multiple propositions might be contained in a single sentence, or a proposition may stretch over more than one sentence (Stede and Schneider, 2019). Multiple arguments can enforce each other in so called compound argumentations (Palau and Moens, 2009; Stab and Gurevych, 2017) and have to be recognized as being part of the same segment. Further, segments can be embedded into another (Lawrence and Reed, 2020) so that they cannot be separated appropriately. Another challenge are implicit statements which are difficult to capture on text-level, for example enthymemes (implicit premises that are considered obvious), rhetorical questions or sarcasm (Lawrence and Reed, 2020; Trabelsi and Zaïane, 2019; Hasan and Ng, 2014). Sometimes, propositions require knowledge beyond the text span under consideration, such as back-references to (parts of) previous statements (Lawrence and Reed, 2020), or missing co-references that have to be resolved. Finally, there is the problem of segment evaluation since humans often disagree on the exact boundaries, and the importance of different types of errors might depend on the application of the resulting segments (Pevzner and Hearst, 2002; Ghosh et al., 2014).

[1] Our code is available at https://github.com/webis-de/argmining25-argument-segmentation.

Related Work Approaches that tackle the argument segmentation task, usually process a text on either sentence or token level. On sentence level, argument segmentation is typically approached as classification task, labeling a sentence as argumentative (probably even more fine-granular, for example as claim or premise, pro or con) or as not argumentative (Reimers et al., 2019; Lippi and Torroni, 2015; Moens et al., 2007). On token level, several approaches are based on BiLSTM architectures or BERT, sometimes in combination with Conditional Random fields or other additional components (Fu et al., 2023; Alhindi and Ghosh, 2021; Trautmann et al., 2020; Chernodub et al., 2019). For example, Ajjour et al. (2017) use a BiLSTM model with different textual features including POS-tags, information about clauses, phrases, and sentences as well as a list of discourse markers. Others propose rule-based approaches (Fujii and Ishikawa, 2006) or use the parse tree representations of the sentences (Guilluy et al., 2023; Dumani et al., 2020; Persing and Ng, 2016). Recent approaches also use LLMs for the segmentation task (D'Agostino et al., 2024). All approaches have in common that they extract argument units with specific boundaries.

3 Conceptualizing Key Statement Segmentation

The extraction of argumentative text units has been addressed under varying terms and definitions and with different scope. Against this background, we formalize the segmentation task for our use case.

3.1 Defining Key Statements

In order to describe, illustrate, and categorize the concept of key statements of a text, we relate and contrast it with existing concepts.

Key statements are argument discourse units Stede and Schneider (2019) define an argumentative discourse unit (ADU) as a text segment "that plays a single role for the argument being analyzed, and is demarcated by neighboring text spans that play a different role, or none at all [for the argumentation.]" The nature of "role" can vary between analyses and ADUs can thus span multiple sentences, or be shorter than a sentence. ADUs are in this sense the argumentative counterpart to the elementary discourse units (EDUs) in rhetorical structure theory (see Taboada and Mann (2006) for an introduction). Typically, ADUs are a text's statements (Lawrence and Reed, 2020) and can be seen as nodes in a tree in which the edges indicate support and attack relationships and with the topic statement as the tree's root node. In this view, key statements are a subset of all ADUs in a text, namely the ADUs at depth (or level) one, i.e., the children of the root node.

Key statements are linked to key points In argumentation, one distinguishes between the written or spoken words (statement) and their abstract meaning (proposition). Key statements are the salient statements in an argumentative text. As statements, they are linked to the abstract propositions a reader forms in their mind while comprehending the text. In this sense, the concept of "central propositions" of a text, introduced by Misra et al. (2015) and extracted by means of abstractive summarization, coincides with the propositions of key statements. Furthermore, the concept of "key points" of a topic, introduced by Bar-Haim et al. (2020a,b); Friedman et al. (2021), follows the same idea, but defines salience with respect to a topic—described by a collection of texts—and not single texts. Key statements can thus be used to infer central propositions and potential key points.

Key statements are not aspects Though seemingly related, key statements are not the salient parts of single statements or propositions. For example, typical aspect terms in statements on minimum wage increases are "job" and "economy," which indicate that the statements concern effects on the respective aspect (Trautmann, 2020). The same concept for segments longer than single words has been coined "point at issue" by Fujii and Ishikawa (2006). The corresponding concept for propositions has been coined "argument facet" by Misra et al. (2015). In contrast to these, key statements are complete statements.

3.2 Formalizing Key Statement Segmentation

Having defined key statements, we define the task of segmenting by key statements as follows:

> Given an argumentative text and the controversial topic it discusses, segment the text such that each segment contains exactly one key statement (as per the topic).

The most important difference compared to previous argument segmentation approaches is that this task definition allows segments to encompass more text than just the key statement. Instead of defining specific segment boundaries, we permit some variability in the segments in order to account for the ambiguity of the segmentation task, as explained in Section 1. Key statements only define a minimum set of ADUs that the segments must cover in terms of content, and they must be correctly separated from each other.

3.3 Segmentation Approaches

We apply a range of different approaches to the segmentation task. Based on the structural text features, we apply a segmentation at sentence boundaries using NLTK's sentence tokenizer, and at each new paragraph based on HTML tags (`<br>` and `<p>`). Additionally, we apply a re-implementation of the unit segmentation by Ajjour et al. (2017), and TARGER (Chernodub et al., 2019) which is usable via an API. Finally, we prompt PaLM and GPT-4 as representatives of LLMs.[2] The prompt used for the segmentation with PaLM (provided in Figure 4 in Appendix A) is derived from a prompt by Chen et al. (2024) for the segmentation of Wikipedia pages into propositions. For GPT-4, the prompt is subtly varied for better results. We also tested prompt optimization with DSPy (Khattab et al., 2022, 2023), but did not achieve further improvements by this. For all created segments, we automatically filter those with less than three whitespaces in order to reduce noise without potential argumentative content.[3] We further test the effect of filtering segments classified as non-argumentative by the model provided by Reimers et al. (2019),[4] since the applied approaches do not necessarily distinguish between argumentative and non-argumentative propositions of a text.

4 Developing an Evaluation Framework for Key Statement Segmentation

To evaluate the coverage of the key statements by predicted segments, we provide a test set with manually extracted key statements, and propose an automatic matching approach that assigns segments to semantically equivalent key statements (indepen-

[2]PaLM 2 and GPT-4o mini

[3]For example, for the sentence approach, this removes segments like "It's that simple.", "1.2 Contention 1" or links.

[4]github.com/UKPLab/acl2019-BERT-argument-classification-and-clustering

The given texts contain arguments on different controversial claims ("topics"). Your task is to annotate the text's key statements.
A key statement is a minimal text passage that expresses exactly one proposition that directly supports or attacks the text's topic. It can range from a single phrase to multiple sentences.
If a key statement is repeated in a similar way, annotate only the occurrence that expresses the statement best.

Figure 2: Instructions for the expert annotators.

Forced marriages are not supported theologically by any of the major religions.$_{[ann2,\ ann3]}$ Whilst different religions may disagree on the nature of marriage and its formation, all are agreed that some level of consent is necessary.$_{[ann1]}$ Forced marriage is no more than a barbaric tribal custom which has no place in a modern society.$_{[ann2]}$

Figure 3: Example annotations for a text on the topic "We should abandon marriage." The brackets show which annotators annotated each sentence as key statement. The first two of the three sentences are semantically very similar and which one to annotate as key statement is somewhat arbitrary.

dent of the specific segment boundaries). Furthermore, we introduce suitable evaluation categories and measures.

4.1 Compiling a Dataset for Key Statement Segmentation

In order to evaluate key statement segmentation approaches on relevant web data and analyze the relationship between the key statements and key points, we create a dataset by sampling texts from the args.me corpus of online discussion forums (Ajjour et al., 2019a). In this sampling process, we focus on texts discussing topics that are related to the topics in IBM's Key Point Analysis Shared Task (Friedman et al., 2021). The dataset consists of 50 texts that comprise 1,263 sentences and 25,201 words in total,[5] and cover 14 different controversial IBM topics. We manually annotated the key statements of these texts, resulting in 147 ground truth segments, covering 204 sentences and 4,019 words (16%). Figure 2 shows the annotation instruction for our three expert annotators.[6] The dataset is available online.[7]

To analyze the ambiguity of the annotation task, ten argumentative texts were annotated independently by all three annotators.[8] A discussion between the annotators revealed a general agreement; a major ambiguity resides in semantically similar sentences that could all be selected as key statements. Due to this ambiguity, traditional measures for inter annotator agreement are unsuitable for the task. For illustration purposes, consider the situation in Figure 3, where it is somewhat arbitrary which of the first two sentences to choose as key statement. Still, Cohen's Kappa would produce a negative score for annotators ann1 and ann3, who both agree that the last sentence is not a key statement. We thus performed a manual matching of annotated key segments between annotators and use the pairwise Jaccard index[9] to assess the agreement, resulting in medium to high scores between 0.47 and 0.80 macro-averaged across the ten texts. Given the ambiguity of the task, moderate agreement in argument segmentation studies is a common result (Habernal and Gurevych, 2017; Ghosh et al., 2014; Palau and Moens, 2008). The amount of words that the annotators marked as key statements is similar (between 41% and 51%). To complete our agreement assessment, Section 4.3 shows that evaluation results vary only slightly when switching between the annotations of the different annotators as ground truth. We thus conclude that a reliable annotation of key statements is possible, except for ambiguities induced by repetitions. For future datasets, one could consider to change the annotation instructions for repetitions (last sentence of Figure 2) to suggest the first occurrence instead of the commonly used but more ambiguous "best" occurrence to potentially reduce these ambiguities.

4.2 Matching Segments to Key Statements

To match predicted segments to ground truth key statements, we require an approach that goes beyond simple string matching for multiple reasons. Firstly, a text may contain paraphrases of the same statement. In such cases, all different formulations should be matched to the corresponding ground truth key statement (see, for example, the highlighted text snippets in Figure 5). Secondly, the ground truth key statements are not necessarily continuous text snippets. However, they should

[5]As per NLTK's word and sentence tokenizer.

[6]Members of our research group

[7]Data: https://doi.org/10.5281/zenodo.14865977

[8]Using doccano (Nakayama et al., 2018)

[9]Jaccard index: $\frac{|\text{segments both annotated}|}{|\text{segments at least one annotated}|}$

still be matched to segments from extractive approaches, such as sentence or paragraph segmentation. Thirdly, using LLMs often results in segments that are not strictly extractive, but these should still be matched to the key statement that is semantically most similar. For example, a ground truth key statement "Prostitution and recreational drugs are totally different: with prostitution you are not really harming anyone and recreational drugs can have a negative effect on people" should be matched with the LLM-generated segment "Prostitution is different from recreational drugs; it doesn't inherently harm others, unlike addictive drugs."

To match segments, we tested different similarity measures at various thresholds (skipped for brevity) against a human matching. We found that a combination of 3-gram overlap (threshold: 0.12), difflib's SequenceMatcher,[10] (threshold: 0.5), and an SBERT sentence transformer model[11] (threshold: 0.9) yields the best performance for PaLM segments and key statements, and outperforms each single measure: Counting it as a match if the similarity is above the threshold for at least one of the three measures, we reach a precision of 0.90, a recall of 0.79, and a very good F1 of 0.84.

4.3 Distinguishing Segment Match Categories

In order to distinguish between different kinds of mismatches between predicted segments and ground truth key statements, we derive different matching categories (Table 1). Key statements are *missed* if they are not covered at all, predicted segments without a corresponding key statement are *spurious*. A *match* between two segments can be *correct* or either *incomplete*, *impure* or *incomplete&impure*. The categories are illustrated with an example in Table 7 (Appendix).

To assess the correct matching category automatically, we build upon the segment matching and corresponding similarity scores. For each predicted segment (precision perspective), we count the number of ground truth segments to which it was matched. If this count is one, we consider the key statement to be correctly covered (*match*), if it is zero, the predicted segment falls in category *spurious*, and if it is greater than one, we assume that the prediction condenses multiple key statements into a single segment (*impure*). Similarly, we count the number of matches for each ground truth segment (recall perspective). Again, it is a *match* if this count is one, if it is zero, the ground truth segment is *missed* by the prediction; if it is greater than one, we assume that the ground truth segment is erroneously divided into multiple predicted segments and therefore only *incompletely* covered. An exception are predictions with a similarity > 0.9 to a key statement for either the SequenceMatcher or SBERT. They are considered as *match* rather than *incomplete*, to take into account that a statement can be repeated with different wording throughout a text, so that multiple matches would be possible. Segment pairs where both ground truth and prediction are matched multiple times are assigned an *incomplete&impure* label. In a strict evaluation, we only consider correct matches, whereas a relaxed evaluation comprises all matched segments (including incomplete and impure ones).

To further extend our assessment of inter annotator agreement, this time with respect to implications of disagreement on segmentation results, we evaluate each approach against the annotations of each annotator separately (cf. Section 4.1). Table 2 shows the mean and standard variation over annotators for relaxed precision, recall, and F1. As the low standard deviation indicates, evaluation results vary only slightly for different annotators, which shows a general agreement among annotators.

4.4 Measuring the Key Point Coverage

In order to assess how critical incomplete, impure and even missed segments are, we can estimate their effect on the end application (as described by Pevzner and Hearst (2002)), which will be the creation of key points in future work. It can be analyzed whether missed predictions lead to a complete loss of key points, or if they are still covered by other texts in the corpus. We therefore map the manually extracted key statements and predicted segments to the key points of the Key Point Analysis Shared Task 2021 (Friedman et al., 2021), which summarize the most important premises for a controversial topic (five pro, five con).[12] We apply the best matching approach (Alshomary et al., 2021) that participated in the shared task to map the segments to their most similar key point, but only if the calculated similarity is > 0.9. Key points covered by key statements should also be covered by the predicted segments.

[10]docs.python.org/3/library/difflib.html

[11]all-mpnet-base-v2, https://www.sbert.net/

[12]github.com/ibm/KPA_2021_shared_task

Category	Explanation
Matched correct	A key statement is covered correctly by a prediction (additional text may be included)
Incomplete	A key statement is covered partially or split into multiple segments
Impure	Different key statements are merged into a single predicted segment
Incomplete & impure	Different (incomplete) key statements are merged
Spurious	A predicted segment matches no key statement (e.g., non-argumentative text, examples)
Missed	A key statement is not covered by any predicted segment

Table 1: Explanation of segment match categories. In the pictogram, blue and and purple rectangles illustrate key statements (ground truth), whereas orange boxes represent predicted segments. For calculating strict precision and recall, only matched correct segments are counted as true positives, whereas the relaxed measures also count incomplete and impure (and both combined) as such.

Measure	Approach					
	PaLM	GPT-4	Paragr.	Sent.	Ajjour	Targer
Precision	0.49±0.02	0.27±0.04	0.50±0.02	0.23±0.00	0.21±0.02	0.17±0.02
Recall	0.66±0.08	0.65±0.03	1.00±0.00	1.00±0.00	0.90±0.02	0.98±0.03
F1 strict	0.47±0.02	0.29±0.05	0.29±0.05	0.26±0.05	0.22±0.04	0.18±0.01
F1 relaxed	0.56±0.03	0.37±0.04	0.67±0.01	0.39±0.00	0.35±0.02	0.28±0.03

Table 2: (Micro-) average and standard deviation for (relaxed) precision, recall, and (strict and relaxed) F1 score calculated by evaluating each approach for each of the three ground truths (one per annotator).

	All		Filtered	
	Man.	Auto.	Man.	Auto.
matched | Precision	0.54	0.56	0.63	0.57
– correct	0.33	0.31	0.44	0.43
– incorrect	0.21	0.25	0.19	0.14
spurious	0.46	0.54	0.37	0.43
matched | Recall	0.84	0.74	0.64	0.59
– correct	0.64	0.58	0.52	0.50
– incorrect	0.20	0.16	0.12	0.09
missed	0.16	0.27	0.36	0.41
F1 micro strict	0.44	0.40	0.48	0.46
F1 micro relaxed	0.66	0.56	0.63	0.58

Table 3: Comparison of automatic (auto.) and manual (man.) matching results using PaLM segments, reporting micro average scores from a precision and recall perspective. Row 'incorrect' summarizes incomplete and impure matches, 'matched' covers all correct and incorrect segments.

5 Results

The evaluation results for the automatic matching approach as well as the effectiveness of the segmentation approaches are reported in the following.

5.1 Matching Categories

The automatic assignment of matching categories is evaluated using the PaLM segments. Table 3 compares the segmentation effectiveness based on the automatic matching procedure with the effectiveness based on a manual matching. The differences in the scores mainly result from a shift of correct or incomplete segments (manually labeled) to spurious or missed (automatically labeled). The overall precision and recall are very similar, the slightly better scores resulting from the manual assignments indicate that we do not erroneously improve the overall results by the automatic estimation of the categories.

5.2 Segmentation

Table 4 shows the effectiveness of the presented segmentation strategies, whose segments are automatically matched to the key statements. Afterwards, the matching categories are assigned automatically. The scores are reported on micro-level, averaging over all predicted and ground truth segments of all argumentative texts together. The upper half of the table presents a precision-oriented evaluation. The matched/precision row shows the relaxed proportion of predicted segments that are matched to a key statement, comprising correct, incomplete and impure segments; the remaining predictions are spurious. The recall-oriented results are similarly arranged in the second half of the table. The precision of the approaches can be improved at the cost of recall by filtering segments classified as non-argumentative by Reimers et al.'s

Measure	Approach							
	PaLM f.	PaLM	GPT-4	Paragr.	Sent. f.	Sent.	Ajjour	Targer
# Segments	173	285	470	347	408	1125	1174	1759
matched I Precision	0.57	0.46	0.28	0.42	0.38	0.22	0.17	0.14
– correct	0.43	0.31	0.18	0.22	0.21	0.08	0.07	0.05 →
– incomplete	0.11	0.13	0.10	0.13	0.16	0.13	0.10	0.09 →
– impure	0.02	0.01	0.00	0.04	0.00	0.00	0.00	0.00 →
– incomplete & impure	0.01	0.01	0.00	0.03	0.01	0.01	0.00	0.00 →
spurious	0.43	0.54	0.71	0.58	0.62	0.78	0.82	0.86 →
matched I Recall	0.59	0.74	0.69	0.93	0.79	1.00	0.90	1.00 →
– correct	0.50	0.58	0.52	0.49	0.56	0.59	0.55	0.53
– incomplete	0.05	0.10	0.14	0.12	0.21	0.38	0.34	0.45 →
– impure	0.03	0.03	0.02	0.25	0.01	0.01	0.00	0.01 →
– incomplete & impure	0.01	0.03	0.01	0.07	0.01	0.02	0.01	0.01 →
missed	0.41	0.27	0.30	0.07	0.20	0.01	0.10	0.00 →
F1 micro strict	0.46	0.40	0.27	0.30	0.31	0.14	0.12	0.09
F1 micro relaxed	0.58	0.56	0.41	0.58	0.52	0.36	0.30	0.25

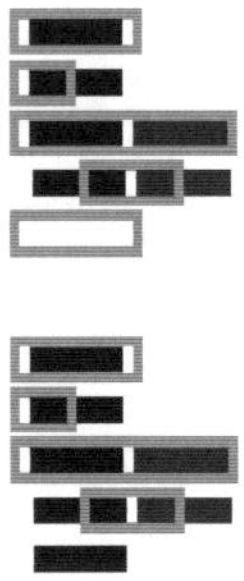

Table 4: Evaluation of different argument segmentation approaches from a precision- and recall-oriented perspective, reporting the micro average scores. The rows 'matched' cover all correct and incorrect segments. The total number of manual reference segments is 147. For PaLM and the sentence approach, the results after filtering (f.) are shown for comparison.

(2019) argument classifier. In Table 4, this is exemplarily shown for the segments created by PaLM and the sentence approach (columns 'PaLM f.' and 'Sent. f.'), the filtering results for all segmentation approaches can be found in Table 8 (Appendix).

Both sentence and paragraph segmentation approaches produce segments that cover almost the complete text (except the filtered short segments) and therefore have a high recall. Accordingly, a high number of spurious segments causes a low precision. The recall of the paragraph segmentation is not a hundred percent because the semantic matching approach may miss a key statement, for example if the segment contains much additional content. Also, the paragraph segments vary considerably in length (depending on the text formatting) and can thereby result in short spurious segments (see example in Table 10 in the Appendix). The two argument unit segmentation approaches, TARGER and Ajjour, create a high number of segments that are usually shorter than a sentence. The created segments are in some cases useful and succinct,[13] but in most of the cases not self-contained and not argumentative (e.g., "agree that would be absurd", "As for lives saved"), resulting in the lowest precision scores of all approaches. PaLM provides a better balance between precision and recall, produces considerably less segments than the sentence approach, TARGER and Ajjour, and does not return the complete text, like paragraph and sentence approach. GPT-4 has a lower precision and recall than for example the paragraph segments, however, it has a higher proportion of correct matches and therefore a comparable strict F1. Still, the segmentation with LLMs has room for improvement.

Measure	Approach			
	PaLM f.	PaLM	GPT-4 f.	GPT-4
matched I Pre.	0.67	0.58	0.53	0.47
– correct	0.32	0.24	0.19	0.14
– incomplete	0.32	0.31	0.34	0.33
– impure	0.03	0.02	0.00	0.00
– inc. & imp.	0.00	0.01	0.00	0.00
spurious	0.32	0.42	0.48	0.53
matched I Rec.	0.62	0.84	0.65	0.90
– correct	0.34	0.45	0.31	0.42
– incomplete	0.20	0.27	0.32	0.45
– impure	0.08	0.10	0.01	0.02
– inc. & imp.	0.00	0.02	0.01	0.01
missed	0.37	0.16	0.36	0.11
F1 micro strict	0.33	0.31	0.24	0.21
F1 micro relaxed	0.65	0.69	0.57	0.62

Table 5: Evaluation with fix boundaries for PaLM and GPT-4 segments (with filtering in columns 'f.').

To compare our evaluation setup with the traditional evaluation based on explicit segment boundaries, we map the key statements and LLM-created segments to the original text, to verify whether the key statements' boundaries are within the bound-

[13] for example, "DP sometimes kills innocents", "Violates the right to life" for the topic "abolish capital punishment"

aries of the predictions. Our evaluation shows that the results with explicit boundaries are less accurate. Key statements or segments by LLMs can consist of disconnected text passages (e.g., leaving out lengthy explanations). Mapping such segments to contiguous text passages to get the exact boundaries, can result in segments much longer than the original one. On the one hand, this produces longer key statements, which are more difficult to cover, on the other hand, it can cause predictions to cover additional content, so that key statements might be matched by mistake. The results in Table 5 show that the number of correctly matched segments is lower than with our proposed evaluation approach. At the same time, the number of incomplete matches is much higher, which results from the changed segment sizes. This leads to an improvement of the relaxed F1, while the strict F1 is clearly lower for the LLM-generated segments.

5.3 Key Point Coverage

Table 6 shows the key point coverage of the different segmentation approaches with the key points covered by the manual segments as reference. Since segmentation approaches with a high output number have a higher probability to cover all key points, we only report the numbers of the more reasonable approaches. Although the paragraph approach covers almost the complete text, it does not cover all key points. As before, this can most probably be explained by the potentially greater length of these segments which might prevent the matching model from a correct mapping, since the matching approach for key points (Alshomary et al., 2021) was trained on segments of sentence length. This might also explain why the filtering approach removes more relevant segments for paragraphs. The highest coverage of key points is achieved for segments from GPT-4, although it has lower F1 scores than PaLM and the paragraph approach. This indicates that an approach can provide a good overall coverage of argumentative propositions in a pool of texts, even if not every single key statement is covered. Also, the filtering approach works very well on the GPT-4 segments, as the key points coverage does not drop here. All in all, using the key points of the IBM shared task gives only an estimation of the covered key points. Ideally, we would generate new key points for the underlying data, however, this is beyond the scope of this work.

PaLM	PaLM f.	GPT-4	GPT-4 f.	Paragr.	Paragr. f.
0.74	0.70	0.87	0.87	0.70	0.57

Table 6: Coverage of key points for segments created by three approaches (with filtering in columns 'f.'), with key points covered by the key statements as reference.

5.4 Qualitative Analysis

Different challenges of the segmentation task that were described in Section 2 are also present in the texts from the args.me corpus. For example, rhetorical question express opinions only implicitly, like "should we ban Kentucky fried chicken because it too can be used as an instrument for terrorists ?" (topic "We should prohibit flag burning"). Another problem is the citation of counterarguments that can result in segments with the opposite stance. In the passage *"hate is the motivational force behind the burning*. Untrue", the contrary proposition is indicated by a single negating word. A sentence segmenter can never capture this, but PaLM creates the following segment: "In the first round, my opponent claimed that hate is the motivational force behind flag burning. This is untrue. [...]". Beyond that, LLMs allow to address most of the other segmentation challenges as well, for example, they can segment texts independently of sentence boundaries, make them self-contained, and filter non-argumentative content (illustrated in Figure 6 for the example text in Section 1). Other text attributes that require reformulations to obtain a meaningful segment are careless mistakes in writing that can distort the meaning and even turn a statement into the opposite, as in the following sentence: "Study shows that there there is not enough evidence to support the fact that the death penalty does not act as a deterrence.", where the writer is actually arguing against the death penalty, but reverses the statement by adding a "not" too many. Implicit references to previous posts, cannot be resolved without further knowledge: "With the Cain and Abel story [...] the bible never said that they were the only people on the earth" (referring to a passage where his opponent argues with illogical parts of the bible). A downside of the use of LLMs are reformulations that change the original content. An example is the generated segment "The Dutch euthanasia's have doubled since 1998.", whereas the text originally states "The euthanasia's in Belgium have doubled since 1998". In our case, this only happens in exceptional cases and is therefore not further considered, but it is important to keep this possibility in mind. Moreover, LLMs have problems with argumentative chains (such as "1: Every state of the universe is caused by another state. 2: If every state of the universe if caused by another state, then an initial state is logically impossible. 3: From 1 and 2, an initial state is logically impossible. 4: From 3, there can be no cause of the initial state. 5: According to the definition of god, god cannot exist.") that are consistently separated rather than kept together.

6 Conclusion

In this work, we formalize the new task of text segmentation by key statements, the most salient argumentative statements in a text that form the basis for an abstract overview of the contained arguments. We provide detailed insights into the theoretical background of the task, and into its evaluation that takes the ambiguity of segmentation into consideration. Moreover, we demonstrate the suitability of the proposed coarse-grained segmentation approach for less structured web documents, such as discussion forums, and apply a range of segmenters of varying complexity. For the evaluation, we provide a first test set with human annotations of key statements in 50 texts. First experiments on this test set show that a segmentation by paragraphs represents a strong baseline for the task. While previous unit segmentation approaches result in a high number of very short segments, LLMs provide the most promising results so far. They additionally have the advantage that they allow subtle adaptations to the text which can be useful in order to tackle segmentation challenges, such as resolving missing co-references or formulating implicit statements more explicitly. All approaches benefit in terms of precision when applying an additional filtering step to remove non-argumentative segments. Our results suggest that a combination of different approaches, such as paragraphs and LLMs, could lead to even better results. Also, chain-of-thought prompting could further improve the effectiveness of LLMs on this task. Apart from that, we plan to investigate the usefulness of key statements for the generation of key points in future work.

7 Limitations

The presented setup for the automatic segmentation of an argumentative text by key statements entails different limitations which are important to consider. First of all, we propose a "stacked" evaluation approach where multiple steps are performed until the final results are available. Although all steps are evaluated, each step is a potential source of error. For example, the quality of the intermediate matching step (and optionally of the classification approach for filtering non-argumentative segments) influences the final effectiveness of the different segmentation approaches. The estimation of the key point coverage additionally relies on the approach for mapping segments and key points. The key point coverage as calculated in this paper, is additionally limited by the number of key points provided in the ArgKP 2021 dataset. Table 9 shows example segments where none of the provided key points is suitable. It is therefore desirable, to extend the existing key points in future work. Regarding the data base, it should be emphasized that working with unstructured documents from the web is always more challenging than with curated data, and that automatic analysis methods can only be applied to a limited extend. Finally, we are aware of the limited size of our test dataset. However, it covers a considerable range of texts with different levels of quality and structuredness, and is thus sufficient to demonstrate the concept of our proposed evaluation setup. Moreover, it can be extended for further evaluations.

8 Ethical Considerations

All annotators gave their consent to the use of their key statement annotations. They all have an academic background, but we collected no further demographic information as they are not relevant in our context, and could not be sufficiently anonymized for three people. Since no personal data were collected, an approval by an ethics review board was not necessary. The texts collected from the debate portals might contain harmful content, but we do not take responsibility for offensive content of any kind. All argumentative texts were processed by annotators and authors independent of their personal opinion on the expressed statements. As already noted, the use of LLMs for the segmentation task has the potential to distort the content, so their output should always be verified. All scientific artifacts used in this work are free to use for research purposes. This mainly concerns the args.me corpus (CC BY 4.0), data from the IBM shared task (Apache License 2.0), the argument classification model by Reimers et al.

(2019) (Apache License 2.0) and the TARGER API (MIT License). All artifacts are used in the context of argumentation mining and analysis which is consistent with their original use.

Acknowledgments

This publication has been partially supported by the European Union's Horizon Europe research and innovation programme under grant agreement No 101070014 (OpenWebSearch.EU), and by the German Federal Ministry of Education and Research (BMBF) through the project "DIALOKIA: Überprüfung von LLM-generierter Argumentation mittels dialektischem Sprachmodell" (01IS24084A-B).

References

Yamen Ajjour, Milad Alshomary, Henning Wachsmuth, and Benno Stein. 2019a. Modeling Frames in Argumentation. In *Proceedings of EMNLP-IJCNLP 2019*, pages 2922–2932.

Yamen Ajjour, Wei-Fan Chen, Johannes Kiesel, Henning Wachsmuth, and Benno Stein. 2017. Unit Segmentation of Argumentative Texts. In *Proceedings of ArgMining@EMNLP 2017*, pages 118–128.

Yamen Ajjour, Henning Wachsmuth, Johannes Kiesel, Martin Potthast, Matthias Hagen, and Benno Stein. 2019b. Data Acquisition for Argument Search: The args.me Corpus. In *42nd German Conference on Artificial Intelligence (KI 2019)*, pages 48–59.

Tariq Alhindi and Debanjan Ghosh. 2021. "Sharks are not the threat humans are": Argument Component Segmentation in School Student Essays. In *Proceedings of BEA@EACL, 2021*, pages 210–222.

Milad Alshomary, Timon Gurcke, Shahbaz Syed, Philipp Heinisch, Maximilian Spliethöver, Philipp Cimiano, Martin Potthast, and Henning Wachsmuth. 2021. Key Point Analysis via Contrastive Learning and Extractive Argument Summarization. In *Proceedings of ArgMining@EMNLP 2021*, pages 184–189.

Roy Bar-Haim, Lilach Eden, Roni Friedman, Yoav Kantor, Dan Lahav, and Noam Slonim. 2020a. From Arguments to Key Points: Towards Automatic Argument Summarization. In *Proceedings of ACL 2020*.

Roy Bar-Haim, Yoav Kantor, Lilach Eden, Roni Friedman, Dan Lahav, and Noam Slonim. 2020b. Quantitative Argument Summarization and Beyond: Cross-Domain Key Point Analysis. In *Proceedings of EMNLP 2020*.

Tong Chen, Hongwei Wang, Sihao Chen, Wenhao Yu, Kaixin Ma, Xinran Zhao, Hongming Zhang, and Dong Yu. 2024. Dense X Retrieval: What Retrieval Granularity Should We Use? In *Proceedings of EMNLP 2024*, pages 15159–15177.

Artem Chernodub, Oleksiy Oliynyk, Philipp Heidenreich, Alexander Bondarenko, Matthias Hagen, Chris Biemann, and Alexander Panchenko. 2019. TARGER: Neural Argument Mining at Your Fingertips. In *Proceedings of ACL 2019*, pages 195–200.

Giulia D'Agostino, Chris A. Reed, and Daniele Puccinelli. 2024. Segmentation of Complex Question Turns for Argument Mining: A Corpus-based Study in the Financial Domain. In *Proceedings of LREC/COLING 2024*, pages 14524–14530.

Lorik Dumani, Christin Katharina Kreutz, Manuel Biertz, Alex Witry, and Ralf Schenkel. 2020. Segmenting and Clustering Noisy Arguments. In *Proceedings of LWDA 2020*, pages 23–34.

Roni Friedman, Lena Dankin, Yufang Hou, Ranit Aharonov, Yoav Katz, and Noam Slonim. 2021. Overview of the 2021 Key Point Analysis Shared Task. In *Proceedings of ArgMining@EMNLP 2021*, pages 154–164.

Yujie Fu, Yang Li, Suge Wang, Xiaoli Li, Deyu Li, Jian Liao, and Jianxing Zheng. 2023. Hierarchical Enhancement Framework for Aspect-based Argument Mining. In *Proceedings of EMNLP 2023*, pages 1423–1433.

Atsushi Fujii and Tetsuya Ishikawa. 2006. A System for Summarizing and Visualizing Arguments in Subjective Documents: Toward Supporting Decision Making. In *Proceedings of the Workshop on Sentiment and Subjectivity in Text 2006*, pages 15–22.

Debanjan Ghosh, Smaranda Muresan, Nina Wacholder, Mark Aakhus, and Matthew Mitsui. 2014. Analyzing Argumentative Discourse Units in Online Interactions. In *Proceedings of ArgMining@ACL 2014*, pages 39–48.

Samuel Guilluy, Florian Méhats, and Billal Chouli. 2023. Constituency Tree Representation for Argument Unit Recognition. In *Proceedings of ArgMining 2023*, pages 35–44.

Ivan Habernal and Iryna Gurevych. 2017. Argumentation Mining in User-Generated Web Discourse. *Comput. Linguistics*, 43(1):125–179.

Kazi Saidul Hasan and Vincent Ng. 2014. Why are You Taking this Stance? Identifying and Classifying Reasons in Ideological Debates. In *Proceedings of EMNLP 2014*, pages 751–762. ACL.

Omar Khattab, Keshav Santhanam, Xiang Lisa Li, David Hall, Percy Liang, Christopher Potts, and Matei Zaharia. 2022. Demonstrate-Search-Predict: Composing Retrieval and Language Models for Knowledge-Intensive NLP. arXiv/2212.14024.

Omar Khattab, Arnav Singhvi, Paridhi Maheshwari, Zhiyuan Zhang, Keshav Santhanam, Sri Vardhamanan, Saiful Haq, Ashutosh Sharma, Thomas T. Joshi, Hanna Moazam, Heather Miller, Matei Zaharia, and Christopher Potts. 2023. DSPy: Compiling Declarative Language Model Calls into Self-Improving Pipelines. arXiv/2310.03714.

John Lawrence and Chris Reed. 2020. Argument Mining: A Survey. *Computational Linguistics*, 45(4):765–818.

John Lawrence, Chris Reed, Colin Allen, Simon McAlister, and Andrew Ravenscroft. 2014. Mining Arguments From 19th Century Philosophical Texts Using Topic Based Modelling. In *Proceedings of ArgMining@ACL 2014*, pages 79–87.

Marco Lippi and Paolo Torroni. 2015. Context-Independent Claim Detection for Argument Mining. In *Proceedings of IJCAI 2015*, pages 185–191.

Amita Misra, Pranav Anand, Jean E. Fox Tree, and Marilyn A. Walker. 2015. Using Summarization to Discover Argument Facets in Online Idealogical Dialog. In *Proceedings of NAACL HLT 2015*, pages 430–440.

Marie-Francine Moens, Erik Boiy, Raquel Mochales Palau, and Chris Reed. 2007. Automatic Detection of Arguments in Legal Texts. In *Proceedings of IAAIL 2007*, pages 225–230.

Hiroki Nakayama, Takahiro Kubo, Junya Kamura, Yasufumi Taniguchi, and Xu Liang. 2018. doccano: Text annotation tool for human. Software available from https://github.com/doccano/doccano.

Raquel Mochales Palau and Marie-Francine Moens. 2008. Study on the Structure of Argumentation in Case Law. In *JURIX 2008*, pages 11–20.

Raquel Mochales Palau and Marie-Francine Moens. 2009. Argumentation Mining: The Detection, Classification and Structure of Arguments in Text. In *Proceedings of ICAIL 2009*, pages 98–107.

Isaac Persing and Vincent Ng. 2016. End-to-End Argumentation Mining in Student Essays. In *Proceedings of NAACL HLT 2016*, pages 1384–1394.

Lev Pevzner and Marti A. Hearst. 2002. A Critique and Improvement of an Evaluation Metric for Text Segmentation. *Comput. Linguistics*, 28(1):19–36.

Nils Reimers, Benjamin Schiller, Tilman Beck, Johannes Daxenberger, Christian Stab, and Iryna Gurevych. 2019. Classification and Clustering of Arguments with Contextualized Word Embeddings. In *Proceedings of ACL 2019*, pages 567–578.

Christian Stab and Iryna Gurevych. 2017. Parsing Argumentation Structures in Persuasive Essays. *Comput. Linguistics*, 43(3):619–659.

Manfred Stede and Jodi Schneider. 2019. Finding Claims. In *Argumentation Mining*, pages 57–76. Springer.

Shahbaz Syed, Roxanne El Baff, Johannes Kiesel, Khalid Al Khatib, Benno Stein, and Martin Potthast. 2020. News Editorials: Towards Summarizing Long Argumentative Texts. In *Proceedings of COLING 2020*, pages 5384–5396.

Maite Taboada and William C. Mann. 2006. Rhetorical structure theory: looking back and moving ahead. *Discourse Studies*, 8(3):423–459.

Amine Trabelsi and Osmar R. Zaïane. 2019. PhAITV: A Phrase Author Interaction Topic Viewpoint Model for the Summarization of Reasons Expressed by Polarized Stances. In *Proceedings of ICWSM 2019*, pages 482–492.

Dietrich Trautmann. 2020. Aspect-Based Argument Mining. arXiv/2011.00633.

Dietrich Trautmann, Johannes Daxenberger, Christian Stab, Hinrich Schütze, and Iryna Gurevych. 2020. Fine-grained argument unit recognition and classification. In *Proceedings of AAAI 2020*, pages 9048–9056. AAAI Press.

Henning Wachsmuth, Martin Potthast, Khalid Al-Khatib, Yamen Ajjour, Jana Puschmann, Jiani Qu, Jonas Dorsch, Viorel Morari, Janek Bevendorff, and Benno Stein. 2017. Building an Argument Search Engine for the Web. In *Proceedings of ArgMining 2017*, pages 49–59.

A Appendix

Decompose the 'content' into clear and simple arguments, ensuring they are interpretable out of context.

1. Maintain the original phrasing from the input whenever possible.
2. Decontextualize each argument by adding necessary modifier to nouns or entire sentences and replacing pronouns (e.g. 'it', 'he', 'she', 'they', 'this', 'that') with the full name of the entities they refer to.
3. Each argument can consist of multiple sentences.
4. Present the results as a list of strings.

Input: Good morning my fine opponent and thank you for this wonderful debate. I will start off with a small overview of my points, and then leave it to you for the next round. [...] Teens should be able to develop self-expression and their personal identity. Instead, they might resort to unconventional piercings and tattoos... School uniforms encourage followers not leaders. The practice discourages independent thinkers. This follower mentality could extend into adulthood. [...]

Output:
- Teens should be able to develop self-expression and their personal identity. With school uniforms, they might resort to unconventional piercings and tattoos...
- School uniforms encourage followers not leaders. The practice discourages independent thinkers. This follower mentality could extend into adulthood.
- ...

Input: *<new text>*
Output:

Figure 4: PaLM prompt for segmentation.

[...] So if there is no evidence left behind and there are scientific explanations for things usually described to god. Than the evidence points more towards there being no god. Just because we can't know absolutely doesn't mean that based on the evidence we can't make an educated guess about what is most likely true. "In short, you have faith God doesn't exist therefore live your life as if he did not. " I don't have faith that he does not exist I have no reason to believe he does [...] We can never know anything absolutely but we do have evidence that that can help us know what is most likely true.

Figure 5: Text on topic 'We should adopt atheism', highlighting two different formulations of the same statement.

- Eating meat isn't necessary for maximum physical development.
- All of the vitamins and minerals in meat can be found in other foods.
- The taste of meat does not outweigh the costs of killing.
- Vegetarianism saves animals' lives.
- Vegetarianism helps one's health.
- Vegetarianism helps the environment.
- Almost all major religions agree that vegetarianism is better than eating meat.

Figure 6: Segments generated by GPT-4o mini for the argumentative text in Section 1, Figure 1.

Match Category	Manual	Model
matched	man	Eating meat isn't necessary for maximum physical development.
matched	man	Eating meat isn't necessary for maximum physical development. All of the vitamins, minerals etc. in meat can be found in other foods.
incomplete (a)	man	Eating meat isn't necessary.
incomplete (b)	man	part 1: Eating meat isn't necessary
		part 2: All of the vitamins, minerals etc. in meat can be found in other foods.
impure	man	Eating meat isn't necessary for maximum physical development. All of the vitamins, minerals etc. in meat can be found in other foods. And does the taste of meat really outweigh the costs of killing?
incomplete & impure	man	Eating meat isn't necessary. And does the taste of meat really outweigh the costs of killing?
missed	man	—
spurious	—	Thanks for the timely response.

Table 7: Examples for different error categories in segment matching. Manually extracted main proposition (man): "Eating meat isn't necessary for maximum physical development."

Measure	Approach					
	PaLM filt.	GPT-4 filt.	Paragr. filt.	Sent. filt.	Ajjour. filt.	Targer. filt.
# Segments	173	272	154	408	413	465
matched | Precision	0.57	0.35	0.63	0.38	0.29	0.30
– correct	0.43	0.24	0.36	0.21	0.18	0.18
– incomplete	0.11	0.10	0.16	0.16	0.11	0.11
– impure	0.02	0.01	0.08	0.00	0.00	0.00
– incomplete & impure	0.01	0.00	0.03	0.01	0.00	0.01
spurious	0.43	0.65	0.37	0.62	0.70	0.69
matched | Recall	0.59	0.52	0.66	0.79	0.64	0.73
– correct	0.50	0.41	0.38	0.56	0.49	0.56
– incomplete	0.05	0.08	0.07	0.21	0.14	0.15
– impure	0.03	0.02	0.18	0.01	0.0	0.01
– incomplete & impure	0.01	0.01	0.03	0.01	0.01	0.01
missed	0.41	0.47	0.33	0.20	0.36	0.27
F1 micro strict	0.46	0.30	0.37	0.31	0.26	0.27
F1 micro relaxed	0.58	0.42	0.65	0.52	0.41	0.44

Table 8: Effectiveness of different argument segmentation approaches after filtering segments labeled as non-argumentative (classification approach by (Reimers et al., 2019)). The evaluation is done from a precision- and recall-oriented perspective, reporting the micro average scores. The rows 'matched' cover all correct and incorrect segments, the total number of manual reference segments is 147.

Segment PaLM	Key Point
Every time the DP is used the right to life is violated.	State-sanctioned killing is principally wrong
Study shows that there there is not enough evidence to support the fact that the death penalty does not act as a deterrence.	The death penalty is ineffective in deterring crimes
88% of expert criminologists concur that the death penalty doesn't deter violent crime, despite what these "flimsy" studies might suggest.	The death penalty is ineffective in deterring crimes
People generally support capital punishment because they believe criminals do not deserve to live.	State-sanctioned killing is principally wrong
The purpose of the justice system is, ideally, to make an impartial decision not to satisfy the lust for vengeance possessed by the victim's loved ones. The "bonus" of satisfying the family is hardly adequate reason to support the death penalty.	The death penalty helps the victim/their family
Pro argues that the death penalty is justified because it is saving money that would otherwise be used for life imprisonment; if anyone is trying to put a dollar value on human life, it would be Pro.	The death penalty saves costs to the state
Even law enforcement admits that the death penalty is "the least efficient use of taxpayers' money".	The death penalty saves costs to the state
The use of the death penalty is actually far more expensive than the maintenance of a LIP inmate.	The death penalty saves costs to the state
What makes it right for the guilty person to be deserved of the same thing he's being executed for? [...] life imprisonment is a better means of punishing the guilty.	
It is exceedingly rare for those confined in prison to escape.	
Justice is not killing people to make ourselves feel at ease. Justice is not an eye for an eye, a tooth for a tooth until we are all blind and toothless.	
...our "justice" system would condemn these men to death without providing a chance for contrition, repentance, or redemption. [...]	
Ethical justifications are not based upon economic gains ([...] human life cannot be compared to material goods).	

Table 9: Examples of segment key point matches for the topic 'We should abolish capital punishment'. The segments in the lower half have no suitable key point in the ArgKP 2021 dataset (Friedman et al., 2021).

#	Segments
0	Viewers keep in mind I will first be finishing addressing my opponents round 2 rebuttal.
1	Defense: C.4, Jury less likely to condemn.
2	I would like some evidence that the jury are able to choose the sentence of the criminal, because I've been searching for it but can't find it.
3	The DP saves only the lives of criminals being murdered, besides cases when murderers are let go with should not happen. The DP sometimes kills innocents.
4	Defense: C.5, Innocence.
5	Here's a case in which a man was framed by the police. [1]
6	This source says that well over eighty people in the past quarter century have been condemned but then released before execution [2]
7	This source shows accounts of 11 innocents being executed. [3]
8	Here is a quote from one study taken.
9	" In my current research into probable innocents that have been executed, I have uncovered at least 74 cases in which wrongful executions have most likely taken place." [2]
10	Let me also add what I said in the previous round. There have undoubtedly been cases in which the innocent have been executed but have not been proved innocent afterwards. After being executed there is usually not much need for someone to try too prove the innocence of someone who is already dead. So there are undoubtedly instances in the past where we have executed an innocent man but did not know so, and still do not know.
11	With life imprisonment there is zero chance of killing an innocent man.
12	Defense: C.6, Life imprisonment just as effective removing those who cause harm.
13	The only people murderers can harm is their fellow inmates, assuming they were not sentenced to solitary confinement. This is far outweighed by the fact that executing innocents is a much bigger a problem than murderers and rapists killing each other.
14	Defense: C.8, Violates the right to life.
15	1. Not outweighed: The lives saved by the DP are the lives of rapists and murderers. The lives saved by life imprisonment are the lives on innocent people wrongly condemned.
16	2. "Not comparable morally": The murderer of course has no right to take another mans life. So what makes it right for us to take his life?
17	3. Murderer is guilty, but not deserved of death: What makes it right for the guilty person to be deserved of the same thing he's being executed for? Of course he's guilty, but life imprisonment is a better means of punishing the guilty.
18	4. DP Vengeful: My opponents analogy's are faulty. His first analogy doesn't even make sense because what he's saying is it would be absurd to kidnap someone to show that kidnapping is wrong. I agree that would be absurd, which is why killing people to show killing people is wrong is also absurd. His second analogy is completely wrong because cops don't punish those who speed by speeding.
19	5. Violating anothers rights does not deprive you of your own: John Stuart Mill is essentially saying the "eye for eye tooth for tooth" concept is right. Proving that the DP is vengeful. This concept is widely accepted as wrong.
20	6. I'm not sure exactly what my opponent means by personal liberty, but putting a man in prison for murder is easily justified while the DP is not.
21	7. The fact of whether war is justified is completely another matter.
22	8. "Protecting the right to life": Every time the DP is used the right to life is violated. As for lives saved, see my first point.
23	It is fallacious reasoning to assume that, because murder rates were dropping at the time the DP was used that means it was because of the DP.
...	...
33	"Prisoners prefer life"
34	I think that it all depends for different people.
35	Being locked in a single small room in solitary confinement for years on end is certainly not very pleasant.
...	...
49	http://beta.nodeathpenalty.org... [1]
50	http://www.the-slammer.org... [2]
51	http://www.justicedenied.org... [3]

Table 10: Examplary paragraph segments. Gray segments are removed since they contain less than 3 whitespaces—the segment at index 33 is the only relevant passage that is lost by this filtering approach.

Overview of the Critical Questions Generation Shared Task

Blanca Calvo Figueras[♠], **Jaione Bengoetxea**[♠], **Maite Heredia**[♠], **Ekaterina Sviridova**[♣], **Elena Cabrio**[♣], **Serena Villata**[♣], **Rodrigo Agerri**[♠]
[♠]HiTZ Center - Ixa, University of the Basque Country, UPV/EHU
[♣]Université Côte d'Azur, Inria, CNRS, I3S, France
blanca.calvo@ehu.eus rodrigo.agerri@ehu.eus

Abstract

The proliferation of AI technologies has reinforced the importance of developing critical thinking skills. We propose leveraging Large Language Models (LLMs) to facilitate the generation of critical questions: inquiries designed to identify fallacious or inadequately constructed arguments. This paper presents an overview of the first shared task on Critical Questions Generation (CQs-Gen). Thirteen teams investigated various methodologies for generating questions that critically assess arguments within the provided texts. The highest accuracy achieved was 67.6, indicating substantial room for improvement in this task. Moreover, three of the four top-performing teams incorporated argumentation scheme annotations to enhance their systems. Finally, while most participants employed open-weight models, the two highest-ranking teams relied on proprietary LLMs.[1]

1 Introduction

In recent years, educators and researchers have expressed growing concern that the widespread use of LLM–based chat systems may encourage superficial learning habits and undermine the development of critical thinking skills (Hadi Mogavi et al., 2024). In response to this challenge, our shared task explores a novel approach: leveraging LLMs to promote critical thinking. Specifically, we propose using LLMs to guide users in formulating critical questions or, in other words, questions aimed at uncovering fallacious reasoning or poorly constructed arguments (Calvo Figueras and Agerri, 2024).

To this end, we introduce the task of Critical Questions Generation (CQs-Gen), a generative task that involves automatically generating useful critical questions for argumentative texts. Critical questions (CQs) are inquiries used to evaluate whether an argument is valid or flawed. These questions serve to expose underlying and spurious assumptions in the argument's premises and to question the inferential relations between premises and conclusions, thereby enabling the identification of potential fallacies and weaknesses in the reasoning (Walton et al., 2008).

This research extends prior work's findings on the fact that critical questions may serve as effective tools for fighting misinformation (Musi et al., 2023) and evaluating argumentative essays (Song et al., 2014) by exposing flawed argumentative structures. Additionally, it draws upon established research in argumentation scheme taxonomy development and argumentative text annotation (Walton et al., 2008; Wachsmuth et al., 2017; Macagno et al., 2017; Visser et al., 2021).

This paper presents an overview of the shared task, including a detailed discussion and analysis of the results obtained by the participants. The shared task was launched in February 2025. Participants were given one and a half months to work on the validation set and later evaluated their systems in the test set. The reference questions for the test set remained hidden. A total of 19 teams registered for the task, 13 submitted system outputs for evaluation, and 12 provided corresponding system descriptions.

Key findings from this shared task include: (i) model selection has a greater impact than prompt engineering, though the benefits of model scaling are limited; (ii) using argumentation schemes helps generate more useful CQs but tends to reduce question diversity; and (iii) there remains significant room for improvement in the task of CQs-Gen.

2 Task Description

To facilitate systematic experimentation and evaluation for the task of CQs-Gen, we developed a dataset comprising debate interventions paired with

[1] https://hitz-zentroa.github.io/shared-task-critical-questions-generation/

Proceedings of the 12th Argument Mining Workshop, pages 243–257
July 31, 2025 ©2025 Association for Computational Linguistics

Walton: Claire's absolutely right about that. But then the problem is that that form of capitalism wasn't generating sufficient surpluses. And so therefore where did the money flow. It didn't flow into those industrial activities, because in the developed world that wasn't making enough money.

(a) **Input**: the intervention

USE: What evidence is there to support the claim that the form of capitalism being used in the developed world was not generating sufficient surpluses?

USE: How is "sufficient surpluses" defined, and how would one measure it?

USE: Are there any alternative explanations for why the money did not flow into industrial activities?

(b) **Output**: Given that all CQs here are useful, this answer has an overall punctuation of 1.

IN: Does this argument support Socialist policies?

UN: How does the speaker define "the developed world", and is this a relevant distinction in this context?

USE: What are the "industrial activities" being referred to, and how do they relate to the form of capitalism in question?

(c) **Output**: This set of questions would get $0.\overline{33}$ points for the useful CQ, 0 for the CQ that is unhelpful, and 0 for the invalid one. Therefore, this answer has a $0.\overline{33}$ punctuation.

Figure 1: Example of candidate outputs with its labels: Useful (USE), Unhelpful (UN), and Invalid (IN).

corresponding critical questions. The dataset contains real debate interventions that have been annotated with argumentation schemes and associated critical question sets. Each intervention includes the speaker's identity, argumentation scheme classifications, and critical questions. The critical questions are labeled according to their effectiveness in challenging the presented arguments, using three categories: Useful, Unhelpful, or Invalid.

In this shared task, participants are asked to develop a system that gets one of the interventions as input and produces three insightful critical questions. The generated questions are compared to the annotated gold references of each intervention, and each generated question inherits the label of the most similar reference CQ. Note that each of these questions is evaluated separately, and that the punctuation is then aggregated.

Useful critical questions are given $0.\overline{33}$ points, and Unhelpful and Invalid CQs get 0 points. Therefore, each output containing 3 CQs is given a score between 0 and 1, depending on the usefulness of the generated questions. The definitions of these categories are described in Section 3. Figure 1 shows two evaluated possible outputs for a given intervention.

Participants were encouraged to engage in the task by either generating multiple critical questions and choosing the top 3, or by developing a system that only outputs useful critical questions.

2.1 Evaluation

The evaluation is performed by comparing the newly automatically generated critical questions with the reference critical questions in the dataset using semantic textual similarity (STS) with Sentence Transformers (Reimers and Gurevych, 2019). The new question inherits the label of its most similar reference. We employ *stsb-mpnet-base-v2* embeddings with a threshold of 0.65, as this approach demonstrated the highest correlation with human evaluation among non-LLM methods in previous research (Calvo Figueras and Agerri, 2025).

If the newly generated questions do not match any of the reference critical questions, in other words, the similarity between the new CQ and each reference CQ is lower than 0.65, the question is tagged as *Not Able to Evaluate* (NAE). In these cases, NAE questions are manually evaluated following the same annotation guidelines employed during reference CQ annotation.

Considering $\{R\}$ as the set of vectors of the reference questions, N the vector of the newly generated question, and T the threshold, the label is computed as:

$$f(N) = \begin{cases} R_{argmax_j cos}(R_j, N) & \text{if } max_j cos(R_j, N) > T \\ \text{NAE} & \text{else} \end{cases}$$

2.2 Baselines

The baselines for the shared task were developed by prompting two LLMs to generate critical questions with the requirement of avoiding non-useful questions (prompt in Appendix A). We used the default hyperparameters and HuggingFace's implementations of:

- run 1: Qwen2.5-VL-72B-Instruct (Qwen et al., 2025)
- run 2: gemma-2-9b-it (Team et al., 2024)

Baseline models undergo identical evaluation procedures as the participants' submissions to ensure methodological consistency and prevent preferential treatment.

3 Data

For this shared task, we use the CQs-Gen benchmark (Calvo Figueras and Agerri, 2025), which was built on top of 4 existing datasets: US2016 (Visser et al., 2021), Moral Maze Debates (Lawrence et al., 2018), RRD (Konat et al., 2016), and US2016reddit. Our CQs-Gen dataset contains 220 argumentative texts, associated with 22.4 questions on average (theoretical and LLM-generated), which have been manually annotated. The dataset is divided between a validation set (186 texts) and a test set (34 texts). The reference questions of the test set are kept private to avoid data contamination (Sainz et al., 2023). Table 1 shows the stats of these two splits.

Set	Nº Int.	Nº CQs	%USE	%UN	%IN
Valid.	186	4,136	67.46	21.59	10.95
Test	34	806	42.68	31.02	26.30

Table 1: Stats of the dataset.

These questions have been annotated by journalists specialized in detecting misinformation. They were asked, "Can this question be used to undermine the arguments given in the intervention?". If they considered that the question is not useful, they could choose between two possibilities: the question not being valid, or the question being unhelpful.[2] The three categories are described in the guidelines as follows:

1. **Useful (USE)**: The answer to this question can potentially challenge one of the arguments in the text.

2. **Unhelpful (UN)**: The question is valid, but it is unlikely to challenge any of the arguments in the text.

3. **Invalid (IN)**: This question is invalid because it cannot be used to challenge any of the arguments in the text. Either because (1) its reasoning is not right, (2) the question is not related to the text, (3) it introduces new concepts not present in the intervention, (4) it is too general and could be applied to any text, or (5) it is not critical with any argument of the text (e.g. a reading-comprehension question).

[2]The guidelines can be found in `https://github.com/hitz-zentroa/shared-task-critical-questions-generation/blob/main/shared_task/utils/guidelines.pdf`

3.1 Training Phase

In the training phase, the participants worked with the validation set (184 interventions). For this dataset, we released the reference CQs and their annotations, the argumentation schemes, and their datasets of origin. This phase lasted a month and a half.

3.2 Evaluation Phase

During evaluation, participants processed the test set containing 34 interventions without access to reference critical questions. Each participant submitted a maximum of three result runs to the organizers, who assessed the generated outputs using the similarity-based automated metric against withheld reference standards. The highest-scoring run from each participating group underwent manual evaluation, wherein three human annotators, the task organizers, assigned labels to the NAE cases based on the established annotation guidelines.

4 Submissions

Nineteen different teams registered for the shared task, of which thirteen submitted their system outputs during the evaluation phase, and twelve submitted a system description, eleven of which were archival submissions. A summary of the submitted papers is provided below.

4.1 System description

ELLIS Alicante Favero et al. (2025) won the shared task. Their approach uses a *Questioner* LLM that generates the questions together with a *Judge* LLM that picks the best 3 candidates. For both components of their pipeline, they try multiple configurations, such as different models, using argumentation schemes, and different numbers of candidates. Their best system uses GPT-4o (OpenAI et al., 2024) for both components, and generates 8 candidates per text, half of which have to be connected to the argumentation schemes.

COGNAC Anjum Islam et al. (2025) experiment with RAG-based approaches to (1) select example CQs of similar interventions for few-shot, (2) incorporate argumentation schemes descriptions, and

(3) again perform few-shot but this time using both the intervention and the reference CQs for computing similarity. Their best system uses approach 1 and GPT-4o-mini. They acknowledge this system might have constrained generalization to texts outside of the dataset.

StateCloud Zhang et al. (2025) investigate both prompt-engineering and model ensembling. Regarding prompts, they try zero-shot, few-shot, oral-expression, and shuffling the order of the instructions. They report that the improvement observed with prompt engineering is largely overshadowed by model selection. Regarding model ensembling, they experiment with sequential and parallel ensembling. Generating CQs by sequentially prompting different models obtains the best results in the validation set. However, their best performing system in the test set combines Qwen2.5-72B, QwQ-32B, and DeepSeek R1 in parallel (Team, 2025; Yang et al., 2024; DeepSeek-AI, 2025).

DayDreamer Zhou et al. (2025) are the most theory-based team. They develop a pipeline that (1) conversationally builds the structure of the arguments in the text (they fill the templates of the argumentation schemes), to then (2) generate the candidate questions, and finally (3) rank them regarding usefulness to choose the top 3. They use LLMs for all these steps, and achieve their best results with GPT-4o-mini. Their analysis shows that the quality of the scheme template can have a great impact on their pipeline.

Webis Kanadan et al. (2025)'s approach consists of a pipeline with two components, namely: (1) a generation LLM, and (2) an encoder fine-tuned to label the questions as Useful or Not-Useful. They try different prompting strategies, such as guidelines-based, chain-of-thought, and few-shot. Additionally, they create new data for fine-tuning. They achieve their best results using Gemma2-9B and Phi-4-14B for generating 3 questions each, and fine-tuning ModernBERT with their new data (Warner et al., 2024).

TriLLaMa Turkstra et al. (2025) explore the use of various sizes of Llama-3.1 models (Grattafiori et al., 2024) for both the generation and classification of CQs. The most effective configuration employs Llama-3.1-405B for few-shot question generation and Llama-3.1-70B for zero-shot classification. Furthermore, two innovative classification strategies yield notable results: (1) debate classification, in which two models debate the usefulness of a CQ and a third model adjudicates the winner; and (2) deliberation classification, where two models vote on the questions they consider to be most helpful.

Mind_Matrix Mahmud et al. (2025) develop a pipeline where critical questions are generated using LLMs and then ranked according to a score. This score is the product of the similarity of the question to the intervention, the coherence, and the relevance. All these metrics are computed using Sentence Transformers. Finally, a last module of the pipeline uses another LLM to rank the effectiveness of the chosen CQs, if the average score of the 3 CQs is lower than a threshold, they rerun the pipeline, lowering the temperature by 0.1. Their best-performing model is DeepHermes-3-Llama-3-8B (Teknium et al., 2025).

CriticalBrew El Baff et al. (2025) employ a machine society simulation approach (Zhang et al., 2024). This approach creates a network of agents that collaborate to reach a conclusion using different personality traits and thinking patterns. They experiment with different configurations and conclude that the number of agents and the thinking patterns significantly impact the results, while the personality traits do not. They also experiment with ranking the CQs using LLMs with different prompts. Their best-performing model uses Mistral-24B with 2 easy-going agents and an overconfident one, with three rounds of discussion, two debate rounds, and one discussion round.

Tndguyen Nguyen and Nguyen (2025) investigate multi step reasoning techniques, namely: chain-of-thought prompting in zero-shot and one-shot, least-to-most settings, and tree-of-thought prompting. Their results show that structured prompting consistently offers performance gains. Their best-performing system is zero-shot chain-of-thought prompting with GPT-4o. Their error analysis highlights that models tend to fail in long and multi-topic interventions, as well as those involving emotionally charged and subjective content.

ARG2ST Ramponi et al. (2025) build a pipeline with an LLM for generation and a fine-tuned encoder for classification. In the generation step, they experiment with modularly extending the prompts with argumentation schemes, guideline descriptions, and few-shot examples. Their ablation study shows that incorporating a classifier consistently improves the performance of their systems and that providing explanations in the prompt on not-useful CQs works better than providing instructions on which ones are useful. Their best performing system is a Llama-3-70B for generation and a BERT-base as classifier (Devlin et al., 2019).

CUET_SR34 Bhattacharjee et al. (2025) fine-tune a Llama-3-8B model using LoRa on a 10% of the validation set and a few-shot prompt. They show that simplifying the text, adding named entities (NER), and the names of the argumentation schemes, gets their best results.

Nompt This team focuses exclusively on two issues in CQs-Gen, namely: questions that do not target the speaker's arguments and instead are in line with them; and questions that introduce new concepts related to some named entity mentioned but not present in the text. They propose 4 stages: (1) argument scheme extraction, (2) speaker anonymization, (3) main points extraction, and (4) questions generation using only the extracted information. While their overall results are low, their manual evaluation shows that their approach solves the phenomena they are targeting.

Team Name	Run	Score	Auto. score
ELLIS Alicante	3	**67.6**	50.0
COGNAC	1	**62.7**	61.8
StateCloud	3	**59.8**	47.1
DayDreamer	1	**58.8**	55.9
Webis	2	**56.9**	52.0
TriLLaMa	1	**55.9**	53.9
Mind_Matrix	1	**55.9**	42.2
CriticalBrew	1	**54.9**	52.0
Lilo&stitch*	2	**53.9**	49.0
baseline	2	**52.9**	52.0
Tdnguyen	1	**52.0**	49.0
ARG2ST	2	**50.0**	45.1
CUET_SR34	1	**48.0**	43.1
baseline	1	**44.1**	41.2
Nompt	1	**38.2**	29.4

Table 2: Official results of the shared task.
* This team did not submit a system description. Therefore, we do not discuss it.

5 Results

The official results of the shared ask are reported in Table 2. Based on the automatic evaluation metric, *COGNAC* was initially ranked first. However, manual evaluation revealed *ELLIS Alicante* as the winner of the shared task, with *StateCloud* in third place. *ELLIS Alicante* employed a strategy that prioritized minimizing Unhelpful and Invalid question categories rather than optimizing for maximum overall scores through NAE reduction. This approach demonstrated superior generalization capabilities on the test set, an effect that was only detectable through manual assessment.

Interestingly, 3 out of the 4 best-performing teams (*ELLIS Alicante*, *COGNAC*, and *DayDreamer*) reported that argumentation schemes improved system performance. Two other teams, *Webis* and *ARG2ST*, also experimented with argumentation schemes but excluded them from their final submissions, determining that the performance gains were insufficient to warrant inclusion. We examine the various methods by which this information is integrated in Section 6.

Multiple teams reported that differences between models had a greater impact than prompt variations. Thus, three of the top 4 teams (*ELLIS Alicante*, *COGNAC*, and *DayDreamer*) relied on GPT-4o or GPT-4o-mini for their submissions. Unsurprisingly, submissions with lower performance typically used smaller and open-weight models, which represented the most frequently selected option among participants.

Several teams implemented classification or ranking methodologies to select the most promising critical questions. All teams using these approaches reported performance improvements. We analyze their methods in Section 6.

6 Additional Evaluations and Analysis

The following sections provide supplementary automated evaluation methods and analyses beyond the official results to examine the implications of participant design choices.

Results on the validation set. During system development, participants had access only to the validation set, which informed their design decisions. Comparison of validation and official test set results (see Table 4 in Appendix) revealed no clear correlation between performance across these datasets. However, each team's best-performing validation submission typically remained their strongest on the test set. Qualitative insights from validation analysis transferred effectively to test performance, with teams conducting more comprehensive qualitative evaluations achieving superior final results.

LLM- and data-enhanced evaluation. Calvo Figueras and Agerri (2025) introduced two evaluation methods that demonstrated better correlation with human judgment and an expanded test set. The extended test set incorporated manual evaluations from this shared task to increase reference CQs and reduce NAE values. The proposed evaluation methods employed LLMs (Claude 3.5 Sonnet[3] and Gemma-2-9B-it (Team et al., 2024)) to compare reference and generated CQs, assigning labels to new questions based on matching references. These automated approaches enabled a comprehensive evaluation of all team submissions, with results presented in the Appendix, Table 5.

The extended dataset includes manually-evaluated questions solely from each team's top-performing run, yielding accurate assessments for these runs but potentially undervaluing other runs. Analysis in Table 5 confirms *ELLIS Alicante*'s third run as the winner across all evaluation metrics. High-performing submissions absent from Table 2 include *COGNAC*'s second and third runs, indicating reliable submission standards from this team.

The effect of incorporating argumentation schemes. Several teams investigated incorporating argumentation schemes as additional context, with three of the four top-performing systems implementing them. However, effective integration proved challenging, as several teams reported no improvement or performance degradation. *ARG2ST* found no benefit from simple scheme references, while *Webis* included both scheme descriptions and associated CQs structures but similarly observed no gains. *Webis*'s analysis revealed that generated questions became excessively rigid and templated when using this approach.

Similarly, *ELLIS Alicante* found that argumentation scheme descriptions improved question quality while decreasing diversity. Their winning run combined dual prompts, with and without scheme descriptions, and employed a third LLM (also informed with argumentation schemes) to select optimal questions from the combined outputs.

[3]Version *claude-3-5-sonnet-20241022*, https://www.anthropic.com/news/claude-3-5-sonnet

Team Name	n-gram	CR-div	USE CR-div
ELLIS Alicante	**3.04**	**0.373**	0.405
COGNAC	2.52	0.287	0.306
StateCloud	2.96	0.350	0.388
DayDreamer	2.71	0.320	0.364
Webis	2.97	0.352	0.392
TriLLaMa	3.01	0.366	0.403
Mind_Matrix	2.84	0.350	0.387
CriticalBrew	2.90	0.349	0.390
Lilo&stitch	2.92	0.353	0.392
Tdnguyen	3.00	0.356	0.400
ARG2ST	**3.09**	**0.383**	0.429
CUET_SR34	2.74	0.331	0.369
Nompt	**3.12**	**0.388**	0.459

Table 3: Diversity scores (the higher the more diverse). Averaged scores between the 3 runs submitted by each team. The last column measures diversity within the Useful CQs.

COGNAC and *DayDreamer* developed two additional effective approaches for incorporating argumentation schemes. *COGNAC* paired scheme descriptions with custom CQ sets from similar interventions to reduce rigidity; *DayDreamer* centered their approach on scheme-based argument extraction followed by CQ generation. *DayDreamer*'s poor performance with *ERPracticalReasoning* and *ERExpertOpinion* schemes indicated that description quality critically affects system effectiveness.

Diversity analysis. Although many system descriptions mention diversity, none of them provide a quantitative assessment of it. To address this gap, we now analyze diversity explicitly. Following Calvo Figueras and Agerri (2025), we adopt two metrics: n-gram diversity and Compression Ratio Diversity, as defined in Shaib et al. (2025). In Table 3, these metrics are applied to the three submissions of each team and then averaged.

The results indicate that *ELLIS Alicante*, the winning team, produced one of the most diverse sets of critical questions, both overall and when considering only the Useful CQs (see last column). According to their system description, they qualitatively analyzed diversity during development and observed that using argumentation schemes for all CQs reduced diversity. Consequently, they opted to include schemes in their prompts for only half of their generated questions. Additionally, despite ranking lower on the performance leaderboard, both *ARG2ST* and *Nompt* also achieved high diversity scores.

In contrast, the least diverse sets of CQs were produced by *COGNAC* and *DayDreamer*, two of the top-performing teams. *DayDreamer* generated their questions using the theoretical CQs in all their runs, which likely contributed to the low variation in their outputs. Similarly, two of *COGNAC*'s submissions used prompts that included argumentation scheme descriptions, which may have constrained their output diversity.

These findings support the conclusion drawn by *ELLIS Alicante*: incorporating argumentation schemes involves a trade-off between usefulness and diversity. Teams aiming to optimize both may benefit from hybrid strategies that balance structured guidance with open-ended generation.

Ranking and classification modules. All teams that incorporated ranking or classification modules into their pipelines reported positive effects. However, since these modules were evaluated differently across teams, it is difficult to quantitatively compare their individual impact. Instead, we describe each team's approach in order, starting with the highest-scoring system.

1. *ELLIS Alicante* prompts an LLM to select 3 out of 8 questions generated by two other models. The prompt includes detailed guidelines and explicitly encourages the model to favor repeated questions, suggesting that repetition may indicate relevance.

2. *DayDreamer* also uses an LLM, but instead of directly selecting questions, they prompt it to rank the candidates and then choose the top 3 from the ranking.

3. *Webis* fine-tune an encoder (ModernBERT), using a dataset of 67.8k additional LLM-generated critical questions, labeled using the official evaluation script. They select the questions classified as Useful with the highest confidence.

4. *TriLLaMa* implements an original classification approach whereby multiple LLMs engage in debate and voting to classify candidate questions. However, this multi-model strategy yields inferior performance compared to zero-shot classification using a single LLM. The authors' analysis indicates that the debate process causes models to lose positional coherence and attempt simultaneous evaluation of all 10 candidates, leading to errors.

5. *Mind_Matrix* applies a handcrafted ranking method, computing a score based on similarity to the intervention, coherence, and relevance, using SentenceTransformers.

6. *CriticalBrew* prompts LLMs to perform selection, scoring, and ranking. They conclude that the specific method used (choosing vs. scoring vs. ranking) does not significantly affect overall performance.

7. *ARG2ST* adopts an approach similar to that of *Webis*, but with key differences: they use BERT-base as the encoder and do not incorporate any additional training data.

Overall, prompt-based approaches tend to yield better results than encoder-based ones. Additionally, several teams report that their classifiers exhibit a bias toward labeling most questions as Useful, a pattern consistent with findings in Calvo Figueras and Agerri (2025).

Few-shot approaches. Including examples in the prompt (i.e., few-shot learning) yielded mixed results. While some teams found it beneficial, others observed no improvement or even performance drops. A few teams included examples in their prompts but did not conduct ablation studies; therefore, we exclude those cases from this discussion.

The most successful applications of few-shot prompting came from *COGNAC*, *TriLLaMa*, and *Tndguyen*. Both *COGNAC* and *Tndguyen* employed a dynamic example selection strategy: for each test instance, they retrieved a similar intervention and used its reference CQs as examples. Additionally, *Tndguyen* augmented this with an automated reasoning path, illustrating how the example CQ related to the intervention. While these techniques are interesting, they might not generalize well to interventions about new topics. In contrast, *TriLLaMa* used a fixed set of three examples presented in a conversational format, where the user provided the intervention and the assistant replied with example CQs.

On the opposite end, *ARG2ST* reported consistent performance degradation when using few-shot prompting. Their approach involved a fixed intervention example, tested with either Useful CQs only or examples from all three categories.

StateCloud followed a similar setup and ultimately chose not to use few-shot, although their results were less conclusive.

A likely explanation for these mixed outcomes is prompt length: including examples significantly increases the prompt size, which can confuse smaller models such as those used by *ARG2ST*. In contrast, the three teams that benefited from few-shot learning used much larger models. Interestingly, *TriLLaMa* did observe some gains with smaller models, suggesting that their conversational prompt structure may have been more manageable for models with limited capacity.

Reasoning approaches Reasoning techniques are currently a topic of active research. Given that CQs-Gen involves substantial reasoning, several teams explored these advanced approaches.

Tndguyen experimented with various reasoning strategies, including Chain-of-Thought (CoT) prompting in zero-shot, few-shot, and least-to-most formats, as well as a Tree-of-Thought approach. Despite the potential of these methods, their performance gains are unexpectedly small. Their analysis identifies several categories of failure: long, multi-topic interventions; emotionally charged content; overly short texts; sensitive topics; and satirical content. *Webis* also explores CoT, but does not use it in their final prompt either.

In a different direction, *StateCloud* evaluated the performance of state-of-the-art open-weight reasoning models (DeepSeek-R1-671B and QWQ-32B). While these models did not surpass general-purpose LLMs in terms of the percentage of Useful CQs, they produced remarkably more NAE values. This suggests that the models may be generating novel, useful critical questions that lie outside the scope of the current reference CQs. However, without further analysis, this remains a hypothesis. A similar pattern was observed in the system developed by *ELLIS Alicante*, which used GPT-4o (a closed-weight reasoning model) and also generated a large number of NAE values that were later found to be useful CQs. These observations suggest that the capabilities of advanced reasoning models in CQs-Gen may currently be underestimated and highlight the need for further manual evaluation and expanded reference sets to fully capture the quality of their outputs.

Model performance Many teams observed that model selection has a greater impact on performance than prompt engineering in this task. However, several teams also noted that the benefits of scaling to larger models are surprisingly limited, often not justifying the increased computational cost. This aligns with the findings reported in Calvo Figueras and Agerri (2025).

Error analysis. Figure 2 shows the distribution of the scores per intervention of all the submissions, as evaluated in Table 5 (Appendix) with Claude. Most interventions received both maximum and zero scores, though difficulty varied considerably. While two interventions had zero as the modal score, most exhibited a median score of 0.66. *RRD* and *US2016* interventions showed distributed score ranges, whereas *Moral Maze* interventions were predominantly difficult. This pattern is interesting given that *Moral Maze* contains the most comprehensive and technical content, but addresses complex topics such as 'state intervention legitimacy' and 'loan morality'. The remaining two datasets featured more accessible topics but employed emotional language and rhetorical devices. Error analysis focused on the six lowest-scoring interventions.

The first intervention (*CLINTON_47*) is very short. In this intervention, Clinton is claiming that she did not support the NAFTA agreement once the terms were laid out. However, the intervention does not mention what agreement she is talking about, and many systems just fabricate that piece of information.

The second and fourth interventions (*pnorton_20* and *REBacon_165*) are a bit more complex. To avoid a lack of context (as in Clinton's text), some interventions in the *RRD* dataset were paired with their previous message using the mark "< *this message is answering to* >". The systems do not always get this differentiation and output questions related to the wrong message. This could be improved in the dataset.

The third intervention (*HOLT_159*) is from the presenter of the presidential debate: Holt. He is asking questions to Trump and claiming he lied for years. Many systems get confused and output questions that are in line with what Holt is saying and directed to Trump. This also happens often in another Holt's interventions (*HOLT_122*), and is one of the issues *Nompt* tried to solve. In fact, none of the CQs generated by this team in these two interventions have this issue.

The fifth intervention (*CLINTON_227*) is very emotional, as Clinton is making her final speech of

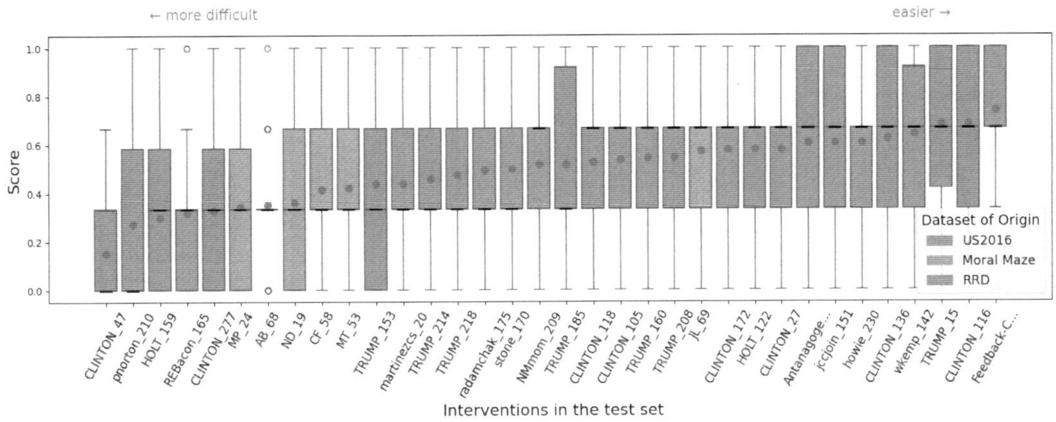

Figure 2: Distribution of the scoring of each run by intervention in the test set as evaluated with Claude in Table 5. Grey dots show the average score per intervention. The median is marked in black. Colors show the dataset of origin.

the debate, and the main points of her arguments are not very clear.

Finally, the sixth intervention (*MB_24*) is about housing loans, and the speaker is defending that laws protect borrowers over lenders. While his argument is clear and complete, the complexity of the topic makes many questions Unhelpful, and the systems often get lost in the speaker's stance.

7 Conclusions

This shared task on Critical Question Generation (CQs-Gen) aimed to promote systems capable of fostering critical thinking by generating insightful questions that challenge weak or fallacious arguments. The task attracted 19 registered teams, with 13 submitting systems and 12 providing descriptions.

The evaluation revealed that strong performance was not solely determined by automated metrics. Manual evaluation played a decisive role in identifying the most effective systems, with *ELLIS Alicante* emerging as the winner due to its focus on reducing Unhelpful and Invalid questions rather than purely optimizing quantitative scores. Their approach also highlighted the value of qualitative analysis in system development.

A key insight from the task was the mixed impact of incorporating argumentation schemes. While three of the top four teams successfully integrated these schemes into their pipelines, others reported performance degradation or reduced question diversity. This suggests that while argumentation schemes can enhance question quality and relevance, they may also limit variability and flexibility if not carefully balanced.

Model choice proved to be more impactful than prompt engineering, with most of the top-performing teams using GPT-4o or GPT-4o-mini. Additionally, classification and ranking modules that were used to select the best questions consistently improved output quality, with prompt-based approaches showing a better performance. Reasoning models did not seem to outperform general models. Nonetheless, further research is required to investigate whether they produce novel but useful CQs that are not captured by the automated evaluation method.

To further analyze system behavior, we applied automatic diversity metrics and extended test set evaluations. Results confirmed that higher-quality CQs often came with reduced diversity, reinforcing the observed trade-off between structure and variability. The winning team successfully navigated this trade-off through a hybrid generation and selection approach.

In sum, the task highlights that combining powerful models, informed prompt design, and thoughtful use of structured knowledge (like argumentation schemes) can yield high-quality critical questions. However, success also depends on careful evaluation, iterative analysis, and balancing competing goals such as diversity and usefulness.

Finally, the results of the shared task also show a big margin for improvement in CQs-Gen, revealing that it remains a challenging task for current LLMs.

Limitations

While this shared task generated valuable insights and fostered creative approaches to Critical Questions Generation (CQs-Gen), several limitations remain.

First, although many promising techniques emerged, the experimental approaches across teams were largely exploratory. A more systematic, controlled evaluation is necessary to draw robust conclusions about what methods are most effective for generating critical questions.

Second, the reliance of top-performing teams on proprietary, closed-weight language models raises concerns for the long-term scalability and transparency of CQs-Gen as an educational tool. Since the original motivation for this task includes real-world educational deployment, further research should explore the performance and adaptability of open-weight models, which may offer greater control and accessibility.

Third, the dataset used in this shared task presents topical and linguistic limitations. It primarily covers discussions related to politics, morality, and airline policies, and is restricted to English. Expanding the dataset to include a broader range of topics and additional languages would improve both the generalizability and inclusivity of future models.

Finally, the evaluation methodology imposed constraints in the validation phase. Since participants could not quantitatively and reliably compare performance due to a high number of NAE values, some systems may have been optimized without clear feedback. Refining the evaluation method would enhance the development process in future iterations.

Acknowledgments

This work has been partially supported by the French government, through the 3IA Cote d'Azur Investments in the project managed by the National Research Agency (ANR) with the reference number ANR-23-IACL-0001. HiTZ's researchers are thankful to the following MCIN/AEI/10.13039/501100011033 projects: (i) DeepKnowledge (PID2021-127777OB-C21) and by FEDER, EU; (ii) Disargue (TED2021-130810B-C21) and European Union NextGenerationEU/PRTR; (iii) DeepMinor (CNS2023-144375) and European Union NextGenerationEU/PRTR. Blanca Calvo Figueras is supported by the UPV/EHU PIF22/84 predoc grant.

References

Azwad Anjum Islam, Tisa Islam Erana, and Mark A. Finlayson. 2025. Cognac at cqs-gen 2025: Generating critical questions with llm-assisted prompting and multiple rag variants. In *Proceedings of the 12th Workshop on Argument Mining (ArgMining 2025)*, Vienna, Austria. Association for Computational Linguistics.

Sajib Bhattacharjee, Tabassum Basher Rashfi, Samia Rahman, and Hasan Murad. 2025. Cuet_sr34 at cqs-gen 2025: Critical question generation via few-shot llms – integrating ner and argument schemes. In *Proceedings of the 12th Workshop on Argument Mining (ArgMining 2025)*, Vienna, Austria. Association for Computational Linguistics.

Banca Calvo Figueras and Rodrigo Agerri. 2025. Benchmarking critical questions generation: A challenging reasoning task for large language models. *Preprint*, arXiv:2505.11341.

Blanca Calvo Figueras and Rodrigo Agerri. 2024. Critical questions generation: Motivation and challenges. In *Proceedings of the 28th Conference on Computational Natural Language Learning*, pages 105–116, Miami, FL, USA. Association for Computational Linguistics.

DeepSeek-AI. 2025. Deepseek-r1: Incentivizing reasoning capability in llms via reinforcement learning. *Preprint*, arXiv:2501.12948.

Jacob Devlin, Ming-Wei Chang, Kenton Lee, and Kristina Toutanova. 2019. Bert: Pre-training of deep bidirectional transformers for language understanding. *Preprint*, arXiv:1810.04805.

Roxanne El Baff, Dominik Opitz, and Diaoulé Diallo. 2025. Criticalbrew at cqs-gen 2025: Collaborative multi-agent generation and evaluation of critical questions for arguments. In *Proceedings of the 12th Workshop on Argument Mining (ArgMining 2025)*, Vienna, Austria. Association for Computational Linguistics.

Lucile Favero, Daniel Frases, Juan Antonio Pérez-Ortiz, Tanja Käser, and Nuria Oliver. 2025. Ellis alicante at cqs-gen 2025: Winning the critical thinking questions shared task: Llm-based question generation and selection. In *Proceedings of the 12th Workshop on Argument Mining (ArgMining 2025)*, Vienna, Austria. Association for Computational Linguistics.

Aaron Grattafiori, Abhimanyu Dubey, Abhinav Jauhri, Abhinav Pandey, Abhishek Kadian, Ahmad Al-Dahle, Aiesha Letman, Akhil Mathur, Alan Schelten, Alex Vaughan, Amy Yang, Angela Fan, Anirudh Goyal, Anthony Hartshorn, Aobo Yang, Archi Mitra, Archie Sravankumar, Artem Korenev, Arthur Hinsvark, and 542 others. 2024. The llama 3 herd of models. *Preprint*, arXiv:2407.21783.

Reza Hadi Mogavi, Chao Deng, Justin Juho Kim, Pengyuan Zhou, Young D. Kwon, Ahmed Hosny Saleh Metwally, Ahmed Tlili, Simone Bassanelli, Antonio Bucchiarone, Sujit Gujar, Lennart E. Nacke, and Pan Hui. 2024. ChatGPT in education: A blessing or a curse? A qualitative study exploring early adopters' utilization and perceptions. *Computers in Human Behavior: Artificial Humans*, 2(1):100027.

Midhun Kanadan, Johannes Kiesel, Maximilian Heinrich, and Benno Stein. 2025. Webis at cqs-gen 2025: Prompting and reranking for critical questions. In *Proceedings of the 12th Workshop on Argument Mining (ArgMining 2025)*, Vienna, Austria. Association for Computational Linguistics.

Barbara Konat, John Lawrence, Joonsuk Park, Katarzyna Budzynska, and Chris Reed. 2016. A Corpus of Argument Networks: Using Graph Properties to Analyse Divisive Issues. In *10th conference on International Language Resources and Evaluation (LREC'16)*, pages 3899–3906.

John Lawrence, Jacky Visser, and Chris Reed. 2018. BBC Moral Maze: Test Your Argument. In *Comma*.

Fabrizio Macagno, Douglas Walton, and Chris Reed. 2017. Argumentation Schemes. History, Classifications, and Computational Applications.

Sha Newaz Mahmud, Shahriar Hossain, Samia Rahman, Momtazul Arefin Labib, and Hasan Murad. 2025. Mind_matrix at cqs-gen 2025: Adaptive generation of critical questions for argumentative interventions. In *Proceedings of the 12th Workshop on Argument Mining (ArgMining 2025)*, Vienna, Austria. Association for Computational Linguistics.

Elena Musi, Elinor Carmi, Chris Reed, Simeon Yates, and Kay O'Halloran. 2023. Developing Misinformation Immunity: How to Reason-Check Fallacious News in a Human–Computer Interaction Environment. *Social Media + Society*, 9(1):20563051221150407. Publisher: SAGE Publications Ltd.

Tien-Dat Nguyen and Duc-Vu Nguyen. 2025. Td-nguyen at cqs-gen 2025: Adapt large language models with multi-step reasoning for critical questions generation. In *Proceedings of the 12th Workshop on Argument Mining (ArgMining 2025)*, Vienna, Austria. Association for Computational Linguistics.

OpenAI, :, Aaron Hurst, Adam Lerer, Adam P. Goucher, Adam Perelman, Aditya Ramesh, Aidan Clark, AJ Ostrow, Akila Welihinda, Alan Hayes, Alec Radford, Aleksander Mądry, Alex Baker-Whitcomb, Alex Beutel, Alex Borzunov, Alex Carney, Alex Chow, Alex Kirillov, and 401 others. 2024. Gpt-4o system card. *Preprint*, arXiv:2410.21276.

Qwen, :, An Yang, Baosong Yang, Beichen Zhang, Binyuan Hui, Bo Zheng, Bowen Yu, Chengyuan Li, Dayiheng Liu, Fei Huang, Haoran Wei, Huan Lin, Jian Yang, Jianhong Tu, Jianwei Zhang, Jianxin Yang, Jiaxi Yang, Jingren Zhou, and 25 others. 2025. Qwen2.5 technical report. *Preprint*, arXiv:2412.15115.

Alan Ramponi, Gaudenzia Genoni, and Sara Tonelli. 2025. Arg2st at cqs-gen 2025: Critical questions generation through llms and usefulness-based selection. In *Proceedings of the 12th Workshop on Argument Mining (ArgMining 2025)*, Vienna, Austria. Association for Computational Linguistics.

Nils Reimers and Iryna Gurevych. 2019. Sentence-bert: Sentence embeddings using siamese bert-networks. In *Proceedings of the 2019 Conference on Empirical Methods in Natural Language Processing*. Association for Computational Linguistics.

Oscar Sainz, Jon Campos, Iker García-Ferrero, Julen Etxaniz, Oier Lopez de Lacalle, and Eneko Agirre. 2023. NLP evaluation in trouble: On the need to measure LLM data contamination for each benchmark. In *Findings of the Association for Computational Linguistics: EMNLP 2023*, pages 10776–10787, Singapore. Association for Computational Linguistics.

Chantal Shaib, Joe Barrow, Jiuding Sun, Alexa F. Siu, Byron C. Wallace, and Ani Nenkova. 2025. Standardizing the Measurement of Text Diversity: A Tool and a Comparative Analysis of Scores. *arXiv preprint*. ArXiv:2403.00553 [cs].

Yi Song, Michael Heilman, Beata Beigman Klebanov, and Paul Deane. 2014. Applying Argumentation Schemes for Essay Scoring. In *Proceedings of the First Workshop on Argumentation Mining*, pages 69–78, Baltimore, Maryland. Association for Computational Linguistics.

Gemma Team, Morgane Riviere, Shreya Pathak, Pier Giuseppe Sessa, Cassidy Hardin, Surya Bhupatiraju, Léonard Hussenot, Thomas Mesnard, Bobak Shahriari, Alexandre Ramé, Johan Ferret, Peter Liu, Pouya Tafti, Abe Friesen, Michelle Casbon, Sabela Ramos, Ravin Kumar, Charline Le Lan, Sammy Jerome, and 179 others. 2024. Gemma 2: Improving open language models at a practical size. *Preprint*, arXiv:2408.00118.

Qwen Team. 2025. Qwq-32b: Embracing the power of reinforcement learning.

Teknium, Roger Jin, Chen Guang, Jai Suphavadeeprasit, and Jeffrey Quesnelle. 2025. Deephermes 3 preview.

Frieso Turkstra, Sara Nabhani, and Khalid Al-Khatib. 2025. Trillama at cqs-gen 2025: A two-stage llm-based system for critical question generation. In *Proceedings of the 12th Workshop on Argument Mining (ArgMining 2025)*, Vienna, Austria. Association for Computational Linguistics.

Jacky Visser, John Lawrence, Chris Reed, Jean Wagemans, and Douglas Walton. 2021. Annotating Argument Schemes. *Argumentation*, 35(1):101–139.

Henning Wachsmuth, Nona Naderi, Yufang Hou, Yonatan Bilu, Vinodkumar Prabhakaran, Tim Alberdingk Thijm, Graeme Hirst, and Benno Stein. 2017. Computational Argumentation Quality Assessment in Natural Language. In *Proceedings of the 15th Conference of the European Chapter of the Association for Computational Linguistics: Volume 1, Long Papers*, pages 176–187, Valencia, Spain. Association for Computational Linguistics.

Douglas Walton, Christopher Reed, and Fabrizio Macagno. 2008. *Argumentation Schemes*. Cambridge University Press, Cambridge.

Benjamin Warner, Antoine Chaffin, Benjamin Clavié, Orion Weller, Oskar Hallström, Said Taghadouini, Alexis Gallagher, Raja Biswas, Faisal Ladhak, Tom Aarsen, Nathan Cooper, Griffin Adams, Jeremy Howard, and Iacopo Poli. 2024. Smarter, better, faster, longer: A modern bidirectional encoder for fast, memory efficient, and long context finetuning and inference. *Preprint*, arXiv:2412.13663.

An Yang, Baosong Yang, Beichen Zhang, Binyuan Hui, Bo Zheng, Bowen Yu, Chengyuan Li, Dayiheng Liu, Fei Huang, Haoran Wei, Huan Lin, Jian Yang, Jianhong Tu, Jianwei Zhang, Jianxin Yang, Jiaxi Yang, Jingren Zhou, Junyang Lin, Kai Dang, and 23 others. 2024. Qwen2.5 technical report. *arXiv preprint arXiv:2412.15115*.

Jinghui Zhang, Dongming Yang, and Binghuai Lin. 2025. Statecloud at cqs-gen 2025: Prompt engineering for critical questions generation. In *Proceedings of the 12th Workshop on Argument Mining (ArgMining 2025)*, Vienna, Austria. Association for Computational Linguistics.

Jintian Zhang, Xin Xu, Ningyu Zhang, Ruibo Liu, Bryan Hooi, and Shumin Deng. 2024. Exploring collaboration mechanisms for llm agents: A social psychology view. *Preprint*, arXiv:2310.02124.

Wendi Zhou, Ameer Saadat-Yazdi, and Nadin Kökciyan. 2025. Daydreamer at cqs-gen 2025: Generating critical questions through argument scheme completion. In *Proceedings of the 12th Workshop on Argument Mining (ArgMining 2025)*, Vienna, Austria. Association for Computational Linguistics.

A Baseline Prompt

You are tasked with generating critical questions that are useful for diminishing the acceptability of the arguments in the following text:
"{intervention}"
Take into account a question is not a useful critical question:

1. If the question is not related to the text.
2. If the question is not specific (for instance, if it's a general question that could be applied to a lot of texts).
3. If the question introduces new concepts not mentioned in the text (for instance, if it suggests possible answers).
4. If the question is not useful to diminish the acceptability of any argument. For instance, if it's a reading-comprehension question or if it asks about the opinion of the speaker/reader.
5. If its answer is not likely to invalidate any of the arguments in the text. This can be because the answer to the question is common sense, or because the text itself answers the question.

Output 3 critical questions. Give one question per line. Make sure there are at least 3 questions. Do not give any other output. Do not explain why the questions are relevant.

Figure 3: Prompt for generating baseline outputs.

B All Test Set and Validation Set Results including NAEs

Team Name	Run	Validation	Test
ELLIS Alicante	1	61.4	36.3
ELLIS Alicante	2	61.0	44.1
ELLIS Alicante	3	**64.4**	**50.0**
COGNAC	1	**83.0**	**61.8**
COGNAC	2	81.0	57.8
COGNAC	3	82.0	60.8
StatetCloud	1	**76.2**	45.1
StatetCloud	2	72.8	42.2
StatetCloud	3	71.3	**47.1**
DayDreamer	1	**72.2**	**55.9**
DayDreamer	2	**72.2**	50.0
DayDreamer	3	62.2	43.1
Webis	1	72.0	49.0
Webis	2	**84.0**	**52.0**
Webis	3	82.0	48.0
TriLLaMa	1	*	**53.9**
TriLLaMa	2	*	37.3
TriLLaMa	3	*	52.0
Mind_Matrix	1	**53.0**	**42.2**
Mind_Matrix	2	46.0	36.3
CriticalBrew	1	**78.0**	**52.0**
CriticalBrew	2	**78.0**	40.2
CriticalBrew	3	71.0	51.0
Tdnguyen	1	70.7	**49.0**
Tdnguyen	2	**71.9**	45.1
Tdnguyen	3	61.3	46.1
ARG2ST	1	**76.2**	44.1
ARG2ST	2	72.8	**45.1**
ARG2ST	3	72.3	40.2
CUET_SR34	1	**71.1**	**43.1**
CUET_SR34	2	69.2	32.4
CUET_SR34	3	70.3	42.2

Table 4: Results of the shared task in the validation and test set using the official shared task evaluation script. The validation set results have been submitted by the participants. Therefore, we can not ensure direct comparison. The table is ordered by teams, starting by the winning team and ending with the lowest performing one. In bold are the highest results from each team.

* this team did not evaluate on the whole validation set.

C Automated-methods Evaluation

Team Name	Run	STS_0.65	Claude	Gemma2
ELLIS Alicante	1	48.04	51.96	61.76
ELLIS Alicante	2	54.90	54.90	53.92
ELLIS Alicante	3*	**67.65**	**67.65**	**66.67**
COGNAC	1*	62.75	64.71	61.76
COGNAC	2	65.69	62.75	**66.67**
COGNAC	3	64.71	60.78	65.69
StateCloud	1	50.00	49.02	53.92
StateCloud	2	51.96	50.00	53.92
StateCloud	3*	59.80	58.82	59.8
DayDreamer	1*	58.82	58.82	56.86
DayDreamer	2	52.94	49.02	54.9
DayDreamer	3	46.08	46.08	46.08
Webis	1	50.00	43.14	44.12
Webis	2*	56.86	56.86	51.96
Webis	3	53.92	52.94	48.04
TriLLaMa	1*	55.88	57.84	54.9
TriLLaMa	2	47.06	40.2	48.04
TriLLaMa	3	54.90	56.86	54.9
Mind_Matrix	1*	55.88	55.88	54.9
Mind_Matrix	2	47.06	40.20	50.98
CriticalBrew	1*	54.90	54.90	54.90
CriticalBrew	2	37.25	41.18	50.0
CriticalBrew	3	55.88	52.94	58.82
Lilo&stitch	1	53.92	52.94	54.9
Lilo&stitch	2*	53.92	52.94	53.92
Lilo&stitch	3	52.94	36.27	48.04
Tdnguyen	1*	51.96	52.94	54.90
Tdnguyen	2	51.96	41.18	47.06
Tdnguyen	3	51.96	46.08	53.92
ARG2ST	1	46.08	40.2	42.16
ARG2ST	2*	50.00	50.00	50.98
ARG2ST	3	46.08	41.18	51.96
CUET_SR34	1*	48.04	48.04	49.02
CUET_SR34	2	37.25	41.18	40.2
CUET_SR34	3	44.12	45.10	52.94
Nompt	1*	38.24	38.24	36.27
Nompt	2	37.25	24.51	36.27
Nompt	3	36.27	30.39	37.25

Table 5: Results of the shared task with the new fully-automated metrics. We kept the order from the ranking of the official shared task results. The table is ordered by teams, starting by the winning team and ending with the lowest performing one.
* runs included in the test set references.

StateCloud at CQs-Gen 2025: Prompt Engineering for Critical Questions Generation

Jinghui Zhang and **Dongming Yang** * and **Binghuai Lin**
jinghui-19@tsinghua.org.cn, yangdongming@pku.edu.cn,
linbinghuai@gmail.com
China Telecom Cloud Technology Co., Ltd

Abstract

This paper presents StateCloud's submission to the Critical Questions Generation (CQs-Gen) shared task at the Argument Mining Workshop 2025. To generate high-quality critical questions from argumentative texts, we propose a framework that combines prompt engineering with few-shot learning to effectively guide generative models. Additionally, we ensemble outputs from diverse large language models (LLMs) to enhance accuracy. Notably, our approach achieved 3rd place in the competition, demonstrating the viability of prompt engineering strategies for argumentative tasks.

1 Introduction

Critical Questions (CQs) play a pivotal role in argumentation by challenging the validity, relevance, or sufficiency of claims. Automated generation of CQs from argumentative texts has emerged as a key task in computational argumentation, enabling systems to engage in nuanced discourse. The CQs-Gen shared task at the Argument Mining Workshop 2025 aims to advance this capability by developing a system model to produce high-quality, contextually relevant CQs.

In this paper, we present StateCloud's submission to the CQs-Gen task(Calvo Figueras et al., 2025). Our approach centers on prompt engineering to guide generative LLMs toward producing critical questions that adhere to domain-specific requirements. While fine-tuning LLMs is a common strategy, we prioritize few-shot learning with carefully curated prompts to leverage pre-trained knowledge efficiently. We further enhance accuracy by ensembling outputs from diverse state-of-the-art LLMs.

The main contributions of this work are:

- A systematic framework for prompt engineering tailored to argumentative CQs generation.
- Empirical validation of model ensembling for improving question accuracy.

Our system achieved 3rd place in the competition, demonstrating the effectiveness of prompt-driven strategies.

2 Related Work

2.1 Critical Question Generation in Argument Mining

CQs-Gen is a specialized task in computational argumentation that focuses on identifying and formulating questions that challenge the validity, relevance, or sufficiency of arguments.

With the advent of machine learning, supervised approaches (Nguyen and Litman, 2016); (Opitz and Frank, 2019) emerged, training classifiers or sequence-to-sequence models on annotated datasets. These methods improved generalization but required substantial labeled data, which is costly to obtain for argumentative tasks.

To address this limitation, researchers have explored transfer learning(Dutta et al., 2022); (Hua and Wang, 2022). Dutta et al. used web data for argumentative knowledge, adapting Transformers via Selective MLM (masking discourse markers instead of random tokens) and prompt-based relation prediction, reducing labeled data needs.

2.2 Prompt Engineering for Generative Tasks

Prompt engineering has emerged as a critical methodology for optimizing the performance of LLMs across diverse domains (Zhang et al., 2023);(Brown et al., 2020). Unlike traditional fine-tuning approaches that require extensive parameter updates, prompt engineering operates through carefully designed input formulations that guide LLMs to produce desired outputs without modifying their underlying architecture.

The concept of prompt engineering originated from observations that LLMs are highly sensitive

*Corresponding Author.

Proceedings of the 12th Argument Mining Workshop, pages 258–264
July 31, 2025 ©2025 Association for Computational Linguistics

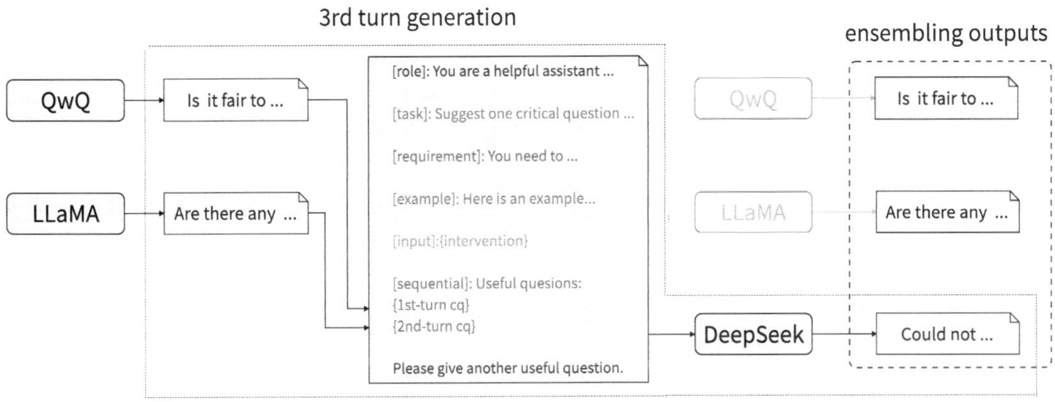

Figure 1: Our framework employs a sequential ensembling approach to integrate the outputs of different LLMs. The output from each preceding model is incorporated into the prompt template for the subsequent generation step.

to input phrasing. Seminal work by (Bsharat et al., 2024) demonstrated how subtle changes in prompt structure could yield dramatically different outputs in creative writing tasks. Their study presents principled guidelines for improving prompt quality, including techniques such as combining affirmative and negative directions, structured formatting, and role assignment.

Subsequent research has introduced more rigorous frameworks for prompt construction, including: Chain-of-Thought (CoT) prompting (Wei et al., 2022); Tree-of-Thoughts (ToT) prompting (Yao et al., 2023); (Long, 2023); Self-Refine prompting (Madaan et al., 2023).

However, robustness issues persist as model outputs remain highly sensitive to subtle prompt variations, necessitating more stable and transferable solutions.

3 Task Description

The CQs-Gen task involves generating meaningful CQs in response to an argumentative text. A dataset of real debate interventions, along with associated CQs, is provided. The validation dataset consists of 186 interventions.

The goal is to develop a system that takes an intervention as input and outputs exactly three CQs, all of which should be effective in challenging the arguments presented.

Each of the three CQs will be independently evaluated by computing the cosine similarity between the embeddings of generated CQs and reference CQs using sentence transformers [1], then assigning one of four labels: Useful, Not-Able-to-Evaluate, Unhelpful, or Invalid. If the similarity score exceeds a predefined threshold, the generated CQ will inherit the same label as its corresponding reference CQ. Otherwise, it will be labeled as Not-Able-to-Evaluate. Finally, the individual question evaluations will be aggregated into an overall score.

4 Methodology

4.1 Framework Overview

Our system generates one question at a time and combines model outputs to produce a specified number of questions. Our scripts are publicly available on GitHub. [2] The framework integrates these key components:

Prompt Engineering We constructed multiple templates with varying structures and linguistic styles, carefully designing the model's role and generation requirements within the prompts. We also evaluated the effectiveness of in-context learning.

Model Ensembling To maintain high-quality question generation while improving output stability, we aggregated outputs from multiple models including QwQ and others. We compared the effects of sequential versus parallel ensemble approaches.

4.2 Prompt Design

We designed four different prompts (shown in Appendix A), all specifying the model's role as a "helpful assistant with critical thinking skills." The variations include:

[1] https://huggingface.co/sentence-transformers/stsb-mpnet-base-v2

[2] https://github.com/QQJellyy/StateCloud-at-CQs-Gen-share-task.git

Models	USE	UNCERTAIN
Llama-3-8B	70.4 %	11.8 %
Llama-3.3-70B	75.8 %	9.1 %
qwen2.5-7B	71.0 %	14.5 %
qwen2.5-14B	64.5 %	18.3 %
qwen2.5-32B	71.0 %	12.9 %
qwen2.5-72B	76.3 %	5.4 %
QWQ-32b-32B	66.7 %	16.1 %
DeepSeek-R1-671B	61.3 %	21.0 %

Table 1: The performance of some open-source general large language models. USE denotes the number of Useful questions. UNCERTAIN denotes the number of Not-Able-to-Evaluate questions.

Zero-shot A zero-shot prompt containing only the target intervention and generation requirements.

Few-shot A few-shot prompt featuring an example intervention with corresponding helpful and unhelpful CQs.

Oral-expression A version with more conversational requirement phrasing to examine the impact of linguistic style.

Requirements-ahead A structurally modified prompt placing requirements earlier to investigate component ordering effects.

4.3 Model Ensembling

We selected n candidate open-source models and evaluated their performance using a calibration dataset. Two ensembling methods were implemented:

Parallel Ensemble The top 3 models each generate one CQ independently, with results combined directly. This configuration operates under the explicit assumption that model diversity inherently produces distinct question formulations, thus intentionally omitting deduplication steps.

Sequential Ensemble A single model generates an initial CQ. Subsequent CQs are produced iteratively by incorporating all previous results into the prompt (similar to few-shot learning). The sequential template is detailed in Appendix A.

5 Experiment Setup

5.1 Dataset

Our experiments utilized two data components.

- A randomly selected intervention from the sample set, paired with its corresponding useful and unhelpful question pairs for few-shot demonstration.

Prompt versions	USE	UNCERTAIN
zero-shot	74.7%	9.7%
requirements-ahead	75.3%	7.0%
oral-expression	75.8%	8.1%
few-shot	76.3%	5.4%

Table 2: The performance of prompt engineering. Here we use the Qwen2.5-72B model. USE denotes the number of Useful questions. UNCERTAIN denotes the number of Not-Able-to-Evaluate questions.

Prompt versions	Combination Strategy	USE	UNCERTAIN
Qwen + R1	parallel	68.8%	13.2%
Qwen→R1	sequential	74.5%	7.6%
Qwen + Qwen	parallel	76.4%	5.4%
Qwen→Qwen	sequential	77.2%	5.9%

Table 3: The performance of model ensembling. USE denotes the number of Useful questions. UNCERTAIN denotes the number of Not-Able-to-Evaluate questions. Qwen denotes Qwen2.5-72B-Instruct. R1 denotes DeepSeek-R1.

- The full validation set comprising 186 interventions, each annotated with multiple *useful*, *unhelpful*, and *invalid* CQs for evaluation. This structure enabled both effective few-shot learning and comprehensive evaluation of model performance.

5.2 Models

We selected eight state-of-the-art open-source models based on three criteria: model size, training data distribution and reasoning capability. Details of the selected models are provided in Tables 1. All models were inferred using HuggingFace Transformers with default generation configurations (temperature, top-p, etc.).

6 Results and Analysis

6.1 Model Comparison

The performance of general and reasoning LLMs on the validation set are presented in Tables 1, respectively. Since neither Unhelpful nor Invalid labels constitute effective challenges, we focus primarily on Useful and Not-Able-to-Evaluate labels to highlight valid or potentially valid critiques. The top-performing model was Qwen2.5-72B-Instruct, generating 142 useful CQs for 186 interventions, with LLaMA-3.3-70B closely following at 141 useful CQs.

Scaling Effects While larger models produced more useful CQs, consistent with expectations, the marginal gains were surprisingly small: both LLaMA and Qwen models at 7B/8B scales gen-

System	Models	USE(val)	UNCERTAIN(val)	USE(test)	UNCERTAIN(test)
System 1	Qwen2.5-72B→72B→72B	**76.2%**	6.1%	45.1%	5.9 %
System 2	Qwen2.5-72B + 32B +7B	72.8%	**10.9%**	42.2%	15.7 %
System 3	**Qwen2.5-72B + QwQ + DeepSeek-R1**	71.3%	10.4%	**47.1%**	**22.5** %

Table 4: Performance of the three final submitted systems on the validation and test sets. "→" denotes sequential ensembling, while "+" indicates parallel ensembling. **Bold** values indicate best performance across systems.

erated approximately 131 useful CQs, while their 70B/72B counterparts produced only about 10 additional useful CQs.

Reasoning Models Underperform Despite reasoning models' strong performance on benchmark tasks, they did not outperform general LLMs in useful CQ generation on validation set. Notably, reasoning models produced significantly more *Not-Able-to-Evaluate* CQs, suggesting they may generate more novel CQs beyond the annotation scope. This leaves open the possibility that their true capability might be underestimated by current evaluation metrics.

6.2 Prompt Design Analysis

Using Qwen2.5-72B-Instruct, we evaluated various prompt designs (Table 2), revealing several insights. The performance variation between prompts proved minimal (142 vs. 139 useful CQs, Δ=2%), significantly overshadowed by model selection impacts. Few-shot prompting demonstrated a clear trade-off: while increasing useful CQ counts, it simultaneously caused a 44% reduction in uncertain questions (from 18 to 10) while increasing unhelpful and invalid outputs.

6.3 Model Ensembling

Our framework implements model ensembling to generate multiple CQs for each intervention. Comparative results for generating two CQs are presented in Table 3, demonstrating the superior performance of sequential ensembling over parallel approaches. The sequential method shows particular effectiveness when applied to reasoning models such as R1, yielding a statistically significant increase in useful CQs generation (114 vs. 135 useful CQs, Δ=18%). Notably, this approach maintains its advantage even when employing identical models, suggesting that the contextual incorporation of previously generated CQs enhances subsequent question quality. This phenomenon indicates that exposing the model to its own outputs creates a beneficial self-refinement mechanism, where each generated question informs and improves subsequent outputs.

7 Submission

We evaluated multiple systems and selected the top three for final submission based on the number of Useful and Not-Able-to-Evaluate CQs generated. The results are presented in Table 4. System 1 employed a sequential approach, where Qwen2.5-72B generated three CQs in succession. System 2 used a parallel ensemble of Qwen2.5-72B, 32B, and 7B models. System 3 combined Qwen2.5-72B, QwQ, and DeepSeek R1 in parallel.

On the validation set, System 1 produced the highest number of Useful CQs, while Systems 2 and 3 generated more Not-Able-to-Evaluate CQs, indicating greater potential for diverse questioning. However, on the test set, System 3 achieved the highest counts for both types of CQs, demonstrating superior overall performance.

8 Conclusion

This paper presented StateCloud's comprehensive framework for the CQs-Gen shared task, integrating innovative prompt engineering with model ensemble techniques. We submitted three different systems, with System 3 emerging as our top performer, ultimately achieving 3rd place in the competition.

Our systematic evaluation yielded several key insights: (1) While larger models (e.g., Qwen2.5-72B-Instruct) achieved marginally better performance, the scaling benefits diminished significantly beyond 7B parameters; (2) Sequential model ensemble demonstrated superior effectiveness over parallel approaches, particularly for reasoning models, which presents a promising direction for enhancing question quality without additional supervision.

9 Limitations

Our study was constrained by the fixed annotation scope of the validation set, which may not fully capture the models' reasoning capabilities. Due to the limited number of systems submitted, we did not evaluate the performance of sequential ensembles with reasoning models.

References

Tom B. Brown, Benjamin Mann, Nick Ryder, Melanie Subbiah, Jared Kaplan, Prafulla Dhariwal, Arvind Neelakantan, Pranav Shyam, Girish Sastry, Amanda Askell, Sandhini Agarwal, Ariel Herbert-Voss, Gretchen Krueger, Tom Henighan, Rewon Child, Aditya Ramesh, Daniel M. Ziegler, Jeffrey Wu, Clemens Winter, Christopher Hesse, Mark Chen, Eric Sigler, Mateusz Litwin, Scott Gray, Benjamin Chess, Jack Clark, Christopher Berner, Sam McCandlish, Alec Radford, Ilya Sutskever, and Dario Amodei. 2020. Language models are few-shot learners.

Sondos Mahmoud Bsharat, Aidar Myrzakhan, and Zhiqiang Shen. 2024. Principled instructions are all you need for questioning llama-1/2, gpt-3.5/4.

Blanca Calvo Figueras, Jaione Bengoetxea, Maite Heredia, Ekaterina Sviridova, Elena Cabrio, Serena Villata, and Rodrigo Agerri. 2025. Overview of the critical questions generation shared task 2025. In *Proceedings of the 12th Workshop on Argument Mining (ArgMining 2025)*, Vienna, Austria. Association for Computational Linguistics.

Subhabrata Dutta, Jeevesh Juneja, Dipankar Das, and Tanmoy Chakraborty. 2022. Can unsupervised knowledge transfer from social discussions help argument mining? In *Proceedings of the 60th Annual Meeting of the Association for Computational Linguistics (Volume 1: Long Papers)*, pages 7774–7786, Dublin, Ireland. Association for Computational Linguistics.

Xinyu Hua and Lu Wang. 2022. Efficient argument structure extraction with transfer learning and active learning. In *Findings of the Association for Computational Linguistics: ACL 2022*, pages 423–437, Dublin, Ireland. Association for Computational Linguistics.

Jieyi Long. 2023. Large language model guided tree-of-thought.

Aman Madaan, Niket Tandon, Prakhar Gupta, Skyler Hallinan, Luyu Gao, Sarah Wiegreffe, Uri Alon, Nouha Dziri, Shrimai Prabhumoye, Yiming Yang, Shashank Gupta, Bodhisattwa Prasad Majumder, Katherine Hermann, Sean Welleck, Amir Yazdanbakhsh, and Peter Clark. 2023. Self-refine: Iterative refinement with self-feedback.

Huy Nguyen and Diane Litman. 2016. Context-aware argumentative relation mining. In *Proceedings of the 54th Annual Meeting of the Association for Computational Linguistics (Volume 1: Long Papers)*, pages 1127–1137, Berlin, Germany. Association for Computational Linguistics.

Juri Opitz and Anette Frank. 2019. Dissecting content and context in argumentative relation analysis. In *Proceedings of the 6th Workshop on Argument Mining*, pages 25–34, Florence, Italy. Association for Computational Linguistics.

Jason Wei, Xuezhi Wang, Dale Schuurmans, Maarten Bosma, brian ichter, Fei Xia, Ed Chi, Quoc V Le, and Denny Zhou. 2022. Chain-of-thought prompting elicits reasoning in large language models. In *Advances in Neural Information Processing Systems*, volume 35, pages 24824–24837. Curran Associates, Inc.

Shunyu Yao, Dian Yu, Jeffrey Zhao, Izhak Shafran, Thomas L. Griffiths, Yuan Cao, and Karthik Narasimhan. 2023. Tree of thoughts: Deliberate problem solving with large language models.

Jinghui Zhang, Dongming Yang, Siyu Bao, Lina Cao, and Shunguo Fan. 2023. Emotion classification on code-mixed text messages via soft prompt tuning. In *Proceedings of the 13th Workshop on Computational Approaches to Subjectivity, Sentiment, & Social Media Analysis*, pages 596–600, Toronto, Canada. Association for Computational Linguistics.

A Prompts

We developed four distinct prompt configurations, with key differentiators highlighted in bold.

Here is the zero-shot prompt:

(1) """You are a helpful assistant with critical thinking skills.

Suggest one critical question that directly challenges an argument in this text:

<text>

{intervention}

</text>

Requirements for the question:

<requirement>

1. Keep the question simple—no explanations or justifications.

2. Ensure logical reasoning aligns with the text.

3. Focus exclusively on content within the provided text.

4. Avoid introducing new concepts or external ideas.

5. Make it specific to the arguments in the text (not generic).

6. Target a single argument critically (e.g., a precise reading-comprehension critique).

</requirement>

"""

Here is the few-shot prompt:

(2) """You are a helpful assistant with critical thinking skills.

Suggest one critical question that directly challenges an argument in this text:

<text>

{intervention}

</text>

Requirements for the question:

<requirement>

1. Keep the question simple—no explanations or justifications.

2. Ensure logical reasoning aligns with the text.

3. Focus exclusively on content within the provided text.

4. Avoid introducing new concepts or external ideas.

5. Make it specific to the arguments in the text (not generic).

6. Target a single argument critically (e.g., a precise reading-comprehension critique).

</requirement>

Here is an example.

<text>

{Intervention example}

</text>

Useful questions:

{Useful question 1}

...

Unhelpful questions:

{Unhelpful question 1}

...

Please give an useful question.

"""

Here is the oral-expression prompt:

(3) """You are a helpful assistant with critical thinking skills.

Suggest one critical question that directly challenges an argument in this text:

<text>

{intervention}

</text>

Requirements for the question:

<requirement>

1. Be useful (challenge one of the arguments in the text).

2. The reasoning should be right.

3. Be related to the text.

4. Do not introduce new concepts not present in the text.

5. Avoid being too general that could be applied to any text.

6. Be critical with one of the argument in the text (e.g. a reading-comprehension question).

</requirement>

Here is an example.

<text>

{Intervention example}

</text>

Useful questions:

{Useful question 1}

...

Unhelpful questions:

{Unhelpful question 1}

...

Please give an useful question.

"""

Here is the requirements-ahead prompt:

(4) """You are a helpful assistant with critical thinking skills.

Suggest one critical question that directly challenges an argument in the given text.

Requirements for the question:

<requirement>

1. Be useful (challenge one of the arguments in the text).

2. The reasoning should be right.

3. Be related to the text.

4. Do not introduce new concepts not present in the text.

5. Avoid being too general that could be applied to any text.

6. Be critical with one of the argument in the text (e.g. a reading-comprehension question).

</requirement>

Here is an example.

<text>

{Intervention example}

</text>

Useful questions:

{Useful question 1}

...

Unhelpful questions:

{Unhelpful question 1}

...

<text>

{intervention}

</text>

Please give an useful question.

""""

1. Be useful (challenge one of the arguments in the text).

2. The reasoning should be right.

3. Be related to the text.

4. Do not introduce new concepts not present in the text.

5. Avoid being too general that could be applied to any text.

6. Be critical with one of the argument in the text (e.g. a reading-comprehension question).

</requirement>

Here is an example.

<text>

{Intervention example}

</text>

Useful questions:

{Useful question 1}

...

Unhelpful questions:

{Unhelpful question 1}

...

<text>

{intervention}

</text>

Useful questions:

{cq}

Please give another useful question.

""""

Here is the prompt for sequential model ensembling:

(5) """You are a helpful assistant with critical thinking skills.

Suggest one critical question that directly challenges an argument in the given text.

Requirements for the question:

<requirement>

Tdnguyen at CQs-Gen 2025: Adapt Large Language Models with Multi-Step Reasoning for Critical Questions Generation

Tien-Dat Nguyen[1, 3], **Duc-Vu Nguyen**[2, 3]
[1]Faculty of Computer Science, University of Information Technology, Ho Chi Minh City, Vietnam
[2]Laboratory of Multimedia Communications, University of Information Technology, Ho Chi Minh City, Vietnam
[3]Vietnam National University, Ho Chi Minh City, Vietnam
21520707@gm.uit.edu.vn vund@uit.edu.vn

Abstract

This paper explores the generation of Critical Questions (CQs) from argumentative texts using multi-step reasoning techniques, specifically Chain-of-Thoughts (CoT) and Tree-of-Thoughts (ToT) prompting frameworks. CQs are essential for enhancing critical thinking and improving decision-making across various domains. Despite the promise of Large Language Models (LLMs) in this task, generating contextually relevant and logically sound questions remains a challenge. Our experiments show that CoT-based prompting strategies, including Zero-shot and One-shot methods, significantly outperform baseline models in generating high-quality CQs. While ToT prompting offers a more flexible reasoning structure, it was less effective than CoT in this task. We suggest exploring more advanced or computationally intense multi-step reasoning techniques, as well as alternative tree structures for the ToT framework, to further improve CQs-Gen systems.

1 Introduction

Generating Critical Questions (CQs) from argumentative texts plays a vital role in enhancing human understanding, promoting critical thinking, specifically in education (Santoso et al., 2018), and improving decision-making processes across domains such as education, law, and policy analysis. These questions aim to identify potential weaknesses, blind spots, or implicit assumptions within arguments, thereby encouraging deeper reflection and discourse. The task draws inspiration from argumentation theory, particularly Walton's argumentation schemes (Walton et al., 2008), where each type of argument is associated with a set of critical questions designed to test its validity (Calvo Figueras and Agerri, 2024).

Despite its importance, Critical Questions Generation (CQs-Gen) remains an underexplored and challenging task. It requires not only an understanding of the structure and content of arguments but also the ability to reason about unstated premises and hypothetical counterpoints. Previous approaches, including prompt-based generation using Large Language Models (LLMs), have shown promise but still struggle with generating questions that are both contextually relevant and logically sound (Calvo Figueras and Agerri, 2024).

In this paper, we explore the use of multi-step reasoning techniques, particularly Chain-of-Thoughts (CoT) and Tree-of-Thoughts (ToT) framework, to improve the performance of LLMs in CQs-Gen. These approaches aim to mimic the step-by-step reasoning process humans use when evaluating arguments, allowing the model to better capture underlying assumptions and generate more insightful critical questions. Through systematic experiments and evaluation, we demonstrate the effectiveness of multi-step prompting in generating high-quality, argument-sensitive critical questions.

2 Related Work

To contextualize our contribution, we examine three foundational pillars: the development of Large Language Models (LLMs), the task of CQs-Gen, and recent advancements in multi-step reasoning techniques.

2.1 Large Language Models

The advent of Large Language Models (LLMs) such as GPT-4o (OpenAI et al., 2024), Deepseek-R1 (DeepSeek-AI et al., 2025), and LLaMA 3 (Grattafiori et al., 2024) has brought significant progress in natural language processing. Trained on vast corpora of diverse text, these models exhibit strong zero-shot and few-shot performance across a wide array of tasks, including question answering, summarization, and reasoning. Notably, models like GPT-4o and Deepseek-R1 demonstrate implicit reasoning capabilities, often reasoning

Proceedings of the 12th Argument Mining Workshop, pages 265–280
July 31, 2025 ©2025 Association for Computational Linguistics

through complex prompts before producing outputs. These characteristics make them strong candidates for tasks that require nuanced comprehension and logical progression, such as multi-step inference and question generation.

2.2 Critical Questions Generation (CQs-Gen)

The CQs-Gen task, introduced by Calvo Figueras and Agerri (2024), involves generating questions that critically engage with the reasoning presented in a given text. CQs-Gen holds potential for applications in combating misinformation and promoting critical thinking, as evidenced by related studies on argument analysis and fallacy detection (Musi et al., 2023; Musi and Reed, 2022). However, the task remains underexplored. Existing LLMs often struggle with generating relevant and coherent critical questions. Common issues include producing questions that are (1) unrelated to the argument, (2) based on introduced but unsupported concepts, (3) overly generic, or (4) grounded in flawed reasoning. Furthermore, the absence of large-scale, high-quality datasets of reference critical questions poses an additional challenge, limiting the development and evaluation of robust CQs-Gen systems (Calvo Figueras and Agerri, 2024).

2.3 Multi-Step Reasoning Techniques

Recent advances in multi-step reasoning have introduced techniques such as CoT prompting (Wei et al., 2023), ToT (Yao et al., 2023; Long, 2023)[1], and Chain-of-Draft (Xu et al., 2025), all of which have demonstrated notable improvements in tasks like arithmetic reasoning, commonsense inference, and symbolic reasoning (e.g., the coin-flip task). More recent work has explored integrating these techniques with decision-making frameworks such as A* search or reinforcement learning to further enhance reasoning performance (Wang et al., 2024a,b).

In this study, we focus on two foundational methods – Chain-of-Thoughts and Tree-of-Thoughts – due to their simplicity, accessibility, and effectiveness, while leaving the exploration of more advanced or computationally intensive approaches to future work.

[1]For a prompt-based implementation of Tree-of-Thoughts, see `https://github.com/dave1010/tree-of-thought-prompting`

3 Methodology

In this section, we present several multi-step reasoning techniques for the CQs-Gen task. An overview of the different prompting strategies is illustrated in Figure 1. All prompts and sample responses can be found in appendix A.

3.1 Chain-of-Thoughts Prompting

To support the generation of critical questions that challenge arguments effectively, we adopt CoT prompting – a technique that decomposes reasoning into intermediate steps (Wei et al., 2023). This structure helps LLMs expose implicit assumptions and reasoning gaps. We evaluate several CoT prompting variants:

- **Zero-Shot CoT Prompting:** Following Kojima et al. (2023), this method appends a trigger phrase to the input to elicit structured reasoning without examples. We use the custom phrasing:

  > "Think about the argument step-by-step. Print your reasoning first in a structured step-by-step format."

  to discourage models from skipping the reasoning phase.

- **One-Shot CoT Prompting:** As proposed in Wei et al. (2023), this variant includes an exemplar that illustrates structured reasoning and CQ derivation. For each intervention, we select a similar – but not identical – example from the validation set to promote unbiased performance (explained in Appendix A.3.2).

- **Least-to-Most CoT Prompting:** Introduced by Zhou et al. (2023), this approach breaks down the task into explicit subtasks, guiding the model step-by-step rather than relying on implicit decomposition.

3.2 Tree-of-Thoughts Framework

To complement linear CoT strategies, we explore Tree-of-Thoughts (ToT) prompting (Yao et al., 2023), which organizes reasoning as a search tree. Inspired by human problem-solving via branching deliberations (Newell, 1959), ToT enables multiple reasoning paths using heuristics such as BFS, DFS, or A*. Our implementation builds a shallow tree via BFS with three stages: (1) generate and rank initial plans; (2) expand top plans into sub-plans; (3) generate critical questions from sub-plans. At each

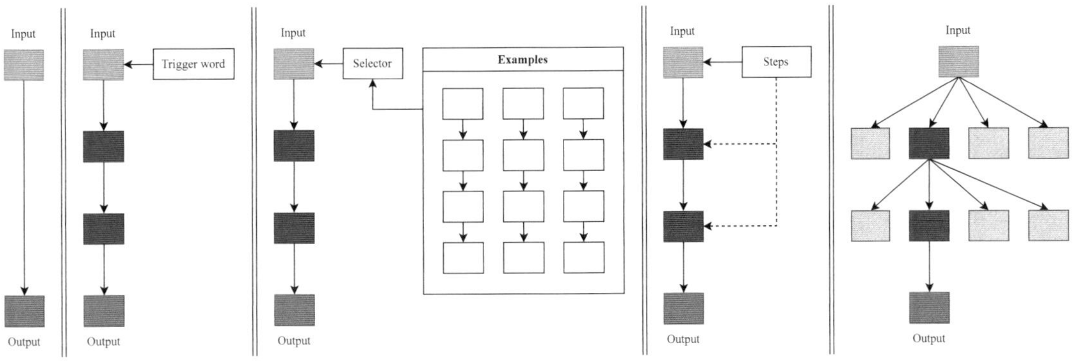

Figure 1: Overview of prompting strategies explored in this work. From left to right: (1) Standard input-output prompting (baseline), (2) Zero-Shot CoT prompting with a trigger phrase, (3) Few-Shot CoT prompting with selected exemplars, (4) Least-to-Most CoT prompting with explicit step guidance, and (5) Tree-of-Thoughts (ToT) prompting using breadth-first exploration of reasoning paths. **Yellow boxes** denote the input, **green boxes** represent intermediate reasoning steps or sub-tasks, **light green boxes** indicate reasoning paths that were pruned in the ToT framework, and **blue boxes** represent the final output (i.e., the generated critical question).

depth, a voting-based mechanism selects the most promising candidates. For simplicity and due to time constraints, we evaluate a single tree structure, leaving broader configurations for future work.

4 Experiments and Results

4.1 Experiments

In this section, we describe the experimental setup used to evaluate the multi-step reasoning strategies introduced in Section 3. We outline the dataset, model configurations, prompting procedures, evaluation protocol, and implementation details.

4.1.1 Dataset

We conduct all experiments using the validation set of the CQs-Gen Shared Task dataset (Figueras et al., 2025; Figueras and Agerri, 2025), which consists of argument-based scenarios paired with corresponding interventions. Each input scenario serves as the context for generating critical questions that challenge the underlying reasoning or assumptions of the argument. For One-shot CoT, for each intervention, we randomly selected three useful representative questions and then used DeepSeek-R1 to generate the reasoning steps that lead to those questions (prompt in Appendix A.3.1).

4.1.2 Model

We evaluate all prompting strategies using GPT-4o mini via the OpenAI API, keeping default parameters (temperature = 1.0) to encourage generation diversity. As baselines, we adopt LLaMA-3-8B and GPT-4o mini, both under standard prompting. While prior work used LLaMA-2-13B and Zephyr-13B (Calvo Figueras and Agerri, 2024), LLaMA-3-8B offers architectural improvements, including enhanced tokenization, instruction following, and reasoning capabilities (Grattafiori et al., 2024). Using GPT-4o mini additionally allows us to isolate the effect of prompting strategies from model capacity, and to assess whether structured reasoning benefits even strong proprietary models. In addition, we conducted tests using DeepSeek-R1, Mistral, and Qwen 3 (locally via Ollama) to explore generalization across different LLMs.

4.1.3 Tree-of-Thoughts Configuration

For the ToT strategy, we construct trees with a maximum depth of 4, where the root node (depth 1) represents the input scenario; we generate 5 candidate initial plans at depth 2; for each selected plan, we generate 3 sub-plans at depth 3, and each sub-plan is used to generate 3 candidate critical questions at the depth 4. At each depth level, we conduct 10 independent voting rounds using the model to evaluate and rank candidates. Based on these votes, we select the top 3 candidates to expand to the next level. The final output is selected from the pool of questions generated at depth 4.

4.1.4 Evaluation

In this study, we perform automatic evaluation due to time constraints. Following the CQs-Gen Shared Task setup (Calvo Figueras and Agerri, 2024), we use automatic evaluation based on similarity between generated and reference questions. For each generated question, we identify the reference question with the highest similarity. If this score is below 0.6, the output is marked as "not evaluable" and assigned a score of 0. Otherwise, we assign the reference label ("Useful," "Unhelpful," or "Invalid") to the generated question. Each intervention yields three questions. The intervention score is the sum of question scores, with "Useful" is 0.33, "Unhelpful" is 0.1, and others is 0. The system's overall score is the mean intervention score across the dataset. Finally, we submit the test set questions generated by the two most promising CoT prompting methods and the ToT framework for official evaluation by the CQs-Gen Shared Task organizers.

4.2 Results

4.2.1 Punctuation Evaluation Results

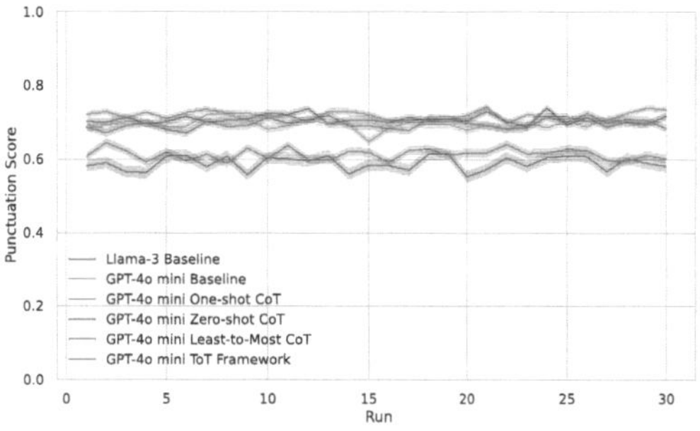

Figure 2: Punctuation score of all methods, including baseline.

Figure 2 and the table 1 presents the punctuation score across 30 runs on the validation set for all prompting strategies, including a baseline using GPT-4o mini. As expected, the baseline using LLaMA-3 8B lags significantly behind all other methods. Notably, the GPT-4o mini baseline demonstrates a strong improvement over the LLaMA-based baseline, confirming that model strength plays a substantial role in performance. However, prompting strategies such as One-shot CoT and Zero-shot CoT still outperform this strong baseline, indicating that reasoning scaffolds continue to provide benefits even when using advanced language models. Least-to-Most CoT performs comparably to GPT-4o mini baseline, while the ToT framework underperforms relative to other CoT-based methods in this setting. These results highlight that while newer models enable implicit reasoning, structured prompting continues to offer performance gains, especially in tasks requiring nuanced argumentative analysis. Results from additional model evaluations using DeepSeek-R1, Mistral and Qwen 3 are provided in Appendix B.

Interestingly, official evaluation on the hidden test set (also shown in table 1) reveals that Zero-shot CoT and the ToT Framework slightly outperform One-shot CoT, despite its superior performance on the validation set. This suggests that simpler or more diverse prompting strategies may generalize better in unseen scenarios.

Method	Validation	Test
Llama-3-8B Baseline	0.589 ± 0.019	
GPT-4o mini Baseline	0.694 ± 0.014	
GPT-4o mini One-shot CoT	0.719 ± 0.011	0.451
GPT-4o mini Zero-shot CoT	0.707 ± 0.013	0.490
GPT-4o mini Least-to-Most CoT	0.695 ± 0.014	
GPT-4o mini ToT Framework	0.613 ± 0.015	0.461

Table 1: Comparison of performance metrics of 30 runs across different prompting and reasoning strategies in validation set and test set.

4.2.2 Error Analysis

Our error analysis examined the top struggling interventions across various prompting strategies and model architectures. We identified several consistent patterns in failure cases: long and multi-topics interventions; emotionally charged or highly subjective content; too brief or ambiguous interventions; interventions involving sensitive themes such as race, health, or politics. Across methods, a common failure mode was the generation of descriptive rather than genuinely critical questions. Although the ToT approach demonstrated more structured reasoning, it continued to struggle with emotionally complex or contextually diffuse inputs. Representative examples of such interventions and model outputs are provided in Appendix C.

5 Conclusion

In this study, we investigated multi-step reasoning techniques, specifically CoT prompting and the ToT framework, for generating critical questions (CQs) from argumentative texts. Experiments show that CoT variants – especially Zero-shot CoT and One-shot CoT – outperform the LLaMA-3 baseline and slightly surpass GPT-4o mini, helping expose underlying assumptions. While the ToT framework supports structured exploration, it proved less effective in this context. Key challenges remain, such as handling emotionally charged or ambiguous content. Future work should explore more advanced multi-step strategies and alternative tree structures for ToT to enhance CQs-Gen performance.

Limitations

One limitation of our work lies in the inference cost associated with multi-step prompting using large language models (LLMs). Although GPT-4o-mini is relatively inexpensive, Table 2 shows that ToT incurred substantially higher cost across 30 runs ($21.10 total), compared to simpler strategies such as Zero-shot CoT ($0.98). While the per-sample cost remains low, the cumulative overhead may become prohibitive for larger-scale deployment. This motivates future exploration into cost-efficient prompting or model distillation techniques.

Method	Input	Output	Cost ($)
Zero-shot CoT	2.17M	1.10M	0.98
One-shot CoT	5.20M	0.90M	1.27
Least-to-Most CoT	2.39M	1.38M	1.19
ToT Framework	97.39M	10.94M	21.10

Table 2: Input/output token usage and total cost (in USD) for 30 runs of each multi-step reasoning technique using GPT-4o-mini on the validation set.

Acknowledgement

This research was supported by The VNUHCM-University of Information Technology's Scientific Research Support Fund. We thank the anonymous reviewers for their time and helpful suggestions that improved the quality of the paper.

References

Blanca Calvo Figueras and Rodrigo Agerri. 2024. Critical questions generation: Motivation and challenges. In *Proceedings of the 28th Conference on Computational Natural Language Learning*, pages 105–116, Miami, FL, USA. Association for Computational Linguistics.

DeepSeek-AI, Daya Guo, Dejian Yang, Haowei Zhang, Junxiao Song, Ruoyu Zhang, Runxin Xu, Qihao Zhu, Shirong Ma, Peiyi Wang, Xiao Bi, Xiaokang Zhang, Xingkai Yu, Yu Wu, Z. F. Wu, Zhibin Gou, Zhihong Shao, Zhuoshu Li, Ziyi Gao, and 181 others. 2025. Deepseek-r1: Incentivizing reasoning capability in llms via reinforcement learning. *Preprint*, arXiv:2501.12948.

Banca Calvo Figueras and Rodrigo Agerri. 2025. Benchmarking critical questions generation: A challenging reasoning task for large language models. *Preprint*, arXiv:2505.11341.

Blanca Calvo Figueras, Jaione Bengoetxea, Maite Heredia, Ekaterina Sviridova, Serena Villata Elena Cabrio, and Rodrigo Agerri. 2025. Overview of the critical questions generation shared task 2025. In *Proceedings of the 12th Workshop on Argument Mining*.

Aaron Grattafiori, Abhimanyu Dubey, Abhinav Jauhri, Abhinav Pandey, Abhishek Kadian, Ahmad Al-Dahle, Aiesha Letman, Akhil Mathur, Alan Schelten, Alex Vaughan, Amy Yang, Angela Fan, Anirudh Goyal, Anthony Hartshorn, Aobo Yang, Archi Mitra, Archie Sravankumar, Artem Korenev, Arthur Hinsvark, and 542 others. 2024. The llama 3 herd of models. *Preprint*, arXiv:2407.21783.

Takeshi Kojima, Shixiang Shane Gu, Machel Reid, Yutaka Matsuo, and Yusuke Iwasawa. 2023. Large language models are zero-shot reasoners. *Preprint*, arXiv:2205.11916.

Jieyi Long. 2023. Large language model guided tree-of-thought. *Preprint*, arXiv:2305.08291.

Elena Musi, Elinor Carmi, Chris Reed, Simeon Yates, and Kay O'Halloran. 2023. Developing misinformation immunity: How to reason-check fallacious news in a human–computer interaction environment. *Social Media + Society*, 9(1):20563051221150407.

Elena Musi and Chris Reed. 2022. From fallacies to semi-fake news: Improving the identification of misinformation triggers across digital media. *Discourse & Society*, 33(3):349–370.

A. Newell. 1959. *Report on a General Problem-solving Program*. P (Rand Corporation). Rand Corporation.

OpenAI, :, Aaron Hurst, Adam Lerer, Adam P. Goucher, Adam Perelman, Aditya Ramesh, Aidan Clark, AJ Ostrow, Akila Welihinda, Alan Hayes, Alec Radford, Aleksander Mądry, Alex Baker-Whitcomb, Alex Beutel, Alex Borzunov, Alex Carney, Alex Chow, Alex Kirillov, and 401 others. 2024. Gpt-4o system card. *Preprint*, arXiv:2410.21276.

T Santoso, L Yuanita, and E Erman. 2018. The role of student's critical asking question in developing student's critical thinking skills. *Journal of Physics: Conference Series*, 953(1):012042.

Douglas Walton, Christopher Reed, and Fabrizio Macagno. 2008. *Argumentation Schemes*. Cambridge University Press.

Chaojie Wang, Yanchen Deng, Zhiyi Lyu, Liang Zeng, Jujie He, Shuicheng Yan, and Bo An. 2024a. Q*: Improving multi-step reasoning for llms with deliberative planning. *Preprint*, arXiv:2406.14283.

Huaijie Wang, Shibo Hao, Hanze Dong, Shenao Zhang, Yilin Bao, Ziran Yang, and Yi Wu. 2024b. Offline reinforcement learning for llm multi-step reasoning. *Preprint*, arXiv:2412.16145.

Jason Wei, Xuezhi Wang, Dale Schuurmans, Maarten Bosma, Brian Ichter, Fei Xia, Ed Chi, Quoc Le, and Denny Zhou. 2023. Chain-of-thought prompting elicits reasoning in large language models. *Preprint*, arXiv:2201.11903.

Silei Xu, Wenhao Xie, Lingxiao Zhao, and Pengcheng He. 2025. Chain of draft: Thinking faster by writing less. *Preprint*, arXiv:2502.18600.

Shunyu Yao, Dian Yu, Jeffrey Zhao, Izhak Shafran, Thomas L. Griffiths, Yuan Cao, and Karthik Narasimhan. 2023. Tree of thoughts: Deliberate problem solving with large language models. *Preprint*, arXiv:2305.10601.

Denny Zhou, Nathanael Schärli, Le Hou, Jason Wei, Nathan Scales, Xuezhi Wang, Dale Schuurmans, Claire Cui, Olivier Bousquet, Quoc Le, and Ed Chi. 2023. Least-to-most prompting enables complex reasoning in large language models. *Preprint*, arXiv:2205.10625.

A Prompts and Sample Responses

All sample responses presented in this section are generated using the following prompt with the specified intervention:

> **MT:**
> *"Claire's absolutely right about that. But then the problem is that that form of capitalism wasn't generating sufficient surpluses. And so therefore where did the money flow. It didn't flow into those industrial activities, because in the developed world that wasn't making enough money."*

A.1 Standard input-output prompting (baseline)

A.1.1 Prompt:

> Suggest exactly 3 critical questions that should be raised before accepting the arguments in this text:
> "{intervention}"
> Make the questions simple, and do not give any explanation regarding why the question is relevant.

A.1.2 Sample response:

> 1. What evidence supports the claim that that form of capitalism wasn't generating sufficient surpluses?
> 2. What specific industrial activities is the speaker referring to, and why were they not profitable?
> 3. Where did the money flow instead, and what were the consequences of that shift?

A.2 Zero-shot CoT

A.2.1 Prompt:

Think about the argument step-by-step. Print your reasoning first in a structured step-by-step format.

Then, from the reasoning, suggest exactly 3 critical questions that should be raised before accepting the arguments in this text:

"{intervention}"

Make the questions simple.

A.2.2 Sample response:

Step-by-Step Reasoning

1. **Identifying the Claim**: The speaker, MT, agrees with Claire regarding a point about capitalism. They assert that a particular form of capitalism ("that form of capitalism") is not generating sufficient surpluses.
2. **Analyzing the Problem**: MT highlights a problem: the insufficient generation of surpluses under the discussed form of capitalism. This implies a need to understand what "that form" refers to and why it fails in this aspect.
3. **Exploring the Consequence**: MT states that because of the lack of surpluses, there is a flow of money that does not enter industrial activities. There is an implication that perhaps money is flowing elsewhere but does not specify where exactly it is going.
4. **Contextualizing Development**: The mention of the "developed world" suggests that the argument is rooted in a specific economic context. It implies that in more economically advanced regions, industrial activities are not lucrative enough to attract investment.
5. **Inquiring About Implications**: MT's point suggests broader implications for capitalism and industrial economies. The argument may require further substantiation to understand the full picture of economic flow and investment in relation to industrial activities.

Critical Questions

1. What specific form of capitalism is being referenced, and why is it deemed ineffective in generating surpluses?
2. Where exactly is the money flowing if it is not going into industrial activities?
3. What evidence is there to support the claim that industrial activities in the developed world are not profitable enough to attract investment?

A.3 One-shot CoT

A.3.1 Prompt for generating contents of One-shot CoT:

Given the following intervention:
{intervention}
And the following reasoning guideline:
- Identify its core claim.
- Identify any assumptions it makes.
- Examine the logical connections between claims.
- Consider what evidence would be needed to support it.
- Identify any missing or unclear aspects.
Use this guideline to generate reasoning steps that lead to these questions:
{questions}

A.3.2 Prompt for generating questions:

* Task: Given an intervention, identify its core claim, assumptions, logical connections, required evidence, and missing aspects. Then, suggest 3 critical questions that should be raised before accepting the argument. Make the questions simple.
* Example:
- Intervention: "{example_intervention}"
- Core claim: {core_claim}
- Assumption: {assumptions}
- Logical connections: {logical_connections}
- Required evidence: {required_evidence}
- Missing or unclear aspects: {missing_or_unclear_aspects}
- From these reasoning, here are the questions: {questions}
* Intervention: "{intervention}"

In this prompt, we use a semantic similarity-based selection approach to retrieve an intervention that is similar – but not identical – to the input, as example intervention. For OpenAI GPT-4o mini, we compute cosine similarity directly between the input and all stored example embeddings. For locally run models (e.g., DeepSeek-R1, Mistral, Qwen3), due to time constraint, we use a FAISS-based vector store to perform similarity search. In both cases, we normalize and filter out exact matches and ensure the selected example is semantically relevant.

A.3.3 Sample response of generating questions:

Core Claim:
The current form of capitalism is not generating enough surplus to support industrial activities in the developed world, leading to a lack of investment in these sectors.

Assumption:
The speaker assumes that a correlation exists between surplus generation and investment in industrial activities, and that the current form of capitalism is inherently insufficient for fostering necessary economic growth within the developed world.

Logical Connections:
The speaker connects the inability to generate sufficient surpluses under the current form of capitalism directly to the lack of funding and investment in industrial sectors. They suggest a causal relationship where inadequate profitability leads to inadequate investment.

Required Evidence:
Evidence would include data comparing surplus generation under different forms of capitalism, examples of industrial investment trends in response to surplus levels, comparisons between developed and developing economies, and studies demonstrating the relationship between profit margins and investment in industrial activities.

Missing or Unclear Aspects:

The speaker does not clarify what specific factors contribute to the lack of surplus generation in current capitalist structures, how these factors impact different sectors, or what alternative economic models might better support surplus generation. The implications of this lack of surplus on long-term economic health are also not discussed.

From these reasoning, here are the questions:

1. What specific aspects of the current form of capitalism are preventing sufficient surplus generation?
2. How does the speaker define "sufficient surpluses," and is there a consensus on what this should be?
3. Are there alternative economic models or strategies that could address this problem, and have they been considered?

A.4 Least-to-Most CoT

A.4.1 Prompt:

First, analyze the argument by breaking it down logically:
- Identify its core claim.
- Identify any assumptions it makes.
- Examine the logical connections between claims.
- Consider what evidence would be needed to support it.
- Identify any missing or unclear aspects.

Print your reasoning first in a structured step-by-step format. Then, suggest exactly 3 critical questions that should be raised before accepting the arguments in this text:

"{intervention}"

Make the questions simple.

A.4.2 Sample response:

Logical Breakdown of the Argument

1. **Core Claim:**
   - The speaker asserts that a specific form of capitalism is ineffective because it fails to generate sufficient surpluses, leading to a diversion of money away from industrial activities.
2. **Assumptions:**
   - There exists a specific form of capitalism being referenced.
   - The speaker believes that the failure to generate surpluses directly correlates with inadequate investment in industrial activities.
   - The claim assumes that sufficient surpluses are necessary for money to flow into industrial sectors.
3. **Logical Connections:**
   - The argument suggests a causal relationship between the insufficiency of surpluses and the lack of investment in industrial activities.
   - It implies that if capitalism were generating sufficient surpluses, then money would flow into the industrial sector.
4. **Evidence Needed:**
   - Data supporting the assertion that the current form of capitalism is inadequately generating surpluses.
   - Examples or statistics that demonstrate how lower surpluses correlate with reduced investment in industrial activities.
   - Analysis of the current financial flow patterns to industrial activities to substantiate claims of diversion.
5. **Missing or Unclear Aspects:**
   - The specific characteristics of the form of capitalism being discussed are not defined.
   - The speaker does not clarify what "sufficient surpluses" means or how it can be measured.
   - There's no mention of potential alternative explanations for the lack of investment in industrial activities, which could dilute the strength of the claim.

Critical Questions to Raise

1. What specific form of capitalism is being referred to, and what differentiates it from other forms?
2. What criteria do you use to define "sufficient surpluses," and how do we measure them?
3. Are there other factors besides surplus generation that could explain why money is not flowing into industrial activities?

A.5 ToT Prompting

A.5.1 Generating plans

Here is the intervention:

"{intervention}"

Generate a one line plan on how you would suggest a critical question that should be raised before accepting the arguments in this text. Do not give the question yet.

A.5.2 Generating sub-plans

Here is the intervention:

"{intervention}"

To suggest a critical question, here is the plan:

{parent_plan}

Generate a one line sub-plan of this plan on how you would suggest a critical question that should be raised before accepting the arguments in this text. Do not give the question yet.

A.5.3 Generating questions

Here is the intervention:

"{intervention}"

To suggest a critical question, here is the plan:

{plan}

From the plan, suggest three critical questions that should be raised before accepting the arguments in that intervention. Make the questions simple, and do not give any explanation regarding why the question is relevant.

A.5.4 Voting for plans

Here is the intervention:

"{intervention}"

To suggest a critical question, here are the plans:

{plans}

Analyze these plans, then conclude which is the most promising for a critical question for the intervention.

A.5.5 Voting for questions

Here is the intervention:

"{intervention}"

Here are the critical questions:

{cqs}

Analyze these questions and choose the three most suitable critical questions that should be raised before accepting the arguments in the intervention.

B Additional Results with Deepseek-R1, Mistral-7B, and Qwen 3-7B

To assess the generalizability of our prompting strategies across different LLM families, we conducted supplementary experiments using DeepSeek-R1, Mistral-7B, and Qwen3-8B, all run locally via the Ollama framework. Due to extensive computational runtime and time constraints during local evaluation, we did not include the Tree-of-Thought (ToT) framework in these supplementary tests. The results are reported below.

Method	**DeepSeek-R1**	**Mistral-7B**	**Qwen3-8B**
Baseline	0.538 ± 0.022	0.631 ± 0.017	0.629 ± 0.018
One-shot CoT	0.472 ± 0.020	0.670 ± 0.018	0.650 ± 0.017
Zero-shot CoT	0.526 ± 0.020	0.677 ± 0.013	0.645 ± 0.021
Least-to-Most CoT	0.434 ± 0.021	0.532 ± 0.019	0.671 ± 0.017

Table 3: Validation results with DeepSeek-R1, Mistral-7B, and Qwen3-8B using local inference (with `enable_thinking=true` in `apply_chat_template` for Qwen3-8B only).

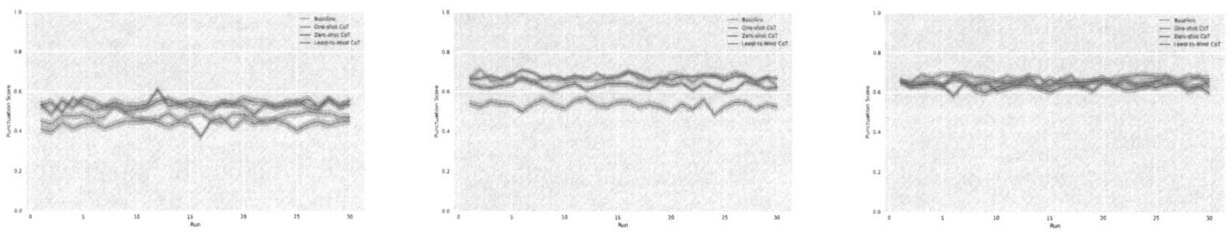

Figure 3: Performance comparison of prompting strategies. From left to right: DeepSeek-R1, Mistral-7B, and Qwen3-8B (with `enable_thinking=true` in `apply_chat_template` for Qwen3-8B only).

C Examples of Model Output on Challenging Interventions

C.1 Long, Multi-Topic Interventions

> **CLINTON**
> *"The central question in this election is really what kind of country we want to be and what kind of future we'll build together. Today is my granddaughter's second birthday... We need new jobs, good jobs, with rising incomes... I also want to see more companies do profit-sharing."*

- **GPT-4o mini Zero-shot CoT:** What specific policies or initiatives will be implemented to ensure new jobs in infrastructure and advanced manufacturing?
- **GPT-4o mini One-shot CoT:** What specific strategies will you implement to ensure new jobs created are of high quality and provide rising incomes for workers?
- **GPT-4o mini Least-to-Most CoT:** What evidence or data do you have to support the claim that increasing investments in certain sectors will lead to job growth and fairer economic conditions?
- **GPT-4o mini ToT Framework:** What impact will raising the national minimum wage have on small business profitability?
- **GPT-4o mini baseline:** What specific policies or measures will be implemented to build a fairer economy?

Despite their structured reasoning design, both CoT and ToT fail to produce useful critical questions in this example, as they focus on the most salient economic claims and neglect the discourse-level structure, resulting in unhelpful or invalid questions that do not fully challenge the argumentative richness of the intervention.

C.2 Emotionally Charged / Subjective Language

> **AllergyDad**
> *"As a parent of a child with severe life-threatening allergies to peanuts and treenuts... a peanut can have the same result [as death]. I urge the DOT to issue the ban, and make traveling safe for everyone."*

- **GPT-4o mini Zero-shot CoT:** What practical implications would banning peanuts and tree nuts on flights have on airlines and food service operations?
- **GPT-4o mini One-shot CoT:** How would the proposed ban on nut products be effectively enforced on flights?
- **GPT-4o mini ToT Framework:** How will a ban on peanut and tree nut products affect passengers with other dietary restrictions and allergies?
- **LLaMA-3 baseline:** What are the current airline policies regarding food allergies on flights?

CoT and ToT fail in this case because they generate operational or policy-related questions that accept the argument's premise, rather than critically examining whether an emotionally driven personal case justifies a general policy ban, rendering their outputs unhelpful or invalid.

C.3 Overly Short / Ambiguous Content

> **CLINTON**
> *"It's a good one, though. It well describes the problem."*

- **GPT-4o mini ToT Framework:** What specific problem is Clinton addressing in his statement?
- **GPT-4o mini baseline:** What specific problem is being referred to in the statement?

ToT fails in this case because the original statement lacks clear argumentative content, leading the model to produce a vague question that could be applied to any text – thus rendering it invalid.

C.4 Sensitive / Politically Charged Topics

> **CLINTON**
> *"It's just a fact that if you're a young African-American man and you do the same thing as a young white man, you are more likely to be arrested... I want to see private prisons ended in the state system... we need commonsense gun safety measures."*

- **LLaMA-3 baseline:** How would Clinton's plan to divert people from the criminal justice system work in practice, and what metrics would be used to measure its effectiveness?

C.5 Satirical / Figurative Language Misinterpreted Literally

> **Antanagoge**
> *"Is it really possible that all blindly partisan advocates of the peanut... are overtaken by such a compulsion... These sound like symptoms of addiction... The only prudent course of action is to discontinue peanuts on airplanes."*
> **howie**
> *"Most food allergies are completely imagined... Peanuts are incredibly nutritious... Leave my peanuts alone!"*

- **GPT-4o mini ToT Framework:** What are the documented cases of severe allergic reactions to peanuts occurring on airplanes?

ToT fails in this case because its multi-path reasoning converges prematurely on a literal interpretation of the text, overlooking its satirical tone.

Webis at CQs-Gen 2025:
Prompting and Reranking for Critical Questions

Midhun Kanadan[1] **Johannes Kiesel**[2] **Maximilian Heinrich**[1] **Benno Stein**[1]

[1]Bauhaus-Universität Weimar, [2]GESIS - Leibniz Institute for the Social Sciences

Abstract

This paper reports on the submission of team *Webis* to the Critical Question Generation shared task at the 12th Workshop on Argument Mining (ArgMining 2025). Our approach is a fully automated two-stage pipeline that first prompts a large language model (LLM) to generate candidate critical questions for a given argumentative intervention, and then reranks the generated questions as per a classifier's confidence in their usefulness. For the generation stage, we tested zero-shot, few-shot, and chain-of-thought prompting strategies. For the reranking stage, we used a ModernBERT classifier that we fine-tuned on either the validation set or an augmented version. Among our submissions, the best-performing configuration achieved a test score of 0.57 and ranked 5th in the shared task. Submissions that use reranking consistently outperformed baseline submissions without reranking across all metrics. Our results demonstrate that combining open-weight LLMs with reranking significantly improves the quality of the resulting critical questions.

1 Introduction

Large Language Models have demonstrated remarkable fluency in generating natural language text, but often struggle with hallucinations, outdated knowledge, or superficial reasoning (McKenna et al., 2023; Li et al., 2023; Islam et al., 2024). Therefore, one can not rely on LLMs to produce factual counterarguments. However, Critical Question Generation offers a different approach for arguing against statements: generating questions that expose an argument's "blind spots"—such as hidden assumptions, missing evidence, or flawed logic—which do not require factual knowledge to ask. Critical questions are thus not counterarguments in the typical sense of statements that are incompatible with the attacked argument. Instead, they are challenges to an argument's reasoning (Walton et al., 2008; Reed and Walton, 2001; Calvo Figueras and Agerri, 2024).

The ArgMining 2025 Shared Task on Critical Question Generation (Figueras et al., 2025) introduced a benchmark for evaluating automated question generation systems. Given interventions (contributions) to a debate, each annotated with argumentation schemes, submissions are required to generate three critical questions per intervention that meaningfully challenge the argument.

In this paper, we present our participating system (team *Webis*), which implements a two-stage pipeline: (1) prompting for critical questions and (2) reranking the generated questions to pick the most useful ones. For prompting, we test strategies ranging from basic zero-shot prompts to few-shot and chain-of-thought templates against multiple open-weight and closed-source models. For reranking, we use a ModernBERT classifier trained to predict usefulness on the shared task's validation dataset, as well as on an augmented version of this dataset of questions we generated and evaluated automatically.

Our system achieved 5th place in the shared task with an official score of 0.569, demonstrating the effectiveness of our two-stage pipeline.

This paper is structured as follows. Section 2 reviews related work on critical question generation and argumentation mining. Section 3 outlines the task definition. Section 4 presents our two-stage pipeline, detailing the prompting strategies and reranking. Section 5 reports our results, showing that reranking—especially when using an augmented training dataset—improved the effectiveness of methods over a baseline without reranking.

2 Related Work

The task of critical question generation is closely related to the notion of argumentation schemes (Walton et al., 2008), which define reasoning patterns

Proceedings of the 12th Argument Mining Workshop, pages 281–288
July 31, 2025 ©2025 Association for Computational Linguistics

and associated critical questions that probe assumptions and implications. While critical questions have been explored in logic and pedagogy (Reed and Walton, 2001; Macagno et al., 2017), their automatic generation remains underexplored. Recent work by Calvo Figueras and Agerri (2024) introduced a shared task on critical question generation, comparing LLM-based generation with template-based instantiation of critical questions. Their study highlights the challenge of producing valid, relevant questions that challenge the logic of an argument.

A significant strand of work in computational argumentation has examined the detection of argumentative components such as claims, premises, and discourse relations (Lawrence and Reed, 2019). However, less attention has been paid to the generation of inferentially challenging questions. While datasets like US2016 and Moral Maze offer valuable annotations for argument structure and schemes (Visser et al., 2021), their limited size and coverage pose challenges for training robust models for critical question generation.

A typical choice of model for argument classification and evaluation tasks is BERT and its variants (Devlin et al., 2019), which have been widely used for stance classification, argument quality prediction, and claim detection. For instance, Favreau et al. (2022) utilized BERT-based learning-to-rank models to evaluate the convincingness of arguments, demonstrating its efficacy in ranking tasks. In our work, we extend this line of research by adapting a fine-tuned ModernBERT classifier to score the usefulness of generated critical questions.

In previous work, the shared task organizers (Calvo Figueras and Agerri, 2024) showed that LLMs can be used for critical question generation, but their outputs often lack inferential validity or relevance. Combining LLM-based generation with downstream filtering or reranking, as explored in this paper, has shown potential for improving quality and consistency (Jain et al., 2024).

3 Task

Given an argumentative text, the task of critical question generation is to generate three questions that directly challenge the argument. These texts are interventions from real-world debates.

To evaluate systems for critical question generation, each generated question for a given argument is matched to a set of reference questions—which were labeled as `Useful`, `Unhelpful`, or `Invalid`—using semantic similarity. Each generated question is assigned the label of its most similar reference question. A system's final score is computed as the proportion of generated questions labeled as `Useful` across all interventions. In addition to the annotated reference questions, the shared task's dataset also contains argument scheme annotations for each argument, which we used in one prompting strategy.

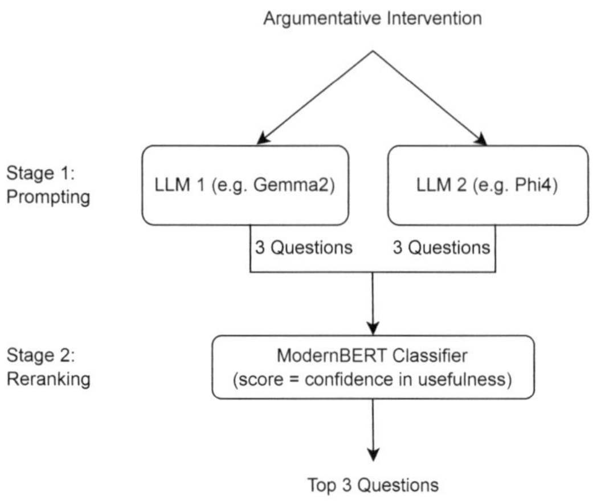

Figure 1: Overview of our evaluation and reranking pipeline. Each intervention is processed by two LLMs, generating six candidate critical questions. These are classified by a fine-tuned ModernBERT model, and the top three useful questions are selected.

4 Our Approach

Our approach is a pipeline of two stages: (1) prompting for critical questions and (2) reranking the generated questions to select the most useful ones. Figure 1 illustrates our pipeline.

4.1 Stage 1: Prompting for Critical Questions

To improve the quality, diversity, and relevance of generated critical questions, we implemented a wide spectrum of prompting strategies,[1] grouped into the following categories:

- *Basic prompting*: Directly asking the LLM to generate critical questions for an argumentative paragraph in a zero-shot manner.

[1] See Appendix B. As prompts are rather long, we only included the prompting strategy that led to the best results. The full set of prompts and code used in our system is available at `https://github.com/webis-de/argmining25-CQs-Gen.git`.

- *Guideline-based prompting*: Incorporating definitions of critical questions and their intended function (also zero-shot).

- *Chain-of-thought prompting*: Prompting the model to reason step-by-step before generating each question, for example by first identifying assumptions or implications in the argument (also zero-shot).

- *Few-shot prompting*: Providing one or more intervention–CQ examples, definitions with illustrative cases, good vs. bad comparisons, and self-assessment checks to guide the model toward higher-quality output.

These strategies were tested across different models and served as building blocks for the final prompt, which combined elements from several strategies—such as few-shot examples, definitions, and self-assessment instructions—to generate critical questions that are coherent, relevant, and inferentially valid.

Model selection: We used both open-weight and closed-source LLMs. The employed open-weight models—Gemma 3 (4B parameters), Gemma 2 (9B), LLaMA 3.2 (3B), Mistral (7B), Phi-4 (14B), and Qwen 2.5 (7B) are the respective default models from Ollama.[2] For comparison, we also included GPT-4o-mini as a closed-source baseline. Appendix B shows the final prompt we used for submission after preliminary evaluations.

Argumentation scheme integration: We also tested an approach that incorporated argumentation schemes from Walton et al. (2008) into the prompting process. These schemes were embedded into prompts, encouraging the model to generate questions targeting assumptions, analogies, consequences, and other reasoning patterns. Although this method aligned with the theoretical foundations of critical question generation, it was not included in the final submission due to lower empirical performance during our preliminary tests on the validation dataset. Appendix A provides more details on this approach.

4.2 Stage 2: Reranking Critical Questions

Model selection and fine-tuning: To select the most useful questions from the set of generated candidates, we implemented an evaluation and reranking pipeline using fine-tuned classification models. We tested BERT, DistilBERT, and ModernBERT, with ModernBERT demonstrating the best performance in our preliminary evaluations.

While BERT and DistilBERT showed some promise in preliminary evaluations, they struggled to process longer interventions and complex critical questions—possibly due to limited context size. In contrast, ModernBERT performed better, likely because it could handle longer inputs—some interventions exceeded the context size limit of standard BERT models—allowing it to consider a more complete argumentative context during classification.

We fine-tuned two variants of ModernBERT. The first was trained on the validation dataset provided by the organizers. The second variant was further trained on approximately 67.8k critical questions generated by the LLMs listed in the model selection section, using the diverse prompting strategies described in Section 3. These questions were automatically labeled using the official evaluation script, which assigns labels based on semantic similarity with reference questions from the validation set. Questions labeled as `not_able_to_evaluate` were discarded, along with duplicate questions generated across different LLMs and prompts, to reduce redundancy in the fine-tuning dataset. This extended version generalized better across different prompt styles and generation patterns in our preliminary experiments.

Training was conducted for 5 epochs using the AdamW optimizer with a learning rate of 5e-5. Evaluation and checkpoint saving were performed at the end of each epoch, with the best model selected based on the F1-score.

Data preparation: We merged the `Unhelpful` and `Invalid` categories into a single `Non-Useful` class to simplify the classification task, since both receive zero points in the evaluation. The dataset was then split into training, validation, and internal test sets. We fine-tuned ModernBERT to perform binary classification, predicting whether a given critical question is `Useful` or `Non-Useful`. This internal test set was used solely for development and is distinct from the official shared task test set.

Evaluation and reranking: To ensure that the final output included the most useful and diverse critical questions, we combined the outputs of two LLMs. For each intervention, three candidates were generated by each model, resulting in six critical questions. These were scored by ModernBERT per its confidence in the predicted usefulness (0 meaning 100% confident it is not useful), and the

[2] `https://ollama.com`

top three were selected. This multi-model generation and reranking strategy leveraged the strengths of different LLMs while ensuring output consistency through a unified reranking mechanism.

We submitted three runs for evaluation, selected based on their performance on the official sample and validation sets. The first submission used output from Gemma 2 with a single prompt; no reranking is needed as only three critical questions are generated. The second submission combined outputs from Gemma 2 and Phi-4, reranked using ModernBERT fine-tuned on both validation data and additional generated critical questions (Reranker-Augmented). The third submission used the same prompting setup but reranked with a model trained only on the validation set (Reranker-Base).

Method / Model	Evaluation Score		
	Sample	Validation	Test
Prompting			
Gemma 2*	**0.53**	**0.72**	0.49
Gemma 3	0.27	0.60	
LLaMA 3.2	0.40	0.58	
Mistral	0.33	0.61	
Phi-4	0.33	0.68	
Qwen 2.5	0.27	0.59	
Prompting + Reranking			
Reranker-Augmented*	**0.67**	**0.84**	**0.57**
Reranker-Base*	0.56	0.82	0.48
Argumentation Scheme Integration			
Gemma 2	0.60	0.72	

Table 1: Evaluation scores on the Sample, Validation, and Test sets for Prompting-only and Prompting + Reranking strategies. Stars (*) mark the three systems submitted to the shared task. The score 0.57 on the test set was partially based on manual evaluation.

5 Results

Table 1 presents the evaluation scores for all systems on the official sample, validation, and test sets. Among the prompting-only models, Gemma2 achieved the highest scores on the sample (0.53) and validation set (0.72). Phi-4, Mistral, Gemma 3, and LLaMA 3.2 showed moderate performance while Qwen 2.5 performed worst.

In contrast, our reranking pipeline significantly improved performance. Reranker-Augmented achieved a test score of 0.57, marking the best result among all our submissions. Reranker-Base, which shared the same LLM generation setup, yielded a slightly lower score of 0.48. These results validate the effectiveness of combining prompt diversity with model-based reranking.

For high-scoring submissions in the automatic evaluation mentioned above, the organizers manually reviewed critical questions that the automated evaluator marked as `not_able_to_evaluate`. For Reranker-Augmented, this included 12 such cases; after manual review, some were relabeled as `Useful`, increasing the total to 58 `Useful` questions, resulting to the final score of 0.57.

It is worth noting that we do not have access to the relabeling outcomes for the other two submissions, which included 12 (Gemma2) and 19 (Reranker-Base) `not_able_to_evaluate` questions. If some of these were similarly reclassified as `Useful`, their final scores would be higher.

6 Conclusion

We presented the submission of team *Webis* to the ArgMining 2025 Critical Question Generation shared task. Our system employed a two-stage pipeline combining diverse prompting strategies with a reranking mechanism powered by ModernBERT. Among our submissions, the best-performing configuration achieved a test score of 0.57 and ranked 5th overall.

As the goal of the task was to automate the generation of critical questions, we did not manually edit or post-process any of the outputs. All results were derived directly from the LLMs and the reranking model without human intervention, ensuring complete pipeline automation.

Our results highlight that even relatively lightweight open-weight models like Gemma 2, when paired with a reranking classifier fine-tuned on extended data, can yield competitive performance in challenging generative tasks such as critical question generation. The effectiveness of our approach stems from leveraging the diversity of LLM generations and then selecting questions through a classifier trained on inferential quality.

However, we observed that short or single-sentence interventions often led to overly generic or unhelpful critical questions, as the models had limited argumentative context to build upon. Additionally, the reliance on similarity-based evaluation can undervalue useful questions that diverge lexically from reference examples.

One idea for future work is to explore agent-based iterative generation strategies, where a critical question generation model and a feedback module interact to improve question quality over multiple rounds. Instruction-tuned models or reinforcement learning setups could also be used to explicitly optimize for the usefulness and specificity of generated questions.

Ethics Statement

We participated in the Critical Question Generation Shared Task using the dataset provided by the organizers, without modifying its content. All experiments were conducted solely for research purposes and in accordance with the ACL Ethics Policy. Our system generates critical questions automatically, but it is not yet suitable for deployment in high-stakes or production environments. The focus of this work is to advance research on critical reasoning and question generation in argumentation settings.

References

Blanca Calvo Figueras and Rodrigo Agerri. 2024. Critical questions generation: Motivation and challenges. In *Proceedings of the 28th Conference on Computational Natural Language Learning*, pages 105–116, Miami, FL, USA. Association for Computational Linguistics.

Jacob Devlin, Ming-Wei Chang, Kenton Lee, and Kristina Toutanova. 2019. Bert: Pre-training of deep bidirectional transformers for language understanding. In *Proceedings of the 2019 Conference of the North American Chapter of the Association for Computational Linguistics: Human Language Technologies*, pages 4171–4186. Association for Computational Linguistics.

Charles-Olivier Favreau, Amal Zouaq, and Sameer Bhatnagar. 2022. Learning to rank with bert for argument quality evaluation. In *Proceedings of the 35th International FLAIRS Conference (FLAIRS-35)*.

Blanca Calvo Figueras, Jaione Bengoetxea, Maite Heredia, Ekaterina Sviridova, Elena Cabrio, Serena Villata, and Rodrigo Agerri. 2025. Overview of the critical questions generation shared task 2025. In *Proceedings of the 12th Workshop on Argument Mining*.

S. M. Towhidul Islam, S. M. Mehedi Zaman, Vinija Jain, Anku Rani, Vipula Rawte, Aman Chadha, and Amitava Das. 2024. A comprehensive survey of hallucination mitigation techniques in large language models. *arXiv preprint arXiv:2401.01313*.

Siddhartha Jain, Xiaofei Ma, Anoop Deoras, and Bing Xiang. 2024. Lightweight reranking for language model generations. In *Proceedings of the 62nd Annual Meeting of the Association for Computational Linguistics (Volume 1: Long Papers)*, pages 6960–6984, Bangkok, Thailand. Association for Computational Linguistics.

John Lawrence and Chris Reed. 2019. Argument mining: A survey. *Computational Linguistics*, 45(4):765–818.

Bangzheng Li, Ben Zhou, Fei Wang, Xingyu Fu, Dan Roth, and Muhao Chen. 2023. Deceptive semantic shortcuts on reasoning chains: How far can models go without hallucination? *arXiv preprint arXiv:2311.09702*.

Fabrizio Macagno, Douglas Walton, and Chris Reed. 2017. Argumentation schemes. *Argumentation*, 31(4):529–563.

Nick McKenna, Tianyi Li, Liang Cheng, Mohammad Javad Hosseini, Mark Johnson, and Mark Steedman. 2023. Sources of hallucination by large language models on inference tasks. *arXiv preprint arXiv:2305.14552*.

Chris Reed and Douglas Walton. 2001. Applications of argumentation schemes. *Argumentation*, 15(3):239–255.

Jacky Visser, John Lawrence, Chris Reed, Jean H. M. Wagemans, and Douglas Walton. 2021. Annotating argument schemes. *Argumentation*, 35:101–139.

Douglas Walton, Chris Reed, and Fabrizio Macagno. 2008. *Argumentation Schemes*. Cambridge University Press, Cambridge, UK.

A Argumentation Scheme Integration

We conducted exploratory experiments integrating *argumentation schemes* from Walton et al. (Walton et al., 2008) into the CQ generation process. We began by identifying and extracting the argumentation schemes present in the sample and validation datasets. For each scheme, we retrieved its associated critical questions from Walton's Argumentation Schemes.

At generation time, we designed a structured prompt that included the intervention text, its corresponding argumentation scheme(s), a brief definition of each scheme, and representative critical questions drawn from Walton's work. This prompt guided the LLM to reason within a specific argumentative structure, aiming to produce more targeted critical questions. For this experiment, we used the Gemma 2 model to generate outputs. The full prompt template is shown in Figure 2.

Despite its theoretical alignment, this scheme-aware prompting approach was not included in the final submission. During preliminary evaluation (scores in Table 1), we observed that it often constrained the model's generative flexibility and led to questions that were overly rigid or templated. In contrast, more general prompting strategies produced more diverse and context-sensitive outputs.

You are an expert in argument analysis and critical reasoning.

Your task is to generate exactly **3 high-quality critical questions** that challenge the argument below.

Argument:
`{intervention_text}`

How to Generate Strong Critical Questions:
Each question must challenge the argument's assumptions, reasoning, evidence, consequences, or alternative solutions.

Relevant Argumentation Schemes & Examples:
Below are the argumentation schemes relevant to this intervention, along with examples of critical questions.

Scheme Name
• Definition: <*scheme definition*>

Good Example:
Argument: "..."
Good CQ: "..."

Bad Example:
Argument: "..."
Bad CQ: "..." (Not helpful)

Walton's Critical Questions:
– Walton CQ 1
– Walton CQ 2
...

Final Self-Assessment:
• "Does this question challenge the argument's assumptions, reasoning, evidence, consequences, or alternatives?"
– If yes, keep the question.
– If no, refine it to make it more impactful.

Your Task:

- Generate exactly 3 critical questions.
- Ensure each question closely follows Walton's Critical Questions.
- Do not introduce new topics or concepts not present in the argument.
- Write each question in one line without additional explanation.

Figure 2: Example of a scheme-aware prompt used in our exploratory experiment integrating argumentation schemes. The prompt includes scheme definitions, examples, and Walton-style critical questions to guide LLM generation.

B Final Prompt Used

You are an expert in argument analysis and critical reasoning.

Your task is to generate **exactly 3 critical questions** that should be asked before accepting the argument below.

Argument:
`{text}`

Definition of Critical Questions (CQs):
Critical Questions are inquiries designed to evaluate the strength and validity of an argument by uncovering and examining the assumptions underlying its premises. They serve as tools to assess whether an argument is sound or fallacious by challenging its reasoning, evidence, and potential implications.

How to Construct High-Quality Critical Questions:

- **Challenge the reasoning** – Does the argument's conclusion logically follow from its premises?
- **Challenge the assumptions** – Is the argument relying on hidden assumptions that might be false?
- **Challenge the evidence** – What proof supports the argument's claims?
- **Challenge the consequences** – Could there be unintended side effects of accepting the argument?
- **Challenge alternative explanations** – Are there better explanations or solutions?

Examples of Strong Critical Questions:
Example 1: Argument from Cause to Effect
Argument: *"If people migrate, unemployment rises."*
Good CQ: *"Are there other economic factors that contribute to unemployment apart from migration?"*
Bad CQ: *"What is the history of migration?"* (Not directly relevant)

Example 2: Practical Reasoning
Argument: *"Raising the minimum wage makes the economy fairer, so we should raise it."*
Good CQ: *"Are there alternative policies that could also achieve economic fairness without raising the minimum wage?"*
Bad CQ: *"What is the history of minimum wage policies?"* (Too broad)

Final Self-Assessment:
After generating the 3 critical questions, apply this check to each one:
"Can the answer to this question diminish the acceptability of the argument?"
- If **yes**, keep the question.
- If **no**, refine the question to make it more impactful.

Your Task:

- Generate exactly **3 high-quality critical questions**.
- **Ensure each question directly relates to the given argument** (avoid generic questions).
- Do not introduce new topics or concepts not present in the argument.
- After generating each question, apply the self-assessment check.
- Write each question in one line without any explanation.

Now, generate the 3 critical questions:

Figure 3: Final prompt used for critical question generation.

DayDreamer at CQs-Gen 2025: Generating Critical Questions through Argument Scheme Completion

Wendi Zhou and **Ameer Saadat-Yazdi** and **Nadin Kökciyan**
School of Informatics,
University of Edinburgh
{wendi.zhou, ameer.saadat, nadin.kokciyan}@ed.ac.uk

Abstract

Critical questions are essential resources to provoke critical thinking when encountering an argumentative text. We present our system for the Critical Questions Generation (CQs-Gen) Shared Task at ArgMining 2025. Our approach leverages large language models (LLMs) with chain-of-thought prompting to generate critical questions guided by Walton's argumentation schemes. For each input intervention, we conversationally prompt LLMs to instantiate the corresponding argument scheme template to first obtain structured arguments, and then generate relevant critical questions. Following this, we rank all the available critical questions by prompting LLMs to select the top 3 most helpful questions based on the original intervention text. This combination of structured argumentation theory and step-by-step reasoning enables the generation of contextually relevant and diverse critical questions. Our pipeline achieves competitive performance in the final test set, showing its potential to foster critical thinking given argumentative text and detect missing or uninformed claims. .

1 Introduction

In this paper, we present a system description for our contribution to the ArgMining 2025 shared task CQs-Gen (Figueras et al., 2025). Critical questions are an approach to evaluating arguments by providing criteria upon which an argument can be accepted. The argument can be considered acceptable if all the critical questions are satisfactorily answered (Walton and Godden, 2005).

In recent years, there has been an increasing interest in developing systems that can automate this process, aiming to improve the efficiency and reliability of argument evaluation. Our approach leverages advanced natural language processing techniques and machine learning algorithms to generate contextually relevant and diverse critical questions.

The system we propose not only identifies key components of an argument but also generates questions that challenge the premises, evidence, and reasoning used in forming conclusions. By doing so, it assists in uncovering potential weaknesses or biases within the argument, thus facilitating more rigorous and comprehensive critical thinking.

Our contribution to the CQs-Gen shared task (Figueras et al., 2025) is rooted in an approach that integrates argumentation theory with a large-scale language model, allowing our system to understand complex argument structures. Our system relies on the identification of argument schemes according to the taxonomy defined by Walton (Walton et al., 2008). Code available at DayDreamer[1].

2 Background

In Walton et al. (2008), the authors develop a comprehensive framework of argument schemes from which critical questions can be derived. An argument scheme is a structured pattern of reasoning associated with a common form of argument. These schemes can be used to analyse and evaluate arguments, particularly in everyday discourse where informal logic is often applied. Not only does this work categorise various types of arguments but it also provides critical questions for each scheme that help in assessing arguments. In their work, 26 Argument Schemes are described with associated critical questions. For example, one common scheme is the *Argument from Expert Opinion* shown in Table 1.

Critical questions are employed to scrutinise and challenge arguments constructed using argument schemes. These questions aim to identify potential weaknesses or gaps in the argument. Each argument scheme has its own set of critical questions. For the *Argument from Expert Opinion*, the critical

[1]https://git.ecdf.ed.ac.uk/s2236454/DayDreamer-CQs-Gen

Proceedings of the 12th Argument Mining Workshop, pages 289–294
July 31, 2025 ©2025 Association for Computational Linguistics

Argument from Expert Opinion	
Premise	E is an expert in domain D.
Premise	E asserts that A is true (false).
Conclusion	A may plausibly be accepted (rejected).

Table 1: Scheme for *Argument from Expert Opinion*

questions are shown in Table 2.

Critical Questions (CQs)
CQ1: Is E a credible expert in domain D?
CQ2: Is A consistent with what other experts assert?
CQ3: Is E's assertion based on reliable evidence?
CQ4: Is there any bias or conflict of interest?
CQ5: Is the argument plausible irrespective of expert opinion?

Table 2: Critical Questions associated with the *Argument from Expert Opinion*

These questions guide the evaluator in determining the robustness of the argument by challenging them to assess the credibility of the expert, the quality of the evidence, and any external influences that may affect the truth value of the expert's assertion.

3 Related Work

Several works approach the automatic identification of argument schemes as a multiclass classification problem. Starting from raw text, the goal is to label the text according to the scheme of reasoning being used (Visser et al., 2018; Rigotti and Greco, 2019). Others take this a step further and seek to instantiate the scheme based on the input text (Saadat-Yazdi, 2024; Jo et al., 2021; Ruiz-Dolz et al., 2024). The latter approach considers the problem of scheme identification as a two-step process of scheme classification, followed by instantiation, or a direct sequence-to-sequence translation problem. We combine these two approaches by choosing scheme labels that describe the set of schemes we wish to identify first. However, our goal is to automatically find the exact span of text to which a particular scheme applies, as well as the instantiation of the scheme.

Automatic critical question generation is less studied, with Calvo Figueras and Agerri (2024) being the only work that explicitly undertakes this investigation. Several other works, however, touch upon aspects of automated question generation in broader contexts. Mulla and Gharpure (2023) survey a number of approaches ranging from rule-based to neural approaches for automatic question generation, finding that modelling the task as a sequence-to-sequence learning problem seems to be the most promising direction.

4 Critical Question Generation Pipeline

We now introduce the three main stages within our critical question generation pipeline: *Argument Extraction*, *Critical Question Generation* and *Ranking*. Since our pipeline relies on chain-of-thought prompting with LLMs, the output of each stage would be the input for the next one. This conversational structure is depicted in Figure 1.

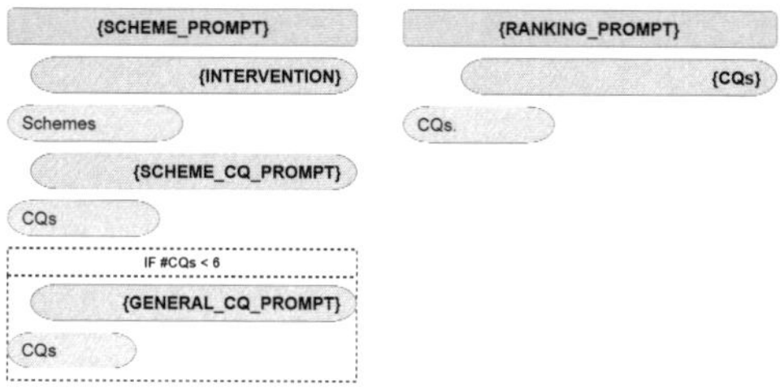

Figure 1: Conversational structure of our approach. The system prompt is shown in green, user prompts in blue, and LLM responses in orange. The text associated with user and system prompts can be found in Appendix A.

Argument Extraction In this stage, we utilised a comprehensive approach to extract arguments with the intervention text as input. Each intervention text was paired with a list of schemes in the provided dataset, which indicates the types of arguments that have been made in the intervention. To utilise this, we collected the definition of all the argument schemes from (Walton et al., 2008) and provided them to LLMs for template instantiation (prompt in Table 4), thereby generating structured arguments. This step provided a structured representation and categorisation of arguments, laying the foundation for critical question generation.

Critical Question Generation After successfully extracting the arguments, the next phase involved generating critical questions pertinent to each scheme. This was also accomplished by referencing Walton's work (Walton et al., 2008), which provides a well-established framework of critical questions for each scheme. With the prompt in Table 5, we complemented the LLMs ability on critical questions generation with this well-defined framework, providing guidance for generating more relevant and helpful questions by helping the models to hallucinate less. Occasionally, this process would result in fewer than three critical questions. To address this, we introduced one more turn (the dash box in Figure 1) that directly prompts LLMs to generate additional critical questions based on the chatting history when the total number of critical questions is insufficient for the next ranking stage (prompt in Table 7).

Ranking of Critical Questions The final stage of our pipeline focused on ranking the generated critical questions. Ranking is done with a new chat history as we are only interested in the original intervention and the generated critical questions. Using the prompt in Table 6, we present these to LLMs and task them with assessing and ranking the questions based on the helpfulness of the questions. Then, LLMs select the top three most helpful questions as the final output. This ranking process was crucial in choosing the most significant critical questions that would contribute to more in-depth critical thinking, considering the intervention.

5 Results

5.1 Final Evaluation

We obtained the 4th place out of 13 teams that participated, having 60 *Helpful* questions, 25 *Unhelpful* questions and 17 *Invalid* questions. This result comes from our first run result using GPT-4o-mini with manual evaluation.

Figure 2 shows the comparison of our three submissions, where our critical question generation pipeline is combined with two backbone models: *GPT-4o-mini* from OpenAI[2] and *LLaMa-3.1-8B-Instruct* (Grattafiori et al., 2024). Runs 1 and 2 use GPT model twice to assess the stability of our results. Overall, `GPT-4o-mini-run1` achieves the best performance, generating more Helpful critical questions while producing fewer Invalid and Unhelpful ones. `GPT-4o-mini-run2` shows a similar but slightly worse profile, suggesting some instability in our pipeline. In contrast, `LLaMa-7B-run3` demonstrated the lowest response quality compared to other runs, with a tendency toward less helpful and more error-prone outputs. These results highlight the better capability of GPT-4o models in critical question generation compared to LLaMa-7B; however, our pipeline fails to achieve consistent performance in unlocking their full potential.

[2]https://platform.openai.com/docs/models/gpt-4o-mini

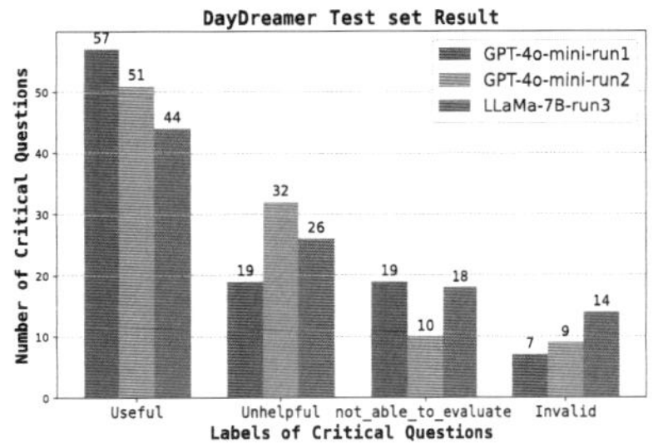

Figure 2: The automated test set evaluation results across three runs. The first two runs are implemented with GPT-4o-mini and the third one is with LLaMa-7B.

5.2 Pipeline Optimization on Validation set

In Table 3, we list all experiment results on the validation set that we conduct to optimize our critical question generation pipeline. Although the baseline method, where we simply prompt the GPT-4o-mini model with the same instruction as (Calvo Figueras and Agerri, 2024), achieves the highest percentage for *Useful* questions, our optimization goal is to minimize the number of *Invalid* and *Unhelpful* critical questions rather than maximize the number of *Helpful* ones. Focusing solely on having a higher number of *Helpful* questions may lead to overfitting, as 75% of the questions in the validation set are generated by LLMs.

We implement our pipeline both with *direct prompting* of the LLMs as well as *conversational prompting*. For direct prompting, we prompt the LLM separately in each stage of our pipeline, which means we take the output of the previous stage and use it together with the instructions of this stage as the input. On the other hand, we prompt LLMs in a conversational manner by keeping a list of chat history messages. In this way, we only provide this stage's instruction and additional helpful information in the prompt because the response of LLMs from the previous stage already exists in the history messages. When comparing the results from *Con* and *Direct Prompting* (in Table 3), we observe a higher percentage of *Useful* critical questions with a similar percentage of *Invalid* and *Unhelpful* ones. Therefore, we build on top of the conversational prompting method to enhance our pipeline.

Each intervention could be related to a long list of scheme names, and we observe that LLMs tend to hallucinate while having more than two scheme templates as input for argument extraction (Section 4). Initially, we feed those schemes into LLMs

Model	Method	Useful	Unhelpful	Invalid	N/A
LLaMa-3.1-8B-Instruct	Baseline	71.68	12.37	3.23	12.72
	$Con_{+ss+rank-er}$	62.21	12.48	2.71	22.60
GPT-4o-mini	Baseline	72.04	13.80	3.94	10.22
	Direct Prompting	56.81	12.19	1.79	29.21
	Con	62.90	13.08	1.25	22.76
	Con_{+ss}	65.41	13.26	3.76	17.56
	$Con_{+ss+rank}$	68.28	12.01	3.94	15.77
	$Con_{+ss+rank-er}$	72.22	8.78	2.87	16.13

Table 3: Validation results to justify our chosen LLMs and the final method of our submitted three run results. All the numbers are the percentage of the number of critical questions with the label. We use **N/A** to represent the fourth label in the automated evaluation: "not_able_to_evaluate". Con is the abbreviation of "Conversational prompting". Con_{+ss} represents that we include "sort scheme" technique on top of the conversational prompting design. Similarly, $Con_{+ss+rank}$ represents that we include prompt tuning for ranking, and $Con_{+ss+rank-er}$ means we remove the scheme templates starting with "ER" as input for LLMs. We choose $Con_{+ss+rank-er}$ as our final submission method for both models we implemented.

with a sliding window where the window size is 2. However, the scheme names within the list are not unique, and the same scheme name could occur in different positions. This window size limits LLMs to extract diverse arguments following the same scheme, as LLMs do not remember what arguments have been extracted with this scheme. To generate more diverse arguments and critical questions, we overcome this challenge with the "sort scheme" technique, where we sort the scheme names in the list and provide all the occurrences of the same scheme names to LLMs together. This approach enables LLMs to estimate the number of argument instances within the intervention that follow the scheme template, thus extracting them all together. There is an evident increase in the number of *Useful* questions and *Invalid* ones from Con to Con_{+ss} in Table 3, justifying that sorting scheme names could result in more diverse critical question generation. Furthermore, we improve the number of *Helpful* questions by modifying the instructions for the ranking stage.

Since our pipeline involves a chain-of-thought prompting, the response of LLMs for each stage could have a great influence on the next stage. We perform a bad case analysis to correlate the quality of the generated critical questions with the scheme types. Unsurprisingly, we notice that most of the *Invalid* critical questions are generated using the schemes that start with "ER" (such as "ERPracticalReasoning", "ERExpertOpinion", etc), which are not defined in (Walton et al., 2008). Since we failed to find the accurate definition, we filled the scheme templates with the corresponding scheme that does not start with "ER". For example, we used the scheme content of "PracticalReasoning" for the scheme "ERPracticalReasoning". However, this inaccurate scheme definition seems to confuse LLMs from extracting correct arguments from the intervention, thus resulting in poor critical question generation. So, we decide not to provide any template to LLMs for these four schemes and let them generate the critical questions based purely on the intervention text. The difference between results from $Con_{ss+rank}$ and $Con_{+ss+rank-er}$ in Table 3 suggests that LLMs can generate higher quality critical questions without misleading scheme templates. Therefore, the quality of the scheme template has a great impact on our pipeline.

6 Conclusion

The findings of our study underscore the significant impact that argument schemes have on the critical question generation process. Our analysis indicates that the accurate definition and implementation of schemes are crucial for extracting valid arguments and enhancing the overall effectiveness of the pipeline. Future work may focus on improving the ability of language models to correctly identify schemes and generate appropriate critical questions accordingly. Constructing a compendium of argument scheme definitions used in the dataset, alongside generating critical questions, would also likely improve results in follow-up work, as it would avoid the issues we found with "ER" schemes.

Limitations

As discussed in our results, the key limitation of this is the lack of definitions of argument schemes for certain cases. We also found that certain schemes used in the dataset were not provided with critical questions in Walton et al. (2008), preventing us from generating critical questions once the scheme has been extracted.

Acknowledgment

This work was supported by the University of Edinburgh-Huawei Joint Lab grants CIENG4721 and CIENG8329.

References

Blanca Calvo Figueras and Rodrigo Agerri. 2024. Critical questions generation: Motivation and challenges. In *Proceedings of the 28th Conference on Computational Natural Language Learning*, pages 105–116, Miami, FL, USA. Association for Computational Linguistics.

Blanca Calvo Figueras, Jaione Bengoetxea, Maite Heredia, Ekaterina Sviridova, Elena Cabrio, Serena Villata, and Rodrigo Agerri. 2025. Overview of the critical questions generation shared task 2025. In *Proceedings of the 12th Workshop on Argument Mining*.

Aaron Grattafiori, Abhimanyu Dubey, Abhinav Jauhri, Abhinav Pandey, Abhishek Kadian, Ahmad Al-Dahle, Aiesha Letman, Akhil Mathur, Alan Schelten, Alex Vaughan, Amy Yang, Angela Fan, Anirudh Goyal, Anthony Hartshorn, Aobo Yang, Archi Mitra, Archie Sravankumar, Artem Korenev, Arthur Hinsvark, and 542 others. 2024. The llama 3 herd of models. *Preprint*, arXiv:2407.21783.

Yohan Jo, Seojin Bang, Chris Reed, and Eduard Hovy. 2021. Classifying Argumentative Relations Using Logical Mechanisms and Argumentation Schemes. *Transactions of the Association for Computational Linguistics*, 9:721–739.

Nikahat Mulla and Prachi Gharpure. 2023. Automatic question generation: a review of methodologies, datasets, evaluation metrics, and applications. *Progress in Artificial Intelligence*, 12(1):1–32.

Eddo Rigotti and Sara Greco. 2019. *Inference in Argumentation: A Topics-Based Approach to Argument Schemes*, volume 34 of *Argumentation Library*. Springer International Publishing, Cham.

Ramon Ruiz-Dolz, Joaquin Taverner, John Lawrence, and Chris Reed. 2024. NLAS-multi: A Multilingual Corpus of Automatically Generated Natural Language Argumentation Schemes. *arXiv preprint*. ArXiv:2402.14458 [cs].

Ameer Saadat-Yazdi. 2024. Beyond Recognising Entailment: Formalising Natural Language Inference from an Argumentative Perspective. In *Procedings of the The 62nd Annual Meeting of the Association for Computational Linguistics.*

Jacky Visser, John Lawrence, Jean Wagemans, and Chris Reed. 2018. Revisiting Computational Models of Argument Schemes: Classification, Annotation, Comparison. In *Computational Models of Argument*, pages 313–324. IOS Press.

Douglas Walton and David M Godden. 2005. The nature and status of critical questions in argumentation schemes. In *OSSA Conference Archive*.

Douglas Walton, Chris Reed, and Fabrizio Macagno. 2008. *Argumentation Schemes*. Cambridge University Press, Cambridge.

A Prompts for LLMs

Extract arguments for each of the scheme in {**scheme_name**} from the input paragraph. These schemes are defined as follows: {**scheme_description**} If no argument can be extracted to fit the scheme, extract the main arguments with premise and conclusion.

Table 4: **SCHEME_PROMPT** Prompt for the **Argument Extraction** stage. {**scheme_name**} is the placeholder for the scheme names paired with this intervention. {**scheme_description**} is the placeholder for the scheme definition in (Walton et al., 2008).

{**cq_template**} With the help of the information above, generate a list of critical questions to ask regarding the extracted arguments. You may rephrase the critical question to make it more fluent. Return only a list questions as defined below: [{"CQ1": "the content of the critical question"}, ...]

Table 5: **SCHEME_CQ_PROMPT** Prompt for the **Critical Question Generation** stage. {**cq_template**} is the placeholder for the defined critical question template related to each scheme.

{**intervention**}

A helpful critical question can potentially challenge one of the arguments in the text.
Rank and select top three most helpful critical questions.
Return ONLY the question id in a Python list:
“‘python
[id_1, ...]

Table 6: **GENERAL_CQ_PROMPT** Prompt for the **Ranking of Critical Questions** stage. {**intervention**} is the placeholder for the original intervention text.

{**intervention**}

A helpful critical question can potentially challenge one of the arguments in the text.
Provide me 3 more critical questions that should be asked given the arguments from the text above.
Return only the questions as following format:
[{"CQ1": "the content of the critical question"}...]

Table 7: **RANKING_PROMPT** Prompt for generating more critical questions when the available critical questions are insufficient for ranking.

CUET_SR34 at CQs-Gen 2025: Critical Question Generation via Few-Shot LLMs – Integrating NER and Argument Schemes

Sajib Bhattacharjee, Tabassum Basher Rashfi, Samia Rahman, Hasan Murad
Department of Computer Science and Engineering
Chittagong University of Engineering and Technology, Bangladesh
{u2004003, u2004004, u1904022}@student.cuet.ac.bd, hasanmurad@cuet.ac.bd

Abstract

Critical Question Generation (CQs-Gen) improves reasoning and critical thinking skills through Critical Questions (CQs), which identify reasoning gaps and address misinformation in NLP, especially as LLM-based chat systems are widely used for learning and may encourage superficial learning habits. The Shared Task on Critical Question Generation, hosted at the 12th Workshop on Argument Mining and co-located in ACL 2025, has aimed to address these challenges. This study proposes a CQs-Gen pipeline using Llama-3-8B-Instruct-GGUF-Q8_0 with few-shot learning, integrating text simplification, NER, and argument schemes to enhance question quality. Through an extensive experiment testing without training, fine-tuning with PEFT using LoRA on 10% of the dataset, and few-shot fine-tuning (using five examples) with an 8-bit quantized model, we demonstrate that the few-shot approach outperforms others. On the validation set, 397 out of 558 generated CQs were classified as Useful, representing 71.1% of the total. In contrast, on the test set, 49 out of 102 generated CQs, accounting for 48% of the total, were classified as Useful following evaluation through semantic similarity and manual assessments.

1 Introduction

Critical Question Generation (CQs-Gen) is the automated process of generating questions to assess the strength, validity, and assumptions of arguments in a text. Instead of simple factual questions, critical questions promote deeper inference and reasoning, essential for critical thinking (Ennis, 2011). With the rise of LLM-based chats, there is concern that students may develop superficial learning habits, weakening their crucial critical thinking abilities. Critical Questions (CQs) sharpen one's mind by exposing weakness in arguments and forging stronger arguments (Walton, 2006).

The CQs-Gen shared task (Calvo Figueras et al., 2025), held as part of the 12th Workshop on Argument Mining (ACL 2025), focused on generating critical questions from argumentative texts. Unlike earlier QG models (Du et al., 2017; Heilman and Smith, 2010) that focused on surface-level question generation, this task emphasizes deeper reasoning. Previous models often missed logical structure and implicit assumptions, lacking the use of tools like NER, text simplification, or argument schemes that could improve understanding.

In this work, we propose a pipeline to generate high-quality CQs by combining diverse strategies to enhance question development. We initiated our experiment by testing some LLMs without any training. Thereafter, we fine-tuned these models on the given dataset, incorporating experiments with and without text simplification and NER. Ultimately, the best result was achieved with few-shot fine-tuning integrating text simplification, NER, and argument schemes, even with just five training examples. Our proposed pipeline generates contextually relevant and logically targeted CQs. We evaluated multiple systems, with our best model generating 397 out of 558 useful CQs (71.1%) on the validation set and 49 out of 102 CQs (48%) on the test set.

Our key contributions include:

- We integrated text simplification, NER, and argument schemes to improve the quality of generated questions.
- Our experiment demonstrated that few-shot fine-tuning with an 8-bit model outperforms traditional fine-tuning approaches.
- We provided a reproducible implementation available at: https://github.com/Sojib001/Critical-Question-Generation

Proceedings of the 12th Argument Mining Workshop, pages 295–300
July 31, 2025 ©2025 Association for Computational Linguistics

2 Related Work

Critical Question Generation (CQs-Gen) is an improvement over standard question generation by generating questions that probe the logical structure and weakness of argumentative texts, which was first introduced by Calvo Figueras and Agerri, 2024.

Transformer-based models have advanced QG by generating grammatically correct questions. Kriangchaivech and Wangperawong (2019) found that these models made a lot of mistakes on the SQuAD dataset. Later, it was pointed out that the models copied parts of the text directly or didn't even form proper questions, mainly because they were too influenced by patterns in their training data (Lopez et al., 2020).

LLMs like GPT-3 and T5 often struggle with understanding deeper context or specialized topics (Cuskley et al., 2024). Cuskley et al. (2024) highlighted LLMs reliance on unimodal text, leading to generic outputs. Pérez-Gállego et al. (2024) demonstrated that LLMs generate questions misaligned with educational goals. Recent multimodal approaches improved distractor generation but still lack focus on argumentative reasoning (Luo et al., 2024). Li and Zhang, 2024 uses LLM in a zero-shot setting to generate questions in a controlled setting. Various QG methods (Duan et al., 2017; Subramanian et al., 2018; Yao et al., 2022) used named entities to guide models in generating contextually relevant questions.

Prior work has not combined text simplification, NER, and argumentation schemes for CQs-Gen, nor explored few-shot learning with quantized LLMs in this context. Our system leverages these techniques with few-shot learning using an 8-bit quantized LLM.

3 Data

We have used the dataset (Figueras and Agerri, 2025) provided under the Shared Task on Critical Question Generation hosted at the 12th Workshop on Argument Mining and co-located in ACL 2025 (Calvo Figueras et al., 2025) which is segmented into a sample set containing 5 interventions with 133 critical questions (CQs) and a validation set comprising 186 interventions with 4,136 CQs. It consists of argumentative texts like political debates, economic policies, social issues, security, foreign policy, and social justice.

4 System

Our task was to generate exactly three critical questions using the given intervention with an LLM. The input is an argumentative text in English and the schemes of the argument.

4.1 Simplifying Text

As Van et al., 2021 suggested, text simplification improves downstream NLP tasks, so we preprocessed the data by simplifying the intervention text, employing the Llama-3-8B-Instruct-GGUF-Q8_0.[1] We fine-tuned the model using a few-shot technique with five examples to illustrate the expected input-output mapping to the model.

4.2 Named Entity Recognition Feature

Following Harrison and Walker, 2018, we used named entity recognition (NER) to boost question relevance. Using the flair/ner-english-large[2] model, we labeled entities as Person, Location, Organization, or MISC and appended them to each input to guide question generation.

4.3 Argument Schemes Feature

Baumtrog, 2021 and Yu and Zenker, 2020 advocate that argument schemes can enhance the generation of CQs by offering a structured framework. So, we integrated this feature in the input intervention across various configurations. For each data instance, argument schemes from the dataset were provided.

An illustration of how we integrated the simplification process, NER, and argument schemes with our input text is seen in Figure 1.

4.4 Initial Experimentation

We initially conducted experiments to fine-tune LLMs with a small portion of our dataset. The models evaluated were Llama-3.2-3B-Instruct,[3] Mistral-7B-Instruct-v0.3,[4] and Llama-3-8B-Instruct.[5] We used 4-bit quantization to reduce the size of the models when importing them from Hugging Face. Additionally, we applied Parameter Efficient Fine Tuning (PEFT) with Low-Rank Adaptation (LoRA) to reduce the number of trainable parameters. Finally, we have used the GGUF version of Llama-3-8B-Instruct, employing a few-shot training approach, which

[1] huggingface.co/bartowski/Meta-Llama-3-8B-Instruct-GGUF

[2] https://huggingface.co/flair/ner-english-large

[3] huggingface.co/meta-llama/Llama-3.2-3B-Instruct

[4] https://huggingface.co/mistralai/Mistral-7B-Instruct-v0.3

[5] huggingface.co/meta-llama/Meta-Llama-3-8B-Instruct

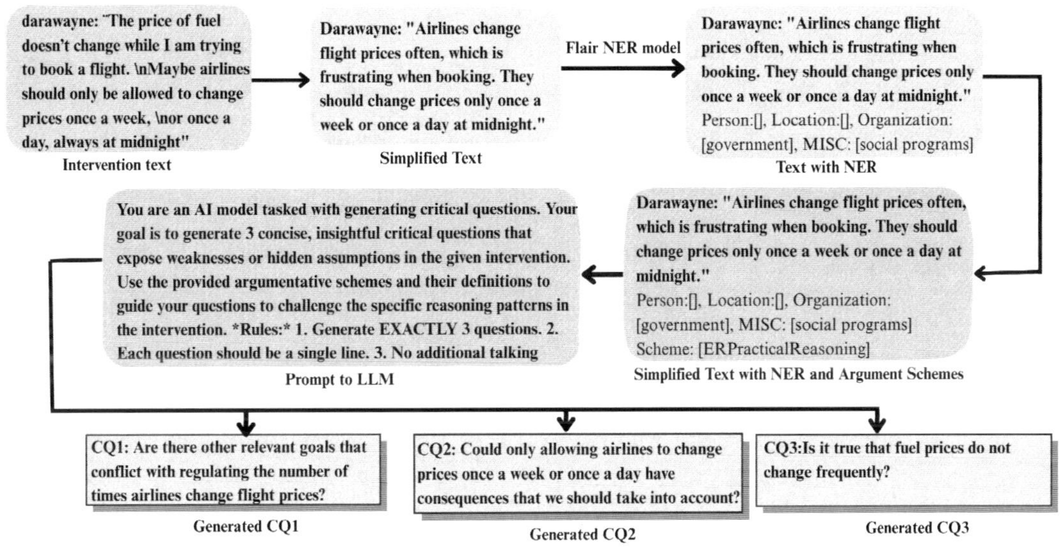

Figure 1: Overview of Our Proposed Critical Question Generation System.

outperformed other models due to its 8-bit quantization as opposed to the 4-bit quantization used in other models.

4.5 Overview of the Adopted Model

We used 8-bit quantized Llama-3-8B-Instruct-GGUF-Q8_0 due to its enhanced quantization compared to previously used models. We have used a few-shot technique to fine-tune it by using five interventions from the validation set and mapping expected input-output. For every example, we have provided the simplified intervention text, a categorized list of named entities, and the argument schemes of that intervention text. Figure 1 illustrates the workflow of our system.

5 Parameter Setting

For traditionally fine-tuned models, we have utilized 10% of our dataset, applying LoRA with a rank of 32 and an alpha value of 64. For our best-performing model, Llama-3-8B-Instruct-GGUF-Q8_0, we have employed a few-shot fine-tuning technique with five examples to map expected input-output. The same prompt was consistently applied throughout the experiment, as illustrated in Figure 1.

6 Evaluation Metric

The evaluation metric is based on semantic similarity with a reference question set. A Sentence-Transformer model (stsb-mpnet-base-v2)[6] was used to check semantic similarity, or the BLEURT score, between the generated CQs and reference CQs. If similarity crosses the predefined threshold of 0.65, the highest-scoring reference CQ is selected, and the corresponding label is assigned to the generated CQ. If the highest semantic similarity falls below the threshold, the question is labeled as "not_able_to_evaluate" and subjected to manual evaluation later.

7 Result and Analysis

The produced CQs were categorized into four classes based on semantic similarity: Useful (USE), Unhelpful (UN), Invalid (IN), and Not Able to Evaluate (NAE). Questions in the last class require manual evaluation. Based on Table 1, five-example few-shot learning outperformed no training and traditional training, producing the most useful CQs.

The number of successful CQs increased with larger model sizes in both no-training and fine-tuned conditions. Fine-tuning on 10% of the data, along with features like NER and text simplification, also improved performance. Llama-3-8B-Instruct showed consistent performance in all conditions, with its quantized GGUF version performing best under few-shot learning. Including the argument schemes as an input feature made the model optimal.

Table 2 presents the test results of our three submitted models, and the optimal performance is from the model with simplified text, NER, and argument schemes. Human assessment of uneval-

[6]https://huggingface.co/sentence-transformers/stsb-mpnet-base-v2

Type	Model	Count			
		USE	UN	IN	NAE
No Training	Llama-3.2-3B-Instruct	100	20	10	428
	Mistral-7B-Instruct-v0.3	248	42	16	252
	Llama-3-8B-Instruct	253	56	15	234
Fine-Tuned	Llama-3.2-3B-Instruct	150	30	11	367
	Mistral-7B-Instruct-v0.3	260	42	16	240
	Llama-3-8B-Instruct	260	50	13	235
	Llama-3-8B-Instruct (original text + NER)	266	47	14	231
	Llama-3-8B-Instruct (simplified text + NER)	267	54	13	224
Few-Shot	Llama-3-8B-Instruct-GGUF-Q8_0 (simplified text + No NER)	386	73	25	74
	Llama-3-8B-Instruct-GGUF-Q8_0 (simplified text + NER)	392	74	19	73
	Llama-3-8B-Instruct-GGUF-Q8_0 (simplified text + NER + schemes)	**397**	**79**	**18**	**64**

Table 1: Count metrics of models on the validation dataset.

uated CQs generated from the model is given in Table 3.

7.1 Error Analysis

While there was consistent overall performance, our model also made some mistakes by generating unhelpful and invalid CQs.

Unhelpful CQs were generated when the model did not fully understand the argument schemes. These questions were well-formed but did not challenge the speaker's reasoning or assumptions. As an example, in the "CLINTON_199_2" intervention, the model asked an abductive question regarding cooperation, missing the chance to challenge the logic or feasibility of Clinton's argument.

Invalid CQs resulted from misunderstanding the argument. For instance, in "CLINTON_25," the model generated a question about inflation and environmental destruction when Clinton actually spoke about clean energy and the economy, which did not match the actual topic.

Examples of both types of errors are shown in Table 4.

Run	Model	Count			
		USE	UN	IN	CAE
Test Run 1	**Llama-3-8B-Instruct-GGUF-Q8_0 (simplified text + NER + schemes)**	**44**	**29**	**17**	**12**
Test Run 2	Llama-3-8B-Instruct-GGUF-Q8_0 (simplified text + No NER)	33	28	17	24
Test Run 3	Llama-3-8B-Instruct-GGUF-Q8_0 (simplified text + NER)	43	24	14	21

Table 2: Count metrics of models on the test dataset.

Run	Model	Count		
		USE	UN	IN
Test Run 1	Llama-3-8B-Instruct-GGUF-Q8_0 (simplified text + NER + schemes)	49	34	19

Table 3: Final metrics of models on the test dataset after manual evaluation.

8 Conclusion

Though the task of critical question generation using LLMs is a new task, we have generated a huge number of useful critical questions using Llama-3-8B-Instruct-GGUF-Q8_0 using features like text simplification, NER, and argumentation schemes. We have contributed by exploring multiple models and enhancing the input by adopting text simplification, NER, and argumentation schemes as a feature. Among all the models, Llama-3-8B-Instruct-GGUF-Q8_0 outperformed others by generating 397 useful CQs (71.1%) in the validation set and 49 useful CQs (48%) in the test dataset after manual evaluation. However, it has struggled to understand the argument schemes and the right interpretation of a given intervention.

9 Limitations

While this study presents useful insights into CQs-Gen with LLMs, it is not without limitations. We were only able to utilize two models, Mistral and Llama, due to time and resource limitations. The fine-tuning was performed using 4-bit quantized models with only 10% of the data. Additionally, we were not able to evaluate the CQs labeled "Not Able to Evaluate (NAE)" because it was done by the task organizers. In the future, we plan to use larger models, train on more data, improve NER, and explore other languages to make our approach more generalizable.

References

Michael D Baumtrog. 2021. Designing critical questions for argumentation schemes. *Argumentation*.

Blanca Calvo Figueras and Rodrigo Agerri. 2024. Critical questions generation: Motivation and challenges. *arXiv preprint arXiv:2410.14335*.

Blanca Calvo Figueras, Jaione Bengoetxea, Maite Heredia, Ekaterina Sviridova, Elena Cabrio, Serena Villata, and Rodrigo Agerri. 2025. Overview of the critical questions generation shared task 2025. In *Proceedings of the 12th Workshop on Argument Mining (ArgMining 2025)*, Vienna, Austria. Association for Computational Linguistics.

Christine Cuskley, Rebecca Woods, and Molly Flaherty. 2024. The limitations of large language models for understanding human language and cognition. *Open Mind*.

Xinya Du, Junru Shao, and Claire Cardie. 2017. Learning to ask: Neural question generation for reading comprehension. *arXiv preprint arXiv:1705.00106*.

Nan Duan, Duyu Tang, Peng Chen, and Ming Zhou. 2017. Question generation for question answering. Association for Computational Linguistics.

Robert H. Ennis. 2011. Critical thinking: Reflection and perspective. *Inquiry: Critical thinking across the Disciplines*.

Banca Calvo Figueras and Rodrigo Agerri. 2025. Benchmarking critical questions generation: A challenging reasoning task for large language models. *arXiv preprint arXiv:2505.11341*.

Vrindavan Harrison and Marilyn Walker. 2018. Neural generation of diverse questions using answer focus, contextual and linguistic features. *arXiv preprint arXiv:1809.02637*.

Michael Heilman and Noah A. Smith. 2010. Good question! statistical ranking for question generation. Association for Computational Linguistics.

Kettip Kriangchaivech and Artit Wangperawong. 2019. Question generation by transformers. *arXiv preprint arXiv:1909.05017*.

Kunze Li and Yu Zhang. 2024. Planning first, question second: An LLM-guided method for controllable question generation. Association for Computational Linguistics.

Luis Enrico Lopez, Diane Kathryn Cruz, Jan Christian Blaise Cruz, and Charibeth Cheng. 2020. Transformer-based end-to-end question generation. *arXiv preprint arXiv:2005.01107*.

Haohao Luo, Yang Deng, Ying Shen, See-Kiong Ng, and Tat-Seng Chua. 2024. Chain-of-exemplar: Enhancing distractor generation for multimodal educational question generation. Association for Computational Linguistics.

Pablo Pérez-Gállego, Marc Franco-Salvador, Luis García-Sardiña, Marco del Tredici, and Roberto Navigli. 2024. Analysis of large language models for educational question classification and generation. *Computers and Education: Artificial Intelligence*.

Sandeep Subramanian, Tong Wang, Xingdi Yuan, Saizheng Zhang, Adam Trischler, and Yoshua Bengio. 2018. Neural models for key phrase extraction and question generation. *arXiv preprint arXiv:1706.04560*.

Hoang Van, Zheng Tang, and Mihai Surdeanu. 2021. How may i help you? using neural text simplification to improve downstream nlp tasks. *arXiv preprint arXiv:2109.04604*.

Douglas Walton. 2006. *Fundamentals of Critical Argumentation*. Cambridge University Press.

Bingsheng Yao, Dakuo Wang, Tongshuang Wu, Zheng Zhang, Toby Jia-Jun Li, Mo Yu, and Ying Xu. 2022. It is AI's turn to ask humans a question: Question-answer pair generation for children's story books. *arXiv preprint arXiv:2109.03423*.

Shiyang Yu and Frank Zenker. 2020. Schemes, critical questions, and complete argument evaluation. *Argumentation*.

A Appendix: Examples of Invalid and Unhelpful CQ Errors

Label	Intervention_ID, CQ_ID	Critical Question (CQ)
Unhelpful	CLINTON_199_2 (CQ_ID 1)	How does Clinton's proposal to work closely with Muslim-majority nations in the Middle East and Europe address the concerns of Muslim communities, and what specific measures does she plan to take to ensure their cooperation?
	CLINTON_223_2 (CQ_ID 2)	What are the consequences of Clinton's approach to diplomacy, and how does she weigh the benefits of building coalitions against the potential risks of relying on other nations' cooperation?
Invalid	CLINTON_25 (CQ_ID 2)	What specific measures will be taken to ensure that the creation of jobs and stimulation of the economy will not lead to unintended consequences, such as increased inflation or environmental degradation?
	Elmattador_92 (CQ_ID 0)	What specific arguments or points made during the debate did Elmattador find unconvincing or problematic, rather than simply attacking the tone or demeanor of the debaters?

Table 4: Representative Examples of Invalid and Unhelpful CQ Errors

ARG2ST at CQs-Gen 2025: Critical Questions Generation through LLMs and Usefulness-based Selection

Alan Ramponi,[1] Gaudenzia Genoni,[2] Sara Tonelli[1]
{alramponi,satonelli}@fbk.eu, gaudenzia.genoni@studenti.unitn.it

[1] Fondazione Bruno Kessler, Italy
[2] University of Trento, Italy

Abstract

Critical questions (CQs) generation for argumentative texts is a key task to promote critical thinking and counter misinformation. In this paper, we present a two-step approach for CQs generation that *i)* uses a large language model (LLM) for generating candidate CQs, and *ii)* leverages a fine-tuned classifier for ranking and selecting the top-k most useful CQs to present to the user. We show that such usefulness-based CQs selection consistently improves the performance over the standard application of LLMs. Our system was designed in the context of a shared task on CQs generation hosted at the 12th Workshop on Argument Mining, and represents a viable approach to encourage future developments on CQs generation. Our code is made available to the research community.[1]

1 Introduction

In the rapidly evolving field of argument mining (Stede and Schneider, 2018; Lawrence and Reed, 2020), the automated generation of critical questions (CQs) for argumentative texts has recently been introduced as a task to foster individuals' critical thinking and counter misinformation (Calvo Figueras and Agerri, 2024). CQs are defined as *the set of inquiries that could be asked in order to judge if an argument is acceptable or fallacious* (Calvo Figueras and Agerri, 2024) and have been proven useful for identifying fallacies (Musi et al., 2022; Ramponi et al., 2025) and evaluating argumentative essays (Song et al., 2014). Unlike automated fact-checking tasks that assign veracity labels to claims (Gupta and Srikumar, 2021; Valer et al., 2023, *inter alia*), CQs generation advances misinformation countering by moving beyond the absolutist notion of truth and offering a means to identify missing or potentially misleading arguments even without access to up-to-date factual knowledge (Calvo Figueras and Agerri, 2024).

To encourage research in this direction, a shared task on CQs generation has been proposed (CQs-Gen; Calvo Figueras et al., 2025) and hosted at the 12th Workshop on Argument Mining. The goal of the shared task is to investigate methods for generating useful CQs given an argumentative text as input. Participants are asked to provide three CQs per argumentative text, which are then subject to semi-automatic evaluation (Section 2).

In this paper, we present our research contribution for CQs generation. Motivated by recent advancements in NLP driven by large language models (LLMs), their pitfalls (e.g., outputs' reliability and consistency), and the shared task requirement of providing exactly $k = 3$ CQs per text, we propose a two-step approach that *i)* uses an LLM for generating n CQs (with $n > k$) and *ii)* leverages a fine-tuned classifier to select the top-k useful CQs to retain based on their confidence scores (Section 3). Results show that our usefulness-based selection leads to performance improvements across all the LLMs tested (Section 4). Finally, we provide a qualitative analysis and insights for future work (Section 5) and outline our conclusions (Section 6).

2 Data and Task Description

In this section, we provide details on the data provided by the shared task organizers (Section 2.1) and describe the task setup (Section 2.2).

2.1 Data Description

The data used for the CQs-Gen shared task is based on Calvo Figueras and Agerri (2025). The validation set provided to participants comprises 186 interventions, either from real debates or online discussions (i.e., argumentative texts). Among these, 80 are drawn from the US2016TV corpus (Visser et al., 2020, 2021), i.e., transcripts from televised debates for the 2016 US Presidential election, 72 from REGULATION ROOM DIVISIVE-

[1] Repository: https://github.com/dhfbk/cqs-gen.

Proceedings of the 12th Argument Mining Workshop, pages 301–313

NESS (RRD) (Konat et al., 2016), a corpus of user comments from the eRulemaking platform RegulationRoom.org, 20 from MORAL MAZE DEBATES (MMD) (Lawrence et al., 2018), a corpus for the homonymous BBC4 radio programme, and 14 from the US2016REDDIT corpus (Visser et al., 2020, 2021), i.e., Reddit posts reacting to the 2016 US political debates. Each intervention is annotated with one or more argumentation schemes based on the Walton et al. (2008)'s taxonomy and is accompanied by a set of CQs, categorized as `useful`, `unhelpful`, or `invalid` according to their effectiveness in challenging the arguments of the intervention (Appendix A). These CQs can be either LLM-generated or manually instantiated by annotators using fixed templates in line with Walton et al. (2008)'s theory, as described in Calvo Figueras and Agerri (2024). The test set instead comprises 34 interventions distributed as follows: US2016TV (17), RRD (11), and MMD (6).

2.2 Task Setup

The CQs-Gen shared task encourages the development of methods to counter misinformation and promote critical thinking. Participants are asked to design a system that, given an argumentative text as input, provides exactly three CQs that challenge the arguments in the intervention. Focusing on the internal structure and content of text, rather than external knowledge, these questions aim to uncover implicit assumptions, expose logical weaknesses, or highlight insufficient evidence.

For evaluation, each generated CQ is assigned the label of the closest reference CQ in the dataset, as determined by semantic similarity (Reimers and Gurevych, 2019).[2] CQs that match `useful` CQs are awarded $0.\overline{33}$ points, while those matching `unhelpful` or `invalid` CQs receive 0 points: therefore, for each intervention, a *punctuation* score between 0 and 1 can be obtained. However, if the similarity between the generated and the most similar reference CQ falls below a given similarity threshold[3] – also when the CQ is useful but it is not included in the reference set – the generated CQ remains unmatched and does not contribute any points to the score, requiring manual evaluation to assess its usefulness. The overall punctuation score for a system is given by the average of all punctuation scores obtained across interventions.

[2]Semantic similarity in the official organizers' evaluation script is computed using the `stsb-mpnet-base-v2` model.

[3]The threshold used in the official evaluation script is 0.60.

3 Methods

Our approach to CQs generation consists of two stages. First, we use an LLM to generate candidate CQs and extract them from the raw output (Section 3.1). Second, we apply a fine-tuned classifier to the CQs, rank them by confidence score, and select the top-k candidate CQs to retain (Section 3.2).

3.1 Generation of Candidate Questions

The generation phase is conducted by prompting an LLM to obtain a raw output containing candidate CQs for a given argumentative text. Models and prompting strategies are described in Section 4.1.

Since LLMs' raw outputs often include extra text before or after the requested output, we carefully curate the post-processing. Specifically, to extract the n CQs from the raw output, we split the text by line breaks and retain only the lines starting with a capital letter that end in a question mark. If less than n CQs are detected, the remaining slots are filled with a placeholder value.

3.2 Usefulness-based Questions Selection

The CQs selection phase leverages a pretrained model that we specifically fine-tune using a dataset of `useful` and `non-useful` (i.e., `unhelpful` and `invalid` merged together) CQs. The fine-tuned model is therefore a binary classifier, and the confidence score for the predicted label is provided. This classifier is applied to all n candidate CQs. Models and dataset compositions that we tested are described in the experimental setup (Section 4.1).

We use the confidence score for the label `useful` as given by the classifier and rank the n candidate CQs by decreasing "usefulness". We then select the top-k CQs and use them as final output.

4 Experiments

In this section, we describe the experimental setup (Section 4.1) and the model selection process (Section 4.2). Then, we present the results (Section 4.3).

4.1 Experimental Setup

Models For the generation of candidate CQs, we experiment with different families of instruction-tuned LLMs of varying sizes in both zero-shot and few-shot settings. Specifically, we use `Llama-3-8B` and `Llama-3-70B` (Grattafiori et al., 2024), `Mixtral-8x7B` (Jiang et al., 2024), and `Qwen-2.5-7B` and `Qwen-2.5-32B` (Qwen et al.,

2025). Hyper-parameter settings for these models are reported in Appendix B.1. For CQs selection, we fine-tune transformer-based models using MaChAmp v0.4.2 (van der Goot et al., 2021) in a single task setting with default hyper-parameter values (Appendix B.1). We employ `BERT-base-uncased` (Devlin et al., 2019) and `RoBERTa-base` (Liu et al., 2019) as encoders, and use `[CLS]` and `<s>` special tokens for classification.

Prompts For CQs generation, we devise a set of prompts that include increasingly-detailed information about the task and the input argumentative text. To isolate the impact of individual information pieces from linguistic variation, we design prompts in a modular fashion (Appendix B.2). Specifically, starting from a prompt with only key information on the task and the desired output (`base`), we experiment with the inclusion of the argumentation schemes associated to the input intervention (`schemes`) and descriptions of what `useful` and `non-useful` CQs are (`desc` in different flavors). The provisionally best-performing prompt is also used for in-context learning experiments (Dong et al., 2024) in few-shot settings. Details on our prompts can be found in Appendix B.2.

Classifier data For fine-tuning the CQs usefulness classifier (Section 3.2), we collect all the CQs in the validation set and their associated labels, and divide the resulting set into 80%/20% train/test portions, i.e., obtaining `gold-train` and `gold-test` splits. We further collect CQs generated by small-sized LLMs (i.e., `Llama-3-8B`, `Qwen-2.5-7B`, and `Mixtral-8x7B`) using the `base` prompt with $n = 3$ across all 5 runs on the validation set (Section 4.2) along with assigned labels, leading to three synthetic sets: `synth-l`, `synth-q`, and `synth-m`, respectively. These different sets, including their concatenation (`all`), are used for determining the best data combination based on macro F_1 score on the `gold-test` split (Section 4.2).

4.2 Model Selection

We use the validation set and the evaluation script provided by shared task organizers[4] for selecting the most promising LLM configurations (i.e., underlying models and prompts) and usefulness-based CQs classifier. To ensure fair comparison between zero- and few-shot settings, we remove from the development set the interventions used in few-shot prompts (Appendix B.2.2). Given the small size of the resulting development set, we run all LLMs with 5 random seeds and select the best approaches based on average punctuation score.

Generation of candidate CQs We start by assessing the performance of small-sized LLMs across all prompts in a zero-shot setting with $n = 3$ to identify promising models and prompts to be used in further experiments. As shown in Appendix C.1, `Mixtral-8x7B` and `Llama-3-8B` outperform `Qwen-2.5-7B` across all prompts; we thus discard the latter from further experimentation. The `base` prompt provides the best overall performance for both `Mixtral-8x7B` and `Llama-3-8B` despite its simplicity. Among prompts with CQ descriptions, providing information only on what `non-useful` CQs are (i.e., $\texttt{desc}_{(\neg U)}$) is more reliable than providing definitions for `useful` CQs (i.e., $\texttt{desc}_{(U)}$) or their combination (i.e., $\texttt{desc}_{(U+\neg U)}$), even when extremely detailed (i.e., $\texttt{desc}_{(FULL)}$). However, $\texttt{desc}_{(\neg U)}$ still lags behind the `base` prompt in terms of performance. We further observe that using `schemes` leads to the worst performance across models. We hypothesize that this is due to the unavailability of precise information about the part of the input intervention where each argumentation scheme occurs. We thus select `Mixtral-8x7B` and `Llama-3-8B` with the `base` prompt for few-shot experiments; however, we observe that this direction is not viable: a substantial performance degradation occurs when including CQs examples in the prompt. Results are in Appendix C.2 to encourage research in this direction.

Selection of useful CQs To choose the CQs selection classifier, we compare the performance of `BERT-base-uncased` and `RoBERTa-base` models when fine-tuned using either `gold-train`, synthetic sets (i.e., `synth-l`, `synth-q`, and `synth-m`), or a combination thereof (i.e., `all`) (Section 4.1). As shown in Appendix C.3, using the `all` set for fine-tuning consistently improves the performance across models, leading to 0.7563 macro F_1 for `BERT-base-uncased` and 0.7341 macro F_1 for `RoBERTa-base`. We therefore select the `BERT-base-uncased` model fine-tuned with the `all` data variant as our CQs selection classifier.

4.3 Results

The best-performing small-sized LLMs and prompts derived from the model selection (Section 4.2) – i.e., `Mixtral-8x7B` and `Llama-3-8B`,

[4] https://github.com/hitz-zentroa/shared-task-critical-questions-generation.

Model	Prompt	n	Selection	Punctuation	
MIXTRAL-8X7B	base	3	no	$0.6758_{\pm 0.01}$	
MIXTRAL-8X7B	base	5	rand	$0.6878_{\pm 0.01}$	
MIXTRAL-8X7B	base	5	yes	**0.7231**$_{\pm 0.02}$	*
LLAMA-3-8B	base	3	no	$0.6510_{\pm 0.01}$	
LLAMA-3-8B	base	5	rand	$0.6058_{\pm 0.01}$	
LLAMA-3-8B	base	5	yes	**0.6790**$_{\pm 0.01}$	
QWEN-2.5-32B	base	3	no	$0.6543_{\pm 0.01}$	
QWEN-2.5-32B	base	5	rand	$0.6499_{\pm 0.02}$	
QWEN-2.5-32B	base	5	yes	**0.6732**$_{\pm 0.02}$	
LLAMA-3-70B	base	3	no	$0.6903_{\pm 0.02}$	
LLAMA-3-70B	base	5	rand	$0.7162_{\pm 0.02}$	
LLAMA-3-70B	base	5	yes	**0.7618**$_{\pm 0.02}$	*
LLAMA-3-70B	$\texttt{desc}_{(U+\neg U)}$	3	no	$0.6958_{\pm 0.02}$	
LLAMA-3-70B	$\texttt{desc}_{(U+\neg U)}$	5	rand	$0.6922_{\pm 0.01}$	
LLAMA-3-70B	$\texttt{desc}_{(U+\neg U)}$	5	yes	**0.7279**$_{\pm 0.02}$	*

Table 1: Results on the development set for different LLMs and the best prompt strategies in a zero-shot setting with/without CQs selection. We report the average punctuation score with standard deviation across 5 runs with different random seeds. Models for which a best run has been selected for testing are indicated with *.

Run	U	UH	I	NE	P (labeled)	P (all)
RUN_1	45	26	10	21	0.5556	0.4412
RUN_2	46	23	14	19	0.5542	0.4510
RUN_3	41	20	16	25	0.5325	0.4020
$\text{RUN}_{2\text{FINAL}}$	51	24	27	–	0.5000	**0.5000**

Table 2: Distribution of CQ labels and results in the test set. **U**: `useful`; **UH**: `unhelpful`; **I**: `invalid`; **NE**: `not_able_to_evaluate`; **P (labeled)**: Punctuation score over labeled CQs only, i.e., U/(U+UH+I); **P (all)**: Official punctuation score over all CQs including those labeled as NE, i.e., U/(U+UH+I+NE). For RUN_2, we also include the final counts after manual review by the shared task organizers ($\text{RUN}_{2\text{FINAL}}$).

both with `base` – as well as large-sized LLMs with promising prompts from preliminary experiments – i.e., `Llama-3-70B` with `base` and $\texttt{desc}_{(U+\neg U)}$ and `Qwen-2.5-32B` with `base` – are finally compared with and without the CQs selection classifier. Specifically, to assess whether a classifier for selecting the most useful CQs helps in improving performance, we compare the results obtained on the validation set by the aforementioned LLMs when *i)* directly instructed to generate exactly $n = 3$ CQs – with no selection (i.e., "no"), *ii)* instructed to generate $n = 5$ CQs followed by random selection of $k = 3$ CQs (i.e., "rand"), and *iii)* instructed to generate $n = 5$ CQs that are then given to the usefulness-based CQs classifier to keep the top-k ($k = 3$) most useful CQs (i.e., "yes"). Results in Table 1 show that using the usefulness-based CQs classifier (i.e., "yes") consistently improves the performance over the "no" and "rand" selection strategies. This indicates that our two-step approach for CQs generation is more effective compared to the standard application of LLMs for the task.

For test set evaluation in the context of the CQs-Gen shared task, we select the best run (among the 5 runs with different random seeds) for the three top-performing models (marked with "*" in Table 1), i.e., `Llama-3-70B` with prompt `base` (RUN_1) and $\texttt{desc}_{(U+\neg U)}$ (RUN_2), and `Mixtral-8x7B` with prompt `base` (RUN_3), all with CQs selection. In Table 2, we report the punctuation scores and the distribution of CQ labels obtained by all runs in the test set. `Llama-3-70B` in RUN_1 and RUN_2 performs similarly, while `Mixtral-8x7B` in RUN_3 yields a slightly lower outcome. All models show a consistent drop in performance compared to their average scores on the validation set (Table 1).[5] Results for RUN_2, which achieved the best score on the test set (i.e., 0.4510), were manually revised by the CQs-Gen shared task organizers to evaluate the remaining 19 unlabeled questions: of these, 5 were classified as `useful`, 1 as `unhelpful`, and 13 as `invalid` ($\text{RUN}_{2\text{FINAL}}$), raising the final punctuation score to 0.50. We should mention that the lack of manual evaluation for the validation set may have impacted the reliability of model selection – a limitation that the shared task organizers aim to resolve through a fully automated evaluation in the future.

5 Qualitative Analysis and Future Work

We conduct a qualitative analysis of the manually reviewed results from RUN_2 (i.e., $\text{RUN}_{2\text{FINAL}}$) on the test set, proposing a classification of the generated CQs according to the type of argumentative gap they attempt to expose. Results are in Table 3. We recall that, for the 34 interventions in the test set, the output of the run consists of 102 questions (3 per intervention) generated by `Llama-3-70B` with prompt $\texttt{desc}_{(U+\neg U)}$ and usefulness-based selection, and that the punctuation score achieved by $\text{RUN}_{2\text{FINAL}}$ is 0.50 (see Table 2).

For the purpose of the analysis, each CQ is assigned a label based on its underlying argumentative function, structure, and semantics. For instance, questions that request supporting data for a specific claim (e.g., one of the CQs generated for the intervention with identifier "HOLT_122":

[5]Note that the similarity threshold was adjusted from 0.60 to 0.65 by shared task organizers for test set evaluation.

Type	# useful	# non-useful
ALTERNATIVE MEASURES	4	2
ALTERNATIVE EXPLANATION	2	2
ASSUMPTIONS	0	1
BASIS/RATIONALE	2	1
CAUSAL FACTORS	0	1
COMPARISON	1	1
CONSEQUENCES	2	4
CREDIBILITY	0	1
DEFINITION	3	1
EVIDENCE	**15**	**9**
EXAMPLES	1	2
EXPLANATION	1	1
GENERALIZATION	2	2
IMPACT/EFFECT	3	0
IMPLICATION	0	3
OTHER	9	10
POLICY DETAILS	1	6
RESPONSE TO CONCERNS	3	2
ROOT CAUSES	2	2
Total	51	51

Table 3: Distribution of the CQs from RUN_{2FINAL} according to the type of argumentative gap they attempt to expose, divided into useful and non-useful categories. EVIDENCE-related CQs represent the most frequent type across both groups (indicated in bold). The row highlighted in gray groups all CQs for which no clear semantic category can be identified.

"What evidence is there to support the claim that race relations are bad in this country?") are labeled as EVIDENCE. When no clear semantic category emerges, the question is classified in the group OTHER (gray row in Table 3). In some cases, a single CQ includes elements that could be associated with multiple labels (e.g., one of the CQs generated for the intervention with identifier "MP_24": *"What would be the consequences of allowing banks to 'crystallise the debts' and how would it affect the economy?"*, which pertains to both CONSEQUENCES and IMPACT/EFFECT categories); for the sake of consistency and simplicity, in this analysis we assign only the most salient type (in this case, CONSEQUENCES), leaving a more granular categorization for future work. The annotation was carried out manually by a native Italian speaker with advanced proficiency in English and background in data science and Italian studies.

Overall, the qualitative analysis aligns well with findings reported by Calvo Figueras and Agerri (2024). In particular, we observe that the most common type of CQ generated by `Llama-3-70B` asks for EVIDENCE to support a claim: 15 out of 51 `useful` CQs (29.40%) fall into this category. This type is also the most frequent among `unhelpful` and `invalid` questions (9 out of 51; 17.64%), representing 24% of the total questions generated for this run. Among the `useful` CQs, other frequent types include ALTERNATIVE MEASURES (e.g., *"Are there other measures* [...]"), though at lower frequencies (4; 7.84%); questions about DEFINITION (e.g., *"How do you define* [...]"), IMPACT/EFFECT questions (e.g., *"How does* [something] *affect* [...]") and RESPONSE TO CONCERNS questions (i.e., *"How does* [someone] *address the concerns of* [...]") each occur 3 times (5.88%). Among `non-useful` questions, the second most common type is POLICY DETAILS (e.g., *"What specific policies* [...]", 6; 11.76%), followed by CONSEQUENCES questions (e.g., *"What are the potential consequences of* [...]", 4; 7.84%).

Beyond these initial observations, however, a larger sample size would be needed to identify broader groupings and statistically determine whether any patterns can be directly linked to either `useful` or `non-useful` questions. Indeed, at this stage, rather than being systematically tied to a specific flawed type, `non-useful` questions appear to reflect broader limitations that LLMs face in generating CQs – namely, the introduction of irrelevant concepts, bad reasoning, and insufficient specificity, as discussed by Calvo Figueras and Agerri (2024).

In future work, we aim to manually inspect automatically evaluated CQs to assess the reliability of semantic similarity-based scoring. We also plan to improve our methodology by combining the usefulness-based CQs selection approach with strategies such as chain-of-thought prompting (Wei et al., 2022) and by fine-tuning LLMs – an approach that has shown state-of-the-art performance on several argument mining tasks (Cabessa et al., 2024) – using low-rank adapters (Hu et al., 2022).

6 Conclusion

We present a two-step approach for CQs generation along with a qualitative analysis and insights on the results obtained in the context of the CQs-Gen shared task hosted at the 12th Workshop on Argument Mining. Our experiments show that usefulness-based CQs selection leads to substantial gains in performance compared to using LLMs only. We hope that our approach may encourage future developments in CQs generation and stimulate research on similar tasks more broadly.

Limitations

The experiments, results, and findings in this paper are based on the dataset of interventions that was provided in the context of the CQs-Gen shared task. Interventions in the dataset are in English, and a large fraction of them concern political topics in the US context. Further research is needed to ensure that results and insights hold for other languages, topics, and contexts that are not represented in the dataset. Due to resource constraints, we employ a limited set of models in our experiments. We are aware that higher results could have been obtained with larger and/or closed-source LLMs. However, our goal was to investigate the effectiveness of a two-step approach for CQs generation using freely available and widely used models.

Acknowledgments

This work has been funded by the European Union's Horizon Europe research and innovation program under grant agreement No. 101070190 (AI4Trust).

References

Jérémie Cabessa, Hugo Hernault, and Umer Mushtaq. 2024. In-context learning and fine-tuning gpt for argument mining. *arXiv preprint arXiv:2406.06699*.

Banca Calvo Figueras and Rodrigo Agerri. 2025. Benchmarking critical questions generation: A challenging reasoning task for large language models. *arXiv preprint arXiv:2505.11341*.

Blanca Calvo Figueras and Rodrigo Agerri. 2024. Critical questions generation: Motivation and challenges. In *Proceedings of the 28th Conference on Computational Natural Language Learning*, pages 105–116, Miami, FL, USA. Association for Computational Linguistics.

Blanca Calvo Figueras, Jaione Bengoetxea, Maite Heredia, Ekaterina Sviridova, Elena Cabrio, Serena Villata, and Rodrigo Agerri. 2025. Overview of the critical questions generation shared task 2025. In *Proceedings of the 12th Workshop on Argument Mining*, Vienna, Austria. Association for Computational Linguistics.

Jacob Devlin, Ming-Wei Chang, Kenton Lee, and Kristina Toutanova. 2019. BERT: Pre-training of deep bidirectional transformers for language understanding. In *Proceedings of the 2019 Conference of the North American Chapter of the Association for Computational Linguistics: Human Language Technologies, Volume 1 (Long and Short Papers)*, pages 4171–4186, Minneapolis, Minnesota. Association for Computational Linguistics.

Qingxiu Dong, Lei Li, Damai Dai, Ce Zheng, Jingyuan Ma, Rui Li, Heming Xia, Jingjing Xu, Zhiyong Wu, Baobao Chang, Xu Sun, Lei Li, and Zhifang Sui. 2024. A survey on in-context learning. In *Proceedings of the 2024 Conference on Empirical Methods in Natural Language Processing*, pages 1107–1128, Miami, Florida, USA. Association for Computational Linguistics.

Robert M Fano. 1961. Transmission of information: A statistical theory of communications. *American Journal of Physics*, 29:793–794.

Aaron Grattafiori, Abhimanyu Dubey, Abhinav Jauhri, Abhinav Pandey, Abhishek Kadian, Ahmad Al-Dahle, Aiesha Letman, Akhil Mathur, Alan Schelten, Alex Vaughan, Amy Yang, Angela Fan, Anirudh Goyal, Anthony Hartshorn, Aobo Yang, Archi Mitra, Archie Sravankumar, Artem Korenev, Arthur Hinsvark, and 542 others. 2024. The Llama 3 herd of models. *arXiv preprint arXiv:2407.21783*.

Ashim Gupta and Vivek Srikumar. 2021. X-fact: A new benchmark dataset for multilingual fact checking. In *Proceedings of the 59th Annual Meeting of the Association for Computational Linguistics and the 11th International Joint Conference on Natural Language Processing (Volume 2: Short Papers)*, pages 675–682, Online. Association for Computational Linguistics.

Edward J. Hu, Yelong Shen, Phillip Wallis, Zeyuan Allen-Zhu, Yuanzhi Li, Shean Wang, Lu Wang, and Weizhu Chen. 2022. LoRA: Low-rank adaptation of large language models. In *International Conference on Learning Representations*.

Albert Q. Jiang, Alexandre Sablayrolles, Antoine Roux, Arthur Mensch, Blanche Savary, Chris Bamford, Devendra Singh Chaplot, Diego de las Casas, Emma Bou Hanna, Florian Bressand, Gianna Lengyel, Guillaume Bour, Guillaume Lample, Lélio Renard Lavaud, Lucile Saulnier, Marie-Anne Lachaux, Pierre Stock, Sandeep Subramanian, Sophia Yang, and 7 others. 2024. Mixtral of experts. *arXiv preprint arXiv:2401.04088*.

Barbara Konat, John Lawrence, Joonsuk Park, Katarzyna Budzynska, and Chris Reed. 2016. A corpus of argument networks: Using graph properties to analyse divisive issues. In *Proceedings of the Tenth International Conference on Language Resources and Evaluation (LREC'16)*, pages 3899–3906, Portorož, Slovenia. European Language Resources Association (ELRA).

John Lawrence and Chris Reed. 2020. Argument mining: A survey. *Computational Linguistics*, 45(4):765–818.

John Lawrence, Jacky Visser, and Chris Reed. 2018. BBC Moral Maze: Test your argument. In *Computational Models of Argument - Proceedings of COMMA 2018*, Frontiers in Artificial Intelligence and Applications, pages 465–466, Amsterdam, The Netherlands. IOS Press.

Yinhan Liu, Myle Ott, Naman Goyal, Jingfei Du, Mandar Joshi, Danqi Chen, Omer Levy, Mike Lewis, Luke Zettlemoyer, and Veselin Stoyanov. 2019. RoBERTa: A robustly optimized BERT pretraining approach. *arXiv preprint arXiv:1907.11692*.

E. Musi, M. Aloumpi, E. Carmi, S. Yates, and K. O'Halloran. 2022. Developing fake news immunity: Fallacies as misinformation triggers during the pandemic. *Online Journal of Communication and Media Technologies*, 12(3):e202217.

Qwen, An Yang, Baosong Yang, Beichen Zhang, Binyuan Hui, Bo Zheng, Bowen Yu, Chengyuan Li, Dayiheng Liu, Fei Huang, Haoran Wei, Huan Lin, Jian Yang, Jianhong Tu, Jianwei Zhang, Jianxin Yang, Jiaxi Yang, Jingren Zhou, Junyang Lin, and 24 others. 2025. Qwen2.5 technical report. *arXiv preprint arXiv:2412.15115*.

Alan Ramponi, Camilla Casula, and Stefano Menini. 2024. Variationist: Exploring multifaceted variation and bias in written language data. In *Proceedings of the 62nd Annual Meeting of the Association for Computational Linguistics (Volume 3: System Demonstrations)*, pages 346–354, Bangkok, Thailand. Association for Computational Linguistics.

Alan Ramponi, Agnese Daffara, and Sara Tonelli. 2025. Fine-grained fallacy detection with human label variation. In *Proceedings of the 2025 Conference of the Nations of the Americas Chapter of the Association for Computational Linguistics: Human Language Technologies (Volume 1: Long Papers)*, pages 762–784, Albuquerque, New Mexico. Association for Computational Linguistics.

Nils Reimers and Iryna Gurevych. 2019. Sentence-BERT: Sentence embeddings using Siamese BERT-networks. In *Proceedings of the 2019 Conference on Empirical Methods in Natural Language Processing and the 9th International Joint Conference on Natural Language Processing (EMNLP-IJCNLP)*, pages 3982–3992, Hong Kong, China. Association for Computational Linguistics.

Yi Song, Michael Heilman, Beata Beigman Klebanov, and Paul Deane. 2014. Applying argumentation schemes for essay scoring. In *Proceedings of the First Workshop on Argumentation Mining*, pages 69–78, Baltimore, Maryland. Association for Computational Linguistics.

Manfred Stede and Jodi Schneider. 2018. *Argumentation Mining*. Morgan & Claypool, San Rafael, CA, USA.

Giovanni Valer, Alan Ramponi, and Sara Tonelli. 2023. When you doubt, abstain: A study of automated fact-checking in Italian under domain shift. In *Proceedings of the 9th Italian Conference on Computational Linguistics (CLiC-it 2023)*, pages 433–440, Venice, Italy. CEUR Workshop Proceedings.

Rob van der Goot, Ahmet Üstün, Alan Ramponi, Ibrahim Sharaf, and Barbara Plank. 2021. Massive choice, ample tasks (MaChAmp): A toolkit for multi-task learning in NLP. In *Proceedings of the 16th Conference of the European Chapter of the Association for Computational Linguistics: System Demonstrations*, pages 176–197, Online. Association for Computational Linguistics.

Jacky Visser, Barbara Konat, Rory Duthie, Marcin Koszowy, Katarzyna Budzynska, and Chris Reed. 2020. Argumentation in the 2016 US presidential elections: annotated corpora of television debates and social media reaction. *Language Resources and Evaluation*, 54(1):123–154.

Jacky Visser, John Lawrence, Chris Reed, Jean Wagemans, and Douglas Walton. 2021. Annotating argument schemes. *Argumentation*, 35(1):101–139.

Douglas Walton, Christopher Reed, and Fabrizio Macagno. 2008. *Argumentation Schemes*. Cambridge University Press, Cambridge, United Kingdom.

Jason Wei, Xuezhi Wang, Dale Schuurmans, Maarten Bosma, Brian Ichter, Fei Xia, Ed Chi, Quoc V. Le, and Denny Zhou. 2022. Chain-of-thought prompting elicits reasoning in large language models. In *Advances in Neural Information Processing Systems*, volume 35, pages 24824–24837. Curran Associates, Inc.

Thomas Wolf, Lysandre Debut, Victor Sanh, Julien Chaumond, Clement Delangue, Anthony Moi, Pierric Cistac, Tim Rault, Remi Louf, Morgan Funtowicz, Joe Davison, Sam Shleifer, Patrick von Platen, Clara Ma, Yacine Jernite, Julien Plu, Canwen Xu, Teven Le Scao, Sylvain Gugger, and 3 others. 2020. Transformers: State-of-the-art natural language processing. In *Proceedings of the 2020 Conference on Empirical Methods in Natural Language Processing: System Demonstrations*, pages 38–45, Online. Association for Computational Linguistics.

Appendix

A Categories of Critical Questions

In their GitHub repository,[6] the organizers of the CQs-Gen shared task have provided guidelines outlining the criteria used to label questions as `useful`, `unhelpful`, or `invalid` in the validation and test sets. As a reference, we summarize the descriptions below. Furthermore, in Table 4 we report the number of interventions per corpus in the validation and test sets, and in Table 5 we show the distribution of the three CQs categories in the validation set, broken down by corpus and distinguishing between LLM-generated and theoretical questions.

Useful *"The answer to this question can potentially challenge one of the arguments in the text. One should not take the arguments in the text as valid without having reflected on this question."*

Unhelpful *"The question is valid, but it is unlikely to challenge any of the arguments in the text. This may be in cases where: a) the answer to the question is common sense; b) the answer to the question is a well-known fact that does not generate controversy; c) the question is very complicated to understand and it would be impractical to question the arguments; d) the question is answered in the text itself."*

Invalid *"A question is invalid when the answer to this question cannot serve to invalidate or diminish the acceptability of the arguments of the text. This can be in cases where: a) the question is unrelated to the text; b) the question introduces new concepts not present in the text; c) the question does not challenge any argument defended in the text (for example, when the question challenges the opposite position to the one defended in the text); d) the question is too general and could be applied to any text; e) the question is not critical of the text (e.g. a reading-comprehension question)."*

Set	Corpus				Total
	US2016tv	RRD	MMD	US2016reddit	
Validation	80	72	20	14	186
Test	17	11	6	–	34

Table 4: Number of interventions per corpus in the validation and test sets.

[6] `https://github.com/hitz-zentroa/shared-task-critical-questions-generation`.

B Further Experimental Details

B.1 Hyper-parameter Values

Generation For the generation of candidate CQs using LLMs, we rely on the default hyper-parameter values as provided in the `transformers` library (Wolf et al., 2020). We only avoid greedy decoding by setting `do_sample = True` and constrain the minimum and maximum number of tokens to generate (using `min_new_tokens` and `max_new_tokens`). Specifically, the maximum number of tokens is set to `128` or `192` when requiring $n = 3$ or $n = 5$ CQs in the output, respectively, whereas the minimum number of tokens is set to `32`. We load `Mixtral-8x7B`, `Qwen-2.5-32B`, and `Llama-3-70B` in 4-bits due to resource constraints, whereas the remaining models are loaded in 8-bits. The five random seeds used for the experiments are `0`, `42`, `101`, `31`, and `4321`.

Classification For the model used in the CQs selection stage, we employ default MaChAmp's hyper-parameter values (van der Goot et al., 2021) as detailed in Table 6. We select the best model to be used based on macro F_1 score on a 20% held-out data split. We use 5 epochs of fine-tuning and {32, 64} as search space for the batch size, of which 64 emerged as the best batch size value.

B.2 Prompts

We here provide details on our modular prompts for the zero-shot setting (Appendix B.2.1) as well as prompts adapted for few-shot experiments (Appendix B.2.2). All prompts are built starting from the prompt template presented in Figure 1.

B.2.1 Zero-shot Setting

Starting from a `base` prompt,[7] we experiment with adding information on either the argumentation schemes of the intervention (`schemes`) or detailed description about what CQs are (`desc`).

Prompt `base` A prompt that provides specific task instructions and clear guidance on the expected output. It includes only the free text of the prompt template in Figure 1 and the input `$intervention`.

[7] Our base prompt led to higher performance in preliminary experiments compared to the baseline prompt provided by shared task organizers. We here provide their prompt for reference: *"Suggest 3 critical questions that should be raised before accepting the arguments in this text:*`\n\n$intervention\n\n`*Give one question per line. Make the questions simple, and do not give any explanation reagrding why the question is relevant."*

Corpus	Useful			Unhelpful			Invalid			Total
	LLM	Theory	All	LLM	Theory	All	LLM	Theory	All	
US2016tv	1117	270	1387	166	283	449	116	169	285	2121
RRD	912	110	1022	217	84	301	71	9	80	1403
MMD	224	24	248	56	15	71	49	4	53	372
US2016reddit	122	11	133	60	12	72	33	2	35	240
Overall	**2375**	**415**	2790	**499**	**394**	893	**269**	**184**	453	**4136**

Table 5: Distribution of CQs categories across corpora in the validation set. For each category, we report the number of LLM-generated CQs, the number of theory-derived CQs, and their combined totals (shown in gray).

Prompt template

You are given an argumentative text in the form of an intervention. Your task is to generate $n useful critical questions that should be raised before accepting its arguments. The intervention is as follows:

`$intervention`

`$additional_context`

`$few-shot_examples`

Provide exactly $n useful critical questions, each strictly on a separate line and ending with a question mark. Keep the questions concise and do not add any comments or explanations.

Output:

Figure 1: Template used for modular prompt construction. The `base` prompt consists of the core text (namely, the task instructions, the `$intervention`, and the output requirements). Modular components – i.e., `$additional_context` (either argumentation `schemes` or CQ `descriptions`) and/or `$few-shot_examples` – can be inserted to extend the `base` prompt. The number `$n` of critical questions to generate is a variable parameter, with $n \geq k$.

Hyperparameter	**Value**
Optimizer	AdamW
β_1, β_2	0.9, 0.99
Dropout	0.2
Epochs	5
Batch size	64
Learning rate	1e-4
LR scheduler	Slanted triangular
Weight decay	0.01
Decay factor	0.38
Cut fraction	0.3

Table 6: Hyper-parameter values employed for fine-tuning the usefulness-based CQs selection classifier.

Prompt `schemes` A prompt where supplementary information on argumentation schemes that occur in the intervention is added to the `base` prompt in place of the `$additional_context` placeholder of the prompt template (Figure 1). The addition is as follows:

> Below are the argumentation schemes associated with the arguments in the intervention:
>
> `$ARG_SCHEMES`

`$ARG_SCHEMES` is a placeholder for the set of argumentation schemes associated with the intervention, automatically extracted from the validation set with duplicates removed. Based on the appendix tables in Calvo Figueras and Agerri (2024), similar scheme names are normalized into a human-readable standard format, following the mapping presented in Table 7.

Normalized name	#	Argumentation scheme(s)
Argument from example	175	Example, ERExample
Practical reasoning	135	PracticalReasoning, ERPracticalReasoning
Argument from cause to effect	55	CauseToEffect
Argument from consequences	38	Consequences, NegativeConsequences, PositiveConsequences
Ad hominem	29	GenericAdHominem, ERAdHominem, Ad hominem
Argument from sign	25	Sign, SignFromOtherEvents
Argument from verbal classification	25	VerbalClassification
Circumstantial ad hominem	22	CircumstantialAdHominem
Argument from fear appeal	14	FearAppeal, DangerAppeal
Argument from analogy	11	Analogy
Argument from expert opinion	10	ExpertOpinion, ERExpertOpinion
Argument from position to know	10	PositionToKnow
Argument from values	10	Values
Argument from popular opinion	8	PopularOpinion
Argument from alternatives	6	Alternatives
Argument from popular practice	6	PopularPractice
Argument from authority	4	ArgumentFromAuthority
Argument from bias	4	Bias
Direct ad hominem	2	DirectAdHominem

Table 7: Normalized names and total number of occurrences for the 28 argumentation schemes in the validation set.

Prompt desc A prompt where supplementary information on critical questions is added to the `base` prompt in place of the `$additional_context` placeholder of the prompt template (Figure 1). The addition is one of the following:

- $\texttt{desc}_{(FULL)}$, i.e., a detailed bulleted description of `useful` and `non-useful` CQs:

  Useful critical questions may:
  - challenge or clarify a claim by asking for evidence or explanation;
  - examine the consequences of the argument;
  - explore alternatives to the proposed idea;
  - check the generalizability beyond the given case;
  - uncover assumptions that may be implicit.

  Non-useful critical questions:
  - ask common sense questions or refer to well-known facts;
  - are overly complex, unclear, or vague;
  - are already answered in the text or are unrelated to the text;
  - introduce new concepts not present in the text;
  - do not challenge the argument or fail to be critical (e.g., reading-comprehension questions).

  You must avoid non-useful questions.

- $\texttt{desc}_{(U)}$, i.e., an abridged description of `useful` CQs:

  Useful critical questions may ask for evidence, examine consequences, explore alternatives, test generalizability, or uncover hidden assumptions.

- $\texttt{desc}_{(\neg U)}$, i.e., an abridged description of `non-useful` CQs:

  You must avoid questions that are vague, overly complex, irrelevant, repetitive, introduce new concepts, restate common knowledge, or fail to critically challenge the arguments.

- $\texttt{desc}_{(U+\neg U)}$, i.e., the combination of $\texttt{desc}_{(U)}$ and $\texttt{desc}_{(\neg U)}$ as a single description:

  Useful critical questions may ask for evidence, examine consequences, explore alternatives, test generalizability, or uncover hidden assumptions.

You must avoid questions that are vague, overly complex, irrelevant, repetitive, introduce new concepts, restate common knowledge, or fail to critically challenge the arguments.

In all four versions, the description of `non-useful` questions is based on the guidelines provided by the shared task organizers (Appendix A), while the description of `useful` CQs is derived by scrutinizing examples labeled as `useful` in the validation set. The $\texttt{desc}_{(FULL)}$ version is more comprehensive, whereas $\texttt{desc}_{(U)}$, $\texttt{desc}_{(\neg U)}$, and $\texttt{desc}_{(U+\neg U)}$ are introduced to facilitate the generation of CQs by small-sized models, which, in our preliminary experiments, we observe may struggle with longer input prompts.

B.2.2 Few-shot Settings

One- or three-shot examples can be added to the `base` prompt in place of the `$few-shot_examples` placeholder of the prompt template (Figure 1), with or without `$additional_context` preceding. Below, example interventions and related CQs are referenced by their identifier in the validation set.

One-shot This setting includes a single example intervention and its corresponding output, matching the format expected in the model's final response. We design two variants:

- *all-useful*, where the intervention is followed by three `useful` CQs:

  Here is an example of an intervention, followed by three useful critical questions:

  $TRUMP_125_1

  Output:

  $TRUMP_125_1_T__1
  $TRUMP_125_1_T__14
  $TRUMP_125_1_T__10

- *mixed*, where three examples of `non-useful` questions are also provided:

  Here is an example of an intervention, followed by three non-useful questions (negative examples) and three useful critical questions (positive examples):

  $TRUMP_125_1

  Non-useful questions:

  $TRUMP_125_1_T__7
  $TRUMP_125_1_T__25
  $TRUMP_125_1_T__0

  Output:

  $TRUMP_125_1_T__1
  $TRUMP_125_1_T__14
  $TRUMP_125_1_T__10

Three-shot This setting includes three example interventions and their corresponding outputs. We design two variants:

- *all-useful*, where each intervention is followed by three `useful` CQs:

  Here are three examples of interventions, each followed by three useful critical questions:

  $CLINTON_130_1

  Output:

  $CLINTON_130_1_T__8
  $CLINTON_130_1_T__7
  $CLINTON_130_1_T__11

  $TRUMP_125_1

  Output:

  $TRUMP_125_1_T__1
  $TRUMP_125_1_T__14
  $TRUMP_125_1_T__10

  $CLINTON_57

  Output:

  $CLINTON_57_T__3
  $CLINTON_57_T__12
  $CLINTON_57_T__10

- *mixed*, where three examples of `non-useful` questions are also provided for each intervention:

Here are three examples of interventions, each followed by three non-useful questions (negative examples) and three useful critical questions (positive examples):

$CLINTON_130_1

Non-useful questions:

$CLINTON_130_1_T__2
$CLINTON_130_1_T__19
$CLINTON_130_1_T__17

Output:

$CLINTON_130_1_T__8
$CLINTON_130_1_T__7
$CLINTON_130_1_T__11

$TRUMP_125_1

Non-useful questions:

$TRUMP_125_1_T__7
$TRUMP_125_1_T__25
$TRUMP_125_1_T__0

Output:

$TRUMP_125_1_T__1
$TRUMP_125_1_T__14
$TRUMP_125_1_T__10

$CLINTON_57

Non-useful questions:

$CLINTON_57_T__5
$CLINTON_57_T__13
$CLINTON_57_T__7

Output:

$CLINTON_57_T__3
$CLINTON_57_T__12
$CLINTON_57_T__10

All questions used in the few-shot settings are selected from theory-derived CQs in the validation set; we exclude LLM-generated CQs to prevent over-amplification of synthetic language use. Since theory-derived CQs are instantiated from templates based on argumentation schemes (Calvo Figueras and Agerri, 2024), we ensure that no template is repeated within the sets of `useful` and `non-useful` example questions. In the *mixed* version, however, we include pairs of a `useful` and a `non-useful` question derived from the same template, encouraging the model to focus on the semantic quality of the question rather than relying on their underlying argumentative structure (see Table 8 for examples).

C Further Experimental Results

C.1 Zero-shot Experiments

In Table 9 we report the results on the development set for small-sized LLMs using all the prompt strategies designed for the zero-shot setting.

C.2 Few-shot Experiments

In Table 10 we report the results on the development set for small-sized LLMs in the one-shot setting using the *all-useful* and *mixed* prompt variants. Since the performance in the one-shot setting proved unsatisfactory, due to limited time and resources we did not proceed further with the prompts designed for the three-shot setting. We leave this additional investigation for future work.

C.3 CQs Classifier Experiments

In Table 11 we report the results of the usefulness-based CQs selection models when using different data variants for fine-tuning.

For usefulness-based CQs selection, we also experimented with a strategy based on the most relevant n-grams for the `non-useful` class (i.e., the `unhelpful` and `invalid` merged together). We computed the weighted, positive, and normalized pointwise mutual information (PMI; Fano, 1961) score for each n-gram ($n \in 1, 2, 3$) and class using Variationist (Ramponi et al., 2024), calculated over the `all` data set variant described in Section 4.1. We then selected the top-k ($k = 20$) unigrams, bigrams, and trigrams associated with the `non-useful` class, for a total of 60 keywords. We used the resulting keywords to match candidate CQs to remove from the $n = 5$ generated ones, if any. As a fallback (i.e., when there were no matches), we simply picked the first three CQs. However, this strategy did not consistently improve the performance over the LLMs' application without any selection; therefore, we discarded it.

Theory-derived CQ template	Argumentation scheme	Useful CQ (ID)	Non-useful CQ (ID)
Are there special circumstances pertaining to `<subjecta>` that undermine its generalisability to other `<subjectx>` that `<featF>`?	Argument from Example	TRUMP_125_1_T__1	CLINTON_57_T__7
Did `<expertE>` really assert that `<eventA>`?	Argument from Expert Opinion	CLINTON_57_T__10	TRUMP_125_1_T__0
Is `<eventA>` consistent with known evidence in `<domainD>`?	Argument from Expert Opinion	CLINTON_57_T__12	TRUMP_125_1_T__25
Are there any events other than `<eventB>` that would more reliably account for `<eventA>`?	Argument from Sign	TRUMP_125_1_T__14	TRUMP_125_1_T__7

Table 8: Four pairs of `useful` and `non-useful` questions, derived from the same theoretical template, are included in the *mixed* version of the prompt for one- and few-shot settings. These examples are intended to help the model to discriminate between `useful` and `not-useful` CQs based on semantic content rather than argumentative structure.

Model	Prompt					
	`base`	`schemes`	`desc`$_{(FULL)}$	`desc`$_{(U)}$	`desc`$_{(\neg U)}$	`desc`$_{(U+\neg U)}$
MIXTRAL-8X7B	**0.6758**$_{\pm 0.01}$	0.6262$_{\pm 0.01}$	0.6557$_{\pm 0.01}$	0.6284$_{\pm 0.02}$	0.6594$_{\pm 0.02}$	0.6452$_{\pm 0.01}$
LLAMA-3-8B	**0.6510**$_{\pm 0.01}$	0.5869$_{\pm 0.03}$	0.6076$_{\pm 0.01}$	0.5982$_{\pm 0.02}$	0.6149$_{\pm 0.01}$	0.5905$_{\pm 0.01}$
QWEN-2.5-7B	0.5359$_{\pm 0.02}$	0.4725$_{\pm 0.02}$	**0.5756**$_{\pm 0.01}$	0.5490$_{\pm 0.01}$	0.5476$_{\pm 0.02}$	0.5359$_{\pm 0.02}$

Table 9: Results on the development set for small-sized LLMs using different prompts in a zero-shot setting. We report the average punctuation score with standard deviation across 5 runs with different random seeds.

Model	Shot variant	
	all-useful	mixed
MIXTRAL-8X7B	**0.5847**$_{\pm 0.02}$	0.5719$_{\pm 0.01}$
LLAMA-3-8B	0.1377$_{\pm 0.02}$	**0.4619**$_{\pm 0.02}$

Table 10: Results on the development set for small-sized LLMs in the one-shot setting with prompt base and different shot variants (cf. Appendix B.2.2). We report the average punctuation score with standard deviation across 5 runs with different random seeds.

Data variant	Model	
	BERT	RoBERTa
`gold-train`	0.6910	0.6946
`synth-l`	0.7365	0.6916
`synth-m`	0.7392	0.7095
`synth-q`	0.7327	0.6999
`all`	**0.7563**	0.7341

Table 11: Results for different classification models when fine-tuned on different data variants for the sake of usefulness-based CQs selection. We report the macro F_1 score on the `gold test` split.

CriticalBrew at CQs-Gen 2025: Collaborative Multi-Agent Generation and Evaluation of Critical Questions for Arguments

Roxanne El Baff **Dominik Opitz** **Diaoulé Diallo**
Institute of Software Technology, German Aerospace Center (DLR), Germany
roxanne.elbaff@dlr.de

Abstract

This paper presents the *CriticalBrew* submission to the CQs-Gen 2025 shared task, which focuses on generating critical questions (CQs) for a given argument. Our approach employs a multi-agent framework containing two sequential components: 1) **Generation**: machine society simulation for generating CQs and 2) **Evaluation**: LLM-based evaluation for selecting the top three questions. The first models collaboration as a sequence of thinking patterns (e.g., *debate* $\rightarrow$ *reflect*). The second assesses the generated questions using zero-shot prompting, evaluating them against several criteria (e.g., depth). Experiments with different open-weight LLMs (small vs. large) consistently outperformed the baseline, a single LLM with zero-shot prompting. Two configurations, agent count and thinking patterns, significantly impacted the performance in the shared task's CQ-usefulness evaluation, whereas different LLM-based evaluation strategies (e.g., scoring) had no impact. Our code is available on GitHub[1].

1 Introduction

Critical thinking is essential in a world overflowing with opinionated texts. Questioning arguments encourages deeper analysis, which can unravel fallacious reasoning (e.g., ad hominem and weak evidence) or strengthen agreement.

Recent research has shown that large language models (LLMs) have excelled in several tasks, including argument mining and question answering. However, it is crucial to acknowledge three issues that arise when using LLMs for generation, as stated by Calvo Figueras and Agerri (2024): hallucination (Huang et al., 2025), the lack of continuous up-to-date knowledge (Gao et al., 2023), and the relativity of what is true (Chang et al., 2024). In their work, Calvo Figueras and Agerri (2024) mitigate these three issues by using LLMs to generate critical questions to uncover the blind spots of argumentative text rather than relying on LLMs' direct answers. For that, they create a reference dataset containing political oral debate arguments (Visser et al., 2021; Lawrence et al., 2018) along with three critical questions by combining a hybrid approach relying on Walton's argumentation theory (Walton et al., 2008) and augmenting their dataset with LLM prompting. The resulting dataset is manually evaluated for relevance and validity. The CQs-Gen 2025 Shared Task (Calvo Figueras et al., 2025) employs this dataset to generate three CQs for an argument.

Building on this task setup, this paper presents our *CriticalBrew* submission to the CQs-Gen 2025 (Calvo Figueras et al., 2025). Our approach employs a collaborative multi-agent framework comprising two sequential components for **generation** and **evaluation**, which aligns with recent trends favoring compound LLM systems over standalone models (Zaharia et al., 2024).

1. Generation. This component builds on the machine society simulation approach by Zhang et al. (2024), originally employed for reasoning tasks (e.g., chess). More precisely, it models agents' collaboration as a sequence of thinking patterns (e.g., *debate* $\rightarrow$ *reflect*) where each agent impersonates a personality trait, either *easy-going* or *overconfident*. For instance, a society simulation uses n agents where each initially solves a *task*; in this case, generating critical questions for an argument. Then, in r subsequent rounds, each agent re-generates CQs by reflecting on previous answers or debating with other agents. Our experiments exploit several settings based on two main attributes: (i) number of agents (1–3), n, with different combinations of personality traits (e.g., one easy-going and one overconfident), and (ii) number of rounds (0–3), r, with different permutations of thinking patterns

[1] https://github.com/roxanneelbaff/critical_questions_generation

Proceedings of the 12th Argument Mining Workshop, pages 314–321
July 31, 2025

(e.g., two rounds where n agents first debate and then reflect). Zhang et al. (2024) adopt the Society of Mind concept (Minsky, 1986): interacting modules lead to emergent intelligence, aligning with the critical thinking needed for CQ generation.

2. Evaluation. This component selects the top three questions from the first component based on quality criteria, using zero-shot prompting. It explores several methods, including ranking a set of CQs, scoring each CQ, and using a two-stage prompting approach for scoring. Each of these methods assesses criteria such as *depth*, *reasoning*, and *specificity*.

To our knowledge, this is the first collaborative multi-agents approach with LLM-based evaluation in the computational argumentation field.

Our experiments use three open-weight LLMs with different size ranges: Llama-3.1 8B, Mistral Small 3.1 (24B), and Llama-3.3 8B. We report their performance using the overall punctuation, the task's evaluation metric. This score is based on the semantic similarity between a generated CQ and reference data, followed by labeling each CQ as useful or not. The score corresponds to the proportion of CQs labeled useful. The highest overall punctuation was **0.78** on the validation and **0.55** on the test sets. Results show that for the **Generation** component, employing more agents improves models' performance. However, the number of rounds has no effect. Additionally, thinking patterns (e.g., only reflecting vs. only debating) significantly impact performance, unlike personality traits.

2 Related Work

Recent research has explored the use of large language models (LLMs) in the field of computational argumentation. Intersecting this trend with the increasing use of multi-agent systems, our approach combines both directions.

LLM in Computational Argumentation. Recent research in computational argumentation explores the potential of LLMs in tackling existing and new problems (Chen et al., 2024; El Baff et al., 2024; Ziegenbein et al., 2024). For example, Chen et al. (2024) assess LLMs on argument mining and generation tasks, showing their effectiveness with little or no training data, using zero- or few-shot prompts. In turn, Calvo Figueras and Agerri (2024) generate critical questions using a hybrid approach boosted by an LLM for a given argument. Our approach leverages large language models (LLMs) without relying on training data.

LLM Agents as Collaborators. Current work shows that compound LLM systems outperform a standalone LLM (Zaharia et al., 2024; Yao et al., 2023). Our approach adapts Zhang et al. (2024)'s approach, which deploys multi-agent LLM societies, impersonating different personality traits and collaborating via thinking patterns (debate or reflection). These simulations are tested on logic-based tasks (e.g., chess). In contrast, we employ this approach within computational argumentation, detailed in Section 4.1.

LLM Agents as Evaluators. LLMs are also increasingly used as evaluators (Kim et al., 2023), with different methods proposed. Liu et al. (2023) scores a text criterion (e.g., "evaluate coherence") per prompt, while Qin et al. (2023) and Sun et al. (2023) use ranking for evaluation. Our use of LLMs as evaluators is not exhaustive. It rather focuses on a subset of methods, such as ranking, scoring, and two-step prompting, to evaluate the critical questions and pick the top ones, as detailed in Section 4.2.

3 Task Description and Data

We describe the CQs-Gen 2025 dataset and evaluation (Calvo Figueras et al., 2025), used in our experiments.

Overview. CQs-Gen promotes critical thinking by automatically generating useful critical questions (CQs) given an argumentative text. More precisely, given a real oral debate intervention, a model generates three CQs to challenge it.

Dataset. The dataset consists of oral debates from the U.S. 2016 elections (Visser et al., 2021) and the Moral Maze (Lawrence et al., 2018). Each entry consists of one intervention, its corresponding CQs, and other metadata, such as argumentation schema. Each CQ is labeled for its *usefulness* in challenging the given intervention. A CQ can be either *useful* if it challenges the argument, *unhelpful* if it is valid but unlikely to challenge the argument, or, otherwise, *invalid*. The validation set comprises 186 labeled entries.

Evaluation. The CQs-Gen evaluation script first checks if the generated CQ is similar to one of the *useful* CQs in the reference data. If similarity is detected, the CQ is then labeled as *useful*, *unhelpful*, or *invalid*.[2] The performance of a model is measured by the *overall punctuation*[3] score defined as the proportion of CQs labeled *useful*. We interpret results using this score.

4 Approach

This section outlines our two-component approach[4]: a **Generation** component that generates critical questions (CQs) for an argument, and an **Evaluation** component that selects 3 questions. Below, we describe each component.

4.1 Generation via Collaboration

The Generation component takes an argument and outputs a set of CQs. Initially, each agent generates three questions using a zero-shot prompt. Then, the system applies a sequence of thinking patterns over r rounds, resulting in $3 \times n$ CQs. This approach is adapted from Zhang et al. (2024). Below, we explain the concepts underlying social simulation and then detail how it works.

The Concepts for Collaboration

Zhang et al. (2024) explore collaboration mechanisms with multiple agents by focusing on three concepts: **individual traits** assigned to each agent, **thinking patterns** applied in each round, and a **collaborative strategy** defining their sequence.

Individual Traits. The framework defines two agent traits: *easy-going* (t_e) associated with democratic harmony (Mutz, 2006; Held, 2006) and *overconfident* (t_o), more resistant to others' opinions (Moore and Healy, 2008).

Thinking Pattern. Zhang et al. (2024) explore two thinking patterns: **debate** (p_d) and **reflect** (p_r). Each pattern defines how an agent regenerates new CQs based on the answers from the previous round. In the debate pattern, each agent considers all the agents' answers, including their own, while in the reflection, they consider only their own.

Collaborative Strategy. A collaborative strategy defines the sequence of thinking patterns applied in rounds. At each round, all agents employ the same thinking pattern, p_r or p_d (Du et al., 2023).

[2]If no similarity is found between the generated CQ and any useful reference CQ, the generated CQ is labeled as *unable to label*, requiring manual evaluation.

[3]*Score* and *overall punctuation* are used interchangeably.

[4]Our initial approach included an *argument mining* step where we transformed each argument into a structured text, decomposed into argument components, but this step did not perform well. See appendix A for more details.

Evaluation	# Prompts	Description
Basic	1	A single prompt selects the top n critical questions (CQs) based on evaluation criteria (depth, relevance, reasoning, and specificity).
Scoring	1	A single prompt scores all CQs from 1–5 across all criteria and averages the result.
Ranking	# criteria	For each criterion, a prompt ranks all CQs in order of quality (e.g., depth).
Two-Step	2 × # criteria × # CQ	For each CQ-criterion, one prompt presents the argument and CQ, then another prompt scores a criterion.

Table 1: Overview of the LLM-based evaluators. For each method (*Evaluation*), we report the number of prompts per argument (*# Prompts*) and a *Description*. $\#criteria$ refers to the number of evaluation criteria, and $\#CQ$ refers to the number of critical questions.

These concepts are employed in a Machine society, as explained next.

Machine Society Simulation

Similar to Zhang et al. (2024), a machine society has n LLM agents, each with a trait (t_e or t_o), collaborating over r rounds of thinking patterns (p_d, p_r). Initially, each agent generates three CQs for an argument. Then, in each round, each agent generates three CQs. If the society has more than one agent, we use the evaluator component (Section 4.2); otherwise, we return the agent's output.

4.2 LLM Agents as Evaluators

A machine society can output more than n critical questions when it includes at least two agents. For that, we employ LLM-based evaluator agents to choose the top 3 CQs (Table 1). We employ four methods, focusing on criteria selected based on findings from Calvo Figueras and Agerri (2024): depth, relevance, reasoning, and specificity. We list the four methods below, ordered by the number of prompts needed per task.

Basic. An agent is prompted with an argument and list of CQs to select the top 3 CQs. Our prompt instructs the agent to select top CQs based on the criteria mentioned (Appendix C).

Scoring. Similar to basic, an agent is prompted with an argument and list of CQs. However, the agent, using one prompt, is instructed to score each criterion for each CQ, similar to (Kim et al., 2023), from 1 to 5. Then, the top 3 CQs are selected based on the highest mean value of criteria scores.

Ranking. We employ one agent per criterion (depth, reasoning, relevance, and specificity) to rank (Sun et al., 2023) the set of CQs. An agent is prompted with an argument and a list of CQs and returns the ranked CQs for a specific criterion. Then, the top 3 CQs are selected based on the highest mean ranks of all criteria.

Two-step Prompting. We employ a two-step prompting strategy designed for complex reasoning tasks (Seo et al., 2025; Hama et al., 2024). The LLM is prompted with the argument and one CQ in the first step. In the second step, given a critical question, we prompt an agent for each criterion: depth, reasoning, and specificity. The top 3 CQs with the highest criteria average are then selected.

5 Experiments and Results

This section reports our experiment settings, results on the validation set, and Gen-CQs 2025 submission results on the test set.

Our experiments simulate machine societies based on two configurations: the number of agents and rounds. More precisely, we employ n agents where $1 \leq n \leq 3$, and r rounds where $0 \leq r \leq 3$. In total, we simulate 113 machine societies[5].

5.1 Settings and Baselines

We run each simulation using three open-weight LLMs, varying in their parameter size: Llama-3.1 8B (L8B), Mistral Small 24B (M24B), and Llama-3.3 70B (L70B) (Touvron et al., 2023). For our implementation, we use the LangGraph Python agent framework[6], along with LangChain, allowing us to output structured data and save each *state* as a JSON object for each LLM answer (Appendix D).

To test the **1. Generation** component, we run all simulations with the *basic* evaluator defined in Section 4.2. The best-performing simulations are defined based on the highest score[7] (§3). Then, to test the **2. Evaluation** component, we rerun the best simulation per LLM type from the previous stage with the evaluation methods defined in §4.2. All our results are reported on the *validation set* with 186 arguments.

[5]We have 9 agent-trait groups and 15 pattern sequences, yielding 135 simulations, but, for single agent (t_e or t_o), 11 of the 15 sequences are excluded for containing p_d, resulting in 135 – 22 = 113 combinations.

[6]`https://langchain-ai.github.io/langgraph/`

[7]Referred to as the *overall punctuation* in CQs-Gen 2025.

LLM		Agents	Rounds	Pattern	Traits	Score	3/3 %
Llama 8B		3	3	$p_r p_d p_d$	$t_e t_e t_e$	0.71	0.40
	↑	3	2	$p_r p_d$	$t_e t_e t_e$	0.70	0.42
		2	2	$p_d p_d$	$t_e t_e$	0.69	0.42
		1	1	p_r	t_o	0.59	0.26
	↓	2	2	$p_r p_r$	$t_e t_e$	0.59	0.23
		2	2	$p_d p_r$	$t_e t_o$	0.60	0.31
		1	0	–	t_e	0.68	0.39
	○	1	0	–	t_o	0.66	0.29
		1	0	–	–	0.68	0.38
Mistral 24B		3	3	$p_d p_d p_r$	$t_e t_e t_o$	**0.78**	0.54
	↑	3	0	–	$t_e t_e t_e$	0.76	0.53
		3	1	p_r	$t_e t_o t_o$	0.76	0.53
		1	3	$p_r p_r p_r$	t_o	0.70	0.42
	↓	2	3	$p_d p_d p_r$	$t_e t_e$	0.70	0.41
		3	3	$p_r p_d p_r$	$t_o t_o t_o$	0.71	0.40
		1	0	–	t_o	0.74	0.45
	○	1	0	–	t_e	0.73	0.47
		1	0	–	–	0.73	0.43
Llama 70B		2	3	$p_d p_d p_d$	$t_e t_e$	**0.78**	0.53
	↑	2	3	$p_r p_r p_d$	$t_e t_o$	0.77	**0.55**
		3	2	$p_d p_r$	$t_o t_o t_o$	0.77	0.53
		3	3	$p_r p_r p_r$	$t_e t_e t_e$	0.71	0.45
	↓	3	3	$p_d p_r p_r$	$t_e t_e t_o$	0.71	0.41
		3	3	$p_d p_r p_d$	$t_e t_e t_o$	0.71	0.39
		1	0	–	t_o	0.73	0.44
	○	1	0	–	t_e	0.72	0.43
		1	0	–	–	0.73	0.44

Table 2: Performance of the three LLMs on the validation set ($N = 186$), showing top (↑), worst (↓), and baseline (○) setups. Each machine society is defined by number of *Agents*, number of *Rounds*, Thinking *Pattern* (p_d, p_r), and Personality *Traits* (t_e, t_o). The overall punctuation (*Score*) is reported as a proportion of *useful* questions, and 3/3 is the argument rate where 3 questions were labeled useful.

Baseline. We use three baselines, each of which is a standalone LLM with zero-shot prompting to generate the three CQs with three settings: with no personality trait, t_o, and t_e. The baselines are shown in Table 2 marked with (○).

5.2 Generation Component Results

Table 2 summarizes the best, worst, and baseline simulation per LLM.

Overview. All three LLM of different sizes outperform their baselines: L8B (0.71) by 3%, and M24B and L70B (0.78) by 4-5%. Despite being significantly smaller, the M24B model performs comparably to the L70B model. Also, for the *3/3 %*, both models achieve a range of $0.53 - 0.55$

LLM	Evaluation	Pattern	Traits	Score	3/3 %
Llama 8B	**Basic**			0.71 (0.78)	0.40
	Scoring	$p_r p_d p_d$	$t_e t_e t_e$	0.69 (0.77)	0.42
	Ranking[3]			0.71 (0.80)	0.42
	2-step			0.66 (0.76)	0.36
Mistral 24B	**Basic**			**0.78** (0.82)	0.54
	Scoring[1]	$p_d p_d p_r$	$t_e t_e t_o$	**0.78** (0.82)	**0.58**
	Ranking			**0.78** (0.82)	0.57
	2-step			0.76 (0.80)	0.52
Llama 70B	**Basic**			**0.78** (0.82)	0.53
	Scoring[2]	$p_d p_d p_d$	$t_e t_e$	**0.78** (0.82)	0.55
	Ranking			**0.78** (0.82)	0.54
	2-step			0.77 (0.80)	0.55

Table 3: Performance of the three LLMs, showing their best machine society configurations (from Table 2) across **Basic**, **Scoring**, **Ranking**, and **Two-step**. Each society is defined by a thinking *Pattern* (p_d, p_r) and Personality *Traits* (t_e, t_o). *Score* is the overall punctuation, and 3/3 is the rate of arguments with all questions useful. Best per-LLM is underlined, overall best in **bold**, and submitted simulations marked with [1,2,3].

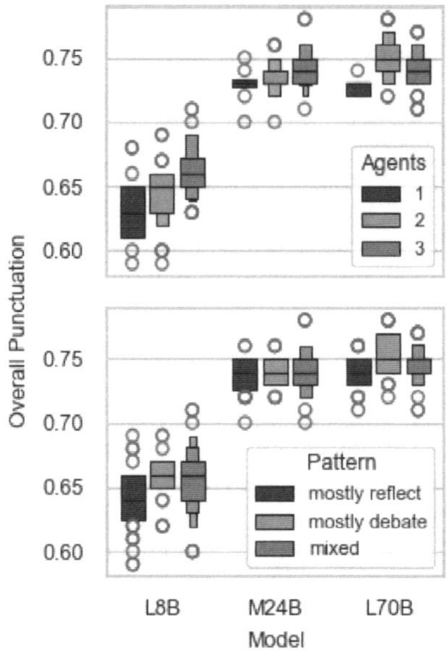

Figure 1: Boxplots for the *Overall Punctuation* per LLM (L8B, M24B and L70B) with two configurations: ***Agent** Counts* (Top) and *Thinking **Pattern*** (Bottom).

compared to 0.42 for the smallest model, L8B.

For each configuration (e.g., number of agents), we measured significance using ANOVA in cases of normality (Kruskal-Wallis otherwise). If $p < 0.05$, we conducted posthoc analysis (independent t-test in case of normality, Mann- Whitney otherwise) with Bonferroni correction. We report below the results where $p < 0.05$.[8]

Number of Agents. Agent count significantly influenced performance for all models; L8B, M24B[9] and L70B ($p < 0.05$). For L70B, both two- and three-agent setups outperformed single-agent. For L8B, three agents performed significantly better than one or two. Figure 1-Top shows score distributions per model and agent count.

Thinking Patterns We compare three types: *mostly debate*, *mostly reflection* and *mixed* (at least one round of each). We report a significant effect for L8B and L70B[9] ($p < 0.05$). For L8B, *mostly reflection* differed significantly from the other two. Figure 1-Bottom shows score distributions per model and pattern type.

5.3 Evaluation Component Results

We re-evaluate the CQs of the best-performing society simulation configurations from Table 2 using the four evaluation methods. The scores shown in Table 3 are similar across all methods within each LLM, especially for *Basic*, *Scoring*, and *Ranking*. A more complex method (two-step) does not yield better results. For the *3/3 %*, M24B achieved the highest score with 0.58.

5.4 Submission

We submit CQs from the best models per LLM type (Table 3). As performance is similar across *evaluators*, we manually inspect the test set ($N = 34$) and choose semantically diverse CQs per argument (submitted simulations are marked with [1,2,3] in Table 3). Only the first submission outperforms the shared task's baselines, with an overall punctuation of **0.55**: **M24B** uses three agents ($2 \times$ easy-going, $1 \times$ overconfident), three patterns (p_d, p_d, p_r), and *scoring* evaluation.

6 Conclusion

In this work, we employed a social machine framework to generate critical questions (CQs) for an argument that had been previously adapted in logical domains. Our approach outperformed standalone LLMs. We found that the number of collaborating agents and the choice of thinking pattern have a positive impact on the generation of CQs. However, alternative evaluation strategies do not show any additional benefit. To enable further investigation, we release our experimental data.

[8]number of rounds, and the personality trait (mixed traits vs. one-type trait) had no to little significant effect.

[9]Posthoc results had no pairwise significance difference.

References

Blanca Calvo Figueras and Rodrigo Agerri. 2024. Critical questions generation: Motivation and challenges. In *Proceedings of the 28th Conference on Computational Natural Language Learning*, pages 105–116, Miami, FL, USA. Association for Computational Linguistics.

Blanca Calvo Figueras, Jaione Bengoetxea, Maite Heredia, Ekaterina Sviridova, Elena Cabrio, Serena Villata, and Rodrigo Agerri. 2025. Overview of the critical questions generation shared task 2025. In *Proceedings of the 12th Workshop on Argument Mining*.

Tyler A Chang, Katrin Tomanek, Jessica Hoffmann, Nithum Thain, Erin MacMurray van Liemt, Kathleen Meier-Hellstern, and Lucas Dixon. 2024. Detecting hallucination and coverage errors in retrieval augmented generation for controversial topics. In *Proceedings of the 2024 Joint International Conference on Computational Linguistics, Language Resources and Evaluation (LREC-COLING 2024)*, pages 4729–4743.

Guizhen Chen, Liying Cheng, Anh Tuan Luu, and Lidong Bing. 2024. Exploring the potential of large language models in computational argumentation. In *Proceedings of the 62nd Annual Meeting of the Association for Computational Linguistics (Volume 1: Long Papers)*, pages 2309–2330, Bangkok, Thailand. Association for Computational Linguistics.

Yilun Du, Shuang Li, Antonio Torralba, Joshua B Tenenbaum, and Igor Mordatch. 2023. Improving factuality and reasoning in language models through multiagent debate. In *Forty-first International Conference on Machine Learning*.

Roxanne El Baff, Khalid Al Khatib, Milad Alshomary, Kai Konen, Benno Stein, and Henning Wachsmuth. 2024. Improving argument effectiveness across ideologies using instruction-tuned large language models. In *Findings of the Association for Computational Linguistics: EMNLP 2024*, pages 4604–4622, Miami, Florida, USA. Association for Computational Linguistics.

Yunfan Gao, Yun Xiong, Xinyu Gao, Kangxiang Jia, Jinliu Pan, Yuxi Bi, Yi Dai, Jiawei Sun, Haofen Wang, and Haofen Wang. 2023. Retrieval-augmented generation for large language models: A survey. *arXiv preprint arXiv:2312.10997*, 2.

Kenta Hama, Atsushi Otsuka, and Ryo Ishii. 2024. Emotion recognition in conversation with multi-step prompting using large language model. In *Social Computing and Social Media*, pages 338–346, Cham. Springer Nature Switzerland.

David Held. 2006. *Models of democracy*. Polity.

Lei Huang, Weijiang Yu, Weitao Ma, Weihong Zhong, Zhangyin Feng, Haotian Wang, Qianglong Chen, Weihua Peng, Xiaocheng Feng, Bing Qin, et al. 2025. A survey on hallucination in large language models: Principles, taxonomy, challenges, and open questions. *ACM Transactions on Information Systems*, 43(2):1–55.

Seungone Kim, Jamin Shin, Yejin Cho, Joel Jang, Shayne Longpre, Hwaran Lee, Sangdoo Yun, Seongjin Shin, Sungdong Kim, James Thorne, et al. 2023. Prometheus: Inducing fine-grained evaluation capability in language models. In *The Twelfth International Conference on Learning Representations*.

John Lawrence, Jacky Visser, and Chris Reed. 2018. Bbc moral maze: Test your argument. In *Comma*.

Jingjing Li, Yifan Gao, Lidong Bing, Irwin King, and Michael R. Lyu. 2019. Improving question generation with to the point context. In *Proceedings of the 2019 Conference on Empirical Methods in Natural Language Processing and the 9th International Joint Conference on Natural Language Processing (EMNLP-IJCNLP)*, pages 3216–3226, Hong Kong, China. Association for Computational Linguistics.

Yang Liu, Dan Iter, Yichong Xu, Shuohang Wang, Ruochen Xu, and Chenguang Zhu. 2023. G-eval: Nlg evaluation using gpt-4 with better human alignment. *arXiv preprint arXiv:2303.16634*.

Marvin Minsky. 1986. *Society of mind*. Simon and Schuster.

Don A Moore and Paul J Healy. 2008. The trouble with overconfidence. *Psychological review*, 115(2):502.

Diana C Mutz. 2006. *Hearing the other side: Deliberative versus participatory democracy*. Cambridge University Press.

Zhen Qin, Rolf Jagerman, Kai Hui, Honglei Zhuang, Junru Wu, Le Yan, Jiaming Shen, Tianqi Liu, Jialu Liu, Donald Metzler, et al. 2023. Large language models are effective text rankers with pairwise ranking prompting. *arXiv preprint arXiv:2306.17563*.

Seongbum Seo, Sangbong Yoo, and Yun Jang. 2025. A prompt chaining framework for long-term recall in llm-powered intelligent assistant. In *Proceedings of the 30th International Conference on Intelligent User Interfaces*, pages 89–105.

Weiwei Sun, Lingyong Yan, Xinyu Ma, Shuaiqiang Wang, Pengjie Ren, Zhumin Chen, Dawei Yin, and Zhaochun Ren. 2023. Is chatgpt good at search? investigating large language models as re-ranking agents. *arXiv preprint arXiv:2304.09542*.

Hugo Touvron, Thibaut Lavril, Gautier Izacard, Xavier Martinet, Marie-Anne Lachaux, Timothée Lacroix, Baptiste Rozière, Naman Goyal, Eric Ramani, Rohan Taori, et al. 2023. Llama 2: Open foundation and fine-tuned chat models. *Preprint*, arXiv:2307.09288.

Jacky Visser, John Lawrence, Chris Reed, Jean Wagemans, and Douglas Walton. 2021. Annotating argument schemes. *Argumentation*, 35(1):101–139.

Douglas Walton, Christopher Reed, and Fabrizio Macagno. 2008. *Argumentation schemes*. Cambridge University Press.

Douglas N. Walton. 1996. *Argumentation Schemes for Presumptive Reasoning*. Lawrence Erlbaum Associates, Mahwah, NJ.

Yiqiu Xu, Alessio Frosini, Mattia Vanni, Anisa Rula, and Roberto Navigli. 2024. Frase: Frame-based semantic enrichment for sparql query generation. *arXiv preprint arXiv:2503.22144*.

Shunyu Yao, Jeffrey Zhao, Dian Yu, Nan Du, Izhak Shafran, Karthik Narasimhan, and Yuan Cao. 2023. React: Synergizing reasoning and acting in language models. In *International Conference on Learning Representations (ICLR)*.

Matei Zaharia, Omar Khattab, Lingjiao Chen, Jared Quincy Davis, Heather Miller, Chris Potts, James Zou, Michael Carbin, Jonathan Frankle, Naveen Rao, and Ali Ghodsi. 2024. The shift from models to compound ai systems. https://bair.berkeley.edu/blog/2024/02/18/compound-ai-systems/.

Jintian Zhang, Xin Xu, Ningyu Zhang, Ruibo Liu, Bryan Hooi, and Shumin Deng. 2024. Exploring collaboration mechanisms for LLM agents: A social psychology view. In *Proceedings of the 62nd Annual Meeting of the Association for Computational Linguistics (Volume 1: Long Papers)*, pages 14544–14607, Bangkok, Thailand. Association for Computational Linguistics.

Timon Ziegenbein, Gabriella Skitalinskaya, Alireza Bayat Makou, and Henning Wachsmuth. 2024. LLM-based rewriting of inappropriate argumentation using reinforcement learning from machine feedback. In *Proceedings of the 62nd Annual Meeting of the Association for Computational Linguistics (Volume 1: Long Papers)*, pages 4455–4476, Bangkok, Thailand. Association for Computational Linguistics.

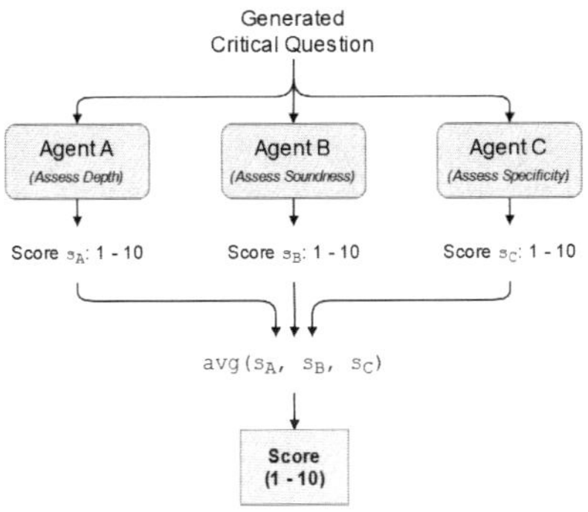

Figure 2: Schematic process of scoring generated questions where an LLM scores one criterion.

A Pre-step - Argument Formulizer

We explored an additional step with a Formulizer agent. Inspired by Walton's Argumentation Schemes (Walton, 1996), the Formulizer transforms each natural-language argument into a structured representation. Specifically, arguments were decomposed into a main claim, explicit supporting premises, implicit assumptions, potential areas of weakness, and conclusions when present. The intuition behind this approach was that structured formulation could help the Generator agent to identify critical questions by explicitly highlighting ambiguous premises, unstated assumptions, and argumentative weaknesses. Prior work in other domains has shown that structured semantic representations can improve generation quality (Li et al., 2019; Xu et al., 2024) of large language models. Our preliminary experiments indicated that large models, such as GPT-based systems, might benefit from this structured context. However, when applying the Formulizer on smaller, open-source models selected for the main experiments, no measurable improvement was found. This suggests that, in the context of critical question generation, additional structured input might help sufficiently powerful models but could introduce confusion or unnecessary complexity for smaller models. Based on our findings, we have not included the Formulizer agent into the final system.

B Evaluator

Within the two-sept evaluator, each LLM evaluate one criterion for each CQ, as shown in Figure 2.

C Prompts

All prompts can be found here: `https://github.com/roxanneelbaff/critical_questions_generation/tree/main/prompts`.

D Technical Details

Implementation We used LangGraph to build the multi-agents workflows for machine societies and for the LLM-based evaluators. Also we use LangChain[10] along with TogetherAI[11]. All three models were loaded via the TogetherAI API and are as follows:

- Llama 3.1 8B: `meta-llama/Llama-3.1-8B-Instruct`
- Mistral Small (24B): $mistralai/Mistral\text{-}Small24BInstruct2501$
- Llama 3.3 70B: meta-llama/Llama-3.3-70B-Instruct

We used the default temperature, 0.7, when running our experiments.

Data For each workflow, representing a machine society, we save each *state*; a state represents the output of all LLMs after being prompted in a round: whether to initially generate the three critical questions, reflect or debate. Also the scores/ranks from the 4 evaluators are saved at each stage. This will allow for expanded analysis.[12]

[10] `https://www.langchain.com`

[11] `https://www.together.ai`

[12] `https://github.com/roxanneelbaff/critical_questions_generation/tree/main/output`

ELLIS Alicante at CQs-Gen 2025: Winning the critical thinking questions shared task: LLM-based question generation and selection

Lucile Favero[1], **Daniel Frases** [2] *, **Juan Antonio Pérez-Ortiz**[3], **Tanja Käser**[4], **Nuria Oliver**[1]

[1] ELLIS Alicante, Spain, [2] Universidad Alfonso X el Sabio, Spain,
[3] Universitat d'Alacant, Spain, [4] École Polytechnique Fédérale de Lausanne, Switzerland

Correspondence: lucile@ellisalicante.org

Abstract

The widespread adoption of chat interfaces based on Large Language Models (LLMs) raises concerns about promoting superficial learning and undermining the development of critical thinking skills. Instead of relying on LLMs purely for retrieving factual information, this work explores their potential to foster deeper reasoning by generating critical questions that challenge unsupported or vague claims in debate interventions. This study is part of a shared task of the 12th Workshop on Argument Mining, co-located with ACL 2025, focused on automatic critical question generation. We propose a two-step framework involving two small-scale open source language models: a `Questioner` that generates multiple candidate questions and a `Judge` that selects the most relevant ones. Our system ranked first in the shared task competition, demonstrating the potential of the proposed LLM-based approach to encourage critical engagement with argumentative texts.

1 Introduction

The intensive use of chatbots based on Large Language Models (LLMs) has been associated with the promotion of superficial learning habits and a decline in critical thinking skills in their users, particularly students (Gerlich, 2025; Schei et al., 2024). Motivated by this fact, rather than relying on LLMs to provide factual answers, there is an opportunity to leverage the sophisticated natural language understanding capabilities of LLMs to foster critical thinking by means of the generation of critical questions.

This paper contributes to the CQs-Gen shared task of the 12th Workshop on Argument Mining, co-located with ACL 2025, which focuses on generating critical questions from debate interventions (Figueras, 2025b). While previous research has extensively explored the automatic generation of questions (Mulla and Gharpure, 2023; Ling and Afzaal, 2024), and current AI systems are capable of detecting misinformation with reasonable accuracy (Guo et al., 2022), relatively little work has leveraged argumentation theory to identify missing claims and misinformation in argumentative text (Figueras, 2024), and to generate relevant critical questions about the text (Favero et al., 2024; Figueras and Agerri, 2024; Ruiz-Dolz and Lawrence, 2025).

To fill this gap, we present an LLM-based framework for generating critical questions from argumentative text, aimed at encouraging users to reflect before accepting a claim. Our approach uses relatively small, open-source[1] LLMs to generate critical questions from a given debate intervention. Figure 1 illustrates the pipeline of the proposed method, detailing each step in the process.

In sum, the main contributions of our work are four-fold: (1) We propose a **Two-Step Framework for Critical Question Generation** composed of a `Questioner-Judge` LLM architecture where the `Questioner`, LLM_Q, generates multiple candidate questions that are evaluated by the `Judge`, LLM_J, which selects the most relevant ones, improving quality through selection; (2) we perform an extensive **empirical evaluation** of several small (7B–14B), open-source LLMs, demonstrating their strong performance despite limited size and without fine-tuning; (3) we explore how integrating **argumentation scheme theory** into prompts —both selectively and systematically— impacts generation quality and diversity; and (4) we highlight the potential of the proposed method to support **educational tools** that can be deployed locally, pre-

*Worked performed during an internship at ELLIS Alicante.

[1]We use the term "small" to refer to LLMs in the 7B-14B range, able to run on a student's laptop, and "open-source" to refer to LLMs that are freely available with at least open weights.

Proceedings of the 12th Argument Mining Workshop, pages 322–331
July 31, 2025 ©2025 Association for Computational Linguistics

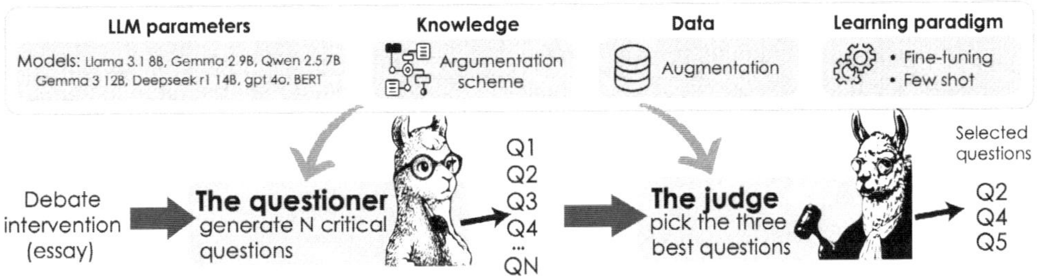

Figure 1: Overview of the proposed framework. Given a debate intervention as input, a first LLM, the `Questioner` LLM_Q, generates several candidate questions, and a second LLM, the `Judge`, LLM_J, chooses the three most useful critical questions among the questions generated.

serving privacy and reducing computational costs.

Our system ranked first in the CQs-Gen 2025 shared task on critical question generation, validating the effectiveness of the proposed approach.

2 Problem definition

2.1 Dataset description

The provided dataset (Figueras, 2025a), $D_{\text{shared train}}$, is composed of:

(1) $D = 189$ **interventions** during real political debate where each intervention consists of a short text of an average of 138 ± 88.4 words;

(2) Their associated **argumentative schemes**, that is "stereotypical patterns of inference that capture common types of defeasible arguments, *i.e.*, arguments that are plausible but open to rebuttal. Each scheme represents a form of reasoning with typical premises and a conclusion" (Walton et al., 2008).[2] Most (62.4%) of the interventions are associated with a single argumentative scheme, although some may have up to six;

(3) A set $\mathcal{R}^j$ consisting of N^j annotated **reference questions** for each debate intervention j, where $j = 1 \dots D$. Each reference question q_i^j is labeled with a label or category $l_i^j \in$ {Useful, Unhelpful, Invalid}, such that $\mathcal{R}^j = \{(q_i^j, l_i^j) \mid i = 1, \dots, N^j\}$. **Useful** questions can potentially challenge one of the arguments in the text; **Unhelpful** questions are valid but unlikely to challenge any of the arguments in the text; and **Invalid** questions cannot be used to challenge any argument in the intervention (Figueras, 2025b).

2.2 Task description

The task consists of automatically generating three *Useful* critical questions, $Qc^j = \{qc_1^j, qc_2^j, qc_3^j\}$ for each debate intervention j. In this context, critical questions are designed to evaluate the strength of an argument by revealing the assumptions underlying its premises (Figueras and Agerri, 2024). The usefulness of each generated critical question qc_i^j is evaluated by measuring its cosine similarity with the annotated reference questions $\mathcal{R}^j$. The label assigned to qc_i^j corresponds to the label of the most similar reference question, provided that it is larger than or equal to 0.6. If no similarity score exceeds this threshold, the question is marked as *Not able to evaluate*. In this case, human evaluators assessed the usefulness of the question during the competition. The final score was computed on the 34 interventions that composed the test set, $D_{\text{shared test}}$. Note that the reference test set, with the labels corresponding to the interventions in $D_{\text{shared test}}$ was not made available.

3 Methodology

As illustrated in Figure 1, the proposed system consists of two large language models (LLMs) used sequentially. (1) The `Questioner` (LLM_Q) which generates candidate critical questions given an intervention and its associated argumentation schemes; and the (2) The `Judge` (LLM_J) which evaluates these candidates and selects those deemed most useful (Li et al., 2024). This architecture is grounded in the framework of critical thinking proposed by Elder and Paul (2020), which comprises analytic, creative, and evaluative dimensions. We operationalize the creative components through LLM_Q (generation), and the analytic and evaluative components through LLM_J (selection).

3.1 The prompts

The prompts provided to the LLMs include: the intervention text, the role of the LLM (*i.e.*, `Questioner` or `Judge`), definitions of critical ques-

[2]See A.3 for a comprehensive list of the annotation schemes included in the dataset.

tion and argumentation scheme, the argumentative schemes present in the intervention along with their definitions (see A.3) and corresponding question templates (see A.4), the task objective, and the expected output. For more details, see A.2.3.

For LLM_Q, each prompt is designed to elicit N questions in a single generation step, rather than prompting the model N times for one question at a time. This strategy effectively reduces question repetition.

Aligned with Guo et al. (2023), we hypothesize that candidate questions exhibiting high similarity are likely to be useful. Thus, the following instruction is added to LLM_J's prompt: *If some questions are redundant, these questions must be important: select the most relevant one.* This modification led to an overall improvement in performance.

3.2 Experimental design

We split $D_{\text{shared train}}$ into training (D_{train}, 74), validation (D_{val}, 33), and test (D_{test}, 79) sets. The size of D_{test} was selected to ensure stable results under the automatic evaluation metric (see A.2.1). We conducted experiments on D_{test} by varying the following parameters to assess their impact on performance: the choice of LLM for each of the roles (`Questioner` and `Judge`), the number of candidate questions generated, and the temperature setting of the LLMs. Additionally, we performed an ablation study to evaluate the role of argumentation schemes in the generation process and address the added value of LLM_J by comparing it with alternative question selection strategies. For more details on the experimental setup and further experiments, including LLM and BERT fine-tuning and data augmentation, see A.2 and A.4.

4 Experiments and results

4.1 Model comparison

We evaluated both LLM_Q and LLM_J using a selection of small, open-source LLMs ranging from 7B to 14B parameters: Qwen 2.5 7B (Yang et al., 2024), Llama 3.1 8B (Dubey et al., 2024), Gemma 2 9B (Team et al., 2024), Gemma 3 12B (Team et al., 2025), and DeepSeek R1 14B (Guo et al., 2025) [3]. We compare their performance with that of GPT-4o (Achiam et al., 2023).

As shown in Table 1, the LLM combination yielding the highest proportion of useful outputs on D_{test} is Llama 3.1 8B as LLM_Q and Gemma 2 9B as LLM_J.

LLM_Q	LLM_J	Use. ↑	Inv. ↓	NoEval
Llama 3.1	-	53.2	3.0	33.8
Gemma 2	-	46.4	3.0	42.6
Gemma 3	-	40.5	**2.5**	46.0
Llama 3.1	Llama 3.1	53.2	3.9	33.0
Llama 3.1	Qwen 2.5	56.8	3.3	28.6
Llama 3.1	Gemma 2	**57.6**	5.2	30.3
Llama 3.1	Gemma 3	57.1	2.6	30.7

Table 1: **Performance on D_{test} for a selection of LLM_Q and LLM_J.** *Use*, *Inv* and *NoEval* are the % of *Useful*, *Invalid*, and *Not able to evaluate* questions, respectively. LLM_Q generates 8 questions of which LLM_J selects the best 3. The argumentative schemes are not given in the prompt. Best results in bold.

4.2 Leveraging argumentation schemes

To assess the impact on performance of adding argumentation scheme theory in the prompts for both LLM_Q and LLM_J, we conducted an ablation study. Table 2 compares the performance of LLM_Q (Llama 3.1 8B, generating six questions) and LLM_J (Gemma 2 9B) with the following configurations: **(1) Without**: No argumentation scheme is provided; **(2) With (one)**: All argumentation schemes relevant to the given intervention are included in a single prompt; **(3) With (mult.)**: Each argumentation scheme is provided in a separate prompt; and **(4) Both** : LLM_Q is prompted independently using the **With (one)** and without argumentation schemes setups. Then the two sets of candidate questions are merged for their selection by LLM_J . Similarly to previous work (Figueras and Agerri, 2024), the best performance is achieved in the **Both** configuration, suggesting that combining scheme-based and non-scheme-based prompts yields the most effective results. Note that 81% of the questions selected by LLM_J were generated with the argumentation scheme in the prompt.

Scheme	LLM_Q			$LLM_Q + LLM_J$		
	Use.↑	Inv. ↓	NoEval	Use.↑	Inv. ↓	NoEval
Without	54.7	3.2	32.7	57.7	3.8	27.4
With (one)	53.4	4.0	32.1	56.5	3.7	28.3
With (mult.)	46.0	4.0	27.0	51.6	3.6	34.2
Both	54.0	3.5	31.0	**62.4**	**2.1**	**25.7**

Table 2: **Performance on D_{test} with different argumentation schemes setups.** LLM_Q: Llama 3.1 generating 6 questions. *Without*: No argumentation scheme is provided;*With (one)*: Argumentation schemes are included in a single prompt; *With (mult.)*: Each argumentation scheme is provided in a separate prompt; and *Both*: LLM_Q is prompted independently with and without argumentation schemes. Best results in bold.

[3]For further details, see Section A.2.2.

4.3 Number of candidate questions

Table 3 presents the effectiveness of the questions as a function of the number of candidate questions generated per prompt. The experiment uses Llama 3.1 8B as LLM_Q—prompted both with and without the schemes—and Gemma 2 9B as LLM_J. Generating four candidate questions per prompt (eight in total) yielded the best performance.

# quest.	Use.↑	Inv. ↓	NoEval
4	**59.3 ± 3.36**	**$2.80 \pm 1.05e^{-1}$**	**22.5 ± 2.13**
6	$57.2 \pm 8.82e^{-1}$	$2.72 \pm 6.38e^{-1}$	25.9 ± 2.91
8	$57.3 \pm 7.58e^{-1}$	$3.22 \pm 2.78e^{-1}$	$25.7 \pm 8.99e^{-1}$

Table 3: **Performance on $D_{\text{Shared train}}$ as a function of the number of candidate questions generated.** LLM_Q: Llama 3.1, LLM_J: Gemma 2. 3 runs.

4.4 Added value of the Judge, LLM_J

Although we observe an improvement in performance when adding LLM_J versus a random selection (see Tables 2 and 3), the results are not directly comparable, as the average usefulness is computed over different numbers of questions (N for LLM_Q and three for LLM_J). To further assess the effectiveness of LLM_J, we compared it against alternative selection paradigms. Table 4 reports the performance LLM_J versus a selection by an oracle and randomly, using Llama 3.1 8B as LLM_Q with four candidate questions per prompt. The oracle selects up to three useful questions. If fewer than three *Useful* questions are available, the remaining slots are filled by *Unhelpful* questions. If still insufficient, *Invalid*, and then *Not able to evaluate* questions are considered, in that order. The oracle illustrates the upper bound of the Judge's potential performance. Results show that LLM_J achieves a usefulness rate that is 3.4 percentage points higher than random selection, a statistically significant improvement ($p < 0.05$, McNemar's test). As expected, the oracle yields the highest usefulness with a gain of 34.2 percentage points.

Selection	Use.↑	Inv. ↓	NoEval
Random	55.9 ± 2.22	$2.7 \pm 7.94e^{-3}$	$25.7 \pm 2.5e^{-2}$
Gemma 2	59.3 ± 3.36	$2.8 \pm 1.05e^{-1}$	22.5 ± 2.13
Oracle	93.5 ± 1.19	$6.68 \pm 8.59e^{-2}$	$1.70 \pm 8.19e^{-1}$

Table 4: **Performance on $D_{\text{Shared train}}$ depending on the method to select the questions.** Comparison between random selection, selection with Gemma 2 as LLM_J or with an Oracle. In all cases, LLM_Q is Llama 3.1 generating $4 + 4$ questions. 3 runs.

4.5 Final submission

Based on the results of the previous experiments, we selected the following setup for our final submission: LLM_Q, Llama 3.1 8B, generating four questions without the scheme and four with the scheme, all within a single prompt; LLM_J, Gemma 2 9B, selecting the three best questions, used without fine-tuning. For comparison, we maintained the same experimental setup but substituted LLM_J with GPT-4o in our second submission, and in the third submission, GPT-4o was used for both LLM_Q and LLM_J under identical prompting conditions. Table 5 shows the performance with the automated evaluation on $D_{\text{Shared train}}$ and $D_{\text{Shared test}}$ for the three final submissions.

Sub.	Valiadation		Test	
	Use. ↑	NoEval	Use. ↑	NoEval
1	61.4	21%	36.3	36%
2	61.0	19%	44.1	36%
3	**64.4**	**19%**	**50.0**	**28%**

Table 5: **Performance with the automated evaluation on the validation set and the test set for the three final submissions.** Bold indicates the winning submission.

After the manual annotation of the questions by the organizers, the score of the best performing submission rose to **67.6**, ranking first in the task.

5 Discussion and conclusion

In this paper, we have proposed a two-step framework for generating critical questions, where one LLM (LLM_Q) generates multiple candidate questions and another LLM (LLM_J) evaluates and selects the most relevant ones (Li et al., 2024). This selection-based approach consistently outperformed direct generation, emphasizing the benefits of separating generation from evaluation. Our experiments show that adding argumentation schemes to the prompts improves the quality of the generated questions. However, strictly enforcing these schemes can reduce diversity. Thus, a selective use of schemes strikes a better balance between structural guidance and creative generation, in line with prior work (Figueras and Agerri, 2024).

Given the small size of the dataset, traditional strategies such as fine-tuning or data augmentation (*e.g.*, using BERT-based methods) yielded limited improvement. Instead, leveraging small, open-source LLMs guided by domain-specific argumentation theory proved more effective in this low-resource setting.

Limitations

This work has several limitations that should be acknowledged.

The first limitation concerns the evaluation methodology, which relies on an automatic comparison with a set of predefined reference questions by means of cosine similarity. Many generated questions did not align with any reference, despite being potentially useful, and hence were labeled as *Not able to evaluate*. This mismatch introduces a risk of mis-estimation of the model's performance and could lead to overfitting.

A second limitation stems from the use of a small, domain-specific dataset focused on political discourse, which at times lacks sufficient context for effective question generation. This narrow scope limits the generalizability of our findings. Future work should aim to evaluate the proposed framework on broader and more diverse datasets to assess its robustness across different domains, like education.

A third limitation lies in the performance of LLM_J, which shows a substantial gap compared to the oracle. This indicates that while some generated questions are *Useful*, the Judge does not consistently identify them, suggesting significant potential for future improvements.

Acknowledgements

L.F. and N.O. have been partially funded by a nominal grant received at the ELLIS Unit Alicante Foundation from the Regional Government of Valencia in Spain (Convenio Singular signed with Generalitat Valenciana, Conselleria de Innovación, Industria, Comercio y Turismo, Dirección General de Innovación). L.F. has also been partially funded by a grant from the Banc Sabadell Foundation.

References

Josh Achiam, Steven Adler, Sandhini Agarwal, Lama Ahmad, Ilge Akkaya, Florencia Leoni Aleman, Diogo Almeida, Janko Altenschmidt, Sam Altman, Shyamal Anadkat, et al. 2023. GPT-4 technical report. *arXiv preprint arXiv:2303.08774*.

Jacob Devlin. 2018. Bert: Pre-training of deep bidirectional transformers for language understanding. *arXiv preprint arXiv:1810.04805*.

Abhimanyu Dubey, Abhinav Jauhri, Abhinav Pandey, Abhishek Kadian, Ahmad Al-Dahle, Aiesha Letman, Akhil Mathur, Alan Schelten, Amy Yang, Angela Fan, et al. 2024. The Llama 3 herd of models. *arXiv preprint arXiv:2407.21783*.

Linda Elder and Richard Paul. 2020. *Critical thinking: Tools for taking charge of your learning and your life*. Rowman & Littlefield.

Lucile Favero, Juan Antonio Pérez-Ortiz, Tanja Käser, and Nuria Oliver. 2024. Enhancing critical thinking in education by means of a Socratic chatbot. *arXiv preprint arXiv:2409.05511*.

Blanca Calvo Figueras. 2024. Using argumentation theory to fight misinformation. *Doctoral Symposium on Natural Language Processing*.

Blanca Calvo Figueras. 2025a. Benchmarking Critical Questions Generation: A Challenging Reasoning Task for Large Language Models — arxiv.org. https://arxiv.org/abs/2505.11341. [Accessed 19-05-2025].

Blanca Calvo Figueras and Rodrigo Agerri. 2024. Critical questions generation: Motivation and challenges. *arXiv preprint arXiv:2410.14335*.

Maite Heredia Ekaterina Sviridova Elena Cabrio Serena Villata Rodrigo Agerri Figueras, Jaione Bengoetxea. 2025b. Overview of the critical questions generation shared task 2025. In *Proceedings of the 12th Workshop on Argument Mining*.

Michael Gerlich. 2025. AI tools in society: Impacts on cognitive offloading and the future of critical thinking. *Societies*, 15(1):6.

Daya Guo, Dejian Yang, Haowei Zhang, Junxiao Song, Ruoyu Zhang, Runxin Xu, Qihao Zhu, Shirong Ma, Peiyi Wang, Xiao Bi, et al. 2025. Deepseek-r1: Incentivizing reasoning capability in llms via reinforcement learning. *arXiv preprint arXiv:2501.12948*.

Shasha Guo, Jing Zhang, Xirui Ke, Cuiping Li, and Hong Chen. 2023. Diversifying question generation over knowledge base via external natural questions. *arXiv preprint arXiv:2309.14362*.

Zhijiang Guo, Michael Schlichtkrull, and Andreas Vlachos. 2022. A survey on automated fact-checking. *Transactions of the Association for Computational Linguistics*, 10:178–206.

Dawei Li, Bohan Jiang, Liangjie Huang, Alimohammad Beigi, Chengshuai Zhao, Zhen Tan, Amrita Bhattacharjee, Yuxuan Jiang, Canyu Chen, Tianhao Wu, et al. 2024. From generation to judgment: Opportunities and challenges of LLM-as-a-judge. *arXiv preprint arXiv:2411.16594*.

Jintao Ling and Muhammad Afzaal. 2024. Automatic question-answer pairs generation using pre-trained large language models in higher education. *Computers and Education: Artificial Intelligence*, 6:100252.

Nikahat Mulla and Prachi Gharpure. 2023. Automatic question generation: a review of methodologies, datasets, evaluation metrics, and applications. *Progress in Artificial Intelligence*, 12(1):1–32.

Ramon Ruiz-Dolz and John Lawrence. 2025. An explainable framework for misinformation identification via critical question answering. *arXiv preprint arXiv:2503.14626*.

Odin Monrad Schei, Anja Møgelvang, and Kristine Ludvigsen. 2024. Perceptions and use of AI chatbots among students in higher education: A scoping review of empirical studies. *Education Sciences*, 14(8):922.

Gemma Team, Aishwarya Kamath, Johan Ferret, Shreya Pathak, Nino Vieillard, Ramona Merhej, Sarah Perrin, Tatiana Matejovicova, Alexandre Ramé, Morgane Rivière, et al. 2025. Gemma 3 technical report. *arXiv preprint arXiv:2503.19786*.

Gemma Team, Morgane Riviere, Shreya Pathak, Pier Giuseppe Sessa, Cassidy Hardin, Surya Bhupatiraju, Léonard Hussenot, Thomas Mesnard, Bobak Shahriari, Alexandre Ramé, et al. 2024. Gemma 2: Improving open language models at a practical size. *arXiv preprint arXiv:2408.00118*.

Douglas Walton, Christopher Reed, and Fabrizio Macagno. 2008. *Argumentation schemes*. Cambridge University Press.

An Yang, Baosong Yang, Beichen Zhang, Binyuan Hui, Bo Zheng, Bowen Yu, Chengyuan Li, Dayiheng Liu, Fei Huang, Haoran Wei, et al. 2024. Qwen2. 5 technical report. *arXiv preprint arXiv:2412.15115*.

A Appendix

A.1 The datasets

Figure 2 shows the distribution of the number of annotated questions per intervention in $D_{\text{shared train}}$, Figure 3 shows the distribution of the number of schemes per intervention in $D_{\text{shared train}}$ and Figure 4 shows the distribution of the labels in $D_{\text{shared train}}$.

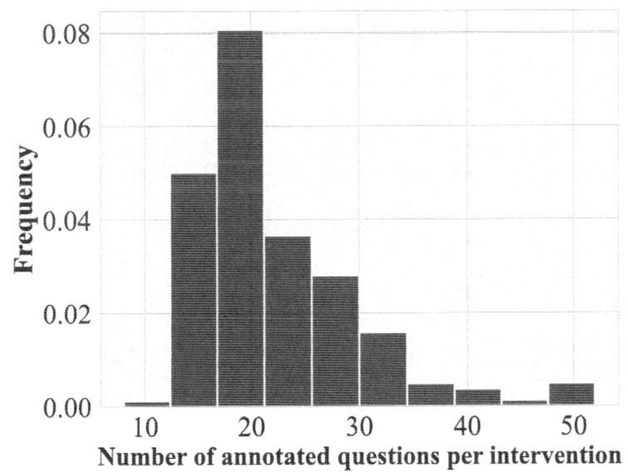

Figure 2: Distribution of the number of annotated questions per intervention in $D_{\text{shared train}}$.

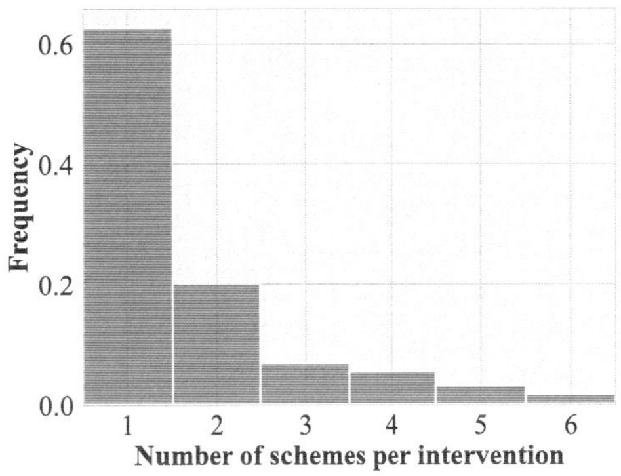

Figure 3: Distribution of the number of schemes per intervention in $D_{\text{shared train}}$.

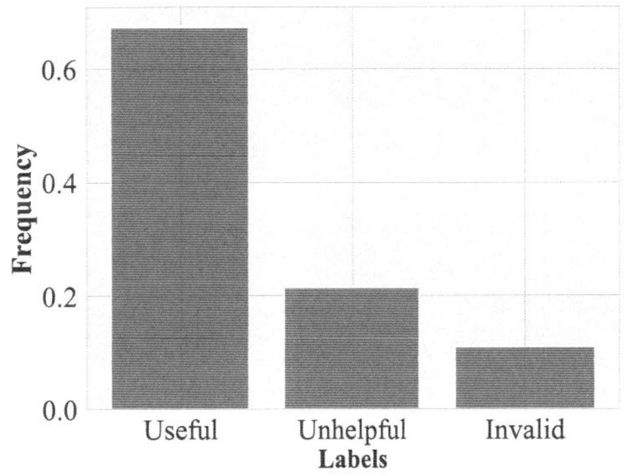

Figure 4: Distribution of the labels in $D_{\text{shared train}}$.

A.2 Experimental setup

Data split To enable training (see A.4), we divided $D_{\text{shared train}}$ (189 interventions) into three subsets: a training set D_{train} (74 interventions), a validation set D_{val} (33 interventions), and a test set D_{test} (79 interventions). The test set was intentionally large to accommodate the variability due to the automatic evaluation metric (see A.2.1), aiming for more stable and reliable results.

Software and hardware setup All experiments were performed on an Apple M1 Pro laptop with 32 GB RAM using Ollama [4], an open-source framework that enables users to run, create, and share LLMs locally on their machines. Our code is available at `https://github.com/lucilefavero/SQ_shared_task`.

[4] `https://github.com/ollama/ollama`, `https://ollama.com`.

A.2.1 Limitation of the automatic evaluation and human evaluation

Due to the nature of the automatic evaluation metric, a substantial proportion of generated questions could not be evaluated (see the column *No* in Tables 1, 2, and 3). Consequently, distinguishing the best-performing configurations was not straightforward. The performance differences across varying numbers of candidate questions were small and overshadowed by significant variance in our test set D_{test}. To improve precision, we repeated the experiment three times on $D_{\text{shared train}}$ (the entire dataset).

Throughout our experiments, we prioritized the quality of critical questions over minimizing the proportion of *Not able to evaluate* labels. We intentionally avoided overfitting to the automatic evaluation metric, under the assumption that some unevaluated questions might still be useful. The primary goal was to reduce the proportion of *Invalid* and *Unhelpful* labels. To ensure quality, we manually evaluate some questions that could not be evaluated by the automatic scoring system.

A.2.2 Additional information on the LLMs

A complete list of the tested models is provided below. The results for the most relevant combinations of LLM_Q and LLM_J are presented in Table 1.

- **Qwen 2.5 7B**. Qwen 2.5 is a multilingual transformer-based LLM with RoPE, SwiGLU, RMSNorm, and Attention QKV bias, released in September 2024 by the Qwen Team. (Yang et al., 2024).
- **Llama 3.1 8B**, Llama 3.1 is a multilingual large language model optimized for dialogue applications. It supports eight languages and offers a context window of up to 128,000 tokens, enabling it to handle extensive conversational contexts. Released in July 2024 by Meta (Dubey et al., 2024).
- **Gemma 2 9B**, Gemma 2 is a text-to-text decoder-only LLM available in English with open weights, released in June 2024 by Google, (Team et al., 2024).
- **Gemma 3 12B**, Gemma 3 is another model from the Gemma family; it has longer context, a different architecture than Gemma 2, and is trained with distillation. It was released in March 2025 by Google, (Team et al., 2025).
- **DeepSeek R1 14B**. DeepSeek R1 is an open-source large language model designed to enhance reasoning capabilities through reinforcement learning. It rivals other advanced models in tasks such as mathematics, coding, and logical reasoning. Released in January, 2025 by the Chinese AI startup DeepSeek (Guo et al., 2025).

A.2.3 Structure of LLM's prompts

The prompt for LLM_Q consists of the following components:

- **The intervention**.
- **Role.** "You are a critical judge."
- **Definition of critical question**: "Critical questions are the set of enquiries that should be asked in order to judge if an argument is good or fallacious by unmasking the assumptions held by the premises of the argument."
- **Definition of argumentation scheme.** "Argumentative schemes are stereotypical patterns of inference that capture common types of defeasible arguments, i.e. arguments that are plausible but open to rebuttal. Each scheme represents a form of reasoning with typical premises and a conclusion."
- **The argumentation schemes present in the intervention with their definition and template of critical questions** see A.3
- **Goal.** "Use the provided scheme and template of critical questions to generate [N] critical questions to evaluate the arguments in the given essay."
- **Expected output.** "Give one question per line. Make the questions simple, and do not give any explanation regarding why the question is relevant."

The prompt for LLM_J consists of the following components:

- **The intervention**.
- **Role.** "You are a very strict critical and sceptical judge."
- **Definition of critical question**: "Critical questions are the set of enquiries that should be asked in order to judge if an argument is good or fallacious by unmasking the assumptions held by the premises of the argument."

- **Definition of argumentative scheme.** "Argumentative schemes are stereotypical patterns of inference that capture common types of defeasible arguments, i.e. arguments that are plausible but open to rebuttal. Each scheme represents a form of reasoning with typical premises and a conclusion."

- **The argumentation schemes present in the intervention with their definition and template of critical questions** see A.3

- **Goal.** "Select the 3 best critical questions that should be raised before accepting the arguments in the essay. If some questions are redundant, these questions must be important: select the most relevant one."

- **Expected output.** "Give one question per line. Make the questions simple, and do not give any explanation regarding why the question is relevant."

A.3 Argumentation scheme definition and template

Table 6 depicts the argumentation schemes identified in the dataset, along with their corresponding critical question templates. The definitions and templates are adapted from Walton et al. (2008).

A.4 Further experiments

Critical questions' templates We examined two approaches for incorporating critical question templates into the prompts: using the template provided by Figueras and Agerri (2024), and utilizing the critical question templates outlined in Table 6. We noted a slight performance improvement with the first template for the configurations employing LLM_Q: Llama 3.1, LLM_J: Gemma 2 or GPT-4o, and with the second template for the configurations involving LLM_Q: GPT-4o and LLM_J: GPT-4o. This approach was adopted in our final submission.

Temperature We also explored modifying the generation temperature from its default setting and observed an overall decrease in performance.

Fine-tuning Attempts to fine-tune both LLM_Q and LLM_J were inconclusive. The resulting model outputs often diverged significantly from the intended instructions and demonstrated poor performance, likely attributable to task complexity combined with the limited size of the training dataset D_{Train}.

We also fine-tuned BERT (Devlin, 2018) to classify candidate questions into three categories: *Useful*, *Unhelpful*, and *Invalid*, selecting the three questions with the highest predicted probability of being *Useful*. However, similar to the LLM fine-tuning, the model failed to outperform a random baseline, likely due to task complexity and the limited size of D_{Train}.

Data augmentation The poor performance of the trained approaches is likely attributable to the limited and highly imbalanced annotated dataset. Specifically, over 67% of annotations in $D_{\text{Shared train}}$ are labeled as *Useful* (see Figure 4). To address this, we augmented D_{Train} with Llama 3.1, generating questions and matching them to reference annotations to balance label distribution across interventions. However, fine-tuning the LLMs and BERT on the augmented data still yielded inconclusive results.

A.5 Further comments on the results

The automatic evaluation scores on $D_{\text{shared test}}$ are lower compared to those obtained on $D_{\text{shared train}}$, likely due to increased variance arising from the test set's smaller size. Additionally, the shared-task organizers indicated, after human evaluation, that the test set presented a higher difficulty.

Name	Scheme's definition	Critical questions template
Ad Hominem	This scheme attacks an opponent's argument by alleging inconsistency between their actions and their stated position.	Is the alleged inconsistency real and relevant to the argument? Does the inconsistency undermine the argument's validity? Could the argument still hold despite the personal inconsistency?
Alternatives	This scheme reasons that one option should be chosen (or avoided) by comparing it to other possible options.	Have all relevant alternatives been considered? Are the alternatives fairly evaluated? Is the chosen alternative clearly superior based on the criteria?
Analogy	This scheme draws a conclusion about one case by comparing it to a similar case where the conclusion is known to hold.	Are the two cases sufficiently similar in relevant respects? Are there significant differences that undermine the analogy? Is the conclusion in the known case well-established?
Bias	This scheme attacks an argument by alleging that the source is biased, thus undermining its credibility.	Is there clear evidence of bias in the source? Does the alleged bias directly affect the truth of the argument's conclusion? Could the argument still hold despite the bias?
Cause to effect	This scheme reasons that if a certain cause occurs, it will lead to a specific effect, based on a causal relationship.	Is there sufficient evidence that the cause reliably produces the effect? Could other factors intervene to prevent the effect from occurring? Is the causal link based on correlation rather than proven causation?
Consequences	This scheme bases a conclusion on the positive or negative outcomes of a proposed action, arguing for or against it based on those consequences.	Are the predicted consequences likely to occur if the action is taken? Are there other consequences (positive or negative) that haven't been considered? Is the evaluation of the consequences as good or bad justified?
Example	This scheme involves reasoning from a specific case or instance to a general conclusion, suggesting that what holds in the example applies more broadly.	Is the example representative of the broader category or situation? Are there significant counterexamples that undermine the generalization? Is the example relevant to the conclusion being drawn?
Expert opinion	This scheme concludes that a proposition is true because an expert in the relevant field asserts it.	How credible is the expert as a source? Is the expert an authority in the field relevant to the proposition? What exactly did the expert assert? Is the expert personally reliable and trustworthy? Is the expert's claim consistent with other experts? Is the expert's assertion backed by evidence?
Fear and danger appeals	This scheme urges action or avoidance based on the fear of a harmful outcome if the action isn't taken or is taken.	Is the feared outcome realistically likely to occur? Is the fear disproportionate to the evidence of danger? Are there other ways to mitigate the feared outcome without the proposed action?
Negative consequences	This scheme argues against an action because it will lead to bad outcomes.	Are the negative consequences probable? Are there positive consequences that might offset the negative ones? Is the judgment of the consequences as negative reasonable?

Continued on next page

Name	Scheme's definition	Critical questions template
Popular opinion	This scheme argues that a proposition is true or should be accepted because it is widely believed by the majority.	Is the opinion truly held by a significant majority? Does the majority have reliable evidence or expertise to justify their belief? Could the majority be mistaken or influenced by bias?
Popular practice	This scheme justifies an action or belief because it is commonly practiced by many people.	Is the practice widespread enough to be considered popular? Does the practice's popularity indicate its correctness or value? Are there reasons the practice might be flawed despite its popularity?
Positive consequences	This scheme argues for an action because it will plausibly lead to good outcomes.	Are the positive consequences likely to occur? Are there potential negative consequences that outweigh the positive ones? Is the assessment of the consequences as positive well-founded?
Position to know	This scheme concludes a proposition is true because the source is in a position to know about it (e.g., firsthand experience).	Is the source genuinely in a position to know about the proposition? Is the source honest and trustworthy? Did the source actually assert the proposition?
Practical reasoning	This scheme involves an agent reasoning from a goal to an action that is a means to achieve that goal (e.g., "I want G, doing A achieves G, so I should do A").	What other goals might conflict with G? Are there alternative actions to A that could also achieve G? Is A the most efficient means to achieve G? Is it practically possible for me to carry out A? What are the potential side effects or consequences of doing A?
Sign	This scheme infers a conclusion based on an observable sign or indicator that suggests the presence of a condition or event.	Is the sign a reliable indicator of the conclusion? Could the sign be present without the conclusion being true? Are there alternative explanations for the sign?
Value	This scheme reasons that an action should be taken or avoided because it aligns with or conflicts with an agent's values (e.g., "V is good, so I should pursue G that promotes V").	Is value V genuinely positive/negative as judged by the agent? Does pursuing V conflict with other values the agent holds? Is the link between the action and the promotion of V well-supported?
Verbal classification	This scheme applies a general rule or property to a specific case based on how the case is classified linguistically.	Is the classification of the case accurate and appropriate? Does the general rule reliably apply to all cases under this classification? Is the classification ambiguous or contested?

Table 6: Argumentation schemes identified in the dataset, along with their corresponding critical question templates. Definitions and templates are adapted from Walton et al. (2008).

Mind_Matrix at CQs-Gen 2025: Adaptive Generation of Critical Questions for Argumentative Interventions

Sha Newaz Mahmud, Shahriar Hossain, Samia Rahman, Momtazul Arefin Labib, Hasan Murad
Department of Computer Science and Engineering,
Chittagong University of Engineering and Technology, Bangladesh
{u2004081,u2004069,u1904022,u1904111}@student.cuet.ac.bd,
hasanmurad@cuet.ac.bd

Abstract

To encourage computational argumentation through critical question generation (CQs-Gen), we propose an ACL 2025 CQs-Gen shared task system to generate critical questions (CQs) with the best effort to counter argumentative text by discovering logical fallacies, unjustified assertions, and implicit assumptions. Our system integrates a quantized language model, semantic similarity analysis, and a meta-evaluation feedback mechanism including the key stages such as data preprocessing, rationale-augmented prompting to induce specificity, diversity filtering for redundancy elimination, enriched meta-evaluation for relevance, and a feedback-reflect-refine loop for iterative refinement. Multi-metric scoring guarantees high-quality CQs. With robust error handling, our pipeline ranked 7th among 15 teams, outperforming baseline fact-checking approaches by enabling critical engagement and successfully detecting argumentative fallacies. This study presents an adaptive, scalable method that advances argument mining and critical discourse analysis.

1 Introduction

Critical Questions (CQs) are designed specifically to challenge argumentative texts by uncovering logical fallacies, unsupported claims, and underlying assumptions (Walton et al., 2008). In accordance with the theory of argumentation, CQs promote rational discourse by stimulating a more detailed evaluation of claims; thus, they are critical to applications such as debate analysis, pedagogy, and policy critique (Lawrence and Reed, 2019). Investigating CQs-Gen is valuable because it adds to computational argumentation, enabling systems to enhance critical thinking and debunk false information without solely relying on fact-checking, which is often limited by consensus or data availability.

The ACL 2025 CQs-Gen shared task (Calvo Figueras et al., 2025) aims to advance computational argumentation by generating CQs that uncover these logical fallacies and assumptions. Previous CQs-Gen systems, which were commonly rule-based templates or early NLP-based, could not produce diverse, context-aware questions, instead yielding imprecise or redundant responses (Cao and Wang, 2021). These limitations necessitate adaptive and scalable solutions.

This paper describes our submission to the CQs-Gen Shared Task, which is designed to generate three high-quality and diverse CQs through a five-stage pipeline: (1) Data Preprocessing to normalize interventions, (2) CQs Generation using a quantized LLaMA-3 model, (3) Post-processing and validation to ensure well-formed questions, (4) semantic ranking to select the top three questions, and (5) an Adaptive Meta-Evaluation Loop to refine question quality, which finalizes and packages three CQs per intervention into a JSON file. This approach ensures contextually appropriate and useful CQs that enhance critical engagement with argumentative text. The implementation details have been provided in the following GitHub repositories[1] for reproducibility purposes.

2 Related Work

CQs are rooted in argumentation schemes that formalize reasoning patterns and associated questions to check assumptions, evidence, and logical consistency (Walton et al., 2008). Computational argumentation CQs assess argument quality and identify fallacies, allowing applications such as educational software (Pinkwart and McLaren, 2012). Corpora such as the Argument Reasoning Comprehension Task (Habernal et al., 2018) and Argument Annotated Essay Corpus (Stab and Gurevych, 2017) support argument mining but rarely include explicit CQs; thus, the CQs-Gen dataset is a new

[1] https://github.com/SM-Shaan/shared-task-critical-questions-generation.

Proceedings of the 12th Argument Mining Workshop, pages 332–339
July 31, 2025

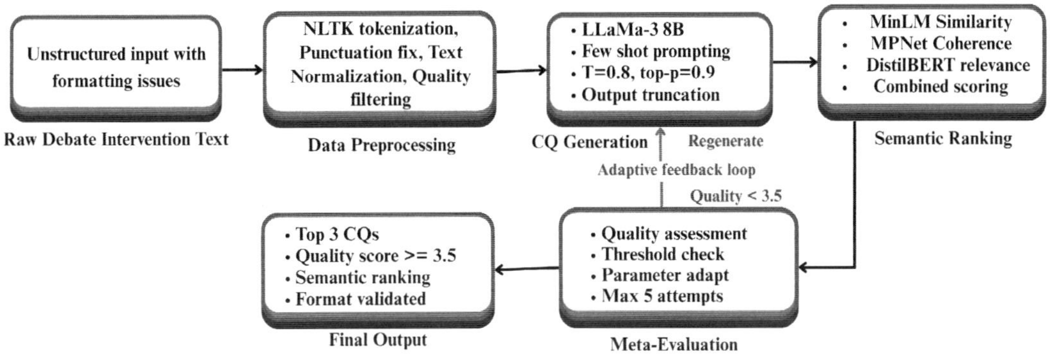

Figure 1: Workflow diagram of our proposed methodology.

contribution. Recent advances in question generation (QG) depend on transformer models to produce controllable questions, such as why-questions and counterfactuals (Cao and Wang, 2021). CQ generation is distinct and must aim at argumentative weaknesses, evaluated using fine-grained metrics such as utility (Scialom et al., 2021). Recent work by (Calvo Figueras and Agerri, 2024) underscores the motivation and challenges of computationally generating critical questions, highlighting the need for systems that produce context-aware, diverse, and argumentatively relevant questions to effectively challenge such claims. This study supplements these studies by employing rationale-augmented prompting and meta-evaluation to enhance the quality of CQs for the CQs-Gen shared task.

3 Dataset Description

The CQs-Gen dataset, as described in (Calvo Figueras and Agerri, 2025), includes debate interventions annotated with argumentation schemes and reference CQs labeled Useful, Unhelpful, or Invalid. Participants were provided with a small development sample and a larger validation set. An overview of the dataset is presented in Table 1. Combining the sample and validation datasets, all the schemes are listed in Figure 2 with their frequencies across the entire dataset.

Set	# Int.	# CQs	% U	% UN	% IN
Sample	6	122	48.36	29.51	22.13
Validation	186	4,136	67.46	21.59	10.95
Test	34	806	42.68	31.02	26.30

Table 1: Statistics of the CQs-Gen dataset.

4 Methodology

In this section, we describe the end-to-end pipeline of our CQs-Gen system, illustrated in Figure 1, organized into five-stage pipeline.

4.1 Data Preprocessing

We begin by normalizing each intervention to ensure well-formed sentence boundaries and punctuation. Raw debate texts often contain line breaks, missing periods, and irregular capitalization, which can confuse the language model. We apply NLTK's sent_tokenize [2] to split the text into sentences, then append a period to any sentence that does not end in one of '.', ';', '!', or '?'. Finally, we recombine the sentences into a single string. This "enhanced_normalize_text" step not only improves downstream tokenization but also maintains a minimum punctuation ratio (default 0.4) to prevent the occurrence of degenerate inputs.

4.2 CQ Generation

Our core generator is a quantized LLaMA-3 (8B, 4-bit GGUF) model. We employ two Appendix B prompts: the Few-Shot Prompt (Short) to support fast generation with few exemplars, and the Structured 3-Q Prompt in order to enforce a strict three-question structure. We sample with temperature $T = 0.8$ and top-$p = 0.9$, truncating at the fourth question indicator ("4.") to ensure three interrogative, numbered items without commentary.

4.3 Post-processing and Validation

The raw model output may contain irrelevant texts or malformed questions. We apply a regular expression (`(?m)^\s*(\d+)\.\s*(.+\?)\s*$`) in multi-

[2] https://www.nltk.org/api/nltk.tokenize.sent_tokenize.html

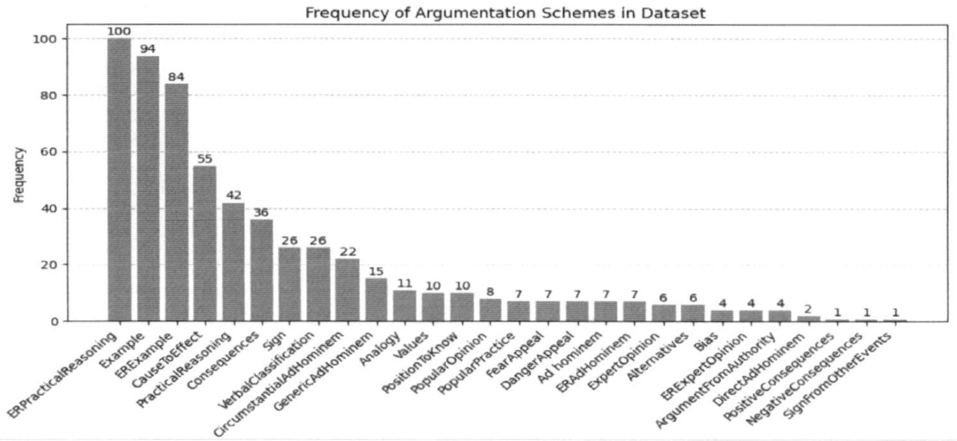

Figure 2: Frequency of argumentation schemes across the full dataset.

line mode to extract lines starting with an integer, followed by a period, and ending with a question mark. If fewer than three questions are found, we split on newlines, retaining only lines ending in a question mark. Each candidate question must have at least six words and be in interrogative form. A heuristic diversity check discards question pairs with a word-overlap ratio above 0.6, promoting varied content.

4.4 Semantic Ranking

To choose the top three questions when more than three pass validation, we embed the intervention and each CQ using three SentenceTransformer models:

- all-MiniLM-L6-v2[3] – measures semantic similarity, ensuring CQs align closely with the intervention's meaning.
- all-mpnet-base-v2[4] – evaluates coherence, assessing the logical clarity of CQs.
- msmarco-distilbert-base-v3[5] – determines relevance, focusing on CQs that target argumentative weaknesses.

We compute the cosine similarities between the intervention embedding and each question embedding and then calculate a weighted sum:

$$\text{score} = 0.4 \times \text{sim} + 0.3 \times \text{coh} + 0.3 \times \text{rel}.$$

Weights were empirically optimized via sensitivity analysis (Section 5.3, Table 3) to prioritize contextual alignment while ensuring clarity and argumentative focus. Then, Questions are sorted by this score, and the top three are retained for final evaluation.

4.5 Adaptive Meta-Evaluation Loop

To further ensure usefulness, we embed a feedback loop: the top three CQs are fed back into the LLaMA-3 (8B, 4-bit) model via a meta-evaluation prompt that asks for a 1–5 rating on how effectively the questions challenge the argument. If the average score is below 3.5 or the heuristic diversity checks (word-overlap ratio >0.6) fail, we adapt the generation parameters—either lowering the temperature by 0.1 (down to 0.5) or switching to the alternate prompt template—and retry up to five attempts. If no set meets the threshold, the highest-scoring set from prior iterations is retained. This loop enhances the relevance and diversity of CQ, addressing the limitations of semantic ranking alone.

Finally, we apply this adaptive pipeline to each intervention in the development or validation sets. The generated CQs (exactly three per intervention) are packaged alongside the intervention metadata into a JSON file conforming to the shared task submission format.

5 Experiments and Results

5.1 Experimental Setup

We evaluated our CQ-Gen pipeline using a quantized LLaMA-3 (8B, 4-bit GGUF) model, DeepHermes-3-Llama-3-8B, which was chosen for

[3] https://huggingface.co/sentence-transformers/all-MiniLM-L6-v2

[4] https://huggingface.co/sentence-transformers/all-mpnet-base-v2

[5] https://huggingface.co/sentence-transformers/msmarco-distilbert-base-v3

its efficiency in few-shot prompting. For the CQs-Gen 2025 shared task, two systems were submitted for testing: DeepHermes-3-Llama-3-8B and TheBloke/Mistral-7B-OpenOrca-GPTQ. In the validation phase, three additional models were evaluated: meta-llama/Llama-2-7b-chat-hf, Zero-Shot LLaMA-3 (as a baseline), and google/flan-t5-large (as baselines). All models were hosted on a 16 GB VRAM GPU. We adopt the shared task's utility-based scoring: each Useful CQ receives 0.33 points, Unhelpful and Invalid receive 0. The per-intervention score is the sum of three questions (max = 1.0).

5.2 Overall Performance

Table 2 lists punctuation-scores for the CQs-Gen task, with test results in Table 4 (similarity metric). DeepHermes-3-Llama-3-8B topped with a validation score of 0.53 and test score of 0.42, surpassing TheBloke/Mistral-7B-OpenOrca-GPTQ (0.46 validation, 0.36 test), meta-llama/Llama-2-7b-chat-hf (0.50 validation), Zero-Shot LLaMA-3 (0.26 validation), and google/flan-t5-large (0.20 validation). In the test phase (similarity metric), it produced 43 Useful, 20 Unhelpful, 32 Not Able to Evaluate, and 7 Invalid CQs, versus Mistral-7B's 37 Useful, 14 Unhelpful, 43 Not Able to Evaluate, and 8 Invalid. Under the manual metric for ACL 2025 CQs-Gen, DeepHermes scored 0.559, with 57 Useful (55.88%), 27 Unhelpful (26.47%), and 18 Invalid (17.65%) CQs ($57 \times 0.33 \approx 0.559$).

Model	Punctuation Score
DeepHermes-3-Llama-3-8B	**0.53**
Mistral-7B-OpenOrca-GPTQ	0.46
meta-llama/Llama-2-7b-chat-hf	0.50
Zero-Shot LLaMA-3	0.26
google/flan-t5-large	0.20

Table 2: Validation results

5.3 Sensitivity Analysis

To justify the semantic ranking weights ($0.4 \times$ sim + $0.3 \times$ coh + $0.3 \times$ rel), we tested alternative configurations and ablations on the dataset, as shown in Table 3.

5.4 Error Analysis

Despite strong overall performance, our system made errors in three key areas (Appendix A): (1) vague questions missing the intervention logic due to fallback or prompt drift, (2) redundant CQs by-

Config	W(Sim, Coh, Rel)	Utility	3 Useful
Original	**(0.3, 0.4, 0.3)**	**0.53**	**61.54%**
Equal	(0.5, 0.25, 0.25)	0.47	53.85%
Sim-Heavy	(0.6, 0.2, 0.2)	0.46	53.84%
No Sim	(0.75, 0.0, 0.25)	0.26	26.67%
No Rel	(0.57, 0.43, 0)	0.2	23.08%

Table 3: Sensitivity analysis for ranking weights.

Model	Test	U	UN	I
DeepHermes-3-Llama-3-8B	**0.42**	**43**	**20**	**7**
Mistral-7B-OpenOrca-GPTQ	0.36	37	14	8

Table 4: Test run results based on similarity metric

passing word-level diversity filters, and (3) misaligned scoring from hallucinated outputs. Future work should explore embedding-based diversity re-ranking and CQs-Gen-aware external judges.

6 Conclusion

We present an adaptive CQs-Gen system using few-shot prompting, semantic ranking, and meta-evaluation to enhance output diversity, relevance, and specificity. Achieving a punctuation score of 0.559 on the ACL 2025 shared task dataset, our system demonstrates the effectiveness of hybrid generation-evaluation loops for argument mining. Future studies will explore rationale-conditioned decoding, structured decoding, and human-in-the-loop refinement.

7 Limitations

Although our system is strong, it suffers from timely sensitivity, considering that the generated quality for important questions largely relies on short, few-shot, well-crafted prompts and thus limits new domain applicability. LLaMA-generated hallucinations during generation and meta-evaluation result in questionable question quality scores. Moreover, the use of iterative generation, multi-model encoding, and meta-evaluation introduces considerable inference time and resources.

References

Blanca Calvo Figueras and Rodrigo Agerri. 2024. Critical questions generation: Motivation and challenges. In *Proceedings of the 28th Conference on Computational Natural Language Learning*, pages 105–116, Miami, FL, USA. Association for Computational Linguistics.

Blanca Calvo Figueras and Rodrigo Agerri. 2025. Benchmarking critical questions generation: A challenging reasoning task for large language models. *arXiv preprint arXiv:2505.11341*.

Blanca Calvo Figueras, Jaione Bengoetxea, Maite Heredia, Ekaterina Sviridova, Elena Cabrio, Serena Villata, and Rodrigo Agerri. 2025. Overview of the critical questions generation shared task 2025. In *Proceedings of the 12th Workshop on Argument Mining (ArgMining 2025)*, Vienna, Austria. Association for Computational Linguistics.

Shuyang Cao and Lu Wang. 2021. Controllable open-ended question generation with a new question type ontology. In *Proceedings of the 59th Annual Meeting of the Association for Computational Linguistics and the 11th International Joint Conference on Natural Language Processing (Volume 1: Long Papers)*, pages 6424–6439, Online. Association for Computational Linguistics.

Ivan Habernal, Henning Wachsmuth, Iryna Gurevych, and Benno Stein. 2018. The argument reasoning comprehension task: Identification and reconstruction of implicit warrants. *Proceedings of NAACL-HLT*.

John Lawrence and Chris Reed. 2019. Argument mining: A survey. *Computational Linguistics*, 45(4):765–818.

Niels Pinkwart and Bruce M. McLaren, editors. 2012. *Educational Technologies for Teaching Argumentation Skills*. Bentham Science Publishers.

Thomas Scialom, Paul-Antoine Dray, Sylvain Lamprier, and 1 others. 2021. Questeval: Summarization asks for fact-based evaluation. *EMNLP*.

Christian Stab and Iryna Gurevych. 2017. Parsing argumentation structures in persuasive essays. *Computational Linguistics*, 43(3).

Douglas Walton, Chris Reed, and Fabrizio Macagno. 2008. *Argumentation schemes*. Cambridge University Press.

A Appendix A: Examples of Error Types in Generated CQs

Error Type	Example (Intervention_CQ ID)	Critical Question (CQ)
Vague or Generic	CLINTON_47 (id 1)	"Were there alternative ways to negotiate or resolve the issue without having to come to an agreement on the terms you disagreed with?"
	CLINTON_47 (id 0)	"Can you provide specific examples of where the terms of the negotiated agreement were not accurate?"
Overlapping or Redundant	Feedback-Commenter_183 (id 0)	"What specific evidence or data supports the claim that airlines treat passengers as a 'nuisance'?"
	Feedback-Commenter_183 (id 2)	"What specific examples or data support the claim that Southwest Airlines is a 'shining example' of how legacy airlines should treat customers?"
Scoring Misalignment	CLINTON_277 (id 1)	"Does Clinton address the potential for voter suppression or other issues that might prevent people from voting?"
	AB_68 (id 2)	"How does the argument define 'domination' in the context of family dynamics, and what criteria are used to determine when intervention is necessary?"

Table 5: Representative Examples of Common CQ Error Types

B Appendix B: Prompt Variations

ID	Prompt Type	Description and Format
1	Basic Prompt	Generate three CQs to challenge the following argument: {text}.
2	Varied 3-Q Prompt	Multiple paraphrased instructions asking for three CQs to reveal fallacies, unsupported claims, and hidden assumptions. Each prompt ends with a numbered list starting from 1.
3	Varied 8-Q Prompt	Similar to Prompt 2, but requests exactly eight CQs. The format and objective remain the same: to highlight weaknesses in reasoning.
4	Few-Shot Prompt (Long)	Includes labeled examples of "Useful" questions and defines what makes CQ effective. Then asks the model to generate at least 5 diverse CQs for a new intervention.
5	Structured 3-Q Prompt	Direct instruction to write exactly three CQs focusing on fallacies, missing evidence, and hidden assumptions. The output must be a numbered list (no explanations).
6	Few-Shot Prompt (Short)	Includes a short example with three questions. Then prompts the model to generate exactly 3 CQs following similar logic with no added explanation.
7	Scheme-Guided Prompt (Walton)	Incorporates our own modified version of Walton's argumentation scheme to guide question generation, ensuring that questions map to specific schemes (see Appendix C).
8	Zero-Shot Prompting	Direct prompt without examples, instructing the model to generate CQs solely based on the instruction.
9	Chain-of-Thought Prompting	Prompts the model to articulate its reasoning process step-by-step before generating CQs, enhancing the depth and transparency.
10	Role-Based Prompting	Specifies a persona or expert role (e.g., "As a Critical thinker…"), steering tone and depth of the generated questions.
11	Iterative Refinement Prompting	Uses previous outputs as feedback to iteratively improve and refine CQs over multiple turns.
12	Dynamic Few-Shot Selection	Automatically selects and rotates few-shot examples based on similarity to the target argument for more tailored prompting.

Table 6: Prompt variations used for CQs-Gen.

C Appendix C: Walton-Style Argumentation Schemes

Argumentation Scheme	Critical Questions
Sign	Is this sign always a reliable indicator of an underlying condition? Could there be alternative explanations for this? Is there evidence that contradicts the suggested interpretation of the sign?
Practical Reasoning	Are there other actions that could achieve the same goal more effectively? What are the potential risks or downsides of taking these actions? Is there strong evidence that this action will lead to the expected outcomes?
Expert Opinion	Are the experts truly qualified in this specific domain? Do the experts have any biases or conflicts of interest? Is the expert's opinion supported by strong evidence?
Danger Appeal	Is the danger real and supported by the evidence? Are there alternative ways to mitigate this danger? Is the warning of danger exaggerated for persuasive effect?
Bias	Does the alleged bias undermine the argument? Can the claim be independently verified? Is the same standard applied to all arguments or just this one?
Popular Opinion	Are people who believe this claim knowledgeable about the topic? Can the claim be supported by objective evidence? Has popular opinion been incorrect on similar issues in the past?
Generic Ad Hominem	Does this attack address the substance of the arguments? Could the personal characteristics of the arguer be irrelevant to the claim itself? Is there independent evidence to support or refute this argument?
Example	Are the examples provided representative of the general case? Could there be counterexamples that weaken this argument? Is there statistical or empirical evidence supporting this claim beyond these examples?
Negative Consequences	Are the predicted negative consequences likely to occur? Is there evidence supporting this cause-and-effect relationship? Could other factors influence the outcome?
Fear Appeal	Is the fear induced proportionate to the actual risk involved? Could the threat be exaggerated to manipulate public opinion? Are there alternative interpretations of the risk that are less alarming?
Verbal Classification	Is the classification accurate and relevant to the argument? Could the labels be misleading or oversimplified? Does the classification obscure the important nuances?
Sign from Other Events	Are the other events sufficiently similar to justify this inference? Could these similarities be coincidental rather than causal? Is there direct evidence linking these events to the condition?
Popular Practice	Does popular practice imply that the practice is correct or effective? Are there cultural or contextual reasons for this practice that might not apply universally? Is this practice supported by empirical evidence?
Consequences	Are the predicted consequences likely to occur? What evidence supports the causal link between the action and its outcomes? Could alternative actions lead to different consequences?
Analogy	Are the two cases truly comparable in terms of relevant aspects? What are the key differences that might undermine this analogy? Is the analogy oversimplifying complex issues?
Circumstantial Ad Hominem	Do the arguer's circumstances actually bias their arguments? Is the argument being dismissed solely on personal circumstances? Can the claim be evaluated independently of the arguer's situation?
Argument from Authority	Is the authority figure truly an expert on the subject? Does the authority provide evidence beyond their status? Can the claim be validated using independent evidence?
Alternatives	Are the alternatives plausible in the given context? What evidence supports these proposed alternatives? Could the original claim still hold despite these alternatives?
Positive Consequences	Are the predicted positive consequences likely to be realized? What evidence supports the link between the action and positive outcomes? Could there be unforeseen negative effects despite positive predictions?
Position to Know	Does the arguer's position guarantee an accurate insight? Could their proximity to the issue bias their perspectives? Is there independent evidence supporting the arguer's claims?

Table 7: Templates of CQs for selected Walton-style argumentation schemes.

COGNAC at CQs-Gen 2025: Generating Critical Questions with LLM-Assisted Prompting and Multiple RAG Variants

Azwad Anjum Islam*, Tisa Islam Erana* and Mark A. Finlayson
Florida International University
Knight Foundation School of Computing and Information Sciences
11200 SW 8th Street, Miami, FL 33199, USA
{aisla028, tisla016, markaf}@fiu.edu

Abstract

We describe three approaches to solving the Critical Questions Generation Shared Task at ArgMining 2025. The task objective is to automatically generate critical questions that challenge the strength, validity, and credibility of a given argumentative text. The task dataset comprises debate statements ("interventions") annotated with a list of named argumentation schemes and associated with a set of critical questions (CQs). Our three Retrieval-Augmented Generation (RAG)-based approaches used in-context example selection based on (1) embedding the intervention, (2) embedding the intervention plus manually curated argumentation scheme descriptions as supplementary context, and (3) embedding the intervention plus a selection of associated CQs and argumentation scheme descriptions. We developed the prompt templates through GPT-4o-assisted analysis of patterns in validation data and the task-specific evaluation guideline. All three of our submitted systems outperformed the official baselines (0.44 and 0.53) with automatically computed accuracies of 0.62, 0.58, and 0.61, respectively, on the test data, with our first method securing the 2nd place in the competition (0.63 manual evaluation). Our results highlight the efficacy of LLM-assisted prompt development and RAG-enhanced generation in crafting contextually relevant critical questions for argument analysis.

1 Introduction

While LLM-based chat interfaces (e.g., ChatGPT, Gemini) provide convenient access to information, they can inadvertently promote superficial learning habits by delivering direct answers and hindering critical thinking. The *Critical Questions Generation (CQs-Gen) Shared Task* (Figueras et al., 2025) addresses this concern by challenging participants to build systems to generate insightful critical questions (CQs) about argumentative texts. Such questions serve to probe the underlying premises and implications of arguments, thereby encouraging deeper engagement and analytical reasoning. These questions are then evaluated based on their strength, relevance, and validity, and are categorized as *Useful*, *Unhelpful*, or *Invalid*.

Our approach to the task includes a series of prompting-based strategies using large language models (LLMs). First, we used a state-of-the-art model (GPT-4o) (OpenAI, 2024a) to analyze the validation data which we used to generate high-quality prompt templates. We then experimented with multiple variants of Retrieval Augmented Generation (RAG) (Lewis et al., 2021) with a smaller, less resource intensive model (GPT-4o-mini) (OpenAI, 2024b). Our RAG-based approaches include (1) few-shot prompting with in-context example selection based on embedding similarity of the interventions, (2) incorporation of manually curated argumentation scheme descriptions as supplementary context to the first approach, and (3) few-shot prompting with in-context example selection based on embedding similarity of the intervention plus a selection of associated CQs and argumentation scheme descriptions. Our experiments showed that these approaches significantly outperformed baseline prompting techniques. Our best-performing system (approach 1) achieved a maximum validation accuracy of 0.83—defined as the proportion of generated questions labeled as useful—and secured second place overall in the official evaluation with a test accuracy of 0.63.

The remainder of the paper is structured as follows. We first provide background on the task of critical question generation and related work on prompt-based and retrieval-augmented approaches (§2). We next describe the dataset and task formulation provided by the shared task organizers (§3).

*The first two authors shared equally in the ideation, implementation, and writing.

Proceedings of the 12th Argument Mining Workshop, pages 340–348
July 31, 2025 ©2025 Association for Computational Linguistics

We then detail our methodology and experimental setup (§4). Section §5 presents the results from our experiments as well as official submissions. Finally, we summarize our contributions and discuss key findings, limitations, and directions for future research (§6).

2 Related Work

The concept of Critical Questions (CQs) comes from argumentation theory, designed to expose the "blind spots" or missing information in an argument by questioning the validity of assumptions and inference (Calvo Figueras and Agerri, 2024). Walton et al.'s work provided a theoretical foundation with a comprehensive catalog of argumentation schemes each accompanied by a set of critical questions. Computational approaches to automatically generating CQs have only been explored in the past few years. Calvo Figueras and Agerri introduced *CQs-Gen* as a new NLP task. They leveraged LLMs to generate questions that dig into the hidden assumptions behind an argument. They built datasets in two ways: using templates from Walton's theory and prompting LLMs to produce critical questions. Their findings showed that only 27% of CQs generated by LLMs were valid in relation to the argumentative texts.

Beyond CQs-Gen, recent advances in LLMs have highlighted the importance of prompt engineering in guiding the model for complex reasoning tasks. Early methods such as Shin et al. (2020) showed that task-specific prompts could be optimized automatically, while more recent work like Zhou et al. (2023) demonstrated that LLMs themselves can iteratively propose and evaluate improved prompts that outperform manually written prompts. Building on this insight, we used a state-of-the-art model (GPT-4o) (OpenAI, 2024a) to analyze validation data and systematically derive better prompt structures for CQs-Gen.

Parallel to prompt development, Retrieval-Augmented Generation (RAG) (Lewis et al., 2021; Gao et al., 2024) has emerged as a powerful framework to enhance LLM performance by conditioning generation in retrieved external knowledge. A RAG framework consists of two steps: retrieval and generation. RAG provides richer context at inference time by retrieving semantically similar examples that are incorporated into the prompt, helping the model generate more relevant critical questions. This aligns with the findings by Zebaze et al. (2024); Liu et al. (2021), who showed that similarity-based in-context example selection can substantially improve LLM outputs in low-resource settings.

3 Shared Task Data

CQs are defined as inquiries that help determine whether an argument is acceptable or problematic by challenging inferences and exposing assumptions (Calvo Figueras and Agerri, 2024). The dataset consists of real debate interventions annotated with argumentation schemes and associated with sets of CQs. The validation set includes 186 interventions, each with 8 to 56 annotated CQs, while the test set comprises 34 interventions with no labeled CQ. Each annotated intervention includes the name of the speaker, annotated argumentation scheme(s), and a set of CQs labeled as:

- **Useful (USE):** The answer to this question can potentially challenge one of the arguments in the text.
- **Unhelpful (UN):** The question is valid, but unlikely to challenge the argument.
- **Invalid (IN):** The question is flawed—unrelated, overly general, or non-critical.

Participating systems were required to generate exactly three CQs per intervention, all intended to be *Useful*. Each CQ is evaluated independently: 0.33 for useful, and 0 for unhelpful or invalid CQs, with three *Useful* CQs achieving a score of 1.

The debate interventions in the validation set were also annotated with argumentation scheme labels such as *Bias*, *AdHominem*, *ArgumentFromAuthority*, etc.. While many of these tags correspond to well-known argumentative structures, no official documentation, list, or definitions were provided as part of the task. The full list of argument structures named in the data is found in Appendix A.

4 Our Approaches

As a baseline system for generating CQs with LLMs, we first developed a simple zero-shot prompt using the information provided on the task description website. The prompt is given in Appendix B. We then used a state-of-the-art LLM model, GPT-4o (OpenAI, 2024a), to analyze and identify the distinguishing characteristics of *Useful* CQs—both in terms of their semantics and syntactic patterns—by feeding it the validation data and the evaluation guidelines using the ChatGPT[1] interface. The prompt used for this step is shown in Appendix C. This step unearthed some key characteristics of *Useful*, *Unhelpful*, and *Invalid* questions, as shown in Table 4 in the Appendix F. We then manually incorporated these insights into a modified prompt template, given in Appendix D. While some of the findings were questionable—such as categorizing *"If...then...?"* style questions as indicative of *Invalid*, while this style of questions also appear as *Useful* in the data—Table 1 shows that including these findings into the prompt resulted in a significant boost in overall performance. This revised prompt template formed the foundation for all our subsequent experiments. Although we used GPT-4o for the purpose of a one-time analysis of the validation data, we conducted the rest of our experiments on a much smaller and less resource-intensive model, GPT-4o-mini (OpenAI, 2024b), due to compute limitations.

4.1 Approach 1: RAG on Interventions Alone

We experimented with few-shot prompting strategies to provide the model with contextual examples of high- and low-quality critical questions. Our baseline setup for a few-shot configuration includes augmenting the prompt with two randomly selected example interventions from the validation data. For each example, we included three random *Useful* CQs as well as one *Unhelpful* and one *Invalid* CQs.

In the first method, for each intervention, we identified the most similar interventions other than itself in the validation set using cosine similarity between intervention embeddings. We computed embeddings using the `stsb-mpnet-base-v2` sentence-transformer model (Reimers and Gurevych, 2019), which is the same model used in the official evaluation script. Note that in this method we only compared embeddings of the interventions, not the associated CQs. In a standard RAG the retrieval step fetches top-k similar documents using cosine similarity over the text embeddings. We experimented with the value of k and found that fetching the top-2 relevant documents performed best (the value of k=2 was optimal for all the methods discussed below as well). We then included these two similar interventions in the prompt as examples, along with three useful, one unhelpful, and one invalid CQs associated with each identified example, selected at random.

4.2 Approach 2: RAG on Interventions plus Argumentation Schemes

In our second method, we experimented with incorporating information about identified argumentation schemes to the selections of the first method. However, the lack of official definitions for the argumentation schemes identified in the validation data was a problem. Thus, we wrote brief descriptions for the argumentation schemes found in the validation dataset using external resources such as Walton (2013), and GPT-4o (OpenAI, 2024a). These descriptions explain the core reasoning behind each scheme and also highlight the types of concerns or weaknesses that a critical question should explore. For instance, we described *Argument from Authority* as "Argument that relies on the credibility of an expert or authoritative figure. Critical questions may examine if the authority cited is credible and relevant." For schemes without an obvious meaning—such as *ERPracticalReasoning*—we approximated their meaning by categorizing them under broader, more familiar scheme types[2]. In this case, *ERPracticalReasoning* was treated as a variant of *Practical Reasoning*. All the argumentation scheme descriptions are provided in Appendix A. We then included the scheme descriptions of the target interventions in the prompt as additional information with the goal of grounding the model in the underlying reasoning structure. However, Table 1 shows that inclusion of argumentation schemes in the prompt did not result in any noticeable improvement.

4.3 RAG on Annotated Examples Alone

Another approach we explored, but which we ultimately did not submit to the competition, was a standard RAG pipeline that retrieves semantically similar examples based on an embedding interventions along with their CQs. To generate embeddings of the documents, we used OpenAI's *text-embedding-3-large* (OpenAI, 2024c) model. Each document in the RAG vector store combines the original intervention with a set of labeled CQs: three *Useful*, one *Unhelpful*, and one *Invalid*, selected at random. We carried out the generation step using the GPT-4o-mini model using the prompt shown in Appendix E.

[1] chat.openai.com

[2] There were four schemes in this category: ERExpertOpinion, ERPracticalReasoning, ERAdHominem and SignFromOtherEvents.

Experiment Setup	Useful	Unhelpful	Invalid	Unable to Evaluate	Score
Baseline prompt	348	85	19	106	0.62
Baseline zero-shot prompting	424	54	43	37	0.76
2-shot prompting with random examples	435	50	32	41	0.78
RAG on interventions alone	**463**	38	23	34	**0.83**
RAG on interventions + argumentation schemes	**452**	55	29	22	**0.81**
RAG on annotated examples alone	440	55	31	32	0.79
RAG on annotated examples + argumentation schemes	**457**	21	29	51	**0.82**

Table 1: Detailed results of our different approaches on the validation dataset

4.4 Approach 3: RAG on Annotated Examples plus Argumentation Schemes

For our final approach, we enhanced the methods outlined in Section 4.3 by incorporating descriptions of the argumentation schemes associated with each target intervention as shown in the prompt template in Appendix E. These descriptions aimed to clarify the reasoning structure and guide the generation of more targeted questions. We formulated the scheme descriptions as detailed in 4.2. This method improved generation quality compared to using annotated examples alone.

5 Evaluation and Results

Automatic evaluation is conducted by comparing each generated question against the set of reference questions for that intervention using a sentence similarity model. If a generated question is sufficiently similar to a labeled reference question based on a predefined similarity threshold, it inherits the corresponding label. The scoring mechanism for different labels is described in Section 3. If no reference exceeds the similarity threshold, the generated question is flagged for manual evaluation.

All experiments described in Section 4 were conducted on the validation dataset, with results summarized in Table 1. Our three best approaches that we submit for official evaluation on the test data are highlighted in bold. These scores are conservative, treating all interventions flagged for manual evaluation as failures. The findings highlight that LLM-assisted prompt development yielded the greatest performance boost, with retrieval-augmented generation providing additional gains.

Table 2 shows the final score of the top-5 teams in the competition along with the distribution of *Useful* (USE), *Unhelpful* (UN), and *Invalid* (IN) CQs after manual evaluation by the task organizers. The results show that all three of our submissions—scoring 0.62, 0.61, and 0.58 with only automatic evaluation—would place in the top-5.

Team	USE	UN	IN	Score
ellisalicante	69	18	15	0.68
COGNAC*	64	24	14	0.**63**
CtCloud	61	25	16	0.60
DayDreamer	60	25	17	0.59
gottfried-wilhelm-leibniz	58	23	20	0.57

Table 2: Official final results on test data (top-5). Our submission is marked with an asterisk(*) symbol

6 Conclusion and Limitation

In this paper, we presented a set of RAG-based approaches for CQs-Gen using LLMs as part of the ArgMining 2025 Shared Task. Our methods focused on creating high-quality prompt using LLM-assisted data analysis and incorporating contextual supervision via retrieval-augmented generation (RAG). We submitted three RAG-based variant systems in the competition, all of which produced competitive performance against other participating systems. Our approach of in-context example selection using semantic similarity on the intervention alone produced the best score (0.63) on the test data and secured second place in the official evaluation.

While our approaches demonstrated strong performance, we acknowledge several limitations. First, our reliance on the validation set for example retrieval may have constrained generalization to novel argument types or schemes underrepresented in the data. This limitation is evident in the significant difference between the validation and test scores. Second, the lack of standardized definitions for argumentation schemes limited the effectiveness of scheme-based guidance. Our manually curated descriptions may not have captured the nuances of each scheme. Lastly, it was not qualitatively evaluated how effectively LLMs could identify the characteristics of different CQ labels. Complete reliance on LLMs at this stage risks overgeneralization.

References

Blanca Calvo Figueras and Rodrigo Agerri. 2024. Critical questions generation: Motivation and challenges. In *Proceedings of the 28th Conference on Computational Natural Language Learning*, pages 105–116, Miami, FL, USA. Association for Computational Linguistics.

Blanca Calvo Figueras, Jaione Bengoetxea, Maite Heredia, Ekaterina Sviridova, Elena Cabrio, Serena Villata, and Rodrigo Agerri. 2025. Overview of the critical questions generation shared task 2025. In *Proceedings of the 12th Workshop on Argument Mining*.

Yunfan Gao, Yun Xiong, Xinyu Gao, Kangxiang Jia, Jinliu Pan, Yuxi Bi, Yi Dai, Jiawei Sun, Meng Wang, and Haofen Wang. 2024. Retrieval-augmented generation for large language models: A survey. *Preprint*, arXiv:2312.10997.

Patrick Lewis, Ethan Perez, Aleksandra Piktus, Fabio Petroni, Vladimir Karpukhin, Naman Goyal, Heinrich Küttler, Mike Lewis, Wen tau Yih, Tim Rocktäschel, Sebastian Riedel, and Douwe Kiela. 2021. Retrieval-augmented generation for knowledge-intensive nlp tasks. *Preprint*, arXiv:2005.11401.

Jiachang Liu, Dinghan Shen, Yizhe Zhang, Bill Dolan, Lawrence Carin, and Weizhu Chen. 2021. What makes good in-context examples for gpt-3? *Preprint*, arXiv:2101.06804.

OpenAI. 2024a. Gpt-4o: An omnimodal ai model. Accessed: 2025-04-02.

OpenAI. 2024b. Gpt-4o mini: Advancing cost-efficient intelligence. Accessed: 2025-04-02.

OpenAI. 2024c. Openai text-embedding-3-large model. Accessed: 2025-04-01.

Nils Reimers and Iryna Gurevych. 2019. Sentence-bert: Sentence embeddings using siamese bert-networks. In *Proceedings of the 2019 Conference on Empirical Methods in Natural Language Processing*. Association for Computational Linguistics.

Taylor Shin, Yasaman Razeghi, Robert L. Logan IV, Eric Wallace, and Sameer Singh. 2020. Autoprompt: Eliciting knowledge from language models with automatically generated prompts. *Preprint*, arXiv:2010.15980.

Douglas Walton. 2013. *Argumentation schemes for presumptive reasoning*. Routledge, New York.

Douglas Walton, Chris Reed, and Fabrizio Macagno. 2008. *Argumentation Schemes*. Cambridge University Press, Cambridge.

Armel Zebaze, Benoît Sagot, and Rachel Bawden. 2024. In-context example selection via similarity search improves low-resource machine translation. *Preprint*, arXiv:2408.00397.

Yongchao Zhou, Andrei Ioan Muresanu, Ziwen Han, Keiran Paster, Silviu Pitis, Harris Chan, and Jimmy Ba. 2023. Large language models are human-level prompt engineers. *Preprint*, arXiv:2211.01910.

A Argumentation Schemes Description

Argumentation Scheme	Description
Example	Relies on specific instances/examples as evidence. Critical questions may ask if examples are representative or sufficient.
CauseToEffect	Draws a causal connection between events. Critical questions may challenge the causal link or suggest alternatives.
PracticalReasoning	Appeals to practical considerations; weighing costs, benefits, or feasibility. Critical questions may ask for evidence that the action will achieve the outcome.
Consequences	Focuses on predicted outcomes. Critical questions may query likelihood, scope, or unintended side effects.
PopularOpinion	Appeals to what is widely believed or done. Critical questions may ask if popular sentiment justifies the claim.
Values	Based on ethical or normative standards. Critical questions may challenge how these values are defined or whether they are universally accepted.
Analogy	Makes a comparison between two cases. Critical questions may ask if the analogy holds and whether differences matter.
Sign	Uses observable indicators as evidence. Critical questions may ask if the sign reliably implies the conclusion.
FearAppeal	Employs threats or fear to persuade. Critical questions may evaluate whether the fear is justified or exaggerated.
DangerAppeal	Uses potential dangers to motivate. Critical questions may examine the realism and evidence behind the danger.
VerbalClassification	Categorizes an issue in a particular way. Critical questions may ask if the classification is appropriate or arbitrary.
ExpertOpinion	Cites expert testimony. Critical questions may scrutinize the credibility and potential bias of the expert.
Bias	Explores prejudices or preconceptions influencing the argument. Critical questions may assess their source and impact.
Alternatives	Suggests the existence of alternatives. Critical questions may ask if alternatives are viable or properly considered.
ERExpertOpinion	An elaborated form of expert opinion. Critical questions may probe the details and context of the expert evidence.
ERPracticalReasoning	An elaborated form of practical reasoning. Critical questions may examine thoroughness and realism.
AdHominem	Attacks the opponent's character instead of addressing the argument. Critical questions may challenge the relevance of the attack.
ERAdHominem	An extended ad hominem attack. Critical questions may examine whether the personal attack detracts from the actual argument.
CircumstantialAdHominem	Attacks based on opponent's circumstances. Critical questions may assess relevance to the argument.
GenericAdHominem	Makes a general personal attack. Critical questions may evaluate relevance to the argument's substance.
DirectAdHominem	A direct personal insult. Critical questions may examine if it distracts from the argument's merits.
NegativeConsequences	Highlights potential harmful outcomes. Critical questions may assess the likelihood and evidential support for these predictions.
PositiveConsequences	Highlights potential beneficial outcomes. Critical questions may examine whether these benefits are realistically attainable.
PositionToKnow	Assumes that holding a certain position grants special insight. Critical questions may assess whether the position truly provides reliable knowledge.
SignFromOtherEvents	Draws parallels between signs observed in different events. Critical questions may challenge whether the comparison is appropriate and meaningful.
ArgumentFromAuthority	Appeals to an authority's credibility to support a claim. Critical questions may evaluate the authority's reliability, expertise, and relevance.
PopularPractice	Bases claims on the commonality of a behavior or practice. Critical questions may examine whether popularity alone justifies the claim.

Table 3: Summary of argumentation schemes and associated critical questioning strategies.

B Baseline Prompt

```
You are a critical thinker. Your task is to generate three critical questions about a political or argumentative text. These questions are meant to help students evaluate the strength, validity, and credibility of the argument.
As an expert, you know that a critical question is a question that challenges the argument – it should make a thoughtful reader pause and reconsider the truth, logic, or assumptions behind the claims.
Now generate three useful critical questions, 20-30 words long, for the following text. Output should be in the format:
CQ: <Critical question>
```

C Prompt for Extracting Validation Set Commonalities

```
You are a smart, intelligent data analyst.
I want you to look through this data and find patterns or characteristics of different types of CQs. What do useful CQs have in common? What makes a CQ unhelpful or invalid? etc.
Focus on both semantic and syntactic characteristics and differences.
Use the guideline PDF for additional insight.

Uploaded files:
<validation.json>
<guidelines.pdf>
```

D Prompt Template

```
You are a critical thinker. Your task is to generate three critical questions about a political or argumentative text. These questions are meant to help students evaluate the strength, validity, and credibility of the argument.
As an expert, you know that a critical question is a question that challenges the argument - it should make a thoughtful reader pause and reconsider the truth, logic, or assumptions behind the claims.
Guidelines:
Your questions should:
> Focus only on claims made in the text.
> Target assumptions, evidence, reasoning, or consequences.
> Be specific - not something that could apply to any text.
> Raise issues that, if left unanswered, weaken the argument.
Avoid questions that:
> Ask for definitions or summaries (reading comprehension).
> Introduce new concepts not mentioned in the text.
> Are too general or vague (e.g., "Is the argument strong?")
> Are too obvious or based on common knowledge.
> Merely expand or support the argument without questioning it.
Good question starters may include:
> What evidence is there that...
> How does the speaker justify...
> Could this lead to unintended consequences?
> Are there reasonable alternatives to...
Avoid questions starting with:
> What is "it"...
> Why is this bad...
> Could you summarize...
> If X, then Y?

For example, for the following text:
<Example intervention>
Useful critical questions may look like:
<Useful Example 1>
<Useful Example 2>
<Useful Example 3>
And unhelpful/invalid questions may look like:
<Unhelpful Example 1>
<Invalid Example 1>[a]

As additional information, here are some suggestions based on the argumentation schemes present in the input text:
<Scheme: Scheme Description>[b]

Generate three useful critical questions, each 20-30 words long, for the following text.
Output should be in the format:
CQ 1: <question 1>
CQ 2: <question 2>
CQ 3: <question 3>
```

[a] Text in light blue is only included for few-shot experimental set-up.

[b] Text in dark blue is only included for the experiment that uses argumentation schemes.

E Prompt Template for RAG

```
You are a critical thinker. Your task is to generate three critical questions about a political or argumentative text. These questions are meant to help students evaluate the strength, validity, and credibility of the argument.
As an expert, you know that a critical question is a question that challenges the argument - it should make a thoughtful reader pause and reconsider the truth, logic, or assumptions behind the claims.
Definition of critical question generation:
Critical question generation involves formulating insightful and challenging questions that encourage deep analysis of a text. These questions should probe assumptions, evaluate evidence, and explore underlying reasoning, thereby fostering a critical engagement with the material.
Guidelines:
Your questions should:
> Focus only on claims made in the text.
> Target assumptions, evidence, reasoning, or consequences.
> Be specific - not something that could apply to any text.
> Raise issues that, if left unanswered, weaken the argument.
Avoid questions that:
> Ask for definitions or summaries (reading comprehension).
> Introduce new concepts not mentioned in the text.
> Are too general or vague (e.g., "Is the argument strong?")
> Are too obvious or based on common knowledge.
> Merely expand or support the argument without questioning it.
Good question starters may include:
> What evidence is there that...
> How does the speaker justify...
> Could this lead to unintended consequences?
> Are there reasonable alternatives to...
Avoid questions starting with:
> What is "it"...
> Why is this bad...
> Could you summarize...
> If X, then Y?

Suggestion based on argumentation schemes:
<Scheme explanations>[a]

Retrieved examples:
<Example interventions and labeled CQs>

Now generate three useful critical questions, 20-30 words long, for the following text.
The output must be a valid JSON string in the following format:
{ "CQ 1": "<Critical question 1>" },
{ "CQ 2": "<Critical question 2>" },
{ "CQ 3": "<Critical question 3>" }
```

[a] Text in dark blue is only included for the experiment that uses argumentation schemes.

F Identifying Characteristics of Different Type of CQs, Extracted by GPT-4o

Category	Key Features	Common Starters
Useful	Targets core claims or reasoning, demands clarification or evidence, explores alternatives, challenges assumptions or generalizations, tightly grounded in argumentation structure, precise and contextual	*How...?, What evidence...?, Could...?, Are there alternatives...?*
Unhelpful	Vague or generic, lacks critical engagement, exploratory tone, restates parts of the argument without probing deeper, often misses logical flaws or assumptions	*Is it true...?, What other...?, Are there...?, Can it be argued...?*
Invalid	Illogical or malformed structure, ambiguous references, speculative beyond the argument's scope, context-insensitive, grammatically or logically flawed, often confusing to interpret	*If... then...?, What is "it"?, Is it practically possible...?*

Table 4: Summary of identifying characteristics of different type of CQs, extracted using GPT-4o.

TriLLaMA at CQs-Gen 2025: A Two-Stage LLM-Based System for Critical Questions Generation

Frieso Turkstra * **Sara Nabhani** * **Khalid Al-Khatib**
University of Groningen
{f.turkstra,s.nabhani,khalid.alkhatib}@rug.nl

Abstract

This paper presents a new system for generating critical questions in debates, developed for the Critical Questions Generation shared task. Our two-stage approach, combining generation and classification, utilizes LLaMA 3.1 Instruct models (8B, 70B, 405B) with zero-/few-shot prompting. Evaluations on annotated debate data reveal several key insights: few-shot generation with 405B yielded relatively high-quality questions, achieving a maximum possible punctuation score of 73.5. The 70B model outperformed both smaller and larger variants on the classification part. The classifiers showed a strong bias toward labeling generated questions as *Useful*, despite limited validation. Further, our system, ranked 6th, outperformed baselines by 3%. These findings stress the effectiveness of large-sized models for question generation and medium-sized models for classification, and suggest the need for clearer task definitions within prompts to improve classification accuracy.

1 Introduction

The ability to critically question arguments is essential for structured reasoning, debate, and discourse analysis. Argumentation schemes, reusable patterns of reasoning, present a systematic framework for constructing sound arguments. Arguments built on these schemes can be critically assessed using targeted questions that reveal hidden assumptions, logical gaps, or weak reasoning. Automating the generation of such critical questions has promising applications in various domains of computational argumentation. Yet, it remains a complex challenge due to the contextual and logical understanding required to produce truly *useful* critiques.

This paper presents a new system for generating critical questions that challenge arguments in real-world debates. The proposed system was submitted to the Critical Questions Generation shared task (Calvo Figueras et al., 2025).[1] The system is based on a two-stage approach involving question generation followed by classification. Evaluation was conducted on a dataset of debate interventions annotated with argumentation schemes and labeled questions (*Useful*, *Unhelpful*, *Invalid*). The usefulness of the generated questions was assessed based on their semantic similarity to reference questions.

The system employs LLaMA 3.1 Instruct models (8B, 70B, 405B) with both zero-shot and few-shot prompting. For generation, few-shot prompting with the 405B model produced reasonable numbers of high-quality questions, highlighting the potential of large models in generating useful critiques. For classification, the 70B model outperformed smaller and larger variants. The classification module showed a strong bias toward labeling the generated questions as *Useful* (75–85%), despite only 44.4% of them being validated as such. Deliberation- and debate-based classification strategies were explored, but simple zero-shot prompting yielded superior performance, indicating that prompt design can be effective, whereas complex reasoning strategies require more careful implementation.

The system ranked 6th in the shared task, outperforming baseline models by 3%. Overall, the findings highlight the effectiveness of medium-sized models with optimized prompts and emphasize the importance of clearer task definitions within prompts to improve classification accuracy.

2 Related Work

Critical questions generation is an emerging task at the intersection of natural language generation and argumentation theory, aimed at producing questions that challenge the reasoning, assumptions, or evidence in argumentative texts. The task is

*Equal contribution.

[1] https://hitz-zentroa.github.io/shared-task-critical-questions-generation/

Proceedings of the 12th Argument Mining Workshop, pages 349–357
July 31, 2025 ©2025 Association for Computational Linguistics

grounded in Walton's argumentation schemes (Walton et al., 2008), which define common structures of arguments and the critical questions used to evaluate them. These theoretical structures were used by Figueras and Agerri (2025) to generate reference critical questions for the task. While effective in producing relevant questions, this method was limited in flexibility and coverage. To complement the theory-based generation, Calvo Figueras and Agerri (2024) also explored the use of two large language models (LLMs), LLaMA-2 and Zephyr (Touvron et al., 2023; Tunstall et al., 2023), to generate critical questions in zero-shot settings. The outputs were then manually reviewed for validity. The results showed that while current LLMs can generate fluent and well-formed questions, they often struggle to produce questions that are truly critical and grounded in the argument. Only 28% of the generated questions were found to be valid, mainly due to issues with relevance, generality, and reasoning.

Beyond argument analysis, several studies examined how critical questions generation can support fact-checking and misinformation detection. For example, Ousidhoum et al. (2022) proposed generating multiple targeted questions from a single claim, each addressing a specific factual aspect such as source credibility, timelines, or implications. Similarly, Setty and Setty (2024) experimented using sequence-to-sequence generative models and LLMs to automate questions generation for fact-checking applications. The results showed improvements in evidence retrieval and verification performance, suggesting that critical questions generation can enhance the effectiveness of claim verification systems. Augenstein et al. (2024) discuss the potential threat of hallucinations and the generation of misinformation when using LLMs for fact-checking. Critical questions generation mitigates this threat by prompting models to question existing claims rather than produce factual knowledge, reducing the risk of hallucinations.

These studies highlight the growing importance of critical questions generation. Yet, current LLM performance and limited resources leave ample room for improvement, especially in generating valid, argument-specific questions.

3 Task Description

In this section, we describe the task goal, data, and the evaluation of system outputs.

Dataset The dataset used for this task is derived from real-world debates, where each data point represents a single speaker's intervention. Interventions are labeled with argumentation schemes following the taxonomy of Walton et al. (2008). In addition to the scheme label, each entry includes a unique identifier and a set of associated critical questions. These questions are labeled for their usefulness in challenging the underlying argument of the intervention. The critical questions are categorized into three labels:

- **Useful**: The question is directly relevant and can effectively challenge an argument in the text.
- **Unhelpful**: The question is reasonable but unlikely to challenge arguments in the text.
- **Invalid**: The question cannot be used to challenge any argument in the text. This may be due to flawed reasoning, lack of relevance, the introduction of unrelated concepts, excessive generality, or a lack of critical focus.

The task includes a validation set and a test set, with 186 and 34 interventions, respectively. The data is provided in JSON format, and can be accessed through the task repository on GitHub.

Task Definition The goal of the task is to generate three critical questions for a given argumentative intervention. These questions should challenge or examine the argument more deeply. The questions can point out missing assumptions, ask for more evidence, or raise possible counterpoints. The main goal is to generate questions that would be considered *Useful* based on the labels in the dataset.

Evaluation The system has to generate three critical questions for each intervention. These questions are evaluated based on their usefulness in challenging the argument in the intervention text. Each *Useful* question gets 0.33 points, while *Unhelpful* and *Invalid* questions get 0 points. The sum of these scores for an intervention is referred to as its *punctuation*. The final system score is calculated as the average punctuation across all interventions in the test set. To evaluate the usefulness of generated questions, each question is compared to a set of reference questions using semantic similarity. The generated question is matched to the most similar reference, and if the similarity score exceeds a threshold of 0.65, it is assigned the label of that reference question. If the score falls below 0.65, the question is labeled as *Not Able to Evaluate*.

Task	Setting	Small	Medium	Large
Gen	Zero-shot	61.5	67.8	66.3
	Few-shot	67.2	66.7	**68.5**
Cls	Zero-shot	58.2	**65.8**	62.4
	Few-shot	60.9	64.4	59.2

Table 1: Validation results for generation (Gen) and classification (Cls) modules. Generation scores use overall punctuation with a similarity threshold of 0.6. Classification scores are binary accuracy.

4 Methodology

We decompose the task of critical questions generation into two subtasks: question generation and question classification. Accordingly, our pipeline is structured into two main modules. The first module takes an argumentative text as input and generates ten critical questions related to it. The second module then classifies these questions into one of three categories: *Useful*, *Unhelpful*, or *Invalid*. The questions are sorted by their usefulness, and the top three questions are selected as the final output.

For each module, we evaluated three models from the LLaMA 3.1 Instruct family: the small (8B), medium (70B), and large (405B) variants. These models were tested across two prompting techniques: zero-shot and few-shot, resulting in six experimental conditions per module. For few-shot prompting, the generation module was provided with three example interventions, each accompanied by one useful critical question. The classification module was given one example intervention with three critical questions, each representing a different category. The validation results for each configuration are presented in Table 1.

The optimal settings for the test set were achieved using few-shot prompting with the large model for question generation and zero-shot prompting with the medium-sized model for classification. The inference parameters were kept consistent across all conditions, with a temperature of 0.5, a maximum generation length of 1024 tokens, and the top_p parameter set to 0.9.

We experimented with two alternative classification strategies: debate and deliberation. These methods redefine the task as a binary classification, where the goal is for multiple models to determine whether each of the ten questions is useful or not. *Debate Classification:* In this approach, two LLMs engage in a traditional debate format. In the opening statement, each model presents the questions it considers useful, along with justifications. Disagreements are addressed during the rebuttal round. The debate concludes with closing statements from both models. Thereafter, a third model, acting as a judge, determines the winner. The final output comprises the questions deemed useful by the winner of the debate. *Deliberation Classification:* This approach involves three LLMs which engage in up to three rounds of deliberation to identify useful questions. In each round, the models can propose a classification, justify their choices, critique others' proposals and collaborate to reach consensus. After the first round, the participants vote on which questions they consider useful. If they unanimously agree on three questions, the deliberation ends. If no agreement is reached, a second round of discussion follows, which ends with a majority vote. If disagreement persists, a third and final round is initiated, after which a judge selects the most useful questions based on the entire deliberation.

The complete set of prompts used in the experiments is provided in Appendix A.

5 Results

Our system ranked 6th out of thirteen participating teams, demonstrating a modest improvement of three percentage points over the baseline scores. The test set results are presented in Table 2. As the question generation module remained consistent across all three submissions, any variation in performance can be attributed solely to differences in the classification modules. The best-performing classifier was LLaMA 3.1 70B Instruct with the zero-shot method, closely followed by the debate-based classification approach. In contrast, the deliberation-based classification yielded significantly lower performance, as a substantial number of questions were labeled as *Not Able to Evaluate*.

The generation module produced ten questions for each of the 34 debate interventions, resulting in 340 generated questions. Out of these, only 180 were included in at least one of the three official submissions. This subset received gold labels during the official evaluation and thus serves as the basis for our assessment of the quality of the generation module. Within this subset, 44.4% of the questions were labeled as *Useful*, 22.8% as *Unhelpful*, and 15% as *Invalid*, while the remaining 17.8% were unable to be evaluated. Assuming a perfect classifier operating on this subset, the maximum

Method	Useful	Unhelpful	Invalid	Not able to evaluate	Score
Zero-shot (Manual)	57	28	16	0	55.9
Zero-shot	55	25	12	9	53.9
Debate	53	26	13	10	52.0
Deliberation	38	22	16	26	37.3

Table 2: Test set results. Scores represent the ratio of achieved punctuation to the maximum possible punctuation. "Manual" indicates that the scoring involved manual evaluation.

achievable punctuation score would be 73.5.

On average, the best classification module labeled 8.4 out of 10 questions as *Useful*, while the debate-based module classified 7.6 out of 10 questions as *Useful*. The debate-based and zero-shot prompt-based modules showed strong alignment, agreeing on 2.6 out of every 3 questions. In contrast, agreement between the deliberation-based approach and the prompt-based or debate-based methods was substantially lower, with agreement scores of 0.9 and 1, respectively. The agreement across all three classifiers was 0.8.

6 Discussion & Analysis

The generation module employed few-shot prompting with the large 405B parameter model. Competitive scores were also achieved by zero-shot prompting the medium-sized model (70B) and few-shot prompting the small model (8B). In particular, scaling from 8B to 405B, a 50-fold increase in model size, resulted in only a 1.3 percent point increase in the overall punctuation score. Such a relatively small gain may not justify the substantial increase in computational cost. Relatedly, no clear benefits of model scaling were observed in the classification module, where the 70B model outperformed both the 8B and 405B models. Interestingly, the small model seemed to benefit from in-context examples in the few-shot setting, while the larger models performed better under zero-shot prompting. This suggests that the smaller model, with less internal world knowledge, gains more from external context than its larger counterparts.

All classifier modules show a strong bias toward labeling questions as *Useful*: 75–85% of generated questions were classified as such, though only 44% were actually validated as useful. This suggests that classifiers often assess surface-level relevance to argumentative text rather than true criticality, struggling to distinguish genuinely critical questions from those merely contextually related. The high number of questions labeled *Unhelpful* supports this. Possible remedies include enriching prompts with more discriminative examples and providing clearer definitions to distinguish the two categories.

Both the debate and deliberation approaches failed to outperform the zero-shot prompting. We initially hypothesized that the structured discussion would guide the model's reasoning and improve overall performance. If anything, the debate and deliberation formats simply allowed the models to generate more tokens, which by itself could potentially lead to better results. However, our error analysis showed two areas for improvement. First, prompt complexity posed a challenge: the models occasionally lost track of their position within the debate or deliberation and failed to consider their opponent's responses. Second, the models attempted to discuss all ten questions simultaneously, preventing them from engaging with the arguments beyond a surface level. Both limitations may be addressed by improvements to the current implementation, e.g. by structuring discussions around a single intervention and question and refining the prompts to enhance flow awareness. With these adjustments, the underlying approaches still hold potential for improving classification performance.

7 Conclusion

This paper presents our two-stage system for critical questions generation, developed for the shared task using LLaMA 3.1 Instruct models. The system ranked 6th, outperforming the baseline. Key challenges include classifier bias toward labeling questions as *Useful* and limited benefits from scaling or complex reasoning. Future work will refine prompt and interaction design to support robust debate and deliberation, including prompts based on argumentation schemes and improved focus on addressing each question individually.

Acknowledgments

This work was partially supported by the AKASE third-party project under the OpenWebSearch.eu project. The OpenWebSearch.eu project is funded by the EU under Grant Agreement No. 101070014, and we thank the EU for their support.

References

Isabelle Augenstein, Timothy Baldwin, Meeyoung Cha, Tanmoy Chakraborty, Giovanni Luca Ciampaglia, David Corney, Renée DiResta, Emilio Ferrara, Scott Hale, Alon Halevy, Dirk Hovy, Heng Ji, Filippo Menczer, Rafael Miguez, Preslav Nakov, Dietram Scheufele, Sapna Sharma, and Giorgio Zagni. 2024. Factuality challenges in the era of large language models and opportunities for fact-checking. *Nature Machine Intelligence*, 6(8):852–863.

Blanca Calvo Figueras and Rodrigo Agerri. 2024. Critical questions generation: Motivation and challenges. In *Proceedings of the 28th Conference on Computational Natural Language Learning*, pages 105–116, Miami, FL, USA. Association for Computational Linguistics.

Blanca Calvo Figueras, Jaione Bengoetxea, Maite Heredia, Ekaterina Sviridova, Elena Cabrio, Serena Villata, and Rodrigo Agerri. 2025. Overview of the critical questions generation shared task 2025. In *Proceedings of the 12th Workshop on Argument Mining (ArgMining 2025)*, Vienna, Austria. Association for Computational Linguistics.

Banca Calvo Figueras and Rodrigo Agerri. 2025. Benchmarking critical questions generation: A challenging reasoning task for large language models. *Preprint*, arXiv:2505.11341.

Nedjma Ousidhoum, Zhangdie Yuan, and Andreas Vlachos. 2022. Varifocal question generation for fact-checking. In *Proceedings of the 2022 Conference on Empirical Methods in Natural Language Processing*, pages 2532–2544, Abu Dhabi, United Arab Emirates. Association for Computational Linguistics.

Ritvik Setty and Vinay Setty. 2024. Questgen: Effectiveness of question generation methods for fact-checking applications. In *Proceedings of the 33rd ACM International Conference on Information and Knowledge Management*, CIKM '24, page 4036–4040. ACM.

Hugo Touvron, Louis Martin, Kevin Stone, Peter Albert, Amjad Almahairi, Yasmine Babaei, Nikolay Bashlykov, Soumya Batra, Prajjwal Bhargava, Shruti Bhosale, Dan Bikel, Lukas Blecher, Cristian Canton Ferrer, Moya Chen, Guillem Cucurull, David Esiobu, Jude Fernandes, Jeremy Fu, Wenyin Fu, and 49 others. 2023. Llama 2: Open foundation and fine-tuned chat models. *Preprint*, arXiv:2307.09288.

Lewis Tunstall, Edward Beeching, Nathan Lambert, Nazneen Rajani, Kashif Rasul, Younes Belkada, Shengyi Huang, Leandro von Werra, Clémentine Fourrier, Nathan Habib, Nathan Sarrazin, Omar Sanseviero, Alexander M. Rush, and Thomas Wolf. 2023. Zephyr: Direct distillation of lm alignment. *Preprint*, arXiv:2310.16944.

Douglas Walton, Chris Reed, and Fabrizio Macagno. 2008. *Argumentation Schemes*. Cambridge University Press, New York.

A Prompts

Model-specific tokens have been replaced with simpler tags to improve readability. The few-shot tags indicate the additional context with regards to the zero-shot prompt. Placeholder values are marked using double curly brackets.

A.1 Question Generation Prompt

<system>You are a critical thinker who asks critical questions to evaluate the validity and soundness of arguments. Critical questions are designed to uncover the underlying assumptions and scrutinize the reasoning process of an argument. Read the given paragraph carefully and generate a set of critical questions that challenge the premises, assumptions, and inferences made in the argument. Respond with the critical questions directly, without any preamble or explanation. Ensure your questions are probing and insightful to thoroughly assess the argument's acceptability or potential fallacies. Answer as accurately and critically as possible!</system>

<fewshot>
<user>TRUMP: "A lot of people even within my own party want to give certain rights to people on watch lists and no-fly lists. I agree with you. When a person is on a watch list or a no-fly list. These are very, very good people. They're protecting the Second Amendment. I have the endorsement of the NRA. I'm very proud of. We have to look very strongly at no-fly lists and watch lists. When people are on there, even if they shouldn't be on there, we'll help them, we'll help them legally, we'll help them get off. I tend to agree with that quite strongly. You were the one that brought up the words super-predator about young black youth. That's a term that I think was a—it's—it's been horribly met. You've apologized for it."</user>

<assistant>What are the potential consequences of removing people from watch lists and no-fly

lists without proper vetting, and how would Trump mitigate these risks?</assistant>

<user>HOLT: "We're talking about the burden that Americans have to pay, yet you have not released your tax returns. The reason nominees have released their returns for decades is so that voters will know if their potential president owes money to—who he owes it to and any business conflicts. Don't Americans have a right to know if there are any conflicts of interest?"</user>

<assistant>How would releasing tax returns guarantee that voters would be aware of all potential conflicts of interest, considering that tax returns may not reveal all relevant information?</assistant>

<user>CLINTON: "In fact, his cavalier attitude about nuclear weapons is so deeply troubling. That is the number-one threat we face in the world. It becomes particularly threatening if terrorists ever get their hands on any nuclear material."</user>

<assistant>What specific actions or policies has Clinton's opponent proposed or supported that demonstrate a "cavalier" attitude towards nuclear weapons?</assistant>
</fewshot>

<user>Generate critical questions for this text: {{intervention}}. For the output, print only the top 10 questions generated with each question on a separate line without numbering.</user>

A.2 Question Classification Prompt

<system>You are a critical thinker whose task is to evaluate and classify critical questions. Read the given critical questions carefully and classify them into three categories: useful, unhelpful, or invalid. Follow these definitions:

1. Useful question: One should not take the arguments in the text as valid without having reflected on this question.

2. Unhelpful question: The question makes sense, is related to the text, and in some exceptional cases, the answer could invalidate or diminish the validity of the arguments in the text, but this is unlikely. This may be in cases where:
   (a) The answer to the question is common sense.
   (b) The answer to the question is a well-known fact that does not generate controversy.
   (c) The question is very complicated to understand, and it would be impractical to question the arguments.
   (d) The question is answered in the text itself.

3. Invalid question: A question is invalid when the answer to this question cannot serve to invalidate or diminish the acceptability of the arguments in the text. This can be for several reasons:
   (a) Unrelated: The question is unrelated to the text.
   (b) New concept: The question introduces new concepts that were not in the text.
   (c) Bad reasoning: The question does not challenge any argument defended in the text. For example, when the question challenges the opposite position to the one defended in the text.
   (d) Very general: The question is very vague and does not ask about anything specific in the text. This question could be asked of any argument.
   (e) Non-critical: Although the question asks about something in the text, it is not critical of any argument. For example, when the question is a reading-comprehension one. A question is only critical if the answer to the question can potentially reduce the validity of the argument.

Provide only the predicted labels in the format of a valid Python list of strings, without any preamble or explanation.</system>

<fewshot>
<user>TRUMP: "A lot of people even within my own party want to give certain rights to people on watch lists and no-fly lists. I agree with you. When a person is on a watch list or a no-fly list. These are very, very good people. They're protecting the Second Amendment. I have the endorsement of the NRA. I'm very proud of. We have to look very strongly at no-fly lists and watch lists. When people are on there, even if they shouldn't be on

there, we'll help them, we'll help them legally, we'll help them get off. I tend to agree with that quite strongly. You were the one that brought up the words super-predator about young black youth. That's a term that I think was a—it's—it's been horribly met. You've apologized for it." Questions:

- How does Trump's stance on watch lists and gun control align with his broader views on national security and individual rights?
- What are the potential consequences of removing people from watch lists and no-fly lists without proper vetting, and how would Trump mitigate these risks?
- What are the potential consequences of restricting gun ownership based on watch lists or no-fly lists, and are they justified by the potential benefits?

</user>

<assistant>["Invalid", "Useful", "Unhelpful"]</assistant>
</fewshot>

<user>Classify the following critical questions: {{questions}}</user>

A.3 Debate Prompts

Each round uses a different user prompt but they all share the same system prompt, as defined in A.3.1.

A.3.1 System Prompt

General Instructions
You are an expert debater tasked with critically analyzing a set of questions related to an argument. Your role is to determine whether each question is Useful, Unhelpful, or Invalid for evaluating the validity and acceptability of the argument.

Definitions

1. Useful question: A question that must be reflected upon, as failing to consider it could lead to accepting a potentially fallacious argument.
2. Unhelpful question: A question that is related to the argument but unlikely to invalidate or diminish its validity, often because:
   (a) The answer is common sense or a well-known fact.
   (b) The question is overly complicated or impractical.
   (c) The question is already answered in the argument text.
3. Invalid question: A question that cannot serve to invalidate or diminish the acceptability of the argument, due to reasons such as:
   (a) Being unrelated to the argument.
   (b) Introducing new, unmentioned concepts.
   (c) Exhibiting faulty reasoning or challenging the opposite position.
   (d) Being too vague or general.
   (e) Being a simple reading comprehension question rather than a critical one.

A.3.2 Opening Statement Prompt

Task
You will be provided with:

1. An argument text or context.
2. A set of 10 critical questions related to the argument.
3. (Optional) An opening statement from an opposing debater.

Your task is to analyze each of the 10 critical questions and provide an opening statement arguing whether each question is Useful, Unhelpful, or Invalid for evaluating the argument's validity and acceptability.

Argument and critical questions (and optionally, the opposing opening statement):
{{context}}

Now, provide your opening statement analyzing each critical question as Useful, Unhelpful, or Invalid, and provide arguments for your decisions.

A.3.3 Rebuttal Prompt

Task: Provide a concise rebuttal to the opponent's arguments in the given debate context.

Instructions:

1. Read the debate context carefully to understand the arguments made by both sides.
2. Identify weaknesses, logical fallacies, or inconsistencies in the opponent's case.

3. Formulate a rebuttal that directly responds to and challenges the opponent's previously stated points.

4. Do not introduce any new arguments or claims. Focus solely on critiquing the opponent's existing arguments.

5. Keep the rebuttal concise and to-the-point, without unnecessary elaboration.

Context:
{{context}}

Rebuttal:

A.3.4 Closing Statement Prompt

Task: Summarize the given debate context and provide a concise closing statement reinforcing your main arguments.

Context:
{{context}}

Closing Statement Guidelines:

1. Read and understand the full debate context provided above.

2. Identify the key arguments and evidence presented in support of your position.

3. Summarize those main points concisely in 1-2 sentences.

4. Reinforce why your arguments are stronger and more persuasive than the opposing side.

5. The closing statement should be a brief but impactful conclusion aimed at convincing the audience/judges that you should win the debate.

A.3.5 Judge Prompt

Instruction
You are a judge in a traditional 1v1 debate. Your role is to critically assess proposals on the classification of ten critical questions by evaluating the arguments and rebuttals to ensure robust decision-making. Follow these steps:

1. Parse the input discussion to identify premises, conclusions, and argument structure.

2. Map the argument to one of Walton's argumentation schemes (e.g., expert opinion, analogy, cause-effect).

3. For the identified scheme, apply its specific critical questions (e.g., "Is the expert credible?" for expert opinion scheme).

4. Highlight any missing premises, weak evidence, or fallacies in the argument.

5. Provide a structured critique of the argument (e.g., "This argument assumes X but lacks evidence for Y").

6. Determine the winning side based on logic, evidence and persuasion.

Context
{{context}}

Output Format
Provide your response as a Python list containing the numbers of the sentences that, according to the winner, are Useful, without any preamble or additional information.

A.4 Deliberation Prompts

A.4.1 General Prompt

<system>### Instruction
You are an expert deliberator tasked with critically analyzing a set of questions related to an argument. Your role is to determine, together with another deliberator, whether each question is Useful, Unhelpful, or Invalid for evaluating the validity and acceptability of the argument.

Definitions

1. Useful question: A question that must be reflected upon, as failing to consider it could lead to accepting a potentially fallacious argument.

2. Unhelpful question: A question that is related to the argument but unlikely to invalidate or diminish its validity, often because:

   (a) The answer is common sense or a well-known fact.

   (b) The question is overly complicated or impractical.

   (c) The question is already answered in the argument text.

3. Invalid question: A question that cannot serve to invalidate or diminish the acceptability of the argument, due to reasons such as:

(a) Being unrelated to the argument.
(b) Introducing new, unmentioned concepts.
(c) Exhibiting faulty reasoning or challenging the opposite position.
(d) Being too vague or general.
(e) Being a simple reading comprehension question rather than a critical one.

</system>

<user>### Context
{{context}}

Actions
<propose> Generate clear and concise proposals aligned with the core objectives of the deliberation. Present your proposals in a well-structured way. </propose>

<argue> Build arguments to support your proposals that are grounded in the definitions of the types of questions. Ensure your arguments are logical, well-structured, and clear. </argue>

<counter> Address critiques from other deliberators by acknowledging weaknesses, updating proposals, or offering compromises. Respond respectfully and constructively, demonstrating openness to refinement and collaboration. </counter>

<collaborate> Engage with critiques from other agents, stress-test ideas, and work towards aligning priorities. Actively participate in the discussion, considering different perspectives and fostering a shared understanding. </collaborate>

Guidelines

- Engage directly with critiques from the other Deliberator (e.g., "To address your concern about X, we could...").
- Prioritize brevity: Avoid repetition and focus on key trade-offs and innovations.
- Signal resolution or deadlock clearly.

Provide your response immediately without any preamble or additional information:</user>

A.4.2 Label Extraction Prompt

Instruction
Analyze the provided deliberation between two deliberators who aimed to determine the usefulness, unhelpfulness, or invalidity of questions. Your task is to identify the final labels assigned by each deliberator to each question after their discussion.

Deliberation
{{deliberation}}

Output Format
Provide your response as two valid Python dictionaries, one for each deliberator, with the following structure: ["1": "[label]", "2": "[label]", ..., "10": "[label]"] Replace [label] with one of the following values for each question number from 1 to 10:

- "Useful"
- "Unhelpful"
- "Invalid"

Do not include any additional text or explanation. Return only the two Python dictionaries separated by a comma, without any preamble or additional information.

Overview of MM-ArgFallacy2025 on Multimodal Argumentative Fallacy Detection and Classification in Political Debates

Eleonora Mancini[1*], Federico Ruggeri[1], Serena Villata[2], Paolo Torroni[1]

[1]DISI, University of Bologna
{e.mancini, federico.ruggeri6, p.torroni}@unibo.it
[2]Université Côte d'Azur, Inria
serena.villata@inria.fr

Abstract

We present an overview of the MM-ArgFallacy2025 shared task on Multimodal Argumentative Fallacy Detection and Classification in Political Debates, co-located with the 12th Workshop on Argument Mining at ACL 2025. The task focuses on identifying and classifying argumentative fallacies across three input modes: text-only, audio-only, and multimodal (text+audio), offering both binary detection (AFD) and multi-class classification (AFC) subtasks. The dataset comprises 18,925 instances for AFD and 3,388 instances for AFC, from the MM-USED-Fallacy corpus on U.S. presidential debates, annotated for six fallacy types: Ad Hominem, Appeal to Authority, Appeal to Emotion, False Cause, Slippery Slope, and Slogan. A total of 5 teams participated: 3 on classification and 2 on detection. Participants employed transformer-based models, particularly RoBERTa variants, with strategies including prompt-guided data augmentation, context integration, specialised loss functions, and various fusion techniques. Audio processing ranged from MFCC features to state-of-the-art speech models. Results demonstrated textual modality dominance, with best text-only performance reaching 0.4856 F1-score for classification and 0.34 for detection. Audio-only approaches underperformed relative to text but showed improvements over previous work, while multimodal fusion showed limited improvements. This task establishes important baselines for multimodal fallacy analysis in political discourse, contributing to computational argumentation and misinformation detection capabilities.

1 Introduction

This paper presents an overview of MM-ArgFallacy2025: multimodal argumentative fallacy detection and classification on political debates; the task is organized for the first time.

In the past decade, several studies have highlighted the importance of Argument Mining on semantic textual analysis, leading to a broad set of applications, including legal analytics, social media, and biomedicine, to name a few. However, past research has also theorized the importance of including paralinguistic features in argumentative discourse analysis to capture additional dynamics that cannot be extracted from text alone. Consequently, Multimodal Argument Mining (MAM) emerged, aiming to validate these propositions empirically and gain a more comprehensive understanding of argumentative discourse by integrating multiple modalities. So far, core argument mining tasks like argument detection, component classification, and relation classification have been mainly explored, where the integration of audio modality has proved to be effective. Recently, other tasks like fallacy detection and classification have been investigated in the context of MAM, but they are still underexplored.

MM-ArgFallacy2025[1] aims to advance research in this latter area by providing a platform for the development and the evaluation of systems capable of detecting and classifying argumentative fallacies using different modalities. Specifically, MM-ArgFallacy2025 challenges participants to distinguish whether a given sentence from a political debate contains an argumentative fallacy and, if any, which type of logical inconsistency is observed. This research is crucial for advancing NLP technologies and accelerating adoption for user benefit, contributing to the development of systems for aiding users in knowledge acquisition and awareness of controversial topics, consistent with AM contributions in social media (Dusmanu et al., 2017; Lytos et al., 2019) and debates (Carstens et al., 2014; Swanson et al., 2015; Haddadan et al., 2019).

[1]https://nlp-unibo.github.io/mm-argfallacy/2025/

Proceedings of the 12th Argument Mining Workshop, pages 358–368
July 31, 2025 ©2025 Association for Computational Linguistics

With the integration of audio modality, we enrich the spectrum of available features for studying human fallacies, fostering the development of more accurate models. We build on existing work and focus on the political debates, where argumentative content and reasoning fallacies are abundant. The task concerns two sub-tasks: detecting argumentative fallacious sentences and classifying them. We follow (Mancini et al., 2022) and consider three input modes in each sub-task for assessing individual modalities in addition to the multimodal setting: **text-only**, where only an input textual sentence from a political debate dialogue is provided; **audio-only**, where only an audio sample corresponding to a textual sentence from a political debate dialogue is provided; **text-audio**, where an input textual sentence from a political debate dialogue and its aligned audio sample are provided.

We evaluate the participating systems based on binary F1 score for fallacy detection and macro-averaged F1 score for fallacy classification. The latter metric balances precision and recall across fallacious categories, ensuring a fair assessment of system performance. The task's comprehensive evaluation framework, coupled with the diverse multimodal datasets, provides a rigorous benchmark for advancing the state-of-the-art in MAM and, in particular, in multimodal fallacy recognition.

In the rest of the paper, we offer an overview of MM-ArgFallacy2025, detailing the datasets, the evaluation measures, and the submission guidelines. We also present the results and the methodologies of the participating systems, highlighting the progress and the challenges when developing robust MAM solutions. By fostering collaboration and innovation in this critical area, MM-ArgFallacy2025 contributes to the broader goal of enhancing the reliability of automated content analysis in the digital age.

2 Related Work

The study of fallacies is deeply rooted in argumentative theory, which dates back to Aristotle [2]. The utility of recognizing and studying fallacies mainly emerged in the '70-80s (Hamblin, 2022). Moreover, fallacy detection is directly related to human reasoning, where communication can often degenerate into conflicts, disagreements, and debates due to logical fallacies in discourse (Jin et al., 2022). Detecting and classifying fallacies in discourse is a valuable tool in several applications, including analyzing human behavior in dialogical settings, preventing misinformation spread in fact-checking systems, and evaluating generative models' reasoning. Research on fallacy detection and classification is not limited to text analysis, but could encompass other modalities too, such as audio, where paralinguistic features can often be associated with specific fallacy types (Kišiček, 2020a).

Research on the interplay between arguments and emotions in speech began with Benlamine et al. (Benlamine et al., 2015). Subsequently, further studies focused on multimodality in argumentation, showing the correlation of paralinguistic features with argumentative discourse in various domains, including advertisements, news coverage, and legal analytics (Kišiček, 2014; Groarke and Kišiček, 2018; Kišiček, 2020b). These findings led to the development of Multimodal Argument Mining (MAM), where Lippi and Torroni (2016) conducted the first study in political debates, focusing on UK ministerial elections but limited to a single debate.

Interest in political debates motivated further research for argumentative tasks like argument component detection and classification (Haddadan et al., 2019), argumentative fallacy classification (Goffredo et al., 2022a, 2023), and argumentative relation identification (Mestre et al., 2023). Recent work has particularly focused on multimodal approaches to these argumentative tasks in political contexts (Mancini et al., 2022, 2024b; Mestre et al., 2023).

3 Problem Formulation

MM-ArgFallacy2025's subtasks are formulated as follows.

Argumentative Fallacy Detection (AFD). The input is a sentence, in the form of text or audio or both, extracted from a political debate. The objective is to determine whether the input contains an argumentative fallacy.

Argumentative Fallacy Classification (AFC). The input is a sentence, in the form of text or audio or both, extracted from a political debate, containing a fallacy. The objective is to determine the type of fallacy contained in the input, according to the classification introduced by (Goffredo

[2] https://plato.stanford.edu/entries/fallacies/

Snippet	Fallacy Category
the same kind of woolly thinking	Appeal to Emotion
As George Will said the other day, "Freedom on the march; not in Russia right now."	Appeal to Authority
Governor Carter apparently doesn't know the facts.	Ad Hominem
We won the Cold War because we invested and we went forward.	False Cause
And if we don't act today, the problem will be valued in the trillions.	Slippery Slope
We have to practice what we preach.	Slogan

Table 1: Examples of annotated fallacies.

et al., 2022a).[3] In particular, the fallacy categories are: Appeal to Emotion, Appeal to Authority, Ad Hominem, False Cause, Slippery Slope, and Slogan. Table 1 reports examples of each fallacy category.

For each sub-task, participants can leverage the debate context of a given input: all its previous sentences and corresponding aligned audio samples. For instance, consider the **text-only** input setting. Given a sentence from a political debate at index i, participants can use sentences with indexes from 0 to $i-1$, where 0 denotes the first sentence in the debate.

4 Data

We describe the available training data for the challenge and the data collection process to curate the test set used to evaluate participants' submissions in the challenge (hereinafter, denoted as **secret test set**). All datasets are made available through MAMKit (Mancini et al., 2024a)[4]. Since most of these multimodal datasets cannot release audio samples for copyright reasons, MAMKit provides a simple interface to dynamically build them and foster reproducible research.

4.1 Training Data

The primary training dataset is **MM-USED-fallacy** (Mancini et al., 2024b). The data provides annotations for AFC and AFD subtasks. The dataset comprises 1,228 fallacies with corresponding context information from the dataset of (Haddadan et al., 2019) on US presidential elections. The fallacies are labeled as argumentative fallacies belonging to six categories introduced in (Goffredo et al., 2022a). Additionally, inspired by (Goffredo et al., 2022a)'s observations on the benefits of employing other argument mining tasks like component detection for fallacy detection and classification, participants could use the following datasets to encourage multi-task training approaches (see Table 2 for a summary).

UKDebates (Lippi and Torroni, 2016). A dataset of 386 sentences and corresponding audio samples about three candidates for the UK Prime Ministerial elections of 2015. Sentences are annotated for argumentative sentence detection: a sentence is labeled as containing or not containing a claim.

M-Arg (Mestre et al., 2021a). A multimodal dataset built around the 2020 US Presidential elections for argumentative relation classification: a sentence can attack, support, or have no relation with another sentence. The dataset contains 4,104 sentence pairs and corresponding audio sequences of four candidates and a debate moderator concerning 18 topics. A high-quality subset of M-Arg is also provided, containing 2,443 sentence pairs with high agreement confidence.

MM-USED (Mancini et al., 2022). A multimodal extension of the USElecDeb60to16 dataset introduced in (Haddadan et al., 2019). It contains presidential candidates' debate transcripts and corresponding audio recordings aired from 1960 to 2016. The dataset contains 26,781 labeled sentences and corresponding audio samples from 39 debates and 26 distinct speakers for argumentative sentence detection and argumentative component classification: a sentence can contain a claim, a premise, or neither of them.

Text to Audio Alignment Corrections. Compared to the initial release of MAMKit (Mancini et al., 2024a), we introduce an improved text-to-audio alignment framework based on WhisperX (Bain et al., 2023), a state-of-the-art speech recognition model that allows for precise and fine-grained audio-to-text alignment. We use this framework to address some well-known alignment issues in MM-USED (Mancini et al., 2022) and MM-USED-fallacy (Mancini et al., 2024b), allowing to integrate previously discarded debates and favouring the collecting of novel data (4.2). The updated datasets are available through MAMKit.

[3]We only refer to macro categories while sub-categories are left for future work.

[4]https://nlp-unibo.github.io/mamkit/

Name	No. Samples	Task[α]	Domain
Primary			
MM-USED-fallacy	18,925; 3,338	AFD; AFC	US Presidential Elections
Supplementary			
UKDebates	386	ASD	UK Prime Ministerial Elections
M-ARG	4,104 / 2,443	ARC	US Presidential Elections
MM-USED	26,781	ASD, ACC	US Presidential Elections

Table 2: Available datasets for MM-ArgFallacy2025 shared task.
[α]Following (Mancini et al., 2024a), we denote tasks as Argumentative Fallacy Detection (AFD), Argumentative Fallacy Classification (AFC), Argumentative Sentence Detection (ASD), Argumentative Relation Classification (ARC), Argumentative Component Classification (ACC).

4.2 Test Data

Data Collection. We collect and annotate novel debates from US politics available in The American Presidency Project[5]. In particular, we consider the first presidential debate of the election cycle in Atlanta between Trump and Biden, aired on 28th June 2024, and the first presidential debate between Trump and Harris, aired on 11 September 2024. We follow the data collection pipeline proposed by Mancini et al. (2022) to retrieve original audio recordings, but improve the text-to-audio alignment by leveraging WhisperX (Bain et al., 2023) for transcription, alignment and diarization. We follow Goffredo et al. (2022a) and split debates into paragraphs, where each paragraph corresponds to a speaker turn. We use our text-to-audio alignment framework to pair paragraphs and corresponding textual sentences with related audio chunks. In total, we obtain 134 paragraphs for the first debate and 163 for the second one.

Data Annotation. For the annotation, we instruct two annotators with expertise in AM tasks and near-to-native English proficiency. We provide annotators with the guidelines of Goffredo et al. (2022a) for detecting and classifying argumentative fallacies. This is required to ensure annotation consistency with existing datasets (e.g., MM-USED-fallacy). We remove paragraphs (i.e., dialogue turns) that do not belong to the main speakers of the debate (i.e., Trump, Biden and Harris). In total, we obtain 154 paragraphs for annotation, equivalent to 2154 sentences. We rely on Label Studio[6] for annotation, an open-source data annotation platform. For AFD and AFC subtasks, we provide annotators with the same instructions described in Section 3. In particular, for AFD, annotators label each sentence in a given paragraph from a debate as containing a fallacy. In case an annotator labels a sentence as fallacious, they also provide the corresponding logical fallacy category to address AFC subtask.

Inter-Annotator Agreement. Since fallacies can span multiple sentences (Goffredo et al., 2022a), we report the rate of exact and partial overlaps between annotations. An exact overlap is when both annotators agree on all sentences constituting a fallacy. In contrast, a partial overlap is when annotators agree on a subset of sentences constituting a fallacy. We observe 236 overlaps, 110 of which are exact, while the remaining 126 are partial. The agreement rate measured as the number of sentences detected as fallacious of the same category by both annotators is 67.37%. Moreover, we compute inter-annotator agreement (IAA) at sentence level, measured as Cohen's Kappa (Cohen, 1968). For AFD, the IAA is 0.4787 (*moderate agreement*), while, for AFC, the IAA is 0.4954 (*moderate agreement*). Additionally, regarding AFC, the per category IAA is as follows: 0.411 Appeal to Emotion, 0.337 Appeal to Authority, 0.357 Ad Hominem, 0.224 False Cause, and 0.712 Slogan. No annotator labeled a fallacy instance as Slippery Slope.

Resulting Dataset. Table 3 reports the statistics of the resulting secret test set. We observe that a large majority of fallacies belong to Appeal to Emotion, followed by Ad Hominem. These findings are in line with annotations reported in previous work on argumentative fallacy classification (Goffredo et al., 2022a). Regarding AFD, the collected secret test set contains 229 fallacies and 1,946 non-fallacious sentences.

[5]`https://www.presidency.ucsb.edu/`
[6]`https://labelstud.io/`

Fallacy Category	No. Instances
Appeal to Emotion	142
Appeal to Authority	16
Ad Hominem	46
False Cause	16
Slippery Slope	0
Slogan	9
Total	229

Table 3: Secret test set statistics for Argumentative Fallacy Classification.

5 Overview of the Systems and Results

Three teams participated in the AFC subtask, while two teams participated in the AFD subtask. In total, participants submitted 25 valid runs. No team participated in both subtasks.

Table 4 shows the results achieved by the individual teams for each subtask. Regarding AFC, we observe that only one team, Team NUST (Tahir et al., 2025), beats baselines on the text-only modality with a F1-score of 0.4856. This result shows that even a simple baseline like a BiLSTM is a strong competitor. In contrast, all participants improved over the baselines when considering the audio modality, while two teams surpassed the transformer baseline in the multimodal setting. Regarding AFD, Team Ambali_Yashovardhan reaches comparable performance to baselines in the text-only input setting, achieving rank 2. Nonetheless, despite reporting significant results in the audio-only setting where baselines fail the task, their solution is outperformed by both baselines in the multimodal setting.

All teams used neural networks, with transformer-based models being the most frequent choice. Some teams also employed machine learning classifiers like XGBoost on top of neural network models. Moreover, several teams explored a wide set of solutions to account for class imbalance, a well-known challenge in fallacy detection (Goffredo et al., 2022a).

5.1 Baselines

For both tasks, we employ the same set of baselines: a feature-based BiLSTM (Mancini et al., 2024b) and a transformer-based model (Mancini et al., 2024a). Regarding the BiLSTM model, the baseline uses GloVe embeddings for text inputs and extracted MFCCs features for audio recordings. Conversely, the transformer-based model uses RoBERTa (Liu et al., 2019)[7] for encoding text and WavLM (Chen et al., 2022)[8] for audio. Both architectures employ a late fusion strategy for the multimodal setting, where text and audio embeddings are concatenated and fed to a final classification layer. Independently of the given input setting, we denote the baselines as **Baseline BiLSTM** and **Baseline Transformer**, respectively.

5.2 System Descriptions and Task-Specific Results

Below, we describe the approaches of all participating systems; see also Table 5 for an overview.

5.2.1 Argumentative Fallacy Classification.

Team **NUST** (Tahir et al., 2025) employ RoBERTa (Liu et al., 2019) for text encoding and Whisper (Radford et al., 2023) for audio encoding. The two encodings are combined in a late fusion fashion without requiring joint end-to-end training and fed to a XGBoost (Chen and Guestrin, 2016) classifier. To account for label imbalance, they propose several solutions, including generating synthetic samples via GPT 4.0, class weighting, SMOTE (Chawla et al., 2002) in which synthetic samples are generated for minority classes in the fused feature space via interpolation, and focal loss (Lin et al., 2017) to handle hard-to-classify instances.

Team **AlessioPittiglio** (Pittiglio, 2025) explore a wide set of transformer-based text and audio encoders. For text, they evaluate BERT (Devlin et al., 2019), RoBERTa (Liu et al., 2019), DeBERTa (He et al., 2023) and ModernBERT (Warner et al., 2024). In particular, the authors propose three different strategies to integrate context information by (i) concatenating tokens during tokenization, (ii) concatenating pooled embeddings, and (iii) leveraging cross-attention. For audio, they evaluate Wa2Vec 2.0 (Baevski et al., 2020), WavLM (Chen et al., 2022) and HuBERT (Hsu et al., 2021). Regarding multimodality, they build an ensemble of the best text (RoBERTa with context information) and audio (HuBERT) models via a weighted average of individual encoder logits. Weights are calibrated via Bayesian optimization (Snoek et al., 2012).

Team **CASS** (Kalyan et al., 2025) encodes texts with RoBERTa (Liu et al., 2019) and audio

[7] *FacebookAI/roberta-base*

[8] *patrickvonplaten/wavlm-libri-clean-100h-base-plus*

Team	Rank	Text	Rank	Audio	Rank	Text-Audio
			AFC			
Team NUST	1	**0.4856**	2	0.1588	1	**0.4611**
Team AlessioPittiglio	3	0.4444	1	**0.3559**	2	<u>0.4403</u>
Team CASS	5	0.1432	4	0.0864	5	0.1432
Baseline BiLSTM	2	<u>0.4721</u>	3	0.1582	4	0.2191
Baseline Transformer	4	0.3925	5	0.0643	3	0.3816
			AFD			
Team Ambali_Yashovardhan	2	<u>0.2534</u>	1	**0.2095**	3	0.2244
Team EvaAdriana	4	0.2195	2	<u>0.1690</u>	4	0.1931
Baseline BiLSTM	3	0.2462	3	0.0000	2	<u>0.2337</u>
Baseline Transformer	1	**0.2770**	3	0.0000	1	**0.2848**

Table 4: Results for multimodal argumentative fallacy detection on political debates. For AFC, we report the macro F1-score, while for AFD, we report the binary F1-score. Best results per subtask are in **bold**, second best results are <u>underlined</u>.

Team	Task		Text							Audio					MAM			Misc				
	AFC	AFD	BERT	RoBERTa	DeBERTa	ModernBERT	SBERT	ALBERT	DeepSeek R1	Whisper	Wav2Vec	WavLM	HuBERT	MFCCs	Late Fusion	Early Fusion	Mid Fusion	Data Augmentation	Class Weighting	Bayesian Optimization	Focal Loss	Context
NUST (Tahir et al., 2025)	✓			✓						✓					✓			✓	✓			
AlessioPittiglio (Pittiglio, 2025)	✓		✓	✓	✓	✓					✓	✓	✓		✓	✓	✓	✓	✓	✓		✓
CASS (Kalyan et al., 2025)	✓			✓							✓			✓	✓							
Ambali_Yashovardhan		✓		✓									✓		✓						✓	
EvaAdriana (Larumbe and Vendrell, 2025)		✓	✓	✓			✓	✓	✓		✓			✓	✓							

Table 5: **Overview of the approaches.** The numbers in the language box refer to the position of the team in the official ranking.

recordings using a BiLSTM with extracted Mel-Frequency Cepstral Coefficients (MFCCs) features as input (Mancini et al., 2024b). For multimodality, they concatenate the pooled embeddings of RoBERTa for text and Wav2Vec (Baevski et al., 2020) for audio. The concatenated embedding is eventually fed to a logistic regression classifier.

5.3 Argumentative Fallacy Detection

Team **Ambali_Yashovardhan** uses RoBERTa (Liu et al., 2019) for processing text inputs and DistilHuBERT (Chang et al., 2022) for encoding audio recordings. Due to memory constraints, they limit audio sequence length to 320,000 samples (approximately 20 seconds at 16 kHz), truncating longer files. Regarding multimodality, the authors adopt a late fusion strategy where a weighted average of each modality model's logits is computed. The weights are learnt during training. To handle class imbalance, they adopt focal loss (Lin et al., 2017).

Team **EvaAdriana** (Larumbe and Vendrell, 2025) explore five transformer-based models for text modality: BERT (Devlin et al., 2019), RoBERTa (Liu et al., 2019), SBERT (Reimers and Gurevych, 2019), ALBERT (Lan et al., 2020), and DeepSeek R1 (DeepSeek-AI et al., 2025). Up to the last four layers of encoder-based transformers are unfrozen for fine-tuning on the task, while DeepSeek is 4-bit quantized to account for the available computational budget. Regarding audio modality, the authors evaluate two models: a CNN with MFCCs features as inputs and Wav2Vec 2.0 (Baevski et al., 2020). Lastly, they combine the best-performing models for text (RoBERTa) and audio (Wa2Vec 2.0) for multimodality. In particular, they concatenate the output of each modality encoder and feed it to a classification head.

6 Main Findings

The MM-ArgFallacy2025 shared task revealed key insights about multimodal fallacy analysis through binary detection and multi-class classification tasks, highlighting both capabilities and fundamental limitations in this field.

Textual Dominance. Text-based approaches consistently outperformed audio and multimodal alternatives across all teams in AFC. Team NUST achieved a 0.4856 F1-score for classification, establishing transformer-based models, particularly RoBERTa variants, as the most effective. Team EvaAdriana's comparative evaluation in AFD revealed that fine-tuned transformer models substantially outperformed zero-shot approaches, with their task-specific RoBERTa achieving 0.3393 F1-score compared to DeepSeek-R1's zero-shot performance of 0.1567 on the validation set, underscoring the importance of domain-specific adaptation for specialised argumentation tasks.

Audio Processing Challenges. Audio-only approaches consistently underperformed, with Team AlessioPittiglio's best performance of 0.3559 remaining substantially below text baselines despite employing state-of-the-art models including HuBERT, Wav2Vec2, and Whisper. However, the results achieved by the participants demonstrate progress over previous work in extracting fallacy-relevant acoustic features. Technical constraints forced audio truncation to 15-20 seconds, but more fundamentally, acoustic signatures of fallacious reasoning appear too subtle for current speech processing models to reliably capture.

Limited Multimodal Gains. Multimodal approaches failed to deliver expected performance improvements. Team NUST's late fusion achieved 0.4611, only modestly improving over text baselines while requiring significant computational cost. This suggests simple fusion strategies are insufficient to capture complex relationships between semantic content and paralinguistic delivery, with textual information overwhelming rather than complementing audio features.

Effective Strategies. Team NUST's success stemmed from prompt-guided augmentation using GPT-4. Team AlessioPittiglio's context integration (3-4 previous sentences) contributed to strong performance, though benefits were primarily textual, suggesting modality-specific strategies are needed.

Class Imbalance Challenge. Severe class imbalance emerged as the primary technical challenge. Binary detection faced 90.8% vs. 9.2% distribution, while classification presented "double imbalance" with *Appeal to Emotion* comprising 59% of fallacious samples versus <3% for minority classes. Team NUST's synthetic data generation proved more effective than algorithmic adjustments, indicating quality augmentation outperforms technical modifications for addressing imbalance.

7 Discussion

The MM-ArgFallacy2025 shared task established important baselines while revealing both progress and limitations in multimodal fallacy analysis.

Audio Improvements. While text-based methods achieved the highest performance across both detection and classification tasks, teams demonstrated notable improvements in audio-only approaches compared to previous work, with Team AlessioPittiglio achieving a 0.3559 F1-score for classification using HuBERT-based models. These advances suggest that audio modalities contain valuable information for fallacy detection, though current extraction techniques remain limited.

Speaker Dependency. The challenges in audio-only approaches may also be attributed to the inherently speaker-dependent nature of acoustic cues. As noted by previous work, different speakers have varying skills in using vocal cues such as articulation, sonority, and tempo, and possess different levels of persuasive power, with vocal characteristics directly affecting the clarity, credibility, and receptivity of a speaker's message (Lippi and Torroni, 2016).

Multimodality Fusion Strategies. The reliance on simple concatenation and late fusion approaches in the proposed multimodal systems reveals fundamental gaps in current methodologies. These approaches fail to capture complex interdependencies between linguistic content and paralinguistic delivery, which likely explains the limited performance of many multimodal systems. Rather than indicating the non-effectiveness of multimodal integration itself, these results highlight the need for more sophisticated fusion architectures that can jointly learn complementary cues from both modalities during training. Future work should prioritise advanced fusion architectures that enable joint learning across modalities, moving beyond late fusion toward cross-attention mechanisms and early integration strategies.

Conditional Audio Generation. Key contributions of this shared task include successful prompt-guided data augmentation and systematic context integration strategies that proved effective for addressing severe class imbalance and improving classification performance. Building on the success of synthetic textual data generation, a possible direction involves controllable conditional audio generation that transcends the basic text-to-speech approaches employed by teams in this shared task. Drawing inspiration from recent advances in signal-to-language augmentation (Kumar et al., 2024) that enable fine-grained control over acoustic parameters such as loudness, pitch, reverb, brightness, and duration, future research could develop fallacy-aware audio generation systems. Such approaches go beyond traditional digital signal processing by incorporating learned representations that capture how acoustic characteristics convey persuasive intent and logical flaws in context. For appeals to emotion, generation could emphasize particular intonation patterns and vocal intensity, while deceptive reasoning patterns could incorporate vocal stress indicators, hesitation markers, or pitch variations suggesting uncertainty.

8 Conclusion

The MM-ArgFallacy2025 shared task demonstrates that fallacy detection and classification remain challenging problems with significant potential for advancement. Text-based approaches currently show the most promise, while audio and multimodal systems require architectural innovations to realise their full potential. The ultimate goal remains developing integrated systems that effectively leverage both semantic and paralinguistic cues to support democratic discourse and critical thinking education.

Limitations

Annotations. In alignment with (Mancini et al., 2024b), we advocate for approaching fallacy classification as a multimodal problem. Nonetheless, the annotation methodology employed in this study mirrors that of (Goffredo et al., 2022b), relying solely on textual information for both training data preparation and secret test set creation. This text-centric approach potentially overlooks crucial information embedded in the acoustic characteristics of spoken debates, such as intonational patterns, emphasis, and other paralinguistic features that could indicate fallacious arguments. Achieving the full potential of multimodal fallacy detection will require developing new annotation protocols that systematically integrate both linguistic and acoustic dimensions from the ground up.

MAMKit. MAMKit remains an evolving toolkit with several acknowledged limitations that reflect its ongoing development status. The platform currently supports only PyTorch, which may present integration challenges for researchers working with alternative frameworks or seeking to incorporate existing work built on different architectures. Additionally, the toolkit's coverage of multimodal argumentation resources is non exhaustive, as several established datasets (e.g., VivesDebate-Speech (Ruiz-Dolz and Iranzo-Sánchez, 2023), ImageArg (Liu et al., 2022), MMClaims (Cheema et al., 2022)) and models (e.g., M-ArgNet (Mestre et al., 2021b)) have not yet been integrated. Furthermore, the current scope is restricted to text and audio modalities, excluding visual argumentation mining despite its growing importance in the field. Nevertheless, deploying MAMKit to deliver the datasets used in this shared task provided valuable opportunities to gather community feedback and identify priority areas for future development, informing our roadmap for expanding both framework compatibility and multimodal coverage.

Dataset Scale and Imbalance. The MM-USED-fallacy dataset faces dual constraints that significantly impact model development and evaluation. First, with only 3,388 instances for the AFC task, the dataset represents a relatively small scale for training robust deep learning models, a limitation characteristic of specialised argumentation tasks where high-quality annotations are resource-intensive to obtain. The expansion conducted for this shared task, while methodologically sound, added only 229 fallacious instances from two 2024 debates, maintaining the dataset's modest scale. Second, severe class imbalance permeates both detection and classification tasks, with fallacious sentences comprising merely 9.2% of instances in binary detection, while classification exhibits "double imbalance" with Appeal to Emotion representing 59% of fallacious samples versus minority classes accounting for less than 3% each. Some fallacy types, such as Slippery Slope, are completely absent from the test set, preventing comprehensive evaluation. These scale and distribution constraints compound each other, limiting model generalization capabilities across diverse speaking styles, debate formats, and political contexts while making robust performance assessment particularly challenging for underrepresented fallacy categories. Future work should prioritize systematic dataset expansion across multiple election cycles and speaker demographics while developing targeted annotation strategies to achieve more balanced fallacy type distributions.

Acknowledgments

This work was partially supported by project "FAIR - Future Artificial Intelligence Research" – Spoke 8 "Pervasive AI", under the European Commission's NextGeneration EU programme, PNRR – M4C2 – Investimento 1.3, Partenariato Esteso (PE00000013). F. Ruggeri is partially supported by the European Union's Justice Programme under Grant Agreement No. 101087342 for the project "Principles Of Law In National and European VAT".

References

Alexei Baevski, Henry Zhou, Abdelrahman Mohamed, and Michael Auli. 2020. wav2vec 2.0: a framework for self-supervised learning of speech representations. In *Proceedings of the 34th International Conference on Neural Information Processing Systems*, NIPS '20, Red Hook, NY, USA. Curran Associates Inc.

Max Bain, Jaesung Huh, Tengda Han, and Andrew Zisserman. 2023. Whisperx: Time-accurate speech transcription of long-form audio. In *Interspeech 2023*, pages 4489–4493.

M. Sahbi Benlamine, Maher Chaouachi, Serena Villata, Elena Cabrio, Claude Frasson, and Fabien Gandon. 2015. Emotions in argumentation: an empirical evaluation. In *Proceedings of the Twenty-Fourth International Joint Conference on Artificial Intelligence, IJCAI 2015, Buenos Aires, Argentina, July 25-31, 2015*, pages 156–163. AAAI Press.

Lucas Carstens, Francesca Toni, and Valentinos Evripidou. 2014. Argument mining and social debates. In *Computational Models of Argument - Proceedings of COMMA 2014, Atholl Palace Hotel, Scottish Highlands, UK, September 9-12, 2014*, volume 266 of *Frontiers in Artificial Intelligence and Applications*, pages 451–452. IOS Press.

Heng-Jui Chang, Shu-wen Yang, and Hung-yi Lee. 2022. Distilhubert: Speech representation learning by layer-wise distillation of hidden-unit bert. In *ICASSP 2022 - 2022 IEEE International Conference on Acoustics, Speech and Signal Processing (ICASSP)*, pages 7087–7091.

Nitesh V. Chawla, Kevin W. Bowyer, Lawrence O. Hall, and W. Philip Kegelmeyer. 2002. Smote: synthetic minority over-sampling technique. *J. Artif. Int. Res.*, 16(1):321–357.

Gullal Singh Cheema, Sherzod Hakimov, Abdul Sittar, Eric Müller-Budack, Christian Otto, and Ralph Ewerth. 2022. MM-claims: A dataset for multimodal claim detection in social media. In *Findings of the Association for Computational Linguistics: NAACL 2022*, pages 962–979, Seattle, United States. Association for Computational Linguistics.

Sanyuan Chen, Chengyi Wang, Zhengyang Chen, Yu Wu, Shujie Liu, Zhuo Chen, Jinyu Li, Naoyuki Kanda, Takuya Yoshioka, Xiong Xiao, and 1 others. 2022. Wavlm: Large-scale self-supervised pretraining for full stack speech processing. *IEEE Journal of Selected Topics in Signal Processing*, 16(6):1505–1518.

Tianqi Chen and Carlos Guestrin. 2016. Xgboost: A scalable tree boosting system. In *Proceedings of the 22nd ACM SIGKDD International Conference on Knowledge Discovery and Data Mining*, KDD '16, page 785–794, New York, NY, USA. Association for Computing Machinery.

Jacob Cohen. 1968. Weighted kappa: Nominal scale agreement provision for scaled disagreement or partial credit. *Psychological bulletin*, 70(4):213.

DeepSeek-AI, Daya Guo, Dejian Yang, Haowei Zhang, Junxiao Song, Ruoyu Zhang, Runxin Xu, Qihao Zhu, Shirong Ma, Peiyi Wang, Xiao Bi, Xiaokang Zhang, Xingkai Yu, Yu Wu, Z. F. Wu, Zhibin Gou, Zhihong Shao, Zhuoshu Li, Ziyi Gao, and 81 others. 2025. Deepseek-r1: Incentivizing reasoning capability in llms via reinforcement learning. *CoRR*, abs/2501.12948.

Jacob Devlin, Ming-Wei Chang, Kenton Lee, and Kristina Toutanova. 2019. BERT: Pre-training of deep bidirectional transformers for language understanding. In *Proceedings of the 2019 Conference of the North American Chapter of the Association for Computational Linguistics: Human Language Technologies, Volume 1 (Long and Short Papers)*, pages 4171–4186, Minneapolis, Minnesota. Association for Computational Linguistics.

Mihai Dusmanu, Elena Cabrio, and Serena Villata. 2017. Argument mining on Twitter: Arguments, facts and sources. In *Proceedings of the 2017 Conference on Empirical Methods in Natural Language Processing*, pages 2317–2322, Copenhagen, Denmark. Association for Computational Linguistics.

Pierpaolo Goffredo, Mariana Chaves, Serena Villata, and Elena Cabrio. 2023. Argument-based detection and classification of fallacies in political debates.

In *Proceedings of the 2023 Conference on Empirical Methods in Natural Language Processing*, pages 11101–11112, Singapore. Association for Computational Linguistics.

Pierpaolo Goffredo, Shohreh Haddadan, Vorakit Vorakitphan, Elena Cabrio, and Serena Villata. 2022a. Fallacious argument classification in political debates. In *Proceedings of the Thirty-First International Joint Conference on Artificial Intelligence, IJCAI 2022, Vienna, Austria, 23-29 July 2022*, pages 4143–4149. ijcai.org.

Pierpaolo Goffredo, Shohreh Haddadan, Vorakit Vorakitphan, Elena Cabrio, and Serena Villata. 2022b. Fallacious argument classification in political debates. In *Proceedings of the Thirty-First International Joint Conference on Artificial Intelligence, IJCAI 2022, Vienna, Austria, 23-29 July 2022*, pages 4143–4149. ijcai.org.

Leo Groarke and Gabrijela Kišiček. 2018. Sound arguments: An introduction to auditory argument. In *Argumentation and inference: Proceedings of 2nd European Conference on Argumentation*, pages 177–198. London: Collage Publications.

Shohreh Haddadan, Elena Cabrio, and Serena Villata. 2019. Yes, we can! mining arguments in 50 years of US presidential campaign debates. In *Proceedings of the 57th Annual Meeting of the Association for Computational Linguistics*, pages 4684–4690, Florence, Italy. Association for Computational Linguistics.

Charles Leonard Hamblin. 2022. Fallacies. In *Advanced Reasoning Forum*. Advanced Reasoning Forum.

Pengcheng He, Jianfeng Gao, and Weizhu Chen. 2023. Debertav3: Improving deberta using electra-style pretraining with gradient-disentangled embedding sharing. In *The Eleventh International Conference on Learning Representations*.

Wei-Ning Hsu, Benjamin Bolte, Yao-Hung Hubert Tsai, Kushal Lakhotia, Ruslan Salakhutdinov, and Abdelrahman Mohamed. 2021. Hubert: Self-supervised speech representation learning by masked prediction of hidden units. *IEEE/ACM Transactions on Audio, Speech, and Language Processing*, 29:3451–3460.

Zhijing Jin, Abhinav Lalwani, Tejas Vaidhya, Xiaoyu Shen, Yiwen Ding, Zhiheng Lyu, Mrinmaya Sachan, Rada Mihalcea, and Bernhard Schoelkopf. 2022. Logical fallacy detection. In *Findings of the Association for Computational Linguistics: EMNLP 2022*, pages 7180–7198, Abu Dhabi, United Arab Emirates. Association for Computational Linguistics.

Warale Avinash Kalyan, Siddharth Pagaria, Chaitra V, and Spoorthi H G. 2025. Multimodal argumentative fallacy classification in political debates. *"Proceedings of the 12th Workshop on Argument Mining (ArgMining 2025)"*.

Gabrijela Kišiček. 2014. The role of prosodic features in the analysis of multimodal argumentation. In *International Society for the Study of Argumentation (ISSA), 8th international conference on argumentation*. Rozenberg Quarterly, The Magazine.

Gabrijela Kišiček. 2020a. Listen carefully! fallacious auditory arguments. In *Proceedings of the 12th Conference of the Ontario Society for the Study of Argumentation*, OSSA 12, pages 17–32. University of Windsor.

Gabrijela Kišiček. 2020b. Listen carefully! fallacious auditory arguments. In *Proceedings of the 12th Conference of the Ontario Society for the Study of Argumentation*, OSSA 12, pages 17–32. University of Windsor.

Sonal Kumar, Prem Seetharaman, Justin Salamon, Dinesh Manocha, and Oriol Nieto. 2024. Sila: Signal-to-language augmentation for enhanced control in text-to-audio generation. *Preprint*, arXiv:2412.09789.

Zhenzhong Lan, Mingda Chen, Sebastian Goodman, Kevin Gimpel, Piyush Sharma, and Radu Soricut. 2020. ALBERT: A lite BERT for self-supervised learning of language representations. In *8th International Conference on Learning Representations, ICLR 2020, Addis Ababa, Ethiopia, April 26-30, 2020*. OpenReview.net.

Eva Cantín Larumbe and Adriana Chust Vendrell. 2025. Argumentative fallacy detection in political debates. *"Proceedings of the 12th Workshop on Argument Mining (ArgMining 2025)"*.

Tsung-Yi Lin, Priya Goyal, Ross Girshick, Kaiming He, and Piotr Dollár. 2017. Focal loss for dense object detection. In *2017 IEEE International Conference on Computer Vision (ICCV)*, pages 2999–3007.

Marco Lippi and Paolo Torroni. 2016. Argument mining from speech: Detecting claims in political debates. In *Proceedings of the Thirtieth AAAI Conference on Artificial Intelligence, February 12-17, 2016, Phoenix, Arizona, USA*, pages 2979–2985. AAAI Press.

Yinhan Liu, Myle Ott, Naman Goyal, Jingfei Du, Mandar Joshi, Danqi Chen, Omer Levy, Mike Lewis, Luke Zettlemoyer, and Veselin Stoyanov. 2019. Roberta: A robustly optimized bert pretraining approach. *Preprint*, arXiv:1907.11692.

Zhexiong Liu, Meiqi Guo, Yue Dai, and Diane Litman. 2022. ImageArg: A multi-modal tweet dataset for image persuasiveness mining. In *Proceedings of the 9th Workshop on Argument Mining*, pages 1–18, Online and in Gyeongju, Republic of Korea. International Conference on Computational Linguistics.

Anastasios Lytos, Thomas Lagkas, Panagiotis Sarigiannidis, and Kalina Bontcheva. 2019. The evolution of argumentation mining: From models to social media and emerging tools. *Information Processing & Management*, 56(6):102055.

Eleonora Mancini, Federico Ruggeri, Stefano Colamonaco, Andrea Zecca, Samuele Marro, and Paolo Torroni. 2024a. MAMKit: A comprehensive multimodal argument mining toolkit. In *Proceedings of the 11th Workshop on Argument Mining (ArgMining 2024)*, pages 69–82, Bangkok, Thailand. Association for Computational Linguistics.

Eleonora Mancini, Federico Ruggeri, Andrea Galassi, and Paolo Torroni. 2022. Multimodal argument mining: A case study in political debates. In *Proceedings of the 9th Workshop on Argument Mining*, pages 158–170, Online and in Gyeongju, Republic of Korea. International Conference on Computational Linguistics.

Eleonora Mancini, Federico Ruggeri, and Paolo Torroni. 2024b. Multimodal fallacy classification in political debates. In *Proceedings of the 18th Conference of the European Chapter of the Association for Computational Linguistics (Volume 2: Short Papers)*, pages 170–178, St. Julian's, Malta. Association for Computational Linguistics.

Rafael Mestre, Stuart E. Middleton, Matt Ryan, Masood Gheasi, Timothy Norman, and Jiatong Zhu. 2023. Augmenting pre-trained language models with audio feature embedding for argumentation mining in political debates. In *Findings of the Association for Computational Linguistics: EACL 2023*, pages 274–288, Dubrovnik, Croatia. Association for Computational Linguistics.

Rafael Mestre, Razvan Milicin, Stuart Middleton, Matt Ryan, Jiatong Zhu, and Timothy J. Norman. 2021a. M-arg: Multimodal argument mining dataset for political debates with audio and transcripts. In *ArgMining@EMNLP*, pages 78–88. Association for Computational Linguistics.

Rafael Mestre, Razvan Milicin, Stuart E. Middleton, Matt Ryan, Jiatong Zhu, and Timothy J. Norman. 2021b. M-arg: Multimodal argument mining dataset for political debates with audio and transcripts. In *Proceedings of the 8th Workshop on Argument Mining*, pages 78–88, Punta Cana, Dominican Republic. Association for Computational Linguistics.

Alessio Pittiglio. 2025. Leveraging context for multimodal fallacy classification in political debates. *"Proceedings of the 12th Workshop on Argument Mining (ArgMining 2025)"*.

Alec Radford, Jong Wook Kim, Tao Xu, Greg Brockman, Christine Mcleavey, and Ilya Sutskever. 2023. Robust speech recognition via large-scale weak supervision. In *Proceedings of the 40th International Conference on Machine Learning*, volume 202 of *Proceedings of Machine Learning Research*, pages 28492–28518. PMLR.

Nils Reimers and Iryna Gurevych. 2019. Sentence-BERT: Sentence embeddings using Siamese BERT-networks. In *Proceedings of the 2019 Conference on Empirical Methods in Natural Language Processing and the 9th International Joint Conference on Natural Language Processing (EMNLP-IJCNLP)*, pages 3982–3992, Hong Kong, China. Association for Computational Linguistics.

Ramon Ruiz-Dolz and Javier Iranzo-Sánchez. 2023. VivesDebate-speech: A corpus of spoken argumentation to leverage audio features for argument mining. In *Proceedings of the 2023 Conference on Empirical Methods in Natural Language Processing*, pages 2071–2077, Singapore. Association for Computational Linguistics.

Jasper Snoek, Hugo Larochelle, and Ryan P. Adams. 2012. Practical bayesian optimization of machine learning algorithms. In *Proceedings of the 26th International Conference on Neural Information Processing Systems - Volume 2*, NIPS'12, page 2951–2959, Red Hook, NY, USA. Curran Associates Inc.

Reid Swanson, Brian Ecker, and Marilyn Walker. 2015. Argument mining: Extracting arguments from online dialogue. In *Proceedings of the 16th Annual Meeting of the Special Interest Group on Discourse and Dialogue*, pages 217–226, Prague, Czech Republic. Association for Computational Linguistics.

Abdullah Tahir, Imaan Ibrar, Huma Ameer, Mehwish Fatima, and Seemab Latif. 2025. Prompt-guided augmentation and multi-modal fusion for argumentative fallacy classification in political debates. *"Proceedings of the 12th Workshop on Argument Mining (ArgMining 2025)"*.

Benjamin Warner, Antoine Chaffin, Benjamin Clavié, Orion Weller, Oskar Hallström, Said Taghadouini, Alexis Gallagher, Raja Biswas, Faisal Ladhak, Tom Aarsen, Nathan Cooper, Griffin Adams, Jeremy Howard, and Iacopo Poli. 2024. Smarter, better, faster, longer: A modern bidirectional encoder for fast, memory efficient, and long context finetuning and inference. *Preprint*, arXiv:2412.13663.

Argumentative Fallacy Detection in Political Debates

Eva Cantín Larumbe and Adriana Chust Vendrell
Universitat Politècnica de València, Spain
{ecanlar, achuven}@etsinf.upv.es

Abstract

Building on recent advances in Natural Language Processing (NLP), this work addresses the task of fallacy detection in political debates using a multimodal approach combining text and audio, as well as text-only and audio-only approaches. Although the multimodal setup is novel, results show that text-based models consistently outperform both audio-only and multimodal models, confirming that textual information remains the most effective for this task. Transformer-based and few-shot architectures were used to detect fallacies. While fine-tuned language models demonstrate strong performance, challenges such as data imbalance, audio processing, and limited dataset size persist.

1 Introduction

Recent advances in Natural Language Processing (NLP) have enabled substantial progress in understanding and generating human language. Within this context, fallacy detection has gained attention as a means to promote critical thinking and mitigate the spread of misinformation. Fallacious arguments—persuasive yet logically flawed—can contribute to the circulation of deceptive content, especially in politically charged discourse.

Automatic fallacy detection in political discourse could support content moderation, enhance public debate quality, and foster critical thinking by identifying manipulative rhetorical strategies at scale.

Fallacies have been studied extensively in argumentation theory. Informally, they are arguments that appear sound but contain subtle logical flaws (Breslin, 2023). Walton (2006) defines a fallacy as "an argument that seems valid on the surface but is flawed when examined more closely."

In this paper, we address fallacy detection (AFD) in the domain of political debates. This work is part of the MM-ArgFallacy2025 Shared Task on Multimodal Argumentative Fallacy Detection and Classification on Political Debates, co-located with the 12th Workshop on Argument Mining in Vienna, Austria.

We investigate the performance of Transformer-based and few-shot models, across three input configurations: text-only, audio-only, and a novel multimodal setting that combines both modalities. Our contributions are threefold: (1) we apply argumentation theory to fallacy detection in political discourse; (2) we evaluate and compare the performance of text-only, audio-only, and multimodal Transformer-based architectures; and (3) we analyze key challenges in fallacy detection, including data imbalance, the limited contribution of audio features, and practical constraints related to computational resources and training time.

2 Related Work

Recent advances in fallacy detection span from supervised learning with curated datasets to zero-shot prompting with Large Language Models (LLMs), as well as emerging multimodal approaches.

Chaves et al. (2025) introduced FALCON, a multi-label, graph-based dataset focused on fallacies in COVID-19 and politically charged discourse on Twitter. Annotated by experts across six fallacy types, the dataset supports multiple labels per instance. Among the models evaluated, a dual-transformer architecture augmented with sentiment scores and contextual cues achieved the best performance, with a macro F1 score of 48.8%.

Similarly, Atarama et al. (2024) developed F-Detector, a BERT-based classifier for detecting ten fallacy types in digital texts. Leveraging advanced NLP preprocessing and dataset expansion via generative techniques, their system attained a substantial improvement over previous models—achieving an F1 score of 74%, significantly outperforming GPT-based baselines.

Moving toward generalization, Pan et al. (2024)

Proceedings of the 12th Argument Mining Workshop, pages 369–373
July 31, 2025

explored the use of LLMs as zero-shot fallacy classifiers, mitigating the reliance on annotated datasets. They proposed single-round and multi-round prompting strategies to enhance fallacy reasoning. Evaluating models like GPT-4 across seven benchmark datasets—including political debates and COVID-19 discourse—they found that LLMs outperformed fine-tuned models (e.g., T5) in out-of-distribution (OOD) settings, especially when multi-round prompting was used to aid smaller models.

In the specific domain of political discourse, Cruz et al. (2025) introduced the FallacyES-Political dataset, comprising 1,965 annotated fallacies from 30 years of Spanish electoral debates. Their study compared zero-shot GPT-4o and a fine-tuned RoBERTa-base-BNE model, with the latter achieving superior performance (F1 score of 0.641 vs. 0.570), underscoring the value of domain-specific fine-tuning on curated data.

Finally, in a novel direction, Mancini et al. (2024) proposed a multimodal framework for fallacy classification, introducing MM-USED-fallacy, the first dataset combining text and audio from U.S. presidential debates. Their experiments showed that integrating audio features—especially for fallacies like Appeal to Emotion and Appeal to Authority—can yield significant gains, with multimodal models outperforming text-only baselines by up to 8 percentage points in F1 score.

In contrast to previous approaches, our work is among the first to address the detection of fallacies in political debates using a multimodal framework that integrates both textual and audio features.

3 Data

We utilized the MM-USED-fallacy dataset (Mancini et al., 2024), which includes 17,118 instances, with 15,550 labeled as non-fallacious and 1,568 containing a fallacy. The test set comprises 2,175 samples.

The task was approached using three distinct data configurations: text-only, audio-only, and multimodal (text + audio). This setup allowed for an evaluation of the performance of each modality individually, as well as an exploration of the potential synergies from combining text and audio information.

In our methodology, we did not incorporate contextual information in the experiments. This was primarily due to constraints in available computational resources and limited time, which prevented us from implementing and testing models that consider extended discourse context.

For the text modality, no additional preprocessing was applied beyond tokenization using the pretrained model's tokenize. For the audio modality, two approaches were used. In the mel-spectrogram + CNN setup, audio was loaded at 22,050 Hz, trimmed or zero-padded to 3 seconds, converted to 128-band mel spectrograms (fmax=8,000 Hz), normalized to [0, 255], resized to 128×128 pixels, and stacked into 3 channels. In the Wav2Vec 2.0 setup, raw audio was loaded at 16,000 Hz and processed using the facebook/wav2vec2-base processor, which handled feature extraction and padding. For the combined text-audio setting, we adopted a frozen RoBERTa (base) encoder for text and Wav2Vec 2.0 for audio. The text data were tokenized using the RobertaTokenizer, and the audio inputs were processed with the Wav2Vec2Processor.

Finally, data was split consistently. The training and validation sets were obtained using an 80/20 stratified split to maintain label distribution.

4 Experiments

4.1 Method

To build upon previous experimental findings in the literature, we implemented a series of deep learning models. Specifically, we explored five different models for the text-only modality: BERT (uncased) (Devlin et al., 2018), RoBERTa (base and large) (Liu et al., 2021), SBERT (Reimers and Gurevych, 2019), ALBERT (Base v2) (Lan et al., 2019), and DeepSeek-R1-Distill-Llama-8B (Guo et al., 2025).

For BERT and ALBERT, we unfroze the last two hidden layers of the encoder in addition to the classification layer. In the case of RoBERTa and SBERT, we unfroze the last four hidden layers. Regarding DeepSeek-R1-Distill-Llama-8B, we loaded the model with 4-bit quantization using the NF4 scheme and bfloat16 computation, following QLoRA best practices. This quantization approach substantially reduced memory usage and computational overhead, enabling efficient fine-tuning of large-scale models on consumer-grade hardware. Despite the reduced precision, the NF4 scheme preserved high performance by employing a non-uniform quantization grid optimized for downstream tasks.

For the fallacy detection task, the prompt designed for DeepSeek-R1-Distill-Llama-8B was inspired by Ruiz-Dolz and Lawrence (2023):

```
Your task is to detect the type
of fallacy in the Text. The label
should be 1 (it is a fallacy) or
0 (it is not a fallacy)
Text Snippet: [SAMPLE]
```

For the audio-only approach, we tested two models: MFCC + CNN and Wav2Vec 2.0 (Schneider et al., 2019). The MFCC + CNN model uses handcrafted audio features, while Wav2Vec 2.0 processes raw audio waveforms with a pretrained deep learning model. This comparison helps evaluate traditional feature-based methods versus end-to-end representation learning for fallacy detection.

For the text-audio approach, we used a combined model of RoBERTa (base) (Liu et al., 2021) and Wav2Vec2-Base-960h (Schneider et al., 2019). We selected this combination because RoBERTa and Wav2Vec2-Base-960h were the best-performing models in the text-only and audio-only settings, respectively, providing a strong foundation for the multimodal setup. Features from both encoders were concatenated and passed through a classification head. To reduce computational cost, only the classification layers were unfrozen.

4.2 Experimental Setup

Hyperparameter selection was performed based on validation performance. The best model per configuration was retrained during 3-5 epochs on the full training set and evaluated on the test set. Finally, this retrained model was used to generate predictions on the test set.

Text-Only Models. We experimented with five Transformer-based models: BERT (uncased), RoBERTa (base and large), SBERT, ALBERT (Base v2), and DeepSeek-R1-Distill-Llama-8B. For BERT, class imbalance was addressed using weighted loss: we used weights of 0.2 for the non-fallacious class and 0.8 for the fallacious class. These weights were selected empirically based on preliminary validation performance, aiming to improve the F1-score for the minority class. This approach allowed us to balance sensitivity to both classes during optimization.

All models, except for DeepSeek, were trained using a learning rate of 2e-5, cosine learning rate scheduling, a weight decay of 0.1, and 10 epochs. For DeepSeek, a linear classification head was added on top of mean-pooled hidden states, and the prompt used is described in the Method Section 4.1.

Audio-Only Models. For audio-only models, raw audio samples were converted into 128×128 mel-spectrogram images, which were then used to train a CNN composed of three convolutional blocks followed by max-pooling, dropout, and dense layers. The CNN was optimized for binary classification using the Adam optimizer. In parallel, a Wav2Vec2.0-based model was fine-tuned to perform classification directly from raw audio waveforms. The audio files were first loaded and preprocessed using a pre-trained Wav2Vec2 processor, which performed feature extraction and normalization. The extracted features were then passed to a Wav2Vec2 model with a classification head adapted for binary classification.

Multimodal Model. The model was trained for 10 epochs using a class-weighted Cross-Entropy loss with weights of 50 for class 1 and 1 for class 0. These weights were selected empirically based on preliminary validation experiments to better handle class imbalance. Optimization was performed using AdamW and a ReduceLROnPlateau scheduler with an initial learning rate of 2e-5.

5 Results

5.1 Validation Results

All performance metrics were computed on the validation set. We report Accuracy (Acc.) and Binary F1-score. Results for the task are presented in Table 1.

As shown in Table 1, the best performance was obtained by RoBERTa in the text-only setting, achieving the highest Binary F1-score. Other Transformer-based models performed similarly, while the DeepSeek-R1 zero-shot model lagged considerably. This can be attributed to its zero-shot nature: unlike models like RoBERTa or BERT, which were fine-tuned on the task-specific data, DeepSeek-R1 was evaluated without any additional training. Since fallacy detection requires nuanced, context-aware understanding of argumentative language, zero-shot models often fail to capture task-specific patterns, resulting in lower performance. Fine-tuning DeepSeek-R1 on task-specific fallacy detection data could significantly improve its performance.

Model	Acc.	Binary F1
Text-only		
BERT	0.9042	0.3037
RoBERTa	0.9033	**0.3393**
ALBERT	0.9004	0.2816
SBERT	0.9077	0.2956
DeepSeek-R1	0.8814	0.1567
Audio-only		
MFCC+CNN	0.3902	0.1618
Wav2Vec2	0.0938	**0.1683**
Text-audio		
RoBERTa+Wav2Vec2	0.4866	**0.1831**

Table 1: Accuracy and Binary F1-score for the fallacy detection task (validation set).

Audio-only models yielded substantially lower performance across both metrics, with Wav2Vec 2.0 slightly outperforming the CNN-based approach. This limited effectiveness of audio features may be due to several factors: first, fallacy detection primarily relies on semantic and contextual understanding, which is inherently stronger in textual data than in acoustic signals. Second, the acoustic cues relevant to detecting fallacies—such as tone, emphasis, or hesitation—might be too subtle or inconsistent to be reliably captured by current audio representations.

The multimodal configuration (RoBERTa + Wav2Vec 2.0) showed marginal improvement over audio-only models but remained well below the performance of text-only models. These results suggest that semantic cues in text are more informative for fallacy detection, while the additional acoustic features did not contribute significantly under the current setup.

5.2 Official Test Set Results and Shared Task Ranking

Table 2 presents the performance of our best model on the official test set provided by the MM-ArgFallacy2025 shared task. These results reflect the final evaluation submitted to the organizers and were used to determine our ranking in the competition.

6 Conclusion

This work presented a comprehensive evaluation of deep learning models for the detection of logical fallacies in political debates, leveraging both text and audio modalities. Our best-performing model—a fine-tuned RoBERTa variant—achieved an accuracy of 90.33% and a binary F1 score of 0.3393.

Modality	Model	Binary F1	Ranking
Text-only	RoBERTa	0.2195	4th
Audio-only	Wav2Vec2	0.1690	2nd
Text-Audio	RoBERTa + Wav2Vec2	0.1931	4th

Table 2: Binary F1-score and ranking on the official test set for the fallacy detection task, grouped by modality.

Our findings support and extend previous work such as Mancini et al. (2024), while offering new insights. Unlike prior approaches that emphasize multimodal fusion, our experiments indicate that text-only models consistently outperform audio-only and multimodal models for both tasks. In particular, RoBERTa achieved the highest score, underscoring the strength of contextualized language representations in reasoning-based classification tasks.

The proposed model has the potential to be deployed in various applications, such as automatic detection of fallacious reasoning in online forums, academic writing, or news articles. This could aid in improving the quality of discourse in these environments by flagging problematic arguments. Additionally, educational tools could benefit from such a model to help students learn to identify and avoid common logical fallacies in their reasoning.

The code, trained models, and detailed experimental results presented in this work are publicly available at our GitHub repository, facilitating reproducibility and further research in fallacy detection.

7 Limitations

While our proposed model achieved promising results for fallacy detection, several limitations must be acknowledged. The dataset was highly imbalanced, with a significantly larger number of non-fallacious examples compared to fallacious ones. This imbalance likely impacted the model's ability to generalize effectively across both classes, causing it to be biased toward the majority non-fallacious category.

Computational constraints also posed significant challenges. The majority of experiments were conducted using limited GPU resources—dual T4

GPUs on Kaggle (restricted to 30 hours per week) and a local RTX 4070 setup. These limitations prevented thorough hyperparameter tuning and restricted the number of training epochs, particularly for computationally intensive models such as Wav2Vec2 and multimodal architectures. Audio-only and text-audio models were disproportionately affected, as their training was slower and more resource-intensive.

Additionally, time constraints further limited the breadth of our experimentation. In some cases, a single training epoch required up to 30 minutes, significantly curtailing our ability to explore alternative architectures and training strategies. As a result, the full potential of multimodal learning in this context remains underexplored.

These limitations are consistent with broader challenges reported in the field of fallacy detection. Many prior studies also rely on small or imbalanced datasets, limiting generalizability across fallacy detection or application domains. Model performance tends to vary significantly depending on the modality used—text, audio, or multimodal—which complicates cross-study comparisons.

Future work should address these issues by expanding and balancing the dataset across binary fallacy detection categories, optimizing training efficiency, and leveraging more robust computational infrastructure. Exploring a wider range of multimodal architectures with better scalability would also be essential for capturing nuanced fallacious patterns beyond textual content alone. Additionally, an ablation study that systematically repeats all experimental settings while incorporating contextual information—such as preceding or surrounding sentences—could help quantify the impact of context on fallacy detection performance and better inform future model designs.

References

Diego Atarama, Diego Pereira, and Cesar Salas. 2024. F-detector: Design of a solution based on machine learning to detect logical fallacias on digital texts. In *2024 11th International Conference on Soft Computing & Machine Intelligence (ISCMI)*, pages 216–221. IEEE.

Frank Breslin. 2023. Fallacy Detection: Part 1 — frankbreslin41. `https://medium.com/@frankbreslin41/fallacy-detection-part-1-2e5047c335b9`.

Mariana Chaves, Elena Cabrio, and Serena Villata. 2025. Falcon: A multi-label graph-based dataset for fallacy classification in the covid-19 infodemic. In *SAC'25-ACM/SIGAPP Symposium on Applied Computing*.

Fermín L Cruz, Fernando Enríquez, F Javier Ortega, and José A Troyano. 2025. Fallacyes-political: A multi-class dataset of fallacies in spanish political debates. *Procesamiento del Lenguaje Natural*, 74:127–138.

Jacob Devlin, Ming-Wei Chang, Kenton Lee, and Kristina Toutanova. 2018. BERT: pre-training of deep bidirectional transformers for language understanding. *CoRR*, abs/1810.04805.

Daya Guo, Dejian Yang, Haowei Zhang, Junxiao Song, Ruoyu Zhang, Runxin Xu, Qihao Zhu, Shirong Ma, Peiyi Wang, Xiao Bi, and 1 others. 2025. Deepseek-r1: Incentivizing reasoning capability in llms via reinforcement learning. *arXiv preprint arXiv:2501.12948*.

Zhenzhong Lan, Mingda Chen, Sebastian Goodman, Kevin Gimpel, Piyush Sharma, and Radu Soricut. 2019. Albert: A lite bert for self-supervised learning of language representations. *arXiv preprint arXiv:1909.11942*.

Zhuang Liu, Wayne Lin, Ya Shi, and Jun Zhao. 2021. A robustly optimized bert pre-training approach with post-training. In *China national conference on Chinese computational linguistics*, pages 471–484. Springer.

Eleonora Mancini, Federico Ruggeri, Paolo Torroni, and 1 others. 2024. Multimodal fallacy classification in political debates. In *Proceedings of the 18th Conference of the European Chapter of the Association for Computational Linguistics (Volume 2: Short Papers)*, pages 170–178. Association for Computational Linguistics.

Fengjun Pan, Xiaobao Wu, Zongrui Li, and Anh Tuan Luu. 2024. Are llms good zero-shot fallacy classifiers? *arXiv preprint arXiv:2410.15050*.

Nils Reimers and Iryna Gurevych. 2019. Sentence-bert: Sentence embeddings using siamese bert-networks. *arXiv preprint arXiv:1908.10084*.

Ramon Ruiz-Dolz and John Lawrence. 2023. Detecting argumentative fallacies in the wild: Problems and limitations of large language models. In *Proceedings of the 10th Workshop on Argument Mining*. Association for Computational Linguistics.

Steffen Schneider, Alexei Baevski, Ronan Collobert, and Michael Auli. 2019. wav2vec: Unsupervised pre-training for speech recognition. *arXiv preprint arXiv:1904.05862*.

Douglas Walton. 2006. *Fundamentals of Critical Argumentation*. Cambridge University Press, New York.

Multimodal Argumentative Fallacy Classification in Political Debates

Warale Avinash Kalyan, Siddharth Pagaria, Chaitra V, Spoorthi H G
Presidency University, Bengaluru, India
warale.avinash@gmail.com

Abstract

Argumentative fallacy classification plays a crucial role in improving discourse quality by identifying flawed reasoning that may mislead or manipulate audiences. While traditional approaches have primarily relied on textual analysis, they often overlook paralinguistic cues such as intonation and prosody that are present in speech. In this study, we explore how multimodal analysis, in which we combine textual and audio features, can enhance fallacy classification in political debates. We develop and evaluate text-only, audio-only, and multimodal models using the MM-USED-fallacy dataset to assess the contribution of each modality. Our findings indicate that the multimodal model, which integrates linguistic and acoustic signals, outperforms unimodal systems, underscoring the potential of multimodal approaches in capturing complex argumentative structures.

1 Introduction

Argumentative fallacies are the reasoning errors that may appear rhetorically persuasive yet lack logical validity. They pose a significant challenge to both critical thinking and automated discourse analysis. In high-stakes communicative contexts such as political debates, these fallacies (e.g., *ad hominem, appeal to emotion, slippery slope, false cause*) are frequently employed to sway audiences while circumventing sound logic. Automatically identifying such flawed reasoning patterns, a task known as argumentative fallacy classification, is increasingly recognized as a crucial objective in computational argumentation with implications for misinformation detection, media literacy, and democratic accountability.

Recent work has demonstrated the potential of large-scale pretrained language models for detecting fallacies in text. Jin et al. (2022) introduced a benchmark taxonomy and showed that transformer-based models such as RoBERTa outperform traditional classifiers. Goffredo et al. (2022) extended this research to political discourse, annotating U.S. presidential debates and highlighting the importance of nuanced semantic understanding for identifying reasoning flaws. These contributions underscore the ability of neural models to capture structural properties of argumentation when grounded in high-quality text data.

Fallacious reasoning often depends not only on what is said but also on how it is delivered. Paralinguistic features such as intonation, stress, and rhythm convey speaker intent and emotional appeal. Early multimodal work like M-Arg (Mestre et al., 2021) combined audio and transcripts to enhance argumentative analysis, while (Mancini et al., 2022) showed how prosodic signals complement lexical cues in detecting fallacies.

Building on this, Mancini et al. (2024a) introduced MAMKit, which includes the MM-USED-fallacy dataset (Mancini et al., 2024b), annotated with aligned audio and text across six fallacy types. In this paper, we evaluate a broad set of models and focus on three best-performing configurations based on validation performance: text-only (RoBERTa), audio-only (BiLSTM with MFCC), and multimodal (RoBERTa with Wav2Vec2), assessed under a unified framework for comparative analysis. [1]

2 Related Work

The classification of argumentative fallacies has evolved from early rule-based and shallow learning methods to modern neural architectures built on large-scale pre-trained language models. Jin et al. (2022) framed fallacy detection as a structured classification task and demonstrated the advantages of transformer-based approaches, such as RoBERTa, in capturing complex reasoning patterns. Goffredo et al. (2022) extended this line of work to political

[1] https://github.com/p4rz1v4l26/Multimodal-Argumentative-Fallacy-Classification-in-Political-Debates

Proceedings of the 12th Argument Mining Workshop, pages 374–380
July 31, 2025 ©2025 Association for Computational Linguistics

discourse, introducing a richly annotated corpus of U.S. presidential debates and showing that encoding argument structure improves textual fallacy classification.

Beyond text, multimodal approaches have gained traction as researchers increasingly recognize the role of delivery in persuasive discourse. Mestre et al. (2021) introduced M-Arg, a dataset that combines transcripts and aligned audio from political debates, showing that models incorporating both modalities outperform unimodal baselines. Mancini et al. (2024b) released the MM-USED-fallacy corpus, which includes six fallacy categories annotated over real-world political debate clips. This was followed by the release of MAMKit (Mancini et al., 2024a), a toolkit that provides standardized preprocessing and modeling routines for this dataset. Their work highlighted how prosodic cues can complement lexical signals in fallacy detection.

While prior studies highlight the potential of multimodal approaches, they often lack systematic comparisons across modalities. In our work, we evaluate several transformer-based text models and audio models, ultimately selecting RoBERTa for text and BiLSTM for audio based on validation performance. For the multimodal setup, we combined RoBERTa with Wav2Vec2.0. These three configurations were chosen for their strong performance under consistent settings on the MM-USED-fallacy dataset, forming the basis of our controlled comparison across the modalities.

3 Data

We performed the experiments on the **MM-USED-fallacy** dataset (Mancini et al., 2024b), a multimodal resource released as part of the MAMKit toolkit for argument mining. This dataset is specifically designed for the **Argumentative Fallacy Classification (AFC)** task and contains aligned textual and audio segments drawn from political debates. Each snippet is annotated with one of six fallacy types: *ad hominem*, *appeal to authority*, *appeal to emotion*, *slippery slope*, *slogans*, and *false cause*.

Inspired by the setup in Mancini et al. (2024b), our work leverages both linguistic and paralinguistic information from the MM-USED-fallacy dataset. Table 1 presents the count of instances for each fallacy type. This distribution provides insight into the prevalence of each class within the dataset and informs model training, particularly in terms of addressing class imbalance. Notably, some categories such as *appeal to emotion* and *ad hominem* occur more frequently, whereas others like false cause and slogans are relatively underrepresented, potentially impacting classification performance.

Fallacy	**MM-USED-fallacy**
Appeal to Emotion	800
Appeal to Authority	191
Ad Hominem	149
False Cause	56
Slippery Slope	46
Slogans	36
Total Count	**1,278**

Table 1: Distribution of fallacy types in the MM-USED-fallacy dataset.

We employed a stratified data splitting strategy using the `mm-argfallacy-2025` custom dataset splitter, introduced (Mancini et al., 2024a) as part of the MAMKit toolkit. This splitter partitions the data into non-overlapping train, validation, and test sets while maintaining label distribution. The final evaluations were conducted on a held-out secret test set to ensure unbiased assessment of model performance. For further details refer Appendix B.

3.1 Preprocessing and Cleaning

The preprocessing pipeline was tailored to meet the requirements of unimodal and multimodal classification models:

Text Modality.

BERT Text was tokenized using the `BertTokenizer`. Inputs were lowercased (for `bert-base-uncased`), tokenized using WordPiece encoding, and padded or truncated to a fixed sequence length.

RoBERTa We used the `RobertaTokenizer` from Hugging Face. To incorporate broader context, each sentence was concatenated with its preceding and following sentences. Standard text normalization procedures were applied to eliminate inconsistencies, special characters, and formatting noise.

DeBERTa The `DebertaTokenizer` was used for tokenization. Similar to RoBERTa, preprocessing included sentence normalization and cleaning. The pipeline was adapted to accommodate DeBERTa's disentangled attention mechanism.

Audio-Modality.

BiLSTM + MFCC Audio recordings were converted to mono-channel at 16 kHz and standardized to a duration of 5 seconds via padding or truncation. We extracted 13-dimensional Mel-Frequency Cepstral Coefficients (MFCCs) using Librosa, followed by mean-variance normalization to stabilize training.

Wav2Vec2 Raw audio waveforms sampled at 16 kHz were fed directly into the `wav2vec2-base-960h` model without handcrafted feature extraction. Padding or truncation was applied to conform to model input constraints.

Text-Audio Modality.

RoBERTa + Wav2Vec2 Text and audio inputs were preprocessed independently, following the procedures described in the respective unimodal sections. Text was tokenized using the `RobertaTokenizer`, with adjacent sentences concatenated to provide contextual information. Audio inputs were raw waveforms sampled at 16 kHz and padded or truncated to a fixed length of 5 seconds before being passed to the `wav2vec2-base-960h` model. This ensured consistency in input dimensions across both modalities.

4 Experimental Setup

This section outlines the overall architecture and training configuration of models developed for argumentative fallacy classification using text, audio, and multimodal inputs. The models are evaluated using the MM-USED-fallacy dataset, which comprises annotated conversational data collected from political discourse. As illustrated in Figure 1, the multimodal framework integrates a text module and an audio module, whose respective feature representations are concatenated and passed through a classifier to predict the fallacy label.

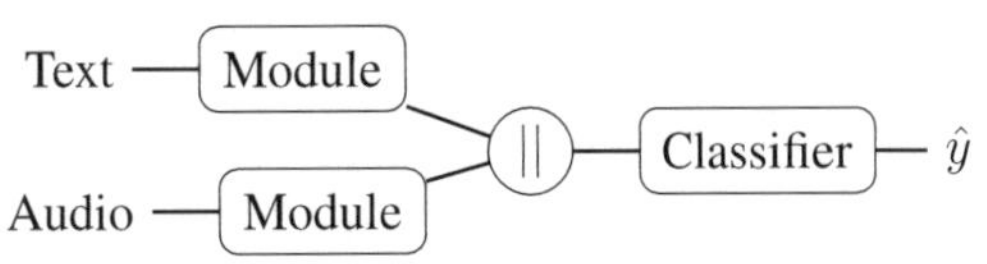

Figure 1: The schema for multimodal Argumentative Fallacy Classification model.

4.1 Model

We evaluated three distinct model configurations for fallacy classification: a Text-Only Model, an Audio-Only Model, and a Text-Audio Model. Each model is trained independently and assessed on the validation dataset to enable comparative analysis. Based on the results achieved and displayed in Table 2, we elected to proceed with the model that demonstrated the highest F1-score across labels on the validation set.

Model	AH	AE	AA	FC	SS	S	Average ($\bar{x} \pm \sigma$)
Text-only							
RoBERTa	**.10**	**.81**	**.22**	**.19**	**.11**	**.03**	**.24 ± .26**
BERT	.09	.74	.2	.16	.12	.02	.22 ± .13
DeBERTa	.06	.13	.12	.08	.07	.01	.078 ± .08
Audio-only							
BiLSTM w/ MFCC	**.00**	**.76**	**.05**	**.11**	**.06**	**.00**	**.16 ± .38**
Wav2Vec2	.00	.56	.04	.11	.05	.00	.12 ± .06
Multi-Modal							
RoBERTa + Wav2Vec2	**.09**	**.79**	**.19**	**.09**	**.07**	**.06**	**.22 ± .27**

Table 2: Macro F1-scores across fallacy types for each model configuration. AH: Ad Hominem, AE: Appeal to Emotion, AA: Appeal to Authority, FC: False Cause, SS: Slippery Slope, S: Slogans.

4.1.1 Text-Only Model

The text-only models are trained to classify fallacies using only the linguistic content of annotated snippets. We experiment with three transformer-based architectures: DeBERTa, BERT, and RoBERTa, each trained on the fallacy-labeled text segments. These models enable a comparative analysis of how different pretrained language encoders capture argumentative patterns in political discourse. The results presented in Table 2 are based on validation data and reflect the performance of the models under a standardized training setup. As seen in Table 2, RoBERTa and BERT outperform the other models, achieving the highest validation F1-score. Based on this observation, we selected RoBERTa as the final text encoder for our text-only and multimodal configurations due to its consistent performance.

4.1.2 Audio-Only Model

We evaluated two audio-only pipelines: one using MFCC features with a BiLSTM classifier, and another using raw audio with a pretrained Wav2Vec2 encoder. In the MFCC-BiLSTM setup, audio clips were converted to 16 kHz mono and standardized to 5 seconds by padding or truncation. We extracted 13-dimensional MFCC features using Librosa, which capture tone and rhythm patterns, and fed them into a BiLSTM for temporal modeling, followed by a dense classification layer (Aldeneh and Provost, 2017). The Wav2Vec2 pipeline, by contrast, operated directly on raw audio to extract high-level embeddings. As shown in Table 2, the MFCC-BiLSTM model outperformed Wav2Vec2 on the validation set and was selected for further experimentation.

4.1.3 Text-Audio Model

The multimodal architecture integrates both textual and audio modalities to enhance fallacy detection performance. For the textual modality, we employ a pre-trained RoBERTa model as the unimodal text encoder, extracting contextual embeddings from input sequences. For the audio modality, we utilize Wav2Vec2 to encode raw audio signals into high-level feature representations. The outputs from both unimodal encoders are then concatenated and fed into a logistic regression meta-classifier, which performs the final classification. This late fusion strategy allows the model to leverage complementary information from both text and audio streams, facilitating more robust fallacy identification. The validation F1-score of the text-audio model is shown in Table 2.

4.2 Model Training

Model training was conducted under constrained computational resources, without access to a dedicated GPU. This limitation imposed significant restrictions on batch size, model complexity, and training time, thereby influencing design choices throughout our experiments. Due to these software and hardware constraints, lightweight architectures and efficient preprocessing pipelines were prioritized. Kindly refer to Appendix A for more details on training configuration and hyperparameter settings.

4.3 Role of the Meta-Classifier

For the multimodal pipeline, we adopted a late fusion strategy, where a logistic regression *meta-classifier* combines the feature representations from the unimodal text and audio encoders. While this approach allows aggregation of complementary representations, its benefits were limited under current conditions, likely due to weak individual model confidence on rare classes and high modality noise. Future work could explore deeper fusion strategies to improve effectiveness.

5 Results

We evaluated three distinct configurations for the task of argumentative fallacy classification in political debates: a text-only model, an audio-only model, and a multimodal text-audio model. Model performance was assessed on the test set. Table 3 shows the macro F1 scores values of our proposed models, alongside results from other participating teams in the shared task, enabling a direct comparison of system performances, alongside their respective baselines.

Team Name	F1-Score
Text-only	
Team NUST	0.4856
Baseline BiLSTM	0.4721
Alessiopittiglio	0.4444
Baseline RoBERTa	0.3925
Team EvaAdriana	0.3746
Team CASS	**0.1432**
Audio-only	
Alessiopittiglio	0.3559
Team EvaAdriana	0.1858
Team NUST	0.1588
Baseline BiLSTM + MFCC	0.1582
Team CASS	**0.0864**
Baseline WavLM	0.0643
Text-Audio	
Team NUST	0.4611
Alessiopittiglio	0.4403
Baseline RoBERTa + WavLM	0.3816
Team EvaAdriana	0.3746
Baseline BiLSTM + MFCC	0.2191
Team CASS	**0.1432**

Table 3: Performance (F1-score) of our models (Team CASS) on the shared task test set, compared with other participating systems and official baselines

Overall, the classification results reveal relatively low performance across all models, with macro-F1 scores ranging from 0.08 to 0.14 (Table 3). While the audio-only model produced slightly different results compared to the text-only and multimodal configurations, it exhibited a significantly lower F1-score, indicating imbalanced precision and recall across classes. This may hinder consistent fallacy classification performance, especially in the presence of class imbalance.

5.1 Analysis of Results

These outcomes suggest that **textual cues remain the most reliable modality** in fallacy classification, aligning with findings from Jin et al. (2022) and Mancini et al. (2024b). Despite employing pretrained architectures for both text and audio modalities (Mancini et al., 2024b), our models exhibited relatively low macro-F1 scores across all configurations. This underperformance, detailed in Tables 2 and 3, is not merely an artifact of architecture selection but reflects deeper challenges inherent in the dataset and experimental constraints. Factors that may contribute to this are as follows:

Overfitting and Generalization Failure. We observe a significant discrepancy between validation and test performance, largely due to overfitting. As shown in Table 2, models achieve high F1-scores for the dominant class *Appeal to Emotion* (over 70%), and fail to generalize fallacy types, which constitutes the majority of both validation and test data. Consequently, when the test distribution slightly shifts or includes more ambiguous examples, performance drops sharply. This overfitting is likely exacerbated by severe class imbalance, which causes the model to memorize rather than learn fallacy-specific patterns.

Class imbalance and Limited Training. As shown in Table 1, the MM-USED-fallacy dataset is heavily skewed towards "Appeal to Emotion," which comprises over 60% of the samples. This imbalance likely biases model predictions toward dominant classes and penalizes underrepresented ones like "Slogans" or "Slippery Slope." The models were trained under constrained computational settings, with only 3–5 training epochs per configuration. In contrast, prior baselines, such as those reported in Mancini et al. (2024b) were trained for up to 500 epochs. Kindly refer to Appendix A for more details on training configuration.

Multimodal misalignment. Although the dataset contains aligned audio and text, the quality of alignment can vary. Minor temporal mismatches or noisy segments may hinder the effectiveness of Wav2Vec2 embeddings, especially when combined with textual representations.

Limited dataset size. With only 1,278 samples and significant class disparity, models especially with deep architectures like RoBERTa and Wav2Vec2, may be prone to overfitting or undergeneralization.

5.2 Label-Wise Performance

Detailed class-wise performance (Table 2) further confirms that models struggle to predict minority classes. For example, "Slogans" and "Slippery Slope" received near-zero F1 scores across all models, while "Appeal to Emotion" showed high F1 scores. Table 3 reports the macro f1-score for each fallacy category, averaged across all models. These scores reflect model performance on the validation set and illustrate the impact of class imbalance on model behavior.

5.3 Data and Alignment.

During preprocessing, we identified instances of misaligned or corrupted audio-text pairs, similar to the alignment issues noted by Mancini et al. (2024b). One notable case involved the audio file `653.wav` under the dialogue folder 46_2020, which was found to be corrupted and unreadable. According to the dataset, this sample was labeled as *Appeal to Emotion*, and the corresponding dialogue was the phrase *"Excuse me"*. Due to the corrupted audio and the impossibility of establishing a valid alignment, we excluded this sample from our corpus. This exclusion was part of a broader quality control effort aimed at ensuring the reliability of audio-text pairs used in our unimodal and multimodal models. Model performance is influenced by the quality of text-audio alignment. Imperfect or noisy alignments can lead to incomplete multimodal inputs, negatively affecting classification accuracy.

6 Conclusion

This study underscores the enduring primacy of textual semantics in argumentative fallacy classification, while also illuminating the potential and current limitations of multimodal integration. Despite modest gains, the multimodal model's performance reveals unresolved challenges in aligning linguistic and acoustic signals, particularly under class imbalance and data sparsity (Mancini et al., 2024b; Mestre et al., 2021). These findings call for deeper representational synergy across modalities and more robust, corpora rich in argumentative discourse to advance the frontier of computational argumentation in real-world settings.

References

Zakaria Aldeneh and Emily Mower Provost. 2017. Using regional saliency for speech emotion recognition.

In *2017 IEEE International Conference on Acoustics, Speech and Signal Processing (ICASSP)*.

Pierpaolo Goffredo, Shohreh Haddadan, Vorakit Vorakitphan, Elena Cabrio, and Serena Villata. 2022. Fallacious argument classification in political debates. In *Proceedings of the Thirty-First International Joint Conference on Artificial Intelligence (IJCAI-22)*.

Zhijing Jin, Abhinav Lalwani, Tejas Vaidhya, Xiaoyu Shen, Yiwen Ding, Zhiheng Lyu, Mrinmaya Sachan, Rada Mihalcea, and Bernhard Schölkopf. 2022. Logical fallacy detection. *arXiv preprint arXiv:2202.13758*.

Eleonora Mancini, Federico Ruggeri, Stefano Colamonaco, Andrea Zecca, Samuele Marro, and Paolo Torroni. 2024a. MAMKit: A comprehensive multimodal argument mining toolkit. In *Proceedings of the 11th Workshop on Argument Mining (ArgMining 2024)* pages, Bangkok, Thailand. Association for Computational Linguistics.

Eleonora Mancini, Federico Ruggeri, Andrea Galassi, and Paolo Torroni. 2022. Multimodal argument mining: A case study in political debates. In *Proceedings of the 9th Workshop on Argument Mining*.

Eleonora Mancini, Federico Ruggeri, and Paolo Torroni. 2024b. Multimodal fallacy classification in political debates. In *Proceedings of the 18th Conference of the European Chapter of the Association for Computational Linguistics: Short Papers*.

Rafael Mestre, Razvan Milicin, Stuart E Middleton, Matt Ryan, Jiatong Zhu, and Timothy J Norman. 2021. M-arg: Multimodal argument mining dataset for political debates with audio and transcripts. In *Proceedings of the 8th Workshop on Argument Mining*.

A Training Details

This appendix outlines the implementation framework and experimental configurations used to conduct our study on multimodal argumentative fallacy classification. All experiments were conducted on a system equipped with an Intel Core i5 processor and 8 GB of RAM. The system used an integrated Intel Iris Xe graphics card, which handled all computational tasks during model training and inference. Each model required approximately 6 hours to complete training.

Despite the absence of a dedicated GPU, the experiments were optimized to run efficiently within these hardware constraints. The following tables present the detailed hyperparameter configurations used across our experiments:

Modality	Model	Ep.	BS	LR
Text	RoBERTa	3	8	2e–5
Audio	BiLSTM + MFCC	5	8	1e–3
Text+Audio	RoBERTa + Wav2Vec2	5	16	2e–5

Table 4: Hyperparameters used for each model. Ep: Epochs, BS: Batch Size, LR: Learning Rate.

B Data Loading

To facilitate standardized experimentation, we adopted the data loading and splitting utilities introduced by (Mancini et al., 2024a) for the MM-USED-fallacy dataset, targeting the task of Argumentative Fallacy Classification (AFC). The loader initializes the dataset with the task parameter set to 'AFC'. For consistency in evaluation, we utilize the custom dataset split defined as `mm-argfallacy-2025`, accessed through the get_splits() method. This splitter provides a 70:15:15 ratio for training, validation, and test sets, ensuring dialogue-level separation to prevent context leakage. The use of this academically validated split facilitates meaningful comparisons with prior work. By leveraging this modular and well-supported pipeline, we ensure that our experiments conform to the dataset's structure and are directly comparable with established baselines in the field.

Prompt-Guided Augmentation and Multi-modal Fusion for Argumentative Fallacy Classification in Political Debates

Abdullah Tahir[*], **Imaan Ibrar**[*], **Huma Ameer**[*], **Mehwish Fatima**[*] **and Seemab Latif**[†]
School of Electrical Engineering and Computer Science,
National University of Sciences and Technology, Islamabad, Pakistan
{abtahir.bese21seecs, iibrar.bese21seecs, hameer.msds20seecs,
mehwish.fatima, seemab.latif}@seecs.edu.pk

Abstract

Classifying argumentative fallacies in political discourse is challenging due to their subtle, persuasive nature across text and speech. In our MM-ArgFallacy Shared Task submission, Team NUST investigates uni-modal (text/audio) and multi-modal (text+audio) setups using pretrained models—RoBERTa for text and Whisper for audio. To tackle severe class imbalance, we introduce Prompt-Guided Few-Shot Augmentation (PG-FSA) to generate synthetic samples for underrepresented fallacies. We further propose a late fusion architecture combining linguistic and paralinguistic cues, enhanced with balancing techniques like SMOTE and Focal Loss. Our approach achieves top performance across modalities, ranking 1st in text-only and multi-modal tracks, and 3rd in audio-only, on the official leaderboard. These results underscore the effectiveness of targeted augmentation and modular fusion in multi-modal fallacy classification.

1 Introduction

Argumentative fallacies—reasoning patterns that appear logically sound but are actually flawed—are frequently employed in political discourse to mislead audiences and manipulate opinions (Goffredo et al., 2022). Their subtle persuasive nature can distort public perception and potentially lead to misguided policy decisions. As political debates continue to be a major platform for shaping public opinion, the automatic detection and classification of such fallacies is crucial for fostering transparency and informed democratic dialogue.

While prior work has focused predominantly on textual data using transformer-based models like BERT and RoBERTa (Goffredo et al., 2022, 2023), fallacies are not purely linguistic. Paralinguistic cues such as intonation, pitch, rhythm, hesitation

Fallacy Type	Description
Ad Hominem	Personal attacks instead of addressing the argument.
Appeal to Authority	Unjustified reliance on authority as evidence.
Appeal to Emotion	Persuasion by emotional manipulation rather than logic.
False Cause	Incorrect causal attributions without sufficient evidence.
Slogan	Use of catchphrases lacking argumentative substance.
Slippery Slope	Assuming one action leads to extreme outcomes without basis.

Table 1: Macro-level argumentative fallacy types and their descriptions (Goffredo et al., 2022).

are critical in signaling fallacy types, especially in speech. Emotional appeals and ad hominem attacks often rely heavily on such acoustic features (Mancini et al., 2024b). This motivates a multi-modal perspective for fallacy detection.

To address these challenges, the *12th Workshop on Argument Mining* introduces the MM-ArgFallacy Shared Task[1], targeting fallacy detection and classification in political debates under three input settings: text-only, audio-only, and text+audio. Subtasks include binary fallacy detection and multi-class classification into macro-level fallacy types (Table 1).

In this paper we are targeting fallacy classification and present Team NUST's submission to the shared task. Our key contributions are:

1. We evaluate traditional (SVM, XGBoost) and deep learning models (RoBERTa, Whisper) across uni-modal and multi-modal setups.
2. We propose Prompt-Guided Few-Shot Augmentation (PG-FSA) using GPT-based generation to synthesize fallacy-specific samples for minority classes.
3. We design a late fusion framework combining RoBERTa text and Whisper audio embeddings, enhanced with SMOTE and Focal Loss for better class balance and performance.

We evaluate our framework on the MM-USED-Fallacy dataset under the shared task. Across all three modalities—text-only, audio-only, and text-audio—our method achieved state-of-the-art per-

[*]Equal contribution.
[†]Corresponding author.

[1]MM-ArgFallacy Shared Task

Proceedings of the 12th Argument Mining Workshop, pages 381–387
July 31, 2025

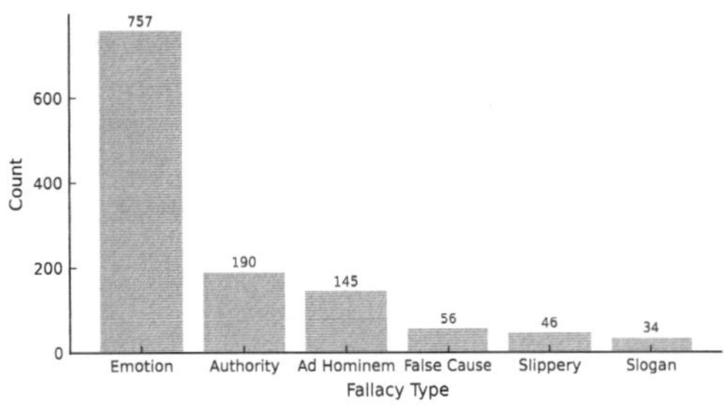

Figure 1: Distribution of fallacy types the training set.

formance, ranking 1st in text-only and multi-modal, and 3rd in audio-only categories. These results validate the effectiveness of our prompt-guided augmentation and modular fusion design.

2 Dataset

The MM-USED-Fallacy dataset, introduced by Mancini et al. (2024b), builds upon textual and audio excerpts from U.S presidential debates. The dataset is obtained using opensource MAMKit tooklkit[2] (Mancini et al., 2024a). Table 1 shows the annotations of dataset into six macro-level fallacy types. Designed for both detection and classification tasks, the dataset supports three modalities: text-only, audio-only, and text+audio.

3 Multi-Class Fallacy Classification

Our proposed framework[3] addresses the dual challenges of data imbalance and modality integration for fallacy classification. It comprises two core components: (1) Prompt-Guided Few-Shot Augmentation (PG-FSA) for data-level augmentation, and (2) Late Fusion Modeling for multi-modal integration. Figure 3 provides an overview of the framework across all modalities.

3.1 Prompt-Guided Few-Shot Augmentation

To mitigate the challenge of class imbalance dataset, we propose Prompt-Guided Few-Shot Augmentation (PG-FSA). This method uses generative capabilities of GPT-4.0, to synthesize high-quality instances for underrepresented fallacy classes. For each minority fallacy category, we engineered a structured prompt which includes formal definition of fallacy from (Goffredo et al., 2022), followed by 15 examples drawn from original training split. Hence, the language model is guided to

[2]MAMKit Link

[3]Github Link: Source code

Fallacy Type	Original	PG-FSA	Total
Ad Hominem	145	52	197
False Cause	56	51	107
Slippery Slope	46	50	96
Slogan	34	80	114

Table 2: Sample counts before and after PG-FSA for minority fallacy types.

produce new samples that remain in the semantic boundaries of the target class. To preserve the integrity of the generated samples, all outputs are human-evaluated, the evaluation method and score is discussed in Appendix A.1. This hybrid human-and-model approach allows us to improve minority class representation. The structure of our prompt is given below:

Prompt

Task:
I want to perform data augmentation because of class imbalance, and this class has very few examples. I want to generate 30 more examples of the class *class_name*.

Class Definition:
definition of class

Instructions:
I have given you 15 examples below from the dataset for your understanding. Study the examples and follow their structuring and other characteristics to generate new examples that align with this definition in the context of the slogans in political debates dataset.

Examples (15 total):
Example 1
Text: *sample from training data 1*
Fallacy Type: *class_name*

Example 2
Text: *sample from training data 2*
Fallacy Type: *class_name*

Figure 2: Prompt for data augmentation in fallacy classification task

Table 2 presents the class-wise augmentation statistics resulting from PG-FSA. We augment the generated samples in the training split given by the organizers. In addition, we also convert these generated textual samples into speech[4] using Eleven Labs[5].

3.2 Methodology

We formulate fallacy classifications as a six-way multi-class classification task spanning three input modalities: text-only, audio-only, and multi-modal (text+audio). The objective is to classify each input instance into one of the six fallacy categories: *Ad Hominem*, *Appeal to Authority*, *Appeal to Emotion*, *False Cause*, *Slippery Slope*, and *Slogan*.

[4]By including the synthetic audio clips, the results didn't improve, therefore in the proposed methodology, we employ the orignal data audio clips.

[5]ElevenLabs

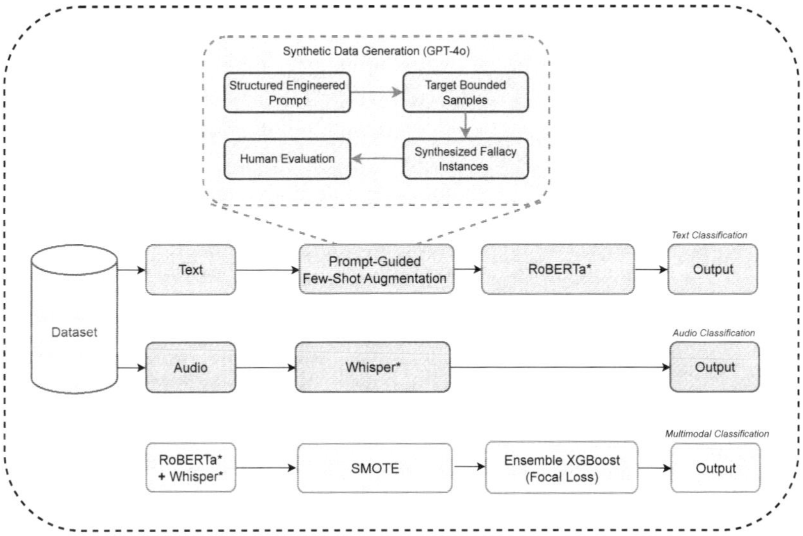

Figure 3: Proposed of Multi-Modal Fallacy Classification Framework.

3.2.1 Text-Only Classification

We fine-tune multiple transformer-based language models for text-only fallacy classification, including RoBERTa-small[6] (RoBERTaS), RoBERTa-base[7] (RoBERTaB), RoBERTa-large[8] (RoBERTaL), DeBERTa-base (DeBERTaB), Electra-base (ElectraB), BERT-base[9] (BERTB), and DistilBERT-base[10] (DistilBERTB). Among all models, RoBERTa-base[7] (RoBERTa) model (Liu et al., 2019) with PG-FSA augmentation showed the best performance and is used in the final system. Input utterances are truncated or padded to a maximum sequence length of 128 tokens. A single-layer classification head with six output neurons is appended to the final $[CLS]$ token representation from RoBERTa.

Class Imbalance Mitigation: To address the skewed class distribution, we apply weighted cross-entropy loss. Class weights are inversely proportional to class frequencies, encouraging the model to prioritize minority classes by penalizing their misclassification more heavily. We also experimented with Focal Loss for text only and found it to perform similarly to weighted cross-entropy. To ensure clarity and maintain simplicity in our final presentation, we chose to report only the weighted cross-entropy results.

[6]smallbenchnlp/roberta-small

[7]FacebookAI/roberta-base

[8]MidhunKanadan/roberta-large-fallacy-classification

[9]mempooltx/bert-base-fallacy-detection

[10]q3fer/distilbert-base-fallacy-classification

3.2.2 Audio-Only Classification

We explore both classical and transformer-based pipelines for audio-only classification. For the classical approach, we combine Mel-Frequency Cepstral Coefficients (MFCCs) Feature Extraction (FE) with 2D-CNNs, Gaussian Naive Bayes, Logistic Regression, and SGD Classifier. For transformer-based approach, we fine-tune Whisper (tiny, small, base) (Radford et al., 2022) and Wav2Vec2.0 (Baevski et al., 2020).

We also use PG-FSA augmented data to address class imbalance. We also generate synthetic speech for the augmented textual examples using ElevenLabs[5]' Text to Speech, enabling Whisper and Wav2Vec2.0 to train on both original and synthesized samples. Whisper-small fine-tuned on original data samples gave the best results. We adapt it as an encoder for classification by replacing the decoder with a feedforward layer predicting over six fallacy categories.

All audio inputs are standardized to a sampling rate of 16kHz and fed directly to the Whisper encoder. No text transcriptions are used in this modality.

3.2.3 Multi-modal Fusion

For multi-modal classification, we adopt a late fusion strategy. We encode each modality independently and concatenate them prior to classification. We incorporate RoBERTa-base[7], DistilBERT-base, and their task-specific variants as our text encoders. We use Whisper-small (WhisperS), Whisper with CNN, and Wav2Vec2.0 as our audio encoders. All the combinations of models used are presented in Table 5.

For fusion of modalities, we first concatenate representations and then we pass the fused representation to a lightweight neural module. It consists of linear projection, layer normalization, ReLU activation and dropout. Final two-layers are feedforward classifier with ReLU activation and dropout regularization. This modular fusion setup enables flexible experimentation with different encoder combinations. Further, we also experiment with various Machine Learning classifiers i.e. Logistic Regression, Random Forest, Gradient Boosting, SVM, and XGBoost+FL. Thus, We evaluate fusion of RoBERTa variants with Whisper, Whisper+CNN, and Wav2Vec2.0 using simple concatenation, XGBoost, and neural projection heads. RoBERTa-base + Whisper-small fused via XGBoost with SMOTE and Focal Loss gave the highest macro-F1 score.

Class Imbalance Mitigation: We adopt two strategies in the multi-modal setting. First, we apply SMOTE (Chawla et al., 2002) in which synthetic samples are generated for minority classes in the fused feature space via interpolation. Second, we use Focal Loss (FL) (Lin et al., 2017) which is used to handle hard-to-classify instances, focal loss down-weights easy examples and focuses the model on minority and ambiguous cases. This dual strategy is chosen to address the increased complexity introduced by the multi-modal setup. The combination of SMOTE and Focal Loss helps balance both underrepresented classes and hard-to-classify examples in the fused feature space.

4 Experimental Setup

This section details the evaluation setup used to benchmark models across three modalities: text-only, audio-only, and multi-modal (text+audio). We organize our discussion into model configurations, fusion strategies, and evaluation metrics.

4.1 Dataset

The official split includes 1,228 training and 2,160 test instances. We use MAMKit loader to obtain the data splits. After applying PG-FSA, the final dataset comprises 1,461 instances. We partition it into training and validation subsets stratified splits. The generated instances are included only in training split.

Model	M-F1
Text	
BiLSTM+GloVe	0.4721
RoBERTa	0.3925
RoBERTaB+aug. (Ours)	**0.4856**
Audio	
BiLSTM+MFCCs	0.1582
WavLM	0.0643
WhisperS+aug. (Ours)	**0.1588**
Multi-modal	
BiLSTM-GloVe+MFCCs	0.2191
MM-RoBERTa+WavLM	0.3816
RoBERTaB+WhisperS+XGBoost (Ours)	**0.4611**

Table 3: Macro-F1 scores across modalities. Models marked (Ours) are Team NUST submissions. RoBERTa-base with augmentation (aug.), Whisper-small and RoBERTa-base+Whisper-small+XGBoost performed best.

4.2 Classification Models

We conduct all experiments on a Tesla T4 GPU with 16 GB memory. For text-only models, we use a batch size of 16, max sequence length of 128, and learning rates of 1e−5 or 2e−5 depending on model stability. For audio models, the sampling rate is set to 16kHz and maximum audio length is set at 20 seconds, with a batch size of 8. We use AdamW optimizer with early stopping based on validation macro-F1. We use PyTorch and HuggingFace Transformers libraries for all these experiments.

4.3 Evaluation

We use Macro F1 score (M-F1) as the primary evaluation metric due to its robustness in imbalanced multi-class settings. It gives equal importance to each class, making it suitable for assessing performance across both majority and minority fallacy types.

5 Results and Analysis

We evaluate model performance on both validation and official test splits. Table 3 presents the results of the official test set using only the best-performing configurations. Table 3 also presents the baselines are those provided by the shared task organizers. Our models consistently outperform all provided baselines across text-only, audio-only, and multi-modal settings, underscoring the effectiveness of our design choices.

Text-only	M-F1	Audio-only	M-F1
RoBERTaB[7]	0.5441	WhisperS	**0.3168**
RoBERTaL[8]	0.4439	WhisperT	0.1800
DistilBERTB[10]	0.4369	WhisperB w/ FE	0.1275
BERTB[9]	0.3939	Wav2Vec2.0	0.1262
ElectraB	0.3945	Whisper+aug.	0.1260
DeBERTaB	0.4856	Wav2Vec+aug.	0.2400
RoBERTaS	0.4418	MFCC+2D-CNN	0.1281
RoBERTaB (aug. data)	**0.5786**	MFCC+GaussianNB	0.1764
DistilRoBERTaB (aug. data)	0.4418	MFCC+Logistic Regression	0.1622
		MFCC+SGDClassifier	0.1622

Table 4: Macro-F1 scores for various text-only & audio-only models for fallacy classification on the validation set.

5.1 Text-Only

Table 3 shows that our proposed RoBERTa-base[7] model augmented with GPT-generated synthetic data achieves an F1 score of 0.4856 on the test set. This represents a moderate decrease from its validation performance of 0.5786 (reported in Table 4). It is expected given potential variability and distributional differences between the splits. Despite the drop, the model maintains its lead over baselines. This result highlights the benefit of large-scale language models that demonstrate their capabilities through well-structured prompt-driven few-shot generation. Thus, it can mitigate data scarcity and enhance minority class representation.

5.2 Audio-Only

Whisper-small attains a test F1 of 0.1588, down from 0.3168 on the validation split (Appendix, Table 4). While the model slightly outperforms baselines, overall performance remains weak. This suggests that fallacies often lack discriminative acoustic cues, and performance is further degraded by noise, speech clarity issues, and accent variability in the dataset.

5.3 Multi-Modality

Our late fusion model RoBERTa+Whisper with XGBoost achieves F1-score of 0.4611 on the test set (vs. 0.5586 on validation; see Table 5). The model surpasses all baselines, but gains from audio remain limited. Textual features dominate the predictive signal, while simple concatenation may not fully capture cross-modal interactions, particularly for confounding classes like Appeal to Emotion and Slogan. More advanced fusion mechanisms could better align multi-modal features.

5.4 Takeaways

Overall, while all models show some test-time degradation, they consistently outperform baselines. These results emphasize the role of targeted data augmentation and modular design in improving generalization. However, the persistent class imbalance constrains further gains. Future work should focus on advanced augmentation, data cleaning, and robust fusion strategies to unlock better cross-modal alignment and minority class recognition.

Multi-modal Models	M-F1
Pre-Trained	
RoBERTaB[7]+WhisperS	**0.5594**
RoBERTaL[8]+WhisperS	0.5590
DilBERTB[10]+WhisperS	0.4531
RoBERTaB+2D-CNN+Whisper	0.4456
ML Classifiers	
Logistic Regression	0.5438
Random Forest	0.5174
Gradient Boosting	0.5277
SVM	0.5600
XGBoost+FL	**0.5586**

Table 5: Macro-F1 scores for multi-modality models for fallacy classification on the validation set. Fine-tuned neural models and ML classifiers are evaluated using RoBERTa-base and Whisper-based embeddings. Note: RoBERTa and Whisper embeddings are finetuned on MM-Used Fallacy dataset.

6 Conclusions

We tackle the task of fallacy classification across text, audio, and multi-modal inputs under class imbalance constraints. Our framework integrates pre-trained models (RoBERTa, Whisper) with prompt-guided few-shot augmentation and late fusion strategies. Experiments on the MM-USED-Fallacy dataset demonstrate strong validation and test performance across all modalities. RoBERTa-base[7] with augmentation proves most effective for text, Whisper-small performs best for audio, and late fusion with XGBoost yields the highest multi-modal gains. Future directions include modality alignment, adaptive fusion, and contrastive learning to enhance cross-modal reasoning and representation.

Limitations

While our framework achieves strong performance across modalities, a few limitations remain:

Simple Fusion Strategy: We adopt a late fusion approach using feature concatenation followed by XGBoost. While effective, this strategy may not fully capture fine-grained inter-modal dependencies. More advanced fusion techniques (e.g., cross-attention or tensor fusion) could potentially yield better alignment between modalities.

Limited Use of Context: Although contextual utterances are provided in the dataset, our current setup does not explicitly model discourse-level dependencies. Incorporating contextual reasoning (e.g., via hierarchical transformers or dialogue-aware models) may improve understanding of fallacies with pragmatic cues.

Synthetic Data Quality: Prompt-guided augmentation boosts performance, especially for underrepresented classes, but generated samples may vary in linguistic quality or realism. Filtering or scoring mechanisms could help ensure higher fidelity in future iterations.

Underperformance in Audio Modality: Despite outperforming baselines, audio-only models remain weaker due to the inherently low signal-to-noise ratio in acoustic fallacy cues. Improvements could be made via better preprocessing (*e.g.*, noise suppression, speaker normalization) or pretrained models fine-tuned for prosodic features.

References

Alexei Baevski, Yuhao Zhou, Abdelrahman Mohamed, and Michael Auli. 2020. wav2vec 2.0: A framework for self-supervised learning of speech representations. *Advances in neural information processing systems*, 33:12449–12460.

Nitesh V Chawla, Kevin W Bowyer, Lawrence O Hall, and W Philip Kegelmeyer. 2002. Smote: Synthetic minority over-sampling technique. In *Journal of Artificial Intelligence Research*, volume 16, pages 321–357.

Pierpaolo Goffredo, Mariana Chaves, Serena Villata, and Elena Cabrio. 2023. Argument-based Detection and Classification of Fallacies in Political Debates. In *ACL Anthology*, volume 2023.findings-emnlp.684 of *Findings of the Association for Computational Linguistics: EMNLP 2023*, pages 11101–11112, Singapore (SG), Singapore. Association for Computational Linguistics.

Pierpaolo Goffredo, Shohreh Haddadan, Vorakit Vorakitphan, Elena Cabrio, and Serena Villata. 2022. Fallacious argument classification in political debates. In *Proceedings of the Thirty-First International Joint Conference on Artificial Intelligence, IJCAI-22*, pages 4143–4149. International Joint Conferences on Artificial Intelligence Organization. Main Track.

Tsung-Yi Lin, Priya Goyal, Ross Girshick, Kaiming He, and Piotr Dollar. 2017. Focal loss for dense object detection. In *Proceedings of the IEEE International Conference on Computer Vision (ICCV)*, pages 2980–2988.

Yinhan Liu, Myle Ott, Naman Goyal, Jingfei Du, Mandar Joshi, Danqi Chen, Omer Levy, Mike Lewis, Luke Zettlemoyer, and Veselin Stoyanov. 2019. Roberta: A robustly optimized bert pretraining approach. *arXiv preprint arXiv:1907.11692*.

Eleonora Mancini, Federico Ruggeri, Stefano Colamonaco, Andrea Zecca, Samuele Marro, and Paolo Torroni. 2024a. MAMKit: A comprehensive multimodal argument mining toolkit. In *Proceedings of the 11th Workshop on Argument Mining (ArgMining 2024)*, pages 69–82, Bangkok, Thailand. Association for Computational Linguistics.

Eleonora Mancini, Federico Ruggeri, and Paolo Torroni. 2024b. Multimodal fallacy classification in political debates. In *Proceedings of the 18th Conference of the European Chapter of the Association for Computational Linguistics (Volume 2: Short Papers)*, pages 170–178, St. Julian's, Malta. Association for Computational Linguistics.

Alec Radford, Jong Wook Gao, Greg Brockman, Vicki Narasimhan, Aditya Ramesh, Gabriel Goh, Sandhini Agarwal, Girish Sastry, Amanda Askell, Pam Mishkin, and 1 others. 2022. Robust speech recognition via large-scale weak supervision. *Preprint*, arXiv:2212.04356.

A Appendix

A.1 Human Evaluation

To ensure the quality of the augmented examples, we use a two-stage human evaluation process. Two independent annotators assess each example against a predefined evaluation criterion to determine whether it matches the intended class. Examples with mutual agreement on label 1 are retained, while those with agreement on label 0 are discarded. In cases of disagreement, the annotators conduct a follow-up discussion to reach a consensus, and the agreed label is marked as the final evaluation. The final augmented dataset includes only examples with a final label of 1. An inter-annotator agreement, measured as raw percentage agreement (due to the absence of negative examples), is 87.55%.

Leveraging Context for Multimodal Fallacy Classification in Political Debates

Alessio Pittiglio
DISI, University of Bologna, Bologna, Italy
alessio.pittiglio@studio.unibo.it

Abstract

In this paper, we present our submission to the MM-ArgFallacy2025 shared task, which aims to advance research in multimodal argument mining, focusing on logical fallacies in political debates. Our approach uses pretrained Transformer-based models and proposes several ways to leverage context. In the fallacy classification subtask, our models achieved macro F1-scores of 0.4444 (text), 0.3559 (audio), and 0.4403 (multimodal). Our multimodal model showed performance comparable to the text-only model, suggesting potential for improvements.

1 Introduction

Politicians have always resorted to stratagems in an attempt to convince as many people as possible to vote for them. In recent years, there have been initiatives aimed at verifying the truthfulness of politicians' statements. However, this type of verification, although useful, is not sufficient: many persuasive techniques do not rely on false facts, but on misleading reasoning, such as logical fallacies.

We address the MM-ArgFallacy2025 shared task[1], which focuses on multimodal detection and classification of argumentative fallacies in political debates. It proposes two tasks: Argumentative Fallacy Detection (AFD) and Argumentative Fallacy Classification (AFC). In this work, we focus on the AFC task. The classes for the AFC are those proposed by Goffredo et al. (2022). For both subtasks, three input settings are provided: text-only, audio-only, and a combination of both (text+audio). The dataset used is MM-USED-fallacy (Mancini et al., 2024b), which is available via MAMKit (Mancini et al., 2024a). Initially, only the training set was released, so we created our own validation split for internal evaluation. The official test set, released later without labels, was used for the final submission. The primary assessment criterion for AFC is the macro F1-score.

We propose a system that leverages Transformer-based models for both text and audio modalities. For text input, we experiment with a range of architectures, including a simple concatenation of text input and its previous context, a context pooling model, and a cross-attention model with a gating mechanism for context integration. Among these, the context pooling model combined with RoBERTa-large (Liu et al., 2019) yielded the best performance. For audio input, we use a fine-tuned HuBERT Base model (Hsu et al., 2021), applying temporal average pooling to obtain global embeddings. We also experiment with a variant that combines embeddings from the audio input and its context, following a strategy similar to the context-pooling approach used for text. For multimodal integration, we explore ensemble strategies that combine the outputs of the text and audio models using weighted averaging and majority voting. The main contribution of this work is an investigation into how context from previous sentences can be effectively incorporated across both modalities. While textual context consistently improved performance, the impact of audio context was less significant. Finally, we suggest some possible directions for future improvements. Our code is publicly available [2].

2 Related Work

Until a few years ago, most research in the field of argument mining in political debates focused exclusively on text data. More recently, it has been shown that the use of audio data can also be informative. In Lippi and Torroni (2016), the authors introduced a dataset based on the 2015 UK elec-

[1] https://nlp-unibo.github.io/mm-argfallacy/2025/

[2] https://github.com/alessiopittiglio/mm-argfallacy

Proceedings of the 12th Argument Mining Workshop, pages 388–397
July 31, 2025

tions and demonstrated that the inclusion of audio features improves claim extraction.

In Haddadan et al. (2019), the authors addressed the problem of recognizing argumentative components in political debates. They created a new corpus, USElecDeb60To16, and highlighted that a key factor in argumentative mining is the use of context.

In Goffredo et al. (2022), the dataset proposed by Haddadan et al. (2019) was extended with annotations for six fallacy categories: Ad Hominem, Appeal to Authority, Appeal to Emotion, False Cause, Slogan, and Slippery Slope. A model based on Longformer (Beltagy et al., 2020) was proposed. The model was trained to classify fallacies using debate context, fallacy snippets, and argumentative components and relations from the original dataset.

Recent studies in multimodal argument mining have highlighted the benefits of combining text and audio inputs for improved performance. In Mancini et al. (2022), the authors showed that features extracted from pretrained models outperform traditional features (e.g., MFCCs) in tasks such as claim detection and argumentative relation classification. However, their effective integration with text inputs remains an open problem. Mancini et al. (2024b) introduced MM-USED-fallacy, the first multimodal corpus for classifying argumentative fallacies, extending the USED-fallacy dataset (Goffredo et al., 2022). Their proposed architecture combines pretrained models for text and audio using a fusion approach, achieving significant improvement over text-only models like BERT (Devlin et al., 2018) and RoBERTa (Liu et al., 2019).

Despite these advances, the usage of context in multimodal argument mining remains unexplored. Prior work has primarily focused on classifying sentences without evaluating how context from preceding sentences influences performance across modalities. In this work, we address this gap by investigating context-aware architectures for both text and audio, as part of the AFC shared task.

3 Input Settings

For the challenge, we had access only to the training set. The train split we worked on was composed of 1278 sentences. It is relatively small and highly imbalanced dataset. To prepare a validation set, we performed an 80/20 train/validation split at the sentence level, using the stratify option to keep the same class distribution as the original dataset.

3.1 Text

Data processing. The text was not preprocessed in any way. We directly used the tokenizer of each backbone model to tokenize the text.

Data encoding. We used a range of backbones varying in size. These include smaller models such as BERT-base (Devlin et al., 2018), RoBERTa-base (Liu et al., 2019), and DeBERTaV3-base (He et al., 2023), as well as larger ones like RoBERTa-large, DeBERTaV3-large, and the recent ModernBERT-large (Warner et al., 2024). The latter integrates new features, such as FlashAttention 2 (Dao, 2023), and has the largest context window (4080 tokens). Compared to other backbones like Longformer (Beltagy et al., 2020), ModernBERT-large was chosen for its more efficient training. All encoders were fine-tuned with all layers unfrozen.

Architectures. To incorporate context, three approaches were used:

1. **Concat**, involving the concatenation of the text and its context, separated by the tokenizer's separator token.

2. **ContextPool**, based on pooled embeddings obtained from a shared transformer to classify the text based on its context.

3. **CrossAttn**, which uses a cross-attention mechanism to integrate text and context, followed by a gating mechanism for fusion.

See Appendix A.1 for more details about the architectures. The model that performed better was **ContextPool-RoBERTa**, which combines the ContextPool architecture with RoBERTa-large. To maximize performance, we submitted an ensemble composed of our three best models trained using this successful combination. Two of the models were trained with the same hyperparameters, while the third used a larger context window size of 5, with all other parameters kept identical (see Table 5). At inference time, predictions from the three models were combined by averaging their predicted logits, using the weights reported in Table 7, which were obtained via Bayesian optimization.

3.2 Audio

Data processing. For the audio processing, we used a custom processor component, based on the one from the MAMKit library (Mancini et al., 2024a), to handle the audio and its context. We implemented a function that returns 100 ms of silence for empty inputs. Valid audio files are loaded, resampled to 16 kHz, and concatenated along the time axis if multiple files are provided. Instead of using the built-in collator provided by MAMKit, which was implemented for training another transformer starting from the features extracted from a backbone, we decided to fine-tune a model directly for this task. Therefore, we implemented a new collator specifically for this purpose. Each input is optionally truncated to a maximum length of 15 seconds. This is done because processing very long audio causes an out-of-memory error. When context is available, it is processed in the same way.

Data encoding. We evaluated the following backbones, also used by Mancini et al. (2024b): Wav2Vec 2.0 Base (Baevski et al., 2020) fine-tuned on 960 hours of LibriSpeech, WavLM Base+ (Chen et al., 2021) fine-tuned on 100h of LibriSpeech clean, and HuBERT Base (Hsu et al., 2021). Despite similar training setups, Wav2Vec 2.0 Base and WavLM Base+ did not perform well in early experiments, while HuBERT Base showed promising results.

Architectures. We used two architectures. The first architecture is **HuBERT-Base fine-tuned**, which is simply a fine-tuned version of the backbone. Our idea was to unfreeze only some layers. With audio, we cannot use the same mechanism used for text (pooling embeddings), so we used the temporal average (average along the sequence dimension) of the embeddings. The result is a global embedding for each audio sample without completely losing the temporal dimension. Inspired by the results obtained with text, the second architecture we implemented is **TemporalAvg** which combines the mean pooling of the audio snippet with that obtained from the audio of the context.

3.3 Text-Audio

In order to obtain the best possible results, we decided to create an ensemble of our best text model (ContextPool-RoBERTa) and audio model (HuBERT-Base fine-tuned). Taking an arithmetic average of the logits of each model is the simplest way to do it, but there are more effective methods to improve it. One such method is to use a weighted average. The optimization was performed using the Bayesian optimization technique (Snoek et al., 2012). The metric we aimed to maximize was the F1 score calculated on the validation set. The validation set used was the same one used during the training of the models. Each model was trained using the same train/validation split; otherwise, this could distort the metric. The optimization was performed with 20 iterations and 15 initial points (see Table 8 for the final weights). Additionally, we tested a technique based on majority voting across three models. These included: (1) our best text-only model (ContextPool-RoBERTa) (2) our best audio-only model (HuBERT-Base fine-tuned), and (3) the ensemble combining our best text and audio models. This majority voting ensemble was used for the final submission.

4 Experimental Setup

4.1 Context Usage

Following the definition provided in the challenge specifications, we define the *debate context* of a given input as the sequence of previous sentences in the debate, aligned with their corresponding audio segments. For a sentence at index i in a political debate, the context consists of all preceding sentences, i.e., those from 0 to $i-1$, where 0 denotes the first sentence in the debate. For text, we experimented with the three previously mentioned architectures: Concat, ContextPool and CrossAttn. For the audio, we used only TemporalAvg, as it is an adaptation of ContextPool, the one that performs best on text. To adapt ContextPool for audio, we slightly modified the architecture, while maintaining the core idea of concatenating audio and context. Since Audio Transformers downsample raw waveforms into shorter sequences, masking padded tokens isn't directly possible; instead, we apply average pooling over time. To assess the contribution of context, we conducted ablation studies across different configurations (see Table 1 and Table 2). We tested all combinations of window sizes and architectures, with window sizes ranging from 1 to 6.

We observed that the Concat approach did not yield improvements over the model without context. ContextPool achieved the highest F1 score with a context size of $N = 4$. One interesting observation is that the improvement does not scale linearly with increasing context. For instance, ContextPool performance slightly drops after $N = 4$.

Vanilla CrossAttn remains below the baseline until $N = 3$. After that, adding context becomes beneficial. With CrossAttn using attentive pooling, we observe immediate improvements that re-

Architecture	N=0 (No Ctx)	N=1	N=2	N=3	N=4	N=5	N=6
Transformer (No Context)	0.6131	-	-	-	-	-	-
Concat	-	0.5538	0.5932	0.4767	0.5331	0.5941	0.5431
ContextPool	-	**0.6636**	0.6479	0.5786	**0.6983**	0.6542	**0.6494**
CrossAttn	-	0.5699	0.6086	0.5395	0.6304	0.6344	0.6219
w/ Gate	-	0.5867	0.6171	0.5487	0.5388	0.6181	0.6032
w/ Attentive Pooling	-	0.6603	**0.6527**	0.6227	0.6590	**0.6579**	0.6383
w/ Gate & Attentive Pool	-	0.6280	0.6520	**0.6407**	0.6261	0.3701	0.6377

Table 1: Ablation study on context integration strategies and window size (N) for text modality (F1-Macro).

mains relatively stable across different values of N. It demonstrates performance comparable to ContextPool but does not reach its peak. In contrast, CrossAttn with gate fusion and attentive pooling shows more inconsistent behavior, achieving the lowest overall score at $N = 5$.

For the audio modality, the ablation results reported in Table 2 reveal that adding context does not consistently improve performance. The TemporalAvg architecture shows fluctuating F1 scores across different values of N, with no clear rising trend. The baseline Hubert model, fine-tuned without additional context, outperforms all TemporalAvg configurations.

4.2 Training

The training was conducted using an NVIDIA RTX 3090 GPU. When available, we utilized FlashAttention (Dao, 2023) to accelerate training. To investigate whether a positive correlation exists between the input and the context window size, we experimented with varying context lengths. The models were trained with bf16 mixed precision, and AdamW (Loshchilov and Hutter, 2019) was used as the optimizer. A linear learning rate scheduler was used, with the warmup phase set to 30% of the total training steps. To mitigate overfitting and prevent wasting computational resources, early stopping based on the validation loss with a patience of 5 was applied during all training runs. For class weights, we used those also used by Mancini et al. (2024b). We also attempted to dynamically compute class weights from our training split but observed no significant improvements. For each model, we tested a range of learning rates, determined based on the model's response to an initial learning rate. Each learning rate was evaluated across three independent experiments with different random seeds, and the optimal rate was selected based on the average performance on the validation set. Hyperparameter tuning was conducted using W&B Sweeps (Biewald, 2020). A detailed list of hyperparameters and training configurations is provided in Appendix A.2 (see Table 5 and Table 6).

5 Results

The results for the final submitted models are reported in Table 3. Observing the ranks, our audio model (HuBERT-Base fine-tuned) performs particularly well compared to other models. Moreover, the multimodal model did not outperform the text and audio models. We hypothesize that the lack of interaction between modalities during training may have limited the model's ability to exploit cross-modal correlations, thereby reducing potential gains. Overall, We conclude that our technique for combining text and audio was not effective.

Since no detailed results for each class were provided, we evaluated the same model checkpoints on our validation set to analyze class performance (Table 4). *Appeal to Emotion* achieves the highest F1 score for both text and audio, likely due to its high concentration in the dataset. In the text modality, the model also performs well on *Slippery Slope*, likely benefiting from lexical patterns that indicate causality or escalation. However, performance drops on *False Cause*, probably due to the complexity of the reasoning required.

In the audio modality, the second highest class is *Slogan*, as it is easily recognizable and strongly dependent on vocal pitch. In contrast, the model struggles with *Slippery Slope*, where increased use of context might improve performance. However, audio was truncated to 15 seconds due to memory constraints.

Interestingly, the text-audio model performs like a "faded" version of the text-only model. This suggests that the current fusion approach may dilute strong unimodal signals rather than enrich them with additional information. Improvement is ob-

Architecture	N=0 (No Ctx)	N=1	N=2	N=3	N=4	N=5	N=6
Hubert Base fine-tuned	0.48061	-	-	-	-	-	-
TemporalAvg	-	0.4282	0.4149	0.3856	0.4460	0.4553	0.4518

Table 2: Ablation study on context window size (N) for audio modality (F1-Macro).

Input	Team	F1
Text-Only	Team NUST	0.4856
	Baseline BiLSTM	0.4721
	Our team	0.4444
Audio-Only	Our team	0.3559
	Team EvaAdriana	0.1858
	Team NUST	0.1588
Text-Audio	Team NUST	0.4611
	Our team	0.4403
	Baseline RoBERTa + WavLM	0.3816

Table 3: External evaluation of submissions on the test set. Reported F1 scores are macro-averaged.

Class	Text-only	Audio only	Text-audio
AE	0.8802	0.7616	0.8519
AA	0.7105	0.3636	0.6667
AH	0.6909	0.4444	0.6667
FC	0.6316	0.3636	0.6316
SS	0.7500	0.3333	0.7500
S	0.6667	0.5455	0.7143

Table 4: F1 scores for each class on the validation set. AE: Appeal to Emotion, AA: Appeal to Authority, AH: Ad Hominem, FC: False Cause, SS: Slippery Slope, S: Slogans

served only in *Slogan*, indicating that integration can be beneficial when modalities contribute complementary.

This provides fundamental insight into the fact that features are orthogonal across modalities, suggesting that a more complex fusion strategy might better leverage the strengths of each.

6 Conclusion

Our main contribution is having explored how to leverage information from previous sentences. Our second approach, ContextPool-RoBERTa, proved more effective than the other methods we tested. In contrast, for the audio setting, we successfully trained a model (HuBERT-Base fine-tuned) capable of distinguishing different fallacies. Furthermore, our decision to fine-tune a model and unfreeze certain layers proved more efficient and merits further exploration. We believe the reason for this efficiency lies in the improvement of the feature extractor when fine-tuned on the specific argument domain.

We also explored a late fusion approach to combine the predictions and majority voting in an attempt to improve performance. However, we found this technique to be less effective. Additionally, we noted that features learned from the text and audio models capture distinct aspects; thus, further exploration of techniques to combine these features in a more complex manner could be promising.

Limitations

Dataset. Duplicate samples were present in the dataset. Specifically, we identified 66 duplicate phrases (10 repeated three times, 1 repeated four times) and 16 inconsistent samples. By "inconsistent", we mean that the phrase and the context are the same, but the labels differ. While we acknowledged their presence, we did not actively resolve or mitigate their impact during training. The dataset was subsequently updated by the organizers to remove duplicates, but the 16 inconsistencies persisted.

Audio processing. Due to out-of-memory errors encountered during the training of the audio model, we adopted a truncation strategy. All audio samples in our dataset were truncated to a maximum of 15 seconds. Truncation is applied at the sample level: if the audio exceeds 15 seconds in length (corresponding to 240000 samples at a 16 kHz sampling rate), it is truncated. The same applies to the context.

This choice, although necessary for experimental feasibility, could have introduced potential implications for model performance. We conducted an analysis of the audio length distribution in the MM-USED-fallacy dataset (see Appendix A.3). Although the average duration of the input samples is 9.51 seconds, 17% of the samples exceeded the threshold, suggesting that a significant portion of the dataset was truncated. Moreover, truncating audio to 15 seconds imposed limitations on context exploitation. Table 11 reports the average duration of the context audio as a function of the window size. For instance, a context window of 6 spans 31.44 seconds, necessitating truncation to fit the limit. This may have impaired the model's performance, particularly for fallacies like Slippery Slope, where extended context could improve classification.

Table 10 shows the length distribution for each class. Classes such as FC and SS have a longer average length compared to other classes. Truncating all audio inputs to 15 seconds disproportionately affects these classes, potentially discarding informative content and introducing a bias toward shorter utterances.

One minor adjustment that could help mitigate the issue is to truncate from the beginning of the audio, as the truncation was applied to the end of the audio sequence. An empirical analysis comparing performance across different strategies for handling audio length could represent an important direction for future work. Such a study could precisely quantify the trade-off between computational efficiency and information fidelity.

Fusion strategy. The late fusion of text and audio models did not outperform individual text- or audio-only models. This suggests that the current fusion approach is suboptimal, and more advanced techniques, should be explored to better integrate modalities.

References

Alexei Baevski, Henry Zhou, Abdelrahman Mohamed, and Michael Auli. 2020. wav2vec 2.0: A framework for self-supervised learning of speech representations. *CoRR*, abs/2006.11477.

Iz Beltagy, Matthew E. Peters, and Arman Cohan. 2020. Longformer: The long-document transformer. *CoRR*, abs/2004.05150.

Lukas Biewald. 2020. Experiment tracking with weights and biases. Software available from wandb.com.

Sanyuan Chen, Chengyi Wang, Zhengyang Chen, Yu Wu, Shujie Liu, Zhuo Chen, Jinyu Li, Naoyuki Kanda, Takuya Yoshioka, Xiong Xiao, Jian Wu, Long Zhou, Shuo Ren, Yanmin Qian, Yao Qian, Jian Wu, Michael Zeng, and Furu Wei. 2021. Wavlm: Large-scale self-supervised pre-training for full stack speech processing. *CoRR*, abs/2110.13900.

Tri Dao. 2023. Flashattention-2: Faster attention with better parallelism and work partitioning. *Preprint*, arXiv:2307.08691.

Jacob Devlin, Ming-Wei Chang, Kenton Lee, and Kristina Toutanova. 2018. BERT: pre-training of deep bidirectional transformers for language understanding. *CoRR*, abs/1810.04805.

Pierpaolo Goffredo, Shohreh Haddadan, Vorakit Vorakitphan, Elena Cabrio, and Serena Villata. 2022. Fallacious argument classification in political debates. In *Proceedings of the Thirty-First International Joint Conference on Artificial Intelligence, IJCAI-22*, pages 4143–4149. International Joint Conferences on Artificial Intelligence Organization. Main Track.

Shohreh Haddadan, Elena Cabrio, and Serena Villata. 2019. Yes, we can! mining arguments in 50 years of US presidential campaign debates. In *Proceedings of the 57th Annual Meeting of the Association for Computational Linguistics*, pages 4684–4690, Florence, Italy. Association for Computational Linguistics.

Pengcheng He, Jianfeng Gao, and Weizhu Chen. 2023. Debertav3: Improving deberta using electra-style pretraining with gradient-disentangled embedding sharing. *Preprint*, arXiv:2111.09543.

Wei-Ning Hsu, Benjamin Bolte, Yao-Hung Hubert Tsai, Kushal Lakhotia, Ruslan Salakhutdinov, and Abdelrahman Mohamed. 2021. Hubert: Self-supervised speech representation learning by masked prediction of hidden units. *Preprint*, arXiv:2106.07447.

Marco Lippi and Paolo Torroni. 2016. Argument mining from speech: Detecting claims in political debates. *Proceedings of the AAAI Conference on Artificial Intelligence*, 30(1).

Yinhan Liu, Myle Ott, Naman Goyal, Jingfei Du, Mandar Joshi, Danqi Chen, Omer Levy, Mike Lewis, Luke Zettlemoyer, and Veselin Stoyanov. 2019. Roberta: A robustly optimized bert pretraining approach. *Preprint*, arXiv:1907.11692.

Ilya Loshchilov and Frank Hutter. 2019. Decoupled weight decay regularization. *Preprint*, arXiv:1711.05101.

Eleonora Mancini, Federico Ruggeri, Stefano Colamonaco, Andrea Zecca, Samuele Marro, and Paolo Torroni. 2024a. MAMKit: A comprehensive multimodal argument mining toolkit. In *Proceedings of the 11th Workshop on Argument Mining (ArgMining 2024)*, pages 69–82, Bangkok, Thailand. Association for Computational Linguistics.

Eleonora Mancini, Federico Ruggeri, Andrea Galassi, and Paolo Torroni. 2022. Multimodal argument mining: A case study in political debates. In *Proceedings of the 9th Workshop on Argument Mining*, pages 158–170, Online and in Gyeongju, Republic of Korea. International Conference on Computational Linguistics.

Eleonora Mancini, Federico Ruggeri, and Paolo Torroni. 2024b. Multimodal fallacy classification in political debates. In *Proceedings of the 18th Conference of*

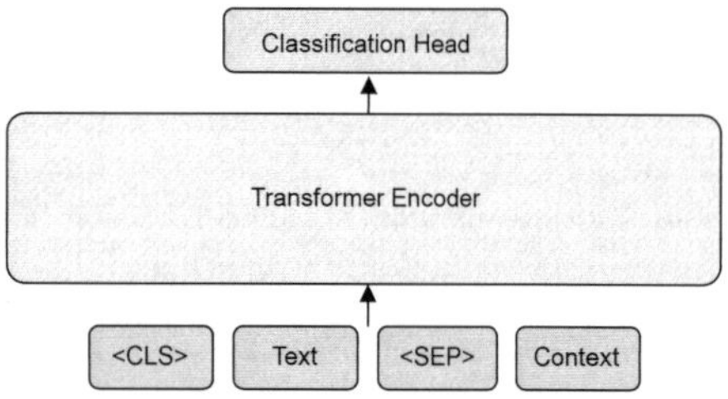

Figure 1: The Concat architecture.

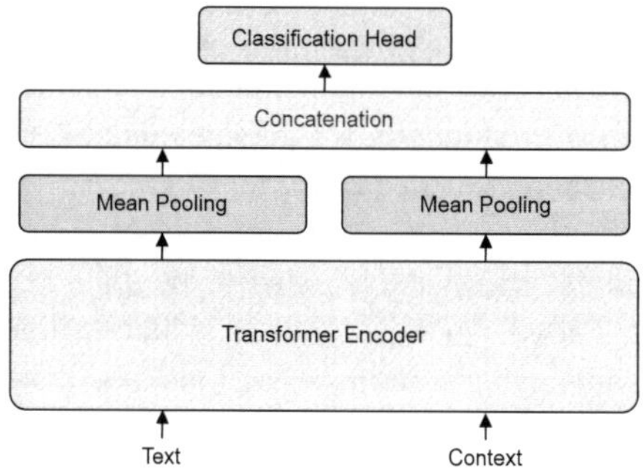

Figure 2: The ContextPool architecture.

the European Chapter of the Association for Computational Linguistics (Volume 2: Short Papers), pages 170–178, St. Julian's, Malta. Association for Computational Linguistics.

Nils Reimers and Iryna Gurevych. 2019. Sentence-BERT: Sentence embeddings using Siamese BERT-networks. In *Proceedings of the 2019 Conference on Empirical Methods in Natural Language Processing and the 9th International Joint Conference on Natural Language Processing (EMNLP-IJCNLP)*, pages 3982–3992, Hong Kong, China. Association for Computational Linguistics.

Jasper Snoek, Hugo Larochelle, and Ryan P. Adams. 2012. Practical bayesian optimization of machine learning algorithms. *Preprint*, arXiv:1206.2944.

Benjamin Warner, Antoine Chaffin, Benjamin Clavié, Orion Weller, Oskar Hallström, Said Taghadouini, Alexis Gallagher, Raja Biswas, Faisal Ladhak, Tom Aarsen, Nathan Cooper, Griffin Adams, Jeremy Howard, and Iacopo Poli. 2024. Smarter, better, faster, longer: A modern bidirectional encoder for fast, memory efficient, and long context finetuning and inference. *Preprint*, arXiv:2412.13663.

A Appendix

A.1 Architectures details

Concat. We use the separator token to divide the text and its context and let the model decide how to attend to each token (see Figure 1). Whether the context appears before or after the text is a matter of choice. The downside of this approach is that it creates very long token sequences. With too much context, the transformer may lose focus on what the task requires, i.e., classifying the text. On the positive side, however, it allows the transformer to decide how to allocate attention to different tokens.

ContextPool. The idea is similar to the one presented in Reimers and Gurevych (2019): a Siamese BERT-base network. Text and context pass through the encoder. Then, for both, we perform mean pooling and concatenate the information. Finally, there is a classification head (see Figure 2).

ContextAtt. It's a transformer with a cross-attention mechanism for integrating text and context (see Figure 3). This model processes text and context inputs separately through a shared transformer, then applies cross-attention to integrate context information into the text representation. This enriched embeddings are fused with the original text embeddings through a gate and compressed into a global embedding via attentive pooling.

The fusion gate is nothing more than an MLP that takes as input the text vector and the context vector concatenated and projected into a space of dimension equal to the hidden size. A sigmoid function was then applied, returning values between 0 and 1. In this way, we obtain a mask that weights the importance of the context inputs during fusion. In our implementation, the text embedding was always assigned full weight, while the context-aware embedding provides an additive contribution modulated by the gate. Finally, a normalization layer was applied at the end of the fusion phase.

Moreover, instead of using average pooling, in this case we implemented attentive pooling, a type of pooling that allows the model to learn which tokens to attend to. For this, we created a small MLP to compute attention scores for each token. The scores are then normalized using softmax. Applying these weights to the embedding tokens, we obtained a global weighted embedding.

A.2 Training details

We tracked all the experiments using Weights & Biases. To manage all the different configuration, we used YAML files. The default class `MAMKitLightingModel` has been expanded by adding more features. First, we added the support for a learning rate scheduler. Another addi-

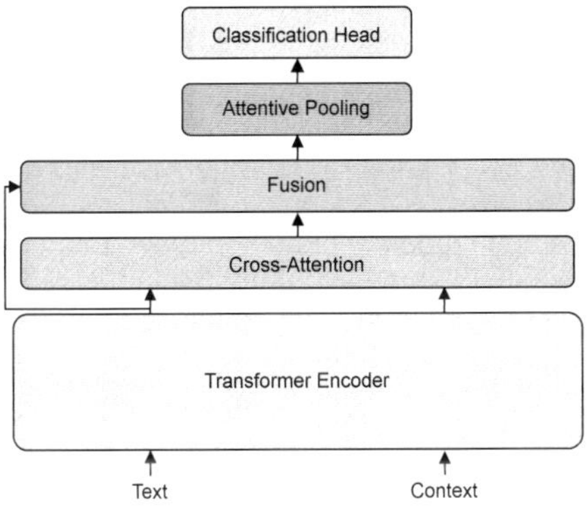

Figure 3: The ContextAtt architecture.

tion was a hook to log total gradient norm at each step. This addition has been very useful in helping us understand how large the gradient norm was. Specifically, using this graph, we were able to detect that applying gradient clipping was harmful in our case, as every time we tried it, we observed very large spikes in the gradient that damaged the learning process. For the audio, we implemented a different version of the `MAMKitLightingModel` that supports differential learning rates. This allowed us to train the head and the backbone of the model with different learning rates, even though the final model was trained using the same learning rate for both the head and the backbone. Two schedulers were tried: a linear scheduler and a cosine scheduler, both with warmup. Also, we tried different warmups. Initially, we set it to 10% of the total number of steps, but then, we noticed that increasing the warmup to 30% allowed us to obtain better results. Furthermore, during model training we applied high internal precision to all float32 matrix multiplications, trading off precision for performance.

A.3 Audio Length Distribution Analysis

Table 9 reports the distribution of audio sample lengths in the dataset. Notably, 216 samples (approximately 17%) have a duration longer than 15 seconds.

Hyperparam	**ContextPool-RoBERTa (N=1)**	**ContextPool-RoBERTa (N=5)**
Backbone	RoBERTa large	RoBERTa large
Model Type	ContextPoolingTextModel	ContextPoolingTextModel
Hidden Layers	[100, 50]	[100, 50]
Dropout	0.1	0.1
Context Window	1	5
Optimizer	AdamW	AdamW
Learning Rates	3.4e-5	1.5e-5
Weight Decay	8.05e-5	3.9e-7
Learning Rate Decay	Linear	Linear
Warmup Steps	258	258
Batch Size	8	4
Gradient Accumulation	3	3
Max Steps	860	860
Precision	bf16-mixed	bf16-mixed
Seed	20	20

Table 5: Hyperparameters of our best text-only models.

Hyperparam	**HuBERT-Base fine-tuned**
Backbone	HuBERT base
Model Type	BaseModel
Hidden Layers	[50]
Layer to Finetune	3
Dropout	0.1
Context Window	0
Optimizer	AdamW
Learning Rates	2e-4 (backbone), 2e-4 (head)
Weight Decay	0.01
Learning Rate Decay	Linear
Warmup Steps	258
Batch Size	4
Gradient Accumulation	3
Max Steps	860
Precision	bf16-mixed
Seed	20

Table 6: Hyperparameters of our audio model.

Model	**Weight**
ContextPool-RoBERTa (N=1)	0.4256
ContextPool-RoBERTa (N=1)	0.3723
ContextPool-RoBERTa (N=5)	0.2021

Table 7: Weights for ensemble predictions of text-only models.

Model	**Weight**
ContextPool-RoBERTa (N=1)	0.8128
HuBERT-Base fine-tuned	0.1872

Table 8: Weights for ensemble predictions of best text and audio models.

Length Interval (s)	Number of Samples
0–1	18
1–3	201
3–5	231
5–10	399
10–15	213
15+	216

Table 9: Distribution of audio samples by length intervals (in seconds).

Class	Avg. Length (s)	Std (s)	Max Length (s)
AE	9.11	8.88	123.79
AA	10.80	12.10	137.27
AH	9.14	10.49	83.98
FC	11.28	7.16	39.75
SS	10.64	7.45	46.00
S	8.97	10.69	39.59

Table 10: Length distribution statistics (average, standard deviation, and maximum) of audio samples for each class.

Context Window	Average Duration (s)
1	5.74
2	11.29
3	16.63
4	21.76
5	26.69
6	31.44

Table 11: Average duration of the context as a function of the context window size.

Author Index

Association for Computational Linguistics
209 N. Eighth Street
Stroudsburg, Pennsylvania 18360

CURRAN ASSOCIATES INC.
proceedings.com

ISBN 979-8-3313-2400-1